CONTEMPORARY BUSINESS

Third Edition

Louis E. Boone
University of Central Florida

David L. Kurtz
Seattle University

THE DRYDEN PRESS

Chicago   New York   Philadelphia   San Francisco   Montreal   Toronto
London   Sydney   Tokyo   Mexico City   Rio de Janeiro   Madrid

Editor—Anne Smith
Development Editor—Lauren S. Bahr
Cover and Interior Designer—Diane Daugherty
Photo Researcher—Inge King
Production Manager—Pat Sarcuni

Address orders to: 383 Madison Avenue, New York, NY 10017

Address editorial correspondence to: 901 Elm Street, Hinsdale, IL 60521

CBS COLLEGE PUBLISHING
The Dryden Press
Holt, Rinehart and Winston
Saunders College Publishing

To Pat and Marcia

PREFACE

The 1980s are exciting times in which to begin a study of business. Never before have organizations—from the smallest businesses to the largest corporations—placed greater emphasis on business knowledge.

Contemporary Business, Third Edition is designed to be the textbook for the 1980s. During the first six years of its existence, more students began their formal study of business with *Contemporary Business* as their text than with any other text-book published. It has become the standard to which other texts are compared.

Improvements in the Third Edition

Although the text has received unprecedented acceptance from professors and students, the business and economic developments of recent years require examination, explanation, and interpretation if *Contemporary Business* is to continue to be worthy of its name. The text has been thoroughly revised, and the latest developments have been incorporated into the new edition. It is packed with current, up-to-date examples, illustrations, cases, and trends designed to provide students with a clear picture of business in the mid-1980s.

In addition, feedback was obtained from dozens of reviews by professors—users and nonusers—and extensive marketing research by the publisher. Respondents indicated that the following items should be incorporated in the new edition:

- additional coverage of small business
- greater emphasis on the current issues of productivity and inflation
- increased attention to the service sector of business
- greater emphasis on business terminology and vocabulary building

As a result of these suggestions, "Small Business and Franchising" is now covered in Chapter 4, and many of the profiles of businesspeople focus on the small business sector. A section on productivity appears in Chapter 1, and inflation is introduced in Chapter 2 "Societal Issues and Business" and discussed throughout the text where applicable. Services are discussed in the marketing section and receive considerable attention in Chapter 14 "Production and Operations Management" which has been thoroughly revised to treat the production of services as well as goods. A newly added feature designed to assist in developing business terminology is the inclusion of a running glossary in the margins of the text.

The extensive revisions are designed to provide users of *Contemporary Business, Third Edition* with the most current and complete teaching package available for the first business course. The text provides both instructors and students with several strengths not found in competing books.

Stresses Pedagogical Soundness

Contemporary Business is written to help students learn about business. Each chapter begins with a list of specific learning objectives, a profile of a real businessperson, and a short case to illustrate in a novel fashion the application of each chapter's subject matter. For example, chapters dealing with organization, human resources, production, labor-management relations, and finance begin with such opening cases as:

- how organization helped land a U.S. astronaut on the moon
- how the University of Wyoming discourages its head football coach from leaving through a novel compensation plan
- how robots are used in factories
- how Solidarity—the Polish labor union—came into existence
- how Christopher Columbus' trip to the New World was financed

Vocabulary-building—a critical concern in the first business course—is stressed by the inclusion of definitions in the margins adjacent to the introduction and discussion of the term in the text. In addition, key terms are listed at the end of each chapter, and all terms are listed and defined in an alphabetical glossary at the end of the book.

Each chapter is well illustrated with tables, figures, examples, and boxed focus items that provide real-life examples of the application of text material. A summary, a list of key terms, review questions, discussion questions and exercises, and two cases dealing with actual people and real organizations conclude each chapter.

Emphasizes Business Concepts with Real-world Examples

Perhaps the most important feature that distinguishes *Contemporary Business* from other texts is that students enjoy reading and studying it. Business concepts are presented in a lively and engaging manner. Hundreds of real-world examples breathe life into these concepts for students. Business profiles, controversial issues, boxed items, cases, and numerous current examples on every page are designed to illustrate the application of business principles discussed in the text.

Focuses on Small Business

Too many business students are introduced to business of only one size—large. *Contemporary Business* recognizes students' growing interest in small business and the many career opportunities found in organizations other than giant corporations. A balanced presentation of applications and examples from both small and big business is maintained throughout the text. Many of the chapter profiles deal with individuals who have developed successful small businesses. Discussions of business careers at the end of each part and in Chapter 25 focus on career opportunities in small businesses as well as in larger organizations. In addition, an entire chapter (Chapter 4) is devoted to small business and franchising.

Highlights Business Careers

In addition to conveying to students the excitement and challenges of business and to developing a foundation in the basic concepts and terminology of business, *Contemporary Business* also provides students with detailed, current information on different careers in business. The text offers descriptions of careers in each functional area, explanations of available positions, and employment forecasts for each career area at the end of each part. Chapter 25, "Careers in Business," is devoted exclusively to helping students evaluate possible careers and to guiding them through each step in the career search process.

Provides a Text Written by Business Professors Who Have Taught the Course

Another critical factor affecting the success of *Contemporary Business* is that its authors are business professors who have taught the introductory business course. Although the text reflects suggestions, reviews, critiques, and recommendations of dozens of business faculty reviewers, it is written by professors who teach business students. The feedback from actually teaching the basic business course can never be duplicated.

Offers the Most Complete Teaching/ Learning Package in Business

The third edition of *Contemporary Business* is a comprehensive teaching/learning package that is unparalleled in its completeness. While the textbook is undoubtedly the most critical element in the package, it is only one part. It is supplemented by the widely acclaimed *Study Guide,* prepared by Professors Steven L. Shapiro of Queensborough Community College, Roderick D. Powers of Iowa State University, and Joseph T. Straub of Valencia Community College, and thoroughly revised and updated. An entirely new supplement, *Cases in Contemporary Business,* written by Professor James M. Higgins of Rollins College, provides more than 50 short, one-to-three-page cases, focusing on many well-known companies and is designed to reinforce concepts in the text.

The Organizer

Although it can be argued that the first business course is the most important in the business curriculum, it is often taught by professors with large classes and heavy teaching loads. Because the authors recognize the challenges facing the instructor of this course, much of this challenge is met with *The Organizer. The Organizer* is a total resource kit for the instructor and includes the following:

Guide to Supplements—a separate explanation of each of the supplements in *The Organizer* with suggestions for using each in developing a complete course in introductory business

Instructor's Manual—written by the authors to provide instructors with teaching objectives, lectures, new examples, student exercises, novel suggestions for teaching the course, and answers to questions and cases in the text

Test Bank—2,000 new questions written by business instructors with each question keyed to chapter learning goals, text page number, minor subject area, and type of question—knowledge or application; available in both a printed and computerized format

Transparencies—100 original transparency acetates of material not included in the text

Supplemental Lecture Topics—25 separate lectures—one for each chapter—on current, high-interest topics

Film Guide—a current list of several hundred films for classroom use organized by chapter

Portfolio of Business Papers—50 examples of actual business documents to introduce students to the mechanics of business

Experiential Exercises for Contemporary Business—the newest addition to the package includes mind teasers, concept games, class experience games, business projects, and development games that offer a hands-on, experiential dimension to teaching business principles; prepared by Professor William Rice of the College of William and Mary

Solutions Manual to Cases in Contemporary Business

Additional Features

As an exciting new aid to instructors, the package also features a newly created *Slide/ Lecture Series in Contemporary Business* developed by Professors Don Sciglimpaglia of San Diego State University and John McMillin of Point Loma College.

The series consists of five lecture modules, each illustrated by approximately 50 four-color, 35mm. slides and accompanied by a written commentary for instructors. The entire series contains 250 slides and covers the following business subjects:

- What is Business?
- Small Business and Franchising
- Sources and Uses of Funds
- Computers and Business
- International Business

Acknowledgements

The authors gratefully acknowledge the contributions of a large number of people—colleagues, students, practitioners in businesses and nonprofit organizations, and the fine professionals at The Dryden Press—for their invaluable critiques, questions, and advice in making *Contemporary Business, Third Edition* a reality. We are particularly grateful to our editor, Lauren S. Bahr, for her suggestions, encouragement, and hours of hard work. For their reviews of all or part of the manuscript or assistance in developing test materials, we would especially like to thank the following dedicated business professionals:

Saul W. Adelman (Miami University), Al Agbay (Wayne County Community College), Margaret Alexander (North Harris County College), Jolene T. Anders (Northwestern State University of Louisiana), Charles Armstrong (Kansas City Kansas Community College), Edwin C. Aronson, Jr. (Golden West College), B. Toby Atkinson (Brevard Community College), Raymond F. Attner (Brookhaven College), Carlson D. Austin (South Carolina State College), W. Gary Bacon (North Lake College), Francis Byron Ballard (Florida Junior College), William Grady Barnhart (El Centro College), Robert L. Bartholomew (College of Boca Raton), James Baylor (Riverside City College), Alec Beaudoin (Triton College), Kay Berry (Kansas City, Kansas Community College), Leonard Bethards (Miami-Dade Community College—North Campus), Robert H. Boatsman (Seattle Central Community College), Anthony Boratta (Laney College), Robert W. Braid (Atlantic Community College), Stephen C. Branz (Triton College), Vera Brooks (Motlow State Community College), J. G. Bryson (West Georgia College), John J. Buckley (Orange County Community College), Clara Buitenbos (Pan American University), Walter Bunnell (Sinclair Community College), Carroll Burrell (San Jacinto College), Donald Cappa (Chabot College), Hugo Carlson (Northern State College), James Cockrell (Chemeketa Community College), Jerry Cohen (Somerset County College), Terry Comingore (Brazosport College), Curt Cremean (Jackson Community College), Linda Culicetto (Prince Georges Community College), D. Dexter Dalton (St. Louis Community College at Meramec), Kathy Daruty (Los Angeles Pierce College), Ted Dedowitz (State University of N.Y. Agricultural and Technical College at Farmingdale), Jack Howard Denson (Fullerton College), Gordon Di Paolo (College of Staten Island), Michael Dougherty (Milwaukee Area Technical College), Gervase A. Eckenrod (Fresno City College), John J. Elliott (San Joaquin Delta College), Douglas A. Elvers (The University of North Carolina at Chapel Hill), Ted Erickson (Normdale Community College), Robert Fishco (Middlesex County College), George Fitchett (Bridgewater College), Fred E. Folkman (Queensborough Community College), Roger Fremier (Monterey Peninsula College), William M. Friedman (Fontbonne College), Barbara J. Frizzell (Macon Junior College), Judith Furrer (Inver Hills Community College), Marlin Gerber (Kalamazoo Valley Community College), Robert Googins (Shasta College), Donald J. Green (Chabot College), Joe Grissom (Tarrant County Junior College), John W. Hagen (California State University—Fresno), Arthur L. Hardy (San Jacinto College), James W. Hariston (South Carolina State College), Susan Harrison (Parkersburg Community College), Larry Helderth (Danville Community College), Larry Henderson (National College), James M. Higgins (Rollins College), Fred E. Hild (Valencia Community College), Harald Hillmer (Riverside City Community College), Nathan Himelstein (Essex County College), Jane Jackson (Eastern New Mexico State University), Dana J. Johnson (Virginia Polytechnic Institute and State University), Edwin Johnson (Parkersburg Community College), Chad Jones (National College), Francis L. Jones (Cypress College), Bernard Karne (Laney College), Bernard V. Katz (Oakton Community College), Louis C. Kaufman (Fordham University—Graduate School of Business), Warren Keller (Grossmont College), Stanlee Kissel (Somerset County College), Derwin Koleada (Menershe State University), John Krane (Community College of Denver), David Krohn (Kirkwood Community College), Fran Kubicek (Kalamazoo Valley Community College), John Leahy (Palomar College), James Lentz (Moraine Valley Community College), Robert J. Lewis (Indiana University—Purdue University at Indianapolis), Paul N. Loveday (University of Nevada/Las Vegas), Charles Lowery (Technical College of Alamance), James Macnamara (Brevard Community College), Edward G. Magruder (Virginia Western Community College), Joel Mansfield (Central Missouri State University), Martin K. Marsh (Humboldt State University), Frank D. Mason (California State University—Northridge),

Sylvia B. Mays (Kirkwood Community College), Martin McKell (College of the Desert), John McMillan (Point Loma College), Thomas Bradford Metcalf (University of Houston—College of Technology), Henry Metzner (University of Missouri—Rolla), Emerson Milligam (Carlow College), Keith Mills (Chemeketa Community College), Edwin Miner (Phoenix College), Robert Moore (Imperial Valley College), Robert Mueller (Olive Harvey College), Dick Mulkey (Eastern New Mexico University—Roswell Campus), William Murray (University of San Francisco), Helen Nabors (Shelby State Community College), James Nestor (Daytona Beach Community College), La Jean Nichols (Alabama Christian College), Robert O. Nixon (Pima Community College), Gerald O'Boyle (St. John's University), G. Dean Palmer (University of Northern Colorado), Dennis Pappas (Columbus Technical Institute), Norman Petty (Central Piedmont College), Stanley Phillips (Tennessee Technological University), Arnold Pisani (Berkshire Community College), Johnette Plantz (College of the Mainland), Noel G. Powell (West Georgia College), Roderick D. Powers (Iowa State University), John K. Preston (North Seattle Community College), James R. Prucnal (Gadsen State Junior College), Richard Randall (Nassau Community College), Robert A. Redick (Lincoln Land Community College), James Reinemann (College of Lake County), William Rice (College of William and Mary), Robert Rizzo (Indian River Community College), Richard S. Robertson (retired) (Jackson Community College), Bernice B. Rollins (Prairie View A & M University), Walter Richard Rooney (University of Houston—Downtown Campus), James J. Runnalls (University of Wisconsin—Stout), Celene Sanders (Radford College), Fernando Santamaria (Fiorello La Guardia Community College), Jean M. Saunders (Virginia Western Community College), Thomas C. Schaber (Miami University—Ohio), Dennis E. Schmitt (Emporia State University), Bill Schwartz (Temple University), Don Sciglimpaglia (San Diego State University), Jon E. Seely (Tulsa Junior College), Barry Shane (Oregon State University), Steven L. Shapiro (Queensborough Community College), David E. Shepard (Virginia Western Community College), Thomas Shockney (Ashland College), James Simpson (College of the Mainland), Clay Sink (University of Rhode Island), Glenn Smith (Marshall University), W. Nye Smith (Clarkson College of Technology), J. Wayne Spence (North Texas State University), Richard J. Stanish (Tulsa Junior College—Metro Campus), Herbert Stuart Stegenga (Housatonic Community College), Randy Stegner (Jefferson Community College), Harold Sternbach (University of Rhode Island), Dewayne Stonebarger (Indiana-Purdue University), Joseph T. Straub (Valencia Community College), William Sidney Sugg, Jr. (Lakeland Community College), Ray Tewell (American River College), Lula Thomas (Southern University A & M College), Richard Trower (Danville Junior College), William C. Tustin (Jackson State Community College), Robert Vaughn (Lakeland Community College), C. Thomas Vogt (Allan Hancock College), Robert Wagley (Wright State University), John F. Warner (University of New Mexico), Irving Wechsler (City University of New York—Borough of Manhattan Community College), Gerry Welch (St. Louis Community College at Meramec), William A. Weller (Modesto Junior College), Susan Wessels (Meredith College), Stephen L. West (Daytona Beach Community College), Clark W. Wheeler (Sante Fe Community College), Charles A. White (Edison Community College), Eugene White (Community College of Denver), Sally Sue Whitten (West Virginia State College), Terrell Williams (Utah State University), Wayne Roy Wilson (Cameron University), Wallace Wirth (Thornton Community College), William Wright (Mt. Hood Community College), Edward Yost (Ohio State University).

Maitland, Florida   Louis E. Boone

Bellevue, Washington   David L. Kurtz

CONTENTS

PART ONE
BUSINESS AND ITS ENVIRONMENT

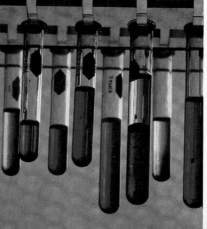

PART TWO
ORGANIZATION AND MANAGEMENT
OF THE ENTERPRISE

PART THREE
MANAGEMENT OF HUMAN RESOURCES

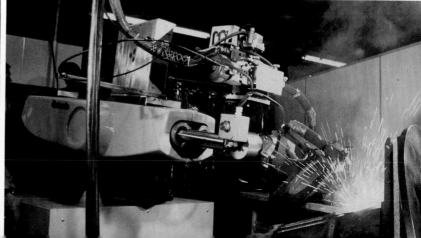

PART FOUR
MARKETING MANAGEMENT

PART FIVE
PRODUCTION AND INFORMATION

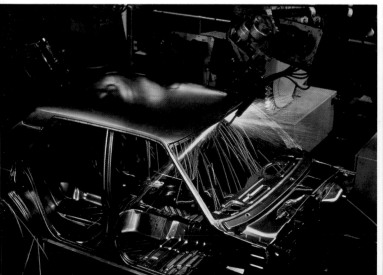

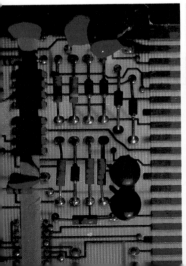

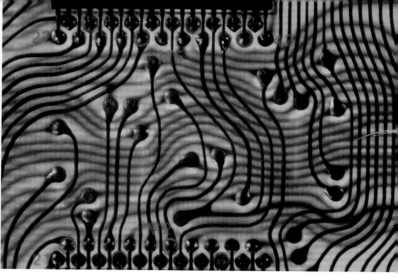

PART SIX
FINANCING THE ENTERPRISE

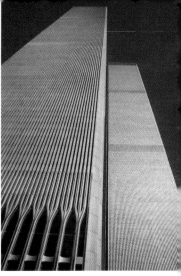

PART SEVEN
ADDITIONAL DIMENSIONS

23 *Business and the Legal System* 577

Contemporary Business

PART
ONE

BUSINESS
AND ITS
ENVIRONMENT

1

The Foundations of Business

Learning Goals

1. To explain what a business is and how it operates within the private enterprise system

2. To define the role of competition and of the entrepreneur in a business enterprise system

3. To understand the concept of productivity and why it is important

4. To analyze how the historical development of the U.S. economy influences contemporary business

5. To identify the different types of economic systems

6. To explain the role of business, labor, and government in modern society

7. To recognize how to study business and why

8. To analyze how contemporary business operates

9. To explain the meaning of each of the key terms introduced in this chapter

Profile: Frank Jarecki
From MIG Pilot to Machine Shop Entrepreneur

Frank Jarecki has every reason to love America. It gave him a home after he fled communist Poland. And it gave him the chance to become a millionaire.

"America is truly the land of opportunity," says Jarecki as he reflects on his life. "No other country in the world could have given me the chances I've had here."

Frank Jarecki's story began on March 5, 1953 when as a twenty-one-year-old pilot in the Polish Air Force, he flew his Soviet-made MIG fighter across the border to the safety and freedom of Denmark.

"I had to leave," says Jarecki, "even though the government took care of everything for pilots like me. We had comfortable lives. But we paid a very high price.

"I was told to join the espionage unit and spy on my friends," continued Jarecki. "I had to report anyone I believed wasn't loyal to the Party. When this happened, I knew I had to get out."

Jarecki's escape made him a Cold War hero, honored by President Dwight D. Eisenhower and by all who loved freedom. It also gave him a chance to see how different life could be in a free enterprise economy.

"Two months after my escape I came to the States for the first time," says Jarecki. "I remember looking out of my window from my room in Chicago and seeing a parking lot filled with thousands of cars—and every one was different. I had never seen anything like it in Poland. I knew then that I could make a good life for myself here. All I needed was talent and a little luck."

Frank Jarecki made the "American dream" come true for himself. He attended Alliance College in Cambridge Springs, Pennsylvania and learned to speak English as well as a native-born American. (Jarecki graduated from Alliance in 1957 and now sits on its board of directors.) Then he spent twelve years selling and working in a machine shop. By 1969 Jarecki had saved enough money to open his own business—a machine shop that manufactured heavy precision valves for power plants, industry, and the government.

"When I opened my first shop in Franklin, Pennsylvania," says Jarecki, "I worked seven days a week, twenty hours a day. I wanted to get ahead more than anything else in the world. The banks believed in my future too. They loaned me the start-up money I needed. I couldn't have made it without their help."

Within two years, Jarecki opened a second shop in Erie, Pennsylvania, where he soon won a reputation for quality work delivered on time. Today, Jarecki Industries bills more than $4 million in sales annually.

When Jarecki reflects on his life in the United States he is sure of one thing. "The free enterprise system is the greatest system on earth. It gives people like me a reason to work hard—to build something out of nothing.

"It's so different in Poland. The people have nothing to look forward to. Why should they put in extra time or take pride in what they do if the government owns everything? Communism takes the spirit out of business people. It kills something in their soul."

The system into which the United States wished to go was that of freeing commerce from every shackle.

—Thomas Jefferson

Professional football is big business in the 1980s. Many franchises experience sell-out crowds at each game. Lucrative television contracts provide substantial monies to the teams, much of which is then paid out to players who command six-figure salaries. Professional football is a business!

Let's begin our study of contemporary business by identifying the logos (symbols) of the professional football franchises that appear below. How many teams can you identify? Even if you are an avid professional football fan, you probably failed to identify most of these logos. Why? All of the logos were used by teams in the World Football League (WFL) that failed in 1975. The answers appear below. The more important issue concerns the WFL as a business enterprise.

The World Football League folded on October 22, 1975, only part of the way through its second season. The league had been established to compete with the National Football League (NFL). The

From left to right, 1975 WFL teams (with original nicknames in parentheses): Southern California Sun, Hawaiians, Chicago Winds (Fire), Portland Thunder (Storm), Philadelphia Bell, Shreveport Steamer (Houston Texans), Jacksonville Express (Sharks), Charlotte Hornets (New York Stars), San Antonio Wings, Memphis Southmen (Toronto Northmen), and Birmingham Vulcans (Americans).

growing interest in professional sports made the WFL an excellent business opportunity in the minds of many of its backers.

The league adopted many football innovations in an attempt to appeal to fans. Coaches wore matched outfits in team colors. Some of the color combinations were quite interesting: the Southern California Sun team was attired in orange pants and hot-pink football jerseys. Even the football was colorful: palomino-colored with orange strips. The new league also used the Dicker rod—an innovative L-shaped device to measure first downs. Many first-rate players were signed, and over 100 of them—including Danny White, Pat Haden, Paul Warfield, and Larry Csonka—ended up in the NFL.

Despite its innovations, the World Football League was a business enterprise that failed. As the end neared, many of the signs of business failure were evident. As soon as the Birmingham Americans whipped the Shreveport Steamers in the WFL's only World Bowl game, an Alabama sheriff seized their uniforms for nonpayment of the team's dry-cleaning bills. Just before their last game, the Honolulu Hawaiians asked their players to sell tickets. And pay days with the Portland Thunder used to end up in near riots. Players would race from the practice field to their banks, fearing that if they delayed their payroll checks would not be cashed.[1]

Not all businesses are as hectic as the World Football League was, but contemporary business is every bit as dynamic and challenging. So let's begin our study of this fascinating subject by defining what the term *business* really means.

Mention the word *business,* and you will get varied responses. Some people think of their jobs, others of the firms they deal with as consumers. And rightly so. This broad, inclusive term can be applied to many kinds of enterprises. Business provides the bulk of our employment as well as the goods and services we seek.

What Is Business?

Business comprises all profit-seeking activities and enterprises that provide goods and services necessary to an economic system. It is the economic pulse of a nation, the means through which society's standard of living gets better. Profits are a primary mechanism for accomplishing these goals. Accountants and business people define **profit** as the difference between a company's revenues (receipts) and expenses (expenditures).

Businesses must serve their customers in some way if they are to survive in the long run. Some businesses produce tangible products,

business
All profit-seeking activities and enterprises that provide goods and services necessary to an economic system.

profit
The difference between a company's revenues (receipts) and expenses (expenditures).

such as automobiles, light bulbs, and aircraft. Others provide services, such as insurance, car rentals, and lodging. The Coca-Cola Co. is a classic example of a business that succeeded by satisfying the needs of the public through the pursuit of profits (see Focus 1–1).

FOCUS 1–1
The Coca-Cola Co.

It all began in a downtown Atlanta drugstore on May 8, 1886. Coca-Cola sold for five cents a glass at the soda fountain and was promoted in the *Atlanta Journal* as "the new and popular soda fountain drink, containing the properties of the wonderful Coca plant and the famous Cola nuts."

Some say Coca-Cola was a mistake. John S. Pemberton may have been trying to develop a headache tonic with syrup he mixed in a three-legged kettle. But the product was soon marketed as a thirst quencher. At first plain water was combined with the syrup. But this was changed to carbonated water after a soda fountain worker mixed it by mistake, and the customer approved of the new mix.

Health problems soon caused Pemberton to take on a partner, Asa G. Candler. For $2,300 and other considerations, Candler became the sole owner within three years. The company prospered primarily because of Candler's endless promotion of the new product.

Benjamin Franklin Thomas and Joseph B. Whitehead obtained exclusive bottling and distribution rights from Coca-Cola in 1899. These rights covered most of the United States. Coca-Cola also began to be sold abroad in Canada, Cuba, Puerto Rico, and England.

The Coca-Cola Co. was sold to an Atlanta investment group led by Ernest Woodruff in 1919. Woodruff's son, Robert, became president in 1923. The younger Woodruff expanded the international segment of the business and emphasized a quality control program to assure that each Coke met the company's high standards. Woodruff also saw bottle sales move ahead of fountain sales in 1928.

The Coca-Cola Co. relied on Coke for 64 years before it expanded into other items. Today the company offers 250 products, but Coke remains the the major offering. New flavors were added—Fanta, TAB, Fresca, Sprite, Mr. PiBB. Various mergers and acquisitiions took place—Minute Maid, Duncan Foods, Aqua-Chem, and Taylor Wine. Over 190 million eight-ounce servings of Coke are consumed in 135 nations daily. The Coca-Cola Co. now has annual sales of about $5 billion and stands as a monument to the American economic system and the people who made it work.

A business has to be continually aware of new opportunities to satisfy customer needs. Often it must modify its traditional operating methods in order to remain competitive. Winnebago Industries is an excellent example of a firm that turned to alternative markets (see Focus 1–2).

FOCUS 1–2
Winnebago Industries, Inc.

Like other motor home manufacturers, Winnebago Industries has been hard hit by rising gasoline prices. Large motor homes that get about five miles per gallon are no longer popular with American consumers. Winnebago has had to report losses to its stockholders, sell a plant, and curtail employment elsewhere. Its stock plunged from $70 to $2 per share.

But Winnebago is making a comeback. It is planning a lightweight mobile home weighing about half that of the standard model. The firm is also working on a fuel conversion kit for existing motor homes. The kit would allow these vehicles to run on propane.

Winnebago has also moved into other lines of business. It now builds stills for making fuel alcohol and manufactures window parts, basketball backboards, wood-burning stoves, bus chassis, and even a tram trailer for Universal Studios. Winnebago is also making equipment for converting pickup trucks into dump trucks. These changes clearly suggest that Winnebago Industries intends to stay in business—with or without its traditional product line.

The Private Enterprise System

private enterprise system
The system under which firms operate in a dynamic environment where success or failure is determined by how well they match and counter the offerings of competitors.

competition
The battle among businesses for consumer acceptance.

Most U.S. businesses, large or small, belong to what is called the **private enterprise system.** This means simply that firms operate in a dynamic environment where success or failure is determined by how well they match and counter the offerings of competitors. **Competition** is the battle among businesses for consumer acceptance. Sales and profits are the yardsticks by which such acceptance is measured.

The business world has abundant examples of firms that were once successful but that failed to continue satisfying consumer demands. Competition assures that, over the long run, firms that satisfy consumer demands will be successful and those that do not will be replaced. The failures of Robert Hall, W. T. Grant, and Studebaker illustrate the need to continue a strong consumer orientation.

The private enterprise system requires that firms continually adjust their strategies, product offerings, service standards, operating procedures, and the like. Otherwise the competition will gain higher shares of an industry's sales and profits. Consider the following cases. A & P was long the largest supermarket chain. Now Safeway is the largest, and A & P is attempting a recovery. Ford once was the dominant automaker. Today, it is second to General Motors, among domestic producers. Montgomery Ward used to be a near-equal rival of Sears; now it lags behind J. C. Penney, K mart and Sears among general merchandisers. These events suggest the dynamic environment of the private enterprise system.

Competition is a critical mechanism for guaranteeing that the private enterprise system will continue to provide the goods and services that make for high living standards and sophisticated life styles. Few organizations that offer a product or service can escape the influence of competition. The American Cancer Society competes for contributions with the American Heart Association, your own college, and other nonprofit enterprises. The armed forces compete in the labor market with private employers. Even the U.S. Postal Service faces competition. United Parcel Service competes for package shipments. Express Mail faces competition from Western Union's mailgrams. And firms like The Mailbox, which rents post office boxes in the Seattle area, compete for the post-office-box business.[2]

The Entrepreneur's Role in the Private Enterprise System

entrepreneur
A risk taker in the private enterprise system.

An **entrepreneur** is a risk taker in the private enterprise system, a person who sees a profitable opportunity and then devises a plan and an organization designed to achieve the objective. Some entrepreneurs set up new companies and ventures; others revitalize established concerns.

John D. MacArthur, an eighth-grade dropout, became a successful entrepreneur and one of the world's richest individuals. He was a risk taker in the truest sense of the word, always striving to upgrade what became a vast financial network of 45 firms with 15,000 employees (see Focus 1–3).

The entrepreneur is at the heart of the American economic system. Without the willingness to take risks, there would be no successful businesses, and the private enterprise system could not exist.

FOCUS 1-3
John D. MacArthur, Entrepreneur

When John D. MacArthur died in 1978, he was one of only two U.S. billionaires (the other is Daniel K. Ludwig). MacArthur's wealth was so vast that, in connection with a legal case, one aide claimed: "It would take a battery of accountants, perhaps 20 of them working full time for several months, to figure it out." But MacArthur was not always that prosperous.

After dropping out of school, MacArthur held a variety of jobs—insurance sales representative, newspaper reporter, and wartime pilot and flight instructor. He started his rise in 1928 by buying Marquette Life Insurance Co., a firm whose assets, MacArthur reported, got as low as $15! MacArthur bought Banker's Life and Casualty in 1935 for $2,500. It is now the nation's leading stockholder-owned seller of individual health and accident insurance. MacArthur built Banker's Life into its current position through newspaper advertisements for $1 insurance policies, an industry first. Still MacArthur kept up his entrepreneurial fervor. Eventually he acquired 13 insurance companies; vast landholdings in Florida, Illinois, Arizona, Georgia, Colorado, Michigan, and Wisconsin; hotels; farms; paper mills; golf courses; 61 New York City buildings; an automobile rental company; oil wells; utility companies; restaurants; real estate firms; a liquor company; and the second largest bank in Illinois.

But John D. MacArthur always remained a frugal entrepreneur. He and his wife, Catherine, lived in a modest home, later moving to an apartment at a Palm Beach hotel that MacArthur owned. MacArthur managed his vast empire from a corner table at the hotel's coffee shop. He refused bodyguards and chauffeurs, flew tourist class, and even asked a fellow air traveler if he could have his slice of pecan pie—which he is reported to have wrapped in a napkin and taken with him.

Despite cancer of the pancreas and a stroke, John D. MacArthur continued to work until his death. Characteristically, he gave his body to science. One of America's great entrepreneurs was gone!

The Operation of the Private Enterprise System

capitalism
The system founded on the principle that competition among business firms best serves the needs of society.

The private enterprise system, or **capitalism,** is founded on the principle that competition among business firms best serves the needs of society. Adam Smith, often called the father of capitalism, first de-

A clear example of competition at work may be seen in this array of shampoos from which a consumer may select any kind imaginable.

invisible hand of competition
Description by Adam Smith of how competition regulates the private enterprise system and assures that consumers receive the best possible products and prices.

antitrust laws
Laws that prohibit attempts to monopolize or dominate a particular market.

scribed this process in his book *Wealth of Nations,* published in 1776. Smith said that an economy is best regulated by the **invisible hand of competition.** By this he meant that competition among firms would assure that consumers received the best possible products and prices, because the less efficient producers would gradually be eliminated from the marketplace.

The invisible hand concept is the basic premise of the private enterprise system; competition is the primary regulator of our economic life. Sometimes, however, the public, through its elected representatives, has passed laws designed to strengthen the role of competition. These laws, called **antitrust laws,** prohibit attempts to monopolize, or dominate, a particular market. Two antitrust laws, the Sherman Anti-Trust Act (1890) and the Clayton Act (1914), are described in Chapter 23. Antitrust legislation outlaws efforts to monopolize markets and preserves the advantages of competition for society.

Basic Rights of the Private Enterprise System

Certain rights crucial to the operation of capitalism are available to citizens living in a private enterprise economy. They include rights to private property, to profits, to freedom of choice, and to competition.

Private Property

The private enterprise system guarantees people the right to own, use, buy, sell, and bequeath most forms of property—including land, buildings, machinery, equipment, inventions, and various intangible properties. The right to **private property** is the most fundamental of all rights under the private enterprise system. Most people in our society believe that they should have the right to any property they work to acquire and to all benefits resulting from this ownership.

private property
Property that can be owned, used, bought, sold, and bequeathed under the private enterprise system.

Profits

The private enterprise system also guarantees the risk taker the right to all profits (after taxes) that are earned by the business. There is, of course, no guarantee that the business will earn a profit; if it does, the entrepreneur has a legal and ethical right to it.

Freedom of Choice

Under private enterprise the people have the maximum amount of freedom of choice in employment, purchases, and investments. This means that people can go into (or out of) business with a minimum of government interference. They can change jobs, negotiate compensation levels, join labor unions, and quit if they so desire. Consumers can choose among different breads, furniture, television programs, magazines, and so on.

We are so used to this freedom of choice that we sometimes forget its importance: that the private enterprise economy tries to maximize human welfare and happiness by providing alternatives. Other systems sometimes limit freedom of choice to accomplish the government's goals, such as production increases.

Competitive Ground Rules

The private enterprise system also guarantees the public the right to set ground rules for competitive activity. Speaking for the public, the U.S. government has passed laws to prohibit "cutthroat" competition—excessively competitive practices designed eventually to eliminate competition. It has also established ground rules that prohibit price discrimination, fraudulent dealings in financial markets, and deceptive practices in advertising and packaging.

Factors of Production

The private enterprise system requires certain inputs if it is to operate effectively. Economists call these inputs the **factors of production.** Not all enterprises require exactly the same combination of elements. Each business has its own mix of the four factors of production: natural resources, labor, capital, and entrepreneurship.

factors of production
The basic inputs into the private enterprise system, including natural resources, labor, capital, and entrepreneurship.

natural resources
Everything useful as a productive input in its natural state, including land and everything that comes from the land.

labor
All individuals who work for a business.

capital
The funds necessary to finance the operation of a business.

entrepreneurship
The taking of risks to set up and run a business.

Natural resources refers to everything useful as a productive input in its natural state including agricultural land, building sites, forests, mineral deposits, and so on. Natural resources are basic resources required in any economic system.

Labor is a critical input to the private enterprise system. The term refers to everyone who works for a business, from the company president to the production manager, the sales representative, and the assembly line worker.

Capital is defined as the funds necessary to finance the operation of a business. These funds can be provided in the form of investments, profits, or loans. They are used to build factories, buy raw materials, hire workers, and so on.

Entrepreneurship is the taking of risks to set up and run a business. As defined earlier, the entrepreneur is the risk taker in the private enterprise system. In some situations the entrepreneur actively manages the business; in others this duty is handed over to a salaried manager.

All four factors of production must receive a financial return if they are to be used in the private enterprise system. These payments are in the form of rent, wages, interest, and profit (see Table 1–1). The specific factor payment received varies among industries, but all factors of production are required in some degree for all businesses.

TABLE 1–1
The Factors of Production and Their Factor Payments

Factors of Production	Factor Payments
Natural Resources	Rent
Labor	Wages
Capital	Interest
Entrepreneurship	Profit

Productivity

The four factors of production just discussed contribute to the productivity of our economy. **Productivity** is a measure of the efficiency of production. It relates to the amount of goods or services a worker produces in a given period of time. The availability of the resources and capital needed to produce these goods and services is also an important factor.

productivity
A measure of the efficiency of production. It relates to the amount of goods or services a worker produces in a given period of time.

The United States today is experiencing what many observers are calling "a crisis in productivity." Annual productivity gains have been decreasing in recent years. The most recent U.S. productivity increase was only 1.5 percent compared to Italy's 8.7 percent, Japan's 8.3

percent, France's 5.4 percent, West Germany's 5.2 percent, and the United Kingdom's 2.2 percent.[3]

Productivity gains are what allow people to receive higher real wages—those that are rising faster than the cost of living. If wages go up 15 percent in a year and productivity only 2 percent, then prices will go up approximately 13 percent. Productivity increases must exceed wage increases if workers are to receive what are known as real wage increases.[4]

Various reasons have been given for the low rate of productivity growth in the U.S. These include: a decline in the work ethic or basic desire to work, failure to invest in new plants and equipment, the difficulty of increasing productivity in service-oriented industries, excessive government regulation, inadequate research and development of new products, the high cost of energy, and the lack of availability of capital. But perhaps the most damaging factor of all is that most Americans do not realize that the U.S. is lagging behind in this crucial area. One recent survey reported that 60 percent of the respondents thought the U.S. had the highest productivity rate in the world.[5]

Types of Competition

Four basic types of competition exist in a private enterprise system: perfect (or pure) competition, monopolistic competition, oligopoly, and monopoly. Firms fall into one of these categories on the basis of the relative competitiveness of their particular industry.

Perfect competition is a situation where the firms in an industry are so small that none of them can individually influence the price charged in the marketplace. Price is thus set by total market demand and total market supply—the **law of supply and demand.** *Supply* is a schedule of what sellers will offer in the market at various price levels; *demand* is a schedule showing what consumers will buy at various price levels. The intersection of the supply and demand curves is the price level that will prevail (see Figure 1–1).

Perfect competition involves similar products, ones that cannot be differentiated from those of a competitor. Agriculture is probably the closest example of perfect competition (although government price-support programs make it somewhat less competitive), and wheat is an example of a product that is similar from farm to farm. Finally, the small size of the firms involved in a perfectly competitive market makes it relatively easy for any firm to enter or leave that market.

Monopolistic competition arises in an industry where somewhat fewer firms than would exist in perfect competition produce and sell products that are different from those of their competitors. Monopo-

perfect competition
A situation where the firms in an industry are so small that none of them can individually influence the price charged in the marketplace.

law of supply and demand
An economic law that says market price is determined by the intersection of the supply and demand curves.

monopolistic competition
A situation where somewhat fewer firms than would exist in perfect competition produce and sell goods that are different from those of their competitors.

FIGURE 1–1
Supply and demand determine price.

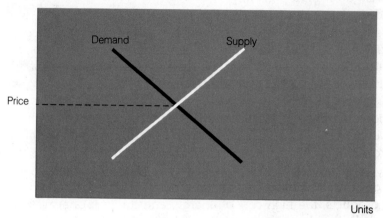

listic competition gives the firm some power over the price it charges. A good example is retailing, where the price can vary among, say, different brands of aspirin, toothpaste, or gasoline. The relatively small size of these retailers also makes it easy for any firm to enter or leave the industry.

oligopoly
A market where there are few sellers.

Oligopoly is a market where there are few sellers. In some oligopolies (such as steel) the product is similar; in others (such as automobiles) it is different. The entry of new competitors is restricted by the huge investments required for market entry. But the primary difference between oligopoly and the previously mentioned markets is that the limited number of sellers gives the oligopolist substantial control over the product's price. In an oligopoly the prices of competitive products are usually quite similar because substantial price competition would lessen every firm's profit. Price cuts by one firm in the industry are typically met by all competitors.

monopoly
A market situation where there are no direct competitors.

Monopoly is a market situation where there are no competitors. Since the Sherman and Clayton acts prohibit attempts to monopolize markets, nearly all the monopolies that do exist are regulated monopolies, such as the public utilities. Firms selling electricity, natural gas,

TABLE 1–2
Major Characteristics of Perfect Competition, Monopolistic Competition, Oligopoly, and Monopoly

Type of Competition	Characteristics			
	Number of Firms	Product	Control over Pricing	Ease of Entry
Perfect competition	Many	Similar	None	Easy
Monopolistic competition	Many	Different	Some	Relatively easy
Oligopoly	Few	Similar or different	Substantial	Difficult
Monopoly	One	No readily available substitite	Usually regulated by government	Virtually impossible

and telephone service are usually regulated by agencies of the state government. These agencies have power over many aspects of the regulated monopolies, including pricing and profits. In a pure monopoly the firm would have substantial control over pricing, but in a regulated monopoly pricing is subject to rules imposed by the regulatory body. There are no directly competitive products in a regulated monopoly, and entry into the industry is restricted by the government. In fact, in some states a public utility must periodically seek voter approval to continue its service.

Table 1–2 summarizes the most important characteristics of the four types of industry structures.

Development of the U.S. Economy

The United States has a fascinating business history. Business has significantly influenced customs, politics, and even family living. The historical development of the U.S. economy continues to affect the way business operates today.

Colonial Society

Colonial society was primarily agricultural—built on the products of its farms and plantations. The nation's prosperity depended on the success of its crops, and most people lived in rural areas. The cities—quite small in comparison to those of Europe—were the marketplaces and residences of craft workers, traders, bankers, and government officials.

But the real economic and political power of the nation was centered in rural areas. The population was tied to the land socially as well as economically. The colonies looked to England for manufactured products and capital with which to finance infant industries.

Even after the Revolutionary War (1776–1783), the United States maintained close economic relations with England. Indeed, British investors provided much of the money needed to finance the developing business system. This financial influence remained well into the nineteenth century.

The Industrial Revolution

The **Industrial Revolution** began in England around 1750–1775. The traditional manufacturing system of independent skilled workers individually pursuing their specialties was replaced by a factory system that mass-produced items by bringing large numbers of semiskilled workers together.

Industrial Revolution
The shift to a factory system of manufacturing that began in England around 1750–1775.

The factory system profited from savings that were created by large-scale production (for example, raw materials could often be purchased cheaper in large lots) and from the specialization of labor (each worker concentrated on one specific task or job). Production efficiency was improved substantially, and the factory system revolutionized business.

Influenced by the events occuring in England, the United States soon began its march toward becoming an industrialized nation. Agriculture became mechanized, and factories sprang up everywhere. But most business historians agree that real progress did not occur until railroads provided a fast, economical method of transporting the goods produced by businesses.

The rapid construction of railroad systems during the 1840s and 1850s was really the U.S.'s "industrial revolution." Not only did the railroads provide the necessary transportation system, they also created the need for greater quantities of lumber, steel, and real estate.

The Age of the Entrepreneur

The nineteenth century saw business make sizable advances in the United States. Eli Whitney introduced the concept of interchangeable parts, an idea that would later facilitate mass production. Peddlers,

The completion of railroads spanning the country in the 1850s marked the real beginning of the Industrial Revolution in the United States.

the salespeople of the day, operated throughout the country. Financiers became less dependent upon England, and the banking system became better established after some early problems. Inventors created a virtually endless array of commercially usable products.

People were encouraged to take risks and become entrepreneurs. Vanderbilt, Rockefeller, Morgan, and Carnegie—all became wealthy because of their willingness to take business risks during this period. Admittedly, some people were hurt by the speculation that characterized industry during the 1800s, but, on balance, the entrepreneurial spirit of the age did much to advance the business system and raise the standard of living.

Production Era

The early part of the twentieth century—the **production era**—was a period when business managers concentrated almost solely on the firm's production tasks. Industry was under considerable pressure to produce more and more to satisfy growing consumer demand and to correct product shortages.

Work assignments became increasingly specialized. Assembly lines, such as the one introduced by Henry Ford, became common. Owners turned over management responsibilities to a new class of managers, who specialized in operating established businesses rather than in starting new ones.

Marketing tended to be viewed strictly as selling. Fields like consumer research were not yet accepted by business. In other words, marketers were those individuals responsible for distribution after the production function had been performed. Business was internally oriented rather than consumer oriented.

production era
The early part of the twentieth century, when business managers concentrated almost solely on the firm's production tasks.

The Marketing Concept

The post-World War II era was influenced by an important new concept in management. The **marketing concept,** which became the prevalent business philosophy, advocated that all activities and functions of the organization be directed toward the identification and satisfaction of consumer wants. Thus, consumer orientation became the principal goal of companies.

New jobs sprang up throughout business organizations as marketing research departments began to analyze what the consumer would buy before the company produced the item. This concept was in marked contrast to the earlier philosophy of producing a product, then trying to sell it to the consumer. Advertising reached ever larger numbers of consumers and increased the efficiency of firms' promotional efforts. Today, firms must have a strong consumer orientation if they are to remain competitive in the marketplace.

marketing concept
A business philosophy advocating that all activities and functions of the organization be directed toward the identification and satisfaction of consumer wants.

The Current Business Era

Challenge after challenge has confronted business in recent years. Consumer critics have noted several failures in the economic system. Concern over large numbers of industrial accidents and illnesses has resulted in passage of federal legislation concerning occupational safety and health. Financial scandals have touched off public demand for greater government regulation of businesses' finances. Millions of people have been shocked by the ecological reports of environmentalists. Higher fuel costs have made energy-saving programs priority items at management meetings.

These challenges have produced several noticeable trends in the business world. Business has become more socially responsible; the impact on society of a business decision is now weighed in most management decision making. Business has become more conscious of its operating costs, particularly energy costs. More minorities and women have business careers today. Management continues to struggle with the problem of predicting and then reacting to new government regulations and requirements. Business has found new markets abroad (some in communist nations) but has encountered increasing competition from foreign producers at home. Writers may someday describe the current business era as one of the most challenging for the private enterprise system.

Alternative Economic Systems

Many people fail to realize that a large part of the world lives under economic systems other than capitalism. The number of countries with communist and socialist systems makes it important to learn the primary features of these alternative economies. The concern here is the economic aspects of socialism and communism; political questions are beyond the scope of this book.

Communism

communism
An economic theory, developed by Karl Marx, under which private property is eliminated and goods are owned in common.

Communist theory was the product of Karl Marx, a nineteenth century economist. Marx believed that the laboring classes were being exploited by capitalists (entrepreneurs and managers). He said that eventually there would be a class struggle, and a new form of society would emerge. Marx labeled his new order **communism.** He believed that the people should own all of a nation's productive capacity but conceded that the government would have to operate businesses until a classless society could evolve. He also adhered to the principle that people should receive according to their needs and give according to their abilities.

A perfect communist state does not exist, because even the Soviet Union and the People's Republic of China have managerial and professional classes, and because the government owns the means of production. The people, in turn, work for the government. There is no freedom of choice in terms of employment, purchases, or investments. The government plays a major role in determining what kinds of work people will do. It also decides what people can buy because it dictates what will be produced, and consumer goods generally rate a low priority. Workers are unable to invest in business enterprises because the government owns them all.

There is no such thing as profits under communism. And there is little or no reward for doing a job well. In the Soviet Union and the People's Republic of China, however, managers and workers are now beginning to receive some incentives for exceeding production quotas. But a promotion to a higher-level job usually still means taking on more responsibility without an increase in pay. Workers are denied the right to strike or to bargain for benefits. The 1980–1981 revolt of workers in Poland reflects continuing unrest within communist states.

FOCUS 1–4
Now Let Us All Laugh Comrades

Officially, as the Russians and their East European satellites see it, inflation is a disease unique to capitalism. "With the exception of the war years," triumphs Nikolai Glushkov, chaiman of the Soviet State Committee on Prices, "there has never been any inflation in the U. S. S. R., nor does any exist today . . ." Now . . . the East bloc, like the West, is suffering a severe dose of rapidly rising consumer prices. It is not called inflation but "an adjustment in the state pricing structure. . . ."

Since 1977 Russia has ordered four waves of price increases covering everything from books and cut glass to gasoline, plane fares and chocolate. . . . Soviet cars jumped 18% and carpets and restaurant meals rose 50%. Czechoslovakia lifted its rate for children's clothing, fuel, postage, and rents, while Hungary raised the price of bread, flour, sugar, and some meats by up to 50%. . . .

Buyers also suffer from hidden prices that the state slides in without fanfare. A product—for example, a $45 electric razor—suddenly might be given a new model number, a different color or a fresh package, and a new price: $58. . . .

Communists believe that centralized management of all productive activity results in less waste than the competition of free enterprise. They admit that a consumer's freedom of choice has to be sacrificed in the interest of production efficiency (see Focus 1–4). Capitalists counter with the argument that government-operated industries soon become inefficient bureaucracies because of a lack of employee incentive. Capitalists believe that competition promotes efficiency by providing incentive to achieve and by eliminating inefficient producers from the marketplace.

Socialism

socialism
An economic system that advocates government ownership and operation of all basic industries (with private ownership continuing to exist in smaller businesses).

Socialism is an economic system that exists in countries where the government owns and operates all the basic industries, such as banking, transportation, and large-scale manufacturing. Private ownership still exists in smaller businesses such as shops and restaurants. Socialists believe that major industries are too important to be left in private hands. They argue that government-owned industries are more efficient and serve the public better. Again, the capitalist counterargument is that state-run industries become massive bureaucracies that are insensitive to consumer needs.

Socialist economies usually follow some master plan for the use of the nation's resources. Workers are free to choose their employment, but the state often encourages people to go into areas where they are needed. As a result most citizens work for some government enterprise. And these government-owned enterprises are often rather inefficient and lacking in leadership. People in leadership positions usually change when new politicians come into office. Also, people are often placed in important jobs on the basis of personal friendship or as a reward for political help and not on the basis of ability to do the job.

Mixed Economies

mixed economies
Economies consisting of a mix of socialism and private enterprise.

The term **mixed economy,** which has become popular in recent years, is used to describe economies having a mix of socialism and free enterprise. Sweden and the United Kingdom are often given as examples of nations that have a traditional philosophy of private enterprise but that also have a high degree of government ownership. The United Kingdom's coal, steel, and communications industries are government enterprises.

Private enterprise proponents often classify these mixed economies as socialist because of the high degree of public ownership. But such countries still have a far greater degree of private ownership than is found in socialist nations. In fact, the United States might be considered a mixed economy in that some public utilities are government owned.

THE WALL STREET JOURNAL

"Capitalism is a failure, socialism is a failure, the welfare state has failed but martinis *never* fail."

One person's view of the world's major economic systems.

Cartoon Features Syndicate

A Comparative Note

Private enterprise has proved to be a very effective economic system for the United States and other countries. It has provided a high degree of economic freedom, a low cost of living, substantial product choice, high earnings, considerable public welfare, and many other economic benefits. The United States became a world power because of the private enterprise system and the businesses that operate within its framework.

Other economic systems aspire to the high levels already achieved by our business system. This is not to say that other systems are always wrong, but the vast majority of U.S. citizens are proud of U.S. business accomplishments and thoroughly support the continuation of the private enterprise system.

Big Business! Big Labor! Big Government!

The United States is the world's leading industrial power primarily because it has a highly developed system of business enterprise. Our leading firms are among the world's leading firms. Industry in the United States is extremely diversified. Thousands of business enterprises exist in nearly every conceivable commercial activity. Table 1–3 shows the number of firms in each of our major industries.

Business has given us the highest standard of living ever known in the world. We are offered a wide variety of high quality goods and services; more importantly, we have the purchasing power to obtain the benefits provided by such items. The size of our business system has affected other areas of society. Big business has created the need for big labor and big government. Today, economists and politicians refer to big business, big labor, and big government as the three **countervailing powers** in our nation. This means that the size and strength of each allows it to balance the economy so that no single sector will ever totally dominate the society. This unique situation is the leading characteristic of today's economy.

countervailing powers
Big business, big labor and big government are the countervailing powers that balance the economy so that no single sector will ever totally dominate the society.

TABLE 1–3
The Number of Firms in Major U.S. Industries

Industry	No. of Firms
Agriculture, forestry, and fishing	3,650,000
Mining	94,000
Construction	1,219,000
Manufacturing	467,000
Transportation and public utilities	443,000
Wholesale and retail trade	3,113,000
Finance, insurance, and real estate	1,686,000
Services	3,826,000

A later chapter will describe the tremendous growth of the U.S. labor movement. Government has also become big; in fact, many people believe it has become too big. The federal government now spends over $1.3 million every minute.[6]

Economic size also raises many complex social and ethical questions. While people generally are proud of the high standard of living produced by industry, many raise questions about its size: "How big is too big?" "Should General Motors be split into several corporations?" "Does Exxon's size allow it to be too profitable?" But the countervailing powers remain an effective balance, allowing the continued operation of the most productive and equitable economic system in the world.

The Study of Business: Why? And How?

Many people are actively involved in studying the U.S. business system. Senior business executives are constantly learning how to become more effective managers. Many consumers are examining how business decisions affect their daily lives. Many students are enrolled in business administration courses. With this much activity, it is fitting that attention be given to why and how people study business.

Why Study Business?

People study business for a number of reasons. Some plan a business career. Others want to learn how the business system affects them in their role of wage earner or consumer. Still others are curious about what business actually means. Certainly, business affects all of us in some manner; and the more we know about the subject, the better able we will be to cope with some of our most common everyday problems. Some specific reasons for studying business are given below.

Career selection. Most students do not spend adequate time in selecting their careers. Many drift from one curriculum to another and then from one kind of job to another. The study of business allows a student to consider various occupational possibilities. The bulk of career possibilities are in private industry, but many similar possibilities are available in government agencies and in other forms of public employment.

The study of business allows the student to consider various kinds of jobs—the work required, the available rewards, the necessary training, and the relative advantages and disadvantages of each. This text includes sections describing jobs that can be found in each major area of business. Chapter 25 is devoted entirely to careers in business. Employment trends, job sources, employment search strategies, resume preparation, and other useful topics are explored.

Self-employment. Some students will decide to work for themselves and establish their own businesses. Since most business concepts and principles are the same regardless of the size of the firm, studying business can be an invaluable first step in setting up a business.

Self-employed persons are actively and personally involved in business. A knowledge of successful business practices becomes even more crucial for those who risk their own funds. The solution—study business!

Tackling the problems of society. Business puts people on the firing line for most of today's pressing societal problems. Alternative energy sources, resource conservation, pollution, minority hiring and affirmative action programs, consumerism, and industrial safety are problems encountered on a daily basis by the business person.

A business career is likely to place an individual in a position of responsibility earlier than most other occupations. Many experts believe that business careers are an excellent choice for activists who want to improve their society.

Better consumer decisions. Business decisions create consumer decisions. A certain stereo comes with three options for accessory equipment. An executive decides to pass on a recent union wage increase to the consumer by raising a product's price. These are typical business decisions that call for related decision making by consumers.

The study of business provides an appreciation of the background for many consumer decisions. Consumer advocates often point out that an informed consumer is a better consumer.

Business is relevant. Students often argue that some fields of study simply are not relevant to life today. Perhaps this is so. But few students believe that business is not relevant. Regardless of opinions about business, executive behavior, and the private enterprise system, the study of business is the study of what is happening today. Business is probably one of the most relevant and fascinating subjects the student will ever study.

How to Study Business

Business can be studied through formal programs of instruction such as those offered at various colleges. These programs teach the basic concepts, methods, principles, and practices used in modern business. The formal study of business provides the framework for later experiences; together they build toward a well-rounded management education.

The study of business, or business administration as it is often called, has grown more formalized and systematic over the years. In the past, many managers achieved their positions on the basis of practical experience in a given area rather than through formal study. But times have changed, and formal education in business has become a recognized early step to a business career. Business leaders of earlier decades would be amazed to see the modern classrooms and instructional methods used by contemporary business students.

The study of business has become one of the most popular programs at colleges and universities. More and more students want to enter this challenging career field.

Business programs are usually organized around functional areas. Typically, courses are offered in such subjects as accounting, finance, management, personnel, marketing, sales, and data processing. Most business programs require students to take at least one course in each major area of study.

This book, combined with an introductory business course, will give the student a broad overview of the field of business. The information acquired here will allow for a better selection of business courses in the future.

While students can learn the basics of business in a classroom setting, it is impossible to learn all that is needed in this manner. Informal study—reading and various job-related experiences—can further a business education. Meaningful part-time and summer work experiences can be invaluable. Internships, study tours, visits to manufacturers, and the like are also vital. Serious business students should pursue knowledge through extensive reading of authoritative sources such as the *Wall Street Journal, Business Week, Fortune,* and *Forbes.* Much can be learned outside the classroom.

A Diagram of Contemporary Business

It is helpful to visualize contemporary business as a system designed to satisfy the needs of society. Business continues to function only if it achieves consumer acceptance for its products. Firms that fail in this objective soon disappear from the marketplace.

Figure 1–2 is a simplified diagram of contemporary business; it shows that a business's objective is to make a profit by serving the needs of its markets. The manager has several variables to control in operating the firm. These variables, the **five Ms,** are manpower, ma-

five Ms
The basic resources of any firm—manpower, materials, money, machinery, and management.

FIGURE 1-2
A diagram of contemporary business: a business's objective is to make a profit by serving the needs of its markets.

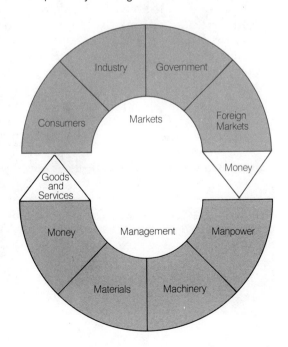

Controversial Issue

Should International Trade Be Used as a Political Weapon?: The U.S.-U.S.S.R Case

On January 4, 1980, then President Jimmy Carter cut off U.S. shipments of grain and high technology to the Soviet Union after its invasion of Afghanistan. Nearly one year later, on December 23, John R. Block, then the Secretary of Agriculture designate, said that food was America's greatest diplomatic weapon.

The use of international trade as a political weapon is not new to the Carter or Reagan administrations. Economic trade sanctions have been part of U.S. foreign policy since the War of 1812 and show no sign of becoming less popular today. But do they work? Or are they an obsolete and in some ways self-defeating weapon that should be packed in mothballs along with old Sherman tanks and propeller-driven fighter bombers?

To find the answer, one must first understand why the United States has turned to economic trade sanctions to influence world affairs. According to Princeton University Professor Robert Gilpin, historically, the United States found itself in an uneven relationship with other countries. They wanted more of our exportable goods such as wheat and high technology than we wanted of theirs. As a monopolistic power in foreign trade, we controlled vital world resources, and any boycott almost certainly had a meaningful effect on foreign affairs.

Opponents of trade embargoes argue that today the situation has all but reversed itself. Instead of powerful weapons of coercion against transgressing nations, trade sanctions are little more than symbolic acts. Toppled from our singular role as supplier to the world, we are now one of many with resources to spare. If we cut off a country's order of grain, others will be waiting to supply its needs. Opponents also point out that food helps create an economic interdependence between the U.S. and other nations, which makes war less likely.

It is of little surprise then that the U.S. grain and technology boycott of the Soviet Union has failed. The 17 million tons of grain we refused to send the Soviets in 1980 may serve only to raise the price the average Soviet citizen must pay for bread. It will not stop the Soviets from buying all the grain they need from other suppliers including Argentina, Canada, and Brazil. Likewise, the Soviets have suffered little from our high technology ban. They have obtained what they want of our products from such NATO allies as Italy and France.

Embargo advocates contend that food is a major bargaining tool that can bring about changes in foreign policy. They argue that the Soviet presence in Afghanistan is incompatible with world peace and that a food embargo may influence future Soviet actions. In addition, supporters argue that the ban has cost the Soviets a lot. In 1980 alone, says the Defense Intelligence Agency, the U.S.S.R. had to pay an additional $1 billion to obtain products from other foreign sources. The shortfall in feed grains has also caused the Soviets to use even more of their scarce foreign currencies to import meat from western producers. Supporters lament the fact that the embargo's power was reduced by our allies who transshipped American grain to the Soviets. In their view, had there been a determined, unified effort, the Soviets would have suffered far more for their foreign transgressions.

The fact that for the most part we stand alone in the world in our trade boycotts is a major reason for their failure. Our European and Japanese allies believe that symbolic acts of this kind are meaningless. "And," says Princeton professor Henry Bienen, "even if you get Canada and Australia and Brazil and Argentina to agree not to ship directly to the Soviet Union, there's nothing that says they can't ship to Czechoslovakia or Poland who then can ship to the Soviet Union."

With these harsh realities staring us in the face, we must reconcile our internal political need to use economic sanctions as a statement of American strength and determination with our need to export an increasing amount of goods. We cannot at one and the same time extend the use of trade sanctions to include acts of aggression such as the Soviet invasion of Afghanistan, human rights abuses, and terrorist activity and hope to maintain our balance of trade throughout the world. Although the embargo may make a symbolic impact against Soviet aggression, it has also had a financial impact on U.S. farmers, grain traders, and industrial exporters who have lost money.

The arguments for and against using trade as a political weapon boil down to one question: can the impact of cutting off trade to transgressing nations bring about a change in their policies or is it a futile effort that will increase tension? President Ronald Reagan skirted this question when he ordered an end to the Soviet grain embargo. He did, however, retain the option of reinstituting an embargo again if he deemed it necessary.

terials, money, machinery, and management.[7] The manager combines them into a proper mix to produce goods and services that satisfy markets.

There are four major markets for the products of industry—consumers, industry, government, and foreign markets. Some businesses serve all four markets; others serve only one or a few. In any case, the provision of satisfactory goods and services to the markets means that the firm will receive funds necessary to operate the business, pay its taxes, and perhaps earn a profit.

The diagram will be used throughout the text. As each part of the business organization is studied, it will be useful to relate it to the model shown here. This will clarify the complex but exciting world of business.

Summary

Business comprises all profit-seeking activities and enterprises that provide goods and services necessary to an economic system. U.S. businesses are part of a private enterprise system in which success is determined by competition among firms. An entrepreneur is a risk taker in this type of economic system. Profits are the rewards for a successful entrepreneur.

Certain basic rights are available to citizens living in a free enterprise economy: the right to private property; the legal and ethical right to any profits that might result from an enterprise; the freedom of choice in purchases, employment, and investments; and the right to set ground rules for competitive activity.

Four factors of production provide the necessary inputs for the operation of private enterprise: natural resources, labor, capital, and entrepreneurship. Each factor receives a payment, such as rent, wages, interest, or profits.

These four factors also contribute to productivity—a measure of the efficiency of production. Productivity relates to the amount of goods or services a worker produces in a given period of time. The availability of necessary resources and capital is also an important factor. The U.S. productivity rate has been declining in recent years.

The four basic types of competition are perfect competition, monopolistic competition, oligopoly, and monopoly. The development of the current U.S. economy has been influenced by colonial society, the Industrial Revolution, the age of the entrepreneur, the production era, and the post-World War II marketing concept.

Many U.S. citizens fail to realize that a large part of the world lives under economic systems other than capitalism—primarily communism, socialism, and mixed economies.

Large-scale business dominates many aspects of American industry. Leading U.S. firms are among the world's largest companies. But big business has also led to the development of big labor and big government. As a result, economic size has become a crucial public issue.

Following are several reasons why the study of business is important:

1. It assists in career selection.
2. It gives opportunities for self-employment.
3. It tackles the problems of society.
4. It leads to better consumer decisions.
5. It is one of the most relevant studies in contemporary society.

The study of business often begins in a classroom and continues in a less formal manner in the world of business.

A simple diagram shows how the five *M*s of business can be used to reach the four major markets—consumers, industry, government, and foreign markets.

Key Terms

business
profit
private enterprise system
competition
entrepreneur
capitalism
invisible hand of competition
antitrust laws
private property
factors of production
natural resources
labor
capital
entrepreneurship

productivity
perfect competition
law of supply and demand
monopolistic competition
oligopoly
monopoly
Industrial Revolution
production era
marketing concept
communism
socialism
mixed economies
countervailing powers
five *M*s

Review Questions

1. Explain each of the terms listed on the previous page.

2. Comment on this statement: All businesses must serve their customers in some way if they are to survive.

3. Explain the entrepreneur's role in the private enterprise system.

4. Outline the basic rights that exist in the private enterprise system.

5. Describe the four factors of production, and explain what productivity is and why it is a problem in the U.S. today.

6. The four basic types of competition are perfect competition, monopolistic competition, oligopoly, and monopoly. Match these types with the businesses listed below:
   a. Consolidated Edison, New York's electric utility
   b. J. C. Penney
   c. American Motors
   d. Harold Clawson's 640-acre farm in southern Iowa

7. Trace the historical development of the American economy.

8. Describe the three alternative economic systems discussed in this chapter.

9. List some specific reasons for studying business.

10. Explain the diagram of contemporary business that appears in this chapter.

Discussion Questions and Exercises

1. Evaluate the pros and cons of the controversial issue that appears in this chapter.

2. Make a list of all the businesses that serve students on your campus. Then prepare a brief evaluation of how effectively they serve their customers.

3. Prepare a short report on a person who has influenced the development of the U.S. business system.

4. Explain how government can help improve the private enterprise system.

5. Set up a panel discussion of instructors and advanced students to explain the business curriculum at your school.

Case 1-1: Pennwalt Corporation Talks About the Right to Fail

Most introductory discussions of contemporary business focus on the tremendous opportunities available in the private enterprise system. Chapter 1 has cited Frank Jarecki, The Coca-Cola Co., and John D. MacArthur as examples of success within our economic system. But remember that the chapter began with the story of the World Football League, a business failure.

The private enterprise system does not guarantee rewards to any person or business venture. It simply provides the opportunity to succeed or fail. This free market system is supported by Reginald Jones, former chairman of General Electric, who remarked, "One of the aspects of the free enterprise system is that you should be allowed to succeed, and you should also be allowed to fail."[8]

A similar viewpoint is expressed in an advertisement run by Pennwalt Corporation (see page 34) in which Pennwalt notes the vitality of the private enterprise system: ". . . for every eight businesses that close, ten new businesses open."

Questions

1. Can you identify some top executives who might disagree with the view expressed by Reginald Jones? Why would they hold differing views?

2. Do you agree with the basic theme of the Pennwalt Corporation advertisement? Why or why not?

3. Are there any instances when the government should guarantee the continuation of an otherwise failing business? Discuss.

Case 1-2: The American Productivity Center

Chapter 1 has noted that the United States is now lagging behind in increases in productivity, the accepted measure of efficiency of pro-

The only way to make sure business survives is to make sure some businesses can fail.

Every time a business opens there's a chance it will fail.

That may seem tragic, especially if the failure affects your life.

But the alternative—government intervention to keep failing businesses afloat—is even worse. For then the public will often just continue to endure inferior products or services.

Being free to take risks in order to earn rewards is what keeps the competitive enterprise system enterprising.

At Pennwalt, we've been enterprising enough to know what risk and reward is.

In the early 60's, while we were still basically a chemical company, we decided to enter several emerging markets that we thought would later become important. Among them: environmental cleanup, health care and plastics.

First we acquired the Sharples

Centrifuge Company, a pioneer in pollution control equipment. A few years later, conservation became a major political and social issue.

Our plan to enter the health care market was advanced when we purchased the S.S. White Dental Company. This, coupled with Wallace & Tiernan's well respected pharmaceutical division, gave us a foothold in one of the fastest growing segments of the economy, not only in America, but worldwide.

When we entered the plastics business, we took a double risk. We not only bought F. J. Stokes, a plastics molding machine company; we also introduced our own high performance plastic resins—Kynar 500® and Tetran®.

In each of these ventures, there were risks. And indeed, Tetran was a failure. But, overall,

the rewards were substantial enough to make the risks worth taking.

Our sales since 1962 have increased more than eightfold. And all the companies we purchased have grown much faster than they had been growing before we acquired them.

Our diversification program could have failed, of course. But isn't it better to be faced with the possibility of failure than to be faced with no possibilities at all?

Apparently, much of America feels the same way.

Because for every eight businesses that close, ten new businesses open.

To learn more about us, send for our "Pennwalt Products & Markets" brochure. Write to: Pennwalt Corporation, Box 102, Three Parkway, Philadelphia, Pa. 19102.

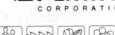

For 129 years, we've been making things people need—including profits.

duction. Productivity can be defined in terms of the amount of goods and services a worker produces in a given period of time. It is what allows people to receive real wage increases, those that exceed the cost of living.

The American Productivity Center of Houston, Texas is a non-profit organization whose objective is to improve the productivity of U.S. industry. It was founded in 1977 by C. Jackson Grayson, the former Dean of the Business School at Southern Methodist University. Grayson headed the Federal Price Commission, the agency responsible for wage and price controls during the administration of President Richard M. Nixon.

After working with wage and price controls, Grayson became convinced that government decrees to hold down prices were ineffective. He also found that 34 nations had national productivity centers. Grayson decided to create a similar group in the United States.

Some $10 million was contributed by 75 separate corporations to get the American Productivity Center started. The center's primary activities are to:

1. Publicize the importance of productivity.
2. Study the concept of productivity and ways to improve it.
3. Develop an adequate measure of productivity.
4. Devise methods by which an industry's or company's productivity potential can be assessed.
5. Provide programs that companies can use for meeting productivity targets.
6. Instill management-labor cooperation so as to improve industrial productivity.
7. Develop ways to make people more efficient in their jobs.

Grayson explains his goals this way: "World records show that the market system, with its sense of private property and capitalism, is more productive than any other system tried by mankind because it encourages and rewards individual initiative . . . . Working together we can get America going again."

Questions

1. Assume you are a worker who annually receives a cost of living adjustment. Why should you be concerned about the concept of productivity?

2. Assume that you head the American Productivity Center. In what areas would you want to concentrate your efforts?

3. What role should the government play in the battle to increase the productivity of American Industry?

2

Societal Issues and Business

Learning Goals

1. To explain how contemporary business faces a dynamic societal environment that is often difficult to predict

2. To explain the concept of societal responsibility as an accepted business policy

3. To describe the major societal issues confronting business: inflation, people-oriented management, ecology and environmental protection, consumerism, and the energy crisis

4. To analyze the ethical questions facing management in its relations with consumers, with other company personnel, with business associates, and with investors and the financial community

5. To explain the meaning of each of the key terms introduced in this chapter

Profile: George Johnson
Putting Social Responsibility into Action

Being a black businessperson is as important to George E. Johnson as increasing sales and company profits. It enables him to help improve the economic and social clout of the black community by aiding other black businesspeople.

Johnson, who is the founder and president of Johnson Products Company, manufacturers of hair products and cosmetics for the black consumer, has taken the idea of black self-interest and made it an integral part of his business. Without black business, Johnson feels, blacks are doomed to remain bottom- and middle-level workers and consumers, who are not going to have any clout unless they work together. With that goal in mind Johnson believes in producing high-quality products to replace the crude formulas that were once all that were available to black consumers. He also has put into operation a business assistance plan to help his hair salon clientele.

Johnson, who is the grandson of a Mississippi sharecropper, began his beauty products business in 1954 with a total capitalization of $500, $250 of which was borrowed from a commercial finance company, and a formula to manufacture an improved hair straightener for blacks. Over the years, Johnson built a line of 38 personal care products, including the company's leading product Ultra Sheen No-Base hair relaxer—the first formula to use a protective cream to shield the scalp from harmful chemicals.

As the nation's third largest black-owned business, Johnson Products has long been a leader in its field. One of the reasons is Johnson's insistence on quality to meet the needs of the black consumer who is quality oriented and full-service minded. Johnson feels a strong obligation to measure up to the standards of those his company serves.

With the introduction in 1980 of a new patented hair relaxer—Ultra Sheen Precise Conditioning Relaxer—Johnson took his philosophy of black excellence along with product information and a unique business management program to his immediate public—the thousands of black beauty salon owners across the country. Aware that black-owned salons were rapidly losing business to white-owned chains courting black women and that 80 to 90 percent of black salon owners had no training in basic business management skills, Johnson believed that it was in his company's and the black community's best interest to provide sorely needed financial, legal, and business advice to help black hairstylists beat the competition.

In a series of 100 all-day seminars held in cities throughout the United States and Canada, company financial experts helped approximately 25,000 black beauticians learn the basic financial and legal tools of running a business. Johnson Products' Grayson Mitchell explained the goals of these seminars. "We've always had product information seminars, but this time we decided to devote half the day to such business skills as pricing, advertising, inventory control, insurance, and bookkeeping. It was a great success."

Helping black beauty salons achieve success is surely in Johnson Products' best interest. According to Mitchell, it's Johnson Products' way of being a socially responsible firm.

I have no complex about wealth. I have worked hard for my money, producing things that people need. I believe that the able business leader who creates wealth and employment is more worthy of historical notice than politicians or soldiers.

—J. Paul Getty

The management of League General, the automobile insurance affiliate of the Michigan Credit Union League, recently decided to offer free children's car seats to its policyholders. The company gave out thousands of the seats, which were designed to protect small children in an automobile accident. Each car seat cost League General nearly $40, but the firm calculated that reduced claims more than paid for the program. In addition, the National Highway Safety Administration gave League General its highest public service award in recognition of its efforts to promote car safety for children.[1]

The concept of **social responsibility** refers to management's consideration of the social as well as economic effects of its decisions. It applies to all businesses regardless of size, location, or industry. Social responsibility is an important part of contemporary business. League General's experience provides an excellent example of how a socially responsible decision can pay off, and clearly illustrates that being socially responsible is also good business!

social responsibility
Consideration by management of social as well as economic effects inits decision making.

Social Responsibility Questions Facing Business

Social responsibility has become a popular term in today's business vocabulary. Society is calling on private enterprise to be more socially conscious and to adopt a higher level of management ethics. Production managers are asked to make assembly-line jobs more meaningful. Personnel officers have been called on to revise many of their procedures.

Retail executives are questioned about their store policies in low-income areas. And credit departments have to answer charges concerning the invasion of personal privacy.

All organizational levels must deal with these kinds of vital questions. Middle managers, production managers, district sales managers, and staff personnel must all be involved in a company-wide effort to raise the firm's level of business ethics and corporate responsibility.

Most companies have adopted social responsibility as the proper business philosophy. It has become standard corporate policy. But its acceptance at this level does not mean that it is always practiced. A divergence between policy and practice is common in modern business. It can best be overcome by assuring that every policy adopted also contains a set of procedures for putting it into practice.

And once a program is put into operation, there must also be provisions for evaluating its results on a continuing and regular basis. New technology, new laws, and new ideas and attitudes present business with an environment that is often difficult to predict (see Focus 2–1).

It is essential for the businessperson to realize that public outcry for increased social responsibility will not disappear. When industry fails to respond to the challenge posed by society, the public will is typically enforced through other means, namely the government. Some children's toys have been banned because of their dangerous features. And government now regulates the type of information that can be requested on job applications. Intelligent managers realize the need for self-regulation by industry. It has become a prerequisite for corporate survival!

How Can We Evaluate Social Performance?

While critics demand higher levels of social responsibility for business, management is faced with the dual problems of implementation and evaluation. The implementation of socially oriented objectives requires a careful analysis to determine whether the benefits deriving from the action exceed the cost. A current public debate centers on whether the United States should strive for completely safe work and living environments. Many argue that such goals are unobtainable and that the related costs are prohibitive.

Business also faces the question of how to evaluate a firm's social performance. Critics readily point out that the private enterprise system is oriented toward quantity, not quality. In other words, modern society tends to confuse new houses, automobiles, dishwashers, vacation cottages, and the like with the true quality of life, however that is defined.

Historically, methods of evaluating social performance were usually based on the firm's contribution to national output and the provision of employment opportunities. Items such as weekly wage payments were often used as crude measures of social performance. However, such methods ignore the other areas of business responsibility—industrial safety, assembly-line drudgery, product safety, minority hiring, affirmative action, and pollution. Industry has tradition-

FOCUS 2–1
The Reserve Mining Company

The Silver Bay, Minnesota, plant of the Reserve Mining Company was opened in 1955 to provide its owners, Armco Steel Corporation and Republic Steel Corporation, with a supply of iron ore pellets for their blast furnaces. The iron, obtained from a rock known as taconite, is rolled into pellets. The extraction process creates 67,000 tons of waste rock each day.

When the plant opened, both state and federal authorities had approved Reserve's plan to dispose of waste rock in Lake Superior. Several of Reserve's competitors sent their managers through the plant to view its modern dust controls. Reserve also had built Silver Bay as a model community. The bulk of its inhabitants are dependent upon the company for their livelihoods.

Silver Bay's tranquility was suddenly disrupted in April 1974, 27 years later, when a U.S. district judge ordered the plant closed as a health hazard. Minnesota and federal authorities had charged that Reserve was polluting Lake Superior with its waste rock and the air with its dust emissions. There were fears that the waste rock and dust contained asbestos-like particles that might cause cancer. Balanced against these fears was the fear of loss of 3,000 jobs and a $350 million capital investment.

The case was reviewed, and the litigation dragged on for several years. Reserve remained open as the legal battles ensued. Divorce, alcoholism, and tension were commonplace in Silver Bay, a town most people considered doomed. The courts finally announced a decision in 1977 whereby Reserve would continue to operate while developing an inland disposal site at a cost of $370 million, more than the original cost of constructing the plant. A 50 percent rise in the price of iron ore pellets contributed significantly to Reserve's acceptance of the plan. The new disposal site opened in 1980. The tailings are now transferred via rail and pipeline to a six-square-mile basin where they are dropped into ten feet of water, a procedure designed to prevent the spread of the asbestos-like dust. Silver Bay and Reserve Mining were saved, but the difficult questions the case posed for both society and business remain.

The Reserve Mining Company case has become a classic example of how societal influences can affect business behavior. *The Wall Street Journal* summarized the case this way:

> By any yardstick, it is a milestone in the changing environment in which U.S. industry operates these days—a classic illustration of how shifting public opinion, changing laws and new scientific discoveries can make a plant that is perfectly acceptable today an outlawed despoiler of the environment and a threat to public health only a few years down the road.[2]

ally been unable to answer its critics because it has lacked adequate measures of social performance.

Some companies are now developing means of assessing social responsibility. General Motors, for example, publishes an annual *Public Interest Report* that outlines the corporation's accomplishments in areas such as improved fuel efficiency, minority contracting, vehicle safety, studying alternative fuels, quality of work life, industrial pollution control, and substance-abuse recovery programs for employees.[3] No generally accepted format has emerged, but the work is encouraging. Environmental, church, and public interest groups are also attempting to create measures of corporate performance. And it is important that this development continue and accelerate in the future. Accomplishing meaningful social goals may be retarded by the lack of an adequate evaluation system for corporate social performance.

What Are the Societal Issues Facing Business?

Business today is confronted with five major groups of societal issues: inflation, people-oriented management, ecology and environmental protection, consumerism, and the energy crisis. Nearly all specific societal questions fall into one of these general areas. Some issues are interrelated. The energy crisis, for example, has led to concern over the use of petroleum resources, but it also has raised important consumer, ecological, and inflation issues.

Inflation: A Contemporary Business Issue

Inflation can be defined in terms of either rising prices or the decreasing purchasing power of a nation's currency. Inflation has often been a critical economic problem for both consumers and businesses. The two traditional types of inflation are demand-pull and cost-push. **Demand-pull inflation** occurs when there is too much money relative to products available. In other words, if consumer demand for a product is greater than its supply, the price of the item will tend to go up. **Cost-push inflation** results from rising costs (labor, raw materials, interest rates, and the like) that are passed on to the consumer.

A Historical Perspective

Consider the situation in post-World War I Europe. Both victors and losers suffered the agony of unprecedented inflation. In Austria and Hungary the currency fell to a 15,000th of its former worth, and in Poland it fell to a 2,000,000th of its prewar value. The Soviet Union's currency dropped to a 50,000,000,000th of its former value. But the

inflation
A decrease in the purchasing power of a nation's currency, often defined in terms of rising prices.

demand-pull inflation
A rise in prices caused when consumer demand for a product exceeds its supply.

cost-push inflation
Results when a rise in operating costs is passed along to the consumer.

ZIGGY

..TODAY YOU CAN BUY ANYTHING YOU WANT ON THE EXCUSE OF BUYING IT BEFORE THE PRICE GOES UP...

...IF YOU CAN AFFORD IT !!

©1980 Universal Press Syndicate

Inflation is a major, ongoing problem for everyone—businesses, and consumers alike.

greatest inflation hit Germany, where the amount of money in circulation reached hundreds of trillions of marks. And because German industry and agriculture were unable to provide the food and other goods that people needed, prices skyrocketed. Consider these German prices: one egg for 80,000,000,000 marks, one match for 900,000,000 marks, and one newspaper for 2,000,000,000 marks. When the German mark reached an unbelievable 1,000,000,000,000th of its prewar value, the government finally took measures to stabilize its worth.[4] Although the current situation has not reached these proportions, inflation is a serious economic problem throughout the modern world.

A Current Perspective

Compared to the German and Hungarian examples cited above, price rises of recent years seem miniscule. Yet inflation remains a major problem for the United States and the rest of the world. To put the situation into perspective, let's assume inflation in the United States was to continue at a double-digit rate of say, 13 percent. By 1990 a ticket to a first-run movie would cost $17; the average U.S. car, $29,700; a stamp, 50 cents; a pound of bacon, $6.00; and a gallon of gasoline, $4.00. In addition, McDonald's would be selling its Quarter Pounder with cheese for $5.00 and a milk shake for $2.55.[5]

The problem of inflation in the United States is complicated by the problem of unemployment. The relatively high level of unemployment means that many people do not have much money to spend. At the same time, rapid inflation is eating away at the purchasing power of earnings and savings. Cost pressures have forced prices up, even though demand has decreased. This has caused significant problems for the business community as well as for consumers. Economists now use the term **stagflation** to describe the dual economic problem of high unemployment and a rapidly rising price level.

stagflation
The dual economic problem of high unemployment and a rapidly rising price level.

Unfortunately, few people can agree on the causes of inflation. One recent study found that Americans considered too much government spending as the primary cause of inflation. It was followed by labor demands, energy costs, business profits, and excessive government regulations.[6]

Consumer Responses to Inflation

Rising consumer prices have forced people to make a number of changes in their daily lives. Soybeans became popular as meat extenders when meat prices went to record levels. High housing costs have forced many people to seek alternatives to single-family homes. Some housing experts now believe that single-family units will make up only one-third of all housing starts by 1990.[7] Many people see borrowing as a means of countering inflation. Others argue that they should buy things now, because prices will be 10 to 20 percent higher next year. The increased use of credit has created even more economic problems, including a high rate of bankruptcy.[8]

Inflation calls for adjustments on the part of consumers, who for the most part have reacted sensibly and blunted its worst effects. People have cut expenses where possible, and many have delayed purchases. They have also begun to take direct action where they see pricing abuses. For instance, consumer boycotts of various products and sellers became commonplace during the past decade. But producers have also boycotted the marketplace. Farmers, for example, have tied up traffic in several cities with their slow-moving tractors in an effort to get higher prices for their products.

Management Responses to Inflation

Businesspeople must also deal with the rising price spiral. Higher costs must be absorbed or passed on to the consumer in the form of higher prices. Management has had to adopt innovative responses to the problems of inflation and tight budgets. Eastern Airlines eliminated 300 telephone lines at its Miami headquarters. Richmond's A. H. Robbins Company decided to wash the firm's windows only half as frequently as in the past. Hardee Food Systems put one of its corporate airplanes up for sale. Deseret Pharmaceutical ordered its division managers to fly coach class rather than first class on plane trips. Glen Gery Corporation of Reading, Pennsylvania, now gives 12-pound instead of 16-pound turkeys to its employees at Christmas. And Virginia Electric & Power Company cut costs by turning off its Muzak system.[9]

Inflation does not have a negative impact on all firms. American Greeting's Corporation reports many consumers are turning to expensive greeting cards—some costing up to $5.00—in place of gifts. Discount stores, do-it-yourself kits, energy-saving items, secondhand outlets, and generic drugs all do well in an inflationary economy.[10] Consumers are adapting to inflation, and businesses must make similar adaptations to remain in operation.

People-oriented Management

Business executives must strive to maintain a people-oriented philosophy of management. The daily press of commercial activity often makes it easier to deal with numbers, organization charts, interoffice memos, and administrative procedures. But industry is not the only segment of society that should pay greater attention to people. Complaints about government employees are also commonplace. U.S. Senator Howard Metzenbaum of Ohio put it this way: "My major complaint is that most bureaucrats forget there is a real, live, usually hurting, human being waiting out there for what is his right."[11] Insensitivity to human needs is a critical problem in nearly all organizations; yet, a humanistic approach to management is always good business, regardless of the industry.

The special needs of some people have been neglected. The physically handicapped have had to overcome some managerial barriers in order to achieve occupational dignity. Individuals who have served time in jails or prisons need jobs that will keep them from returning to criminal activity. Coal miners are often affected by "black lung," an occupational disease of their industry.

These situations reflect dissatisfaction on the part of people involved in or affected by business organizations. Such people argue that business has been too concerned about short-run profitability, machinery, evaluation, and control of corporate personnel and not concerned enough about the people involved. One of the aims of social responsibility is the achievement of a new concept of management that will take into account people-oriented concerns.

Workers are more productive when they have a sense of participation in the decisions affecting them. Human resource development has thus become a major organizational objective for many businesses. West German firms have labor representation on management boards. Swedish automobile manufacturers have pioneered the concept of job enrichment for assembly line workers. American companies have substantially upgraded their equal opportunity employment and affirmative action hiring programs.

People-oriented management requires a careful balance between productivity and profitability objectives on the one hand and employee desires on the other. Is the four-day workweek (four working days of ten hours each) as productive as the traditional five-day, forty-hour workweek? This is the type of question that must be answered by management. Several human relations questions will be discussed in detail later in the book.

Ecology and Environmental Protection

Reserve Mining's story (Focus 2–1) shows what a vital issue ecology and environmental protection can be in modern business. **Ecology**—the relationship between people and their environment—is an important managerial consideration from a legal as well as a societal viewpoint.

ecology
The relationship between people and their environment.

Nearly everyone accepts the premise that we should maintain an ecologically sound environment. But the achievement of this goal requires trade-offs that we are not always willing to make. For example, although we fear the oil spill danger of supertankers, we insist upon readily available supplies of gasoline at reasonable prices. Coal-burning boilers were once converted to oil-using furnaces in order to cut air pollution. But coal is relatively plentiful in the United States, so now some plants are switching back to it.

Ecological goals are important. However, the real issue is whether we can coordinate these goals with other societal and economic objectives. No clear consensus has emerged on this matter.

Pollution—the tainting or destroying of a natural environment—is the major ecological problem today. We are constantly being reminded of the dangers of water and air pollution. Automobiles now have elaborate emission control devices. Smoke-belching factories are fined by environmental protection authorities. Municipal water and sewer treatment systems are being improved.

pollution
The tainting or destroying of a natural environment.

Society faces two major questions about pollution. One is whether the benefits of cleaning up any particular form of pollution are worth the costs involved. The other is whether we are willing to pay now for a future ecological benefit. While most of us recognize the current pollution problems, our willingness to pay for corrections is sometimes doubtful. Gulf Oil, for example, had to withdraw unleaded gasoline when it first appeared because of low sales.

Disposable packaging (such as throwaway plastic bottles) has created a major ecological problem. Trash of this type continues to pile up, showing an amazing resistance to decomposition. Some states have taken action to reduce accumulations of trash. Several have passed legislation requiring deposits on soft drink and beer bottles. But the most logical approach, recycling, remains underutilized. It has been estimated that **recycling**—the reprocessing of used materials for reuse—could provide two-fifths of the materials required in our man-

recycling
The reprocessing of used materials for reuse.

Air and water pollution are major ecological problems today.

ufacturing sector.[12] While the recycling concept has received considerable public support, a comprehensive system has yet to be implemented. The basic question "Who is going to pay for it?" remains unanswered.

Consumerism

consumerism
The demand that businesses give proper consideration to consumer wants and needs in making their decisions.

Consumer demands are another pressing issue facing business. Businesspeople often see the consumer as unpredictable, emotional, and sometimes irrational. Certainly, some consumer demands are unusual and unexpected. For example, the Royal National Institute for the Blind once reported a demand by blind British men for "girlie" magazines printed in Braille.[13] But most of the time consumer demands are not so unusual.

Consumerism—the demand that businesses give proper consideration to consumer wants and needs in making their decisions—has become a major social and economic movement within the United States and other industralized nations. Ralph Nader has been a leading contributor to this movement. His book *Unsafe at Any Speed* was one of many consumer criticisms leveled against industry. Some were justified; others were not.

Since the emergence of consumerism in the 1960s, consumer groups have sprung up throughout the country. Some concentrate on an isolated problem such as excessive pricing by a local service industry, while others are more broadly based. The net effect has been the passage of consumer protection laws covering everything from unethical sales practices to the licensing of persons in the repair business. There is little doubt that more consumer protection laws will be passed in the years ahead, and business would be well advised to heed the warnings of the consumerism movement.

An excellent description of consumer rights was put forth by President John F. Kennedy in 1962:

1. The consumer has the right to safety.
2. The consumer has the right to be informed.
3. The consumer has the right to choose.
4. The consumer has the right to be heard.[14]

Much of the post-1962 consumer legislation has been based on these rights. They are an excellent set of guidelines for business to use in assessing various consumer demands.

In fact, many companies have gone to considerable effort to assure that consumer complaints are given a full hearing. Ford Motor Company, for example, has set up a Consumer Appeals Board to resolve service complaints.

Energy: A Contemporary Business Challenge

Olympia Brewing is making a unique contribution to solving America's energy crisis. Olympia built a $6.5 million plant to produce ethanol—the grain alcohol used in gasohol—from spilled beer and other fermentable wastes. Olympia's spilled beer creates seven million gallons of gasohol annually. The brewer's decision to produce ethanol not only helps alleviate the nation's energy problem; it also has struck a blow for ecology. The new plant has cut the sewage discharge of some wastes by 70 percent.[15]

The **energy crisis** refers to the world's diminished ability to provide for its current and future energy needs. The U.S. energy demand will grow by over 25 percent during 1980–2000. Approximately 42 percent of this energy will come from natural gas and oil in the year 2000, down from 75 percent in 1980. In the year 2000, synfuels (synthetic fuels made from either coal or shale oil) are expected to account for 8 percent of our energy supplies. Also during 1980–2000, coal use is expected to rise from 18 percent to 33 percent, nuclear from 3 percent to 12 percent, and hydropower and geothermal from 4 percent to 5 percent.[16]

energy crisis
The world's diminished ability to provide for its current and future energy needs.

The Impact on Business

The energy crisis has had an enormous impact on business. Consider the case of Detroit Diesel Allison, a division of General Motors. Sales of engines for trucks and construction equipment declined when fuel costs went up, but demand for diesel and gas turbine engines used on oil rigs increased. Detroit Diesel Allison has also benefited from the increased demand for its helicopter engines used in the aircraft carrying workers to and from ocean drilling platforms.[17]

The energy crisis has had a significant effect on the travel, lodging, and automobile industries. Many of these industries have experienced a sharp decline in the demand for their products. But businesses have also been affected in other ways. All firms have felt pressure to curtail their own use of energy. Even office temperatures have been lowered by federal mandate. Virtually all major energy users have instituted programs to cut energy usage and, thus, moderate the tremendous escalation of the costs involved.

Components of the Energy Problem

conservation
The preservation of declining energy resources.

Energy is certainly a complex societal issue. The problem can be divided into its short-run and long-run components. In the short run, the issue is one of **conservation**—the preservation of declining energy resources. A myriad of conservation programs have been proposed or implemented, including fuel oil allocation plans, contingency rationing schemes, shorter workweeks, voluntary energy cuts by industry, and the 55-mile-per-hour speed limit. The success of these plans has been mixed. Some programs have not been as effective as people had hoped; others have been widely ignored by the public. For example, the advocates of the 55-mile-per-hour speed limit now emphasize its safety advantages rather than gasoline savings.

Another oil embargo could bring conservation measures to the forefront again. But the emphasis for now has shifted to seeking long-term solutions to the nation's energy dilemma. The long-run problem can be divided into two critical questions:

1. How can we best discover and develop alternative energy resources?
2. How do we coordinate our growing need for energy resources with other societal goals?

It is evident to most people that the United States and other nations will need to develop alternative energy resources. Nuclear power, wind, sun, synfuels, coal, even garbage and other waste products (see Focus 2–2)—all have been suggested as possible substitutes for oil and natural gas. While the search for new energy sources generates considerable public interest, the basic question of how to discover and develop them remains unresolved.

The second question—how to coordinate our growing need for energy resources with other societal goals—is also important. Sometimes national energy needs clash with ecological and environmental objectives. One such situation arose with the construction of the Alaskan oil pipeline. The nation's gasoline needs had to be balanced against the preservation of the natural environment of our forty-ninth state. The bulk of the ecological questions were resolved, and the Trans-Alaska Pipeline began its flow of oil on June 20, 1977.

Similar questions have been raised about plans to move Alaskan oil to the east via pipeline. Conflicts are to be expected. They are a natural aspect of contemporary business, and one which must be dealt with if management is to prove effective.

FOCUS 2–2
Getting High on Energy

U.S. Customs officials seize 2,500 tons of marijuana a year in Florida, presenting them with a disposal problem that is literally too hot to handle; marijuana burns at such high temperatures that conventional incinerators can be damaged. So, as a favor, the Florida Power and Light Co. has offered to turn the confiscate pot into kilowatts at its Port Everglades power plant.

The marijuana will be pulverized and blown into the plant's furnaces, which now burn either natural gas or oil. Company officials figure that each ton of pot equals 2.7 barrels of oil and will produce 2,000 kilowatt hours of electricity—only a tiny fraction of the plant's daily output, so pot power will not significantly reduce customers' bills. Officials also believe that smoke from the generator's 350-foot stack will not turn on passersby. But just to be sure, they plan to conduct test burns. Until then, the *Miami News* advised readers, "hold your breath"—or, as the case may be, "breathe deeply."

Ethical Questions Facing Business

Societal and ethical issues are closely related and similar in meaning and impact. Generally, however, societal issues are somewhat broader in that they are usually directed at all areas of business enterprise. By contrast, it is possible to isolate specific ethical issues for various segments of a company.

Management is required to resolve specific ethical questions dealing with right and wrong that arise in any work environment. Some-

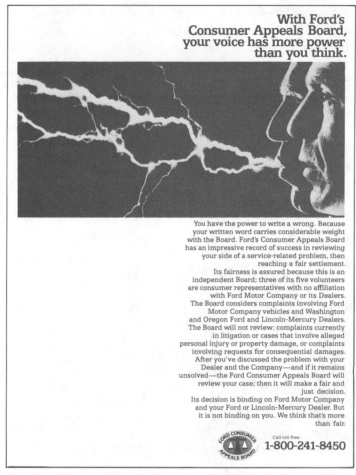

The Ford Motor Company has set up Consumer Appeals Boards throughout the country to handle consumer complaints.

times a conflict exists between an ideal decision and one that is practical under certain conditions. But it is important that companies evaluate their ethical responsibilities in decision making. A recent study found that 73 percent of the firms examined had developed written codes of ethics.[18]

How businesspeople deal with ethical questions was the subject of a study outline in the *Harvard Business Review*. Businesspeople were presented with hypothetical situations where some actions would normally be right, others wrong. Half the sample were asked, "What would you do?" while the other half were asked, "What would the average businessperson do?" The answers to the second question indicated more unethical behavior than did responses to the first question. Businesspeople apparently think their peers are less ethical than they themselves are.[19]

Businesses face numerous ethical questions every day. Some of the more frequently encountered ones are discussed below.

Relations with Customers

The possibility of ethical abuses is quite evident in relations with customers. A multitude of package sizes makes price comparison difficult for the consumer. High-pressure sales tactics have led to cooling-off laws that allow consumers to cancel sales contracts within a certain period of time. The acceptable degree of advertising aimed at children is being questioned.

Promotional strategy is the basis of most ethical questions involved in relations with consumers. The personal sales process has always been open to some form of ethical criticism, but in recent years advertising has been subjected to close scrutiny because of its vast reach. Advertising has become an increasingly pervasive force in our lives.

Pricing is an area that has an immediate, direct effect on the consumer. It is also the most regulated of the firm's relations with consumers. Chapter 22 describes many of the laws that affect pricing strategy.

Relations with Company Personnel

Some of the most difficult ethical questions deal with companies' relations with their employees, because decisions in this area affect people's work environment for years to come. Managers are required to make hiring, promotion, transfer, compensation, and dismissal decisions. Consider the ethical dilemma of a manager forced to promote either a rising young executive with potential for further development or a long-service employee nearing retirement who has performed faithfully, if not sensationally, over the years. Promotion of the older person may cause the younger one to move to a competing firm. Selection of the younger person may be regarded as breaking faith with senior people in the organization. Many complex and vital ethical questions are involved in such decisions.

Ethical questions also arise in the course of a manager's other relationships with people in the organization. For example, consider the situation where one executive keeps important information from a peer so as to enhance his or her own chances for promotion and to lessen the advancement opportunity of the other manager.

Relations with Business Associates

Relations with business associates are another area of possible ethical conflict. Many interpersonal relationships in business include important ethical considerations. For example, an executive may ask, "Am I Nancy's friend because I like her as a person or because she is sometimes a good source of competitive information?"

Another important question is: When does a gift and/or business entertainment become a bribe? Most firms have clear policies prohib-

Controversial Issue

Who Pays the Cost of Love Canal?

There are few people in the United States who have not heard of the small area in upstate New York called Love Canal. A middle-class community, Love Canal would never have come to national attention had it not been for the fact that Hooker Chemical Company used it as a chemical waste dump site for two decades.

The problem began in the 1930s when Hooker Chemical started dumping thousands of 55-gallon drums filled with toxic chemicals into an abandoned canal near Niagara Falls. In 1953, Hooker sold part of the land to the Niagara Falls Board of Education as the site for a neighborhood elementary school and playground and the remaining part to a home developer. Years went by with only an occasional sign of trouble—children developed strange skin rashes, dogs lost their hair—until 1976, when the metal drums, eroded by heavy rains, poured their toxic chemicals into the basements of the Love Canal homes.

The result was a series of medical problems among residents of Love Canal: birth defects, miscarriages, epilepsy, liver abnormalities, cancer, sores, bleeding, headaches. The findings of the New York State Health Department were so dire that in August, 1978 President Carter declared Love Canal a federal emergency. Hundreds of homes were boarded up and residents evacuated.

Love Canal residents contended that Hooker Chemical, now a subsidiary of Occidental Petroleum, should pay for the damage. They charged Hooker with negligence for failing to monitor the toxic chemicals it buried in Love Canal, even though it knew these substances were hazardous. Evidence presented before the House Commerce Committee suggested that the company was well aware of the time bomb ticking away under Love Canal as early as 1958 and chose to do almost nothing about it.

Hooker contends that when it dumped the toxic chemicals into Love Canal it had no idea of the potential problems it was creating. To force it to pay for damages based on information obtained

iting the outright payment of bribes to purchasing directors, government officials, and competitors' employees. On some occasions these restrictions have not been effective in stopping ethical abuses, but most of the time they work. However, often a very fine line exists between a business gift and a bribe. Some organizations have prohibited their employees from giving or receiving *any* business gift; others have set limits on the value of gifts to their employees. One guide in this area is the Internal Revenue Service regulation that allows a tax deduction for business gifts up to $25 per recipient per year. Gifts exceeding this amount are not tax deductible.

decades after it completed the dumping is, in Hooker's view, completely unjust. In addition, Hooker claims that its liability is diminished by the length of time it did not own the property. According to Hooker, the problems began to develop when Love Canal was owned by the Board of Education. The legal questions are very complex. If Hooker knew what the effects of the buried wastes were likely to be and did not inform the Board of Education before the land was sold, then Hooker might well be liable. On the other hand, if there was no "hidden defect" in the land, then liability for future harm might well have passed to the Board of Education under current law.

While the lawsuits against Hooker continue, Love Canal residents have turned to the federal and state governments for help. In the residents' view, if Hooker will not take responsibility for its actions, it is up to government to step in and protect its citizens from a further harm to their health and well-being.

Both the state and federal governments have met many of the residents' demands. In August, 1978, New York State agreed to relocate and buy the homes of 239 residents whose property immediately bordered the dump site. And two years later, the federal government loaned the state $15 million for the purchase of as many as 550 more homes. In addition, the state agreed to pay for relocation housing for an interim period, while Love Canal residents tried to find new homes. Despite all this, residents complain that aid has been slow in coming and that much still needs to be done.

Whether Hooker Chemical or the state and federal governments ultimately bear the burden of paying for Love Canal depends on how the courts view Hooker's responsibility for acts it committed years earlier. If Hooker's liability is limited, then residents may look for even more help from government. The question of Hooker Chemical's legal and social responsibility in this matter is still unsettled.

Relations with Investors and the Financial Community

Throughout history there have been financial scandals. The financial health of firms has been misrepresented, numerous land swindles have been perpetrated, savers have lost millions of dollars due to embezzlement, and nonexistent assets have been reported to the financial community.

Each of these types of financial abuse has been dealt with by the government, so that we now have a comprehensive, well-developed set of laws regulating financial affairs. (These laws will be outlined later in the text.) But business management has also moved to a higher level of ethical behavior. Few firms would now permit financial misconduct by their personnel. Professional organizations and societies such as the Certified Public Accountants have also worked to improve financial ethics.

There is probably no place where the public expects a higher level of business ethics than in the arena of financial transactions. Public attention goes beyond the illegitimate activites identified by statutes. Financial executives such as bankers are expected to exhibit the highest standards of ethical behavior in order to justify the public trust placed in them.

The Scorecard on Social Responsibility in Business

We have briefly explored the various aspects of the social responsibility puzzle facing business, suggesting several areas where management needs to improve. But let us look at the overall scorecard for business.

Certainly there have been failures, particularly in earlier years, when less exacting standards were commonplace. Even today critics can point to overseas payoffs and illegal political contributions as violations of contemporary guidelines for social responsibility. Yet, on balance, business has to be judged one of the most socially responsible segments of our society. The vast majority of business decisions are responsible, and the level of this achievement continues to climb each year. Most businesspeople know that socially responsible behavior is simply good business.

Social responsibility is an inherent part of a businessperson's job, because commercial decisions affect virtually all elements of society. Responsible actions are expected of everyone working in business today. And with very few exceptions, social responsibility has become the norm by which all executives function!

Summary

Contemporary business faces a dynamic societal environment that is often difficult to predict. Social responsibility has become accepted business policy, but its actual implementation has often lagged. As a result, there is a real need to develop an effective method of evaluating a firm's societal performance.

There are five major groups of societal issues confronting business today: inflation, people-oriented management, ecology and environmental protection, consumerism, and the energy crisis. The rising prices caused by inflation are of concern to both consumers and businesses alike. In addition to economics, business must also be more aware of and responsive to the needs and problems of people in the workplace. At the same time, business cannot ignore the environment in which it operates, paying particular attention to pollution and its effects on the ecology of an area. Nor can business turn its back on its consumers, who are demanding to be treated fairly and to have their rights protected. Finally, business, like everyone else, must look for ways to conserve or to find alternate sources of energy on which to run.

Societal and ethical issues are closely related and similar in meaning and impact. Societal issues are somewhat broader in that they are usually directed to all areas of business enterprises. By contrast, it is possible to isolate specific ethical issues for various segments of a company. Ethical questions face management in its relations with consumers, company personnel, business associates, and investors and the financial community.

A brief assessment of business's societal responsibility scorecard shows that most business people today are socially responsible decision makers.

Key Terms

social responsibility	stagflation	consumerism
inflation	ecology	energy crisis
demand-pull inflation	pollution	conservation
cost-push inflation	recycling	

Review Questions

1. Explain each of the terms listed above.

2. Relate League General's decision to offer free children's car seats to its policyholders to the material in this chapter.

3. Outline what you see as the moral of the Reserve Mining Company story.

4. Discuss the need for social performance measures in business.

5. Outline the five major groups of societal issues facing business.

6. What basic consumer rights were suggested by President Kennedy in 1962?

7. Contrast the short-run and long-run components of the complex energy question.

8. Identify the various ethical questions facing business.

9. Why do we state: "Businesspeople know that socially responsible behavior is simply good business"?

10. Identify several reasons why social responsibility has become so important in business today.

Discussion Questions and Exercises

1. Evaluate the pros and cons of the controversial issue that appears in this chapter.

2. Describe the major societal and ethical issues facing:
   a. automobile manufacturers
   b. real estate developers
   c. detergent manufacturers
   d. drug firms selling birth control products
   e. corporate attorneys

3. Do you support a nationwide ban on throwaway bottles? Outline the pros and cons of this issue.

4. Identify two or three societal issues facing business in your local area. How have local firms responded to them? How have local government agencies and officials responded?

5. Prepare a two-page paper on how inflation has affected the college student of the 1980s.

Case 2–1: Civic Affairs and Top Management

When Cleveland's Mayor George Voinovich asked for help, he got it. The financially troubled city benefited from the work of a task force of top executives from the Cleveland business community. Headed by E. Mandell De Windt, chairman of Eaton Corp., the mayor's task force toiled for three months and produced some 800 guidelines for streamlining Cleveland's affairs. Some of the executives paid a significant price for their civic involvement. Herbert E. Strawbridge, who heads Higbee Co., a Cleveland-based operator of retail stores, was criticized because his company's performance suffered while he was helping Mayor Voinovich.

The Cleveland experience is repeated every day throughout the United States. Top executives are spending more and more time on civic affairs not directly related to the operation of their companies. One survey found that 92 percent of these executives said they were more involved in external affairs than they had been three to five years before. Another survey of 41 chief executive officers found that 27 of them went to Washington, D.C. at least twice a month.

Contemporary business has responded in a variety of ways to this additional pressure on executive time. Many top managers have increased their workweek to accommodate these new civic responsibilities. But this can have a severe impact on the physical, mental, and financial well-being of the people and companies involved. Some executives have adjusted by delegating more responsibilities to subordinates. Still others, such as Fletcher C. Byron of Koppers Co., have resigned from the outside groups in order to give their total efforts to their firms.

New organizational formats have sprung up as a result of this trend. Public affairs departments have been added to numerous organizations. The office of the chairman—a new organizational concept that brings together several top executives who share the outside duties that used to be handled by the chief executive alone—is now commonplace. However it is handled, it is certain that top management will become more involved in civic affairs in the 1980s.

Questions

1. Assess the impact on contemporary business of corporate executives, becoming more involved in civic affairs.
2. Study a local company to find out how it deals with civic matters. Report your findings to the class.
3. Assume you are the chief executive officer of a major corporation. How would you cope with this issue?

Case 2–2: Jane Fonda, Dow Chemical, and Central Michigan University

---

Actress and political activist Jane Fonda's speech at Central Michigan University (CMU) created a stir on the Mount Pleasant campus and elsewhere. Fonda had been paid $3,500 by two CMU feminist groups to speak on the Equal Rights Amendment. The popular actress directed a portion of her remarks to an attack on the free enterprise system, big business, and Dow Chemical. Dow, a long-time CMU supporter headquartered in nearby Midland, responded quickly. Dow President Paul F. Oreffice cut the firm's cash contributions (approximately $70,000 the previous year) to Central Michigan.

In a letter to the University's president, Oreffice said:

> It is your prerogative to have an avowed communist sympathizer like Jane Fonda or anyone else speak at your university and you can pay them whatever you please. I have absolutely no argument with that.
>
> I consider it our prerogative and obligation to make certain our funds are never used to support people intent on destruction of freedom.

Fonda later described Dow's action as corporate blackmail and responded to Oreffice's allegations: "I am not proposing destruction. I am proposing that we extend democracy to our economy and put the quality of life, jobs and safety above corporate greed."

Dow's response to the Fonda speech heightens the debate concerning the extent and responsibilities associated with corporate giving. Federal law permits a 5 percent maximum tax deduction for charitable contributions, but industry has traditionally given only 1 percent.

Now with President Reagan's drive to cut the federal budget, the administration is asking Congress to cut more than $22 billion in social programs and aid to the arts and humanities. Charitable contributions from individuals have been declining in recent years, and despite the fact that business donations grew faster than any other area of private-sector contributions during the 1970s, corporations are not expected to fill in much of the gap left by the federal budget cuts.

Most executives agree that their first responsibility is to stockholders and employees, and increased charitable contributions might force management to hike prices in order to meet these responsibilities. According to William D. Ruckelshaus, president of the Weyerhaeuser Foundation, the Weyerhaeuser Co. subsidiary that reviews and coordinates company contributions, the hard part is balancing increasing requests for contributions with profit and dividend motives. Many executives also believe they have a responsibility to evaluate the usage of the monies they donate.

Questions

1. Do you approve of Dow's reaction to the Fonda speech? Explain.

2. Why are corporate charitable contributions less than the maximum permitted by tax law?

3. Do corporations have a right to "attach strings" to their gifts? Do they have an obligation to do so?

4. Why do so relatively few businesses contribute to charity, and of those that do, why do they give such a relatively small amount of money?

5. Should public institutions and charitable groups refuse to accept gifts that are subject to external review?

3

Forms of Business Ownership

Learning Goals

1. To explain the three basic forms of business ownership and the advantages and disadvantages of each

2. To analyze how a corporation is organized and operated

3. To identify the differences among private ownership, public ownership, and collective ownership (cooperatives)

4. To explain the meaning of each of the key terms introduced in this chapter

Profile: Richard W. Sears and Alvah C. Roebuck
A Highly Successful Partnership

Richard W. Sears

Alvah C. Roebuck

WANTED: Watchmaker with references who can furnish tools. State age, experience and salary required. *ADDRESS:* T39, Daily News

When Richard W. Sears ran this ad in the *Chicago Daily News* in 1887, he had no idea that he was about to launch one of the most successful partnerships in American business history.

Sears, a Chicago watch salesman, began selling watches in his spare time when he was a railroad station master in North Redwood, Minnesota. When he moved his business to Chicago, volume expanded, and he discovered he needed a watch repairer. Alvah C. Roebuck, a watchmaker, traveled from Hammond, Indiana, to answer Sears's ad. In 1893 they formed Sears, Roebuck and Company.

Sears, Roebuck and Company opened its doors when the United States was still made up of rural hamlets and towns, general stores, and railroads. Richard Sears understood the needs of farmers and small-town Americans and began marketing merchandise through mail-order catalogs, thereby eliminating middlemen and their profits. The earliest catalogs featured only watches, and Roebuck's skills as a watchmaker were heavily utilized. Thanks to volume buying, Chicago's superior rail system, and the postal system that linked Chi-

cago to every part of the country, company profits boomed.

Because of ill health, in 1897 Roebuck sold out his one-third interest in the company. But, at Sears's request, he took charge of a division that handled watches, jewelry, and optical goods, which he managed for several years, adding phonographs, magic lanterns, and moving picture machines to the product line. Eventually, however, he left Sears, Roebuck and Company to organize and finance two enterprises of his own—one engaged in the manufacture and the other in the distribution of moving picture machines and accessories—which he later sold to acquire real estate holdings in Florida. In February, 1933, he rejoined Sears, Roebuck and Company in the public relations department, and he retired in 1940.

Throughout the company's long history, Richard Sears was the guiding business force. He was a genius at selling, advertising, and merchandising through mail-order catalogs, but he was not an organizer. In 1895 he brought in Julius Rosenwald as part-owner of the business. Rosenwald reorganized the company, including opening an office in Dallas, so that it could service its expanding mail-order business. In 1906, with the sale of common and preferred stock, Sears, Roebuck and Company became publicly owned.

You can spend years tinkering with a partnership or marriage, trying to make it work, but you know in your stomach from the beginning whether it will work or not.

—Gerry Kingen
—President, Red Robin Company,
Seattle, Washington

Koniag, Inc. of Kodiak, Alaska, is one of the nation's exceptional business organizations. It is a corporation—a legal entity separate from its owners—that was set up by Congress, along with 12 other regional native corporations, to settle Alaskan native land claims. The legislation also provided for several village-level corporations, which Koniag is now merging into its own organizational structure. Koniag's net worth of $36 million consists of assets in cash, timber, equipment, office buildings, a marine supply firm, apartment houses, and a fish-processing plant. It also has a share in Beaufort Sea Oil leases.[1]

All businesses, whether Exxon or a native Alaskan firm, must be structured according to the form of business ownership that best meets their needs: sole proprietorship, partnership, or corporation. Selection of a legal form of business organization is a complex and critical decision for the owners of any enterprise. Sometimes it even takes an act of Congress to settle the matter.

A sole proprietorship is a business owned and operated by a single individual.

Forms of Private Ownership

Each of the three forms of private ownership—sole proprietorship, partnership, and corporation—has its own unique advantages and disadvantages. A summary of these features appears in Table 3-1.

TABLE 3–1
Advantages and Disadvantages of
Each Form of Private Ownership

Form of Ownership	Advantages	Disadvantages
Sole Proprietorship	1. Retention of all profits 2. Ease of formation and dissolution 3. Ownership flexibility	1. Unlimited financial liability 2. Financing limitations 3. Management deficiencies 4. Lack of continuity
Partnership	1. Ease of formation 2. Complementary management skills 3. Expanded financial capacity	1. Unlimited financial liability 2. Interpersonal conflicts 3. Lack of continuity 4. Complex dissolution
Corporation	1. Limited financial liability 2. Specialized management skills 3. Expanded financial capacity 4. Economies of larger-scale operation	1. Difficult and costly ownership form to establish and dissolve 2. Tax disadvantage 3. Legal restrictions 4. Alienation of some employees

Sole Proprietorships

Sole proprietorship is the original form of business ownership. It is also the simplest, because there is no legal distinction between the sole proprietor as an individual and as a business owner. A **sole proprietorship** is an organization owned and usually operated by a single individual. Its assets, earnings, and debts are those of the owner.

Today, sole proprietorships are still the most common form of private business ownership in the United States. While they are used in a variety of industries, they are concentrated primarily among small businesses such as repair shops, small retail outlets, and service organizations.

Advantages of sole proprietorships. Sole proprietorships offer advantages not found in other forms of business ownership, such as retention of all profits, ease of formation and dissolution. and ownership flexibility. All profits—as well as losses—of a sole proprietorship belong to the owner (except, of course, that part going to the government for personal income taxes). If the firm is very profitable, this can be an important advantage. Retention of all profits (and respon-

sole proprietorship
Ownership (and usually operation) of an organization by a single individual.

sibility for all losses) provides sole proprietors with the incentive to operate the business as efficiently as possible.

A minimum of legal requirements makes it easy to go into (and out of) business. Usually the only legal requirements for starting a sole proprietorship are registering the business name at the county courthouse (this guarantees that two firms do not use the same name) and taking out any necessary licenses (restaurants, motels, barbershops, retail stores, and many repair shops require certain kinds of licenses).

The fact that it is easy to discontinue a business set up as a sole proprietorship is an attractive feature for certain types of enterprises. This is particularly true for businesses that are set up for a limited time period and are involved in a minimum of transactions—for example, the business created by an individual to organize a rock concert at a local sports arena.

Ownership flexibility is another advantage of sole proprietorships. The owner has no one to consult about management decisions. He or she can take prompt action when needed and can preserve trade secrets where appropriate. Such flexibility can also contribute to the proprietor's personal satisfaction as exemplified by the common saying, "I like being my own boss."

Disadvantages of sole proprietorships. Disadvantages associated with sole proprietorships include unlimited financial liability, limitations on financing, management deficiencies, and lack of continuity. Because there is no legal distinction between the business and its owner, the sole proprietor is financially liable for all debts of the business. If the firm's assets cannot cover its debts, the owner is required to pay them with personal funds. A sole proprietor may even be forced to sell personal property—home, furniture, and automobile—to pay off business debts. The unlimited liability of a sole proprietorship can mean financial ruin to an owner if the business fails.

The financial resources of a sole proprietorship are limited to the owner's personal funds and money that can be borrowed. Sole proprietors usually do not have easy access to large amounts of capital, because they are typically small businesspeople with limited personal wealth. Banks and other financial institutions are often reluctant to risk giving loans to such small organizations. Financing limitations can sometimes retard the expansion of the sole proprietor's business.

The manager of the sole proprietorship is usually the owner. This person has to be able to handle a wide range of managerial and operative activities. As the firm grows, the owner may be unable to handle all duties with equal effectiveness and may also be unable to attract managerial personnel. Sole proprietorships typically offer little hope of promotion (except for the owner's offspring), fewer fringe benefits than can be found in other organizations, and less employment security. But they do offer employees an excellent chance to learn about a particular type of enterprise.

Finally, sole proprietorships lack long-term continuity. Death, bankruptcy, retirement, or change in personal interests can terminate a business organized as a sole proprietorship.

Partnerships

partnership
An association of two or more persons who operate a business as co-owners by voluntary legal agreement.

Partnerships are another form of private business ownership. As defined by the Uniform Partnership Act, they are associations of two or more persons who operate a business as co-owners by voluntary legal agreement. Partnership has been a traditional form of ownership for professional service organizations of such people as doctors, lawyers, and dentists.

general partnerships
A partnership in which all partners carry on the business as co-owners and are liable for the business's debts.

General partnerships are those in which all partners carry on the business as co-owners and all are liable for the business's debts. Some states also permit **limited partnerships** composed of one or more general partners and one or more limited partners. A limited partner is one whose liability is limited to the amount of capital contributed to the partnership.

limited partnership
A partnership composed of one or more general partners and one or more limited partners (those whose liability is limited to the amount of capital contributed to the partnership).

Joint ventures, another type of partnership, occur when two or more people form a temporary business for a specific undertaking—for example, a group of investors who import a shipment of high-quality wine from France and then resell it to wine dealers in the United States. Joint ventures are often used in real estate investments.

joint venture
A partnership in which two or more people form a temporary business for a specific undertaking.

Advantages of partnerships. Partnerships offer the advantages of ease of formation, complementary management skills, and expanded financial capability. It is relatively easy to establish a partnership. As with sole proprietorships, the legal requirements usually involve registering the business name and taking out needed licenses. Limited partners must also comply with state legislation based on the Uniform Limited Partnership Act.

It is usually wise to establish written articles of partnership specifying the details of the partners' agreement. This helps clarify the relationship within the firm and protects the original agreement upon which the partnership is based.

A common reason for setting up a partnership is the availability of complementary managerial skills. If the people involved were to operate as sole proprietors, their firms might lack some managerial skills, but by combining into a partnership, each person can offer his or her unique managerial ability. For example, a general partnership might be formed by an engineer, an accountant, and a marketer who plan to produce and sell a particular product or service. If additional managerial talent is needed in the business, it may be easier to attract people as partners than as employees.

Partnerships offer expanded financial capability through money invested by each of the partners. They also usually have greater access to borrowed funds than do sole proprietorships. Because the individual partners are subject to unlimited financial liability, financial insti-

A partnership is an association of two or more people who operate a business as co-owners by voluntary legal agreement.

tutions are often willing to advance loans to partnerships. Involvement of additional owners may also mean that additional sources of loans become available.

Disadvantages of partnerships. Like other forms of business ownership, partnerships have some disadvantages, including unlimited financial liability, interpersonal conflicts, lack of continuity, and complexity of dissolution. Each partner is responsible for the debts of the firm, and each is legally liable for the actions of the others. This holds true not only for debts in the name of the partnership but also for lawsuits resulting from any partner's malpractice. As with sole proprietors, partners are required to pay the total debts of a partnership from private sources if necessary. In other words, if the debts of a partnership exceed its assets, then creditors will turn to the personal wealth of the partners. If only one general partner has any personal wealth, that person may be required to pay *all* the debts of the partnership. Limited partners lose only the amount of capital they invested in the firm.

Interpersonal conflicts may also plague partnerships. All partnerships, from barbershops to rock groups, face the problem of personal and business disagreements among the participants. If these conflicts cannot be resolved, it is sometimes best to dissolve the partnership because continuation could adversely affect the business.

Continuity of a partnership is disrupted when a partner is no longer able (or willing) to continue in the business. Then the partnership agreement is terminated, and a final settlement is made.

It is not as easy to dissolve a partnership as it is to dissolve a sole proprietorship. Instead of simply withdrawing the investment in the business, the partner who wants to leave must find someone (perhaps an existing partner or perhaps an outsider who is acceptable to the remaining partners) to buy his or her interest in the firm. Sometimes it is very difficult to transfer an investment in a partnership to another party.

Corporations

corporation
An association of persons created by statute as a legal entity with authority to act and to have liability separate and apart from its owners.

A **corporation** is "an association of persons created by statute as a legal entity (artificial person) with authority to act and to have liability separate and apart from its owners."[2] Because corporations are legal organizations apart from their owners, the liability of each owner is limited to the amount that person invests.

Corporate charters are granted through state legislation. Corporate ownership is represented by shares of stock in the firm. Types of stock and their issuance are discussed later in the chapter. Anyone who holds one or more shares of a corporation's stock is considered a part owner of the business. Shares can usually be bought and sold readily on the open market.

Advantages of corporations. Corporate ownership offers considerable advantages, including limited financial risk, specialized management skills, expanded financial capability, and economies of larger-scale operation.

Because corporations are considered separate legal entities, the stockholders (owners) have limited financial risk. If the firm fails, they can lose only the amount of their investments. Personal funds of owners cannot be touched by creditors of the corporation. The limited risk of corporate ownership is clearly designated in the names used by firms throughout the world. U.S. corporations often use the designation "Incorporated" or "Inc." Corporate enterprises in Canada and the United Kingdom use "Limited" or "Ltd." In Australia, limited risk is shown by "Proprietary Limited" or "Pty. Ltd." This limited risk is the most significant advantage of corporate ownership over other forms of ownership.

The managerial skills of sole proprietorships and partnerships are usually confined to the abilities of the owners. Corporations can more easily obtain specialized managerial skills, because they offer longer-term career opportunities for qualified people. Employees may be able to concentrate their efforts in some specialized activity or functional area, because corporations are often larger than partnerships or sole proprietorships.

Expanded financial capability is usually another advantage of corporate ownership. This may allow the corporation to grow and become more efficient than it would if the business were set up as a sole proprietorship or partnership. Because corporate ownership is divided into many small units (shares), it is usually easier for a firm to attract capital. People with both large and relatively small resources can invest their savings in corporations by buying shares of stock. Corporate size and stability also make it easier for corporations to borrow additional funds. Large, financially strong corporations can often borrow money at lower rates than can smaller businesses. Of course, not all corporations are large; many small firms are also set up in the corporate form.

The larger-scale operation permitted by corporate ownership has several advantages. Employees can specialize in the work activities they perform best. Many projects can be internally financed by transferring money from one part of the corporation to another. Longer manufacturing runs usually mean more efficient production and lower prices, thus attracting more customers. The largest U.S. industrial corporations are listed in Table 3-2. The top three—Exxon, Mobil, and General Motors—combined employ more workers than the populations of Alaska, Delaware, Hawaii, Idaho, Maine, Montana, Nevada, New Hampshire, North Dakota, Rhode Island, South Dakota, Vermont, and Wyoming.[3]

While corporate size may be an advantage from a business viewpoint, some economists, attorneys, political figures, and business ex-

TABLE 3-2

The 25 Largest U.S. Corporations by Sales and Earnings

By Sales			By Earnings		
Company	Millions of dollars	Rank	Company	Millions of dollars	Rank
Exxon	$110,469	1	American Telephone & Telegraph	$6,043	1
Mobil	63,652	2	Exxon	5,660	2
General Motors	57,728	3	International Business Machines	3,562	3
Texaco	52,486	4	Mobil	2,820	4
American Telephone & Telegraph	50,233	5	Standard Oil Co. of California	2,401	5
Standard Oil Co. of California	42,900	6	Texaco	2,240	6
Ford Motor	37,086	7	Standard Oil (Indiana)	1,915	7
Standard Oil (Indiana)	27,800	8	Standard Oil (Ohio)	1,811	8
Gulf Oil	26,884	9	Atlantic Richfield	1,651	9
Engelhard Minerals & Chemicals	26,570	10	Shell Oil	1,542	10
International Business Machines	26,213	11	General Electric	1,514	11
General Electric	24,960	12	Gulf Oil	1,407	12
Atlantic Richfield	24,156	13	Eastman Kodak	1,154	13
International Telephone & Telegraph	23,819	14	Phillips Petroleum	1,070	14
Sears, Roebuck	23,037	15	Conoco	1,027	15
Shell Oil	19,959	16	Schlumberger	994	16
Conoco	18,800	17	Getty Oil	872	17
Safeway Stores	15,103	18	Dow Chemical	805	18
Citicorp	14,211	19	International Telephone & Telegraph	804	19
K mart	13,847	20	Tenneco	726	20
Du Pont	13,653	21	Sun	723	21
Phillips Petroleum	13,377	22	Du Pont	716	22
Aetna Life & Casualty	13,318	23	Occidental Petroleum	711	23
Tenneco	13,226	24	Minnesota Mining & Mfg.	678	24
Sun	13,200	25	Union Carbide	673	25

ecutives have begun to question whether there should be limits on corporate size to protect the interests of society.

Disadvantages of corporations. Some disadvantages are also inherent in corporate ownership. Corporations are the most difficult and costly ownership form to establish, they are usually at a tax disadvantage, they often face a multitude of legal restrictions, and their impersonality can alienate some employees.

Each state has different incorporation laws, some of which are quite technical and complex. Establishing a corporation usually requires the services of an attorney and legal fees. States also charge incorporation fees that add to the cost of setting up this type of business. Delaware, however, has traditionally attracted corporations because it has relatively easy requirements and low costs for incorporation.

As separate legal entities, corporations are subject to federal and state income taxes. Corporate earnings and any **dividends**—payments from earnings—to stockholders are taxed on an individual basis. From the viewpoints of stockholders who receive dividends, this is effectively double taxation of corporate earnings. By contrast, the earnings of sole proprietorships and partnerships are taxed only once, because they are treated as personal income. Many states provide tax relief to corporations meeting certain size and stock ownership requirements by recognizing them as **Subchapter S corporations**. These corporations can elect to be taxed as partnerships while maintaining the advantages of incorporation.

Corporate ownership faces a multitude of legal problems not encountered by sole proprietorships and partnerships. Corporate charters restrict the type of business activity in which the corporation can engage. Corporations must also file various reports about their operations. The number of laws and regulations affecting corporations has increased dramatically in recent years.

dividend
Payment from earnings of a corporation to its stockholders.

Subchapter S corporation
A corporation that can elect to be taxed as a partnership while maintaining the advantages of incorporation.

FIGURE 3-1
The ownership structure of U.S. business.

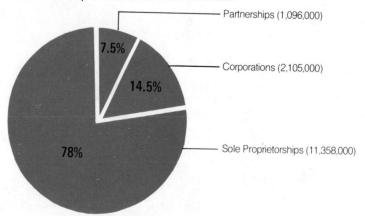

Partnerships (1,096,000)

7.5%

Corporations (2,105,000)

14.5%

78%

Sole Proprietorships (11,358,000)

Big corporations, like other large organizations, sometimes suffer from the impersonality of management. Employees become alienated because they do not feel any close ties with the corporation or its management. By being limited to doing one of many specialized jobs within a corporation, employees often do not develop a sense of identity with the firm. Some managers lack the initiative and sense of self-achievement found in sole proprietorships and partnerships. Employee morale, productivity, volume, and profitability can all be affected if steps are not taken to reduce the problem.

Current Ownership Structure of U.S. Business

Figure 3-1 shows the actual ownership structure of U.S. business. There are more than 11 million sole proprietorships, and they comprise 78 percent of all businesses, by far the most widely used form of business ownership. Corporations rank second, with about 14.5 percent of businesses using this form of organization. Partnerships, the smallest segment, are used by about 7.5 percent. Furthermore, because most states have liberalized the requirement that professional service groups must be partnerships, it seems likely that this form of ownership may decline as more and more professional workers decide to incorporate. The designations "P.C." (professional corporation), "S.C." (service corporation), or "P.S." (public service) have become common for law firms and the like.

Organizing and Operating a Corporation

Suppose you decide to start a business and you believe that the corporation is the best form of ownership for your enterprise. How should you go about setting up this corporation?

Your first step should be to consult an attorney. While it may be possible to incorporate the business by yourself, most people hire a lawyer so they can be assured that all necessary requirements are met.

Your second step should be to select a state in which to incorporate. This is an extremely important decision, because regulations, incorporation costs and other fees, taxes, and ownership rights vary widely among the 50 states. If you intend to operate primarily within the Commonwealth of Massachusetts, for example, you should prob-

domestic corporation
A firm doing business in the state in which it is incorporated.

foreign corporation
A corporation doing business in a state other than the one in which it is incorporated.

alien corporation
A corporation organized in another country but operating in the United States.

ably incorporate in that state. But if your principal business will be in Harris County, Texas, you should probably become a Texas corporation. Aside from the convenience of incorporating in your home state, if the business involves state-awarded contracts, many state governments specify that local firms be given preference. The selection of a state in which to incorporate should be made only after careful research.

A firm is considered a **domestic corporation** in the state where it is incorporated. If it expects to do business in states other than the state of incorporation, it must register as a **foreign corporation** in those states. A corporation organized in another nation but operating in the U.S. is known as an **alien corporation.**

Incorporating the Business

Most states designate a certain official or state agency (usually the secretary of state) to administer corporations. Blank articles of incorporation, corporation charters, or incorporation certificates (depending on the terminology used in a particular state) can be obtained from this official or agency. These forms must be filed with the appropriate state agency.

Corporation charters of the various states usually include similar information. Michigan articles of incorporation show the corporate name, corporate purposes, authorized capital stock, registered office and agent, and name of the incorporator. New York's certificate of incorporation shows the name of the proposed corporation, its purposes, its location, the number of shares of stock it will have the authority to issue, the address to which any process against the corporation should be sent, and the incorporator's name.

Stockholders

stockholders
The people who acquire the shares (and therefore are the owners) of a corporation.

Stockholders are those people who acquire the shares of the corporation; they are its owners. Some corporations such as family businesses are owned by relatively few stockholders. In these firms—known as **closed corporations**—the stockholders also control and manage the corporation's activities. But in larger corporations—sometimes described as **open corporations**—the ownership is widely diversified.

closed corporation
A corporation owned by relatively few stockholders, who control and manage the corporation's activities.

American Telephone & Telegraph Corporation (AT&T), for example, has over three million stockholders.[4] These people obviously have little individual control over the giant corporation. But there is a ready market for their shares if they decide to sell. Adequate markets are available for the stock of large corporations, so the individual stockholder can sell the stock more easily than if the shares held were in a small firm with no public market for its stock.

open corporation
A large corporation where ownership is widely diversified.

Corporations usually hold an annual stockholders' meeting during which management presents reports on the firm's activities. Any de-

"To you, the stockholders—better luck next time!"

Corporations usually hold an annual stockholders' meeting to report on the firm's activities, which are not always positive.
Drawing by Ross; © 1980 The New Yorker Magazine, Inc.

cisions requiring stockholder approval are put to a vote at this time. The election of certain directors (discussed in the next section) and the choice of an independent public accountant are two matters that must be voted on at nearly all stockholder meetings.

Stock is usually classified as common or preferred. Owners of **preferred stock** have the first claim to the corporation's assets after all debts have been paid, but they usually do not have voting rights at the stockholder meetings. Owners of **common stock** have only a residual claim (after everyone else has been paid) to the firm's assets, but they do have voting rights in the corporate system. When a vote is taken, each share of common stock is worth one vote; thus, a person with 225 shares has 225 votes. If people cannot attend the stockholder meetings, they can give their **proxy** (authorization to vote the shares as the owner has instructed) to someone who will attend.

Small stockholders generally have little influence on corporate managment. A holder of 200,000 shares has 200,000 votes for each director, while a holder of 50 shares has only 50 votes for each director. As a result, the issue of cumulative voting has come before many stockholder meetings. **Cumulative voting** allows smaller stockholders to have a greater influence on the selection of directors by enabling them to combine their votes. If, say, 3 director positions are to be filled, cumulative voting allows the holder of 50 shares to cast 150 votes (50 × 3) for 1 person rather than 50 votes apiece for all 3. The shareholder could, of course, allocate the votes any way desired.

Issues of corporate social responsibility have also come before recent stockholder meetings. Many churches, labor unions, and college and university trust funds invest in common stock. The trustees

preferred stock
Stock whose owners have the first claim to the corporation's assets after all debts have been paid but who usually don't have voting rights at stockholder meetings.

common stock
Stock whose owners have only a residual claim (after creditors and preferred stockholders have been paid) to the firm's assets, but who have voting rights in the corporation.

proxy
Authorization by stockholders for someone else to vote their shares, as instructed, at stockholder meetings.

cumulative voting
The practice of enabling stockholders to combine their votes in selecting the board of directors.

FOCUS 3–1
Watchdogs of Corporate Social Responsibility

At a recent International Harvester annual meeting, the Sisters of Charity of the Blessed Virgin tied up the proceedings by forcing a discussion of the company's multimillion-dollar truck operation in South Africa. And at the annual meetings of both Rockwell International and Emerson Electric, stockholders from the Dominican Order questioned production of nuclear weapons by military contractors.

These are only 2 of 187 church groups—170 Roman Catholic orders and 17 Protestant denominations—that have formed a coalition called the Interfaith Center on Corporate Responsibility (I.C.C.R.), a New York-based organization that monitors and attacks what it considers unethical corporate behavior. Its influence comes from its estimated $6 billion holdings of corporate stocks and bonds.

Because the coalition's impact on corporate policies has been minimal to date, many companies do not see its activities as threatening. However, Sister Arlene (Arlene Woelfel), a Franciscan nun and the coalition's board director, claims victories of sorts: a moral victory in voicing social concerns and a tactical victory in being able to get its voice heard.

In 1981 the I.C.C.R. placed 88 resolutions on the ballots of 60 large corporations. And even if it has not yet succeeded in significantly changing corporate policy, its strategy has at least enlivened some usually dull annual meetings and made managers sometimes give second thoughts to the consequences of their business practices.

As Tim Smith, a Protestant layman and executive director of I.C.C.R., summed it up, "We get a lot more attention holding several thousand shares of company stock and a little faith than with just faith alone."

of these organizations have sometimes used their voting power to raise questions about a corporation's social performance (see Focus 3–1).

Board of Directors

The stockholders elect a **board of directors,** which becomes the governing authority for the corporation. The board elects its own officers—usually a chairperson, a vice-chairperson, and a secretary. Most states require a minimum of three directors and at least one annual meeting of the board. Most corporations, other than small or closely held ones, have large boards of directors that meet at least quarterly.

The board of directors must authorize major transactions involving the corporation and must set overall corporate policy. It is concerned

board of directors
The governing authority of a corporation (most states require a minimum of three directors and at least one annual meeting of the board) elected by the stockholders.

with changes in areas such as the firm's stock, financing arrangements, dividends, and major shifts in corporate holdings. But its most important role is that of hiring the corporation's top management. Even the company president is an employee of the board. Although the board hires the top executive officers, it usually leaves the selection of other managers to those executives.

In some corporations (particularly smaller ones) the board of directors plays an active role in the management of the organization, but in most corporations it acts more as a review panel for management decisions. Most boards are composed of both corporation executives and **outside directors** (people not employed by the organization). Sometimes the corporation president is also the chairman of the board.

outside director
A member of the board of directors of a corporation who is not employed by the organization.

Top Management

Top management people, including the president and most vice-presidents, are responsible for the actual operation of the corporation, subject to board approval. They make most of the major corporate decisions and delegate other tasks to subordinate managers. They are responsible to the board of directors, and, indeed, they often sit on the board themselves. State legislation usually defines the duties of such corporate officers as president, secretary, and treasurer, but other executive posts are created by the board.

Subsidiary Organizations

Many corporations own other organizations, called **subsidiaries.** Allstate Insurance Company is a subsidiary of Sears, Roebuck and Company. Dryden Press, the publisher of this book, is a division of Holt, Rinehart and Winston, which is a subsidiary of CBS Inc.

When all or a majority of a corporation's stock is owned by another corporation, it is a subsidiary of that corporation. The owner is usually called the **parent company.** Typically, the management of the subsidiary is appointed by the chief executive of the parent company, subject to the approval of the parent's board. Many well-known corporations are actually subsidiaries of other corporations.

subsidiary
A corporation with all or a majority of its stock owned by another corporation. Management is appointed by the chief executive of the parent company subject to the approval of the parent's board of directors.

Corporate Growth

Corporate growth has become a major economic, political, and social issue in recent years. Successful corporations traditionally have been able to expand through effective business management practices. In some cases, however, they have grown by acquiring other firms. A **merger** occurs when one firm buys the assets and liabilities of another company.

Historically, corporate growth has been seen as desirable, provided it does not restrain competition. But today some people are questioning the need for such growth. Typically, these critics argue that further enlargement will not significantly improve the firm's pro-

parent company
A corporation that owns all or a majority of another corporation's stock (called a subsidiary).

merger
The event that occurs when one firm buys the assets and liabilities of another.

Controversial Issue

Should Monopolies Be Allowed To Exist?: The Case Against AT&T

In 1974, the Justice Department filed an antitrust suit against American Telephone & Telegraph (AT&T), the largest privately owned company in the world, charging it with illegally monopolizing the telecommunications and telecommunications equipment markets in violation of Section 2 of the Sherman Act. The government insisted that AT&T divest itself of Western Electric, the manufacturing arm of the Bell system; parts of Bell Labs, its research arm; and its 23 local or regional operating companies.

Would the breakup of this giant monopoly serve the needs of the business community and the public at large? Would more competition in the telecommunications industry translate into more efficiency?

AT&T sees itself as carrying out the monopoly mandate of the Communications Act of 1934, which still stands as the basic principle of national telecommunications policy. The Act states that the telephone industry should "make available, so far as possible, to all the people of the United States, a rapid, efficient, nationwide and worldwide wire and radio communications service with adequate facilities at reasonable charge."

AT&T contends that only an integrated system can meet this mandate and that its record of success is truly astounding: nearly every home and business in America, it proudly declares, has a telephone.

Regulated by the Federal Communications Commission, AT&T claims that it has modulated its profits, encouraged technological innovation, and attempted to provide the best possible service to its customers. It points to its role in correcting the de-

ductivity, and it may reduce competition in the marketplace. Corporate executives usually reply that significant economies are still available if the firm expands. No consensus has emerged on this question, and it is likely to remain a critical public issue in the decade ahead.

Alternatives to Private Ownership

While most business organizations are owned privately by individuals or groups of individuals, some are owned by either municipal, state, or federal governments and some are owned collectively by a number of people.

structive competition that sprang up following the expiration of Alexander Graham Bell's patents in the 1890s, when companies battled over customers and the need for two phones hooked into two different systems serving different areas was not uncommon. The confusion that arose from this situation led to the recognition that in the area of telephone service, it seemed that one company could serve the public's needs better than many.

The Justice Department charged that AT&T abused its monopoly power during the 1960s and 1970s by setting out to inhibit competition in the telecommunications market. According to the Justice Department lawsuit, AT&T discouraged smaller companies from marketing competitive telephone equipment by requiring its 23 operating companies to buy only Western Electric equipment, regardless of price and quality, even though other companies offered alternatives. AT&T is also charged with failing to comply immediately with orders to connect to local Bell lines long-distance telephone service supplied by its competitors. The old, familiar antitrust question emerged in this lawsuit but this time with a different twist: because of its size alone, did AT&T drive competitors out of business?

In the end, the courts will decide whether AT&T violated the principles of the free marketplace by shutting other, smaller companies out of the telecommunications business or whether it reasonably carried out its obligation to provide telephone service to the nation. Whatever the court decision, the case against AT&T has once again raised the question of whether monopolies are necessary for the provision and efficient operation of certain vital services.

Public Ownership

One alternative to private ownership is some form of **public ownership,** where a government unit or its agency owns and operates an organization on behalf of the population served by that unit. While public ownership is more common abroad, it has been used in several places and at several times in the United States. For example, parking structures and water systems are often owned by local governments. The Pennsylvania Turnpike Authority operates a vital highway link across its state, the federal government established the Tennessee Valley Authority to provide electricity in that region, and the Federal Deposit Insurance Corporation insures bank savings deposits.

When is public ownership used? Sometimes public ownership comes about when private investors are unwilling to make investments because they believe the possibility of failure is too high. An example of this situation is the 1930s rural electrification program that signifi-

public ownership
The ownership and operation of an organization by a government unit or its agency on behalf of the population served by that unit.

cantly expanded utility lines in lightly populated areas. At other times public ownership replaces privately owned organizations that fail. After the Penn Central Railroad financial collapse, proposals to set up a government passenger railway system were considered. Some governments have reasoned that certain activities are so important to public welfare that they should not be entrusted to private ownership. Turnpikes and municipal water systems are examples. Finally, some nations have used public ownership to foster competition by operating public companies as competitive business enterprises. Canadian National Railroad (publicly owned) competes with Canadian Pacific Railroad (privately owned) in a wide range of travel activities. Trans-Australia Airlines (publicly owned) competes against Ansett Airlines of Australia (privately owned).

The operation of publicly owned organizations also varies. Some are supposed to make a profit for their government unit; others are viewed entirely as public services that will operate at a loss. Canadian National Railroad and Trans-Australia Airlines are economically viable organizations, while Japan's well-publicized train system requires a substantial government subsidy. Subsidies are also common in many publicly owned bus systems in the United States. For instance, a sales tax partially subsidizes the Seattle area bus network.

Cooperatives

cooperative
An organization whose owners band together to operate collectively all or part of their company or industry.

Another alternative to private ownership is collective ownership of production, storage, transportation, and/or marketing activities. **Cooperatives** are organizations whose owners band together to collectively operate all or part of their industries. They are often created by large numbers of small producers who want to be more competitive in the marketplace (see Focus 3–2). The well-known Sunkist brand is used to identify the products of Sunkist Growers, a cooperative.

FOCUS 3–2
REI: An Exception to the Rule

Recreational Equipment, Inc. (REI), is a relatively rare organization in contemporary business. REI is the biggest consumer cooperative—with one million members—in the United States. Annual sales exceed $50 million a year from REI outlets in Seattle, Portland, Berkeley, Los Angeles, Anchorage, and Minneapolis. The cooperative—originally founded by Jim Whitaker, the first American to climb Mount Everest—has three separate divisions: manufacturing, retail, and mail order.

Recreational Equipment, Inc., is in business to serve its owners—even to the extent of providing dividends. REI president Jerry Horn puts it this way: "Our membership is our market, and we care about addressing members' concerns."

Some cooperatives have become large economic units that exert considerable power. The Mesta was a Spanish sheep-owners' cooperative formed in the 1200s. By the sixteenth century it was the biggest economic organization in Spain, herding three million sheep. Its size allowed it to exert considerable influence on government policy.[5] By contrast, cooperatives have never reached significant proportions in the United States. U.S. businesses have traditionally operated as independent economic entities.

Summary

Selection of a legal form of business organization is a complex and critical decision for the owners of any enterprise. There are three forms of private business ownership: sole proprietorship, partnership, and corporation.

The advantages of sole proprietorships are retention of all profits, ease of formation and dissolution, and ownership flexibility. Their disadvantages are unlimited financial liability, financing limitations, management deficiencies, and lack of continuity.

The advantages of partnerships are ease of formation, complementary managment skills, and expanded financial capability. The disadvantages are unlimited financial liability, interpersonal conflicts, lack of continuity, and complex dissolution.

The advantages of corporations are limited financial liability, specialized management skills, expanded financial capability, and economies of larger-scale operation. The disadvantages are the difficulty and cost of establishing the company, high taxes, legal restrictions, and possible alienation of some employees.

The most widely used current ownership structure is the sole proprietorship. In organizing a corporation, consideration should be given to hiring an attorney, selecting the state in which to incorporate, and following the correct legal procedures for incorporating. Registration as a domestic, foreign, or alien corporation is also important.

Stockholders own the corporation, the board of directors governs it, and top management is responsible for its actual operation. Subsidiaries are corporations owned by other (parent) corporations. The ongoing growth of corporations has become a major issue today.

One alternative to private ownership of business organizations is public ownership, where a government unit or its agency owns and operates an organization on behalf of the population served by that unit. Another alternative is the cooperative, where there is collective ownership of production, storage, transportation, and/or marketing activities.

Key Terms

sole proprietorship
partnership
general partnership
limited partnership
joint venture
corporation
dividend
Subchapter S corporation
domestic corporation

foreign corporation
alien corporation
stockholders
closed corporation
open corporation
preferred stock
common stock
proxy
cumulative voting

board of directors
outside director
subsidiary
parent company
merger
public ownership
cooperative

Review Questions

1. Explain each of the terms listed above.

2. Identify the advantages and disadvantages of the three forms of business ownership.

3. Why are complementary management skills so important to a successful partnership?

4. Distinguish between a general partner and a limited partner.

5. What is the most commonly used form of business ownership? Why?

6. List the steps in the incorporation process.

7. What is a subsidiary? List several subsidiary companies that operate in your area. Where are their parent companies located?

8. What is the status of cooperatives in the United States?

9. Assume that you are involved in establishing the following businesses. What form of business ownership would you employ?
   a. roadside fruit stand (assume you own an orchard)
   b. barbershop
   c. management consulting firm
   d. small foundry

10. Compare Table 3–2 to earlier listings of the largest U.S. industrial corporations. What major changes have taken place over the past ten years?

Discussion Questions and Exercises

1. Evaluate the pros and cons of the controversial issue that appears in this chapter.

2. Identify a cooperative in your immediate area. What are its primary objectives? How is it organized? Evaluate the effectiveness of its operations.

3. Ask a local attorney to speak to your class about how to set up a corporation in your state.

4. Secure announcements of future stockholder meetings of corporations located in your area. Analyze the types of issues that are scheduled to be debated at these meetings. Can you make any generalizations about them?

5. Invite a director of a firm in your area to speak to the class. Ask this person to describe (a) how the firm's board of directors operates, and (b) what his or her personal philosophy is regarding the role of the board in corporate affairs.

Case 3–1: Big League Baseball— Form of Business Ownership

Major league baseball teams provide entertainment to millions, but for their owners the teams are also business enterprises. Once the domain of wealthy sports enthusiasts, professional baseball has become a big—if not always profitable—business.

Most major league teams are organized in one of three ownership arrangements. The Baltimore Orioles are really the Baltimore Baseball Club, Inc., a traditional corporation. Others are Subchapter S corporations, organized as corporations but taxed as partnerships. The Kansas City Royals team is an example of a Subchapter S corporation. Another possibility is a limited partnership arrangement. The Milwaukee Brewers, for instance, is owned by 16 partners.

Regardless of the form of business ownership employed, professional baseball teams are often unprofitable. The 1980 New York Mets, for example, are estimated to have lost over $3 million.

Questions

1. What are the advantages and disadvantages of the three typical forms of ownership in major league baseball?

2. Assume you were part of a group that wanted to acquire a big league team. How would you organize the ownership structure? Why?

3. Many baseball teams are unprofitable. Does this situation affect the form of business ownership that is selected?

Case 3–2: God Bless You, Mr. Rosewater

God Bless You, Mr. Rosewater is a stage adaptation of a Kurt Vonnegut novel that tells the story of an eccentric and emotionally troubled philanthropist. Eliot Rosewater, head of the $87 million Rosewater Foundation, bankrolls the "useless and unattractive Americans" who would otherwise have no dignity. He does this to the distress of his wife, who suffers four nervous breakdowns (three of them offstage) before divorcing him to become a nun; his father, a craggy fixture of the Establishment; and his psychiatrist, who at one point dismisses him as incurable. A young lawyer, meanwhile, attempts to prove Eliot insane, to transfer control of the Foundation to the branch of the Rosewater clan in Rhode Island, and to collect a handsome fee.

The play is produced by Vonnegut's daughter Edie, who is currently attempting to take it to Broadway.

Like most theatrical productions, *God Bless You, Mr. Rosewater*'s $400,000 budget was financed primarily through the sale of limited partnerships (partial units went for as little as $1,000). Warner Communications chipped in $100,000 for a 25 percent equity position and identification as associate producer. Net profits in most Broadway shows are split 50-50 between the producer and the investors.

Most limited partners will never recover their investments. In fact, the success rate for plays is only about 25 percent, while it is 37 percent for musicals. Why then do people become limited partners in Broadway shows? Most explanations center around an appreciation of the theater or personal desire to be involved in such a venture. Few expect to profit from their investment. Maybe that is why the theater crowd refers to the limited partners as "Broadway Angels."

Questions

1. Why are limited partnerships used for theatrical productions?

2. Research Broadway's financial successes. Is there a common characteristic for these productions?

3. What other types of entertainment have used the limited partnership organizational arrangement?

4

Small Business and Franchising

Learning Goals

1. To explain the vital role played by small business in the economy

2. To define *small business* and to know where most small firms are established

3. To compare the advantages and the disadvantages of small businesses

4. To describe franchising and its advantages and disadvantages

5. To analyze the small business opportunities for women and minorities and to understand the special problems faced by these entrepreneurs

6. To describe how the Small Business Administration functions

7. To explain the meaning of each of the key terms introduced in this chapter

The authors acknowledge the collaborative efforts of Lawrence A. Klatt of Florida Atlantic University. Dr. Klatt is a recognized authority in the field and the author of textbooks dealing with small business management.

Profile: Female Entrepreneurs
Starting Businesses

Lore Harp and Carole Ely

The decade of the woman entrepreneur may be here. Women who climbed the corporate ladder during the 1970s are now ready to apply what they learned to their own businesses—and make it big.

"We see an increasing number of women going after businesses that can really develop into something," says Joseph R. Mancuso, president of the Center for Entrepreneurial Management, Inc., in Worcester, Massachussetts. This new generation of female entrepreneurs is aiming at high technology and manufacturing businesses that were once the exclusive domain of men. Here are two examples:

• Lore Harp and Carole Ely, two Southern California housewives, used $6,000 of personal savings to launch Vector Graphic Inc., a company that markets a memory board for microcomputers designed by Harp's husband, Robert. Today, Vector employs 125 workers and expects $18 million worth of sales.

• With $2,000 of her own money, Sandra L. Kurtzig opened ASK Computer Services, Inc. Today this computer software company expects $12 million in sales and pretax profits of 20 percent.

Today's female entrepreneurs deal for high stakes. They are learning how to handle merger bids, compete with experienced male executives, and get financing through bankers and venture capitalists. But the road is not all smooth. "The biggest obstacle women entrepreneurs face," says Mancuso, "is dealing with a 99 percent male banking and financial community."

Bias is still part of the picture, but bias aside, many female entrepreneurs doom themselves. With unstructured business plans ("I know the business will grow, but I don't know exactly how much," says one company president), women find themselves on the outside of the normal channels of capital formation looking in.

Female business leaders are convinced that this situation is only temporary. As more and more women leave corporate management positions and apply their years of experience to their own businesses, they will operate with the same sophisticated skills as men.

And they may have one important advantage. According to Beatrice Fitzpatrick, chief executive officer of the American Woman's Economic Development Corp. (AWED), a program designed to train and counsel female entrepreneurs, women "simply will not let their businesses die." Regarding their businesses as their "babies," women tend to hold on harder than men. But, cautions Marilyn French Hubbard, a Detroit consultant, when women's grip gets too tight, they can miss the chance to move their companies out of the small business class. According to French, many women "must learn to think bigger and riskier."

To be successful you have to have a goal other than money. My goal is to give blacks an opportunity. The fact that in five years I've built the seventh largest black business in America speaks for itself.

—George Smith
President, Smith Pipe & Supply, Inc.

As a boy, Hector Guevara was always fascinated by the concept of solar energy. Later, after college and stints with the military and two large firms, Guevara opened his own business—Alternate Energy Industries Corp. He concentrated on custom engineering solar hot water systems. Most of Guevara's work has been for private residences, although recently he has branched out into major buildings and restaurants. Alternate Energy Industries' best-known customer is a home located at 1600 Pennsylvania Avenue, Washington, D.C. Guevara, a minority small businessperson, won the $35,000 contract to install a 32-panel solar system at the White House. About 75 percent of the water used at the White House is now heated by the new solar system.[1]

Importance of the Small Business Sector

Guevara is typical of many small businesspeople. The successful installation of the White House solar energy system by a small firm indicates the vital role small business plays in the economy. Americans have long advocated a strong small business sector as the backbone of the private enterprise system. Small businesses provide much of the competitive zeal that keeps the system effective. And much has been done to encourage the development and continuity of small firms. Antitrust legislation, for example, was designed to maintain the competitive environment in which small companies thrive. A separate federal agency—the Small Business Administration—was set up in 1953 to assist smaller firms.

Small business is a vital segment of the U.S. economy; 96.7 percent of all nonfarm businesses are considered small by the federal government. Approximately 10.2 million small companies provide 43 percent of the national output of goods and services and employ about 58 percent of all private, nonfarm workers. Ninety percent of all new jobs are in small business.[2]

Firms with fewer than 100 employees create about two-thirds of all new jobs in the U.S. labor force. Overall, these employers account for 55 percent of the total labor force.[3]

These statistics suggest the vital role that small business plays in contemporary business. Aside from the many services they provide to consumers, small businesses also help large businesses function efficiently. Many suppliers to large manufacturers are small firms attempting to offer a product or service better than that of their competitors.

Our private enterprise system started with the small shops and workrooms of colonial times, and we still depend on such independent entrepreneurs today. They are the very heart of the private enterprise system.

How Do We Define Small Business?

American Motors is small in comparison to General Motors. But with sales of around $3.1 billion, it can hardly be considered small when compared to the vast majority of U.S. businesses. For instance, it is larger than Campbell Soup, a giant in its own industry.[4]

Any conception of a small business is dependent on comparisons with other businesses. Sales, number of employees, assets, net worth, market share, and relationship to competitors have all been used to make this determination. There are probably as many ways to define *small business* as there are people wanting to do so.

The Small Business Administration says that a **small business** is one that is independently owned and operated, is not dominant in its field, and meets a variety of size standards.[5] A recent White House

small business
A business that is independently owned and operated, is not dominant in its field, and meets a variety of size standards.

Service operations, such as barbershops, are most often small businesses.

conference on small business added another dimension to the definition by setting up different classes of small businesses according to the number of people employed: class A firms employ 0–9 people; class B, 10–49; class C, 50–249; and class D, 250–400 persons.[6] From still another perspective, management characteristics are what set small businesses apart from larger ones.

Probably the most workable concept of a small business is the one suggested some years ago by the Committee for Economic Development. To qualify as a small firm under its definition, a business must have had at least two of the following characteristics: (1) independent management with the managers often owning the firm, (2) the capital contribution coming from a limited number of individuals—perhaps only one, (3) the firm operating in a local area, and (4) the firm representing a small part of the overall industry.[7]

Popular Small Business Ventures

Small businesses are found in nearly every industry in the United States. They often compete against some of the nation's largest organizations as well as against a multitude of other small companies. Retailing and service establishments are the most common small businesses. New-technology companies also often start as small organizations.

While general merchandise giants like Sears, J. C. Penney, and K mart are the most significant firms in this area of retailing, they are far outnumbered by small, privately owned retail enterprises. Small business, in fact, characterizes the retailing of shoes, jewelry, office supplies and stationery, apparel, flowers, drugs, convenience foods, and thousands of other products.

Service-oriented industries and individuals—such as restaurants, funeral homes, banking establishments, movie theaters, dry cleaners, carpet cleaners, shoe repairers, attorneys, insurance agents, automobile repairers, public accountants, dentists, and doctors—also abound in our private enterprise economy. There are relatively few national sellers of services, except in the case of insurance. Seven out of ten jobs (and 70 percent of the new ones) are in service industries.[8]

Many new-technology firms—those striving to produce and market some scientific innovation—typically start as small businesses, and many great inventors and technical geniuses began their businesses in barns, garages, warehouses, and attics. Small business is often the best (or only) option available to a scientist who seeks to make an idea into a commercial reality.

Although most new businesses, including a variety of retail and service enterprises, appear in industries that have limited capital re-

Most retail operations, such as shoe stores, and service operations, such as laundries, are small businesses.

quirements, some technical firms require substantial capital to get off the ground. Initial capital requirements of $1 million or more are not at all uncommon in such industries. The high entry cost is primarily due to the long time lag between start-up and receipt of sales revenue.

Many small firms fail when they attempt to operate the way large firms do. They are not simply smaller versions of large corporations. Their legal organization, market position, staff capability, managerial style and organization, and financial resources generally differ from bigger companies, which gives them some distinct advantages and disadvantages.

Advantages of a Small Business

Small size may provide some unique competitive advantages over larger size. Innovative behavior, lower costs, and the filling of isolated market niches are some of the most important of these advantages.

Innovative Behavior

Small firms are often the ones to offer innovations, new concepts, and new products in the marketplace. Genentech, Inc., and Apple Computer, Inc., are two recent success stories. In fact, it is estimated that the formation of small high-technology firms doubled in recent years.[9]

Scientific innovations are not the only concepts offered by small business entrepreneurs. Atlanta's Bill Mc Daniel opened a dry cleaning business in a shopping center near some offices and apartment complexes. His firm now does $130,000 annually. Mc Daniel had been unsuccessful with earlier ventures in real estate leasing and carpet cleaning. An earlier attempt to operate a dry cleaning establishment had also failed, partially because of the growth of wash-and-wear

"Let's just admit that the drive-thru salad bar is an idea whose time has not yet come."

Small firms are often the ones to offer innovations and new concepts in the marketplace.
Drawing by Stevenson; © 1980 The New Yorker Magazine, Inc.

fabrics. Mc Daniel's recent success can be traced largely to his personal interest and hard work in the business.[10]

Innovative behavior is also found in the marketing strategies of smaller firms. U.S. Mills sells Skinner's, the nation's first raisin bran cereal (introduced in 1926), through some clever methods. A privately owned firm, U.S. Mills is quite small in comparison to its raisin bran competitors—Kellogg and General Foods. Rather than spend huge amounts on advertising, it works closely with supermarkets. U.S. Mills tries to improve its minuscule 3 percent market share by offering lower prices to retailers. Another marketing strategy is to use boxes a quarter inch wider than others to give more shelf space exposure in the supermarket.[11]

Lower Costs

Small firms can often provide a product or service cheaper than large firms. They usually have fewer overhead costs—those not directly related to providing the goods and services—than large firms. Thus, they may be able to earn a profit on a price lower than a large company can offer.

Small businesses have leaner organizations with smaller staffs and fewer support personnel. The lower overhead costs resulting from fewer permanent staff people can provide a distinct advantage to small businesses. Small businesses tend to hire outside consultants or specialists, such as attorneys and certified public accountants, only during periods when their assistance is needed. As a general rule, all growing organizations add staff personnel faster than line (management) personnel. Larger organizations tend to maintain such specialists on their permanent staffs.

Small businesses also often have the services of a great deal of unpaid labor. Entrepreneurs themselves are usually willing to work long hours on their pet projects, and no one pays them for overtime or holidays. And family members contribute a significant amount of unpaid labor as bookkeepers, laborers, receptionists, delivery personnel, and the like.

Filling of Isolated Niches

Big businesses are excluded from some commercial activities because of their size. High overhead costs force them to set minimum targets at which to direct their competitive efforts. Some large publishers, for example, have identified minimum acceptable sales figures that take into account their overhead costs. Editorial and production expenses for a certain type of book may not be justified unless the publisher can sell, say, 7,000 copies. This situation allows substantial opportunities for smaller publishers with lower overhead costs.

In addition, certain types of businesses lend themselves better to smaller firms. Many services illustrate this point. Marybeth Armitstead runs a successful men's fashion consulting and wardrobe service in Seattle called the Gentlemen's Agreement. Armitstead meets with her clients away from the office and then decides on a wardrobe to match their needs and lifestyles. She supervises the clothes selection process taking into account what the man already owns. Some of her clients never get near a store.[12] Finally, economic and organizational factors may dictate that an industry consist essentially of small firms.

Disadvantages of a Small Business

A variety of disadvantages face smaller firms, including poor management, inadequate financing, and government regulation. While these problems often can be overcome, they should be considered by anyone contemplating a small business venture.

Poor Management

It is a simple fact that most people who start small businesses are ill prepared to function as managers. Successful small businesspeople are almost always good managers, but they are a minority compared to the failures. Thousands of small businesses open every year. Thirty percent fail within the first year, and half within two years. A Bank of America study blamed poor management for most failures.[13]

Since *poor management* is a vague term, it is important to look at the types of management shortcomings that characterize small business. Often, people who start small firms have little, if any, training or education in running a business. They have an idea for a product or service and assume that they will learn about business matters as they carry on the business. Bankruptcy is often the result. A word of caution is in order: Any budding entrepreneur is well advised to acquire as sound a foundation in basic business principles as possible before initiating any small business venture.

Another cause of failure is that small businesspeople sometimes let their entrepreneurial optimism run wild. Kenneth Eaton, head of Associated Business Consultants, puts it this way:

> An entrepreneur is an optimist by definition, and overoptimism is what does companies in. When things are going well, the average businessman assumes they will continue to go well. When a problem arises, he assumes it will go away quickly by itself. By the time he wakes up to the fact that he really has a problem, it's often too late to do anything about it.[14]

A closely related reason for failure results from not doing needed homework before starting the small business. Entrepreneurs may believe that others will see their product or service as unique or better than that of the competition, but basic research is needed before any action is taken on this assumption. Essentially, what the individual must find out is whether a market exists for the proposed product or service. This information can be secured in many ways: through published sources, surveys, in-depth interviews, competitive analyses, observation, or a number of other techniques.

Inadequate Financing

Many small businesses start with inadequate capital and soon run into a shortage of funds. They often lack the resources to carry them over rough spots or to expand if they are successful. Inadequate financing is generally listed as a leading cause of small business problems.

Banks, venture capitalists, and the Small Business Administration are traditional sources of small business funding—after personal or family funding. Banks are usually quite careful about loaning money to small businesses because of their high failure rate. Banks and most other small business lenders require detailed information in order to justify such loans.

Venture capitalists are groups of private individuals or business organizations that invest in promising new businesses. Sometimes they loan the business the money; at other times they become part owners of the new or struggling firm. Venture capital has been an important source of funds, particularly for firms offering a creative new concept or product.

venture capitalists
Groups of private individuals or business organizations that invest in promising new businesses. Sometimes they loan money, and sometimes they become part owners of the firm.

The Small Business Administration (which will be discussed in detail in a later section of the chapter) offers a variety of loans for small businesses, primarily through banks. These loans are used for business construction, expansion, or conversion; for purchasing machinery, equipment, facilities, supplies, or materials; and for working capital.[15]

Government Regulation

Like most executives, small businesspeople complain bitterly of excessive government regulation and red tape. The U.S. Commission on Federal Paperwork estimates that the paperwork cost for small firms is about $15 billion to $20 billion annually. Furthermore, the regulation of small companies accounts for a large portion of the government's own paperwork expenditure. A Louis Harris survey found that regulatory paperwork was the most common complaint about government among small- and medium-sized businesses.[16]

Most small businesses are not equipped to handle the paperwork necessitated by government regulation (see Focus 4–1). Larger firms with substantial staff can usually cope with the blizzard of required forms and reports, but for many small business owners, it is often the force that drives them out to look for salaried positions. Many experts within and outside government believe that a major effort must be made to reduce the paperwork load for small businesses.

FOCUS 4–1
That New Santa Fe Travail

With $18,000 from a second mortgage on his house, a few hand tools, and his wife as bookkeeper, Robert Ozuna in 1967 founded an electrical contracting firm in his garage. Today his New Bedford Panoramex Corp. of Santa Fe Springs, Calif., occupies an 18,000-sq.-ft. building, employs 41 people and . . . [has] sales of $3.5 million. Ozuna assembles the instrument panels that monitor nuclear plants, oil drilling rigs and other high-technology hardware. Firms working the Alaskan oil pipeline use his products. . . .

A Mexican American raised in Los Angeles, Ozuna, 50, gained his expertise on the job. While working for small West Coast electronics companies in the '50s and '60s, he slogged through night-school classes to pick up engineering skills. Now that his perseverance has paid off, Ozuna is unhappy about what the economy is doing to his business. His chubby face sags as he grumbles: "We're working harder and selling more but making less money."

Unpredictable jumps in raw material prices constantly sabotage his planning. His suppliers have slowed their deliveries, and customers have stretched out their payments. The bank charges him 24% on loans to maintain his inventories. Since oilmen buy his control consoles, the energy boom has put Ozuna in better shape than most entrepreneurs to endure the recession, but his profit margin has plunged from 12% of sales . . . to 4%.

Landing federal contracts would help, but Ozuna complains that the truckloads of paper work required give the advantage to big firms, which have bureaucracies to fill out the forms. He is disenchanted enough to envision building a new plant in Mexico. In the land of his ancestors, he says, government funds flow more freely, and oil money now gushes out of the ground.

franchising
A contractual arrangement between a manufacturer or other supplier and a dealer that sets the methods to be used in selling a product.

franchisee
The dealer in a franchise operation; a small businessperson who is allowed to sell a product or service of a supplier, or franchisor, in exchange for some payment—usually a flat fee plus future royalties or commissions.

franchisor
The supplier of a franchise who typically provides building plans, site selection research, managerial and accounting procedures, and other services to assist the franchisee—and who receives payment, usually in the form of a flat fee and royalties or commissions.

The Franchising Concept

Franchising, legally a contract between a manufacturer or other supplier and a dealer that sets the methods to be used in selling a product, has proved very effective for small businesses. The dealer, or **franchisee,** is a small businessperson who is allowed to sell a product or service of a supplier, or **franchisor,** in exchange for some payment—usually a flat fee plus future royalties or commissions. The franchisor typically provides building plans, site selection research, managerial and accounting procedures, and other services to assist the franchisee.

TABLE 4–1
Advantages and Disadvantages of Franchises

Advantages	Disadvantages
Performance record on which to make comparisons and judgments.	High cost of obtaining a franchise.
Widely recognized name.	Consumer judgment of the business on the basis of other, similar franchises.
Tested management system.	Restrictions on business decisions.

Franchising has come to dominate certain segments of retailing—fast food restaurants, car rentals, motels, weight reduction programs, health spas, and so on. Names like Avis, Holiday Inn, Weight Watchers, and Vic Tanney are widely recognized today.

The franchises associated with the various fast food chains are truly household words. Some, such as Kentucky Fried Chicken, have been around for a long time. Others are relative newcomers. Dozens of others have failed.

Franchising has proven very effective, and many people have become wealthy as a result of their decision to purchase a franchise. Consider the case of Richard Cooper, who accidentally struck a pedestrian while bicycling in New York's Central Park. Cooper and the pedestrian, a Weight Watchers International lawyer, became friends. This relationship led to Cooper quitting his job and buying the Chicago franchise for Weight Watchers. By age 29, Richard Cooper was a millionaire.[17]

A franchise is like any other business property: it is the buyer's responsibility to know what he or she is buying. Poorly financed or poorly managed franchise systems are no better than poorly financed or poorly managed nonfranchise businesses. The advantages and disadvantages of franchises are compared in Table 4–1.

Existing franchises have a performance record on which the small businessperson can make comparisons and judgments. The likelihood of success in the proposed venture can be assessed by looking at earlier results. This requires careful study and hard work on the part of the franchisee. In addition, a widely recognized name gives the franchisee a tremendous advantage. Car dealers, for instance, know that their brand name products will attract a given clientele. A franchise also gives the small businessperson a tested management system. The prospective franchisee usually does not have to worry about setting up an accounting system, calculating quality control standards, or designing employment application forms. These things are typically provided for in the franchise arrangement.

Franchising, however, does not eliminate all the risks of a small business investment. On the negative side, franchise fees and future payments can be very expensive. Good franchises with tested management systems, proven performance records, and widely recognized names usually sell for more than those lacking these characteristics. The prospective franchisee must determine whether the expenses in-

The number of women who own their own small businesses, such as this grocery store, is increasing every year.

volved are fair compensation for what will be received. Another potentially negative factor is that a successful franchise can be pulled down by similar but less successful franchises. An inherent disadvantage of the franchise system is that the franchisee is judged by what his or her peers do. A strong, effective program of managerial control is essential to offset any bad impressions given by unsuccessful franchises. A last possible disadvantage of a franchise is that the franchisor's management system may restrict many decisions. The franchisee may not have the independence that most small business-people seek.

Purchasing a good franchise requires careful study of these advantages and disadvantages. The correct decision in one set of circumstances may be wrong under a different set of circumstances. The franchising concept does not solve the problem for someone considering a small business investment; it merely adds alternatives.

Small Business Opportunities for Women and Minorities

Small firms offer excellent opportunities for women and minorities to enter the business world. Currently these two groups have only a modest share of business ownership; yet both are making significant advances.

Women-owned Businesses

Consider the situation with women-owned businesses. Government statistics indicate that women own only about 7.1 percent of all U.S. firms. Table 4–2 shows that their ownership varied from less than 2 percent in construction to more than 10 percent in certain other areas. Most such firms are quite small, as evidenced by the fact that women's 7.1 percent ownership share often translates into a disproportionately smaller share of all receipts within an industry.

TABLE 4–2
Women-owned Firms in the United States

Industry	Percent of All Firms Owned by Women	Percent of All Industry Receipts Going to Women-owned Firms
Construction	1.9	4.0
Manufacturing	6.6	9.4
Transportation and public utilities	2.9	5.7
Wholesale and retail trade	8.8	8.0
Finance, insurance, and real estate	4.7	3.2
Selected services	8.7	5.9
Other industries and industries not classified	10.2	5.7
Total for all industries	7.1	6.6

More women are setting up their own firms these days. While they are beginning to make their mark in the world of small business, the advances are not without major problems for the people involved.

Some small business problems affect women in particular. Prejudice in varying degrees is always a factor for women-owned firms. Many prospective female entrepreneurs lack business training or experience. College-educated women have typically studied in traditional career areas such as teaching, nursing, and home economics. Today, many of these people are retraining themselves through programs offered by colleges, universities, and other groups interested in furthering female entrepreneurship. Future generations of small businesspersons may include better prepared women, judging by the number flooding into college classrooms to study business administration. Women also encounter all the problems faced by their male competitors. Like their male counterparts, the good entrepreneurs usually survive, and those who cannot adjust or satisfy their markets eventually fail.

Minority-owned Businesses

Minority-owned businesses account for only 5.7 percent of all U.S. firms. Blacks own about 41 percent of all minority businesses. Spanish-origin owners account for another 39 percent. Table 4–3 shows that the percentage of minority ownership varied from 2.0 percent in

Minority-owned businesses in the wholesale and retail sector, such as this shoe repair shop, represent 6 percent of all such firms in the U.S.

TABLE 4–3
Minority-owned Firms in the United States

Industry	Percent of All Firms Owned by Minorities	Percent of All Industry Receipts Going to Minority Firms
Construction	4.7	2.9
Manufacturing	4.2	2.3
Transportation and public utilities	8.6	3.9
Wholesale and retail trade	6.0	3.7
Finance, insurance, real estate	2.0	1.1
Selected services	6.5	4.9
Total for all industries	5.7	3.5

finance, insurance, and real estate to 8.6 percent in transportation and public utilities.

Minority-owned businesses fare worse than women-owned businesses in terms of receipts; their ownership share is about 3.5 of all receipts within an industry. Most of the minority-owned businesses are also small; over 80 percent of them have no paid employees.[18]

All small businesses face a high failure rate in their initial year of operation, but minority-owned firms exceed even these high averages.[29] Minority businesspeople have a variety of special problems, starting with a lack of training or education in business-related fields. Often they are the first in their family to enter the business world. This disadvantage is being countered by training programs sponsored by government, industry, professional business groups, colleges, and others. Like women, younger members of minority groups are also seeking the opportunities that can be found in business administration curricula.

Minority-owned enterprises are often underfinanced, because minority entrepreneurs typically come from poorer families than their counterparts.[20] While this balance is shifting, such firms still tend to have fewer resources than their competitors. Lack of adequate financing is one of the most critical problems facing minority business.

Minorities have traditionally gone into businesses where the opportunities for making large profits may be limited. An example is businesses whose trade is restricted to nonwhite areas. The government's **Minority Business Development Agency** (formerly the Office of Minority Business Enterprise, or OMBE) has encouraged minority business persons to enter more profitable fields.[21] The agency, which is part of the Department of Commerce, is also involved in various assistance programs for minority businesspeople. As more and more minority firms are created, there should be a greater minority representation in the most profitable industries.

No one expects this underrepresentation of women and minority entrepreneurs to be eliminated quickly, but many people are working to correct the inequity. It is now realistic for women and minorities to seek equal opportunities in the small business sector.

Minority Business Development Agency
An agency of the U.S. Department of Commerce that provides financial assistance and advice to minority-owned businesses: often encourages minority businesspeople to enter more profitable fields.

The Small Business Administration

The **Small Business Administration (SBA),** set up in 1953, is the principal government agency concerned with small U.S. firms. The Small Business Act clearly stated Congress's intentions regarding this vital sector of the private enterprise system:

> It is the declared policy of the Congress that the Government should aid, counsel, assist, and protect, insofar as is possible, the interests of small business concerns in order to preserve free competitive enterprise . . . to maintain and strengthen the overall economy of the Nation.

The SBA is small business's advocate within the federal government. A relatively small agency in the government bureaucracy, it has 4,300 employees spread out among its Washington headquarters, 10 regional offices, and 96 field offices.

The primary operating functions of the SBA are providing financial assistance, helping with government procurement matters, and offering management training and consulting.[22] The SBA has several loan programs to help small businesses—both established and planned ones. Small firms also can receive help in securing a share of government contracts. The SBA provides management advice through various publications and programs. It has, for example, established a special outreach program to alert female entrepreneurs to its activities. Its hundreds of business publications can be ordered for little or no

Small Business Administration (SBA)
The principal government agency concerned with small U.S. firms. Set up in 1953, it provides financial assistance and offers management training and consulting and other services to small businesses in order to preserve free competitive enterprise.

The Service Corps of Retired Executives (SCORE) has volunteer management consultants to advise on business problems.

Controversial Issue

Should Government Subsidize Small Business?

Many of the over 14 million small businesses in the United States face a grim future. Pushed to the wall by skyrocketing inflation, high interest rates, low availability of capital, rising operating costs for labor and energy, mounting inventories, low productivity, and customers who are slow to pay their bills, small businesses are going bankrupt at an increasingly alarming rate. According to Small Business Administration (SBA) estimates, bankruptcies were up 48 percent in one recent six-month period. "The failure rate is increasing, and there is no way of telling when it will level off," said Robert Berney, SBA chief economist. The failures "are due to a significant shift in the economy. Something serious is happening to small business."

The Small Business Administration, which was created in 1953 to provide economic assistance to the nation's small businesses, channels money in the form of loan guarantees into those small businesses that have a reasonable prospect of success. Economic development, not rescue, is the goal.

Is this limited action enough? Or should the government directly subsidize companies on the brink of bankruptcy? This question is at the heart of a heated debate.

Those who support government subsidy of small business point to small business's crucial economic role. Because small businesses employ 58 percent of all private, nonfarm workers and account for 96.7 percent of all nonfarm business, supporters of small businesses claim that they are the lifeblood of the American economy. They are also least able to withstand the double-barreled assault of inflation and high interest rates. "Big companies can just pass on extra labor and business costs to the consumer," says George W. Combs, a Houston steel fabricator. "We can't do that. Our prices are controlled by our competitors."

Service Corps of Retired Executives (SCORE)
Groups of volunteer management consultants who assist people with small business problems. A program of the SBA.

Active Corps of Executives (ACE)
Groups of volunteer management consultants who assist people with small business problems. A program of the SBA.

cost, and its conferences and seminars are widely available. Management counseling is done through a variety of programs, including:

1. The **Service Corps of Retired Executives (SCORE)** and the **Active Corps of Executives (ACE).** These groups have volunteer management consultants who assist people with small business problems.

2. The **Small Business Institute (SBI).** The SBI sends out senior and graduate business students as consultants on small business problems at no cost to the firm requesting help. The SBI program operates under faculty supervision at hundreds of schools in the United States.[23]

3. **Small Business Development Centers.** These centers are part of a program aimed at using qualified personnel to assist small businesses

When interest rates skyrocket, small business interest costs, which are usually two to three points above the rate for big business, reduce profit margins and force the cancellation of growth plans. "We are seeing very limited borrowing," says James Phelps, executive vice-president of the First Security Bank of Idaho. "Some of the SBA-guaranteed loan applications are coming through for debt consolidation and working capital. None is for expansion." Faced with these circumstances, small businesses look at the federal government's bail out of Chrysler and Lockheed and ask, "Why not me?"

Opponents of federal subsidy of small business believe as Senator William Proxmire does that it is "a mistake for the federal government to bail out a failing corporation." Our free enterprise system is based on personal initiative, say critics. If businesspeople know what they are doing, have good management skills and a product or service the public wants, they will make it. If they do not, their businesses deserve to fail.

"When government chooses, unnecessarily, to bail out firms that have failed because of incompetence," says Senator Proxmire, "the incompetence and lack of judgment remain." And according to Proxmire such a policy would enable people who have neither good judgment nor capital nor a product in demand to continue in business. Whenever the going got tough, they would only have to call for help, and the government would take care of the rest.

As the economy worsens, the pressure to come to the aid of small businesses will surely increase. Whether government decides that small business survival depends on an infusion of government funds or that a direct subsidy would undermine the free enterprise system is a question that will be debated over the coming years.

through research and consulting activities. Fees are charged to offset the costs involved.[24]

Some Concluding Thoughts on Small Business

Despite the many difficulties encountered by small business, owning and operating a business remains part of our way of life. Small business offers many promises and hopes beyond those of a financial nature. Independence, self-fulfillment, self-respect, and contributions to society are but a few.

Small Business Institute (SBI)
An organization (part of the SBA) that sends out senior and graduate business students as consultants on small business problems at no cost to the firm.

Small Business Development Centers
Centers that are part of a federal program aimed at using qualified faculty personnel and others to assist small businesses through research and consulting activities.

Small business has long been an integral part of the private enterprise system, the cradle of great industries, great companies, and great business leaders. It remains a vital mechanism for the release of competitive energy. People who see a chance for personal achievement are usually more productive than those who see their work as boring or routine and with no chance of improvement. Small business offers the opportunity for personal achievement. It always has offered this opportunity, and it probably always will!

Summary

Small businesses have been an important part of the private enterprise system. They have been looked upon favorably because of the independence they provide and the competitive fervor they bring to the private enterprise economy. Small firms account for the bulk of all U.S. commercial enterprises and provide a major portion of our national output and employment.

A small business is one that is independently owned and operated and is not dominant in its market. Most small companies are concentrated in the retailing and service sectors of our economy, although many new-technology firms have also begun as small businesses. Most new companies crop up in industries with low entry-level capital requirements.

Small businesses have some distinct advantages over larger competitors, including innovative behavior, lower costs, and the filling of isolated niches. They also have disadvantages, including poor management, inadequate financing, and government regulation.

Franchising is a contract between a manufacturer or other supplier and a dealer that sets the methods to be used in selling a product. Franchising now dominates the retailing of some products. The advantages of the franchising approach to small business are performance records on which to make comparisons and judgments, a widely recognized name, and tested management systems. The disadvantages include the high cost of obtaining a franchise, consumer judgment of the business on the basis of other, similar franchises, and restrictions on business decisions.

Women account for only a 7.1 percent ownership share of all U.S. firms, and minorities account for a similarly low 5.7 percent share. In recent years, however, both groups have begun making significant advances in small firms, and greater growth is expected.

The Small Business Administration (SBA) was set up in 1953 to assist small firms. The SBA is small business's chief advocate in government circles. Its primary operating functions are providing financial assistance, helping with government procurement matters, and offering management training and consulting to small businesses.

Key Terms

small business
venture capitalists
franchising
franchisee
franchisor
Minority Business
    Development Agency

Small Business Administration (SBA)
Service Corps of Retired
    Executives (SCORE)
Active Corps of Executives (ACE)
Small Business Institute (SBI)
Small Business Development Centers

Review Questions

1. Explain each of the terms listed above.

2. Describe the importance of small business to the total U.S. economy.

3. List the characteristics of small business as identified by the Committee for Economic Development.

4. In what sectors of the economy is small business most important? To what do you credit its strength in these areas?

5. List the advantages and disadvantages of small businesses.

6. Identify the usual sources of financing available to small businesses.

7. Discuss the advantages and disadvantages of buying a franchise.

8. Describe the current status of women in small business.

9. Describe the current status of minorities in small business.

10. Explain the functions performed by the Small Business Administration.

Discussion Questions and Exercises

1. Evaluate the pros and cons of the controversial issue that appears in this chapter.

2. Some lawmakers have proposed that the post of administrator of the SBA be raised to cabinet rank in order to give small firms a greater voice in government. What is your opinion of this proposal?

3. Contact some small businesses in your area. Make up a list of the specific problems they face. Are any of them common problems?

4. Visit the owners of one or more local franchise businesses. Ask these people why they decided to buy a franchise rather than start an independent business of their own. Find out what problems (if any) they are having with their franchisor.

5. Prepare a two-page report on the services available from the Small Business Administration and the Minority Business Development Agency.

Case 4–1: "Fortune 500"— A Small Business?

Some of the biggest firms in the United States paid $30,000 each to get in on a game created by two small businesspersons—Gavin Brackenridge and Richard Fenwick. The young entrepreneurs market a board and dice game about business, featuring pitfalls, such as inflation, strikes, and regulatory changes as well as rising interest rates and the like. Originally marketed in France as "Business," the game sold 250,000 copies. When they brought it to the United States, Brackenridge and Fenwick decided to retitle the game "Fortune 500." However, this name was the property of Time, Inc., the publisher of *Fortune* magazine, which publishes a list of the nation's top 500 companies. The two entrepreneurs convinced Time, Inc., to let them use the name in exchange for a royalty.

Brackenridge and Fenwick then approached large U.S. firms and suggested that they chip in $30,000 each for the privilege of having their name and logo imprinted on the game board. Many corporate giants ignored the request. But others saw it as an advertising opportunity and paid the fee suggested. Chase Manhattan, Alcoa, Pan Am, Aetna, Mobil, and Southern Pacific are among the 20 firms that appear on "Fortune 500's" four-inch panels. With $600,000 in revenues before they sold a single game in the United States, Brackenridge and Fenwick were fast leaving the world of small business!

Questions

1. Why do you think Brackenridge and Fenwick's small business was successful?

2. Would a large corporation have been able to market this product as successfully as Brackenridge and Fenwick?

3. Identify other small businesses that are based on a similar type of creative idea as "Fortune 500."

Case 4–2: Speakerlab

With $6 million in annual sales and a market share at times as high as 50 percent, Speakerlab is one of the leaders in the kit stereo speaker market. The Seattle-based company also sells finished speakers and assorted stereo components. Pat Snyder started Speakerlab with a total capital investment of $1,500. Total additional cash contributions from the owners over the nine years of the firm's existence amounted to only $15,000.

Snyder's approach, which he now advocates on the lecture circuit, is to begin a business with minimal capitalization. Speakerlab's founder thinks the key is to start a small business with a high sales/total assets ratio and work to keep it that way. Snyder started his company with set financial goals and comprehensive financial statements. The objectives were stated as financial ratios. The financial statements allowed him to obtain credit, a problem for many small firms. Snyder has even claimed that it is possible to start a business without any money.

Other major elements of Snyder's business strategy include the extensive use of leasing, an employee stock option plan that allows Speakerlab workers to share in the ownership of the firm, a continuous research and development effort, and an emphasis on quality. All of Snyder's decisions are based on his firm's overall financial plan. His basic philosophy is: "Re-think the obvious. Do not let assumptions create obstacles."

Questions

1. What is your opinion of Pat Snyder's approach to starting a small business?

2. Why do you think Speakerlab has been successful?

3. Develop a plan for a small business venture along the lines suggested in this case.

Careers in Selected Aspects of Business and Its Environment

Business is the primary employer in our private enterprise system. *Contemporary Business* introduces the reader to a wide range of future business careers. Each major part of the text is followed by a career section featuring employment opportunities in that particular functional area. The careers discussed here are in selected aspects of business and its environment.

The Bureau of Labor Statistics has projected the employment outlook to 1990. Its forecasts for selected business careers appear in the following table. The bureau expects all occupations to add 20.8 percent to the work force between 1978 and 1990. Several business-related careers currently available appear below.

Attorney. Most legal firms are extensively involved in business problems. Some attorneys work directly for a firm, but most are independent contractors. Because so much of most attorneys' work is in business law, it is advisable for them to have a business as well as a legal education.

Banker. The term *banker* applies to a number of people in banking positions. Most top bank executives have had experience in all aspects of bank management and operations. Banking is a prestigious, rewarding career field.

Owner/manager. The ownership and management functions are often performed by the same person in a small business, where people are "their own bosses." This is a rewarding experience for many people.

Public accountant. Public accountants are independent business-people who provide accounting services to firms and individuals. These services range from setting up accounting systems to preparing tax forms. Professional certification for public accountants is indicated by the title Certified Public Accountant (CPA).

Sales representative. Sales representatives are the people who handle the personal selling aspects of the firm's marketing program. They call on prospective buyers, explain the firm's products, and secure orders. They are also responsible for seeing that customers are satisfied with their purchases and become repeat buyers.

Supervisor. A supervisor is a manager of a particular work area within a plant. This person directly supervises employees such as assembly line workers, welders, cutters, and others. The supervisor is at the first level of management in a factory.

Systems analyst. Systems analysts are well-trained computer experts who develop the various computer-based information systems needed in an organization. They determine which information is required and how best to obtain it.

EMPLOYMENT OUTLOOK TO 1990							
		Changes in Employment					
Occupations in Selected Aspects of Business and Its Environment	Recent Employment Figures	Much Faster than the Average for All Occupations	Faster than the Average for All Occupations	About as Fast as the Average for All Occupations	More Slowly than the Average for All Occupations	Little Change Expected	Expected to Decline
Accountants	980,000		X				
Bank Officers and Managers	330,000	X					
Blue Collar Work Supervisors	1,670,000			X			
Economists	130,000		X				
Health and Regulatory Inspectors Government	100,000		X				
Lawyers	480,000			X			
Manufacturers' Sales Workers	400,000			X			
Occupational Safety & Health Workers	80,000		X				
Systems Analysts	182,000		X				

Source: U.S. Department of Labor, Bureau of Labor Statistics, *Occupational Outlook Handbook, 1980–1981,* Bulletin 2075, pp. 5, 55–56, 100–101, 103–105, 113–115, 122–125, 165–170, 195–197, 419–421.

PART
TWO

ORGANIZATION AND MANAGEMENT OF THE ENTERPRISE

5

Introduction to Management

Learning Goals

1. To describe how management is important in all types of organizations, whether profit-seeking or nonprofit

2. To identify the steps in the decision-making process

3. To define the basic functions performed by all managers—planning, organizing, directing, and controlling

4. To describe the three levels of managers in a firm and to analyze which of the managerial functions are likely to be important to each level

5. To explain the importance of objectives in establishing standards by which management performance is measured

6. To explain the meaning of each of the key terms introduced in this chapter

Profile: Tom Wyman
Filling the Top Spot at CBS

Six-foot-three-inch Thomas H. Wyman cuts an imposing figure. Phi Beta Kappa graduate of Amherst College (as an English major he wrote his senior thesis on the poetry of William Butler Yeats), Wyman spent ten years at the Polaroid Corp. as a senior vice-president, general manager, and heir-apparent to Polaroid Chairman Edwin H. Land. Tired of waiting for Land to retire, Wyman moved on to the presidency of the Green Giant Company where, under his direction, sales leaped from $293 million to $485 million in 1978, when Green Giant merged with the Pillsbury Co.

As the number-two man at Pillsbury, Wyman was ready for another move, when, on May 15, 1980, William S. Paley, chairman and founder of CBS, Inc., tapped him for the presidency of the $3.7 billion communications giant. The pot sweetened by an annual salary of $800,000, a three-year contract, and a $1 million bonus, Wyman accepted Paley's offer.

Was Wyman an unusual choice for CBS? Wyman himself conceded that Paley's pick may have raised a few eyebrows. "I haven't had any broadcast experience, or publishing or toy-business experience and I don't know much about music." Apparently Wyman's liberal arts, consumer-oriented background was just what Board Chairman Paley wanted. "A Harvard Business School degree might be more suitable for someone running General Electric than CBS," said Paley.

Wyman's reputation as a professional, highly skilled manager helped convince Paley that he was the person for the job. Wyman's marketing and policy making experience as well as his intelligence and proven ability to run a major organization were attested to by former colleagues. "He's very good with people," said William H. Spoor, chairman of Pillsbury. "He's a team builder . . . a professional executive."

David McLaughlin, president of the Minnesota-based Toro Company, on whose board Wyman sits, added, "He's a very quick learner and an excellent analyzer of problems. There's no question that he makes the decision, but he builds confidence by giving people responsibility."

Aside from his spectacular business achievements at Polaroid and Pillsbury, Wyman's sense of social responsibility and proven history of social activism made him an even more attractive candidate for the CBS top slot. "I've always been interested not just in business in the ingrown sense," explained Wyman, "but in how business can have an impact on the community and world we live in." Paley shares Wyman's view. Running CBS as a big business is only part of Paley's vision for the network. In Paley's view, CBS is also a powerful instrument for cultural and social improvement.

As the fifth man to take over the presidency of CBS in nine years, Wyman welcomes his new challenge. "I've tried it both ways, being No. 1 and No. 2," he said, "and No. 1 is more fun."

Wyman's move to CBS placed him at the helm of a highly successful organization. In other instances, however, managers find themselves using all of their talents and the talents of others in nursing sick organizations and returning them to health.

All mankind is divided into three classes: those who are immovable; those who are movable; and those who move.

—Benjamin Franklin

I've always set high standards for myself and no one expects as much from me as I do. Whatever pressure I feel is self-imposed.

—Christie Hefner
Vice-President, Playboy Enterprises

When Alan Ladd, Jr., son of the late movie actor, joined Twentieth-Century-Fox Corporation as head of the film division in the early 1970s, he joined an organization with an unenviable reputation for producing such costly turkeys as "Dr. Doolittle," "Tora! Tora! Tora!," and "Hello Dolly." Ladd's managerial talents coupled with the financial skills of his boss Dennis Stanfill quickly converted Fox from a consistent loser to a profitable company.

Ladd recognized the need for an appropriate blending of creativity and financial controls in filmmaking, and he followed the practice of using talented professionals in such areas as reviewing scripts, selecting stars, and maintaining overly tight controls over the director, but he held his producers and directors responsible for results.

Ladd would become involved with unusual problems or projects. When young George Lucas approached him in 1973 with a movie idea—a "Western" filled with spaceships, robots, villainous villains, and heroic heroes and a theater filled with special effects at a price tag of at least $10 million in production costs—Ladd listened and liked what he heard.

Although Ladd knew that Universal had already rejected the proposal, he realized that managers must sometimes take risks, and he convinced his boss that this one should be taken. The rest is history. Although the worldwide rental income continues to be counted, "Star Wars" is approaching $500 million in rentals and ranks as the most successful film made so far. Its successors are enjoying similar returns.

After a few years, Ladd left Twentieth-Century-Fox to start his own operation. He recognized the importance of effective management in the movie industry but was also convinced that creative people are often self-motivated and identify their work not with a company but with themselves. As patron-manager of his own firm, he felt it would be easier to provide his creative people with applause and rewards for good work and protection for failures. He understood management concepts, but he also recognized the importance of fitting them to the special characteristics of his organization.[1]

Different Problems, Different Goals . . . But All Managers

Paul W. (Bear) Bryant, Beverly Sills, and William Paley have at least one thing in common. They are all managers. Bryant is head coach of the University of Alabama's Crimson Tide football team, Sills is the general director of the New York City Opera Company, and Paley is chairman of the board of CBS. Other managers preside over organizations such as the local Red Cross office, city governments (many cities are led by a city manager), and colleges or universities.

What Is Management?

Management is the achievement of organizational objectives through people and other resources. The manager's job is to combine human and technical resources in the best way possible to achieve these objectives. Managers are not directly involved in production; they do not produce a finished product. Instead they direct the efforts of others toward the company goals. As Figure 5–1 indicates, management is the critical ingredient in the five *M*s—management, manpower, materials, money, and machinery—the basic resources of any firm.

management
The achievement of organizational objectives through people and other resources.

Management Principles Are Universal

The management principles and concepts to be discussed are applicable—even fundamental—not only to profit-seeking firms but also to nonprofit organizations. The local hospital administrator, the head

FIGURE 5–1
The five *M*s—basic resources of the organization.

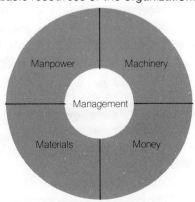

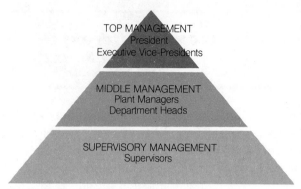

FIGURE 5–2
The management pyramid.

of the United Fund, and the PTA president all perform managerial functions similar to those performed by their counterparts in industry.

Businesses are only one form of enterprise, distinguished from others in terms of objectives. Businesses are profit-oriented, while non-profit organizations such as hospitals, city governments, and charitable agencies are service-oriented. But both benefit from effective management.

The Management Pyramid

management pyramid
The various levels of management, or hierarchy, in an organization—supervisory, middle, and top management.

top management
The highest level of the management pyramid, composed of the president and other key company executives who develop long-range plans for the company and interact with the government and community.

middle management
The second level of the management pyramid, including executives, such as plant managers and department heads, who are responsible for developing detailed plans and procedures to implement the general plans of top management and are involved in specific operations within the organization.

The local Burger King franchise has a very simple organization—a manager and an assistant manager or two. In contrast, CBS has a president, several vice-presidents, department heads, plant managers, and supervisory personnel. Are all these people managers? The answer is yes. Since they are all engaged in combining human and other resources to achieve company objectives, they are all managers.

The various levels of management form a **management pyramid,** or hierarchy, in an organization. As Figure 5–2 indicates, a firm's management can be divided into three categories: top management, middle management, and supervisory management. Although all three categories contain managers, each level of the pyramid stresses different activities.

Top management, the highest level of the management pyramid, is composed of the president and other key company executives. These people devote their time to developing long-range plans for the company. They make broad decisions such as whether to manufacture new products, to purchase other companies, or to begin international operations. A considerable amount of their time is directed to outside activities involving government and community affairs.

Middle management, the second level of the management pyramid, includes such executives as plant managers and department heads. Middle management is more involved than top management in specific operations within the organization. Middle managers are responsible for developing detailed plans and procedures to implement the general plans of top management. They may, for example, determine the number of salespeople for a particular territory, operate a branch of a department store chain, select equipment for a new facility, or develop techniques for evaluating employee performance.

Supervisory mangement, the third level of the management pyramid, includes people who are directly responsible for details of assigning workers to specific jobs and evaluating daily—even hourly— performance. They are in direct and continuing contact with production personnel and are responsible for putting into action the plans developed by middle management.

At any level, managers need certain skills, including the ability to work in a team, the ability to formulate and carry out long-range plans, the courage to take risks, and interpersonal skills, in order to succeed. Lack of some of these abilities often prevents people from moving up the managerial ladder (see Focus 5-1).

supervisory management
The third level of the management pyramid, including people who are directly responsible for the details of assigning workers to specific jobs and evaluating performance.

Importance of Objectives

The old maxim "if you don't know where you are going, any road will get you there" applies to business as well as to individuals. Both need definite objectives in order to be successful. **Objectives** are guideposts used by managers to define standards of what the organization should accomplish in such areas as profitability, customer service, and social responsibility. Managers can continually evaluate performance in terms of how well the organization is moving in the direction of its objectives.

objectives
Guideposts used by managers to define standards of what the organization should accomplish in areas such as profitability, customer service, and social responsibility.

Objectives Serve as Standards

Objectives often become standards for the manager by their definition of excellence in organizational performance. Without such standards, the manager possesses no tools for evaluating performance—no means of deciding whether work is good or bad. Thus, objectives provide not only a definite statement of what the organization wants to accomplish but also a means of evaluating progress toward its goals: If performance appears unsatisfactory, management can take corrective action, refocusing the organization in the direction of its objectives.

Examples of Objectives

The belief that the purpose of a business is to make a profit is accepted by most people—whether they are defenders or critics of business. Newspaper accounts of the success of, say, Walt Disney Enterprises or Levi Strauss are typically stated in terms of annual earnings, which is the most straightforward measure of business performance.

FOCUS 5–1
Women: Making It as Managers

Although opportunities for women in management have increased in recent years, the fact is women make up only 2.3 percent of those earning over $25,000 a year. According to Margaret Henning and Anne Jardin, authors of *The Managerial Woman,* the absence of women in top management is a result of more than male bias. Most corporations were built by men, and women who try to succeed in management must contend with an alien male environment. Doctors Henning and Jardin interviewed thousands of female and male managers and found some striking differences in the two groups:

• While most women view their job as a way of earning a living, men see their job as a means of advancing their careers.

• Women tend to focus on short-run planning, but men focus on long-run career goals.

• Men see risks as both a danger and an opportunity, while women see risk only as involving failure, loss, or danger.

• Men tend to concentrate on their bosses' expectations of them, but women focus on their own self-concept.

• Because boys learn early about being members of a team, male managers have experiences valuable in working in committees and operating in business meetings where teamwork is important. By contrast, popular sports for girls stress individual performance, often leaving them unprepared for team efforts in management.

    The authors believe that male executives have an advantage over females in the world of corporate management. Women are forced to operate in a largely male world, and often they are unprepared to pay the price of success. For those who want to make it to the top, here are some suggestions offered by Henning and Jardin:

• Decide what you want from a career. Objectively evaluate your skills, knowledge, and experience, and prepare a five-year plan for reaching your goal.

• Try to gain experience in key management skills such as group leadership, planning, and problem solving.

• Expand your contacts in the organization. A system of informal relationships can provide helpful information and support.

• Emphasize your competence, not your personality.

• Learn by your mistakes, and use criticism as a tool for self-improvement.

• Control your career by letting people know what you want.

But a statement that profits are the *only* objective of business is clearly misleading. Profits are obviously necessary for survival. A company must be profitable in order to attract additional capital and to satisfy its owners with an adequate return for their invested funds. But other objectives are equally important. The company must, for example, provide its customers with needed goods and services, or it will not make any profits.

A firm's mere existence usually results in the achievement of a number of social objectives as well. These include the provision of job opportunities, good wages, safe working conditions, job training (often for the hard-core unemployed), and good corporate citizenship within the community.

Decision Making: Vital Task of Every Manager

The most important task of managers is decision making. Managers earn their salaries by making decisions that enable their firms to solve problems as they arise. In addition, managers are continually involved with anticipating and preventing future problems. The decision-making process can be described in five steps. Figure 5–3 shows how the manager systematically progresses through each step ultimately to reach a decision aimed at solving a specific problem or taking advantage of a particular business opportunity.

The following hypothetical Flavorfest story illustrates a problem to which the decision-making process can be applied.

The Flavorfest Meat-Packing Company is a leading firm in the meat-packing industry, with annual sales in excess of $800 million. Its brand name is well known in the areas of canned meat products and frozen meats. Although the brand is highly regarded by consumers, Flavorfest's management has recently become concerned about the growing price difference among domestic meat products. Large food chains are increasingly marketing meat products under their own brand names, often at prices as much as 10 to 15 percent

FIGURE 5–3
Steps in the decision-making process.

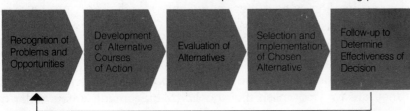

Recognition of Problems and Opportunities

Development of Alternative Courses of Action

Evaluation of Alternatives

Selection and Implementation of Chosen Alternative

Follow-up to Determine Effectiveness of Decision

lower than national brands because of their large purchases from countries such as Argentina. The imported meats are identical in quality with domestic meats, because the U.S. Department of Agriculture controls grading.

Consumers appear to be gradually turning away from the Flavorfest brand because of the price differential. Flavorfest has been approached by two South American meat suppliers to contract for future beef imports.

Flavorfest probably first learned of its problem (and potential opportunity) when it compared company sales with organizational goals for the current year. Now that management is aware of the problem, it can list and evaluate alternative courses of action. It will want to consider such factors as consumer reaction to imported meats, labeling requirements, and dependability of the South American suppliers. Information on these factors will enable management to assess the merits of the various alternatives.

After this assessment, management can choose one of the alternatives and put it into action. It must also, of course, devise methods of follow-up to determine whether its decision will prove effective in solving the problem or taking advantage of the new opportunity. Feedback on the correctness of this decision will be extremely useful to management when it has to make similar decisions in the future.

decision making
Choosing among two or more alternatives by following these steps: recognizing the problem, identifying and evaluating alternatives, selecting and implementing alternatives, and obtaining follow-up on the effectiveness of the decision.

In a narrow sense, **decision making** is choosing among two or more alternatives—the chosen alternative being the decision. But in a broader sense, decision making involves problem recognition, identification and evaluation of alternatives, selection and implementation of an alternative, and follow-up (in the form of feedback) on the effectiveness of the decision. Whether the decision to be made is routine or unique (such as a decision to construct a major new manufacturing facility), the systematic step-by-step approach will be effective.

Management Functions

Management has been defined as the achievement of objectives through people and other resources. This definition implies that it is a *process*—a series of actions that result in a certain end. A manufacturer converts a series of inputs in the form of raw materials, machinery, workers, and other ingredients into finished products designed to satisfy the firm's customers. Completion of this process allows the firm to achieve its objectives.

Managers perform four basic functions—planning, organizing, directing, and controlling—and they must be skillful in performing them if they are to accomplish their goals. (Management writers differ on

FIGURE 5–4
The functions of management.

both the number of management functions and the specific lists of them. Writers who choose to define them more narrowly include such functions as staffing, communicating, motivating, innovating, coordinating, and evaluating—all of which must be accomplished by managers. The four functions listed here are broadly conceived and are assumed to include these more specific functions.) Although Figure 5–4 shows these functions as separate, they really are interdependent, and it is up to the manager to coordinate them. (The arrows in the figure indicate that management is a continual process.) Thus, as managers develop plans, they become involved in organizing to carry them out. They also have to consider methods of directing and controlling the operations during the planning process. Careful coordination of these functions leads to effective decisions and the accomplishment of organizational objectives. As Focus 5–2 shows, the four management functions are necessary for any enterprise to work successfully.

The basic management functions are performed at *all* levels of the management pyramid, although top and middle managers devote more time to the planning function and supervisory managers spend more time on the directing function.

Planning

Planning is the management function of anticipating the future and determining the best courses of action to achieve company objectives. It encompasses decisions about the activities the organization should perform; how big it should be; the production, marketing, and financial strategies it should use in reaching its objectives; and the resources needed to accomplish its goals. Thus, planning involves the determination of courses of action to answer the questions of what should be done, by whom, where, when, and how. In the same way that an architect designs a blueprint, a manager constructs a plan for the organizational activities necessary to reach objectives.

Planning is a continual process. The statement "the only thing constant is change" is undeniably true in today's business world. Busi-

planning
The management function concerned with anticipating the future and determining the best courses of action to achieve organizational objectives.

FOCUS 5–2
Applying Management Concepts in a Commune

Although most people think of communes as pastoral settings where people ignore such worldly considerations as money, planning, organizing, and the other trappings of modern society, the communal failures of the 1970s have led to a desire to learn from past mistakes. As *U.S. News & World Report* noted recently, the communes of the 1980s bear a striking resemblance to any other enterprise.

> Many of the estimated 1 million people in communal arrangements are in groups organized more along free-enterprise lines than in the past. One example is the Renaissance Community, Inc., in Turners Falls, Massachusetts. What started as a backwoods farming commune with eight people in 1968 has evolved into a multifaceted business group that supports 80 adults and 50 children.
>
> Among the commune's activities: a bus company, a greeting-card business, a restaurant, a crafts operation, and several construction businesses. Sales from these enterprises in 1979 totaled more than $750,000. . . .
>
> Also watching its dollars and cents closely is another Massachusetts group—the 3HO Foundation, a Boston commune grounded in Sikhism, a religion founded in India. The commune's 50 adults and 11 children live in four large Victorian houses in the Dorchester section and depend for their livelihood on two shops and a combination restaurant and health-food store. Members aren't required to pool their money, as in many communes, and if someone lends money to one of the businesses, he receives a note for the sum at the prevailing interest rates.
>
> "Unless you do everything in a legal and businesslike fashion, then everything becomes quite confused when emotions change around," says Dr. Gurushabd Singh Khalsa, the group's regional minister. . . ."

The 35-member Twin Oaks commune, located near Louisa, Virginia, has an organizational structure that rivals many major profit-seeking concerns. *The Wall Street Journal* described the operation as follows:

> Members are paid in "labor credits" for their various chores: the more distasteful the task, the higher its credit rating and the less time needed to earn the weekly quota of 40 credits. . . . Overseeing the awarding of credits and other administrative tasks are managers—one for every communal sector . . . who are appointed by a *board of planners* that acts much like a corporate board.
>
> The planners at Twin Oaks consult with the membership as a whole prior to making decisions, but unanimity of opinion isn't required. "Group consensus becomes a silly forum for people fond of their own voices," a spokesperson says. "My solution: Let them talk—then have experienced and responsible people make decisions."

ness conditions change; laws change; organizations change. Managers must continually monitor their own operations and the business environment and make necessary adjustments to their plans. This ongoing analysis and comparison of actual performance with company objectives allows the manager to adjust plans before problems become crises. Successful accomplishment of other managerial functions is unlikely without sound and continual planning.

Organizing

Once plans have been developed, the next step typically is organization. **Organizing** is the means by which management blends human and material resources through the design of a formal structure of tasks and authority. It involves classifying and dividing work into manageable units by:

1. determining specific work activities necessary to accomplish the organizational objectives,
2. grouping work activities into a logical pattern or structure, and
3. assigning the activities to specific positions and people.

Included in the organizing function are the important steps of staffing the organization with competent employees who are capable of performing the necessary activities, and assigning authority and responsibility to these individuals. Organizing is discussed in more detail in Chapter 6, and staffing is dealt with in Chapter 8.

organizing
The means by which management blends human and material resources through the design of a formal structure of tasks and authority.

Directing

Once plans have been formulated and an organization has been created and staffed, the task becomes that of directing people toward achievement of organizational goals. **Directing** is the accomplishment of organizational objectives by guiding and motivating subordinates. It includes assigning work, explaining procedures, issuing orders, and seeing that mistakes are corrected.

The directing function is particularly important at the supervisory level, because the greatest number of employees are concentrated

directing
Guiding and motivating subordinates to accomplish organizational objectives.

Directing people toward the achievement of organizational goals—by assigning work, explaining procedures, issuing orders, and so on—is not unlike conducting a symphony orchestra.

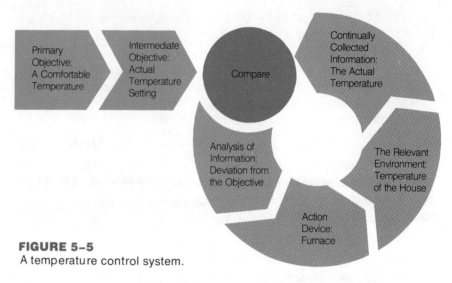

FIGURE 5-5
A temperature control system.

there. If supervisors are to accomplish the task of "getting things done through people," they must be effective leaders. Directing—sometimes referred to as motivating, leading, guiding, or human relations—is thus the "people" function of management. It is discussed at length in Chapter 7.

Controlling

controlling
The management function involved in evaluating the organization's performance to determine whether it is accomplishing its objectives.

Controlling is the management function involved in evaluating the organization's performance to determine whether it is accomplishing its objectives. Controlling is linked closely to planning; in fact, the basic purpose of controlling is the determination of how successful the planning function has been. The three basic steps in controlling are:

1. setting standards
2. collecting information to discover any deviations from standards, and
3. taking corrective action to bring any deviations into line.

The temperature control system shown in Figure 5-5 provides a good illustration of the controlling function. Once the objective of a temperature setting, say 68°F. or 20°C., has been established, information about the actual temperature in the house is collected and compared with the objective, and a decision based on this comparison is made. If the temperature drops below 68°F. or 20°C., the decision is to activate the furnace until it reaches the established level. If the temperature goes too high, the decision is to turn off the furnace and start the cooling system.

Deviation from a firm's goals or profitability, return on investment, or market share may require changes in price structures, new sources of raw materials, changes in production methods, new package design, or a number of other changes. The firm's control system must provide the necessary information from sales records, production cost

FOCUS 5-3

Time Management: Making Certain That Managers Have Time to Manage

Managers often find that their workdays are so filled with momentary activities, problems, telephone calls, conferences, and other aspects of the daily routine that they frequently encounter difficulty in finding the time to devote to planning, organizing, and the other management functions. The following tips from *U.S. News & World Report* can be applied profitably:

Saving Time. To use time effectively, define your goals. How do you really want to live in the year ahead—or the next five years?

Make a List. Write down every possible objective. Then narrow the list down to the practical. Important questions: will the benefits outweigh the disadvantages? What resources of time, effort, and money will be needed? What are the rewards for success? What are the risks in case of failure?

Set Priorities. Evaluate the activities required to achieve your goals. Some will be long range and large scale. Others will be small but necessary. Rank tasks in order of importance and urgency. Update this list of priorities from time to time.

Allocate Time. Make two "to do" lists, one for each week and one for each day. Decide how long it will take to complete an activity and allot only the time necessary. But be realistic, and allow for unexpected events. Set deadlines for all projects, and stick to them even if the result isn't perfect. Break large tasks into small parts, deciding which parts to do today and which later. Refrain from doing easiest tasks first, unless they head your list.

Delegate. Productivity can be increased by delegating tasks to others—subordinates at work and family members or hired help at home. To delegate effectively: give a clear description of the task and what it involves, check to see that your instructions are understood, set a deadline for completion, check on progress from time to time to avoid disaster, and allow for mistakes.

Timesaving Techniques. Group your activities—reading mail, running errands, making phone calls—to eliminate unnecessary duplication of effort. Use a detailed appointment calendar to plan your schedule by the hour. Plan to do the hardest jobs during your most productive times of the day. Use your waiting time. If you're on hold on the telephone, write a memo or update your "to do" list.

figures, financial data, or marketing research studies to uncover deviations from organizational goals. This information then becomes the key ingredient for revisions in plans, and the cycle of planning-organizing-directing-controlling continues.

Earlier in the chapter it was pointed out that all four management functions are performed at all levels of management. But as Figure

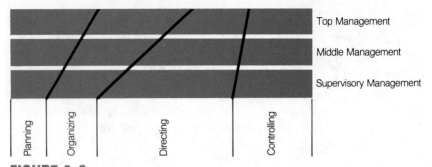

FIGURE 5–6
Relative amount of time spent on each management
function by different levels of management.

5–6 indicates, the amount of time devoted to each function varies by management level. Top management performs more planning than does supervisory management, while supervisors at the third rung of the management pyramid devote more of their time to directing and controlling.

In order to be able to carry out their functions of planning, organizing, directing, and controlling, it is important for managers to use their time well. Time management is an essential part of any manager's job (see Focus 5–3 on page 119).

Leadership

leadership
The act of motivating or causing others to perform activities designed to achieve specific objectives.

great man theory
Leadership theory emphasizing that only an exceptional person is capable of playing a prominent leadership role.

Managers achieve organizational objectives by being good leaders and motivating people to high levels of achievement. **Leadership,** the most visible component of a manager's responsibilities, is the act of motivating or causing others to perform activities designed to achieve specific objectives. Because of the importance of effective leadership in organizational success, it is not surprising that the search for determinants of a good leader has been in process for generations.

Early leadership concepts concentrated on the **great man theory,** which held that remarkable individuals—George Washington, Napoleon Bonaparte, Adolph Hitler, Mahatma Gandhi—emerged and were prepared to play important leadership roles. As a result, the early research attempted to focus on the traits of a good leader. Although the various listings differ, three traits were often mentioned: empathy, self-awareness, and objectivity in dealing with others. These traits are illustrated in Table 5–1.

Obviously these traits do not fit all of the leaders mentioned above. Empathy was hardly characteristic of Adolph Hitler. Other lists proved equally contradictory. Extravertism is an often-mentioned trait, but General George Marshall was an introvert. Height may be character-

TABLE 5–1
Frequently Listed Traits of a Good Leader

A good leader should possess:

1. *Empathy,* the ability to place oneself in another's position
   "How does the worker view this new rule?"
   "Will the worker be able to see its value if I explain it this way?"
   "Whom does the worker trust, and whom does he or she fear?"

2. *Self-awareness,* knowledge of oneself
   "What are my strengths? My weaknesses?"
   "What do my people think of me?" "Do they consider me fair and objective?"
   "Am I too gruff in dealing with others?"

3. *Objectivity in interpersonal relations*
   "Am I objective in dealing with my subordinates, or do I react too emotionally?"
   "Do I maintain a detached view in reacting to subordinates' behavior?"
   "Can I be empathetic and objective at the same time?"

istic of such leaders as Abraham Lincoln and Charles de Gaulle, but what about Napoleon? Leadership is often associated with the experience that often comes with age, but Alexander the Great won some of his most important victories at the age of 18. And in more recent years Senator Charles Percy had already become president of Bell and Howell at age 29.

Gradually leadership research began to focus on different styles of leadership and circumstances under which each style might prove more successful. By considering both alternative styles and a given set of circumstances, it is possible to determine the optimum type of leadership for a particular situation.

Leadership Styles

An effective leader recognizes that there are variations in leadership styles. The three basic styles are autocratic, free rein, and democratic. **Autocratic leaders** make decisions on their own, without consulting others. **Democratic leaders** involve their subordinates in making decisions. (An autocratic sales manager, for example, provides sales personnel with specific sales quotas, while a democratic manager allows them to participate in setting the quotas.) **Free-rein leaders** believe in minimal supervision, leaving most decisions to their subordinates. Figure 5–7 illustrates the continuum of leadership styles.

autocratic leaders
Leaders who make decisions without consulting others.

democratic leaders
Leaders who involve their subordinates in making decisions.

free-rein leaders
Leaders who believe in minimal supervision and who leave most decisions to their subordinates.

FIGURE 5–7
Continuum of leadership behavior.

AUTOCRATIC LEADER
Use of Authority
by the Manager

DEMOCRATIC LEADER
Area of Freedom
for Subordinates

| Manager makes decision and announces it. | Manager "sells" decision. | Manager presents ideas and invites questions. | Manager presents tentative decision subject to change. | Manager presents problem, gets suggestions, makes decision. | Manager defines limits, asks group to make decision. | Manager permits subordinates to function within limits defined by superior. |

Controversial Issue

Should Profits Be the Primary Objective of Business?

Two hundred and twelve life and health insurance companies have been actively involved recently in corporate social responsibility programs. Their social investments alone exceeded $2 billion.

Executives from the Republic National and First National banks in Dallas lent their time and talent to improving predominantly black and Mexican-American high schools.

Thornton F. Bradshaw, president of RCA Corporation and an ardent spokesperson for corporate social responsibility, writes: "Those who believe, as I do, in the intrinsic value of the decentralized market system must act now to develop a more humanistic, responsible and innovative form of capitalism to meet society's demands as well as satisfying its needs."

Are these examples contrary to the primary axiom on which American business was built: roll up your sleeves, put your nose to the grindstone, and make a buck? Not necessarily. As one official of the Milwaukee Association of Commerce said, "Getting involved is not just social responsibility. It is economics and good business."

The concept of corporate social responsibility has been with us for many years. But it was not until the urban riots of 1968 that businesses committed themselves to doing something about the decaying, poverty-ridden cities that housed their factories, to providing minority education and job opportunities, to stopping environmental pollution, to volunteering employee time to community activities, to providing a safe place for employees to work, and more.

Executives asked themselves whether their management decisions were ethical (Are profits really more important than a clean

Which Leadership Style Is Best?

The best leadership style is one that varies with the circumstances, changing according to three elements: the leader, the followers, and the situation. Some leaders are simply unable to encourage or even allow subordinates to participate in decision making. And some followers do not have the ability or the desire to assume such responsibility. Furthermore, the particular situation helps determine which style will be most effective. Problems requiring immediate solutions may have to be handled without consulting subordinates. With less time pressure, participative decision making may be desirable.

A democratic leader may be forced by circumstance to be autocratic in making a particular decision. For example, if there is to be a 10 percent reduction in staff, those subject to being fired are not likely to be consulted on who should go.

environment?) and whether their companies were giving as much to society as they were taking from it. When their answers fell short, many businesses committed resources to socially responsible projects. It was the "right" thing to do, and it also improved companies' public images and potential profits.

One Dallas businessperson has said that helping improve social problems is a matter of "enlightened self-interest." When a company's public image stands in the way of its profits, it makes better business sense to become more sensitive to the community's needs than to try to operate in a hostile environment. Socially responsible behavior also stems the crush of government regulations. When corporations disregard public safety and health, the government has no choice but to step in with stringent rules that affect every company's ability to do business.

Those opposed to corporate social involvement agree with economist Milton Friedman that "there is one and only one social responsibility of business—to use its resources and engage in activities designed to increase its profits so long as it . . . engages in open and free competition, without deception or fraud." Any other focus weakens business's ability to make money and compete in the marketplace. In addition, critics charge that social programs add to the cost of doing business here and abroad and make American products less competitive.

With the potential to produce the environmental nightmare of Love Canal and the highest standard of living in the world, the profit motive has been a mixed blessing to American business. Perhaps that is why more and more business people have expanded their consciousness to include the communities in which they live.

Managers are increasingly moving toward a more democratic style of leadership. They find that workers involved in decision making tend to be more interested in the overall organization and may be more motivated to contribute to organizational objectives than those not involved in decision making.

After devoting many years of research into the best types of leaders, management professor Fred Feidler concluded that no single best style of leadership exists. Feidler feels that the most effective leadership style depends on the power held by the leader, the difficulty of the tasks involved, and the characteristics of the workers. He argues that extremely easy and extremely difficult situations are best handled by leaders who emphasize task accomplishment. Moderately difficult situations are best handled by leaders who emphasize participation and good working relations with subordinates.[2]

Autocratic leaders make decisions on their own.

Drawing by Stevenson; © 1980 The New Yorker Magazine, Inc.

Summary

Management is the achievement of objectives through people and other resources. It is the critical ingredient in the five Ms of an organization: management, manpower, materials, money, and machinery. Management principles are universal, applying equally to profit-seeking and nonprofit organizations.

There are three levels of management in most firms: top management, which includes the president and vice-presidents; middle management, which includes plant managers and key department heads; and supervisory management, which includes first-line managers such as supervisors. These three levels constitute the management pyramid.

Definite organizational objectives are needed by managers in performing their functions. These objectives serve as standards, and their pursuit is the basis of all management efforts. Common organizational objectives include profitability, market share, and societal aims such as providing employment and being a good corporate citizen.

Managers perform four basic functions in attempting to achieve company objectives: planning, organizing, directing, and controlling. Planning involves creating blueprints for future courses of action. Organizing involves grouping work into logical patterns and assigning tasks to specific workers. Directing (the people function of management) involves matching performance with organizational goals. Controlling deals with evaluating actual performance to determine whether the organization is accomplishing its objectives. It involves setting standards, collecting information to discover any deviations from standards, and taking corrective action to bring deviations into line. All four functions involve the manager in the task of decision making.

Although all management levels are involved in each of the managerial functions, top management devotes more of its time to planning and organizing, while the lower levels are more involved with directing and controlling.

Effective leaders often possess three traits: empathy (the ability to look at the situation from another's point of view), self-awareness, and objectivity. The three basic leadership styles are autocratic, democratic, and free rein. The best leadership style depends on three elements: the leader, the followers, and the situation. The general trend is toward greater participation of subordinates in decisions that affect them.

Key Terms

management	decision making	leadership
management pyramid	planning	great man theory
top management	organizing	autocratic leaders
middle management	directing	democratic leaders
supervisory management	controlling	free rein leaders
objectives		

Review Questions

1. Explain each of the terms listed above.
2. How do managers achieve objectives through people and other resources?

3. Comment on the following statement: management principles are universal.

4. Outline the organization of the management pyramid.

5. Why are objectives important to managers?

6. Define the four basic functions of management.

7. Describe the steps in the decision-making process.

8. What are the three basic steps in controlling?

9. What traits are usually associated with effective leadership?

10. Explain the three basic leadership styles.

Discussion Questions and Exercises

1. Evaluate the pros and cons of the controversial issue that appears in this chapter.

2. How much should a corporation president be paid? How should the salary be determined?

3. Murphy Industrial Distributors has long observed St. Patrick's Day as a paid holiday for its employees. Sean Murphy, company president, has noticed that St. Patrick's Day will fall on Wednesday during the next year. He wonders whether the Monday of that week should be declared a company holiday instead. Using each of the steps in the decision-making process, describe how you would make this decision.

4. How would you describe your own leadership style? Has your approach been successful in leadership situations you have faced?

5. Consider a club, sports team, or other group to which you belong. Describe how the basic functions of management have been performed in this group. Has the group's management been effective in accomplishing its objectives? Explain.

Case 5–1: Delta Air Lines

According to the old joke, anyone who dies in the Southeast and goes to Heaven will have to change planes in Atlanta. And the chances are excellent that the plane will belong to Delta Air Lines. Delta, the sixth-largest U.S. air carrier, has moved more than 1 million passengers through Atlanta's giant new terminal in a single month.

Although considerably smaller than such giants as United, American, Pan Am, TWA, and Eastern, Delta is by far the most profitable. It pioneered the concept of developing large numbers of feeder routes to filter passengers into its hub city, Atlanta, and then on to more distant cities aboard other Delta flights. Passengers from Birmingham, Savannah, Memphis, or Jackson bound for New York or Philadelphia are more likely to continue on from Atlanta on a Delta flight boarding at a nearby gate than risk transferring to another airline at a distant gate in the busy airport. In order to minimize "lay-over" time waiting for a connecting flight, Delta schedules several "complexes" of flights each day during which as many as 40 different flights arrive in Atlanta, exchange passengers, baggage, and cargo, and fly out again.

In addition to its location in the fast-growing Southeast, Delta's success is due in a large part to people. The firm benefits from a no-layoff policy and from a policy of promoting from within. Other than professionals with specialized skills, every Delta employee starts at an entry-level position. In addition, each employee is taught to perform at least two or three related functions, thereby producing increased flexibility.

David C. Garrett, Jr., Delta's chief executive officer, is not housed in the palatial office ordinarily expected of the head of a firm that earned about $150 million in 1981. Delta headquarters consist of plain, pipe-rack buildings constructed during the 1930s at the Atlanta airport. The location permits top management to maintain regular and continuing contact with the entire organization. It also facilitates communications among the various divisions. In addition to the offices, the buildings also house the entire maintenance facilities for Delta's fleet of over 200 jets. The firm's total maintenance costs as compared with total revenues are among the lowest in the industry. Equally important is the fact that Delta has the best safety record of any airline.

Although Garrett's counterpart at Eastern Airlines has been to the moon, the Delta leader has never even piloted a plane. He and his top management team have devised plans for moving Delta from sixth to first place among the nation's air carriers by 1990—and continuing to be profitable. Among the first moves are attempts to develop new hub cities in Dallas and, to a lesser extent, in Memphis. Another is to minimize the huge amounts of debt that continue to plague his competitors, while continuing to upgrade the Delta fleet. The 1980s will witness a gradual expansion of the fleet and the purchase of newer, more fuel-efficient planes, requiring hundreds of millions of dollars. These changes are all necessary if Delta is to achieve its goal by 1990.

Questions

1. Relate the discussion of Delta Air Lines to the functions of management described in Chapter 5.

2. What potential dangers can you identify that may prevent Delta from achieving its goal?

3. Select one of the other five leading air carriers and determine what problems face it in competing with Delta. How might these problems be overcome?

Case 5-2: Management—Japanese Style

Time clocks are banned from the premises. Managers and workers converse on a first-name basis and eat lunch together in the company cafeteria. Employees are briefed once a month by a top executive on sales and production goals and are encouraged to air their complaints. Four times a year, workers attend company-paid parties. Says Betty Price, 54, an assembly-line person: "Working for Sony is like working for your family."

Her expression, echoed by dozens of other American Sony workers in San Diego, is a measure of the success achieved at the sprawling two-story plant, where both the Stars and Stripes and the Rising Sun fly in front of the factory's glistening white exterior. In 1981 the San Diego plant turned over 700,000 color television sets, one-third of Sony's total world production. More significantly, company officials now proudly say that the plant's productivity approaches that of its Japanese facilities.

Plant Manager Shiro Yamada, 58, insists that there are few differences between workers in the United States and Japan. Says he: "Americans are as quality conscious as the Japanese. But the question has been how to motivate them." Yamada's way is to bathe his U.S. employees in personal attention. Workers with perfect attendance records are treated to dinner once a year at a posh restaurant downtown. When one employee complained that a refrigerator for storing lunches was too small, it was replaced a few days later with a larger one. Vice-President Masayoshi Morimoto, known as Mike around the plant, has mastered Spanish so he can talk with his many Hispanic workers. The company has installed telephone hot lines on which workers can anonymously register suggestions or complaints.

The firm strives to build strong ties with its employees in the belief that the workers will then show loyalty to the company in return. It carefully promotes from within, and most of the assembly-line supervisors are high school graduates who rose through the ranks because of their hard work and dedication to the company. During the 1973–75 recession, when TV sales dropped and production slowed drastically, no one was fired. Instead, workers were kept busy with plant maintenance and other chores. In fact, Sony has not laid off a single employee since 1972, when the plant was opened. The Japanese managers were stunned when the first employee actually quit within just one year. Says Richard Crossman, the plant's human relations expert: "They came to me and wanted to know what they had done wrong. I had to explain that quitting is just the way it is sometimes in Southern California."

This personnel policy has clearly been a success. Several attempts to unionize the work force have been defeated by margins as high as 3 to 1. Says Jan Timmerman, 22, a parts dispatcher and former member of the Retail Clerks Union: "Union pay was better, and the benefits were probably better. But basically I'm more satisfied here."

Sony has not forced Japanese customs on American workers. Though the company provides lemon-colored smocks for assembly-line workers, most prefer to wear jeans and running shoes. The firm does not demand that anyone put on the uniforms. A brief attempt to establish a general exercise period for San Diego workers, similar to the kind Sony's Japanese employees perform, was dropped when managers saw it was not wanted.

Inevitably, there have been minor misunderstandings because of the differences in language and customs. One worker sandblasted the numbers 1 2 6 4 on a series of parts she was testing before she realized that her Japanese supervisor meant that she was to label them "1 to 64." Mark Dempsey, 23, the plant's youngest supervisor, admits that there is a vast cultural gap between the Japanese and Americans. Says he: "They do not realize that some of us live for the weekend, while lots of them live for the week—just so they can begin to work again." Some workers grumble about the delays caused by the Japanese system of managing by consensus, seeing it instead as an inability to make decisions. Complains one American: "There is a lot of indecision. No manager will ever say do this or do that."

Most American workers, though, like the Japanese management style, and some do not find it all that foreign. Says Supervisor Robert Williams: "A long time ago, Americans used to be more people-oriented, the way the Japanese are. It just got lost somewhere along the way."

Questions

1. How would you describe the Japanese style of management?

2. What is your opinion of this management style?

3. What types of problems would you expect Japanese managers to encounter in the United States?

6

The Role of Organization

Learning Goals

1. To explain why a formal organization structure is needed and what is involved in building it

2. To evaluate the five basic forms of organization: line, functional, line-and-staff, committee, and matrix

3. To define authority and responsibility

4. To analyze the factors that determine how many workers a supervisor should manage

5. To describe Parkinson's Law and how to avoid it

6. To identify both the strengths and the weaknesses of organization charts

7. To recognize the function of informal organizations in a firm

8. To explain the meaning of each of the key terms introduced in this chapter

Profile: Lt. Colonel Yonatan Netanyahu
Organizer at Entebbe

Business success is linked to a well-thought-out, clearly defined organizational structure. This is especially true when normal, everyday business pressures intensify: the organizational structure must respond, or the business will fail. While an effective organizational structure may mean the difference between a healthy firm and a dying one, seldom are human lives at stake when organizational structures are designed. But this was precisely the situation during the 1976 Israeli commando raid on Entebbe.

When the Israeli paratroopers, under the command of Lt. Col. Yonatan Netanyahu, rescued 104 hostages from terrorist hijackers at the Entebbe, Uganda, airfield on July 3, 1976, they depended on an organizational structure so tight that it left little or no room for mistakes. The way the Israelis organized this precise, brilliant, and daring raid, which took them into the heart of Uganda, bears repeating, for it can serve as an example of how a multilayered organizational system can be a pivotal part of a team's success.

When the members of the Israeli Cabinet met on June 28, 1976, they examined the alternative courses of action available to them in accomplishing their objective of freeing the hostages hijacked by terrorists a day earlier. They were being guarded by their captors and by fanatic ruler Idi Amin's Ugandan soldiers.

A special crisis management group was assigned to study the alternatives. They gathered intelligence information about Entebbe Airport from various sources, including 148 nonIsraeli hostages released by the hijackers and aerial reconnaissance and satellite photographs. With this information and permission from Kenya to use Nairobi as a stopping point on the way to and from Entebbe, the group decided on military action.

Chief of Staff Lt. Gen. Mordechai Gur had already chosen the elite 35th Airborne Brigade and the infantrymen of the Golani Brigade to take part in the mission. They would be led in the field by 30-year-old Lt. Col. Netanyahu. Netanyahu's mission was clear, but it had to be accomplished in the incredible time of 55 minutes. He carefully organized his troops, discussed the responsibility of each, drilled them repeatedly, and—just six days after the hijacking began—prepared to carry out the raid.

On July 3, 1976, Netanyahu's commandos accomplished what the world thought was impossible. Under the cover of darkness, two military aircraft landed at Entebbe. (A third aircraft circled the airport acting as a communications center, and a fourth waited in Nairobi to transport the wounded.) They rescued all but four hostages in a raid that took only 50 minutes. The Israeli commandos had one casualty: Natanyahu was shot after he and a small group of soldiers blew up more than ten Ugandan jet fighters, which the Israelis feared would pursue them on their trip home.

The success of the Entebbe mission rests as much on the precise planning and organization of Netanyahu and the crisis management group as on the extraordinary bravery of the Israeli commandos who risked their lives to achieve their goal.

An organization chart strangles profits and stifles people.

—Robert Townsend

The easiest course would be for me to blame those to whom I delegated the responsibility. . . . In any organization the man at the top must bear the responsibility. That responsibility, therefore, belongs here in this office. I accept it.

—Richard M. Nixon

Fifteen years before the success of the Israeli commandos at Entebbe, another organizing attempt was focused on goals equally as dramatic as the hostage rescue. In 1961 President John F. Kennedy committed the United States to the goal of landing a person on the moon before the decade ended. The undertaking, Project Apollo, was an assault of unparalleled magnitude on the unknown. No one at that time knew if a human being could stand the strain of lunar flight or even if the moon could be landed on: many scientists believed its surface to be soft dust that would swallow a landing craft. If all the mysteries could be solved, and the goal achieved, the job of putting together the endeavor would be one of history's greatest organizational challenges.[1]

The trip to the moon would last eight days and cover 245,000 miles. Substandard work by any member of the organization was likely to produce tragic results. The project was coordinated by the Office of Manned Space Flight, a National Aeronautics and Space Administration (NASA) agency. Some 400,000 workers, 16 major industrial firms, and 20,000 subcontractors built rockets and controls, worked singly and jointly to train astronauts, conducted thousands of tests, and finally succeeded. But success was not without cost. A 1967 fire in an Apollo spacecraft killed three astronauts. The accident, a result of defective design and careless workmanship, served to bind the efforts of NASA and its contractors even more strongly to the goal.

The success of this unparalleled effort to organize people and resources in order to achieve specific objectives is summed up in the photo of the first footstep on the moon. On July 20, 1969, astronaut Neil Armstrong planted his boot in lunar dust, and the capabilities of organization were once again dramatically demonstrated.

What Is Organization?

We are constantly confronted with organization in a bewildering variety of activities. Sports teams and social organizations, religious

Astronaut Neil Armstrong's footprint on the moon is a dramatic symbol of the capabilities of organization.

groups and work activities—all include organization. Even groups of animals—bees, ants, baboons, beavers—have organization.

Much of the success of any business depends on organization. Some kind of established structure is necessary to ensure that the manager's plans are carried out.

Organization is a structured process in which people interact to accomplish objectives. Managers must create a formal organization structure in which people and physical resources are properly arranged to carry out plans and achieve overall objectives. The definition of organization includes three key elements: human interaction, goal-directed activities, and structure.

For a small business, the organizing function is fairly simple. The owner-manager of the local dry-cleaning firm employs a few people to sell, to launder and dry-clean clothing, and to make deliveries. The owner usually handles purchases of detergents, plastic wrappers, and other materials; assigns jobs to employees; and personally directs the operation of the business.

But as a company grows, the need for organization increases, as Figure 6–1 illustrates. With increased size come specialization and a larger number of employees. Rather than a single salesperson, the organization employs a large sales force; rather than one bookkeeper, the firm has a sizable accounting department. The large number of personnel and accompanying specialization make it impossible for one person to supervise all operations. Some formal organization is necessary because the manager faces a larger number of specialized employees to supervise.

organization
A structured process in which people interact to accomplish objectives.

FIGURE 6–1
The need for organization increases with increases in the number of employees.

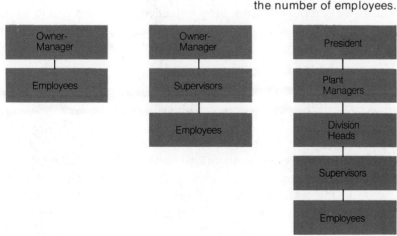

Organizational Structure

Although a small dry-cleaning firm experiences fewer organizational problems than a larger company, both have a formal structure to ensure that people perform tasks designed to accomplish company objectives. In the dry-cleaning company, for example, specific duties are assigned to wrappers, cleaners, and other personnel.

Organizational structure focuses first on the activities necessary to reach goals. Management analyzes the jobs that are to be performed. Then, people with both an interest in and the necessary qualifications for performing the jobs are employed. Coordination of the activities of each worker is another important responsibility of management, because employees must "pull together" if the firm is to operate smoothly.

Well-defined organizational structure should also contribute to employee morale. Employees who know what is expected on the job, who the supervisor is, and how the work fits into the total organizational structure are likely to form a harmonious, loyal work force.

Building the Organizational Structure

The structure of the formal organization is based on an analysis of the three key elements of any organization: human interaction, goal-directed activities, and structure. Management must coordinate the activities of workers to accomplish organizational objectives.

A company objective of "providing our customers with quality products at competitive prices" does not specifically spell out to the mechanic that production machinery should be regularly inspected and defects repaired. Company objectives are often broad in nature and do not specify individual work activities. Consequently, they must be broken down into specific goals for each worker in the organization.

Hierarchy of Objectives

hierarchy of organizational objectives
Levels of objectives that progress from the overall objectives of the firm to the specific objectives established for each employee.

A **hierarchy of organizational objectives** extends from the overall objectives of the firm to specific objectives established for each employee. The broader goals of profitability, sales, market share, and service are broken down into objectives for each division, each factory, each department, each work group, and each individual worker. Once this has been accomplished, each worker can see his or her contribution to the total organizational goals. The number of levels in the hierarchy depends on the size and complexity of the firm. Smaller firms usually have fewer levels than larger ones. Figure 6–2 illustrates this hierarchy of organizational objectives.

FIGURE 6-2
The hierarchy of organizational objectives.

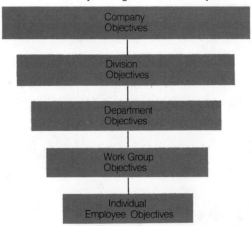

Departmentalization

Building an organizational structure begins with an analysis of the major activities of the organization. In most firms these activities consist of production, marketing, and finance. Each activity is assigned to separate departments in the firm, to both managers and employees.

Departmentalization is the subdivision of work activities into units within the organization. This subdivision allows individual workers to specialize in certain jobs and to become efficient in them. A marketing department may be headed by a marketing vice-president and may include sales, advertising, and market research. A personnel department may include recruitment, training, employee benefits, and industrial relations.

Five major forms of departmentalization exist: product, geography, customer, function, and process. General Motors subdivides its organizational structure on the basis of **products**—the Chevrolet, Pontiac, Oldsmobile, Buick, and Cadillac divisions. The Bell Telephone System is subdivided on a **geographic** basis by regions of the country, as are many railroads, chain stores, and gas and oil distributors. Many sporting-goods stores subdivide on a **customer** basis, with a wholesale operation serving school systems and a retail division serving other customers. Oil companies are sometimes divided on a **functional** basis, with exploration, production, refining, marketing, and finance departments. Machinery manufacturers may departmentalize on the basis of **process.** Manufacturing a product may include cutting the material, heat-treating it, forming it into its final shape, and painting it—all these activities being included in one or more departments.

As Figure 6-3 indicates, a number of different bases for departmentalization may be used within the same company. The decisions on which bases to use are made by balancing the advantages and disadvantages of each. The experience and judgment of top management come into play in such decisions.

departmentalization
The subdivision of work activities into units within the organization.

product departmentalization
Departmentalization organized on the basis of products.

geographic departmentalization
Departmentalization organized by regions of the country.

customer departmentalization
Departmentalization organized on the basis of customer segments.

functional departmentalization
Departmentalization based on the various functions (production, finance, marketing, and so on) of an organization.

process departmentalization
Departmentalization based on the activities being performed (washing, heat treating, painting, packaging, and so on).

FIGURE 6-3
An organization using several bases for departmentalization.

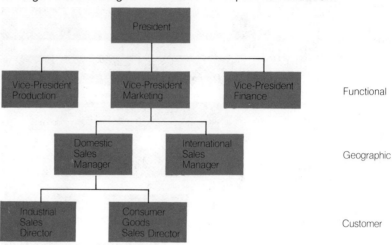

Authority and Responsibility

delegation
The act of assigning part of a manager's activities to subordinates.

responsibility
The obligation of a subordinate to perform assigned duties.

authority
The power to act and make decisions in carrying out assignments.

As the organization grows, the manager must assign part of his or her activities to subordinates in order to have time to devote to managerial functions. The act of assigning activities to subordinates is called **delegation.**

In delegating activities, the manager assigns to subordinates the responsibility to perform the assigned tasks. **Responsibility** is thus the obligation of a subordinate to perform assigned duties. Along with responsibility goes **authority,** the power to act and make decisions in carrying out assignments. Authority and responsibility must be bal-

FIGURE 6-4
The delegation process.

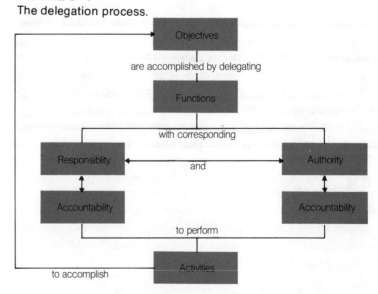

FOCUS 6–1
TWA Managers Bite Financial Bullet to Emphasize Source of Authority and Responsibility

Airline deregulation served to increase competition in a number of lucrative markets as national and regional air carriers began new routes. In many instances, this heightened competition for air passenger business led to such promotional efforts as half-price coupons and super-saver fares. Mergers between former competitors and the discontinuance of service to a number of areas were at least partially the result of the two-way squeeze of major cost increases and the new competition.

Trans World Airlines (TWA) executives decided to demonstrate to its 34,000 employees the seriousness of the problem and the ultimate source of organizational responsibility by reducing salaries of those middle and top managers who were earning more than $35,000 annually. A formula was devised whereby salaries between $35,000 and $60,000 were reduced 10 percent, salaries between $60,000 and $100,000 were cut 15 percent, salaries between $100,000 and $150,000 were dropped 20 percent, and salaries above $150,000 for the most highly paid executives were cut 25 percent. TWA's president Ed Meyer saw his $205,000 salary reduced by $51,250 as a result.

Although the salary cuts did reduce company expenses by approximately $900,000 and were painful to the affected executives, they served more to communicate the seriousness of the problem to TWA employees and to indicate management's willingness to take drastic actions to improve its competitive position. As Meyer stated: "Obviously, this isn't going to save the airline, but it's. . .to emphasize how much we need a turnaround. It's to get people's attention. . . . We just won't sit still and take such losses."

The salary cuts also served to emphasize a fundamental concept of every organization. Although managers may delegate authority and responsibility for the implementation of decisions to subordinates, they do not escape accountability for these actions.

anced so that subordinates are capable of carrying out their assigned tasks. Delegation of sufficient authority to fulfill the subordinate's responsibility in turn makes the subordinate accountable to the supervisor for results. **Accountability** is the act of holding a person liable for carrying out activities for which he or she has the necessary authority and responsibility. This relationship is illustrated in Figure 6–4.

Even though authority is delegated to subordinates, the final responsibility rests with the manager (see Focus 6–1). It is therefore incumbent upon that person to select qualified subordinates who are capable of performing the tasks.

accountability
The liability of a manager for carrying out activities for which he or she has the necessary authority and responsibility.

How Many Subordinates Can a Manager Supervise?

One of the reasons for departmentalization is that managers are limited in the number of activities they can perform and the number of subordinates they can effectively supervise. The **span of control** is the optimum number of subordinates a manager can effectively manage.

Although the optimum number varies from one firm to the next, many management writers agree that top management should directly supervise no more than four to eight people. Supervisory managers, who direct workers performing relatively routine tasks, are capable of effectively managing a much larger number.

The critical factors in determining the optimum span of control are the type of work, the workers' training, the manager's ability, and the effectiveness of communications. An experienced supervisor who manages trained workers performing routine tasks with clear guidelines as to what is expected of them can effectively manage a much larger number of subordinates than can the vice-president of marketing or production.

Ensuring Effective Communications

Communication is a relatively simple task for small organizations. It is often face-to-face, and unclear instructions can be remedied by personal conversation. But communications problems increase with the growth of the organization. Messages, many of which are transmitted in writing, pass through several layers in the formal organization. The sender of the message must thus be continually aware of the recipient and make certain that the message is both clearly written and likely to be interpreted correctly.

At the federal government level, conscious attempts have been made to simplify written communications in order to improve understanding. But bureaucratic language continues, and readers are forced to interpret complex phrases and jargon. *U.S. News & World Report* recently translated some of this bureaucratic babble. Among its choices: a Department of the Interior expression "directly impact the

Clear communications are essential to the smooth functioning of any organization.

Drawing by Stevenson; © 1976 The New Yorker Magazine, Inc.

visual quality of the present environment'' means ''spoil the view.'' A frequently used expression, ''negative saver,'' is a backward label for ''a household that spends more than it earns.'' The House Committee on Aging's ''budgeting restraints and the socioeconomic climate must also be considered in evaluating recommendations and deciding how they should be prioritized'' translates into ''if there's no money, don't spend.'' And the Food and Drug Administration tongue-twister ''innovative processes should be considered to better integrate informed societal judgments and values into the regulatory mechanism'' means ''think''![2]

Centralization versus Decentralization

How much authority are managers willing to disperse throughout the organization? Managers who emphasize **centralization** disperse only the smallest possible amount of authority. Proponents of a centralized management philosophy feel they can most effectively control and coordinate company activities by retaining most of the authority.

Managers who emphasize **decentralization** disperse great amounts of authority to subordinates. Decentralization allows middle and supervisory management more leeway in making decisions than does centralization. For example, middle managers in a decentralized operation are likely to make many financial, production, and personnel decisions themselves rather than obtain approval from their superiors. When such decisions are made by subordinates, higher-level managers can devote their time to more important problems. But decentralization may be carried too far in some situations (see Focus 6-2).

centralization
The practice of managers' dispersing very little authority throughout the organization.

decentralization
The practice of managers' dispersing great amounts of authority to subordinates.

Avoiding Unnecessary Organizational Growth

As the size and complexity of an organization increase, the tendency is to add more supervisory personnel and specialists. This tendency is natural as decentralization occurs and managers recognize their limited span of control. However, the organizational planner should be certain that the new layers of managers and the dozens of technical advisers are really needed, or there will be little increase in production output or efficiency.

British historian-philosopher C. Northcote Parkinson explained this tendency in his book *Parkinson's Law:* ''Work expands so as to fill the time available for its completion.''[3] He applied his law to organizations by illustrating how the number of employees in a firm increases over a period of time regardless of the amount of work to be done. He pointed out, for example, that in 1914 the British navy, the most powerful in the world, contained 2,000 admiralty officials. In 1938 the number had increased to 3,569. By 1954 the ''practically powerless'' British navy was managed by 33,788 members of the admiralty staff. As the British Empire shrank in the period from 1935 to 1954, the number of officials in the British Colonial Office grew from 372 to 1,661—an average annual increase of nearly 6 percent.[4]

> **FOCUS 6–2**
> **Too Much Decentralization Can Prove Disastrous**
>
> Although many managers of large, geographically diverse, multiproduct companies favor the use of decentralization as a means of locating decision making at the place where these decisions must be implemented and as a means of giving subordinate managers more autonomy, this policy has potential dangers.
>
> Some companies have carried decentralization too far—with almost fatal results. Unless control procedures have been developed to keep top management informed of major decisions, the practice of giving subordinate managers the power to make key decisions can prove very costly. One of the greatest losses by a private company in the history of the United States was incurred for this reason. The Convair Division of General Dynamics Corporation acquired so much authority that it was able to lose $480 million on the poorly controlled Convair 880 and 990 jet airplane program. This huge loss almost bankrupted General Dynamics Corporation.

The British government possesses no monopoly on uncontrolled organizational growth. The U.S. Department of Agriculture payroll contains one official for every 24 farmers, and the proportions are even more significant at the Bureau of Indian Affairs (BIA). A tongue-in-cheek story tells of a BIA official sobbing uncontrollably in his office at the Washington headquarters. When asked about the nature of his problem, he responded, "My Indian died!"

Why is there a tendency to add employees at a rate faster than the work is increasing? According to Parkinson, it can be blamed on (a) the selfish desire of managers to build empires by adding subordinates and (b) the paperwork created by the employment of additional workers.[5] Preventing (or minimizing) the occurrence of **Parkinson's Law** requires top management to be constantly vigilant and to give honest appraisals of the need for each proposed new position.

Parkinson's Law
A theory that claims "Work expands so as to fill the time available for its completion."

Forms of Organization Structure

Any group possessing common goals is an organization. But business organizations can be classified according to the nature of their internal authority relationships. Although five forms of organization structure will be discussed, only four forms are in common use today: line, line-and-staff, committee, and matrix. The line structure is the oldest form and is frequently used today in smaller organizations. The line-and-staff form, with its use of specialists to assist line officers, is commonly

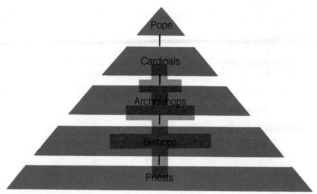

FIGURE 6–5
Line organization used by the Roman Catholic Church.

used in medium- and large-sized firms. The third and fourth types, committees and the matrix organization, exist in many firms but only rarely as the sole types. They are typically used as a suborganizational form within a line-and-staff structure. The final form, the functional organization, represents a transition from pure line to line-and-staff.

Line Organization

The line form of organization is the oldest and simplest form of organizational structure. Caesar's legions used this form; so does the Roman Catholic Church. Figure 6–5 illustrates line organization.

Line organization is the organization structure based on a direct flow of authority from the chief executive to subordinates. It is illustrated by the familiar story of the general who informs the colonel, who tells the major, who instructs the captain, who orders the lieutenant, who yells at the sergeant, who makes an unprintable request of the private, who carries out the order—or else.

The line form is simple. The chain of command is clear, and buck-passing is extremely difficult. Decisions can be made quickly, because the manager can act without consulting anyone other than an immediate superior. But an obvious defect exists within line organization. Each manager has complete responsibility for a number of activities and cannot possibly be an expert in all of them. The supervisor is therefore forced to become a jack-of-all-trades.

This defect is very apparent in medium- and large-sized firms, where the pure line form fails to provide the specialized skills so vital to modern industry. Executives are overburdened with administrative details and paperwork and have little time to devote to planning.

In evaluating the strengths and weaknesses of the line form, the obvious conclusion is that this structure is ineffective in all but the smallest organizations. Beauty shops, cleaning plants, "mom and pop" grocery stores, and small law firms can operate effectively with a simple line structure. CBS, American Motors, and General Electric cannot.

line organization
The organization structure based on a direct flow of authority from the chief executive to subordinates.

Functional Organization

The functional organization form was developed by the father of scientific management, Frederick Taylor, who was attempting to overcome the basic weakness of the line organization form—the concentration of too many duties on a single manager. Taylor divided the work of a single supervisor into components similar to those shown in Figure 6–6. Then he made one supervisor responsible for each individual activity.[6]

Thus, workers become responsible to a specialist in each area such as repair and maintenance, routing, inspection, training, and time and credit. The functional organization does not increase the number of managers: it simply groups them differently. Under the line form each supervisor occasionally is responsible for training. Under the functional form a specialist is placed in charge of all training.

The **functional organization** is the organization structure based on a direct flow of authority for each work activity or function. This form suffers from one critical deficiency. It creates a situation where workers have more than one boss at the same level. Even though each boss should possess authority only in the area of specialization, overlap and conflict are inevitable. And when problems occur, it is extremely difficult to locate the person at fault. With too many masters, production may be slowed rather than speeded up, and disciplinary problems may be difficult to handle. The problems of functional organization are so great that it no longer exists in most organizations. But it did serve a purpose in forcing management to focus on the need for developing an organization structure that would overcome the shortcomings of the pure line form.

Line-and-Staff Organization

The next logical step in organization structure is to combine the strengths of the line and functional organization forms. The **line-and-**

functional organization
The organization structure based on a direct flow of authority for each work activity or function.

FIGURE 6–6
The functional organization form.

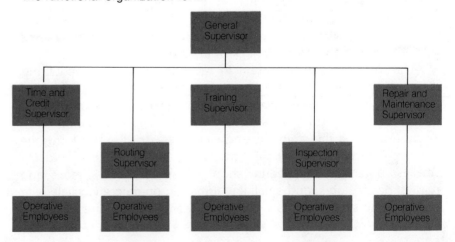

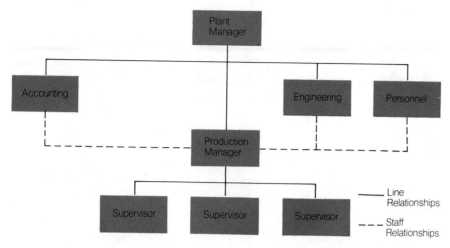

FIGURE 6–7
The line-and-staff organization.

staff organization is the organization structure that combines the direct flow of authority present in the line organization with staff departments that serve, advise, and support the line departments. Line departments are involved directly in decisions affecting the operation of the organization. Staff departments lend specialized technical support. As Figure 6–7 shows, workers receive daily supervision from a line manager and specialized advice and suggestions from staff personnel.

For all practical purposes the line-and-staff and the newer matrix structures are the only forms of organization capable of meeting the requirements of modern businesses. They combine the line organization's rapid decision making and effective, direct communications with the functional organization's expert knowledge needed to direct diverse and widespread activities.

The major difference between a line manager and a staff manager is in authority relationships. Staff managers are expected to make recommendations and to advise line managers. They do not possess the authority to give orders or to compel line managers to take action, although they do have the necessary line authority to supervise their own departments. Table 6–1 lists a few staff managers and their activities.

line-and-staff organization
The organization structure that combines the direct flow of authority present in the line organization with staff departments that service, advise, and support the line departments.

TABLE 6–1
Five Staff Managers and the Line Managers They Advise

Staff Manager	Duties and Line Managers Advised
Controller	Performs financial analyses and makes recommendations to the president and other high-level executives.
Advertising Manager	Assists the marketing director in developing the firm's advertising strategy.
Director of Research	Collects information and advises the firm's president, vice-presidents, and general managers.
Legal Counsel	Advises top management on legal matters.
Director of Engineering	Advises top management on technical and engineering matters.

Committee Organization

Committee organization is the organization structure where authority and responsibility are jointly held by a group of individuals rather than by a single manager. It is proposed not as a separate structure for the entire organization but as part of the regular line-and-staff structure.

In the area of new product introductions, the most common organizational arrangement is the new product committee, which is typically composed of representatives of top management from such areas as marketing, finance, manufacturing, engineering, research, and accounting. In major corporations the inclusion of representatives from all areas involved in developing new products generally improves planning, because diverse perspectives—production, marketing, finance—are considered. Company morale is also usually strengthened when all areas participate in decision making.

But committees tend to be slow and conservative, and decisions are often made through compromise based on conflicting interests rather than by choosing the best alternative. The definition of a *camel* as a horse established by a committee is descriptive of some committee decisions.

The Matrix Organization

During the past two decades a growing number of organizations have utilized a new approach in adjusting their existing structures to changing requirements, particularly in the areas of research and development and new-product development. Operating in coexistence with traditional line-and-staff structures, this new form is referred to as **matrix organization** or project management organization, which may be defined as an organizational structure in which specialists from different parts of the organization are brought together to work on specific projects.

An identifying feature of such organizations is that some members of the organization report to two superiors instead of the traditional single boss.[7] This type of organization exists in companies as diverse as Procter & Gamble, General Electric, NASA, Texas Instruments, Lockheed Aircraft, and the Harvard Business School. In each case, they attempt to focus the activities of several specialists from different functional areas of the organization on a specific problem or project.

Because this structure is designed to tackle specific problems or projects, the identification of such projects is followed by the selection of a team whose members have the appropriate skills. General Motors Corporation's decision to develop a line of economical, front-wheel-drive compacts was followed by the establishment of project teams consisting of specialists from design engineering, finance, marketing, research and development, and electronic data processing.

As Figure 6–8 indicates, the matrix organization produces a combination of dual authority—project members receive instructions from the project manager (the horizontal authority) and maintain their

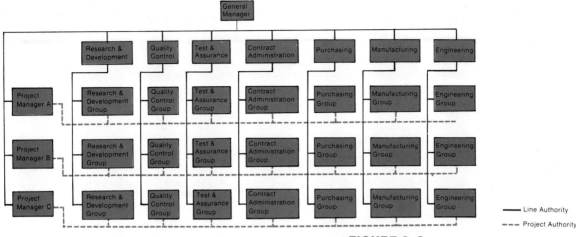

FIGURE 6–8
The matrix organization.

membership in their permanent functional departments (the vertical authority). In order to reduce the potential problems of two bosses, the project manager is typically granted considerable authority for the project and usually reports to the general manager.

The major benefits of the matrix structure lie in its flexibility and the ability to focus resources on major problems or projects. However, it requires coordination on the part of the project manager to mold individuals from diverse parts of the organization into an integrated team. Team members must be comfortable in working for more than one boss. To offset the temporary nature of the matrix team, the project manager is usually granted the authority to make salary decisions, promotion recommendations, and take other personnel actions for team members during the duration of the project.

Comparing the Five Forms of Organization

Although most large companies are organized on a line-and-staff basis, the line organization is usually the best form for smaller businesses. The committee form is also used to a limited extent in major corporations; and some departments (such as legal departments) may be organized on a functional basis. The matrix approach is increasingly used by large, multiproduct firms to focus diverse organizational resources on specific problems or projects. Table 6–2 compares the strengths and weaknesses of the five forms of organization.

The Organization Chart as a Method of Formalization

Most companies use an **organization chart** as their formal outline of authority and responsibility relationships. Such charts provide all employees with a visual statement of these relationships, enabling them

organization chart
The formal outline of authority and responsibility relationships in an organization.

TABLE 6–2
Comparison of Line, Functional, Line-and-Staff, Committee, and Matrix Organizations

Form of Organization	Advantages	Disadvantages
Line	1. Simple and easy for both workers and managers to understand 2. Clear delegation of authority and responsibility for each area 3. Quick decisions 4. Direct communications	1. No specialization 2. Overburdening of top executives with administrative details
Functional	1. The benefits of specialization 2. Expert advice available for each worker 3. Reduced managerial workload	1. Workers having more than one boss 2. Discipline breaking down unless authority is clearly defined 3. Possible conflict due to overlapping of authority
Line-and-Staff	1. Specialists to advise line managers 2. Employees reporting to one superior	1. Conflict between line and staff unless relationships are clear 2. Staff managers making only recommendations to line managers
Committee	1. Combined judgment of several executives in diverse areas 2. Improved morale through participation in decision making	1. Committees slow in making decisions 2. Decisions that are the result of compromises rather than a choice of the best alternative.
Matrix	1. Flexibility 2. Provides method for focusing strongly on specific major problems or unique technical issues 3. Provides means of innovation without disrupting regular organizational structure	1. Problems may result, since this approach violates the traditional unity of command (one boss for each individual) principle 2. Project manager may encounter difficulty in developing cohesive team from diverse individuals recruited from numerous parts of the organization 3. Conflicts may arise between project managers and other department managers

to see how their work relates to the overall operation of the company and to whom they report. The organization chart is thus the blueprint of the organization, indicating lines of authority within it, including staff relationships, line relationships, and permanent committees.

Because the organization chart specifies each area of responsibility and authority, it can also help managers coordinate activities. But it reflects the organization at only one point in time, and it should, therefore, be updated periodically to reflect changing conditions.

Although most organization charts are constructed in the shape of a pyramid, extending downward from the board of directors or president, some firms have adopted the **"doughnut" structure** recommended by Robert Townsend, former president of Avis and author of the business satire *Up the Organization*. Townsend strongly endorses the need for flexible organization charts that reflect a dynamic organization:

> In the best organizations people see themselves working in a circle as if around one table. One of the positions is designated chief executive officer, because somebody has to make all those tactical decisions that enable an organization to keep working.[8]

"doughnut" structure
An organization chart made up of concentric circles that represent top management, staff personnel, and functional areas and that reflect a more flexible structure.

The doughnut design is made up of concentric circles, in which the center ring consists of top management. The second ring is composed of important staff personnel, such as legal, personnel, research and development, and electronic data processing, whose services are used by all departments. The third ring consists of managers of functional areas, while remaining rings comprise department and other supervisory managers. Figure 6–9 shows the construction of a doughnut-shaped organization chart.

The Informal Organization

In addition to the formal lines of authority and responsibility shown in the organization chart, informal channels of communication and contact also exist. The **informal organization** is a self-grouping of employees in the organization who possess informal channels of communication and contact. This type of organization is not formally planned; it develops out of the interactions of people.

Formal organization is the creation of management; informal organization is the result of social and communications relationships. Groups of workers often cut across the formal organizational structure, and informal relationships exist at both managerial and lower levels. Supervisors from a number of departments may take coffee breaks

informal organization
A self-grouping of employees in the organization who possess informal channels of communication and contact.

FIGURE 6–9
A doughnut-shaped organization chart.

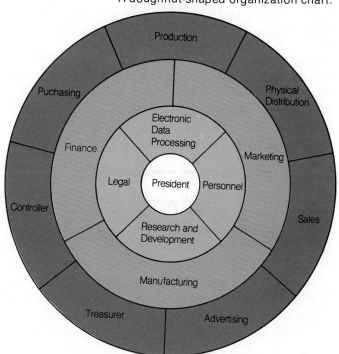

Controversial Issue

Should Company Executives Be Personally Responsible for Illegal Company Activities?

Crime in the executive suite is a lot more common than most business people would care to admit. In a study of 1,043 major U.S. corporations, *Fortune* magazine found that 117 of them—11 percent—had been victims of some form of high-level, domestic corporate corruption since 1970. The crimes included bribery (kickbacks and illegal rebates), criminal fraud, illegal political contributions, tax evasion, and criminal antitrust violations involving price fixing and bid-rigging conspiracies. Had foreign kickbacks and bribes been taken into account, the percentage would have been higher. Here are two examples:

• Bethlehem Steel received a $325,000 fine for a kickback scheme that involved passing hundreds of thousands of dollars in laundered money through Europe and then back again by courier to be distributed as bribes.
• Ashland Oil pleaded guilty to charges of illegal political contributions and, in three cases, to illegally rigging bids for highway construction work in Virginia. It also pleaded *nolo contendre* (no contest) to fixing the price of resins.

Whatever the reason for corporate crimes—whether it be the intense economic pressure that makes managers do almost anything to beat their competitors and turn a profit, or the desire to gain access to government leaders through illegal political contributions—the federal Justice Department and state prosecutors are no longer detoured by the corporate roadblock. They have

together to discuss mutual interests and problems—both company and personal. Two machinists, a drill press operator, a receiving clerk, and a supervisor may form the company basketball team. As part of this regular interaction, they may discuss company operations and communicate the results of their talks to other workers in their areas.

Even though the informal organization is not shown on the organization chart, managers should be aware of its existence. It may even be possible to make use of some aspects of the informal organization in accomplishing organizational objectives such as through the use of the **grapevine**—the informal communications network found in most organizations. In his studies of the grapevine, Professor Keith Davis has found it to be 80 to 90 percent accurate in transmitting noncontroversial information. Because this information travels by word of mouth, the grapevine is faster than formal communications.[9] Recognition of its existence and how it works can enable managers to use the grapevine as a supplement to formal communications channels in dispersing information and in minimizing rumors and incorrect information.

grapevine
The informal communications network found in most organizations.

taken a long, hard look at how responsible white collar executives are for their companies' crimes and decided that some executives should go to jail.

Often people so high up the corporate hierarchy that they probably could not have known about the crimes are being punished. But the statutes and the judges are saying that vicarious responsibility makes them liable whether or not they knew about the wrongdoing. Following this dictum, the courts sentenced more business executives to jail for price fixing in 1978 than in the 89 years since the passage of the Sherman Antitrust Act. The Food and Drug Administration now requires pharmaceutical companies to assign an executive with personal liability for each new drug they put on the market. And the Foreign Corrupt Practices Act of 1977 metes out stiff fines and even stiffer prison sentences for officers and directors found guilty of engaging in bribes. A plea of ignorance is no longer acceptable when corporate wrongdoing comes before the courts. Chief executives who want to keep their noses clean should know every facet of their company's business and the regulations governing it.

As corporations grow larger and corporate life more complex and competitive, the situations where wrongdoing can occur will also grow. Whether executives should be held responsible for this wrongdoing or whether their responsibility should be limited to situations in which they participated first-hand is a question that will be debated in board rooms and judicial chambers over the coming years.

Summary

Organizations provide the necessary structure within which managers work toward the accomplishment of company objectives. The need for structure increases as businesses grow in size. As the numbers of subordinates increase, the responsibility of coordinating their activities through a formal structure also increases.

Formal organizational structure is based on an analysis of the three key elements of an organization: human interaction, goal-directed activity, and structure. Once the activities of the organization have been analyzed, they are grouped into units. This process of departmentalization is based on one of five forms: products, geography, customers, functions, or processes.

Developing a formal organizational structure means that top management must delegate to subordinates the authority and responsibility needed to accomplish assignments. The span of control is the optimum number of subordinates that can be effectively supervised by a manager. It is determined by such factors as the type of work being done, the subordinates' training, the manager's abilities, and the effectiveness of the firm's communications.

Five forms of organization structure have been used: line, functional, line-and-staff, committee, and matrix. The line organization is the simplest form but it suffers from a lack of specialization by management. The functional organization solves the problem of specialization by appointing managers for each specialized activity, but it suffers from the potential problem of multiple bosses for each worker. The most common organization structure is the line-and-staff form, which incorporates the strengths of both line and functional organization structures by assigning authority to line managers and adding staff specialists to provide information and advice. The committee form of organization is rarely used as the sole organization structure, but it is often incorporated to some extent within the line-and-staff structure. Because committees can be composed of representatives of a number of areas in the organization, they ensure that each area is represented in the decision-making process. But they are relatively slow in making decisions, which often end up being compromises among conflicting interests. The matrix approach has evolved in recent years to permit large, multiproduct firms to focus organizational resources on specific problems or projects.

The organization chart is a blueprint of the authority relationships within the organization. It shows functions, formal channels of communication, and line-and-staff relationships. It also indicates the responsibility, authority, and accountability relationships within the firm; it does not reflect the informal groups or lines of communication that exist.

Key Terms

organization
hierarchy of organizational objectives
departmentalization
product departmentalization
geographic departmentalization
customer departmentalization
functional departmentalization
process departmentalization
delegation
responsibility
authority
accountability
span of control

centralization
decentralization
Parkinson's Law
line organization
functional organization
line-and-staff organization
committee organization
matrix organization
organization chart
"doughnut" structure
informal organization
grapevine

Review Questions

1. Explain each of the terms listed on the previous page.

2. What are the purposes of a formal organization structure?

3. What is departmentalization? What are its major forms?

4. Why is it important that authority and responsibility be balanced in an organization?

5. Identify the determinants of the optimum span of control.

6. Distinguish between centralization and decentralization. Under which circumstances might each be preferred?

7. List the types of formal organization.

8. Summarize the major advantages and disadvantages of each type of formal organization structure.

9. What are the major purposes of an organization chart?

10. Explain how the informal organization differs from the formal organization.

Discussion Questions and Exercises

1. Evaluate the pros and cons of the controversial issue that appears in this chapter.

2. Give an example of a firm in your state that should use each of the following forms of departmentalization and explain why it should do so:
   a. product   d. function
   b. geography   e. process
   c. customer

3. Suggest some ways in which Parkinson's Law might be prevented from occurring.

4. Draw an organization chart for your college. Indicate which positions are primarily line and which are primarily staff.

5. The committee structure is rarely used as a separate structure for an entire organization. Suggest several specific ways of improving the committee form of organization structure.

Case 6–1: Choosing the Best Organization Form for a Toy Manufacturer

Fun-For-All is a national manufacturing firm that produces and sells toys and games. Prior to 1968, the company specialized in children's toys. In the late sixties, however, adult games began to gain acceptance and Fun-For-All followed suit. The basic feature of adult games is that they have no single, correct strategy and as a result require a great deal of thought on the part of the participant. For example, *Monopoly,* from Parker Brothers, has a basic strategy that often depends on chance rather than skill. Players who are wise buy as much land as they can and start putting houses, and eventually hotels, on the property. However, true adult games such as chess are much more complex. There is no one correct way to win a chess game: winning depends on what one's opponent does and on one's own skill. The same is true for backgammon.

In 1977 Fun-For-All decided to market an expensive ($100) backgammon set. The company was convinced that with the economy moving along well and people's outlook becoming more positive, demand for such a high-priced game would be sufficient to justify a 25 percent return on investment. By Christmas, thanks to timing and a strong advertising program, the firm had sold four times the number of sets than initially forecasted.

In 1978, because of growing sales, the management of Fun-For-All was considering reorganization. At the time, the firm was organized along the functional lines shown in Figure 6–10. However, the president thought it might be wiser to change to product departmentalization, and he was supported by some of the marketing people who also seemed to think that this would be a good idea. Members of the production department, however, felt there was more to be gained from functional rather than product departmentalization. The finance people seemed indifferent about the matter, but indicated they would make an analysis of the two structures if the president desired.

The president's reorganization plan was to set up three product

FIGURE 6–10
Fun-For-All current organization chart.

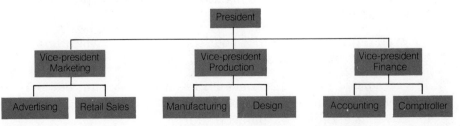

divisions: boy's toys, girl's toys, and adult games. The first two divisions accounted for over 75 percent of the firm's sales, but the latter was growing rapidly and would, according to marketing estimates, account for over 50 percent of all sales by 1983.

Questions

1. Draw the proposed reorganization chart. Be as complete as possible.

2. What are the advantages of product departmentalization over functional departmentalization?

3. What recommendations would you make to the president before he finalized the decision switch from functional to product departmentalization? Explain.

Case 6–2: The Organization of a Professional Sports Team

Professional sports teams in football, basketball, tennis, and hockey are business enterprises that use a simplified organization structure. While not all sports or teams follow exactly the same pattern, most professional teams are owned by wealthy individuals (many of them millionaires) who enjoy being involved with a particular sport. The owners usually make major policy decisions, but a hired general manager handles other managerial duties. The general manager oversees the business side of the operation such as ticket sales, travel, contracts for facilities, equipment, vendors, and personnel matters. He usually also has responsibility for player personnel decisions such as trades, drafts of new players, and assignment of players to minor leagues. The field manager, or head coach, is in charge of the team's actual performance. This person assists the general manager in matters concerning players. In some cases the general manager is also the field manager. Other personnel employed by professional teams include team physicians, assistant coaches, trainers, equipment managers, secretaries, scouts, and ticket sales personnel.

Questions

1. Describe the strengths and weaknesses of the organization structure of professional sports teams.

2. Draw an organization chart for a professional sports team.

3. Can you think of similar organization structures in other businesses? Explain.

Careers in Management

Management offers an exciting array of career opportunities for the person who has the leadership qualities and professional preparation to deal with the complex problems facing the modern executive. Effective managers have numerous career paths available to them, because they can move from one industry or economic sector to another. Good industrial executives, for example, can effectively apply their abilities in service industries, federal agencies, and hospitals.

Most management positions require considerable practical experience. Management is not a beginning job; it is one to work toward as you acquire experience.

The Bureau of Labor Statistics has projected the employment outlook to 1990. Its forecasts for some selected management jobs appear in the table on page 155. The bureau expects all occupations to add 20.8 percent to their work force between 1978 and 1990. Five of the management careers currently available appear below.

General manager. After obtaining substantial practical experience, some people move into general management positions. Titles can range anywhere from president to vice-president to general manager. These positions involve the management of activities that cross functional areas. For example, a general manager of an automobile dealership has overall responsibility for sales (new and\ used vehicles), leasing, service, finance, and personnel.

Department head. A department head is a manager of an organizational unit. Office managers, marketing managers, and production managers are all department heads. These people usually have experience in the areas that are to be managed.

Supervisor. Supervisors are managers of part of a department. They are the first level of management, and they directly supervise employees.

Public administrator. A public administrator is a manager of a government department, bureau, agency, or other division, or of a unit in a hospital or other nonprofit institution. Many local governments have been employing professional public administrators to manage their operations.

Administrative assistant. Administrative assistants are staff personnel who work directly for general management. They often hold the title "Assistant to . . ." Sometimes the position of administrative assistant is used as a training ground for people expected to advance to higher management positions in the firm.

EMPLOYMENT OUTLOOK TO 1990							
		Changes in Employment					
Occupations in Management	Recent Employment Figures	Much Faster than the Average for All Occupations	Faster than the Average for All Occupations	About as Fast as the Average for All Occupations	More Slowly than the Average for All Occupations	Little Change Expected	Expected to Decline
Blue Collar Work Supervisors	1,670,000			●			
City Managers	3,000		●				
Hotel Managers and Assistants	168,000				●		
Health Service Administrators	180,000	●					

Source: U.S. Department of Labor, Bureau of Labor Statistics, *Occupational Outlook Handbook 1980–1981*, Bulletin 2075, pp. 5, 55–56, 117–118, 121–122, 411–412.

MANAGEMENT OF HUMAN RESOURCES

7

Human Relations in Management

Learning Goals

1. To explore different types of needs and to discover what motivates people

2. To distinguish between Theory X and Theory Y managers

3. To analyze a particular job and to point out the factors that serve as motivators

4. To explain the importance of good morale to productivity and the factors involved in achieving it

5. To enumerate the steps involved in installing a management by objectives (MBO) program

6. To explain the meaning of each of the key terms introduced in this chapter

Profile: Guy Odom
Applying Human Relations Concepts to Home Building

Under the leadership of Guy R. Odom, Chairman and Chief Executive Officer since 1977, the U.S. Home Corporation has become the nation's largest on-site manufacturer of single-family homes—a fact that does not surprise anyone who knows him personally. Guy Odom's direction is responsible for turning around the Company's profit picture. An organizational structure that encourages rather than squelches entrepreneurial spirit and a highly sophisticated process for selecting and developing managers are the keys to his success.

Each of the 65 home-building divisions that make up U.S. Home's organizational structure is run by a Division President who in many ways is his own boss. "He's the prima donna in our organization," said Guy Odom. "We give him enough rope to go to the moon—or hang himself."

Division Presidents have the overall responsibility for choosing home sites and home designs, for selecting subcontractors who can build a quality product on schedule, and for marketing their product to the public. When they meet or exceed predetermined profit objectives, they receive generous bonuses based solely on performance that reinforce their willingness to seek higher goals next year. Although Division Presidents are carefully monitored by bottom-line-oriented Corporate Vice Presidents, they feel few restraining tugs if their corporate objectives are being met.

Guy Odom's philosophy is relatively simple: Get the best people. Give them direction and room to grow. Provide the right incentives and growth will follow. He is well aware that none of this would be possible without the right personnel, so he transformed the employee-selection process from a game of chance into a very serious science. Under the U.S. Home system, job applicants are given a series of aptitude and personality surveys to determine the odds toward succeeding at U.S. Home.

The entire corporation places enormous confidence in this process. Employees are not interviewed by field managers prior to hiring, even though they know that not all employees will succeed. "These surveys," says Guy Odom, "are really our only trade secret."

Once hired, employees are then put through the paces of a rigorous management development program. The program consist of bi-weekly meetings in which one of 45 books related directly or indirectly to management and behavioral science are discussed. These books express the Company's management philosophy and become guides to employees.

A high school graduate who schooled himself in management science through reading, Guy Odom has built a company that has few managerial kinks. "I've never been associated with a loss," says Odom. "I don't know what it feels like, and I don't want to find out."

Fairness and decency for American workers means more than simply keeping them alive and safe from injury and disease. It means an effort to make it possible for workers to live not just as robots or machines, but as men and women who are human beings. Additionally, making the assembly line more human and humane is a large and difficult task, but it is at the heart of everything we mean by social justice in America.

—Senator Edward Kennedy

When a three-engine Boeing 727 flying at 40,000 feet loses all three engines at once (under normal circumstances the plane could glide for over 130 miles) the captain has ample time for quickly consulting with his copilot and flight engineer to get their ideas about the cause and remedy, and to discuss emergency procedures with the stewardesses. However, if a similar power loss occurred at 500 feet during a takeoff climb, the captain would be ill advised to practice such participative techniques.

—J. Clayton Lafferty, President Human Synergistics, Inc.

Kockums, a Swedish company that builds supertankers, faced critical personnel problems, that would have shocked Guy Odom, a few years ago. Labor turnover was running at about 50 percent a year, and productivity was down. The firm's management at first turned to efficiency experts who pushed for greater worker output and angered Kockums' production workers.

In desperation, Nils-Hugo Hallenborg, the firm's chief executive officer, made an unusual decision. He turned the problem over to the union and asked union officials to work out a solution. They agreed to tackle the problem and produced a public report that was highly critical of Kockums' management. They also asked for specific changes in working conditions.

Hallenborg again startled observers by implementing the union's report. Wages based on the number of units produced were replaced by hourly rates. Additional medical personnel were hired. Safety standards were upgraded. Saunas were provided. Social workers were made available to deal with workers' personal problems. Vacation cabins were built in Scandinavia, Western Europe, and Africa.

Kockums also tried to give production workers more responsibility. Joint management-labor committees now schedule the construction of the approximately six supertankers built annually. The firm acknowledged that basically "dirty" jobs could not be changed. But management worked to improve nearly everything related to those jobs.

Kockums' employees have enthusiastically supported these reforms. Worker output is up, and turnover is now under 20 percent a year. Kockums' personnel director puts it this way: "People like to work when they know why they are working."[1]

The Hawthorne Studies: Birth of a New Approach to Manager-employee Relations

---

Although the changes in compensation programs and the cooperative efforts of the Swedish shipbuilder may appear unusual (and perhaps impractical) even to workers and managers in the 1980s, striking changes in both the assumptions made by managers about their employees and in the approaches used by managers in motivating employee excellence have occurred over the past half century. The origin of many of these changes can be traced to a series of experiments that later became known as the Hawthorne studies.

In 1927 Elton Mayo and a group of researchers from Harvard University traveled to Chicago to explore the relationship between changes in physical working conditions and employee productivity. They chose the Hawthorne Plant of Western Electric as the subject of their research. The **Hawthorne studies,** a series of investigations that revealed that money and job security are not the only source of employee motivation, led to the development of the human relations approach to motivation.

Asking questions such as "What is the effect of different intensities of light on employee output?" and "How will varying noise levels change worker productivity?" the researchers sought answers by setting up controlled experiments in the relay assembly section of the plant. A group of six female workers was provided with sufficient lighting; then the amount of light was reduced. Mayo and his colleagues were baffled to discover that reducing the amount of light had almost no effect on productivity. In fact, in some cases output actually rose. The light intensity was then reduced to about that of moonlight, and again production increased!

> [Mayo and his colleagues] swooned at their desks. . . . Because of some mysterious X which had thrust itself into the experiment, this group of six girls was pouring 25 percent more relays into the chutes. . . .
>
> What was this X? The research staff pulled themselves together and began looking for it. They conferred, argued, studied, and pres-

Hawthorne studies
A series of investigations that revealed money and job security are not the only sources of employee motivation and that lead to the development of the human relations approach to employee motivation.

ently they found it. It wasn't in the physical production end of the factory at all. It was in the girls themselves. It was an attitude, the way the girls now felt about their work and their group. By segregating them into a little world of their own, by asking their help and cooperation, the investigators had given the young women a new sense of their own value. Their whole attitude changed from that of separate cogs in a machine to that of a congenial team helping the company solve a significant problem.

They found stability, a place where they belonged, and work whose purpose they could clearly see. And so they worked faster and better than they ever had in their lives. The two functions of a factory had joined into one harmonious whole.[2]

What Motivates Workers?

The Hawthorne studies revolutionized management's approach to direction (or motivation) of employees. Prior to the Hawthorne investigation, most organizations had used money as the primary means of motivating workers. Satisfactory wages and job security were assumed to satisfy employees and motivate them to work faster and more efficiently in pursuit of overall organizational objectives. The importance of the Hawthorne findings lies not in denying the effect of money as a motivator but in emphasizing the presence of a number of other sources of employee motivation.

Each individual is motivated to take action designed to satisfy needs. A **need** is simply the lack of something useful. A **motive** is the inner state that directs the individual toward the goal of satisfying a felt need. The individual is moved (the root word for motive) to take action to reduce a state of tension and return to a condition of equilibrium. This motivation process is depicted in Figure 7–1.

need
The lack of something useful; a discrepancy between a desired state and the actual state.

motive
The inner state that directs the individual toward the goal of satisfying a felt need.

FIGURE 7–1
The process of motivation.

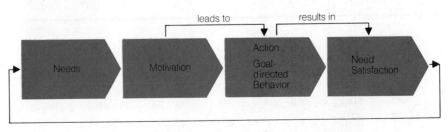

| Self-actualization Needs |
| Esteem Needs |
| Social (Belongingness) Needs |
| Safety Needs |
| Physiological Needs |

FIGURE 7–2
The ladder of human needs.

A Ladder of Human Needs

Psychologist Abraham H. Maslow developed a still widely accepted list of human needs based on two important assumptions:

1. People are wanting animals whose needs depend on what they already possess. A satisfied need is not a motivator; only those needs that have not been satisfied can influence behavior.
2. People's needs are arranged in a hierarchy of importance. Once one need has been at least partially satisfied, another emerges and demands satisfaction.[3]

   Figure 7–2 shows the ladder of human needs with the rungs arranged in order of importance to the individual. Priority is assigned to the basic physiological needs.

Physiological Needs

Physiological needs are the primary needs for food, shelter, and clothing that are present in all humans and that must be satisfied before the individual can consider higher-order needs. A hungry person is possessed by the need to obtain food; other needs are ignored. But once the physiological needs are at least partially satisfied, the other needs come into the picture. Because minimum wage laws and union wage contracts have forced wage levels upward so that most families can afford to satisfy their basic needs, the higher-order needs are likely to play a greater role in worker motivation today.

Safety Needs

The second-level **safety needs** include job security, protection from physical harm, and avoidance of the unexpected. Gratification of these

physiological needs
The primary needs for food, shelter, and clothing that are present in all humans and that must be satisfied before higher-order needs can be considered.

safety needs
The second level of human needs in Maslow's hierarchy, which includes job security, protection from physical harm, and avoidance of the unexpected.

needs may take such forms as guaranteed annual wages, life insurance, the purchase of radial tires, the obeying of job safety rules, or membership in the company health club.

Social Needs

social (belongingness) needs
The desire to be accepted by members of the family and other individuals and groups.

Satisfaction of physiological and safety needs leads to the third rung on the ladder, **social needs** (also known as **belongingness needs**)— the desire to be accepted by members of the family and other individuals and groups. The individual may be motivated to join various groups at the factory, conforming to the standards established and accepted by the informal organization, in order to fulfill these social needs.

Esteem Needs

esteem needs
The human needs for a sense of accomplishment, a feeling of achievement, and the respect of others.

The needs near the top of the ladder, **esteem needs,** are more difficult to satisfy. At this level is the need to feel a sense of accomplishment, achievement, and respect from others. The competitive need to excel—to better the performance of others—is an almost universal human trait.

The esteem need is closely related to belongingness needs. However, at this level the individual wants not just acceptance but also recognition and respect—the desire to stand out from the crowd in some area.

Self-actualization Needs

self-actualization needs
The needs for fulfillment, for realizing one's potential, and for totally using one's talents and capabilities.

The top rung on the ladder of human needs is **self-actualization needs**—the needs for fulfillment, for realizing one's own potential, for using totally one's talents and capabilities.

Maslow defines *self-actualization* this way: "A healthy man is primarily motivated by his needs to develop and actualize his fullest potentialities and capacities." "What man *can* be, he *must* be."[4]

The famous author Robert Louis Stevenson was describing self-actualization when he wrote, "to be what we are, and to become what we are capable of becoming, is the only end of life."[5] For Richard Pryor, self-actualization may mean being the most popular comedian in the United States. The approximately 200 new entries in each revised edition of the *Guinness Book of World Records* represent individuals daring to accomplish what no person has done before.

Applying the Needs Concept

Maslow points out that a satisfied need is no longer a motivator. Once the physiological needs are satisfied, the individual becomes concerned with higher-order needs. There will obviously be periods when an individual is motivated by the need to relieve thirst or hunger, but interest is most often directed toward the satisfaction of safety, belongingness, and the other needs on the ladder.

Business organizations have been extremely successful in satisfying the lower-order physiological and safety needs. The traditional view of workers as ingredients in the productive process—as machines like lathes, drill presses, and other equipment—led management to motivate them with money. The Hawthorne studies showed that people are not like machines and that social and psychological needs are motivators as effective as money. Managers at that point had to reconsider their assumptions about employees and how best to motivate them (see Focus 7–1).

FOCUS 7–1
Motivating the Soviet Worker

As *U.S. News & World Report* observes, Maslow's ladder of needs is not unknown in the Soviet Union.

In Russia, getting Ivan to *work harder* is a big test for managers. Soviet economic growth targets . . . rely almost entirely on more output from labor. But productivity gains are lagging. Any remedy is *worth a try*—

Bonuses for beating production quotas are old hat in Russia but still useful. In addition, many factories now have special *"workers' brigades"* that, in theory, are paid wholly on results. They often set their own output goals. A new award has been adopted for *"shock" workers,* those employees who post outstanding results. Factories, too, may be pitted one against another.

The *Soviet stick* also is used. Workers who damage machinery must pay for repairs. Absentees and people persistently late to work may be shunted to jobs with low pay. Others may be dropped *down the waiting list* for new apartments.

Russian laborers have their gripes, too. One is *"storming"*—having to work flat out at the end of every month to fulfill quotas. Disregard of health and safety rules also irks them. Authorities' advice: *Complain to your union.*

But Soviet unions see their main task as insuring that output meets goals.

Evaluating Theory X: Do People Hate Work?

Theory X is the traditional managerial assumption that employees dislike work and must be coerced, controlled, or threatened to motivate them to work. According to its author, the late Douglas McGregor, Theory X involves the following:

Theory X
The traditional managerial assumption that employees dislike work and must be coerced, controlled, or threatened to motivate them to work.

1. The average human being has an inherent dislike of work and will avoid it if possible.
2. Because of this characteristic, most people must be coerced, controlled, directed, or threatened with punishment to get them to put forth adequate effort toward the achievement of organization objectives.
3. The average human being prefers to be directed, wishes to avoid responsibility, has relatively little ambition, and wants security above all.[6]

If true, this traditional view of workers is a rather depressing indictment of human nature. Managers who accept the view may choose to direct their subordinates through close and constant observation, continually holding over them the threat of disciplinary action and demanding that they closely follow company policies and procedures.

Theory Y: Replacement for Theory X

Theory Y
The newer managerial assumption that workers do not dislike work and that under proper conditions they accept and seek out responsibilities in order to fulfill their social, esteem, and self-actualization needs.

Theory X appears to have a critical deficiency. It focuses strictly on physiological and safety needs while ignoring the higher-order needs. If people behave in the manner described by Theory X, the reason for their behavior may be that the organization only partially satisfies their needs. If, instead, the organization enables them to satisfy their social, esteem, and self-actualization needs, new behavior patterns should develop—and different assumptions should be made.

Theory Y offers a new managerial assumption—that workers do not dislike work and that, under proper conditions, they accept and seek out responsibilities in order to fulfill their social, esteem, and self-actualization needs. Under Theory Y, McGregor points out:

1. Workers do not inherently dislike work. The expenditure of physical and mental effort in work is as natural as play or rest.
2. Employees do not want to be rigidly controlled and threatened with punishment.
3. The average worker will, under proper conditions, not only accept but actually seek responsibility.
4. Employees desire to satisfy social, esteem, and self-actualization needs in addition to security needs.[7]

Unlike the traditional management philosophy that relies on external control and constant supervision, Theory Y emphasizes self-control and direction. Its implementation requires a totally different managerial strategy (see Focus 7–2).

FOCUS 7-2
Applying Theory Y in the Dutch Army

Organizational rules typically take precedence over individual desires. The prevalent image of the military organizational member is a soldier who is highly trained, disciplined, physically fit, well groomed, and willing to follow orders without question. Obviously someone failed to inform the Dutch soldier of that. He makes many old professional soldiers want to cry.

> The hair, long and lank, spills from beneath the helmet. The uniform is rumpled, the demeanor cheerful and offhand. When our hero goes on a field march, he may wear sneakers rather than combat boots; they are more comfortable. Does he salute officers? Hardly ever.

The above description of the 100,000-member Dutch army was made possible by the establishment of a military union in the early 1970s. Regulations concerning hair and hair length were abandoned. And overtime pay has been instituted for situations when Dutch soldiers are required to be on duty during weekends. Late-evening barracks checks and morning reveille have ended. Soldiers simply must be at their posts on time.

The practice of saluting has also changed. Salutes, described by one Dutch soldier as "a strange way of contact between people," are now exchanged between officers and enlisted recruits only during formal ceremonies and at formal appointments.

Strikes, the ultimate threat of any union, are prohibited, and disobedience of commands will result in spelled-out disciplinary actions. One unit that refused to participate in a maneuver because it was too cold received a three-week detention. A soldier who refused to move against hijackers of a Dutch train was discharged from the army.

These Dutch soldiers are members of an honor guard at The Hague.

Maintenance versus Motivational Factors

Over two decades ago, psychologist Frederick Herzberg conducted a study in human motivation of various job factors as sources of satisfaction and dissatisfaction. Based on his research, Herzberg reached two conclusions:

1. Certain characteristics of a job, called **maintenance factors,** are necessary to maintain a desired level of satisfaction. They include such job-related factors as salary, working conditions, and job security. They must be present in order to prevent worker dissatis-

maintenance factors
Job-related factors, such as salary, working conditions, and job security, that must be present in order to prevent worker dissatisfaction but which are not strong motivators.

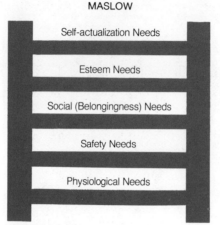

FIGURE 7–3
Comparing Herzberg and Maslow.

faction, but they are not strong motivators. If they are absent or inadequate, they are likely to serve as *dissatisfiers.*

2. Other job-centered characteristics are **motivational factors** such as the work itself, recognition, responsibility, advancement, and growth potential—the key sources of employee motivation.

Thus, although maintenance factors such as money are extremely important when they are lacking, they are of low motivational value when they are present in adequate amounts. Instead, the key motivational factors are related to the job itself. The supervisor motivates the worker not with an additional coffee break but with greater job involvement.[8]

As Figure 7–3 shows, a great deal of similarity exists between Herzberg's two factors and Maslow's ladder of human needs. Herzberg's message is that the lower-rung needs have already been satisfied for most workers, and the manager must focus on the higher-level needs—the primary motivators.

What Factors Influence Employee Morale?

Morale is the mental attitude of employees toward their companies and their jobs. High morale is a sign of a well-managed organization, because the worker's attitude toward the job affects the quality of the work done.

One of the most obvious signs of poor manager-worker relations is poor morale. It lurks behind absenteeism, employee turnover, slowdowns, and wildcat strikes; it shows up in lower productivity, employee grievances, and transfers.

But often management's view of what leads to high employee morale is incorrect. One research study compared how managers and

---

motivational factors
Job-centered characteristics, such as the work itself, recognition, responsibility, advancement, and growth potential, which are the key sources of employee motivation.

morale
The mental attitude of employees toward their companies and their jobs.

TABLE 7–1

Managers' Assessment of Factors Leading to High Morale

Morale Item	Manager Ranking
Good wages	1
Job security	2
Promotion and growth with company	3
Good working conditions	4
Interesting work	5
Management loyalty to workers	6
Tactful disciplining	7
Full appreciation for work done	8
Sympathetic understanding of personal problems	9
Feeling "in" on things	10

workers ranked the importance of various morale factors. Table 7–1 shows how managers ranked these factors.

According to this table, managers chiefly emphasized the lower-order needs of money and job security. But Table 7–2 reveals a quite different ranking by employees. Opinions varied significantly on the importance of such items as job security and appreciation for work done. Other differences included the importance of fair pay, promotion, and understanding of personal problems.

TABLE 7–2

Workers' Assessment of Factors Leading to High Morale

Morale Item	Employee Ranking
Full appreciation for work done	1
Feeling "in" on things	2
Sympathetic understanding of personal problems	3
Job security	4
Good wages	5
Interesting work	6
Promotion and growth with company	7
Management loyalty to workers	8
Good working conditions	9
Tactful disciplining	10

Showing full appreciation for work done is one way to motivate people.
Drawing by Mulligan; © 1975 The New Yorker Magazine. Inc.

"Why, thank you, sir, and I had it in mind to tell you what a bang-up job I think you're doing."

The maintenance of high morale means more than keeping employees happy. A two-day workweek, longer vacations, or almost continual coffee breaks could easily produce happy employees. But high morale results from an environment in which workers obtain satisfaction from their work and are motivated to excel in their assigned duties, which should lead to greater production. Management, therefore, should create a work environment that will result in high employee morale.

Management Techniques Designed to Improve Motivation

Two management techniques are widely used today in an attempt to improve the overall motivation and performance of workers: management by objectives and job enrichment.

Management by Objectives

The management by objectives (MBO) approach was first proposed nearly 50 years ago. It was popularized in the early 1950s by Peter Drucker, who described it this way:

> The objectives of the district manager's job should be clearly defined by the contribution he and his district sales force have to make to the sales department, the objectives of the project engineer's job by the contribution he, his engineers and draftsmen make to the engineering department. . . . This requires each manager to develop and set the objectives of his unit himself. Higher management must, of course, reserve the power to approve or disapprove his objectives. But their development is part of a manager's responsibility; indeed, it is his first responsibility.[9]

management by objectives (MBO)
A program designed to improve employees' motivation through having them participate in setting their own goals and letting them know in advance precisely how they will be evaluated.

Thus, **management by objectives** is a program designed to improve employees' motivation through having them participate in setting their own goals and letting them know in advance precisely how they will be evaluated.

Five steps in an MBO program. Figure 7–4 illustrates the five-step sequence of most MBO programs:

1. Each subordinate discusses the job description with the manager.
2. Short-term performance goals are established.
3. The subordinate meets regularly with the manager to discuss progress toward the goals.
4. Intermediate checkpoints are established to measure progress toward the goals.

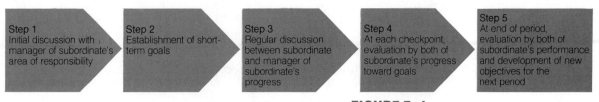

FIGURE 7–4
The management by objectives sequence.

5. At the end of a defined period, manager and subordinate together evaluate the results of the subordinate's efforts.

Management by objectives involves mutual goal setting by manager and subordinate. Both must reach an understanding about the subordinate's major area of responsibility and the acceptable level of performance. These understandings form the basis of the subordinate's goals for the next planning period (usually in about six months).

Goals should be in numerical terms whenever possible—for example, reducing scrap losses by 5 percent or increasing sales of pocket calculators by 15 percent. Once these goals are established and agreed upon, the subordinate has the responsibility for achieving them.

During the interim the subordinate may check often with the manager. At the end of the period a formal progress review is conducted. Both the subordinate and the manager discuss performance and determine whether the goals were achieved. New goals are then established for the next period.

Benefits of an MBO program. The chief purpose of management by objectives is to improve motivation of employees through their participation in setting their own goals. Workers thus know both the job to be done and precisely how they will be evaluated.

An MBO program should improve morale by improving communications between individual employees and their managers. It should also enable workers to relate their performance to overall organizational goals. Finally, it should serve as a basis for decisions about salary increases and promotions.

MBO at all levels. MBO is not limited to any single level in the organization. It should probably begin with the president, who should set some personal job objectives in consultation with the board of directors. The process should then proceed throughout the organization, extending to every employee.

Is MBO for everyone? Experience with MBO programs indicates that they have merit if used with judgment and a great deal of planning. Because changes may have to be made in such areas as the degree of communication between managers and subordinates, MBO will succeed only where both managers and subordinates feel comfortable with it and are willing to participate in it.

Management must also recognize that in many organizations workers' goals are constantly changing. In such situations it is much more difficult to measure results accurately.

Job Enrichment

Most assembly line jobs are likely to have certain common characteristics: mechanically controlled work pace, repetitiveness, minimum skill requirements, predetermined tools and techniques, and minute subdivision of the product that, therefore, requires only surface mental attention.[10] These job characteristics often lead to what is popularly called the blue-collar blues, because workers who cannot control their pace, cannot use judgment, and are not challenged to improve their skills above a minimal level are likely to be poorly motivated at best and suffer from alienation at worst.

job enrichment
Giving workers more authority to plan their work and to decide how it is to be accomplished and allowing them to learn related skills or to trade jobs with others.

Job enrichment means giving workers more authority to plan their work and to decide how it is to be accomplished, and allowing them to learn related skills or to trade jobs with others. Building on Herzberg's ideas, it focuses on motivational factors by designing work that will satisfy individual as well as company needs. Herzberg explains job enrichment this way:

> [It] seeks to improve both task efficiency and human satisfaction by means of building into people's jobs . . . greater scope for personal achievement and recognition, more challenging and responsible work, and more opportunity for individual advancement and growth. It is concerned only incidentally with matters such as pay and working conditions, organizational structure, communications, and training, important and necessary though these may be in their own right.[11]

How can jobs be enriched? A number of companies are using job enrichment with excellent results. For example:

> Chrysler assembly line workers now get the chance to road test cars to help spot quality defects. In one Detroit assembly plant, Chrysler formed a workers' "damage committee" to check welding operations of car bodies. One worker wrote management after his week of moving around the department: "Since that week, I see metal damage, missing welds, and forming fits I never noticed before. This . . . gives me a whole new outlook on body building . . . a sense of real satisfaction . . . using my eyes and mind instead of just my hands."[12]

Two Swedish automobile manufacturers, Volvo and Saab, began a program of job enrichment in 1971. Rather than station each worker on an assembly line to perform one task or a few monotonous operations on each car as it passed by, they decided to have parts brought to the cars and then installed by semiautonomous groups of workers.

In this instance, the enrichment process was accomplished by job enlargement. **Job enlargement** is a method of increasing the number of tasks being performed by individual workers in an attempt to make the job more psychologically rewarding.

An important application of job enrichment took place at the General Foods Corporation manufacturing facility in Topeka, Kansas. The plant, built to process and package Gaines dog food products, was designed specifically with job enrichment in mind. Workers are free to schedule their own hours for starting and stopping work. Production is built around three teams: one processes products, one packages and ships them, and one handles supporting office services. The members rotate jobs within their team. A worker on the packaging and shipping team may operate the forklift truck one day and bag "Gravy Train" the next. Undesirable jobs must be rotated so that each worker does them periodically. Executive parking spaces do not exist. Team members screen job applicants, make employment decisions, and draw up work rules. Because team members are expected to perform numerous functions normally expected of managers, a strong need for training exists. For instance, those team members making personnel decisions must be well versed on federal, state, and local regulations concerning hiring practices. Top management at the Topeka facility recognize the need to provide continual training and to maintain communication systems to keep up the enthusiasm workers bring to their jobs.

During the first ten years of the plant's operation total employment tripled, but the policy of job enrichment continued. In 1981, Randy Castelluzzo, General Foods' manager of personnel services, summarized the benefits of the Topeka "experiment": "higher product quality, lower operating costs, little absenteeism, and productivity per worker averaging 15 to 20 percent higher than similar, conventionally managed plants."[13]

Is job enrichment for everyone? Like MBO programs, attempts at job enrichment have not always been successful. After introducing job enrichment programs in 19 areas at AT&T, management reported that nine were outstandingly successful, one was a complete flop, and the remaining nine were moderately successful.[14] A series of interviews with assembly line workers in an "unenriched" television plant revealed that they did not view their jobs as either frustrating or dissatisfying.[15] One researcher even discovered that some workers prefer routine jobs because it gives them more time to daydream or talk with their fellow employees without hurting their productivity.[16]

job enlargement
A method of increasing the number of tasks performed by a worker in order to make the job more psychologically rewarding.

Controversial Issue

Sexual Harassment: Should Organizations Be Responsible for Preventing Its Occurrence?

On October 30, 1980, CBS president Thomas H. Wyman sent a memorandum on sexual harassment to all CBS employees. In part the memo stated that "it is CBS's position that sexual harassment will not be tolerated. The Company will investigate any issue as it arises and will take appropriate action, including possible termination of employment."

Why did CBS make such a strong statement against sexual harassment—a subject that had always been swept under the corporate carpet? Partially because Equal Employment Opportunity Commission (EEOC) guidelines now hold companies responsible for the acts of their "agents and supervisory employees with respect to sexual harassment." But also because CBS assumed a corporate responsibility for equalizing the treatment of its male and female employees and job applicants.

For years, many working women have been forced to submit to some forms of sexual intimidation and actual physical abuse in order to get and keep their jobs. If they refused to comply with their employers' demands, they would often find themselves harassed, demoted, transferred, or fired. "I started getting demeaned in front of everyone," said one woman who refused her boss's sexual advances, "and no one could account for it because I was always extremely competent. . . . Apparently this man saw me as a powerful figure because I had said no."

To deal with this discriminatory treatment, the EEOC issued guidelines under Title VII of the Civil Rights Act of 1964, which prohibits discrimination in the work place on the basis of sex, race, or national origin, making sexual harassment against the law. Whether these guidelines can solve this nagging problem depends, to a large extent, on how business organizations define their role in controlling sexual harassment.

Employers who question whether the burden of stopping sexual harassment should fall on their shoulders are not necessarily condoning the behavior. Rather, they raise serious doubts as to whether any action they take can affect the status quo. Will a sexually harassed woman, they ask, report the abuse to her employer when she knows that whatever happens she is likely to be labeled

Prospects for job enrichment are good. Although job enrichment programs continue to be relatively rare, their accomplishments in a number of industries and in companies of varying size are indications of the merits of such programs. Even though they are not always successful, their numbers will undoubtedly grow during the 1980s. More and more managers are recognizing that such programs allow an integration of individual and company goals.

as a troublemaker by many in the organization? Or will she be more likely to resign her job and avoid a confrontation with corporate management? Critics charge that most women will choose the path of least resistance, making their employers' attempts to control sexual harassment useless.

Critics also believe that even strong policy statements condemning sexual harassment will not change the tone of the organization nor make women feel more comfortable reporting abuses. With so little chance of success and with so little hard information on how widespread the problem really is (most cases of sexual harassment go unreported), they question whether business should be involved in this matter at all.

Employers who have made a commitment to stopping sexual harassment believe that ignoring this behavior, which robs women of their jobs and puts them on the losing side of a power struggle, is tantamount to accepting it. They believe that only aggressive, diligent actions can change traditional stereotypes that women are sexual objects rather than competent professionals. They are willing to condemn employee abuse, inform workers of EEOC regulations and their consequences, and set up grievance procedures, because they are convinced that it is the right thing to do.

They point to evidence collected by such agencies as the EEOC to show the enormity of the problem. "Sexual harassment in the work place is not a figment of the imagination," said J. Clay Smith, Jr., acting commissioner of the EEOC. Referring to the scores of complaints received by his agency, Smith went on to say, "My instinct tells me this may be the tip of the iceberg." And indeed it may. According to a study done by the United States Merit Systems Protection Board, 42 percent of federally employed women surveyed said they had been sexually harassed on the job.

Neither side in this debate accepts or encourages sexual harassment in the work place. The line is drawn over the issue of the organization's proper role in controlling this behavior. In its simplest terms, the question boils down to whether the organization should step in where it has never been before and, if it does, whether it can be effective.

Summary

The beginning of the human relations movement and the emphasis on employee motivation can be traced to the Hawthorne studies of the 1920s. These studies revealed that employee attitudes and interpersonal relations are important sources of motivation. Although wages and job security are important for all workers, other human needs also require satisfaction.

Abraham Maslow proposed a ladder of human needs extending from (1) the basic physiological needs for water, food, and sex, to (2) safety, (3) social (belongingness) needs, (4) esteem, and (5) self-actualization. He pointed out that satisfied needs are not motivators. Since union contracts, social security, and other benefits have contributed to the satisfaction of lower-order needs, the focus of most individuals is on satisfaction of the top three needs.

The traditional Theory X manager views workers as lazy, disliking work, and requiring close and constant supervision. The new assumptions about workers, termed Theory Y, assume that employees want to satisfy social, esteem, and self-actualization needs through work as well as through other activities. Theory Y emphasizes employee self-control and direction.

The keys to good employee morale appear to lie in job-centered motivational factors, such as the work itself, the potential for achievement, recognition, responsibility, advancement, and growth. Two management techniques designed to improve employee motivation are management by objectives and job enrichment.

Management by objectives (MBO) focuses on employee participation in establishing individual work goals. Manager and subordinate agree on goals, and each participates in evaluating the achievement of predetermined objectives. Employees thus know precisely what is expected of them and on what basis they will be evaluated.

Job enrichment seeks to eliminate worker alienation by making work more interesting (as well as more efficient) through developing employee skills, by increasing individual worker responsibility in the job, and by job enlargement or adding to the number of tasks performed in order to make the job more rewarding.

Key Terms

Hawthorne studies	Theory X
need	Theory Y
motive	maintenance factors
physiological needs	motivational factors
safety needs	morale
social (belongingness) needs	management by objectives (MBO)
esteem needs	job enrichment
self-actualization needs	job enlargement

Review Questions

1. Explain each of the terms listed on page 176.

2. How did the Hawthorne studies revolutionize management's approach to employee motivation?

3. Describe the process of motivation.

4. Outline Abraham Maslow's theory of human needs.

5. What does Frederick Herzberg mean by *dissatisfiers?*

6. List the factors that influence employee morale.

7. Outline the five steps in an MBO program.

8. Can you think of any situations where job enrichment programs would not be effective? List them, and explain your reasoning.

9. How would you classify the management of today's Dutch army as described in this chapter?

10. Do you think the Dutch army would be effective in an emergency? Explain.

Discussion Questions and Exercises

1. Evaluate the pros and cons of the controversial issue that appears in this chapter.

2. Describe a recent decision you have made. What factors motivated you in making this decision?

3. Consider your most recent (or current) job supervisor. Would you describe this person as a Theory X or a Theory Y manager? Why do you think your superior has adopted this management approach?

4. Design an MBO program for the successful completion of a course you are now taking.

5. Prepare a brief report on job enrichment. Describe instances where it has been successful and instances where it has been ineffective.

Case 7-1: Flexitime: An End to the 9-to-5 Day?

At Occidental Life Insurance Company in Los Angeles, employees may show up as early as 6 A.M. or as late as 9, instead of the former 8 A.M. starting time. They may leave any time after 3:15 P.M. Except for their lunch break, workers are expected to be on the job between 9 and 3:15.

The flexible working hours practice, called flexitime, is extremely popular in Europe. An estimated 40 percent of the work force in Switzerland and 25 percent in West Germany use this approach. Most insurance company employees in the United Kingdom and some 700,000 workers in Paris have flexible working hours.

About 6 percent of the United States labor force is currently on a flexitime schedule. Well-known companies adopting the practice include Pitney-Bowes, Hewlett-Packard (which involves all 25,000 employees), Sears, Roebuck (which involves 7,000 workers), and Control Data (which involves 27,000 employees). About 13 percent of all U.S. businesses are currently at least experimenting with flexitime.

Most companies designate certain core hours, such as 9:30 A.M. to 3:30 P.M., when employees are required to be on the job. Beyond those hours workers can adjust their schedules to suit themselves.

Proponents of flexitime cite numerous merits for the concept. Bill Batt, a labor management specialist with the National Center on Productivity, sums up its strengths this way: "Flexitime gives people much more freedom to organize their lives, reduces pressure on transportation systems, and improves productivity. It just makes good sense. It would be my recommendation that more companies should try this."

Flexible work schedules have limited applicability in continuous production operations and in assembly line settings where worker presence at prescribed times is essential. In addition, flexible work schedules may result in increased energy use and problems in situations where key people are not available at crucial times.

Questions

1. How do you account for the high percentage of employees using flexitime in Switzerland and West Germany as compared with the low percentage in the United States?

2. What are the strengths of the flexitime concept?

3. What are its major limitations?

Case 7-2: Motivating Employees by "Well Pay"

Salt shakers have disappeared along with the cigarette and candy machines, and company officers have abandoned sick leave in favor of "well pay" at Scherer Brothers Lumber Co., a firm of 135 employees and annual sales around $30 million.

It's a "wellness program" pioneered by the big lumber yard, which also offers employees free fruit for snacks, an exercise program, and nutritious midday meals. "Everything that's good for people is in one of our programs," boasts Greg Scherer, vice president, director of marketing, and part-owner.

Scherer, 33, began pushing good health in earnest in 1980 after attending a seminar on holistic health and noticing that some employees were developing "corporate waistlines." A six-member "wellness committee" was set up, and "well pay" began, which rewards an employee with two hours extra pay each month that he or she is not absent or late.

Cigarette machines were carted away, and only decaffinated coffee was made available. Fruit juice replaced candy bars in vending machines, and workers can snack on free fruit. Free lunches now feature salads and other wholesome foods. Salt shakers were removed, high-fat foods are avoided, and butter has been discontinued.

The results have not been methodically evaluated, but they are giving Scherer good feelings. There were 15 to 20 smokers in the office before the program began, and only six now. The company's absenteeism rate of 0.3 percent compares with 3 to 4 percent for the industry. For that, Scherer credits "well pay."

Nothing was forced on workers. "We try to offer alternatives," said Scherer. "If people want candy, they can bring their own. We still have smoking areas for those who want to smoke. We provide lunch but we don't make anyone go in there and eat it. If people insist on salting their food, they can bring salt from home."

The cost has not been toted up, but Scherer said the program "didn't cost tons of money." He estimates the figure in the neighborhood of $10,000 a year. Still, there were sacrifices.

"Wellness takes commitment," Scherer said. "It's not fun throwing away salt and butter."

Questions

1. Should companies have programs of a social nature such as Scherer Brothers Lumber Co.? Explain.

2. What other programs might Scherer consider?

8

Personnel: Managing Human Resources

Learning Goals

1. To explain the functions of a specialized personnel department and the continuing responsibilities of all departments for the effective use of human resources

2. To describe how each of the steps in the selection process contributes to finding the right person for the job

3. To evaluate the different methods of training operative employees and present and potential managers

4. To identify the different forms of compensation and to explain when each form should be used

5. To describe the different types of employee benefits and the changes that are likely to occur in future fringe benefit programs

6. To explain the meaning of each of the key terms introduced in this chapter

Profile: Bum Phillips
Football's Free-rein Manager

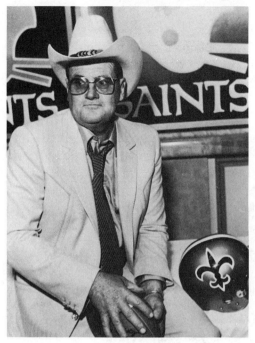

Oail Andrew "Bum" Phillips, the down-home cowboy coach of the New Orlean's Saints and former coach of the Houston Oilers, is just about the most unlikely coach in professional sports. Not because his teams lose—the Oilers won the American Football Conference championship two years in a row—but because, as one of the Oiler players explained, Bum "lets men be their own men."

With curfews, bed checks, all-day workouts, and bans on alcohol, smoking, and getting out of line, individualism is nowhere to be found on most professional football teams. But under Bum Phillips' free-rein management, being your own man is what makes the team tick, along with self-motivation, mutual respect, and just plain having a good time.

"A long time ago," says Phillips, "I gave up the philosophy of not gettin' close to the players. 'Stay away. Keep your distance.' That's a lot of bull. It came home to me when I was coachin' my son and workin' his little fanny off. I was mean and tough. But he knew I was just pretendin'. He knew I loved him. There was never any doubt. I'm around these guys seven months, seven days a week. I laugh with 'em. Cry with 'em. I know 'em. I want 'em to understand my fondness. I want us to be close. I think it helps 'em play better."

Compared to some of the other teams in professional football, under Bum Phillips the Houston Oilers lived on easy street. Their practice sessions never lasted longer than 90 minutes. An 11 P.M. curfew was in force, but there was no bed check. There were few intrasquad scrimmages where Oilers pounded other Oilers into the ground. In short, Bum Phillips ran a team that rose or fell on the players' own willingness to train hard and play harder.

"Discipline?" asks Phillips. "My idea of discipline is not makin' guys do something, it's gettin' 'em to do it. There's a difference in bitchin' and coachin'. Some places the whole damn practice is a constant gripe. All negative stuff. The first thing you know is your people tune you out. Then it becomes a challenge to make them do somethin' they should be doin' on their own all along. The only discipline that lasts is self-discipline."

Bum Phillips demands loyalty and hard work from his players, and he gets it. Maybe it's because they know that he knows that people are a whole lot more important than rules and that when you expect a lot from good people you usually wind up getting even more.

Work is the basis of living. I'll never retire. A man'll rust out quicker than he'll wear out.

—Col. Harland Sanders

Always bear in mind that your own resolution to succeed is more important than any other one thing.

—Abraham Lincoln

The organization had experienced serious turnover problems in one of its most specialized positions. In order to solve the problems and provide more continuity in this position, it decided to use a well-established method: adjust its compensation policy. *Sports Illustrated* described the incident as follows:

> Lashed by frigid winds that whip across the campus from high, virtually treeless plains, the University of Wyoming has a history of losing its football coaches to warm-weather schools. The latest coach to depart for more agreeable climes is Pat Dye, who quit (in December 1980) and went to Auburn after shivering through just one season at Wyoming, during which he guided the Cowboys to a 6-5 record, their first winning season in four years. Forced to hire a new coach for the fourth time in six years, Wyoming tapped Georgia-born Al Kincaid, the team's former offensive coordinator, for the job, then took a step calculated to keep him around a while. The school agreed to pay Kincaid a $45,000 salary, but specified that $700 a month from that amount be placed in an interest-bearing escrow account payable to him only upon completion of his full three-year contract. In other words, now even part of the Wyoming coach's *pay* is frozen.[1]

People—Critical Resource in Every Organization

The emphasis of this chapter is on people—the human element—accomplishing the goals of an organization. The acquisition, training, motivation, and retention of qualified personnel is a critical factor in determining the success or failure of a business.

A hundred years ago companies hired workers by posting a notice outside the gate stating that a certain number of workers would be hired the following day. The notice might have listed skills, say welding or carpentry, or it might simply have listed the number of workers needed. The next morning people would appear at the front gate—a small number in prosperous times, large crowds in periods of unemployment—and the workers would be selected. The choices

TABLE 8–1

Rules for Clerks—in 1882

1. This store must be opened at Sunrise. No mistake. Open 6 o'clock A.M. Summer and Winter. Close about 8:30 or 9 P.M. the year round.

2. Store must be swept—dusted—doors and windows opened—lamps filled, trimmed and chimneys cleaned—counters, base shelves and show cases dusted—pens made—a pail of water also the coal must be brought in before breakfast, if there is time to do it and attend to all the customers who call.

3. The store is not to be opened on the Sabbath day unless absolutely necessary and then only for a few minutes.

4. Should the store be opened on Sunday the clerks must go in alone and get tobacco for customers in need.

5. The clerk who is in the habit of smoking Spanish Cigars—being shaved at the barbers—going to dancing parties and other places of amusement and being out late at night—will assuredly give his employer reason to be ever suspicious of his integrity and honesty.

6. Clerks are allowed to smoke in the store provided they do not wait on women with a "stogie" in the mouth.

7. Each clerk must pay not less than $5.00 per year to the Church and must attend Sunday School regularly.

8. Men clerks are given one evening a week off for courting and two if they go to prayer meeting.

9. After the 14 hours in the store the leisure hours should be spent mostly in reading.

were often arbitrary; the first four in line might be selected or the four people who looked the strongest or the healthiest.

Workers operated under a set of specific rules. One such list is shown in Table 8-1.

What Is Personnel Management?

Personnel management can be viewed in two ways. In a narrow sense it refers to the functions and operations of a single department in a

FIGURE 8–1

Organization of a typical personnel department.

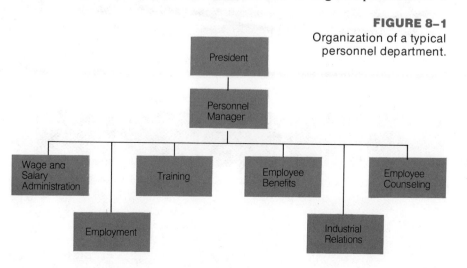

firm—the personnel department. Most firms with 200 or more employees establish a separate department and assign to it the responsibility and authority for selecting and training personnel. A typical personnel department is illustrated in Figure 8-1 on page 183.

In a broader sense personnel management involves the entire organization. Even though a special staff department exists, general management is also involved in the process of training and developing workers, evaluating their performances, and motivating them to do their jobs. **Personnel management** is thus the recruitment, selection, development, and motivation of human resources.

personnel management
The recruitment, selection, development, and motivation of human resources.

Employee Selection

The personnel manager plays a crucial role in selecting employees. The selection process is based on the philosophy: don't fit a square peg into a round hole! Adding new employees is an expensive process. Recruitment costs alone are high. Various interviews and tests are often conducted before new employees are selected. Medical examinations at company expense are often required for applicants. Training new people is also costly, and an inefficient worker wastes money. The personnel manager must ensure that potential employees possess the necessary qualifications for the job. The steps in the selection process are shown in Figure 8–2.

Job Analysis, Job Description, and Job Specification

job analysis
A systematic, detailed study of jobs based on identification and examination of job characteristics and the requirements of the person assigned the job.

In order to match jobs effectively with qualified people, the personnel manager uses three techniques: job analysis, job description, and job specification.

Job analysis is a systematic, detailed study of jobs; it consists of identifying and examining the elements and characteristics of each job and the requirements of the person assigned to the job. From the job

FIGURE 8–2
Steps in the employee selection process.

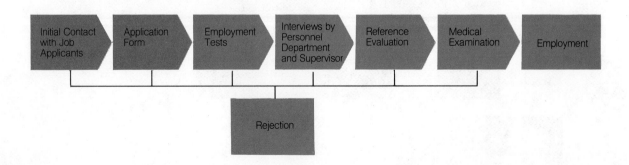

analysis, the personnel department develops a **job description,** which is a document specifying the objectives of a job, the work to be performed, the responsibilities involved, the skills needed, the relationship of the job to other jobs, and the working conditions. Next, the **job specification**—the written description of the special qualifications required of a worker who fills a particular job—is prepared. The specification lists experience, education, special skills, and other requirements.

The job description and job specification are typically combined into one document. This type of document is invaluable to personnel departments seeking qualified applicants for job openings. First used in factory jobs, such combination documents are common today in retail stores, offices, banks, and almost all large organizations.

Avoiding Sexism in Job Specifications

Numerous legislative acts—both federal and state—have been passed to prohibit the use of job specifications that limit employment to men. Employers are not allowed to exclude women from job consideration unless they can demonstrate that the job requires physical skills not possessed by women.

In many countries women are widely employed in occupations that some would label "men's jobs." For example, 90 percent of the physicians in the Soviet Union are women; so too are 70 percent of the overhead crane operators in Sweden.

One well-known result of such job specification laws is the elimination of sex distinctions in the "positions available" sections of newspapers. A second result is the change in job titles. When the U.S. Department of Labor revised its five-pound *Dictionary of Occupational Titles* recently in order to remove sexist job titles, nearly 3,500 of the 35,000 listings had to be changed. Table 8–2 shows some of the revisions.

job description
A document specifying the objectives of a job, the work to be performed, the responsibilities involved, the skills needed, the relationship of the job to other jobs, and the working conditions.

job specification
The written description of the special qualifications required of a worker who fills a particular job.

As a result of federal and state legislation prohibiting the use of job specifications to exclude women from consideration for certain jobs, more and more women are now employed in occupations that were once labeled "men's jobs."

TABLE 8–2
Changes in Job Titles

Former Job Title	New Job Title
Fireman	Firefighter
Policeman	Police officer
Mailman	Mail carrier
Salesman	Sales person
Foreman	Supervisor
Bus Boy	Dining room attendant
Housewife	Homemaker
Congressman	Member of Congress/ Representative
Bat boy	Bat handler
Cameraman	Camera operator
Stewardess	Flight attendant
Headmaster	Principal
Cleaning lady/maid	Housekeeper
Draftsman	Drafter
Song and dance man	Song and dance person

Recruitment

After the job description and job specification are prepared, the next step in the selection process is the recruitment of qualified employees. Personnel departments use both internal and external sources to find candidates for specific jobs.

hiring from within
A policy whereby a firm first considers its own employees for new job openings.

Most firms have a policy of **hiring from within**—first considering their own employees for new job openings. Because the personnel department maintains a file on all employees, its records can be quickly screened to determine whether any employees possess the necessary qualifications for a new opening.

The use of current employees to fill new job vacancies is a relatively inexpensive method of recruitment that also contributes to good employee morale. The railroad industry has long been known for its policy of filling job vacancies with existing workers whenever possible. A railroad personnel manager summarized this policy: "When a president retires or dies, we hire a new office boy."

All firms must utilize external sources to some extent in filling vacancies or in adding new employees for newly created jobs. A company may not have qualified employees to fill a certain position, or better-qualified people may be available from outside the firm. Sources for potential job applicants outside the company include colleges, advertisements in newspapers and professional journals, public employment agencies (such as state employment services), private employment agencies, vocational schools, labor unions, unsolicited applications, and recommendations by current employees. For finding candidates to fill top management positions, a firm may use specialized executive recruiting agencies or advertise in *The Wall Street Journal* or the business section of such newspapers as *The New York Times*.

The Screening Process

Once job applicants have been located, the next step is screening them to determine which candidate is best fitted for the job. The first step of the screening process is to have the applicant complete an application form, which is used to determine whether the applicant meets the general qualifications for the position. The form requests information such as name, address, type of work desired, education, experience, and personal references.

Equal Employment Opportunity Commission (EEOC)
A federal commission created to increase job opportunities for women and minorities and to assist in ending job discrimination based on race, religion, color, sex, or national origin in hiring, promotion, firing, compensation, and other terms and conditions of employment.

The Equal Employment Opportunity Commission

The Civil Rights Act of 1964 ruled that discriminatory practices were illegal. Title VII of the act covered discrimination in employment. To police this part of the act, it set up the **Equal Employment Opportunity Commission (EEOC)**—a federal commission created to increase job opportunities for women and minorities and to assist in ending job discrimination based on race, religion, color, sex, or national origin in hiring, promotion, firing, compensation, and other terms and conditions of employment.

The EEOC has been further strengthened by the passage of the Equal Pay Act of 1963, the Age Discrimination in Employment Act of 1967, the Equal Employment Opportunity Act of 1972, and numerous presidential executive orders. These acts apply to private employers of 15 or more people, private and public educational institutions, state and local governments, and labor unions with 15 or more members.

The EEOC assists employers in setting up **affirmative action programs** to increase job opportunities for women and minorities. Such programs include analysis of the present work force and setting of specific hiring and promotion goals, with target dates in areas where women and minorities are underutilized. Penalties for violations can also be imposed.[2]

affirmative action programs
Programs set up by businesses with the assistance of the EEOC to increase job opportunities for women and minorities through analysis of the present work force and formulation of goals for hiring and promotion within target dates.

The largest penalty to date was included in the consent decree signed by AT&T, in which it agreed to pay approximately $15 million in back wages to employees who had suffered because of discriminatory practices and an estimated $50 million annually for promotion and wage adjustments to women and minority groups.

Employee Testing

Employee testing makes the selection process more efficient. Careful studies determine the tests to be used in measuring the aptitude and abilities required for each job. Some companies with testing programs also administer personality tests.

Employee testing makes the selection process more efficient.

Testing serves two main purposes. It helps eliminate those applicants who are not suited for a particular job, and it helps predict which candidates are likely to become successful employees.

Employee testing became a controversial issue after a number of courts ruled that some intelligence tests are culturally biased and do not predict job success. Because the Civil Rights Act of 1964 prohibits the use of discriminatory tests in hiring workers, considerable effort is being made to evaluate the objectivity of tests currently being used and to design bias-free tests.

Interviewing

The job applicant's first formal contact with a company is usually an interview with a company representative. This face-to-face contact is another step in the screening of candidates for a job. Trained interviewers are able to obtain considerable insight into the prospective employee's goals, attitudes toward others and self, and motivations.

The line manager for whom the prospective employee is to work may also interview the candidate at this stage. Because the line manager will make the ultimate hiring decision (or at least participate in the decision with the personnel department), it is sound practice to involve that person in the screening process.

If the interviewer or the line manager feels that the applicant is unsuitable, the rejection will be made at this stage. An applicant who is acceptable and who has satisfactory references may be subject to a physical examination prior to employment.

The Physical Examination

Most firms include a medical examination as part of the employee selection process for certain jobs. The examination determines whether the applicant is physically capable of performing the job; it also helps protect the company against future claims for disabilities that were already present at the time of employment and, therefore, did not happen on the job. In certain European countries—France, Belgium, and the Netherlands, for example—preemployment physical examinations are required by law.

Orientation of Employees

On-the-job training enables new employees to learn by doing.

Once hired, the employee goes through an orientation program, which is the joint responsibility of the personnel department and the department in which the employee will work. Orientation is likely to include a tour of the building and a meeting with the department head and the employee's immediate supervisor. The personnel department provides the new worker with a copy of the employee manual, which explains company policy on vacations, absenteeism, rest periods, lunch breaks, and so on, and lists employee benefits. The supervisor is responsible for introducing the new employee to fellow workers, explaining the operations of the department, and detailing how the job fits into these operations.

A new employee in a large firm should be put at ease by the supervisor and shown that he or she is needed. The lonely, isolated feelings that often accompany the first days on a new job may lead to frustration, negative attitudes, and poor job performance. The orientation program is designed to convey a sense of belonging and a feeling of personal worth. While the personnel department provides information about company history, products, and benefits, the responsibility for developing a new employee's sense of importance and involvement is primarily that of the immediate supervisor and the other employees in the department.

Employee Training and Counseling

A second major function of the personnel department is the development of a well-trained and productive labor force. Employee training should be viewed as an ongoing process that lasts as long as an employee is with the company. Two types of training programs are common—on-the-job training and classroom training—as well as management development training.

On-the-job Training

For relatively simple jobs, **on-the-job training** is most often used, so workers can learn by doing. In this kind of training, the new employee actually performs the work under the guidance of an experienced worker. The experienced worker, through advice and suggestion, teaches the new worker efficient methods for handling the job.

A variation of on-the-job training is apprenticeship training, which is used in jobs requiring long periods of training and high levels of skill. In **apprenticeship training** programs, the new worker serves for a relatively long time period as an assistant to a trained worker—for example, a carpenter, welder, electrician, or plumber. Employers often use apprenticeship programs in cooperation with trade unions to ensure that skill standards are maintained in these trades.

on-the-job training
An employee training program in which the worker actually performs the required tasks under the guidance of an experienced employee.

apprenticeship training
An employee training program in which the new worker serves as an assistant to a trained worker for a relatively long time period.

Classroom Training

In more difficult jobs, some form of classroom training is used. In this kind of training, employees can acquire the necessary skills at their own pace, without the pressures of the actual job environment. This prior training also minimizes the possibility of wasting materials and time on the job.

Classroom training programs use classroom techniques to teach employees difficult jobs requiring high levels of skill. The training may involve lectures, conferences, films and other audiovisual aids, programmed instruction, or special machines. Some companies establish **vestibule schools,** where workers are given instruction on the operation of equipment similar to that used in their new jobs. Vestibule schools are facsimiles of actual work areas: they duplicate the jobs and machinery found in the plant. New employees are trained in the proper methods of performing a particular job and have an opportunity to become accustomed to the work before actually entering the department.

classroom training
An employee training program that uses classroom techniques to teach employees difficult jobs requiring high levels of skill.

vestibule schools
Company-established schools where workers are given instruction in the operation of equipment similar to that used in their new jobs and are exposed to facsimiles of their actual work areas.

Management Development Programs

While job training is at least as old as recorded history, most **management development programs** have been established within the last 25 years. These programs are designed to improve the skills of present managers and to broaden their knowledge; they also provide training for employees who have management potential.

Management development programs, which usually include formal courses of study, are often conducted off the company premises. General Motors and Texaco have established formal institutes resembling colleges that offer specific programs for current and potential managers. New managers for McDonald's Corporation are required

management development programs
Employee training programs designed to improve the skills and broaden the knowledge of present managers as well as to provide training for employees with management potential.

job rotation
A management development program that familiarizes junior executives with the various operations of the firm and the contributions of each department through temporary assignments in various departments.

coaching
A management development program in which a junior executive works directly under a senior executive.

to complete a three-week intensive program at Hamburger University, the McDonald's training facility in a Chicago suburb.

Two other forms of management development programs are job rotation and coaching. **Job rotation** familiarizes junior executives with the various operations of the firm and the contributions of each department through temporary assignments in various departments. **Coaching** involves a junior executive working directly under a senior executive.

Employee Counseling

Usually employees with personal problems that may adversely affect their job performance will discuss them with their immediate supervisor. But personnel departments are now adding trained specialists to assist workers in solving certain problems—typically family or financial problems.

Another aspect of employee counseling is performance evaluation. While this task is the chief responsibility of the line supervisor, workers occasionally feel that they have been treated unfairly or that the performance standards are too high. In such instances, dissatisfied employees may discuss their objections with a personnel counselor.

One of the chief advantages of the management by objectives program discussed in Chapter 7 is that it provides the employee with specific information on how performance will be evaluated. Because the employee participates in goal setting, there is little uncertainty about what constitutes satisfactory performance.

Promotions, Transfers, and Separations

promotions
Upward movements in an organization to positions of greater authority and responsibility and higher salaries.

seniority
The privileges attained as a result of the length of time an employee has worked at a particular job or in a particular department.

transfers
Horizontal movements in the organization at about the same wage and the same level.

Although four out of every five employees of the U.S. Postal Service are still in their entry positions, most business organizations experience employee movement over a period of time. This movement involves promotions, transfers, and separations.

Promotions are upward movements in an organization to positions of greater authority and responsibility and higher salaries. While most promotions are based on employee performance, some companies and many labor unions prefer to base them on **seniority**—the length of time the employee has worked at a particular job or in a particular department. Managers, however, generally agree that seniority should be the basis for promotion only when two candidates possess equal qualifications.

Transfers are horizontal movements in the organization at about the same wage and the same level. They may involve shifting workers into new, more interesting jobs or into departments where the workers' skills are required.

Separations include resignations, retirements, layoffs, and terminations. Resignations result when employees find more attractive jobs, better-paying positions, or when they move to other cities. Many large firms have had compulsory retirement programs that required employees to retire at age 65. However, Congress recently outlawed mandatory retirement before the age of 70 for most people (see Focus 8–1).

separations
Employee movements resulting from resignations, retirements, layoffs, and terminations.

FOCUS 8–1
The Age Discrimination in Employment Act

The Age Discrimination in Employment Act was passed in 1967 to ban age-related bias against workers between the ages of 40 and 65. It was amended in 1979 to prohibit mandatory retirement before age 70.

Critics of age discrimination practices have long argued that the experience and maturity of older workers and their loyalty to the firm more than compensate for the higher wages they receive as compared with new workers. They also point out that many of the major contributions of such notables as Galileo, Freud, Edison, Baruch, and Shaw occurred after the age of 60.

Approximately 37 million workers, or 40 percent of the total work force, are in the 40-to-65 age category. The extension of the age range to 70 is further indication of the strength of gray power—the growing number of persons aged 65 and over. In 1900, only 4.1 percent of the U.S. population was 65 or over. By 1982, the percentage had grown to 11, and current population trends indicate that one out of every six U.S. citizens alive in the year 2030 will be 65 or older.

The use of 65 as an appropriate retirement age was first proposed by the nineteenth-century German leader Bismarck. It was also used as the eligibility age for benefits when the Social Security Act was passed in 1935 and frequently incorporated into private pension plans as the age for retirement.

Retirement rules vary from country to country. Most nations do not set compulsory retirement ages. In the Societ Union, for example, the typical retirement age is 60 for men, 55 for women. Switzerland has no compulsory retirement age in industry, but civil service employees must retire at 65. Most Japanese employees retire at age 65. In Israel, men must retire at 65 and women at 60, unless both employer and worker agree to extend the worker's career.[3]

"Nothing personal, Carstairs. We're firing all bald personnel."

Employee morale is enhanced through protection against arbitrary dismissal.
Drawing by Ross; © 1976 The New Yorker Magazine, Inc.

layoffs
Temporary separations due to business slowdowns.

Layoffs differ from terminations in that they are considered temporary separations due to business slowdowns. Most employers lay off workers on a seniority basis, letting the newly hired employees go first. When business conditions improve, these workers are the first to be rehired. Some companies help laid-off workers find new jobs (see Focus 8–2 on page 193).

terminations
Permanent separations resulting from inability to perform the work, repeated violations of work rules, excessive absenteeism, elimination of jobs, or the closing of work facilities.

Terminations, or discharges, are permanent separations resulting from inability to perform the work, repeated violations of work rules, excessive absenteeism, elimination of jobs, or the closing of work facilities. Well-run personnel departments have specific employee disciplinary policies that are explained to all workers. The violation of work rules typically results in an oral reprimand for a first offense. Further violations lead to written reprimands and, ultimately, to discharge. Table 8–3 illustrates some typical penalties.

Many personnel managers view the termination of an employee as a failure of the selection process for that individual. Because terminations represent substantial cost to the company, most firms investigate each termination and separation to uncover the cause of failure and improve the personnel selection process.

TABLE 8–3
Typical Penalties for Violating Work Rules, in Order of Severity

Penalties for Violating Work Rules

1. Oral warning
2. Written warning
3. Suspension for a specified length of time
4. Demotion to a less desirable job
5. Termination

FOCUS 8–2
How One Company Helped Its Employees Find New Jobs

When Rockwell International laid off some 8,000 workers a few years ago as a result of then-President Carter's decision to cancel the B-1 bomber production program, it accepted the responsibility for helping these employees find new jobs. One tangible example of Rockwell's attempts to help was this classified advertisement, which appeared in a number of newspapers.

A MESSAGE FROM THE B-1 DIVISION

We assembled some of the world's leading engineers, technicians and production people for the B-1 team.

Due to the cancellation of the B-1 production program, we at Rockwell International are trying to find jobs for our employees affected by the resulting severe reduction in our work force.

As members of one of the finest teams in aviation history, they're primed with the most sophisticated knowledge and techniques anywhere in aerospace.

We urge potential employers to contact us at the address or telephone number shown below. We're anxious to help in any way we can to expedite the transfer of these talented, hard-working men and women to jobs elsewhere in the industry.

Please call or write:

W.W. Ware
B-1 Division
Rockwell International
5701 W. Imperial Highway
Los Angeles, CA. 90009

 Rockwell International

(213) 670-6721

Employee Compensation

One of the most difficult functions of personnel management is the development and operation of a fair and equitable compensation system (see Focus 8–3 on page 194). Because labor costs represent a sizable percentage of total product costs, wages that are too high may result in products that are too expensive to compete effectively in the marketplace. But inadequate wages lead to excessive employee turnover, poor morale, and inefficient production. A satisfactory compensation program should attract well-qualified workers, keep them satisfied in their jobs, and inspire them to produce.

FOCUS 8-3
Women Still Earn Less Than Men

A new Census Bureau study offers a host of reasons—but no final answers—why the 19 million women who work full-time still earn less money than men, even if the women have college degrees.

The study, titled *A Statistical Portrait of Women in the United States,* said the median income for women who worked full-time all year in 1977 was $8,620, compared to $14,630 for men in the same category. That ratio—women earning about 59 percent of what men do—has remained steady for a decade.

The report did, however, offer a few bright spots for women. One is that young women, those 20 to 24 working full-time, earned 75 percent of what their male counterparts made—$7,500 to $9,800—and women 25 to 34 did almost as well, earning 68 percent of their male counterparts—$9,500 to $14,000.

The figures show it is not until men reach their 40s and 50s that they earn peak amounts. During that period, women fall behind the most. The reasons for this, according to the census study, include the fact that women still are concentrated in relatively low-paying clerical jobs even when they work full-time and that on the whole they do not have as much education as working men. Also, they probably do not have the job experience men do because many drop out of the work force to have children.

Consider these figures:

- About 18 percent of the 19 million women working full-time year-round were college graduates compared to 25 percent of the 39 million men in that category.

- While women college graduates earned a median $12,600 for year-round full-time work, men with the same education

wages
Employee compensation based on the number of hours worked or on the amount of output produced.

salary
Employee compensation calculated on a weekly, monthly, or annual basis.

The terms *wages* and *salary* are often used interchangeably, but they do have slightly different meanings. **Wages** are employee compensation based on the number of hours worked or on the amount of output produced. They generally are paid to production employees and maintenance workers. **Salary** is employee compensation calculated on a weekly, monthly, or annual basis. It is usually paid to white-collar workers such as office personnel, executives, and professional employees.

The compensation policy of most companies is based on five factors: (1) salaries and wages paid by other companies in the area that compete for the same personnel, (2) government legislation, (3) the

earned $20,600. But among the graduates 25 to 34, the ratio was closer, with women earning a median $11,300, and men $16,000.

- The median earnings for professional women working full-time were $12,000 compared to $18,000 for men. One explanation is that women in this category were concentrated in teaching and nursing jobs, while men were in higher-paying fields.

- Although there was a 67 percent increase in women managers and administrators during the 1970s, there were still 100 men for every 30 women who held such jobs in 1978.

- There were only 6 women craftworkers for every 100 men.

Taken together, these statistics show younger women appear to be making progress toward income equality with men. But they probably will never catch up unless more break into higher-paying fields and work steadily at building careers, as men have traditionally done.

Another potential factor in the catch-up effort is discrimination, something on which the report provides no statistics. It did comment on the subject, however. "Part of the income differential is attributable to differences in such factors as annual work experience, educational attainment, occupational distribution, industry of employment and extent of life-time work experience," the report said. "However, discrimination in hiring, promotions, hours of work and pay cannot be ruled out as contributing to the differential."

cost of living, (4) the ability of the company to pay, and (5) the workers' productivity.

Job Evaluations Determine Compensation Levels for Different Jobs

In developing compensation programs the personnel department conducts a **job evaluation**—a method of determining salary and wage levels for different jobs by comparing each job on the basis of skill requirements, education requirements, responsibilities, and physical requirements. A monetary scale is then determined for each job. This process attempts to eliminate compensation inequities that exist among jobs. Although the personnel department does not set the

job evaluation
A method of determining wage levels for different jobs by comparing each job on the basis of skill requirements, education requirements, responsibilities, and physical requirements.

specific compensation of employees, it does recommend to line officials rates based on the job evaluation and on surveys of comparable wages and salaries paid by other firms in the area.

Alternative Compensation Plans

piece wage
Employee compensation based on the amount of output produced by a worker.

time wage
Employee compensation based on the amount of time spent on the job.

Employee compensation may be based on the amount of output produced by the worker (a **piece wage**), the amount of time spent on the job (a **time wage**), or some incentive added to a salary or to a time wage or piece wage to reward the employee with extras (such as time off or bonus money) for exceptional performance.

Time wages are usually paid to assembly line workers, clerks, and maintenance personnel. These wages are easy to compute, quickly understood, and simple to administer. Time wage plans assume a satisfactory performance level but include no incentive for outstanding performance by the employee.

Skilled craftworkers are often paid on a piece-rate basis for each unit of output produced. Their wage may be based on individual output or on the production of an entire department. The practice of compensating salespeople with commissions based on sales is an example of the piece-wage form of compensation. This kind of payment plan not only includes an incentive for increased output but also encourages workers to supervise their own activities. It operates well in departments where the work is standardized and the output of each employee or department can be accurately measured.

incentive compensation
Rewarding an employee for exceptional performance by adding something extra to a salary or to a time or piece wage.

Incentive compensation refers to programs designed to reward salaried employees and wage earners for superior performance. Salaried personnel, such as salespersons, may receive a base salary and a commission designed as an incentive. Other types of incentive compensation programs include bonuses and profit-sharing plans.

bonuses
Additions to a salary or time or piece wage that are intended as incentives to increase productivity or as rewards for exceptional performance.

Bonuses are a type of addition to a salary or time or piece wage. Intended as an incentive for increased productivity, they are occasionally used to reward employees for exceptional performance. Eastman Kodak employees, for example, receive annual bonuses equal to the amount of dividends paid to company stockholders.

profit sharing
A type of incentive compensation program where a percentage of company profits is distributed to employees involved in producing these profits.

Profit-sharing plans—a type of incentive compensation program where a percentage of company profits is distributed to employees involved in producing those profits—are used more and more to increase the feeling of belongingness for employees. When Data Terminal Systems of Maynard, Massachusetts, reached its goal of doubling the previous year's profits, the factory closed for a week and all 400 employees who wanted to go—from the president to the assembly line workers—were sent on a company-paid vacation to either London or Walt Disney World in Florida. (Predictably, most of the young singles and older married employees chose London, while workers with young children opted for Disney World.)[4] This kind of partnership between employees and the firm increases employee morale and helps create harmonious working relationships between management and labor.

Employee Benefits

The typical business organization furnishes many benefits to employees and their families, in addition to wages and salaries. These benefits are typically administered by the personnel department. **Fringe benefits** are nonmonetary employee benefits such as pension plans, health and life insurance, sick-leave pay, credit unions, and health and safety programs. Many large companies employ doctors and nurses to investigate working conditions and treat minor illnesses and job-related accidents. Some companies sponsor recreation programs including hobby groups and golf, baseball, and bowling teams, all with separate recreational areas. The latest figures of the U.S. Chamber of Commerce show that wages account for only two-thirds of a worker's earnings; the other third is in the form of fringe benefits, which now average $5,560 per employee in the United Sates. How this figure is broken down is shown in Table 8-4.

TABLE 8-4
Allocation of Employee Fringe Benefits

Benefit	Average Dollar Outlays
Social Security (employers' share)	$ 877
Insurance	861
Pensions	825
Paid vacations	710
Paid rest, lunch periods	539
Paid holidays	482
Worker's compensation	255
Unemployment compensation	229
Profit sharing	216
Paid sick leave	187
Christmas bonuses, suggestion rewards	64
Other benefits	315
Total	$5,560

Industrial Safety

A vital fringe benefit for all workers is the availability of safe working conditions. Industrial accidents result in both suffering for the injured worker and major costs for the employer through loss of experienced employees, increased insurance premiums, and poor morale. Recognition of the importance of a safe work environment led to passage of the Occupational Safety and Health Act in 1970.[5]

This act created the **Occupational Safety and Health Administration (OSHA)**, a federal agency whose purpose is to assure safe

Industrial safety is an important fringe benefit for all workers, particularly those in high-risk jobs.

fringe benefits
Nonmonetary employee benefits such as pension plans, health and life insurance, sick-leave pay, credit unions, and health and safety programs.

Occupational Safety and Health Administration (OSHA)
A federal agency created by the Occupational Safety and Health Act to assure safe and healthful working conditions for the U.S. labor force.

Controversial Issue

Affirmative Action versus the Seniority System

It was an inevitable clash. The seniority privileges of white male workers were incompatible with the demands of minorities and women to get their fair share of the employment pie. The results were also inevitable. After years of discontent, hard-fought battles, and a U.S. Supreme Court decision, many seniority systems remain sticking points in the equal employment opportunity struggle.

In the early 1970s the U.S. government began to enforce federal goals and timetables for the hiring and promotion of minorities and women. The Equal Employment Opportunity Commission (EEOC) and other government agencies now require companies to commit themselves to affirmative action programs that are designed to overcome past discrimination against minorities and women. Failure to meet the goals has led to million-dollar fines in cases involving large companies such as AT&T and the Bank of America. One of the EEOC's targets has been established employee seniority rights programs.

Seniority systems are at the core of the American labor movement. They assign rights and award compensation according to employees' years of service. They protect employees with the most time on the job from being laid off. Because of discriminatory hiring practices against minorities and women, the employees with seniority are almost always white males. But the union struggle to attain seniority rights for workers has lasted many years—and it is a right not easily given up. Without it, union leaders fear a return to worker intimidation and firings without cause.

Supporters of the seniority system also contend that EEOC standards are often impossible to meet. They charge that finding qualified minorities and women to fill high-level jobs is a problem. And, they point out, minority and female employees already working for a company often cannot be promoted because they do not have the background or experience to move into a higher-level job. The alternative is often to promote them and let them fail.

Calling seniority systems just another form of job discrimination, proponents of equal employment opportunity for minorities and women looked to the federal government for help. Specifically, they called for the granting of retroactive seniority to workers who could prove bias.

As minorities and women won institutional recognition and millions of dollars in back pay through court actions, they offered no apologies to the white males who were bumped into lower slots on the seniority ladder—even though these employees were not directly responsible for past discrimination. Herbert Hill, who for many years was the labor director of the NAACP, summed up the viewpoint of blacks and women: "Black workers have not been denied jobs as individuals but as a class—no matter what their personal merits and qualification. Women have not been denied training and jobs as individuals but as a class regardless of their individual talent or lack of it. Correspondingly, white males as a class have benefited from this systematic discrimination. The notion that these white workers are innocent and blameless is a myth."

Feeling the brunt of institutional discrimination, many minority group members and women believe that affirmative action must be seen as part of the cost of doing business. If there are not enough qualified minorities or women available at the top of the seniority ladder, some must be trained, at company expense if necessary, and promoted ahead of white males. Discrimination is illegal as well as unjust, and companies must be forced to revamp their seniority systems, which have excluded certain groups.

The affirmative action tide against discriminatory seniority systems was broken in 1977 when in a 7-to-2 decision the U.S. Supreme Court ruled that a senority system was not necessarily illegal even if its effect was to favor white males over minorities and women. In its majority decision, the Court wrote that a "bona fide" seniority system that was not set up to deny minorities and women equal job opportunities was not unlawful even if its practical result was a clear pattern of discrimination. The Court also denied retroactive seniority prior to the passage of the 1964 Civil Rights Act even if overt racial discrimination was proved. In passing the 1964 Civil Rights Act, Justice Potter Stewart, speaking for the majority of the Court, wrote that it was not the intent of Congress to "destroy or water down the vested seniority rights of employees simply because their employer had engaged in discrimination prior to the passage of the Act." Thurgood Marshall and William J. Brennan, the two dissenting Supreme Court justices, said that because of the decision equal employment opportunity for a full generation of minority workers would remain "a distant dream."

With the seniority issue as the battleground, the rights of older, more experienced workers are lined up against those of minorities and women, long excluded from equal employment opportunity. Both sides have valid arguments to support their cases. Can business help solve the problem without alienating either side?

and healthful working conditions for the labor force. Almost all employers are covered by OSHA: excluded are government bodies and firms covered by specific employment acts such as the Coal Mine Health and Safety Act.

OSHA emphasizes improvement in safety conditions in five industries which have injury rates that are more than double the national average: longshoring, meat and meat products, roofing and sheet metal, lumber and wood products, and miscellaneous transportation equipment—particularly manufacturers of mobile homes, campers, and snowmobiles. Employers are responsible for knowing all mandatory standards under the act. They also must develop and put into action plans that include inspection of work facilities, removal of all hazards, promotion of job safety, and reports to OSHA. Employees must be informed of their rights and responsibilities under the provisions of OSHA.

OSHA typically conducts inspections during normal working hours. A 1978 Supreme Court ruling requires OSHA inspectors to obtain a search warrant before conducting an inspection if the employer denies them entry. The inspections cover both work facilities and records and are followed by a departure briefing that outlines violations and recommended corrective actions. The 1,300 field inspectors inspect about 60,000 work places annually.

Four categories of violations can result from inspections. A *de minimis* is a minor violation not directly job related. A nonserious violation is similar to the *de minimis* but is directly job related and can carry a penalty of up to $1,000. A serious violation is one in which the probability of serious injury or death exists; it is subject to penalties in excess of $1,000. An imminent danger violation is one in which the virtual certainty of serious injury exists; the penalty is assessed by the federal court system.

For any penalty assessed, the employer has the right to an informal appeal hearing with the district or area OSHA director or, in more serious matters, to a formal hearing by the Occupational Safety and Health Review Board. The full rights are outlined in the act itself.

OSHA has been severely criticized by businesses because of its blizzard of required forms and its numerous petty regulations that appear to have little impact on either safety or health. The latter include requirements such as coat hooks on toilet doors, specified heights for fire extinguishers, and the prohibition of ice in drinking water. OSHA also has reportedly spent $466,700 to inform farmers that floors coated with manure tend to be slippery. OSHA officials recently recommended elimination of some of the more petty rules and began to redirect their efforts toward major health and safety hazards.

Fringe Benefits of the Future

Currently most people work a maximum of 240 days out of the 365. By 1989 the 240 workdays may be reduced to 175 through shorter workweeks, longer vacations, and additional paid holidays. Other future fringe benefits are likely to include retirement programs that can be transferred from one company to another, the option of early retirement at age 55, guaranteed lifetime employment, educational benefits for both employees and their families, and a guaranteed annual wage.[6]

Summary

Human resources management can be viewed in two ways. One approach is through the eyes of the personnel department, which is responsible for handling such matters as job descriptions and job specifications, screening of job applicants, development and administration of testing programs, interviewing of prospective employees, training of new employees, and administration of employee compensation and benefit programs.

A second and more complete approach involves the recognition that effective personnel management is the responsibility of every line manager. Although many of the specialized tasks related to locating, training, and compensating employees are assigned as a staff function to the personnel department, the ultimate responsibility for selection, motivation, and retention of qualified workers remains with line managers.

Specialists in the personnel department are involved with all aspects of employee selection, training, and development. The selection process includes locating potential employees, evaluating each applicant's completed application form and references, administering employment tests, arranging for medical examinations, and interviewing. Job orientation is at least partly the responsibility of most personnel departments.

Companies use one of two basic types of training programs—on-the-job and classroom—as well as management development programs. On-the-job training by an experienced worker is typically used for jobs that are relatively simple, while more complex jobs may be taught through a formal classroom training program. Human resources management also involves creating and administering various types of management development programs for current and potential executives.

Employee compensation is, of course, a major company responsibility. Wages can be based on the worker's output (piece wages) or the amount of time spent on the job (time wages) and are usually paid to production employees or maintenance workers. Salaries can be calculated on a weekly, monthly, or annual basis and are usually paid to white-collar workers, including office personnel, executives, and professional employees. In addition, incentive compensation programs, such as bonuses or profit-sharing plans, are often added to a salary or wage in order to reward superior performance and to boost employee morale by sharing the results of the company's success.

An increasingly important function of human resources management is in the area of employee benefits. Fringe benefits, such as pension plans, insurance programs, health and safety programs, credit unions, and sick-leave pay, are typically administered by the personnel department.

Key Terms

personnel management	seniority
job analysis	transfers
job description	separations
job specification	layoffs
hiring from within	terminations
Equal Employment Opportunity Commission (EEOC)	wage
	salary
affirmative action programs	job evaluation
on-the-job training	piece wage
apprenticeship training	time wage
classroom training	incentive compensation
vestibule schools	bonuses
management development programs	profit sharing
	fringe benefits
job rotation	Occupational Safety and Health Administration (OSHA)
coaching	
promotions	

Review Questions

1. Explain each of the terms listed above.

2. Draw an organization chart for the personnel department of a large company. Explain in a sentence or two the functions performed by each unit in the department.

3. Identify the steps in the employee selection process.

4. Why do many firms follow a policy of hiring from within?

5. Compare and contrast the types of employee training programs.

6. Distinguish among promotion, transfer, layoff, and separation.

7. Outline the typical penalties for violating company work rules.

8. Explain how the Occupational Safety and Health Act is enforced. What penalties can be assessed for violations of the act?

9. Give an example of a job in which each of the following employee compensation alternatives would be most appropriate:
   a. piece wage
   b. incentive wage
   c. salary
   d. time wage

10. Describe the typical fringe benefits offered to employees in a large company.

Discussion Questions and Exercises

---

1. Evaluate the pros and cons of the controversial issue that appears in this chapter.

2. What is your opinion of Rockwell International's decision to help laid-off personnel find new jobs? Do companies have an obligation to undertake this task? Explain.

3. Interview an executive at a local firm, and write a brief report about how the firm hires employees.

4. Discuss the type of compensation plan you would recommend for each of the following:
   a. watch repairs
   b. retail salespeople
   c. assembly line workers in a refrigerator factory
   d. professional athletes

5. What unique types of fringe benefits might each of the following companies offer their employees and what are the problems connected with each type?
   a. manufacturing firms
   b. airlines
   c. retail stores
   d. telephone companies
   e. banks

Case 8–1: The Furor over a Lower Minimum Wage for Teenagers

In 1981 the U.S. minimum wage rose to $3.35 per hour. At the time of the increase, more than 7 percent of the nation's work force was out of a job. A disproportionate percentage of the unemployed was comprised of relatively unskilled teenagers. Many observers feared that the increase in the minimum wage would worsen the problem by encouraging current employers of relatively unskilled workers to auto-mate their facilities.

An idea that has been proposed many times during the previous decade is the so-called youth subminimum wage. In 1977, Congress narrowly defeated a bill that would have set teenage minimum wages at 85 percent of the regular minimum wage. Prospects for passage of such a bill brightened in the early 1980s with the election of President Ronald Reagan, a supporter of the idea.

Large numbers of teenage workers are employed in such indus-tries as variety stores, service stations, and the restaurant field. A rep-resentative of the National Restaurant Association estimates that about 24 percent of all food service employees are teenagers and that such a law would save McDonald's about 31 cents a share.

The proposed law is opposed by organized labor, whose spokes-persons argue that the change would generate few additional jobs and would simply lead to a substitution of teenagers for older adults in many jobs. In commenting on McDonald's support for the proposed new law, Ray Dennison, AFL-CIO legislative department director, stated, "They made no bones about it. They wanted to give every-body a break today—mostly them. The real goal here is sheer profit."

Questions

1. Summarize the primary arguments for a youth subminimum wage. What are the major disadvantages of such a law?

2. What is the likely impact of such a law on the economy?

Case 8–2: Adjusting Benefit Programs to Match New Lifestyles

The list of employee fringe benefits contained in Table 8-4 adds $5,560 to the total annual wage for the average employee. However, the mix of benefits is expected to undergo major changes in the years ahead as firms attempt to match benefits to the changing lifestyles of their work force. *Business Week* discussed these changes in a recent report:

"Benefits traditionally have been designed to fit the needs of a breadwinner-dependent spouse family," says Anna Maria Rappaport, a Chicago vice-president of William M. Mercer, Inc., the benefits consulting arm of Marsh & McLennan Cos. "New patterns of benefits are needed to better accommodate the variety of family patterns."

Five important trends have transformed the way of life that traditional benefits were designed to serve:

- Fewer male employees are now the sole support of their families. Statistically, today's married man is more likely to have a wife in the labor force than to have one whose primary occupation is homemaking.

- More couples are remaining childless, and those who do become parents have considerably smaller families than did their predecessors. The number of families having a fourth child has been cut in half in a decade.

- Marriage itself is not the overwhelming norm it once was. At the beginning of the 1970s, 70 percent of all households were maintained by married couples. Today, with growing numbers of Americans living alone or living together without marriage, the figure is just above 60 percent. Former Census Bureau Director Vincent Barabba predicts that the figure will drop to 55 percent by 1990.

- Work spans have become more discontinuous, especially among women. Working women are likely to take sabbaticals during their children's younger years.

- Retirement age is no longer pegged at 65 because of inflation and new legislation changing the rules on mandatory retirement. Today it ranges from 60 to 70.

Questions

1. Identify the fringe benefits that are most likely to be affected by changing lifestyles. Describe in detail the nature of these changes.

2. Some observers have proposed that firms should not attempt to design a single benefit program but should provide a mix of benefit programs designed for different lifestyles or for different age groups and family characteristics (marital status, presence or absence of dependent children, their ages, and so on). Describe two or three alternative programs that might be designed specifically for one of these worker categories.

9

Labor-management Relations

Learning Goals

1. To explain why labor unions were first organized and what their chief objectives are

2. To identify the major federal laws affecting labor unions and to understand the key provisions of each law

3. To analyze the sources of power, or "weapons," of labor and management and how each is used

4. To describe who the union members of the 1980s will be

5. To explain the meaning of each of the key terms introduced in this chapter

Profile: Douglas Fraser
Labor's Voice on the Board

May 13, 1980, is a day that will go down in history for big business and the American labor movement. On that day, the ailing Chrysler Corporation elected Douglas Fraser, president of the United Auto Worker, (UAW), to its board of directors. Some would call Fraser's appointment an ingenious marriage of necessity. Others would call it an outright mistake.

The tall, rugged Fraser, who began his union career in 1935 loading fenders for Chrysler, did not win his seat on the 20-member board under normal circumstances. With a $449 million loss in the first quarter of 1980, Chrysler was fighting for its very life, and putting a representative from the UAW on its board was a small price to pay for the more than $460 million in wage-and-benefit concessions the union gave to Chrysler.

At first this modification of the adversary relationship between labor and management drew little support from either side. Some members of Fraser's own union called it a sellout, and General Motors (GM) Chairman Thomas A. Murphy said, "It makes as much sense as having a member of GM's management sitting on the board of an international union."

Fraser answered these criticisms by citing Chrysler's disastrous decisions that jeopardized the jobs of 100,000 UAW workers. He believes that workers should have a voice in determining their own fates and play a role in the decision-making process instead of just reacting, once the corporation has set its course.

Nearly a year after Fraser's election to the Chrysler board, Chrysler chairman Lee Iacocca admitted that Fraser has been "a surprisingly strong addition . . . who has stimulated our board to think." Union officials are also satisfied that Fraser's position on the board has not compromised his effectiveness in labor-management negotiations. Even though the union was forced to make wage and benefit concessions, Fraser successfully achieved such long-sought union goals as access to sensitive financial data, influence over plant closings and supervisory ratios, and a commitment from Chrysler to negotiate a profit-sharing plan.

Some Chrysler directors believe that Fraser's position on the board helped convince Chrysler workers of the need for labor concessions. Fraser "could speak with credibility to the workers because, as a director, he had seen the detailed financial date," said a Chrysler official.

Despite these initial successes, the question still remains as to whether a union president can effectively bargain with a company while sitting on its board of directors. Even though Fraser claims that he will play absolutely no role in any decisions that involve collective bargaining strategy, he may find himself in the uncomfortable position of being torn between his union ties and his company responsibilities. When closing a plant to ensure Chrysler's survival means the loss of thousands of UAW jobs, Fraser's loyalties will be tested. And so will this uncharted course in labor-management relations.

In Germany, in an arrangement called codetermination, labor sits on the corporate board of directors. Here we still have labor and management as natural enemies—guerrilla warfare, business trying to break the unions, unions trying to beat the management. I don't think that is going to work. Douglas Fraser [head of the United Auto Workers] is on the Chrysler board, because Chrysler is in trouble. When he is on the General Motors board, that will mean something. Business and labor together are the only hope to control inflation.

—*Wassily Leontief*

The players are angry. They want the same employee-employer relationship that is typical of any industry. They want the same rights as any other employee. The issue is an employee-integrity issue beyond compromise.

—*Mike Marshall*
Minnesota Twins Baseball Club player representative

The union was formed for the same reasons that most worker collectives have developed throughout history. The workers faced a deteriorating quality of life as supplies of meat, sugar, and flour became difficult to acquire—even for those workers with sufficient funds. In addition, they wanted the workweek shortened to a 5-day 40-hour week from its present 6 days and 48 hours.

Government officials warned that a reduction in the workweek would be devastating to the already shaky economy. It also pointed, none too subtly, to the thousands of military personnel of an adjacent nation assigned to the border region. But still the workers continued to swell the ranks of the new union, and its numbers grew to eight million members within four months after its formation. Periodic work stoppages were called to demonstrate the union's power.

Although the above description reads like the script for a documentary film on the history of unionism in the United States, the description is both real and current. The union is Solidarity, the first independent trade union in a communist nation. Of the eight million Poles who have joined the union headed by Lech Walesa, it is estimated that some one million of them are also members of Poland's Communist Party. Amid government warnings, Soviet troop concentrations at the Polish border, and domestic rationing programs, the new union takes actions designed to accomplish objectives shared by the founders of other unions organized over the past century.[1]

What Is a Labor Union?

A **labor union** is a group of workers who have banded together to achieve common goals in the key areas of wages, hours, and working conditions. Two types of labor unions exist in the United States: craft and industrial. A **craft union** is a labor union consisting of skilled workers in a specific craft or trade such as carpenters, painters, machinists, and printers.

While a craft union focuses on a trade, an **industrial union** is a labor union consisting of all of the workers in a given industry, regardless of their occupations or skill levels. Industrial unions include the United Auto Workers, the United Mine Workers, and the Amalgamated Clothing Workers Union.

Why Are Labor Unions Needed?

The Industrial Revolution brought the advantages of specialization and division of labor. These factors produced increased efficiency, because each worker could specialize in some aspect of the production process and become proficient at the work. Bringing together numerous workers also resulted in increased output over the individual handicraft methods of production. The factory system converted the jack-of-all-trades into a specialist.

But industrial workers of the nineteenth and the early twentieth centuries discovered that the Industrial Revolution had produced a more sinister impact on their lives. Specialization had resulted in dependence on the factory for their livelihood. In prosperous times they were assured of employment. But when depressions came, they were out of work. Unemployment insurance was a subject for dreamers, and poorhouses represented reality for unemployed workers.

Working conditions were often bad. Workdays were long and safety standards nonexistent in many factories. At the beginning of the nineteenth century, young boys and girls were pressed into the work force to earn a few pennies to help their families. In Boston in 1830, two-fifths of the total number of workers employed were children. The entire cotton and woolen industries were based on the labor of young women. Work hours were from daybreak to dark, and wages were low. In the spinning and weaving mills of New Jersey, children earned an average of a little more than a dollar a week. Imprisonment for debt was common.

By the end of the century, the workweek was typically 60 hours, but in some industries, such as steel, it was 72 or even 84 hours—

In the early 1800s children were employed in many factories, particularly in the textile industry.

seven 12-hour days a week. Working conditions were still frequently unsafe, and child labor was still common.[2]

Workers gradually learned that through bargaining as a unified group they could obtain improvements in job security and better wages and working conditions. The organized efforts of Philadelphia printers in 1786 resulted in the first U.S. minimum wage—one dollar a day. A hundred years later, New York City streetcar conductors banded together in successful negotiations that reduced their workday from 17 to 12 hours. The sweeping changes in labor-management relations that occurred during the past century produced profound changes in wages, hours of work, and working conditions (see Focus 9–1). A visible sign of the success of the labor movement is the presence of Douglas Fraser, the head of the United Auto Workers, on the board of directors of Chrysler Corporation.

FOCUS 9–1
He's Young, His Athletic Talents Are Extraordinary . . .
And He's a Union Man

A millionaire moved to New York City recently. And while he may not sing aloud the union anthem *Solidarity Forever* or name one of his male offspring Marvin Miller, this newcomer is proud to be a card-carrying union member. His name is Dave Winfield, and in exchange for his services as an outfielder for the New York Yankees, he will receive benefits that may total as high as $25 million.

Although the amount is staggering, Winfield is not alone in securing lucrative contracts made possible by the Major League Baseball Players Association. Houston Astro pitcher Nolan Ryan signed a four-year contract at $1 million annually, and the salaries of such players as Pete Rose, Rod Carew, Dave Parker, and J. R. Richard approach that number. Average annual salaries for all major league players are approximately $150,000.

Prior to 1972, major league players were virtual slave-employees bound to one organization for the life of their careers by a 100-year-old agreement called the reserve clause. Unless the player convinced management to sell or trade him for other human merchandise, that player stayed with the organization.

All of this changed under the directorship of Marvin Miller, the attorney who heads the Players Association. The reserve clause no longer exists and veteran players with six years' playing service can become free agents and sell their services to the highest bidder. Miller has also been successful in obtaining impartial arbitration of individual salary disputes and in boosting retirement benefits to the point where a 10-year player may, for example, start collecting $1,276 a month for life at age 55. Clearly, Samuel Gompers would be proud.

The History of U.S. Labor Unions

Although the history of trade unionism in the United States can be traced back prior even to the Declaration of Independence, early unions were loose-knit local organizations that served primarily as friendship groups or benevolent societies to help fellow workers in need. Such unions were typically short-lived, growing during prosperous times and suffering severely during depressions.

The first truly national union was the Knights of Labor, founded in 1869. By 1886 its membership exceeded 700,000 workers, but it soon split into factions. One faction had revolutionary aims, wanting the government to take over production. The second faction wanted the union to continue focusing on the improvement of the economic well-being of union members and opposed the socialist tendencies of some members. This faction merged with a group of unaffiliated craft unions in 1886 to form the **American Federation of Labor (AFL),** which became a national union made up of affiliated individual craft unions.

American Federation of Labor (AFL)
A national union made up of affiliated individual craft unions that later joined with the Congress of Industrial Organizations (CIO) to become the AFL-CIO.

The AFL's first president was Samuel Gompers, a dynamic man who believed that labor unions should operate within the framework of the economic system and who was totally opposed to socialism. In 1903 he stated:

> I want to tell you, Socialists, that I have studied your philosophy; read your works on economics. . . . I have heard your orators and watched the work of your movement the world over. I have kept close watch upon your doctrines for thirty years; have been closely associated with many of you, and know how you think and what you propose. I know, too, what you have up your sleeve. And I want to say that I am entirely at variance with your philosophy. I declare it to you, I am not only at variance with your doctrines, but with your philosophy. Economically, you are unsound; socially, you are wrong; industrially, you are an impossibility.[3]

Gompers' bread-and-butter concept of unionism kept the labor movement focused on the critical objectives of wages, hours, and working conditions. The AFL grew rapidly, and by 1920 three out of every four organized workers were AFL members. The anthem of the labor movement was an emotional description of workers' contributions to society and the battle between labor and management. It proposed a cure for the worker's problems in its words and in its title—"Solidarity Forever!" (see Focus 9–2).

FOCUS 9–2
Solidarity Forever!

(Sung to the tune of ''Battle Hymn of the Republic'')

When the Union's inspiration through the workers' blood shall run,
There can be no power greater anywhere beneath the sun.
Yet what force on earth is weaker than the feeble strength of one?
But the Union makes us strong.

Chorus:
Solidarity forever!
Solidarity forever!
Solidarity forever!
For the Union makes us strong.

Is there aught we hold in common with the greedy parasite
Who would lash us into serfdom and would crush us with his might?
Is there anything left for us but to organize and fight?
For the Union makes us strong.

Congress of Industrial Organizations (CIO)
A national union made up of affiliated individual industrial unions that later joined with the American Federation of Labor (AFL) to become the AFL-CIO.

Union growth was slow in the period between 1920 and 1935. The philosophy of organizing labor along craft lines that had accounted for the AFL's 40-year growth record led to difficulties, because there were few nonunion skilled craft workers left to organize.

Several unions in the AFL began to organize workers in mass-production automobile and steel industries. Successes in organizing the communications, mining, newspaper, steel, rubber, and automobile industries resulted in the formation of a new group, the **Congress of Industrial Organizations (CIO)**—a national union made up of affiliated individual industrial unions. This new technique of organizing entire industries rather than individual crafts was so successful that the CIO soon rivaled the AFL in size.

In 1955, the two groups were united under the presidency of George Meany. The only major national union not affiliated with the AFL-CIO is the two-million-member International Brotherhood of Teamsters, which was expelled in 1957 for alleged corruption. Today, more than 200 separate unions exist in the United States, approximately half of which are affiliated with the AFL-CIO. Figure 9–1 shows the organization of the AFL-CIO.

Currently some 20 million U.S. workers—26 percent of the nonagricultural labor force—belong to labor unions. Unions are particu-

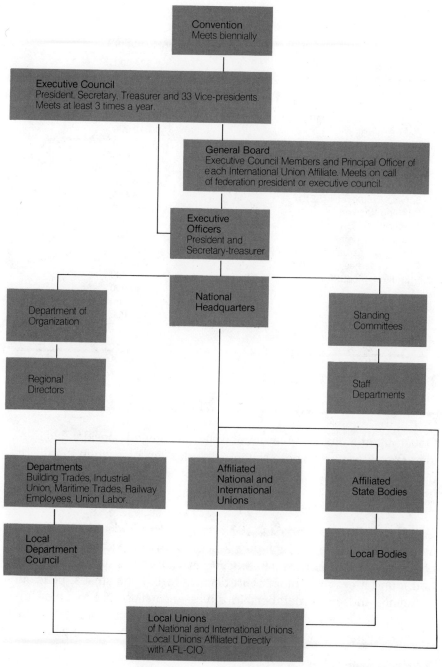

FIGURE 9–1
Organization of the AFL-CIO.

larly strong among blue-collar workers; in the construction and transportation industries, four out of every five blue-collar workers are union members. The 20 largest unions are listed in Table 9–1.

TABLE 9–1
The 20 Largest Unions in the United States

Union	Number of Members
1 Teamsters	1,924,000
2 Automobile Workers	1,499,000
3 Steelworkers	1,286,000
4 Food and Commercial Workers	1,236,000
5 State, county (AFSCME)	1,020,000
6 Electrical (IBEW)	1,012,000
7 Machinists	921,000
8 Carpenters	769,000
9 Communications Workers	625,000
10 Laborers (IUNA)	610,000
11 Service Employees (SEIU)	575,000
12 Clothing Workers	500,000
13 Teachers (AFTU)	500,000
14 Engineers, operating	412,000
15 Hotel and Restuarant	404,000
16 Garment, ladies (ILGWU)	348,000
17 Plumbing, pipefitting	337,000
18 Musicians	330,000
19 Mine workers	308,000
20 Paperworkers	284,000

Labor Legislation[4]

Government attitudes toward unionism have varied considerably during the past century. These shifting attitudes can be seen in the major pieces of legislation enacted during this period.

The Norris-La Guardia Act

Norris-La Guardia Act
Early federal legislation aimed at protecting unions through greatly reducing management's ability to obtain injunctions halting union activities.

The **Norris-La Guardia Act** (1932) is early federal legislation aimed at protecting unions through greatly reducing management's ability to obtain injunctions halting union activities. Before this time, employers had found it easy to obtain court decrees forbidding strikes, peaceful picketing, and even membership drives—activities vital to union effectiveness. Once obtained, such injunctions automatically made the union a wrongdoer in the eyes of the law if it continued the activities.

The Wagner Act

Wagner Act
A federal law that made collective bargaining legal and required employers to bargain with the elected representatives of their employees; also known as the National Labor Relations Act.

In 1935 Congress passed the National Labor Relations Act, or **Wagner Act,** which made collective bargaining legal and required employers to bargain with the elected representatives of their employees and has been called organized labor's Magna Carta. Prior to this time, union activities were often ruled violations of the Sherman Act, which prohibited "attempts to monopolize."

The Wagner Act not only legalized collective bargaining, it actually ordered employers to bargain with their workers' agents if a majority of workers elected to be represented by a union. The act set up the **National Labor Relations Board (NLRB)** to supervise union elections and prohibited management's unfair labor practices such as firing workers for joining a union, refusing to hire those who were sympathetic to unions, threatening to close the firm if workers joined a union, interfering with or dominating the administration of a union, and refusing to bargain with a union.

Fair Labor Standards Act

The **Fair Labor Standards Act** of 1938 continued the wave of pro-union legislation. It set a federal minimum wage and maximum basic hours for workers employed in industries engaged in interstate commerce. It also outlawed the use of child labor. The first minimum wage was set at 25 cents an hour, with exceptions for farm workers and retail employees. By 1981 it had reached $3.35 an hour. The employee groups most likely to be affected by the minimum wage are retail clerks, bellhops, receptionists, and some manufacturing employees in the textile and apparel industries. The act also allows workers to stay on the job longer than 40 hours a week—but only on the basis of overtime pay. Other unions have carried the concept of a minimum hourly wage even further (see Focus 9–3).

National Labor Relations Board (NLRB)
An agency set up by the Wagner Act for the purpose of supervising union elections and prohibiting unfair labor practices on the part of management.

Fair Labor Standards Act
A federal law that sets a minimum wage and maximum basic hours for workers employed in industries engaged in interstate commerce.

FOCUS 9–3
SUB—The United Auto Workers' Answer to a Guaranteed Annual Wage

The concept of a guaranteed annual wage has long been a goal of labor unions as a means of providing income stability to industrial workers. In 1955, contract negotiations between the United Auto Workers and the Big Three auto manufacturers (Ford, General Motors, and Chrysler) resulted in the adoption of a new plan called Supplementary Unemployment Benefits (SUB).

Under this plan, the companies set aside, in the SUB fund, an amount ranging from seven to twelve cents per worker hour. During periods of low production and when the auto plants close each year for new model changeovers, the fund pays the laid-off employees an amount based on their current hourly wages. Each employee first files for unemployment benefits; then SUB pays an additional amount that, added to the unemployment benefits, totals 95 percent of the worker's current take-home pay. At the height of layoffs resulting from auto sales declines in a recent year, GM was paying out $9 million a week from its SUB fund, and Ford and Chrysler were each paying out $5 million weekly. The average laid-off GM worker received $176 a week during this time—$92 from the SUB fund and $84 in state unemployment benefits.

The Taft-Hartley Act

Government support of organized labor produced a generation of growth for the unions. One by one the industrial giants—Ford, General Motors, U.S. Steel—were unionized. For the first time in history they recognized a CIO union as their workers' bargaining agent. Union membership jumped from under 3 million in 1933 to almost 15 million by 1945. In that year union members represented 36 percent of all nonagricultural employees. This percentage figure has never been reached since.

The Wagner Act focused on unfair labor practices by employers; it said nothing about unfair practices by labor. These became the subject of the **Taft-Hartley Act** of 1947 (passed by Congress over the veto of President Truman), which was designed to balance the power of unions and management by prohibiting a number of unfair union practices. The act was passed against the background of a postwar wave of strikes, as the now-giant unions for the first time learned to make full use of their strength. Paralyzing strikes in steel, coal, and shipping alarmed the public. So did **jurisdictional strikes**—those resulting not from disputes with employers but from two unions fighting each other for jurisdiction over a group of workers. Labor, it was argued, had been given an overdose of power, and the new act was designed to curb it.

The closed shop, the union shop, and the agency shop.

A **closed shop** was a business having an employment agreement under which management could not hire nonunion workers. Before being hired, workers had to become union members, and they had to remain union members as a condition of their employment. The closed shop was considered an essential ingredient of union security. If all workers were union members, the union was assured of recognition by the employer. It also had unquestionable power in the areas of wages and working conditions. Finally, because all employees enjoyed the benefits of union contracts, it was felt that they should all support the union.

Employers argued that (1) a fundamental principle of freedom was violated if people were forced to join an organization as a condition of employment, (2) because they could hire only union members, the best, most qualified workers might not be hired, and (3) with a guaranteed membership, union leaders were likely to become irresponsible and to deal dishonestly with their members. Congress apparently favored these arguments because the Taft-Hartley Act made the closed shop illegal.

A **union shop** is a business having an employment agreement whereby all qualified employees can be hired, but they must join the union within a specified time period.

An **agency shop** is a business having an employment agreement whereby all qualified workers can be hired, but nonunion workers

Taft-Hartley Act
A federal law designed to balance the power of unions and management by prohibiting a number of unfair union practices.

jurisdictional strikes
Strikes resulting from disputes between two unions fighting each other for jurisdiction over a group of workers.

closed shop
A place of employment where management cannot hire nonunion workers; prohibited by the Taft-Hartley Act.

union shop
A place of employment where all qualified employees can be hired but where they must join the union within a specified time period.

agency shop
A place of employment where all qualified workers can be hired but those not joining the union are required to pay the union a fee equal to union dues.

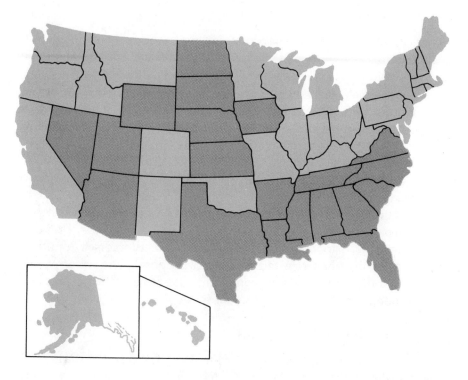

FIGURE 9–2
States with right-to-work laws (shaded areas).

must pay the union a fee equal to union dues. This arrangement eliminates "free riders" who benefit from union negotiations without supporting the union financially.

The Taft-Hartley Act contained a clause permitting states to outlaw the union shop. A total of 20 states, located mainly in the South and in the Great Plains areas, passed these **right-to-work laws.** Figure 9–2 shows the right-to-work states, where compulsory union membership is illegal.

Other unfair union practices. Other unfair union practices outlawed by the Taft-Hartley Act include refusal of the union to bargain with the employer, **featherbedding**—a situation where workers are paid for work not done—(see Focus 9–4), striking without 60 days'

right-to-work laws
State laws prohibiting compulsory union membership.

featherbedding
A situation where workers are paid for work not done.

FOCUS 9–4
Has Anyone Seen Napoleon?

Most writers cite the railroad fireman on diesel locomotives as the best current example of featherbedding. But Robert Townsend found an even better example in England:

> The British created a civil service job in 1803 calling for a man to stand on the Cliffs of Dover with a spyglass. He was supposed to ring a bell if he saw Napoleon coming. The job was abolished in 1945.

secondary boycott
A boycott or work stoppage intended to force an employer to cease dealing in the product of another firm involved in a labor dispute.

cooling-off period
An 80-day suspension of threatened strikes that can be called for by the President of the United States under the Taft-Hartley Act if the threatened strikes could imperil the national health and safety.

Landrum-Griffin Act
A federal law requiring regularly scheduled elections of union officers by secret ballot and increased regulation of the handling of union funds.

collective bargaining
A process of negotiation between management and union representatives for the purpose of arriving at mutually acceptable wages and working conditions for employees.

notice, and **secondary boycotts**—boycotts or work stoppages intended to force an employer to stop dealing in the product of another firm involved in a labor dispute.

Under the Taft-Hartley Act employers can sue unions for breach of contract and can engage (without coercion) in antiunion activities. Unions must make financial reports to their members and disclose their officers' salaries; they cannot use dues for political contributions or charge excessive initiation fees. The act also allows the president of the United States to ask the courts for an 80-day suspension of threatened strikes that "imperil the national health and safety." At the end of this **cooling-off period,** there must be a secret union ballot on the latest company offer. This provision was used by former President Carter in 1978 to order striking United Mine Workers to return to work after they had rejected a contract proposal. The order was ignored by the miners, but an agreement was reached two weeks later that ended the nation's longest coal strike.

The Landrum-Griffin Act

The Taft-Hartley Act was amended in 1959 by the **Landrum-Griffin Act,** which requires regularly scheduled elections of union officers by secret ballot and places added controls on the handling of union funds. Officials handling such funds must be bonded, and federal penalties are imposed for embezzlement. The act was passed against a background of hearings by the McClellan Senate committee investigating labor racketeering. The committee had exposed "gangsterism, bribery, and hoodlumism" in the affairs of some unions. Several union leaders had taken union funds for personal use, had accepted payoffs from employers for union protection, and were even involved in blackmail, arson, and murder.

The Collective Bargaining Process

The primary objective of labor unions is the improvement of wages, hours, and working conditions for its members. This goal is achieved primarily through **collective bargaining,** a process of negotiation between management and union representatives for the purpose of arriving at mutually acceptable wages and working conditions for employees.

Once a union is accepted by a majority of the workers in a firm, it is certified by the National Labor Relations Board and must be recognized by the firm's management as the legal collective bargaining agent for all employees. The stage is then set for representatives of the union and management to meet formally at the bargaining table to work out a collective bargaining agreement or contract.

Union contracts, which typically cover a two- or three-year period, are often the result of days and even weeks of discussion, disagreement, compromise, and eventual agreement. Once agreement has been reached, union members must vote to accept or reject the contract. If the contract is rejected, union representatives may resume the bargaining process with management representatives, or the union members may strike to obtain their demands.

Once ratified by the union membership, the contract becomes the legally binding agreement for all labor-management relations during the period of time specified. Contracts typically include such areas as wages, industrial relations, and methods of settling labor-management disputes. Some are only a few pages in length, while others run more than 200 pages. Table 9–2 lists topics typically included in a union contract.

Union members voting on a proposed new contract.

TABLE 9–2
Topics Usually Included in a Union Contract

Union Activities and Responsibilities

Dues collection
Union bulletin boards
Union officers
Wildcat strikes and slowdowns

Wages

Job evaluation
Wage structure
General wage adjustments
Wage incentives
Time studies
Shift differentials and bonuses

Hours of Work

Regular hours of work
Vacations
Holidays
Overtime rules
Rest periods

Insurance

Medical and life insurance
Pensions

Employee Job Rights and Seniority

Seniority regulations
Transfers
Promotions
Layoffs
Recalls

Grievance Handling and Arbitration

Settling Union-management Disputes

Although strikes make newspaper headlines, 19 out of every 20 union-management negotiations result in a signed agreement without a work stoppage. Approximately 150,000 union contracts are currently in force in the United States. Of these, 147,000 were the result of successful negotiations with no work stoppages.

Mediation

mediation
The process of bringing in a third party to make recommendations for the settlement of union-management differences.

When negotiations do break down, disagreements between union and management representatives may be settled by **mediation**—the process of bringing in a third party, called a mediator, to make recommendations for the settlement of differences.

The Taft-Hartley Act requires labor and management to notify each other of desired changes in union contracts 60 days before the contracts expire. They must also notify a special agency, the Federal Mediation and Conciliation Service, within 30 days after that time if a new contract has not been accepted. The service has a staff of several hundred mediators to assist in settling union-management disagreements that affect interstate commerce. In addition, some states—for example, New York, Pennsylvania, and California—have their own mediation agencies.

Although the mediator does not serve as a decision maker, union and management representatives can be assisted in reaching an agreement by the mediator's suggestions, advice, and compromise solutions. Because both sides must give their confidence and trust to the mediator, that person's impartiality is essential. Mediators are often selected from the ranks of community social or political leaders, attorneys, professors, and distinguished national figures.

Arbitration

arbitration
The process of bringing an impartial third party, called an arbitrator, into a union-management dispute to render a binding, legally enforceable decision.

voluntary arbitration
Arbitration where both union and management representatives decide to present their unresolved issues to an impartial third party.

compulsory arbitration
Arbitration to which both union and management representatives must submit, usually required by a third party (such as the federal government).

The final step in settling union-management differences is **arbitration**—the process of bringing in an impartial third party, called an arbitrator, who renders a binding decision in the dispute. The impartial third party must be acceptable to the union and to management, and his or her decision is legally enforceable. In essence, the arbitrator acts as a judge, making a decision after listening to both sides of the argument. **Voluntary arbitration** occurs when both union and management representatives make the decision to present their unresolved issues to an impartial third party. Ninety percent of all union contracts call for the use of arbitration, if union and management representatives fail to reach an agreement.

Occasionally a third party, usually the federal government, will require management and labor to submit to **compulsory arbitration.**

Although it is rarely used in the United States, there is considerable interest in compulsory arbitration as a means of eliminating prolonged strikes affecting major industries and threatening to disrupt the economy.

Grievance Procedures

The union contract serves as a guide to relations between the firm's management and its employees. The rights of each party are stated in the agreement. But no contract—regardless of how detailed it is—will completely eliminate the possibility of disagreement.

Differences of opinion may arise on how to interpret a particular clause in the contract. Management may interpret the layoff policy of the contract as based on seniority for each work shift. The union may see it as based on the seniority of all employees. Such differences can be the beginning of a grievance.

A **grievance**—whether by a single worker or by the entire union—is a complaint that management is violating some provision of the union contract. Because grievance handling is the primary source of

grievance
An employee or union complaint that management is violating some provision of the union contract.

FIGURE 9–3
The five steps in a grievance procedure (grievances not settled at one level are carried to the next level).

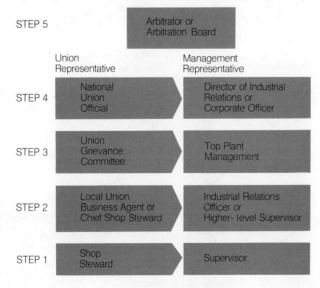

	Union Representative	Management Representative
STEP 5		Arbitrator or Arbitration Board
STEP 4	National Union Official	Director of Industrial Relations or Corporate Officer
STEP 3	Union Grievance Committee	Top Plant Management
STEP 2	Local Union Business Agent or Chief Shop Steward	Industrial Relations Officer or Higher-level Supervisor
STEP 1	Shop Steward	Supervisor

Employee with Grievance

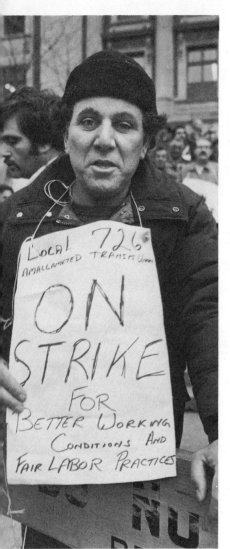

Striking union members often picket outside the employer's facility.

contact between union officials and management from the signing of one contract to the next, the way grievances are resolved plays a major role in the relationship between the employer and the union. Because grievances are likely to arise over such matters as transfers, work assignments, and seniority, almost all union contracts require that these complaints be submitted to a formal grievance procedure. Figure 9–3 shows the five steps involved in a typical grievance procedure. As this figure indicates, the employee's grievance is first submitted by the union representative (the shop steward) to the immediate supervisor. If the problem is solved, it goes no further. But if no satisfactory agreement is reached, a higher union official may take the grievance to a higher manager. If the highest company officer cannot settle the grievance, it is submitted to an outside arbitrator for a final and binding decision.

Weapons of Unions and Management

Although most differences between labor and management are settled through the collective bargaining process or through a formal grievance procedure, both unions and management occasionally resort to tools of power to make their demands known. Table 9–3 lists these weapons.

TABLE 9–3
The Weapons of Unions and Management

Weapons	How Used
Union	
Strike	Refusal to work
Picketing	Discouragement of the firm's suppliers or customers
Boycott	Refusal to do business with the firm
Management	
Lockout	Refusal to let workers enter the plant
Injunction	Stopping union actions, such as strikes
Employers' association	Cooperative, united effort in dealing with unions

Union Weapons

strike
A temporary work stoppage by employees until a dispute has been settled or a contract signed.

The chief weapons of unions are strikes, picketing, and boycotts. The **strike,** or walkout, is one of the most effective tools of the labor union. It involves a temporary work stoppage by employees until a dispute has been settled or a contract signed. Since striking workers are not paid by the company, unions generally establish strike funds to pay them so they can continue striking.

Although the power to strike is the ultimate union weapon, it is not used lightly. In many cases the threat of a strike is almost as effective as an actual work stoppage. The number of worker-days lost

"Ma Bell at your service, Madam."

When union members go out on strike, management personnel sometimes fill in for striking workers.
Drawing by Weber; © 1972 The New Yorker Magazine, Inc.

due to strikes represents slightly more than 1 percent of all lost time—less than the amount of time lost from work due to the common cold.

Picketing—workers marching at the entrances of the employer's plant as a public protest against some management practice—is another effective form of union pressure. As long as the picketing does not involve violence or intimidation, it is protected under the Constitution as free speech. Picketing can take place for a number of reasons: it may accompany a strike, or it may be a protest against alleged unfair labor practices. Because union workers usually refuse to cross picket lines, the firm may be unable to obtain deliveries and other services.

A **boycott** is an attempt to keep people from purchasing goods or services from a company. There are two kinds of boycotts—primary and secondary. In the case of a **primary boycott,** union members are told not to patronize the boycotted firm. Some unions even fine members who buy from such a firm. A secondary boycott, as explained earlier, is a boycott or work stoppage intended to force an employer to stop dealing in the product of another firm involved in a labor dispute.

In the late 1960s César Chavez, head of the United Farm Workers Organizing Committee, became nationally known for his efforts to organize farm laborers. His best-known technique was a call for a nationwide boycott of grapes picked by nonunion workers. People throughout the United States joined in this secondary boycott by purchasing only grapes in produce boxes marked with an Aztec thunderbird, the Farm Workers' union symbol. Although the Taft-Hartley and Landrum-Griffin acts make most secondary boycotts illegal, farm workers are not covered by these acts.

picketing
Workers marching at the entrances of an employer's plant as a public protest against some management practice.

boycott
An attempt to keep people from purchasing goods or services from a company.

primary boycott
A boycott in which union members are told not to patronize the boycotted firm.

The lockout is a management weapon for dealing with organized labor.

Management Weapons

Management also has weapons for dealing with organized labor. In the past it used the **lockout**—in effect, a management strike to bring pressure on union members by closing the firm. The lockout is rarely used today, unless a union strike has partially shut down a plant.

Injunctions—court orders prohibiting some practice—are sometimes obtained by management to prevent excessive picketing or certain unfair union practices. Prior to the passage of the Norris-La Guardia Act, injunctions were frequently used to prohibit all types of strikes. Since then, their use has been limited to restraint of violence, restriction of picketing, and prevention of damage to company property.

Some employers make cooperative efforts to present a united front in dealing with labor unions. These **employers' associations** may even act as negotiators for individual employers who want to reach agreements with labor unions. In industries characterized by many small firms and a single large union, there is an increasing tendency for industry-wide bargaining between the union and a single representative of the industry employers. Although they do not negotiate contracts, the National Association of Manufacturers and the

lockout
A management method to bring pressure on union members by closing the firm.

injunction
A court order prohibiting some practice.

employers' associations
Cooperative efforts on the part of employers to present a united front in dealing with labor unions.

United States Chamber of Commerce are examples of employers' associations. Both groups present the views of their members on key issues.

The Future of Organized Labor

The last two decades have witnessed a lack of union growth. From a peak membership of 36 percent of the nonagricultural U.S. labor force in 1945, union members now represent only 26 percent of nonfarm employment. In addition, the prospect for increasing union membership from traditional blue-collar occupations and industries is bleak for two reasons.

First, most blue-collar workers have already been organized. Almost every employee of the automobile, steel, aerospace, paper, rubber, and brewing industries is a union member. In industrial cities such as Pittsburgh, Seattle, and Detroit, nine out of every ten manufacturing workers are currently members of unions. The days of masses of unorganized blue-collar workers are gone. Union organizers must look elsewhere for additional members.

Second, job-growth projections indicate that blue-collar ranks—the source of union membership strength in the past—will be less important in the future.[5] As factories become more automated, the demand for blue-collar workers decreases. One result of this decline is that labor unions are refocusing their organizing efforts on public (government) employees and white-collar workers.

Prior to President Kennedy's executive order of 1962, federal employees were prohibited from joining unions. Since that time more than half of all federal employees have joined unions. Although they are not allowed to strike, they do have the right to bargain collectively. In a few instances, government employees have resorted to strikes to reinforce their demands for pay increases. Although some union leaders were jailed for an illegal postal strike a few years ago the strikers' wage demands were met.

State and municipal employees have been other targets for union organizing attempts. Strikes have spread to police officers and firefighters, sanitation workers, doctors and hospital employees, zoo keepers, and even prison guards, as these workers seek a dramatic means of obtaining higher wages and other benefits. Mass "sick calls" are often used when strikes are prohibited by law. "Blue flu" is the popular name for strikes by police officers in recent years.

Public school teachers have also used strikes as a means of exerting pressure on state and local officals to meet their demands. While about a half million teachers have joined the American Federation of Teachers (AFT), the most powerful teachers' association is the National Education Association (NEA), with more than 1.6 million members. The NEA often functions as a labor union, calling for strikes and pickets to enforce teacher demands and acting as a bargaining agent for public school teachers and some college faculties.

In fact, the nation's 400,000 college teachers represent another potential source of union membership. About 25 percent of all full-time college faculty members have been brought under formal collective bargaining agreements since the first contract was signed in 1967. The NEA, the AFT, and the American Association of University Professors (AAUP) are the three major bargaining agents for college teachers.

Faculty unionization on college campuses has been hindered by the lack of legislation in more than half the states that would enable employees of public colleges to organize collective bargaining chapters. In addition, many individual faculty members express concern about independence and academic freedom and question the compatibility of organized labor with their profession. More than 500 two- and four-year colleges have already been unionized, including such well-known institutions as the State University of New York system, Boston University, and the University of Wisconsin.[6]

Organizing attempts have also been focused on agricultural workers and white-collar employees. To date, fewer than 40,000 agricultural and fishing workers are union members. White-collar union membership is estimated to be approximately 3.8 million, or one-eleventh of all white-collar workers in the United States.

The success of organizing attempts in these areas—public employees, agricultural workers, and white-collar employees—may ultimately determine whether U.S. labor unions can continue to grow or whether they have already reached their membership peak.

A New Generation of Workers

A major change required of U.S. labor leaders is the recognition that the work force of 1982 is increasingly the product of the baby boom years—a generation that has no memory of the Great Depression and economic hardship. These workers grew up in the affluent and permissive 1950s and 1960s (see Focus 9–5). They often bring to the work-place a demand for challenging work and a dislike for both union and management bureaucracies.

As employment in goods-producing industries continues to decline, the stereotype of the blue-collar industrial worker becomes less valid. For nearly half a century the dominant pattern of bargaining over wages, hours, and working conditions has been set by blue-collar unions such as the United Steelworkers and the United Auto Workers. But a Joint Economic Committee study forecasts that by 1985 eight of every ten workers may be employed in providing services, particularly in information-processing industries such as finance, education, and communications.

The new workers will be better educated than their predecessors. They will also be more militant on the issues of environmental concerns, flexible working patterns, and shared decision making. The future of organized labor will be greatly affected by its responses to these workers.[7]

FOCUS 9–5
Who Are the New Breed of Workers for the 80s?

Over the past half century, cartoonists have portrayed the typical American worker as a Dagwood Bumstead-type figure—a middle-aged man with a tyrannical boss, a stack of unpaid bills, and a wife and two children. But Dagwood Bumstead now represents a dwindling breed. Compared with those of 20 years ago, today's workers are:

- A more diverse group. A record 41 percent are women, 10 percent black, and 23 percent under 25 years old.

- More affluent. Despite inflation, an average worker's real spendable earnings have risen 9 percent since 1960. Working spouses have raised median family income to a record $17,500. Sixty-three percent of all families depend on two wage earners.

- Enjoying more fringe benefits. These extras go beyond the wildest dreams of previous generations and include everything from dental care to club dues.

- Better educated. In 1959, 30 percent of the work force had an elementary education or less. That group has fallen to 10 percent. Meanwhile, high-school graduates rose from 30 percent to 40 percent of the work force and college graduates from 10 percent to 17 percent.

- More likely to work in offices than factories. Half of all workers now hold white-collar jobs.

- Basking in more leisure time. Hours of work have declined. Vacations are more generous. The average office worker enjoys 10 paid holidays per year, versus 7.8 in 1960.

- More mobile. The typical worker in 1963 kept a job for 4.6 years. Now he or she changes jobs every 3.6 years.

These are the new workers of the 1980s—workers who will determine the nature and, indeed, the future of organized labor in the United States.

Controversial Issue

Will Robots and Automation Eliminate Jobs?

At General Electric, hundreds of robots perform heavy industrial jobs that are too hazardous for human workers. At General Motors, robots assigned to the assembly line do their part in putting America on wheels.

At Citibank's Park Avenue office in New York City, 35 four-foot-tall beige robots pick up and deliver mail along preprogrammed routes.

What does this specter of automation and robots mean to the American worker? Opinions vary, but both labor and management agree that the work place will never be the same.

Industry spokespeople see the increasing automation of factories and other industrial environments as a matter of survival, not choice. "Unless we start doing something to increase U.S. productivity," asserts Jules Mirable, director of General Electric's robot program, "the United States will be out of business as a country."

American industrialists are all too painfully aware that their traditionally run factories are no match for Japan's ultramodern industrial facilities. At Nissan Motor's Zama factory in the south of Tokyo, for example, only 67 workers per shift produce a daily output of 1,300 Datsuns. Twenty times as many workers are needed to produce the same number of cars in Detroit.

With the challenge of Japan's productivity revolution staring them in the face, American industrialists turned their technological know-how to the development of reprogrammable, "smart" ro-

Summary

Labor unions have a long and sometimes violent history in the United States. Although they existed even before the Declaration of Independence, they were typically small, weak, and usually short-lived. Serious attempts to form national unions in the late 1800s and early 1900s were met with fierce resistance by both management and government.

The development of the American Federation of Labor (AFL) under the leadership of Samuel Gompers focused union goals on three "bread-and-butter" issues: wages, hours, and working conditions. The AFL grew rapidly until 1920, but its growth slowed considerably from then until 1935, while the Congress of Industrial Organizations (CIO) experienced considerable success in organizing the automobile, mining, and steel industries. The two decades between 1935 and 1955 represented the golden era for union growth. In 1945

bots. A far cry from today's "dumb" robots who are doomed to repeat the same task over and over again, this new generation of automated equipment can adapt to changing situations on the assembly line and can be assigned to jobs too dangerous for human workers. At an average maintenance cost of $4.60 an hour (compared to $16 an hour for human assembly-line workers), they are also one of the few remaining industrial bargains.

Industry spokespeople do not see this growing robot revolution as a real threat to the American worker. On the contrary, they claim that as robots automate boring, hazardous, and repetitive jobs, the workers they replace will move on to more challenging tasks. Displaced assembly-line workers, for example, may take on new quality-control functions, monitoring work as it is done throughout the production process.

Labor leaders have no confidence in these claims. With the cost of microprocessor technology dropping and with Japanese industrial competition intensifying, they foresee the possibility of robots becoming a $2 billion a year industry by 1990 and the displacement of 50 to 75 percent of all factory workers. And, even if new jobs will become available to those displaced workers, the question arises of who will pay the cost of retraining these people to perform the new jobs.

With such contradictory arguments on both sides of the question, the new automation will certainly be a stormy issue at union-management bargaining sessions in the years ahead.

union members represented 36 percent of all nonagricultural workers in the United States. In 1955 the AFL and CIO merged their 18 million members under the presidency of George Meany.

Government attitudes toward unions have varied considerably over the past century as reflected in legislation enacted. The Norris-La Guardia Act of 1932 was one of the first pieces of legislation favoring unions. It aimed at protecting unions by reducing management's ability to stop union activities. The Wagner Act of 1935 has been called the Magna Carta of the union movement. It requires management to bargain collectively with the duly elected representatives of its employees and outlaws a number of unfair management practices. In order to balance the power between labor and management, Congress passed the Taft-Hartley Act in 1947 and the Landrum-Griffin Act in 1959 to outlaw a number of unfair practices on the part of labor unions. The Fair Labor Standards Act of 1938 set a federal minimum wage and maximum basic hours for specified workers and outlawed child labor.

A collective bargaining agreement, or contract, is the basis of relations between management and union. It specifies agreements in such areas as wages, hours of work, employee rights and seniority provisions, and grievance handling. The contract is the result of negotiations among representatives of management and labor. Occasionally, when negotiations break down, a third party—a mediator or an arbitrator—will join the negotiations to assist in reaching an agreement. The mediator offers advice and makes recommendations; the arbitrator listens to both sides and then makes a decision that becomes binding on both sides.

Although most differences between labor and management are settled through the collective bargaining process or through formal grievance procedures, both unions and management have other ways of making their demands known. The chief weapons of unions are strikes, picketing, and boycotts. The main weapons of management are injunctions, lockouts, and employers' associations.

Future union growth will result primarily from organizing attempts in three areas: public employees, agricultural workers, and white-collar employees. Because most of the present union membership comes from the blue-collar ranks, these three relatively unorganized groups of workers represent the greatest source of future union members.

Key Terms

labor union
craft union
industrial union
American Federation of Labor (AFL)
Congress of Industrial Organizations (CIO)
Norris-La Guardia Act
Wagner Act
National Labor Relations Board (NLRB)
Fair Labor Standards Act
Taft-Hartley Act
jurisdictional strikes
closed shop
union shop
agency shop
right-to-work laws
featherbedding

secondary boycott
cooling-off period
Landrum-Griffin Act
collective bargaining
mediation
arbitration
voluntary arbitration
compulsory arbitration
grievance
strike
picketing
boycott
primary boycott
lockout
injunction
employers' associations

Review Questions

1. Explain each of the terms listed above.

2. Trace the development of labor unions in industrialized society.

3. Briefly outline the history of labor unions in the United States.

4. What is the AFL-CIO?

5. What is SUB?

6. Trace the development of labor legislation in the United States.

7. What is the purpose of the cooling-off period that the President of the United States may order under the Taft-Hartley Act? Which party is most likely to benefit from this provision of the act?

8. Describe the collective bargaining process.

9. Outline the steps in the grievance procedure.

10. Will there always be a need for labor unions? Explain.

Discussion Questions and Exercises

1. Evaluate the pros and cons of the controversial issue that appears in this chapter.

2. Suggest an explanation for why major firms like IBM, Sears, Eastman Kodak, and Texas Instruments operate without unions.

3. In 1977 the American Federation of Government Employees revised its constitution to permit membership of military personnel. While it has made no attempt to organize the 2 million men and women in the U.S. armed forces, it has surveyed its own members about this subject. Prepare a list of the advantages and disadvantages to the military of allowing soldiers to join labor unions.

4. Discuss the likely changes in union operations and objectives that may result from the entry of the "baby boom" generation into the labor force.

5. Secure a collective bargaining agreement from a firm. Then divide the class into management and labor bargaining teams and conduct a simulated bargaining session for the next contract. The instructor will act as moderator and set ground rules for the bargaining.

Case 9–1: IBM: Cementing Good Labor-management Relations by Eliminating Layoffs

Security has always been one of the primary motivations for the formation of labor unions. Security clauses are common in bargaining agreements: seniority rights are protected; pension programs are important benefits of union affiliation.

Computer-giant International Business Machines Corporation (IBM) possesses the enviable record of not laying off a single employee for economic reasons in over 35 years. Instead, IBM reassigns and retrains workers no longer needed in one area. Since 1970 it has retrained and physically relocated 5,000 employees as part of the most extensive corporate education program in the United States. The following is an illustration:

> Karyl Nichols worked a routine eight-hour day as a secretary in an office of International Business Machines Corporation in Westchester County, New York. Then she went through a "career bend," as IBM calls it, and became a sales representative in New York City. Today, instead of pounding a typewriter, she sells IBM typewriters and other office equipment. Eager to advance—and to make her sales quota—she voluntarily puts in ten-hour days, or "whatever it takes," and loves it.
>
> The 24-year-old Nichols does not go so far as to sing company songs at lunchtime, but her loyalty and hard work are typical of benefits that IBM gets for offering near-total job security to its employees.

IBM believes that if people are not worried about being laid off, they will be willing to cooperate with the firm in working toward company objectives. This cooperation is reflected at the bottom of the income statement.

On the other hand, the company is quick to point out that it has no place for nonproducers, particularly salespeople and managers. The president has noted that the company will not tolerate unproductive people, yet recognizes the effect that job security can have on the morale of the work force. Therefore an attempt is always made to keep people based on the belief that if you make an employee happy with a new job, when you can fill the old job you also make someone else happy. To make room for these moves, the company fires the nonproducers and encourages older employees to choose early retirement by offering incentive plans.

Is this emphasis on guaranteed job security good for the firm or does it result in a form of paternalism that will eventually backfire? IBM believes that it is a very important step in managing its human assets effectively.

> IBM's way of dealing with its employees does not produce a regimented work force. While protective job security can produce stagnation, IBM insists that it enables employees to be more individualistic and willing to try new ideas. "If you operate in high job security without demanding performance . . . there would be a problem. But we demand performance."

A former IBM executive says a fundamental "attitudinal difference" between IBM and other companies helps explain IBM's success. He says: "IBM knows that you don't keep workers happy by puffing the work force up and down as though it didn't matter what happened to the people."

Questions

1. Does the provision of job security eliminate the need for labor unions?

2. Support or oppose the following statement: "In a high-technology industry, a firm's human assets are its most important resources, so IBM really has no choice—it must treat its people well."

3. If IBM were to change its philosophy and convert to a more autocratic style, what would be the likely impact on employee performance?

Case 9–2: An Incentive to Reach a Bargaining Agreement

The union contract between a local of the Upholsterers' International Union and the Dunbar Furniture Corporation of Berne, Indiana, contained an unusual provision—an incentive for both management and labor to reach an agreement.

Once the old contract expired, union members were to continue working. Half their pay and a matching amount from Dunbar were to go into the bank. If a new contract was agreed upon within six weeks after the old contract expired, the money would be returned to each party. If a settlement was not reached in that time, the percentage of money returned to each party would be progressively reduced, with the remainder going to local public service projects.

If a settlement was not reached by the twelfth week, all the money in the bank would go to such projects. Only then could a strike take place.

Questions

1. As a union member, would you favor such a provision in your contract? What are its advantages? What disadvantages do you see?

2. As a management representative, would you favor such a provision? Explain.

Careers in Human Resource Management

Human resource management involves people management. Admittedly, all managers must deal with people, regardless of the functional areas with which they are associated. But executives directly involved in human resource management have primary responsibility for the administration of people-related activities such as employment, wages and salaries, health, and safety.

The Bureau of Labor Statistics has projected the employment outlook to 1990. Its forecasts for some selected jobs in human resource management appear in the table on page 235. The bureau expects all occupations to add 20.8 percent to their work force between 1978–1990. Some of the careers available in these areas appear below.

Personnel manager. A personnel manager has overall responsibility for the personnel function. This includes recruitment, hiring, training, wage and salary administration, health, and safety. The personnel manager is usually the chief executive involved in human resource management. Sometimes this person has the title of vice-president of personnel.

Director of industrial relations. The director of industrial relations is usually management's representative in dealings with labor unions. He or she is often the spokesperson for management during collective bargaining. In some firms this person also performs the duties of the personnel manager.

Union executive. Many labor unions are starting to employ people with a management education as union executives. While most union leaders still come from the rank and file, more professional managers are entering this field. A labor union career provides many interesting challenges in human resource management.

Wage and salary administrator. Wage and salary administrators are in charge of the compensation plans used in the organization. They are responsible for setting them up, administering them, and studying their effectiveness, so timely revisions can be made as needed.

Industrial counselor or psychologist. Many large firms have added industrial counselors or psychologists to their personnel departments to counsel employees and management on work, career, and personal problems. Such counselors also help determine selection procedures for new employees. Many counselors are qualified industrial psychologists; others hold degrees in guidance and counseling. To be effective, industrial counselors must have a firm business background so they can understand and deal with the problems they encounter.

EMPLOYMENT OUTLOOK TO 1990

Occupations in Human Resource Management and Production Management	Recent Employment Figures	Changes in Employment					
		Much Faster than the Average for All Occupations	Faster than the Average for All Occupations	About as Fast as the Average for All Occupations	More Slowly than the Average for All Occupations	Little Change Expected	Expected to Decline
Blue-Collar Worker Supervisors	1,670,000			X			
Personnel and Labor Relations Workers	405,000		X				
Psychologists	130,000		X				
Sociologists	19,000				X		
Employment Counselors	6,100	Some growth is anticipated					
College Career Planning and Placement Counselors	5,000					X	

Source: U.S. Department of Labor, Bureau of Labor Statistics, *Occupational Outlook Handbook, 1980–1981*, Bulletin 2075, pp. 5, 55–56, 127–129, 428–433, 436–441.

PART
FOUR

MARKETING MANAGEMENT

10

Marketing: Providing for Consumer Needs

Learning Goals

1. To identify the types of utility created by marketing

2. To distinguish between consumer and industrial markets and to identify the major characteristics of these markets

3. To explain how market targets are selected through marketing research

4. To identify the four strategies that make up the marketing mix

5. To classify products and determine their stage in the product life cycle

6. To explain the meaning of each of the key terms introduced in this chapter

Profile: Jerry Buss
Playing the Sports Game to Win

Sports is big business to Jerry Buss, the brilliant multimillionaire who is known as much for his flamboyant lifestyle, Ph.D. in physical chemistry, and uncanny understanding of mathematics as he is for taking the Los Angeles sports scene by storm. It is no understatement to say that Buss changed the face of sports in Los Angeles when in 1979 he consummated what was then the biggest financial deal in sports history. He spent $67.5 million for the National Basketball Association's Los Angeles Lakers, the National Hockey League's Los Angeles Kings, and the 17,505-seat Los Angeles Forum sports arena. "When I first walked into the office of Jack Kent Cooke, who sold me the team," says Buss, "I was totally awed by his power. To control the destiny of a team is a fascinating thing to a sports fan."

The multimillion-dollar deal also fascinated the mass media. "The deal propels to center stage," said *Sports Illustrated* magazine, "one of the most extraordinary entrepreneurs in sport—or in any other category of big dealing for that matter."

Buying a piece of professional sports is a risky business even to someone like Jerry Buss. With spiraling ticket prices and uncontrollable free agent salaries, owners often find a rosy profit picture next to impossible to achieve. Aware of these pitfalls, Jerry Buss plans to bring the fans to the games—one way or another.

Buss believes that winning is infectious and that superstars who can put points on the board are worth their weight in gold. "I don't just want winners," says Buss. "I want champions. Usually that means spending money, and I'm prepared to do that." With players like Kareem Abdul-Jabbar and Earvin "Magic" Johnson, the National Basketball Association Lakers have had little trouble bringing the fans in and making money. The National Hockey League Kings are another story. Playing an icy game in the Los Angeles sun, the Kings lost $2 million in 1979—a figure that disappointed Buss but did not cause him to throw in the towel. "I think you can buy one ball club for fun," says Buss. "But if you're talking about the Lakers and the Forum too, it's clearly a business deal and foolish to assume I bought them as a pastime."

Buss believes in the power of pay television to turn a team's profit picture around. With the possibility of 1½ million television sets in the Los Angeles area hooked up to pay TV, Buss predicts a potential profit boost on the Lakers alone of $2.5 million. As Buss points out, his ownership of the Forum puts him in an even stronger position in his dealings with pay TV. "We're in a controlling position," says Buss, "for all pay TV out of the Forum."

Filling a house and getting it to pay takes as much hard work as a winning season. Once teams understand this, says Buss, they will "see the return of ... huge crowds. And once you have that kind of excitement, ... television follows."

Buss is a fierce competitor who is playing the sports game to win. Owning the Lakers and the Kings is a childhood fantasy come true. Making them profitable is a big and very serious business.

In our business, we are forever trying to see what lies around the corner. We study the ever-changing consumer and try to identify new trends in tastes, needs, environment and living habits. We study changes in the market place and try to assess their likely impact on our brands. We study our competition. Competitive brands are continually offering new benefits and new ideas to the consumer, and we must stay ahead of this.

—Edward G. Harness, Chairman of the Board,
Proctor & Gamble Company

The people in Battle Creek were facing a tough business problem. Kellogg Co., with 42 percent of the market, got 75 percent of its revenues from the sale of cereal. Many of its competitors were more diversified organizations. Post is part of General Foods, and General Mills had built up its noncereal businesses. So any drop in cereal sales would have a disproportionate impact on Kellogg.

Things did not look bright. Population studies predicted fewer children and more 25–50-year-olds in the future. The average child consumes 11 pounds of cereal annually, while the figure for older people is closer to 5 pounds. Lifestyles had changed. Families were not eating breakfast together, and people had turned to other morning foods. And the cereal industry—Kellogg included—had been under attack by nutritionists for the past decade.

Kellogg's solution was to develop a comprehensive marketing plan to counter the negative factors impacting its business. Research and development expenditures were increased 15 percent in an effort to develop new cereals and improve Kellogg's existing brands. One of the results of this effort was the technology capable of encasing the nuts on the flakes in Honey & Nut Corn Flakes. Kellogg also instituted a market segmentation strategy (a concept discussed later in this chapter) that developed new products for specific groups of consumers. For example, Kellogg created a new brand "Smart Start for Women," an iron-enriched product. Kellogg also increased its advertising budget 20 percent and introduced a new promotional theme "It's Gonna Be A Great Day."

The people at Battle Creek recognized that they had a potentially damaging set of business circumstances. An effective marketing strategy allowed them to defuse the problem and register immediate sales increases.[1]

The Definition of Marketing

All organizations must produce and market products or services for use by their consumers. General Motors provides Chevrolets, Cadillacs, Buicks, Pontiacs, and Oldsmobiles. Nationwide Insurance offers a variety of automobile, health, commercial, and life policies. Sinclair Community College provides a quality product (education) for its consumers (students). Top-notch products and services must be effectively marketed as well as produced and developed. **Marketing** is "the performance of business activities that direct the flow of goods and services from producer to consumer or user."[2] Marketing activities are one of the most vital elements of contemporary business.

marketing
The performance of business activities that direct the flow of goods and services from producer to consumer or user.

Creating Utility for the Consumer

utility
The want-satisfying power of a product or service.

time utility
Utility created by having the product available when the consumer wants to buy it.

place utility
Utility created by having the product available at a convenient location when the consumer wants to buy it.

ownership utility
Utility created by arranging for the transfer of title from seller to buyer.

An organization must create **utility**—the want-satisfying power of a product or service—for its consumers. There are four kinds of utility—form, time, place, and ownership.

Form utility is created when the business firm converts raw materials into finished products. This operation is part of the firm's production function (see Chapter 14). The other three kinds of utility are created by marketing.

Time utility—having the product available when the consumer wants to buy it—requires effective marketing research to determine what items the consumer will desire at some future date. **Place utility** is created by having the product available at a convenient location when the consumer wants to buy it. **Ownership utility** is created by arranging for the transfer of title from seller to buyer.

Procter & Gamble's Ivory Soap has been around for over a century. It certainly created utility for the consumer of 1879, and it continues to satisfy the needs of contemporary consumers. Ivory Soap is a classic illustration of a firm correctly matching consumer needs with a product offering (see Focus 10–1).

The Marketing Concept

During the early decades of this century, production management dominated corporate thinking. Manufacturers stressed production of quality products and then looked for people to purchase them. Here is how Robert J. Keith, board chairman, described the Pillsbury Company of that era:

> We are professional flour millers. Blessed with a supply of the finest North American wheat, plenty of water power, and excellent milling machinery, we produce flour of the highest quality. Our basic function is to mill high-quality flour, and of course (and almost incidentally), we must hire salesmen to sell it, just as we hire accountants to keep our books.[3]

Today, the ability to produce a quality product is simply not enough to achieve success. The product must be effectively marketed. Consider the case of Vlasic Foods, the nation's leading pickle marketer. Vlasic has overtaken Heinz, Del Monte, and other food industry leaders and now sells 25 percent of all the pickles retailed in the United States. Robert J. Vlasic explains the firm's success this way: "Most of our competitors were manufacturing-oriented, generations of fine pickle makers and proud of it. We came in exactly the opposite, as marketers who manufactured to have something to sell."[4] Vlasic's tenfold sales increase in a decade attests to the fact that it is an effective marketer as well as producer of quality pickle products.

Most modern firms follow what has been called the marketing concept. Introduced in Chapter 1, the marketing concept says that a firm should adopt a company-wide consumer orientation with the goal of achieving long-run profits.[5] This policy does not mean that marketing personnel will dominate the firm, but it does say that all areas of the business should try to satisfy consumer wants and needs. Most observers believe that the adoption of the marketing concept has resulted in a greater consumer orientation by business in the United States.

What Is a Market?

A **market** consists of people, whether they are consumers, company purchasing agents, or purchasing specialists for a government (local, state, or federal).

But people alone do not make a market. Many people may desire the new $150,000 colonial house on Valley Drive, but not everyone can afford it. A market requires not only people but also purchasing power and the authority to buy. One of the first rules the successful salesperson learns is to determine which person in a firm has the authority to make purchase decisions. Too many hours have been wasted convincing the director of purchasing about the merits of a particular product or group of products when the ultimate buying decision actually rests with the design engineer.

Consumer and Industrial Markets

Products can be classified as consumer or industrial goods. **Consumer goods** are those products and services purchased by the ultimate consumer for his or her own use. **Industrial goods** are products purchased to be used, either directly or indirectly, in the production of other goods for resale. Most of the products you buy—such as pizza, toothpaste, and cassette tapes—are consumer goods. Steel is an industrial product.

Sometimes the same product has different uses, creating a classification dilemma. The bottle of ketchup purchased by a supermarket shopper clearly is classified as a consumer good; yet ketchup bought by McDonald's is considered an industrial good. Proper classification

Consumer goods, such as cosmetics and clothing, are those products purchased by the ultimate consumer from various sources, including, mass merchandise stores like the one shown here.

market
People with the necessary authority, financial ability, and willingness to purchase goods and services.

consumer goods
Products and services purchased by the ultimate consumer for his or her own use.

industrial goods
Products purchased to be used either directly or indirectly in the production of other goods for resale.

of products should be based on the purchaser and the reasons for buying the item. A calculator purchased as a back-to-school gift is a consumer good, but a calculator used by the manager of a nearby Pizza Hut is an industrial good.

Market Segmentation

No marketer can devise a plan to satisfy all consumers. Henry Ford lost his number one position in the automobile industry because he failed to provide the options and colors offered by competitors. Nowadays cars are targeted to a variety of consumers—those seeking fuel efficiency, families, the affluent, second-car buyers, and the like.

The construction company that decides to purchase and market only one style of house to satisfy all home buyers quickly encounters problems concerning floor plans, exteriors, flooring, and so on. In attempting to satisfy the "average" consumer, the builder ends up satisfying no one. Competitors with floor plans appealing to larger families will capture this group of customers. Other builders may adopt specialized strategies to capture submarkets that have significant similarities among members. This process of taking the total market and dividing it into groups with similar characteristics is called **market segmentation**.

market segmentation
The process of dividing the total market into groups with similar characteristics.

Market Characteristics

Marketers must know about the characteristics of the markets they serve, primarily existing population and income patterns, market location factors, and consumption patterns.

Industrial goods, such as these huge pipes for the Alaska oil pipeline, are products purchased to be used in the production of other items.

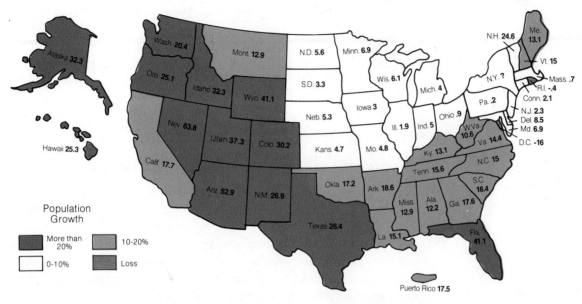

FIGURE 10–1
Population changes: 1970–1980.

Population and Income

Even though the United States has attained the highest standard of living in the history of the world, its population is small compared with the rest of the world. About 5 percent of the world's population lives in the United States. But the United States possesses about two-fifths of the world's income. India has about triple the U.S. population, but its inhabitants must live on a per person income of about $150 a year.[6]

The U.S. population has experienced substantial growth since the 1600s; currently it stands at 226.3 million people.[7] However, recently the birthrate has declined—a drop applauded by proponents of **zero population growth** (that point where live births equal the current death rate). The U.S. birthrate reached its lowest point in history during the 1970s. In 1965, the average woman reported that she wanted 3.1 children, but this figure fell to 2.1 in 1976 and has remained there. There is now evidence that birthrates are rising somewhat as women decide to have the children they delayed having while they established careers, marriages, and financial security.[8] But today's smaller families have forced marketers to change some of their strategies. Some baby powder advertisements, for example, have begun to stress the product's use by adults.

zero population growth
The point where live births equal the current death rate.

Market Location

The population of the United States, like that of the rest of the world, is not distributed evenly (see Figure 10–1). It is concentrated in large metropolitan states such as New York, Pennsylvania, California, Ohio, Michigan, Texas, and Illinois. The population is continually shifting; some states gain population while others lose it.

A migration from farms to metropolitan areas has been a recognized feature of U.S. growth for the bulk of our history. First the central cities grew, then the suburbs. The 1980 census showed that a decided shift to the "Sunbelt" (western and southern states that typically have a mild climate) has also occurred.[9]

Consumption Patterns Vary by Age Group

The population of the United States is expected to grow by almost 20 percent by the year 2050. Two age groups in particular can be highlighted for their importance to contemporary business—young middle-aged persons between the ages of 35 and 54, and senior adults, those over 65. The young middle-aged group, yesterday's young adults, will create a demand for larger homes, better automobiles, second cars, new furniture, and recreational equipment.

Not so many years ago senior adults were of little importance to business decision makers because of their short life expectancies and inadequate retirement income. But there are expected to be more than 49 million senior adults by 2050, and improved pension and retirement arrangements will significantly enhance their purchasing power. Senior adults will certainly represent a profitable market for business firms in the coming decade.[10]

Figure 10–2 shows population projections by age groups to the year 2050. Each age group has different consumption patterns, and marketers must design their strategies accordingly. Food distributors will not use the same promotional appeals for diet-conscious young adults as they will for young children. An insurance company may

FIGURE 10–2
Population projections 1979–2050, by age group.

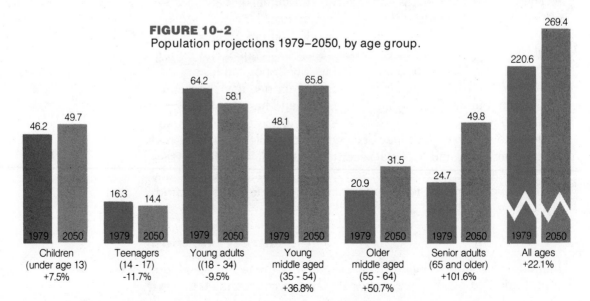

Hey! Leaves it lookin thick and healthy.   Only from Johnson & Johnson.

Because of fewer babies being born, some manufacturers of baby products have begun to target their products for adult use. Johnson & Johnson created a series of advertisements using Fran Tarkenton, the ex-Minnesota Vikings quarterback, to help sell their baby shampoo to adult males.

stress income protection to a young adult and retirement planning to a middle-aged person. Table 10–1 shows some of the types of merchandise most often purchased by or for various age groups.

TABLE 10–1
Merchandise Purchased by or for Specific Age Groups

Age Group	Name of Age Group	Merchandise Purchased
0–5	Young children	Baby food, toys, nursery furniture, children's wear
6–19	Schoolchildren (including teenagers)	Clothing, sports equipment, records, school supplies, food, cosmetics, used cars
20–34	Young adult	Automobiles, furniture, houses, clothing, recreational equipment, purchases for younger age segments
35–49	Younger middle-aged	Larger homes, better autos, second cars, new furniture, recreational equipment
50–64	Older middle-aged	Recreational items, purchases for young marrieds and infants
65 and over	Senior adult	Medical services, travel, drugs, purchases for younger age groups

Income and Expenditure Patterns

Purchasing power is a key part of markets, which are sometimes segmented according to income levels. Retailers often specialize their offerings to appeal to different income groups. Some large retailers offer shoppers three qualities of merchandise—good, better, and best—at three different prices.

Per capita incomes have advanced steadily in the United States, so that today's average family is considerably better off than was the case in an earlier period. Higher income for the typical household means more spending power. A good deal of this increased income

FOCUS 10-2
Marketers Learn to Sell to the Two-income Family

Over half of all U.S. women are now in the labor force. Marketers are now realizing that two-income families are the new affluents. Eighty percent of all families with incomes over $25,000 annually have two incomes. This trend has had a sizeable impact on marketers.

Builders are constructing more luxury townhouses with larger master bedrooms so that two people can dress at the same time to accommodate two-income, childless couples. Status shoes and imported beers are expecting sales hikes. Some power companies are predicting a lowered need for new generating plants because when both members of the family work, they use less gas and electricity.

comes from two-income families—those in which both adult members work (see Focus 10–2). Additional monies are available beyond what is minimally required to maintain a basic standard of living. Marketers must keep track of income and expenditure patterns if they are to achieve their objectives.

Selecting Market Targets through Marketing Research

The key to effective marketing lies in locating unsatisfied customers. Such customers may not be purchasing goods because the goods are not currently available, or they may be buying products that give them only limited satisfaction. In the latter case they are likely to switch quickly to new products that offer greater satisfaction. These unsatisfied consumers should be the targets of consumer-oriented companies. Rosoff's Restaurant in New York City, for example, provides braille menus for blind patrons.

market target
A group of consumers toward which a firm decides to direct its marketing effort.

marketing research
The systematic gathering, recording, and analyzing of data about problems relating to the marketing of goods and services.

A **market target** is a group of consumers toward which a firm decides to direct its marketing effort. Sometimes the firm has several market targets for a given product. The selection of such targets requires considerable research to identify the groups most likely to buy an item. **Marketing research** has been defined as "the systematic gathering, recording, and analyzing of data about problems relating to the marketing of goods and services."[11] Marketing researchers use a variety of approaches to identify market targets, including surveys, consumer panels, direct observation of buying behavior, personal interviews, and analysis of published data.

Marketers need to know about consumer motivation before making business plans. Let's look at what happened in a situation where a company—Ford—did not have a "better idea" (see Focus 10–3). The Edsel did not fail because of an inadequate market. It did not fail because of a lack of consumer income, education, or any of the other

---

FOCUS 10–3
The Edsel

In 1954 Ford Motor Company matched General Motors (GM) in market share of the low-priced auto segment. The Ford car had about 25 percent of the market, GM's Chevrolet had another 25 percent, the Buick-Oldsmobile-Pontiac (or B-O-P) cars a third 25 percent share, and the remaining 25 percent was divided among all other car makes. It appeared certain that any substantial Ford gains would have to come from the B-O-Ps.

Ford, then headed by Lewis Crusoe, put together the following marketing plan:

1. The 1957 and 1958 Ford cars (longer, wider, and more highly styled than any car so far introduced in the low-price field and with two separate body shells) were to attack the Chevrolet at the low end of the GM line.
2. The Mark II Continental (priced at $10,000) and the 1958 Lincoln (a huge, dramatically styled automobile) were to take on the Cadillac at the high end of the GM line.
3. Three entries were planned against the B-O-P cars. First, a four-passenger version of the highly successful Thunderbird would be introduced in 1958. Second, the Mercury line would be completely restyled with a special model called the Turnpike Cruiser. Third was the Edsel.

The results are known to almost everyone. The Edsel, the Mark II Continental, the 1958 Lincoln, the 1958 Mercury, and the 1958 Ford were all product failures. Only the 1958 four-passenger Thunderbird was a marketing success.

What went wrong? Different authorities offer different reasons. Some feel the Edsel was poorly named (but others list Buick as perhaps the ugliest word in the language and Oldsmobile as a silly name). Others point to the "bugs" in the first Edsels as the reason for the subsequent image deterioration. Most seem to agree that the problems resulted from changes in the automobile market. The American love affair with the automobile was undergoing its first rumblings of disenchantment in the late 1950s. The recession of 1958 reduced auto sales substantially, and tail fins, chrome, and other trappings of the 1957–1959 cars were increasingly rejected by purchasers who, in 1959, bought enough American Motors Ramblers to rank that car number 3 behind Ford and Chevrolet in the United States.

variables often used in segmenting markets. It failed because of a misunderstanding of the motivations of consumers. Unfortunately, knowing consumer motivations is perhaps the most difficult task in marketing. Research can provide information about the buying habits of consumers: Who buys? When? Where? What? How? But answers to the question "Why does one buy (or not buy)?" are much more difficult to discover through marketing research.

"Frankly, this is not what we meant when we asked you for a marketing strategy."

A good marketing strategy begins with marketing research.

Cartoon Features Syndicate

The Marketing Mix

marketing mix
The combination of the four strategies of market decision making (product strategy, distribution strategy, promotional strategy, and pricing strategy) in order to satisfy chosen consumer segments.

Once marketing research has identified the firm's market targets, a suitable plan has to be drawn up for reaching the selected market segments. Marketing decision making can be classified into four strategies—product strategy, distribution strategy, promotional strategy, and pricing strategy. The combination of these four strategies forms the **marketing mix**—the blending of product, distribution, promotion,

FIGURE 10–3
The elements of the marketing mix focusing on the consumer.

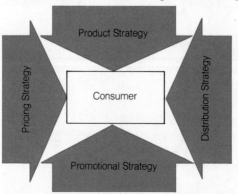

and price to satisfy chosen consumer segments. It is the total package (or mix) that determines the degree of marketing success (see Figure 10–3).

Product strategy includes decisions about package design, brand name, trademarks, warranties, guarantees, product life cycles, and new product development. **Distribution strategy** involves the physical distribution of goods and the selection of marketing channels— the organization of wholesalers and retailers who handle the product's distribution. **Promotional strategy** involves personal selling, advertising, and sales promotion tools. These elements must be skillfully blended to produce effective communication between the firm and the marketplace. **Pricing strategy,** one of the most difficult parts of marketing decision making, deals with the methods of setting profitable and justifiable prices. Both government regulations and public opinion must be considered in pricing decisions.

The marketing mix is the mechanism that allows business to match consumer needs with product offerings. This chapter has already examined how consumer needs are identified; it will conclude by looking at product strategy. The other three elements of the marketing mix— distribution strategy, promotional strategy, and pricing strategy—will be discussed in Chapters 11 to 13.

product strategy
The part of marketing decision making that deals with package design, brand, trademarks, warranties, guarantees, product cycles, and new product development.

distribution strategy
The part of marketing decision making that involves the physical distribution of goods and the selection of marketing channels, and the organization of wholesalers and retailers who handle distribution.

promotional strategy
The part of marketing decision making that involves blending personal selling, advertising, and sales promotion tools to produce effective communication between the firm and the marketplace.

pricing strategy
The part of marketing decision making that deals with the methods of setting profitable and justifiable prices. Consideration is given to government regulations and public opinion.

Classifying Products

Marketers have found it useful to classify products, because each product requires a different competitive strategy. Products are classified as either consumer or industrial goods, depending on the purchaser of the particular item. Each of these categories can be subdivided.

Convenience goods, such as magazines, are products consumers purchase frequently.

Shopping goods, such as washing machines, are products consumers purchase only after having compared competing items in competing stores on the bases of price, quality, style, and color.

Classifying Consumer Goods

A variety of classifications have been suggested for consumer goods, but the system most typically used has three subcategories: convenience goods, shopping goods, and specialty goods. This system, based on consumer buying habits, has been used for more than 50 years.[12]

Convenience goods are products the consumer seeks to purchase frequently, immediately, and with a minimum of effort. Items stocked in 24-hour convenience stores, vending machines, and local newsstands are usually convenience goods. Newspapers, chewing gum, magazines, milk, beer, bread, and cigarettes are all convenience goods.

Shopping goods are products purchased only after the consumer has compared competing goods in competing stores on bases such as price, quality, style, and color. A young couple intent on buying a new color television may visit many stores, examine perhaps dozens of television sets, and spend days making the final decision. The couple follows a regular routine from store to store in surveying competing offerings and ultimately selects the most appealing set.

Specialty goods are particular products desired by the purchaser who is very familiar with the item sought and is willing to make a special effort to obtain it. A specialty good has no reasonable substitute in the mind of the buyer. The nearest Mercedes dealer may be twenty miles away, but the driving enthusiast might go there to obtain what he or she considers one of the world's best-engineered cars.

This classification of consumer goods may differ among buyers. A shopping good for one person may be a convenience good for another. Majority buying patterns determine the item's product classification.

Classifying Industry Products

The industrial market is comprised of manufacturers, utilities, government agencies, contractors, mining firms, wholesalers, retailers, insurance and real estate firms, and institutions such as schools and hospitals that buy goods and services to use in producing other items for resale. The industrial market is concentrated geographically, has a limited number of buyers, and accounts for a considerable portion of all manufactured goods sold in the United States.

Industrial goods can be classified as capital and expense items. **Capital items** are industrial products that are relatively long-lived and that usually involve large sums of money, such as factories, machinery, airplanes, and locomotives. **Expense items** are usually less costly than capital items and are consumed within a year of their purchase. Light bulbs, pencils, and lubricating oil are examples.

capital items
Relatively long-lived industrial products that usually cost large sums of money.

expense items
Usually less costly industrial products than capital items, consumed within a year of their purchase.

The Product Life Cycle

Products, like people, pass through a series of stages from their initial appearance to death; this is known as the **product life cycle.** Humans grow from infants into children, then into adults who gradually move to retirement age and eventually death. The typical path of products from their introduction to their eventual demise is depicted in Figure 10–4. Examples of consumer products in various stages of their life cycles are shown in Figure 10–5.

product life cycle
A series of stages from initial appearance to death that all products pass through: introduction, growth, maturity, decline, and termination.

The Introductory Stage

In the early stages of the product life cycle the firm attempts to promote demand for its new market offering. Because neither consumers

FIGURE 10–4
Stages in the product life cycle.

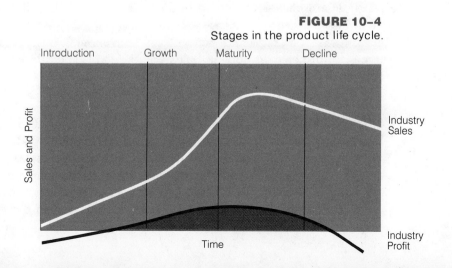

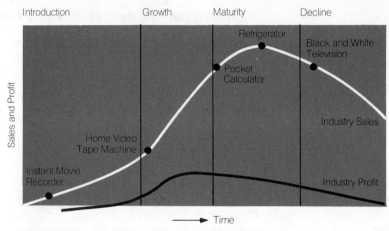

FIGURE 10–5
Life-cycle stages for products selected.

nor distributors are aware of the product, marketers must use promotional programs to inform the market of the item's availability and explain its features.

New product development and introductory promotional campaigns are expensive and commonly lead to losses in the first stage of the product life cycle. This situation is illustrated in Figure 10–5. Yet these expenditures are necessary if the firm is to profit later.

The Growth Stage

Sales climb quickly during the product life cycle's growth stage, as new customers are added to the early users who are now repurchasing the item. Person-to-person referrals and continued advertising by the firm induce others to make trial purchases.

The company also begins to earn profits on the new product. Procter & Gamble, for instance, sets three years as the acceptable time for recouping marketing and development costs on a product.[13]

The Maturity Stage

Industry sales first increase in the maturity stage, but eventually they reach a saturation level where further expansion is difficult. Competition also intensifies, increasing the availability of the product. Firms concentrate on capturing competitors' customers, often dropping prices to further their appeal. Sales volume fades late in the maturity stage.

The Decline Stage

Sales continue to fall in the decline stage of the product life cycle. Profits also decline and may become losses as further price cutting occurs in the reduced market for the item. The decline stage is usually caused by a product innovation (such as skateboards, which replaced frisbees) or a shift in consumer preferences. However, as Figure 10–6 shows, the decline stage of an old product is also the growth stage for a new item.

An A. C. Nielsen Company study reported that 85 percent of new brands will see their market positions deteriorate in less than three years. As a result, manufacturers often try to delay the eventual product withdrawal by new product or package designs or a fresh promotional campaign. But the Nielsen study reports that brand revivals usually succeed for only fifteen months.[14]

Identifying Products—Brands, Brand Names, and Trademarks

Products are identified by brands, brand names, and trademarks. A **brand** is a name, term, sign, symbol, design, or some combination used to identify the products of one firm and to differentiate them from competitive offerings. A **brand name** is that part of the brand consisting of words or letters included in a name used to identify and distinguish the firm's offerings from those of competitors. A **trademark** is a brand that has been given legal protection; the protection is granted solely to the brand's owner. Thus a trademark includes not only the pictorial design but also the brand name.[15] Any five-year-old can spot McDonald's golden arches among other fast-food franchises. Sunkist Growers, a cooperative, brands its oranges with the name *Sunkist.* An industrial purchasing agent can examine a piece of sheet steel and find the name and symbol for, say, Bethlehem Steel. Brand identification of the firm's products is often a critical strategic decision for the marketing manager.

Brands are important in developing a product's image. If consumers are aware of a particular brand, its appearance becomes advertising for the firm. The RCA trademark of the dog at the phono-

brand
A name, term, sign, symbol, design, or some combination used to identify the products of one firm and to differentiate them from competitive offerings.

brand name
That part of the brand consisting of words or letters that make up a name used to identify and distinguish the firm's offerings from those of competitors.

trademark
A brand that has been given exclusive legal protection—protection includes not only the pictorial design but also the brand name.

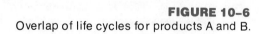

FIGURE 10–6
Overlap of life cycles for products A and B.

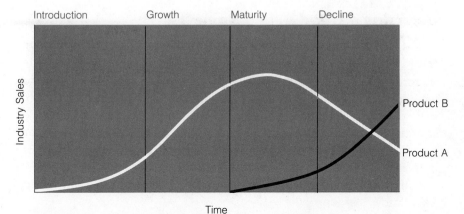

Industry Sales

Introduction   Growth   Maturity   Decline

Product B

Product A

Time

Controversial Issue

Product Recall: Where Does a Company's Responsibility End?

On September 22, 1980, Procter & Gamble Co. (P&G), the country's largest manufacturer of everyday consumer goods, voluntarily withdrew Rely tampons from the market amid growing evidence that Rely was somehow associated with toxic shock syndrome (TSS)—a rare but sometimes fatal disease primarily affecting young women who use tampons. Procter & Gamble's move came at a time when there was no conclusive evidence that Rely caused toxic shock syndrome, despite evidence that Rely users were eight times more likely to develop the disease than nonusers. According to P&G chairman Edward G. Harness, the aim of the withdrawal order was to take Rely out of the controversy "despite the fact that we know of no defect in the Rely tampon and despite evidence that the withdrawal of Rely will not eliminate the occurrence of TSS."

In addition to removing Rely from the shelves—a move that cost company stockholders approximately $75 million or 91 cents a share, Procter & Gamble signed a consent agreement with the Food and Drug Administration (FDA) to run a series of warning and informational advertisements encouraging women to stop using Rely. The commercials also informed women how to obtain refunds for unused packages of Rely and about the relationship of tampon use and TSS. This unprecedented consent agreement was a voluntary action between the FDA and Procter & Gamble. According to an FDA spokesman, Procter & Gamble was willing to do whatever was necessary to take every remaining package of Rely off the shelves.

graph, for example, is instant advertising to shoppers who spot it in a store. Successful branding is also a means of escaping some price competition. Well-known national brands often sell at a considerable price premium over their competition.

Selecting a Good Brand Name

Good brand names are easy to pronounce, recognize, and remember.[16] Short names like Gulf, Crest, Bic, and Kodak meet these requirements. Multinational marketing firms face a real problem in selecting brand names in that an excellent brand name in one country may prove disastrous in another. Every language has "o" and "k" sounds, and *okay* has become an international word. Every language also has a short "a," so that Coca-Cola and Texaco are pronounceable in any tongue. But an advertising campaign for E-Z washing machines failed in the United Kingdom because the British pronounce *z* as "zed."

Why did Procter & Gamble agree to these voluntary steps that cost stockholders millions of dollars in revenues when no hard proof linked Rely to TSS?

One reason was its genuine concern for public safety. "What we are trying to do," said a spokesperson, "is what we think is right." Another reason may have been the desire to protect the Procter & Gamble public image. By agreeing to a voluntary recall, the company avoided the harsh glare of negative publicity that would have undoubtedly accompanied a government order.

According to *The Wall Street Journal,* Procter & Gamble officials were "particularly uneasy over news reports that continue to mention the company's name in connection with the recall. Except for product introductions, Procter & Gamble doesn't make a point of using its name in connection with a product promotion." With $10.8 billion worth of annual sales and dozens of consumer products on the shelves, P&G did not want Rely's bad name to rub off. Their speedy action was intended to inspire consumer loyalty and confidence by making the public forget Rely as soon as possible.

As Procter & Gamble learned, dealing with a possible impending government recall is a no-win situation. The company suffers reduced sales by taking a product off the market before it must and it loses valuable consumer confidence if it holds back until a recall order is issued. Whether other companies facing similar situations make the same decision as P&G is a matter of corporate policy. One thing is certain, however. When public, government, and corporate needs meet head on, there is more than one route to follow.

Brand names should give the right image to the buyer. Accutron suggests the quality of the high-priced and accurate timepiece by Bulova. Miller's Lite creates an image of a beer with reduced calories and carbohydrates.

Avoiding Generic Terms

Brand names cannot contain words in general use such as *television, automobile,* or *suntan lotion.* These are generic words—words that describe a type of product—and they cannot be used exclusively by any company.

Conversely, if a type of product becomes generally known by a certain brand name, it can be ruled generic, and the company that successfully developed the name can lose exclusive rights to it. The generic names *aspirin, cola, nylon, kerosene, linoleum,* and *shredded wheat* were once brand names.

There is a difference between brand names legally judged generic and those viewed as generic by many consumers. Xerox is a brand name; yet many consumers use the term generically to refer to all photocopying processes. The legal brand names Formica, Frigidaire, Kodak, Styrofoam, Kleenex, Scotch tape, Fiberglas, Band-Aid, and Jeep are also often used by consumers as descriptive names.

In order to keep their brand names from being ruled generic, most brand owners take specific steps to inform consumers of their exclusive ownership. The Coca-Cola Company uses ®, the symbol for registration, immediately after the names Coca-Cola and Coke. It also sends letters to newspapers, novelists, and nonfiction writers who use the name Coke with a lower-case first letter, informing them that the name is owned by Coca-Cola.[17] Firms of this sort face the task of attempting to retain exclusive rights to a brand name that is known throughout the world.

Private Brands

private brands
Products that are not identified as to manufacturer but instead carry the retailer's label (often known as house, distributor, or retailer brands).

Not all brand names belong to manufacturers. Some are the property of retailers or distributors. **Private brands** (often known as house, distributor, or retailer labels) are products that are not identified as to manufacturer but instead carry the retailer's label. Private brands have been around since 1859, when the Great Atlantic & Pacific Tea Company began making its own baking powder. Today, A & P supermarkets carry over 1,300 private-label products.[18] Sears, Penney's, and K-mart all have a significant private brand sales volume.

Branding and brand names are the primary means for businesses to identify their products in the marketplace. Marketers must spend considerable time and effort in selecting brand names that enhance the image of their product offerings to consumers.

Summary

Marketing is a basic function of any business firm. It provides time, place, and ownership utilities. Marketing gets the product to the right place at the right time and then arranges the transfer of ownership from seller to buyer.

Most modern firms have adopted the marketing concept. This management philosophy advocates consumer orientation throughout the company.

Products can be classified as consumer or industrial goods. Consumer goods are products and services purchased by ultimate consumers for their own use. Industrial goods are those purchased for use, either directly or indirectly, in the production of other goods for resale. Both consumer and industrial goods can be subclassified. Firms sometimes divide their markets into segments on the basis of market characteristics. The process of designing separate marketing plans for different market segments is known as market segmentation.

A market target is the group of consumers toward which the firm decides to direct its marketing effort. Marketing research is used to identify the market targets most likely to buy an item. Once these targets have been identified, the business person must design a marketing mix composed of four kinds of plans: product strategy, distribution strategy, promotional strategy, and pricing strategy.

All products pass through four stages in their life cycles. In the introductory stage, the firm attempts to secure a demand for the product. In the growth stage, sales climb, and the company earns profits on the product. In the maturity stage, sales reach a saturation level. In the decline stage, both sales and profits decline.

Products are identified by brands, brand names, and trademarks, which are important in developing the products' images. Good brand names are easy to pronounce, recognize, and remember; and they give the right image to the buyer. Brand names cannot contain generic words; conversely, under certain circumstances, companies can lose exclusive rights to their brand, which can be ruled generic. Some brand names belong to retailers or distributors rather than to manufacturers.

Key Terms

---

marketing	zero population	shopping goods
utility	growth	specialty goods
time utility	market target	capital items
place utility	marketing research	expense items
ownership utility	marketing mix	product life cycle
market	product strategy	brand
consumer goods	distribution strategy	brand name
industrial goods	promotional strategy	trademark
market segmentation	pricing strategy	private brands
	convenience goods	

Review Questions

---

1. Explain each of the terms listed above.

2. Describe how marketing creates utility for the consumer.

3. Distinguish between consumer and industrial markets.

4. Outline how the concept of market segmentation might be used in the marketing of:
   a. beer
   b. a headache remedy
   c. pocket calculators

5. How has the population shift from rural to urban-suburban areas affected marketing decision making?

6. Assume you are an executive for a Japanese firm that is considering marketing a line of canned fish products in the United States. What type of market information would you want to have about the U.S. market? Discuss.

7. Comment on the use of marketing research to select market targets.

8. List the last five items you have purchased. Then classify them as convenience, shopping, or specialty goods. Explain why you classified each product as you did.

9. Consider the products shown in Figure 10–5. Explain how the marketing strategies vary for products at different stages of the product life cycle.

10. Suggest a brand name for each of the following new products, and explain why you chose each name:
    a. a development of exclusive homesites
    b. a low-priced, mail order insurance policy for private homes
    c. an extra-durable, single-edged razor blade
    d. a portable drill that is considerably faster than its competition

Discussion Questions and Exercises

1. Evaluate the pros and cons of the controversial issue that appears in this chapter.

2. Figure 10–5 shows black and white televisions in the decline stage of the product life cycle. Color televisions would probably be in the maturity stage. Where would you place the new large-screen television sets? Explain.

3. How would legislation to extend Social Security's retirement age to 68 affect marketers? Discuss the short- and long-term implications of such an action.

4. Many beer drinkers believe they can distinguish among different brands. Yet some research studies have shown that many people are unable to identify brands by taste. Discuss how these studies can affect brewery executives.

5. Prepare a case history of a firm that has successfully matched consumer needs with a new product offering. Also prepare a case history of a firm that has failed in this objective.

Case 10-1: The Reagan Campaign

While Chapter 10 primarily describes the marketing of commercial products, marketing is also important to nonprofit-oriented enterprises. The armed services market enlistments, hospitals market their various medical services, and your college markets its programs and course offerings to the community it serves. Political candidates are another excellent example of nonprofit marketing. Ronald Reagan's landslide victory over Jimmy Carter was no exception.

Reagan's marketing strategists began planning for the general election months before the Republican Convention was held in Detroit. They correctly predicted that the former California governor had the nomination locked up. President Reagan's campaign plans were based on the so-called Black Book, prepared by pollster Richard B. Wirthlin and his associates. This 176-page strategy manual began with some "Conditions of Victory." Some of the more important of these conditions included:

• "The conservative Republican Reagan base can be expanded to include a sufficient number of moderates, independents, soft Republicans and soft Democrats to offset Carter's natural Democratic base and his incumbency advantage.

• "The impact of John Anderson on the race stabilizes, and he ends up cutting more into Carter's electoral vote base than into Reagan's.

• "The campaign projects the image of Gov. Reagan as embodying the values that a majority of Americans currently think are important in their President—namely, strength, maturity, decisiveness, resolve, determination, compassion, trustworthiness and steadiness.

• "The candidate and/or campaign avoid fatal, self-inflicted blunders.

• "The attack strategy against President Carter reinforces his perceived weakness as an ineffective and error-prone leader, incapable of implementing policies and not respected by our allies or enemies.

- "Inoculate the voters against Carter's personal attacks by pointing out in the early stages of the campaign through surrogates that Carter has in the past, and will in the future, practice piranha politics.

- "We can neutralize Carter's October Surprise. (Because of the 7 a.m. press-conference Carter called on the morning of the Wisconsin primary to hint at a hostage solution, the Reagan planners fully believed another such caper would be forthcoming toward the end of the national campaign.)

- "The Governor does not personally answer the Carter attacks; that will be the job of the vice-presidential candidate and other surrogates.

- "He can win the easiest and least expensive minimum of 270 electoral votes with victories in California, Illinois, Texas, Ohio, Pennsylvania, Indiana, Virginia, Tennessee, Florida, Maryland, Idaho, South Dakota, Wyoming, Vermont, Utah, Nebraska, North Dakota, New Hampshire, Kansas, Montana, New Mexico, Nevada, Arizona, Oregon, Alaska, Iowa, Colorado, Washington and Maine (320 electoral votes)."

The Black Book specifically targeted the following opportunities to shift Democratic voters to Ronald Reagan:

- Southern white Protestants

- Blue-collar workers in industrial states

- Urban ethnics

- Rural voters, especially in upstate New York, Ohio and Pennsylvania

The Reagan campaign used marketing research extensively. Studies showed that reducing the size of government ranked first and national defense second in people's minds. These were the issues President Reagan concentrated on in the campaign.

One of the most startling outcomes of the 1980 presidential election was that the close results predicted by most of the major pollsters were swamped along with Jimmy Carter by the Reagan landslide. But Richard Wirthlin's monitoring of the campaign proved correct. In fact, the final computer run at 5 p.m. (California time) the evening before the election showed the "worse case" scenario was that Carter would win 143 electoral votes (13 states and the District of Columbia)—far from the number needed to beat Reagan. When the actual vote was cast the next day, Reagan lost only 49 electoral votes (6 states and the District of Columbia). The marketing strategies outlined in the Black Book were clearly successful, and Ronald Reagan was inaugurated President of the United States on January 20, 1981.

Questions

1. What other marketing factors do you think contributed to President Reagan's election?

2. Evaluate the marketing strategies used in another recent campaign, perhaps for U.S. Senator or Governor of your state.

3. In your opinion, what is the proper role of marketing in a political campaign?

Case 10-2: Levi Strauss & Co.

Levi Strauss & Co. had its origin during the California Gold Rush days. Strauss, a young immigrant, traveled to San Francisco in 1850 with plans to become a dry goods merchandiser. His stock included canvas used for tents and wagon covers. Then a prospector was said to have advised: "You should've brought pants. Pants don't wear worth a hoot up in the diggin's. Can't get a pair strong enough to last." So Levi Strauss ended up in the pants business.

Today Levi Strauss & Co. has annual sales exceeding $2 billion. The firm has shown steady growth in what is regarded as a very cyclical industry. It still leads the jeans market despite the growth of designer jeans such as Calvin Klein, Gloria Vanderbilt, Jordache, and Sasson. Designer jeans now account for only 10 percent of the total jeans market, and many industry experts think this market segment has peaked. Levi Strauss also markets shoes, shirts, jackets, and boys' and women's clothing.

The firm's brand name has an international following. It ranks number 1 in Italy. In Russia, Levis sell for up to $100 even without an official marketing organization. Levis, of course, are a staple for many segments of U.S. society. But perhaps the best indication of Levis' popularity is the listing of the brand name in several dictionaries.

Questions

1. Does the listing of its brand name in dictionaries have any implications for product strategy decisions at Levi Strauss & Co.?

2. Identify some potential marketing research projects that would be of interest to this firm.

3. What (if anything) does the trend toward an aging population suggest about the product's future?

4. Would you classify Levis as a specialty good, a shopping good, or a convenience good? Why?

11

Marketing Channels: Wholesaling, Retailing, and Physical Distribution

Learning Goals

1. To explain the value created by the distribution function through primary marketing channels

2. To identify and understand the functions of the channel middlemen

3. To describe the different degrees of market coverage

4. To explain the role of the physical distribution system

5. To explain the meaning of each of the key terms introduced in this chapter

Profile: Ike Antebi
Owner of the World's Largest Flea Market

"People don't come to the International Indoor Market just to shop," says Ike Antebi, the originator and owner of the world's largest indoor flea market located in East Brunswick, New Jersey. "They also come to have a good time."

With live bands, a roller-skating rink, international restaurants, and a variety of shows highlighting boats, cars, recreational and camping equipment, fashion, and local talent, Antebi is giving people a lot of reasons to return to his market again and again.

"The entertainment draws people in," admits Antebi. "And once they're here, they're likely to spend money in the shops along the mall."

Since the opening of the International Indoor Market in November, 1978, Antebi has tried to provide what he feels people want. "We're located in the flea market belt of New Jersey," says Antebi, "about ten miles away from Englishtown, the 'grandfather' of flea markets on the east coast. But until I came up with the idea of an indoor market, people had no place to search for bargains during the winter. Now they have a place to shop on weekends all year round."

Even in the summer, the "mini-mini mall" concept of the International Indoor Market gives consumers yet another shopping choice. Somewhere between the traditional flea market and the suburban shopping center, the market consists of approximately 500 gaily decorated booths that are really old-time mom and pop stores. "The merchants who rent space from me sell first-quality goods at flea market prices," says Antebi. "They give people the bargains they're looking for. And let me tell you, with prices going through the roof, everyone who comes out here is looking for a good buy." With 60 retail stores open seven days a week, the International Indoor Market also accommodates weekday shoppers.

Antebi feels that in addition to consumers his market is meeting the needs of the merchants as well. "The market is a boon to the small business community in the area," claims Antebi. "It's given a lot of people the chance to open their own shops on the weekends and to run them free of worry. We bring in the customers through ad campaigns and entertainment. We even pay the merchants' utilities bills."

The monthly rent that merchants pay for their space buys them Ike Antebi's good business sense as well. "I try to teach them that in this business volume is the key. Give people a real buy and they'll keep coming back, and that can only be good for everyone involved."

The success of the International Indoor Market is Ike Antebi's success. But it has a formula that others can follow. "Be creative," Antebi advises those just starting out. "And don't hold back. When you have an idea you think will work, move with it while you're filled with excitement. Do it now."

Antebi is currently looking for more sites for his unique concept in retailing.

*I found the greater the volume the cheaper I could
buy and the better value I could give customers.*

—Frank W. Woolworth

Michael Cullen had a plan for a new way to merchandise groceries. He envisioned a store located in a low-rent area, featuring self-service and night hours. Its offerings would be extensively advertised, and about 300 products would be priced at cost. When his employer—a grocery chain—rejected the idea, Cullen decided to open the King Kullen supermarket in Jamaica, New York, in August, 1930. Advertised as "The World's Greatest Price Wrecker," the new concept in food retailing was readily accepted by the Depression-era consumers it served.

At 6,000 square feet this first supermarket was ten times larger than the standard grocery store of 1930. Merchandise was crammed everywhere. Customers used hand-carried baskets. The supermarket concept caught on quickly. Elizabeth, New Jersey's Big Bear Supermarket opened in 1932 in an abandoned automobile factory, and soon after supermarkets began appearing throughout the country. Michael Cullen's idea had clearly changed the face of food marketing forever.[1]

The Dynamic Nature of Distribution

marketing channels
The paths that goods and title to them follow from producer to consumer; the means by which all businesses and public organizations distribute the products or services they are producing and marketing.

Marketing channels are the paths that goods—and title to them—follow from producer to consumer. They are the means by which all businesses and public organizations distribute the products or services they are producing and marketing. They are constantly changing. New channels and marketing institutions replace older methods of wholesaling and retailing. Physical distribution activities are also changing.

A recent example of shifting distribution patterns in the United States is gasoline retailing. The number of U.S. service stations has dropped as a result of gasoline shortages and distribution shifts by major oil companies. Because of their valuable locations, the buildings left by these stations offer considerable marketing opportunities to other forms of retailing. Consumers now find garden shops, used-car dealers, fruit and vegetable sellers, animal hospitals, real estate offices, and fast-food outlets occupying these sites.

This chapter will examine existing channels and distribution patterns as well as the changing aspects of this vital component of marketing management. A thorough understanding of distribution trends is necessary in modern business.

Importance of Distribution

All organizations perform a distribution function. General Motors distributes its products through Chevrolet, Buick, Oldsmobile, Pontiac, Cadillac, and GMC dealers. Del Monte products are distributed in supermarkets and convenience stores across the United States. Various governmental units have set up toll-free numbers and distributed information on car pooling in an effort to cut gasoline consumption.

The distribution function is vital to the economic well-being of society, because it provides the products and services desired by the consumer. Economists often use the terms place, time, and ownership utilities to describe the value of distribution. They mean that the marketer contributes to the product's value by getting it to the right place at the time the consumer wants to buy it and by providing the mechanism for transferring ownership. Firms that do not perform the distribution function effectively usually become business failures.

Distribution also provides employment opportunities. Salespeople, checkout clerks, truck drivers, stevedores, and forklift operators are all involved in distribution. Others service the products provided through a distribution network. Most people involved in distribution are classified as service personnel: their role is to provide service to some other sector of the economy. A considerable part of the labor force is now involved in service-related occupations.

Channels of Distribution

Hundreds of different channels are used to distribute the output of U.S. manufacturing and service industries. Canned food products usually go through wholesalers and retailers to reach the consumer. Some vacuum cleaners and encyclopedias are sold directly to the consumer. No single channel is always the right one: channel selection depends on the circumstances of the market and on consumer needs. Channels for reaching the consumer may vary over time: for example, the channel for distributing beer has changed from taverns to supermarkets. Channels shift, and effective marketers must be aware of consumer needs so they can keep their distribution methods up to date.

Middlemen are persons or firms that operate between the producer and the consumer or industrial purchaser. Such firms perform some type of distribution function and assist in the operation of the channel. Their distribution functions include buying, selling, transporting, and warehousing. The two main categories of middlemen are wholesalers and retailers. **Wholesalers** are persons or firms who sell primarily to retailers and to other wholesalers or industrial users; they do not sell significant amounts to ultimate consumers. **Retailers** are firms that sell products to individuals for their own use rather than for resale.

middlemen
Persons or firms, including wholesalers and retailers, that operate between the producer and the consumer or industrial purchaser.

wholesalers
Persons or firms who sell primarily to retailers and to other wholesalers or industrial users.

retailers
Firms that sell products to individuals for their own use rather than for resale.

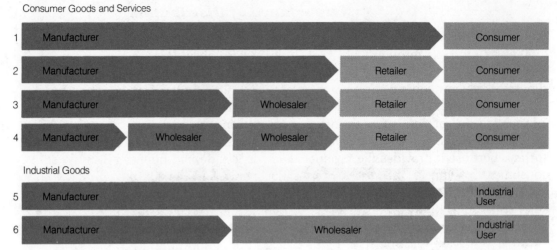

Consumer Goods and Services

1	Manufacturer			Consumer
2	Manufacturer		Retailer	Consumer
3	Manufacturer	Wholesaler	Retailer	Consumer
4	Manufacturer	Wholesaler	Wholesaler	Retailer	Consumer

Industrial Goods

| 5 | Manufacturer | | Industrial User |
| 6 | Manufacturer | Wholesaler | Industrial User |

FIGURE 11–1
The primary channels of distribution.

The primary channels of distribution are shown in Figure 11–1. Channels 1 to 4 are typically used to distribute consumer goods, while channels 5 and 6 are commonly used for industrial goods. Wholesalers of industrial goods are often called **industrial distributors.**

industrial distributors
Wholesalers of industrial goods.

Channel 1. A direct channel from producer to consumer is used for all services but relatively few products. Users include Avon, Fuller Brush, Electrolux, Kirby, and many encyclopedia publishers.

Channel 2. Some manufacturers distribute their products directly to retailers. The clothing industry has many producers who sell directly to retailers through their own sales forces. Some manufacturers set up retail outlets in order to maintain better control over their channels.

Channel 3. The traditional channel for consumer goods, distribution to wholesalers is used by thousands of small manufacturers who cannot afford to maintain an extensive field sales force to reach the retailing sector. Some of these manufacturers employ technical advisers to assist retailers and to secure marketing information, but they are not directly involved in the selling effort.

Channel 4. Several wholesalers are common in the distribution of agricultural—canned and frozen foods—and petroleum products—gasoline. An extra wholesaling level is required to divide, sort, and distribute bulky items.

Channel 5. The direct channel from producer to user is the most common approach to distributing industrial goods. This channel is used for nearly all industrial products except accessory equipment and operating supplies.

Channel 6. The indirect channel from producer to wholesaler to user is used for some industrial goods. It is also used for small accessory equipment and operating supplies that are produced in large lots but sold in small quantities.

Multiple channels. The selection of a particular channel of distribution depends on the market segment the manufacturer is attempting to reach. If the product can be marketed to more than one segment, then multiple distribution channels may be required. In fact, multiple marketing channels have become increasingly popular in recent years.

Tire manufacturers attempt to reach part of the replacement tire market by using wholesalers to distribute their products to service stations and independent garages. At the same time, they may operate their own chain of retail outlets to reach the rest of the replacement market. The original equipment market (OEM) is the automobile manufacturer, which is typically reached through the tire manufacturer's own specialized sales force. Still another direct channel is the institutional market, which includes government motor pools, taxi companies, and motor vehicle fleet operators.

Channels should be chosen on the basis of the markets they serve, with great care used in making this crucial marketing decision. Multiple distribution channels are likely to become even more widespread as marketers try to obtain a competitive advantage within selected consumer segments.

Channel Members

Channel middlemen—including both wholesalers and retailers—perform various marketing functions. They store, transport, and distribute products, and they are often involved in grading and classifying bulk products. Middlemen also perform both a buying and a selling function. By buying a manufacturer's output, they provide the necessary cash flow for the producer to pay workers and buy new equipment. By selling, they provide consumers or other middlemen with want-satisfying products.

Middlemen are able to enter a channel of distribution because they can perform some activities more efficiently than the manufacturer or other channel members. Sometimes their efficiency wanes, and they have to be replaced. But the important thing is that someone must perform these vital marketing functions. Marketers considering a channel change should study the functions currently being performed in the channel and then assess how they would be handled in a revised distribution channel.

Middlemen are
commonplace in today's
marketplace.

Sidney Harris

Wholesalers

Wholesalers are important members of many marketing channels, particularly those for consumer goods. They are often involved in a variety of functional activities—storing, financing, transporting, and the like. The major types of wholesalers are shown in Figure 11–2. Some wholesaling operations are independent businesses; others are owned by manufacturers.

Independent Wholesalers

merchant wholesalers
Independent wholesalers who take legal title to goods.

agent wholesalers
Independent wholesalers who take possession of goods but do not hold legal title to them (typically acting as sales agents).

Independent wholesalers can be classified as either merchant wholesalers or agent wholesalers. **Merchant wholesalers** take legal title to the goods; **agent wholesalers** can take possession of the goods but not legal title. Agent wholesalers usually perform fewer services than merchant wholesalers; they typically act as sales agents.

Sales Offices and Branches

sales branches
Manufacturer-owned wholesalers who stock the items they distribute and process orders from their inventory; often specialize in large-volume, complex, perishable, or highly competitive products.

sales offices
Manufacturer-owned offices for salespeople that provide close local contacts for potential purchasers.

Manufacturers' sales offices and branches tend to be large-volume middlemen specializing in complex, perishable, or intensely competitive products requiring considerable promotional efforts. **Sales branches** stock the items they distribute, and process orders from their inventory. They are common in the chemical, petroleum products, motor vehicle, and machinery and equipment industries. **Sales offices** are exactly what they seem—offices for salespersons. Sales offices do not maintain inventories. They do provide a localized sales effort with distribution being handled from warehouses located elsewhere.

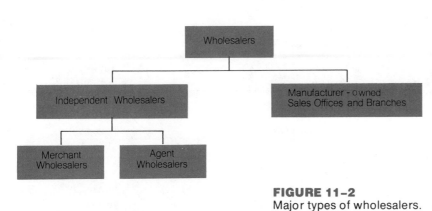

FIGURE 11-2
Major types of wholesalers.

Retailers

In the early 1960s S. S. Kresge (K mart Corp. since 1977) and W. T. Grant were about the same size. Both were variety store chains that faced the problem of deciding what direction to take in the years ahead. Kresge's president, Harry B. Cunningham, decided to take his firm down the discount path. Today, K mart Corp. is the third leading retailer in the United States.

Meanwhile, W. T. Grant watched and then moved to open larger stores and position itself somewhere between discounting and general merchandising. Grant's began to promote big ticket items such as furniture and major appliances in contrast to its traditional soft goods, clothing, and the like. It stimulated sales of the big ticket items by issuing credit cards. The consumer's image of Grant's became confused, and the chain lost $177 million in 1975. New management reversed many of the earlier decisions, but it was too late. W. T. Grant declared bankruptcy in 1976, the same year that K mart replaced J. C. Penney as the nation's third largest retailing company.[2]

Retailers are the final link in the distribution chain. Because they are normally the only channel members with direct customer contact, it is essential that they change with the times and the environment in which they operate. Retailers are part of one of business's most dynamic settings, and special vigilance is required of them if they are to remain competitive.

K mart is a crowning example of a successful retailing company. Certainly its successes are to be admired. But much can also be learned from the study of the failure of W. T. Grant and others.

Size of the Retailing Sector

There are over two million retail stores in the United States.[3] The 20 largest are shown in Table 11-1, ranked by sales.

Fish wholesalers often buy fish from the people who catch them and then sell the fish to retailers and restaurants.

Shopping malls, where many stores are located, have become a major factor in retailing. Many, including the Fairlane Mall in Detroit, are located indoors, thus providing additional comfort to consumers.

TABLE 11–1

The 20 Largest Retailing Companies (Ranked by Sales)

RANK	COMPANY	SALES in Thousands
1	Sears Roebuck (Chicago)	25,194,900
2	Safeway Stores (Oakland)	15,102,673
3	K mart (Troy, Mich.)	14,204,381
4	J.C. Penney (New York)	11,353,000
5	Kroger (Cincinnati)	10,316,741
6	F.W. Woolworth (New York)	7,218,176
7	Great Atlantic & Pacific Tea (Montvale, N.J)	6,684,179
8	Lucky Stores (Dublin, Calif.)	6,468,682
9	American Stores Co. (Salt Lake City)	6,419,884
10	Federated Department Stores (Cincinnati)	6,300,686
11	Montgomery Ward (Chicago)	5,496,907
12	Winn-Dixie Stores (Jacksonville)	5,388,979
13	Southland (Dallas)	4,758,656
14	City Products (Des Plaines, Ill.)	4,462,378
15	Jewel Companies (Chicago)	4,267,922
16	Dayton Hudson (Minneapolis)	4,033,536
17	May Department Stores (St. Louis)	3,172,976
18	Grand Union (Elmwood Park, N.J.)	3,137,612
19	Albertson's (Boise)	3,039,129
20	Wickes Companies (San Diego)	2,876,973

Retailing Concepts

wheel of retailing
A concept that explains how the retail structure is continually evolving as new retailers enter the market by offering lower prices through reductions in service; as the new entries add services and grow, they become targets for competitive assault.

Retail institutions are subject to constant change as new stores replace older establishments. This process, called the **wheel of retailing,** suggests that the retail structure is continually evolving as new retailers enter the market by offering lower prices through reductions in service.[4] Supermarkets and discount houses, for example, gained their initial market footholds through low-price, limited-service appeals. The new entries gradually add services as they grow, and they then become targets for competitive assault. Today's attractive K mart stores, for instance, offer good lighting, wide aisles, adequate paved parking, and services such as credit card purchasing. They are totally unlike those early discounters that often operated from Quonset huts set on unpaved lots in declining factory districts. Some retailers do not survive the evolutionary processes inherent in the wheel of retailing (see Focus 11–1).

scrambled merchandising
Diversification of products offered for sale by retailers in order to preserve or increase their sales volume.

Another factor that makes it difficult to classify retailers is the trend toward **scrambled merchandising.** Many retailers have sought to preserve or increase their sales volume by diversifying the products they offer for sale. Drugstores added soda fountains and then such items as magazines and newspapers. Now they are major retailers of cameras, greeting cards, liquor, tobacco products, cosmetics, and toys. Service stations offer a bewildering array of products—ice, soft drinks, cigarettes, milk, and sometimes toys. Some discount stores have added pharmaceutical departments. Phoenix-based Smitty's has put

FOCUS 11-1
Robert Hall

Robert Hall was founded in 1941 as a discount clothier. The name was invented to suggest a mythical blue-collar bargain-hunter, and the goods were hung on gaspipe racks to underline the absence of expensive extras. For years, the bare-bones clothing chain reigned as chief money-maker for its parent, United Merchants and Manufacturers, Inc. But during the 1960s, Robert Hall failed to move into profitable suburban locations, to keep up with fast-moving fashion trends and to diversify beyond apparel into the more lucrative appliances and hard goods that worked so well for the other discounters [perhaps with the exception of W. T. Grant].

Deficits started piling up; between 1974 and 1977, Robert Hall lost $100 million. [In July 1977] UM&M filed for protection from its creditors under Chapter XI of the Federal Bankruptcy Act, claiming net liabilities of $381 million, and hired the New York auctioneering firm of David Weisz Co. to sell off Robert Hall's inventory in one-store lots.

cocktail lounges in its food-department store.[5] Dental services are offered at some Montgomery Ward stores.[6] The trend toward scrambled merchandising continues in all types of retailing. Possible retail trends and strategies in the 1980s are discussed in Focus 11-2.

Types of Retailers

While it is becoming more difficult to classify stores, the following general categories are usually acknowledged.

General stores. The earliest type of retailers, general stores can still be found in some localities; they offer a wide variety of general merchandise.

Department stores. A. T. Stewart, built in 1863, was the first department store in the United States. The primary strength of department stores has always been the variety of products they offer. Macy's in New York City provides about 400,000 items in its 168 selling departments.

Specialty stores. Some retailers follow a marketing strategy of offering a complete selection in a narrow range of merchandise. By specializing their product offerings, they can concentrate on particular consumer segments and provide technical knowledge and/or services to those segments. Camera and jewelry stores are examples.

FOCUS 11–2
Retail Trends and Strategies in the 1980s

The following retail trends and strategies are forecast for the next decade.

Better market positioning. This involves more careful identification of market segments and providing service superior to that of the competition.

Market intensification. This involves clustering more stores in the same metropolitan area and contiguous markets.

Secondary markets. Expansion will be increasingly focused on secondary markets of under 250,000 population because these investments can be made more cheaply and wage rates are likely to be less.

Differences in store sizes. Retailers will have a more flexible portfolio of different sized stores depending on the size of the community and existing retail competition. More use of second-hand space will occur because this can result in a savings of 30% or more in rent.

Productivity increases. The application of central checkout, self-selection, and low gross margins to areas of trade where these techniques have not been used before will occur. Look now at toy supermarkets, home-decorating centers, and self-service shoe stores.

Fewer product options. Product lines will increasingly be consolidated, and new product development will be cut back.

Services growth. Services retailing will continue to grow as a percentage of total retail sales. Services already represent about 50 percent of the gross national product.

More mergers. Increasingly, smaller and weaker firms will be absorbed as more retail outlets struggle to survive.

Specialty stores, such as produce markets, offer a wide selection of a particular type of product to customers.

Convenience stores. Some retailers focus on convenient locations, long store hours, rapid checkout service, and adequate parking facilities. Local food stores, such as 7–11 stores, gasoline retailers, and some barber shops may be included in this category.

Chain stores. Chain stores are defined as two or more centrally operated stores that offer the same product lines. Chain organization is common among shoe stores, department stores, and variety stores such as the traditional "5 and 10 cent" stores. Many major chain store organizations operate on an international basis.

Discount houses. Most retail discounters have emerged since World War II, traditionally offering lower prices and fewer customer services than other retailers. But, following the wheel of retailing pattern, some of today's discount houses are beginning to resemble general merchandise retailers. Statistics indicate that discount houses are not a major segment of retailing.

Catalog showrooms. One of the major growth areas in retailing during the past ten years has been that of catalog retailing. Catalog retailers send catalogs by mail to their customers who then may come to a showroom in which are displayed samples of each product. Customers select the product or products they wish to buy, and orders are filled from a backroom warehouse. Major catalog showroom retailers include Best Products, Service Merchandise, Giant Stores, Vornado, Zale, and Gordon Jewelry Corporation.

Vending machines. Vending machines are an excellent method of retailing various types of consumer goods. Candy, cigarettes, soft drinks, ice, fruit, ice cream, chewing gum, sandwiches, coffee, milk, hot chocolate, and soup are all available through vending machines. Even entertainment has been packaged for vending operations, beginning with jukeboxes and pinball machines and progressing to the coin-operated video games found in a variety of settings today.

Vending machines serve as retail outlets for various items. A customer can purchase a complete lunch, including soup, a sandwich, coffee, and dessert, from vending machines.

Supermarkets. Supermarkets are large-scale departmentalized stores offering a variety of food products including meats, produce, dairy products, canned goods, and frozen foods in addition to various nonfood items. Supermarkets operate on a self-service basis and emphasize low prices and adequate parking facilities. In an attempt to fight the tendency of consumers to eat many of their meals outside the home, particularly in fast-food restaurants, supermarkets have begun to feature their own delicatessens (see Focus 11–3). The largest supermarket chains in the United States are Safeway, Kroger, Lucky Stores, Jewel, A&P, Winn-Dixie, and Food Fair.

Hypermarkets. Hypermarkets are giant food and general merchandise discount stores. These outlets offer one-stop shopping at discount prices. Hypermarkets, such as the Fred Meyer stores in the Pacific Northwest, are now commonplace in various parts of the United States.

FOCUS 11–3
Byerly's: The Ultimate in Supermarket Chic

Minnesota-based Byerly's is a gourmet's delight. It carries such delicacies as Spanish octopus, killer bee honey, cactus leaves, buffalo meat, taro root, and fried lava worms along with the standard supermarket offerings. Its aisles are carpeted and its walls are papered not painted. Chandeliers provide the lighting. A French pastry chef, a cooking school, and a home economist are available to the chain's discriminating customers. Byerly's also sells postcards featuring pictures of the supermarket. And some people even consider it a status symbol to stow their garbage in one of Byerly's gray grocery bags.

How does Byerly's do it? While the firm's canned and packaged goods sell at competitive prices, Byerly's customers linger longer and buy higher margin items in addition to the staples offered by other supermarkets. Byerly's customers average $19 per visit, compared to an industry average of $12. The firm's founder, Donald D. Byerly, puts it this way: "We have a higher percentage of profit because an imported can of goose-liver pate doesn't have the same price sensitivity as Ajax cleanser." In addition, Byerly's chic appeal allows it to limit advertising to holidays and store openings.

Market Coverage

There is probably only one Chevrolet dealer in your immediate area, but there may be several retail outlets that sell General Electric products. Coca-Cola can be found everywhere—in supermarkets, neighborhood convenience stores, service stations, vending machines, restaurants, and coffee shops. Different types of products require different kinds of distribution coverage. Three categories of market coverage exist—intensive distribution, selective distribution, and exclusive distribution.

Intensive Distribution

intensive distribution
A strategy used to achieve saturation market coverage by placing a product in nearly every available outlet; requires a maximum distribution effort and involves low-priced convenience goods like chewing gum and newspapers.

Intensive distribution is a strategy used by the marketer who tries to place a product in nearly every available outlet. Tobacco products, chewing gum, newspapers, soft drinks, popular magazines, and other low-priced convenience products are available in numerous locations convenient to the purchaser. This kind of saturation market coverage requires the use of wholesalers to achieve a maximum distribution effort.

Exclusive Distribution

Exclusive distribution, the opposite of intensive distribution, occurs when the manufacturer gives a retailer or wholesaler the exclusive right to sell its products in a specific geographical area. Manufacturers sometimes set up effective distribution systems in foreign markets by granting resident firms the exclusive license to import or manufacture their products.

An exclusive distribution contract allows the retailer to carry an adequate inventory and provide the service facilities that might not be possible if competitive dealers existed in the area. Because the dealer has a guaranteed sales area, he or she is likely to make expensive investments in the business. In return, the manufacturer helps the dealer develop a quality image and promote its products effectively. Automobile companies probably provide the best examples of exclusive distribution in domestic markets.

exclusive distribution
The opposite of intensive distribution; occurs when the manufacturer gives a retailer or wholesaler the exclusive right to sell its products in a specific geographical area.

Selective Distribution

Selective distribution, a degree of market coverage somewhere between intensive distribution and exclusive distribution, occurs when a limited number of retailers are selected to distribute the firm's product lines. Television and electrical appliances are often handled in this manner. Manufacturers hope to develop a close working relationship with their dealers and often split advertising expenses with them. Extensive servicing and training facilities are also usually maintained by the manufacturer to help the retailer do a good job of distributing the product.

selective distribution
A degree of market coverage somewhere between intensive and exclusive distribution; occurs when a limited number of retailers are selected to distribute a firm's product lines.

Physical Distribution

All types of market coverage depend on **physical distribution,** the actual movement of goods from the producer to the user, which covers a broad range of activities. These include transportation, warehousing, and materials handling among others. For many years this was a neglected aspect of business management, but since the late 1950s it has become extremely important. Several noticeable trends have occurred. The costs of physical distribution have increased substantially and now exceed 20 percent of the nation's total output. Product lines have been broadened to offer wider consumer choices. This has put a strain on some distribution networks.

Management has sought more efficient inventory practices so as to avoid out-of-stock problems and reduce the financing costs associated with maintaining large inventories. Many experts believe that it may no longer be possible to gain significant cost savings in production. In short, production systems may be near to maximum effi-

physical distribution
The actual movement of goods from producer to user; covers activities such as transportation, warehousing, and materials handling.

ciency, given the present technology. This makes physical distribution a prime candidate for further efficiency improvements.

All these trends are responsible for making physical distribution a critical aspect of modern business. Major gains in efficiency are possible for firms that carefully study their own and alternative physical distribution systems.

Total Cost Approach

The study of physical distribution should include all factors involved in moving goods rather than concentrating on individual aspects of the process. Because the objective of physical distribution is to optimize the level of customer service, total costs should be considered.

Physical distribution costs are often interrelated; a change in one element may affect other elements. Low inventory levels may reduce warehousing costs, but they can result in increases in transportation and order-processing costs. The total cost approach emphasizes the interrelationship of these costs in any physical distribution strategy.

Transportation

The form of transportation used to ship products depends primarily on the kind of product, the distance, and the cost. The physical distribution manager has a number of companies and modes of transportation from which to choose.

common carrier
A transportation company that performs services within a particular line of business for the general public.

contract carrier
A transportation company that carries goods for hire by individual contract or agreement and not for the general public. Their services meet the special needs of their customers.

private carrier
A company that carries its own property in its own vehicles.

freight forwarder
A common carrier that purchases bulk space from other carriers by lease or contract and resells this space to small-volume shippers. The forwarder picks up, loads and delivers the merchandise, and takes care of the billing.

Transportation companies. Transportation companies can be classified into four basic types—common carriers, contract carriers, private carriers, and freight forwarders. A **common carrier** offers to perform services within a particular line of business for the general public. One example is a truckline operating in an area where general merchandise is handled. The truckline is available to serve all the people in the area who offer it general merchandise to haul. However, it may decline to handle such items as liquid petroleum gas or aviation gas. Examples of common carriers are United Airlines and Consolidated Freightways.

Contract carriers transport goods for hire by individual contract or agreement. They do not offer to perform services for the general public; instead they usually offer services that meet the special needs of their customers. Contract carriers are most frequently engaged in business as owner/operator motor carriers. Usually they solicit large shipments from a particular shipper to a particular recipient.

Private carriers transport their own property in their own vehicles. Examples are Safeway Stores, U.S. Steel, Exxon, and mines that operate their own railroads or ships.

Freight forwarders differ from the other carriers in that they do not own any of the equipment used in intercity carriage of freight. They are common carriers that lease or contract bulk space from other carriers such as the airlines and railroads and resell this space to small-volume shippers. The freight forwarder picks up the merchandise from the shipper, loads it into the equipment of whatever carrier is being used, delivers it to its destination, and takes care of all the billing involved.

Freight forwarders provide shippers the advantage of better, less expensive service, and the carriers do not have to handle many small shipments and the billing for them. A further advantage of freight forwarding is that the forwarder knows at all times just where each piece of freight is while it is in transit. The addition of this middleman saves money for everyone and makes for improved service.

Transportation modes. The cost of using a particular transportation mode is usually related to the speed at which it operates. Fast modes typically cost more than slower ones.

Of all domestic intercity freight, a little over 35 percent is carried by the railroads, most of which are common carriers.[7] None are contract carriers, and only a few—owned and operated by mining companies, lumbering operations, and very large industries like steel mills—are private carriers. Railroads are the most efficient mode for transporting bulk commodities over long distances.

Carload freight is the kind of freight railroads prefer to handle. It is provided in shipper-loaded cars to be delivered to someone who will unload the cars, which costs less because railroad personnel do not have to do the loading and unloading. Companion services to carload freight are containerization and trailer-on-flatcar (piggyback) services. Railroads also offer trainload services to shippers of bulk commodities like coal and iron ore. Some trains of this type never stop: they use continuous loading and unloading equipment.

In their recent drive to improve standards and to capture more of the market, railroads have put into effect some new services including run-through trains, which completely bypass congested terminals, and unit trains, which are used exclusively by a single customer who pays lower rates for each shipment.

Highway transportation accounts for just under 25 percent of domestic freight shipping.[8] The principal advantage of highway transportation over the other modes of transportation is flexibility. A truck carrier can operate wherever there is a road, while trains depend on rails and aircraft on airports large enough to accommodate them. Highway carriers are divided into common carriers, contract carriers, and private carriers.

A number of transcontinental highway carriers move freight coast to coast. However, highway carriers are most efficient for distances up to about 300 to 400 miles. For longer distances, railroads are more advantageous.

The typical highway common carrier, with its own pickup and delivery equipment, picks up freight at the shipper's door and delivers it to a freight terminal, where it is loaded into larger trucks for delivery to a terminal in another city. There it is unloaded and delivered by smaller vehicles.

Railroads carry more freight than any other mode of transportation in the United States. They are most efficient for transporting bulk commodities such as automobiles.

Controversial Issue

Foreign Takeover of U.S. Retailers: Should They Be Restricted or Halted?

What could be more American than A & P Supermarkets or the Red Food Store chain of Chattanooga, Tennessee, or Macy's archrival Gimbels? These bulwarks of American retailing are sources of pride to most Americans. They symbolize American big business at its best—homespun success stories that grow bigger with every ring of the cash register. Then why are all these companies foreign owned?

Concerned citizens have been asking this question as an increasing number of American retailers are acquired by British, German, Swiss, French, Dutch, and Belgian companies. The best way to answer it is to look at how Europe's U.S. shopping spree began and where it stands today.

Few would have predicted that the 1962 purchase of Ohrbach's, the New York apparel chain, by the Brenninkmeyer family, wealthy Dutch retailers who already owned clothing stores throughout northern Europe, would open the floodgates to this new European invasion of America. At first few European entrepreneurs followed the Brenninkmeyer's lead. But by the early 1970s, European companies had acquired American retail stores in every part of the country—and their acquisition fever was hardly satisfied. As the 1980s begin, Europeans contined to gobble up the cream of America's retail industry.

Here are only a few examples: The British-American Tobacco Co. (BAT Industries) purchased Gimbel Brothers, owners of Saks Fifth Avenue and Gimbels department stores, headquartered in

Contract highway carriers can frequently offer lower rates than common carriers because they serve a limited number of customers, deal in volume shipments, and operate only when they have a profitable load.

There are many private highway carrier operations. Wholesale grocery companies, supermarket chains, department stores, manufacturing establishments, and mining companies all engage in private-carrier operations when they transport their goods.

Water transportation is one of the least costly of all modes of transportation. There are basically two types of water carriers—the inland or barge lines and the ocean-going deep-water ships.

About 15 percent of the volume of domestic intercity freight is handled through the inland waterways of the United States.[9] The system of waterways includes the Mississippi, Ohio, Tennessee, and other rivers; inland canals; and the Great Lakes. Much of this freight, especially on the rivers and canals, is transported in barges pushed by mammoth tugs. Great Lakes traffic is handled by specially built

New York. The German Tengelmann Group bought A & P Super-markets. Belgium's Delhaize Corporation owns Food Town Stores and Alterman Foods headquartered in Salisbury, North Carolina, and Atlanta, Georgia, respectively. And the Dutch Vroom and Dreesmann acquired the Dillard Department Stores of Little Rock, Arkansas.

According to Gui de Vaucleroy, a director of Delhaize, Euro-peans are flocking to our shores because "the U.S. is the last bastion of capitalism." We offer European entrepreneurs some-thing they cannot find at home: an unrestricted potential for profit. In addition, these foreign businesspeople see less union pressure, fewer government-imposed fringe benefits, access to the latest advances in inventory and checkout systems, and a favorable cli-mate for business and investment in the U.S. Europeans also de-sire the real estate that comes with ownership of a retail chain.

Many American retailers have given a cool welcome to their foreign cousins. Already squeezed by their homegrown competi-tion, many resent the increased competition brought about by the infusion of foreign money. This attitude inevitably breeds the plea for protectionism. Retailers want to know whether foreign control of U.S. business is desirable for the U.S. economy and for the retailing business and, if it is not, whether the federal government should step in to restrict these takeovers or stop them altogether. With the problems facing the inflation-racked U.S. economy, this protectionist plea may not fall on deaf ears.

steamers, some of which are 1,000 feet long. This low-cost type of transportation lends itself mainly to the hauling of bulky commodities.

Ocean-going ships operate on the Great Lakes, between United States port cities, and in international commerce.

About 24.5 percent of intercity freight is handled by pipelines,[10] which convey primarily petroleum products ranging from crude oil to highly refined products and natural gas. Some successful experiments have been made in handling other bulk commodities, such as coal, this way. These commodities are ground into small pieces and mixed with water to form a slurry, which is then pumped through the pipe-lines. Pipelines can transport many liquids and gases cheaper and faster than other modes of transportation.

While still dwarfed by other transportation modes, carrying less than 1 percent of all freight, domestic air freight has become increas-ingly important in recent years.[11] Air freight is usually limited to val-uable and/or perishable products because of the mode's relatively high cost. Live lobsters are flown from the seashore to inland cities.

Detroit automobile manufacturers ship critical parts to assembly plants by air. In some cases air freight costs are offset by lower inventory costs and more efficient manufacturing operations.

The certified airlines of the United States are all common carriers. Some of them (as well as a group of carriers known as supplemental carriers) engage in charter work, which is a form of contract carriage. Many business organizations own or lease aircraft that are operated to transport their personnel or, in some situations, their freight; this is defined as private carriage.

Warehousing

warehousing
The storage of products.

Warehousing is another important part of physical distribution and is involved in the storage of products. There are two types of warehouses: storage and distribution. **Storage warehouses** keep products for relatively long periods of time and are used most often for products that are seasonal in supply or demand such as farm products.

storage warehouse
A place used to store products for a relatively long period of time; usually used for seasonal products.

Distribution warehouses are used to gather and redistribute products. They try to keep products for as short a period of time as possible. They are mainly used by manufacturers that have several small customers in various, distant locations or by firms that have several suppliers in one area.

distribution warehouse
A place used to store products for a short period of time; usually used to gather and redistribute products.

A pharmaceutical manufacturer that ships many small orders to various local stores in an area, for example, might use distribution warehouses. Because the cost of shipping small orders can be quite high, it is cheaper to ship a large quantity to a central distribution warehouse to be broken down into several smaller shipments and delivered to individual customers in the area.

In the case of a supermarket chain that may have several stores in one area and gets its merchandise from various suppliers, a distribution warehouse can be more efficient and less costly than having each of the suppliers ship individual orders separately to each of the stores. Instead, each supplier sends its products to a distribution warehouse where the large order is separated into the quantities needed by each store. Then the correct quantity of each product is put together into one economical shipment and sent to the individual stores.

Materials Handling

materials handling
The moving of items within the customer's warehouse, terminal, factory, or store.

Once a product has been transported from its place of manufacture to the customer, the physical distribution task involves moving the item within the customer's warehouse, terminal, factory, or store. This is known as **materials handling.**

unitization
Combining as many packages as possible into one load that can be handled by a forklift truck.

Two recent innovations—unitization and containerization—have improved materials handling in many firms. **Unitization**—combining as many packages as possible into one load that can be handled by a forklift truck—is sometimes done with steel bands or shrink packing. In the latter case, packages are covered with a plastic sheet and then heated. When the plastic cools, it shrinks and binds the packages together.

Containerization—putting packages, usually made up of several unitized loads, into a form that is relatively easy to transfer—has significantly reduced transporation costs for many products by cutting materials handling time, theft, insurance costs, damage, and scheduling problems. Some containers are designed to be carried via rail, truck, or ship. They can be taken to a rail terminal on a flatbed truck, then placed on a flatbed railway car to be hauled to a seaport, where they can be loaded on an overseas freighter.

containerization
Putting packages, usually made up of several unitized loads, into a form that is relatively easy to transfer.

Summary

All organizations perform a distribution function. The value of a product or service is enhanced by having it available at the right time and in the right place. Distribution also provides considerable employment opportunities.

Marketing channels are the paths that goods and services follow to the final user. Some of them involve middlemen such as wholesalers and retailers; others are direct from manufacturers to consumers. Multiple channels are sometimes used to reach different market segments.

Wholesalers are channel members who sell primarily to retailers and other wholesalers or industrial users and only in insignificant amounts to ultimate users. Retailers, by contrast, are firms that sell products to persons for their own use rather than for resale.

Retail institutions are constantly changing. Two factors make it difficult to describe and classify them—the wheel of retailing and the trend toward scrambled merchandising. Retailers fall into several general categories—general stores, department stores, specialty stores, convenience stores, chain stores, discount houses, vending machines, supermarkets, and hypermarkets.

Three categories of market coverage exist—intensive distribution, where products are placed in many outlets; exclusive distribution, where a firm has exclusive marketing rights in a certain geographical area; and selective distribution, where a limited number of retailers distribute a firm's products.

Physical distribution, the actual physical movement of goods from producer to user, is an important part of the marketing channel. Because the objective of the physical distribution effort is to maximize the level of customer service, total costs must be considered.

There are four types of transportation companies—common carriers, contract carriers, private carriers, and freight forwarders. Transportation modes include rail, highway, water, pipeline, and air.

Warehousing, which involves the storage of products, is usually handled by storage or distribution facilities. Storage warehouses keep products for a relatively long period of time and are generally used for seasonal items. Distribution warehouses are used to gather and redistribute products and are usually used by companies that have several small customers in various, distant locations or by firms that have several suppliers in one area.

Materials handling involves moving an item within the customer's facility. Recent improvements in this area are unitization and containerization.

Key Terms

marketing channels	selective distribution
middlemen	physical distribution
wholesalers	common carrier
retailers	contract carrier
industrial distributors	private carrier
merchant wholesalers	freight forwarder
agent wholesalers	warehousing
sales branches	storage warehouse
sales offices	distribution warehouse
wheel of retailing	materials handling
scrambled merchandising	unitization
intensive distribution	containerization
exclusive distribution	

Review Questions

1. Explain each of the terms listed above.

2. Outline the primary channels of distribution.

3. Why would a firm ever use multiple channels of distribution?

4. Manufacturer-owned wholesalers tend to be large-volume middlemen. Why?

5. What is the primary difference between merchant wholesalers and agent wholesalers?

6. Describe the various types of retail establishments. Which ones appear to be declining? Growing?

7. Which types of market coverage would be best for:
   a. electronic calculators
   b. bubble gum
   c. men's cologne
   d. bulldozers and other earth-moving equipment

8. What is meant by the total cost approach to physical distribution?

9. Differentiate among common, contract, and private carriers.

10. Which transportation mode would you suggest for:
    a. sheet steel
    b. natural gas
    c. premium electronic components
    d. breakfast cereal

Discussion Questions and Exercises

1. Evaluate the pros and cons of the controversial issue that appears in this chapter.

2. Comment on the statement: The functions performed by channel middlemen cannot be eliminated.

3. Research and report on the failure of either W. T. Grant or Robert Hall. What have you learned from your research?

4. A vice-president for United Airlines has predicted that by the year 2026 domestic air travelers will board 1,700-passenger airplanes that fly at 600 miles an hour; and overseas passengers will fly in 500-passenger airplanes that travel at 1,500 miles an hour.[12] If this really happens, how will it affect other modes of transportation?

5. Prepare a report on the physical distribution used by a company in your area. Can you suggest any way(s) to improve its physical distribution efficiency?

Case 11–1: Dr. Pepper Meets "Welch's Sparkling Grape Soda"

The marketing of "Welch's Sparkling Grape Soda" and the firm's other carbonated drinks has involved some critical management de-

cisions. Welch Foods, a cooperative composed of 2,000 grape growers, spent considerable time and expense in formulating just the right
type of carbonated beverage. The company was convinced it could
upgrade the market position of grape soft drinks by targeting its product as a national brand rather than by using the private-brand category. Welch was successful in this effort; their product became the
first major grape soda brand.

Welch Foods set up a distribution system based on 226 licensed
bottlers. These bottlers handled an expanded carbonated beverage
line that included grape, orange, strawberry, and apple drinks. Welch
eventually accounted for 0.5 percent of soft-drink industry sales with
this marketing system.

But in 1981 Dr. Pepper acquired an exclusive manufacturing and
marketing license for all of Welch's carbonated beverages. Both man-
agements believed they had reached a good agreement. Welch gained
Dr. Pepper's marketing clout (Dr. Pepper and 7-UP are both ranked
as the nation's third leading soft drinks), and Dr. Pepper was able to
expand its product line, which had previously consisted of only regular
and diet Dr. Pepper.

Questions

1. Do you agree with the marketing decision reached by Welch Foods
   and Dr. Pepper?

2. Compare the marketing of "Welch's Sparkling Grape Soda" to
   that of other soft drinks.

Case 11–2: Susan McBride Is Losing Her Battle with OPEC

At sunrise one morning . . . Captain Kenneth Redden and his nine-
man crew maneuvered the tugboat *Susan McBride* and her 15 barges,
heading north to take on coal, into a mooring along the Mississippi
River near Alton, Ill. For the next three days, Redden and his men
watched TV and played cards, while waiting to get the vessels through
the antiquated locks that are known as the Turnstyle of the Upper
Mississippi.

Redden's delay was typical of the problems of transporting the
U.S.'s largest potential source of energy. While experts predict that
America's vast coal reserves could become a major alternative to
OPEC oil and an important export product, the use of coal is being

thwarted by the U.S.'s inadequate and outdated system of transporting the valuable black rock. . .

. . . The U.S. lacks the transportation network to move coal rapidly and inexpensively. Coal already is piling up, waiting for barges, railroad cars or ships to carry it. Railroads haul 65% of coal, and the Department of Transportation estimates that the industry will have to spend about $12 billion by 1985 to replace ancient equipment and improve track roadbeds. Yet the railroads are reluctant to spend huge sums until they are certain that the demand for coal will remain strong. Says John Fishwick, president of the Norfolk & Western Railway: "We need long-term contracts if we're to put money into facilities."

Railroaders also argue that if they cannot earn a sufficient profit on a shipment of coal, they will be unable to invest the money needed to keep tracks and cars in good shape. Critics charge, though, that railroads often demand exorbitant rates in areas where there are no good alternatives for moving the bulky product.

Barge and port facilities are also insufficient. The export demand for steam coal in Europe increased by nearly 100% . . . yet buyers are unhappy about the delays in delivery. U.S. piers have little storage capacity, so that railroad cars stocked with the black stuff wait weeks to be unloaded. Port channels are neither large nor deep enough to handle the traffic. Through most of the summer there were about 50 colliers at anchor on any given day at Hampton Roads, Va., the largest coal port on the East Coast.

Eric Thibau, a commercial attaché of the French embassy in Washington, met . . . with Virginia Governor John Dalton and Senator Harry F. Byrd, Jr., to warn them that France, which last year bought $180 million worth of coal through Hampton Roads, would take its business elsewhere unless the port is modernized. Said Thibau: "We are not so much displeased as surprised. When you think that the U.S. put a man on the moon, you'd think that it would have modern railroad and pier facilities. But the technology is 30 to 50 years out of date." Americans, who used to enjoy laughing at the French and their deplorable phone system and bumpy roads, will have to become accustomed to Europeans joking about overaged U.S. transportation facilities.

Questions

1. Analyze the causes of this physical distribution failure.

2. How can these problems be corrected? Who should be responsible for this undertaking?

3. Identify other economic problems that are at least partially caused by an ineffective physical distribution system.

12

Promotional Strategy

Learning Goals

1. To describe how most organizations use some type of promotional strategy in order to reach their goals
2. To enumerate the objectives of promotion
3. To identify the basic elements of promotional strategy
4. To distinguish among the alternative promotional strategies
5. To explain the meaning of each of the key terms introduced in this chapter

Profile: Barbara Proctor
Reaching the Black Consumer

In Barbara Proctor's view, "advertising is the single most important way of reaching everyone in America"—including America's 26 million blacks. Proctor, who is the founder, president, and creative director of the Chicago-based Proctor & Gardner advertising agency, has dedicated herself to marketing corporate America's advertising messages to the black consumer—a job she feels has been placed on the white advertising establishment's back burner for too long.

In 1963 as the first black in the advertising business in Chicago, Proctor quickly realized that advertising could improve the lives of black people, and she determined to play a part in creating the messages blacks saw and heard. She spent the rest of the 1960s learning her craft and in 1970, with the help of the Small Business Administration (SBA), she formed her own full-service advertising agency. Proctor & Gardner received the first service loan guaranteed by the SBA to any business in the country, and now the agency is an $8-million-a-year business.

Creating advertising that is right for the black consumer involves an "accumulation of experiences," says Proctor. "It's not something you can learn in a course in college—how to write black or how to market to the black consumer." Moreover, says Proctor, in general, the corporate community does not understand that black America is at least as diversified as white America and that it is impossible to reach the entire black audience through one message. Nor do many corporations see the futility in simply reshooting with black models ads directed at white consumers. This kind of advertising is "deadly advertising," contends Proctor. "It is worse than no advertising at all." Advertisers must realize that an "insincere message to the marketplace is really a negative message." They're losing far more black consumers than they're gaining.

Proctor cites another problem advertisers face in dealing with black consumers—changing lifestyles and product preferences. "It takes 18 months for the corporate community to get an ad campaign under way," says Proctor. "The black community is a much more quickly moving market." The corporate creative thrust just can't keep up with it.

Proctor contends that radio rather than television is the most effective medium to reach blacks. "Blacks watch less prime-time television than any other English-speaking group," says Proctor, "primarily because prime time does not reflect the black universe. The most effective use of television for blacks is in the late-night fringe, in the newsbreaks, and in those places where blacks go for specific information." If a sponsor's advertising message is placed right alongside the unreality of prime-time programming, its credibility will be lost.

Right now, says Proctor, "media advertising to blacks is abominable." Whether it improves depends on corporate America's awareness of the real differences between black and white consumers and their willingness to trust professionals like Barbara Proctor to create advertising messages that are meaningful to blacks.

If I were starting my life over again I am inclined to think I would go into the advertising business in preference to almost any other.

—*Franklin Delano Roosevelt*

Many readers will recall the television commercial featuring Mean Joe Greene of the Pittsburgh Steelers:

> It opens with Greene, a Goliath of a man, limping down a stadium tunnel, presumably injured, with a jersey slung over his shoulder. A little boy follows him.
>
> The boy says timidly, "Mr. Greene . . . Mr. Greene . . . you need help?"
>
> "Uh, uh," says Greene, too tired and disgusted to bother with the kid.
>
> "I just want you to know . . . I think . . . I think you're the best ever," the boy says and offers Greene his bottle of Coke.
>
> Greene is at first reluctant to accept the Coke; the kid—12-year-old Tommy Oken—persists, and Greene finally takes it. He drinks all of it without putting the bottle down, then calls to the boy as the kid is about to walk away, saying, "Here . . . catch," and throws his jersey to him. The boy catches it and exults, "Wow . . . thanks a million, Joe."[1]

Greene, who once dropped out of a school play because of stage fright, and Oken provide an important element of Coca Cola's promotional strategy. Their television commercial combined with other commercials and forms of advertising, sales promotion, and personal selling efforts on the part of company and bottler personnel make up Coca Cola's promotional strategy.

Most organizations use some type of promotional strategy to reach their goals. **Promotional strategy** is the function of informing, persuading, and influencing a consumer decision. It is as important to nonprofit organizations as it is to Coca Cola.

promotional strategy
The function of informing, persuading, and influencing a consumer decision; the part of marketing decision making that blends personal selling, advertising, and sales promotion tools to produce effective communication between the firm and the marketplace.

Objectives of Promotional Strategy

Promotional strategy objectives vary among organizations. Some use promotion to expand their markets, others to hold their current positions, still others to present a corporate viewpoint on a public issue. Promotional strategies can also be used to reach selected markets. Ronald Reagan's presidential campaign used Chinese-language newspapers to reach this group of voters. An organization can have multiple promotional objectives. Most sources identify the specific promotional objectives or goals of providing information, increasing sales, positioning the product, and stabilizing sales.

Providing Information

In the early days of promotional campaigns (an era characterized by short supply of many items), most advertisements were designed to inform the public of a product's availability. Criers made public announcements of the cargo carried by vessels newly arrived in local ports. General stores on the frontier of a nation advancing westward inserted advertisements in weekly newspapers. These advertisements essentially listed the contents of the latest shipment from the East.

Today, a major portion of advertising in the United States is still informational. A large section of the daily newspapers on Wednesdays or Thursdays consists of advertising that tells consumers which products are being featured by stores, and at what prices, for weekend shopping. Health insurance advertisements in Sunday newspaper supplements emphasize information about rising hospital costs. Industrial salespeople keep buyers aware of the latest technological advances in a particular field.

Providing information about product availability, prices, and other details has always been of primary importance to marketing and promotional strategy. Marketers realize that nearly all promotional messages must have some educational role.

An advertisement for a law firm provides information about the cost of various legal services.

Positioning the Product

Promotional strategy has been used to "position" a product in certain markets. **Positioning** is the strategy of concentrating on specific market segments rather than on trying to achieve a broad appeal. It requires the marketer to identify the market segments that will be likely users of the product. Promotional strategy is then brought into play to differentiate the item from others and to make it appealing to these market segments (see Focus 12–1).

Positioning is also often used for products that are not leaders in their particular fields. Faced with a mouthwash widely accepted for control of bad breath but characterized by medicinal flavor, Scope offered itself as providing "minty fresh breath" instead of "medicine breath."

positioning
The promotional strategy that concentrates on specific market segments rather than on trying to achieve a broad apppeal; often used for products that are not leaders in their particular fields.

Increasing Sales

The ultimate promotional goal for most firms is increased sales, but there are other bases for positioning a product. In a classic promotional campaign Avis positioned itself against Hertz with the theme: "Avis is only number two in rent-a-cars, so why go with us? We try harder." More recently, Hertz has countered by stressing the advantages of its leadership position via the well-known "super star in rent-a-car" advertisements featuring O. J. Simpson flying through airports.

FOCUS 12–1
The We Generation of the 1980s

The 1970s were known as the "Me Decade" in advertising. Themes like "Me and My RC" were commonplace as marketers emphasized a youth cult orientation. People over 40 were virtually ignored by advertisers. But things are changing. Royal Crown now advertises "Me and You and My RC." What happened?

Statistics suggest that the United States has experienced some major population and lifestyle changes. The population is aging. The over-40s constitute 60 percent of the population and the national buying power. Meanwhile, the under-25s constitute less than 9 percent of the U.S. population and a mere 6 percent of all income. Moreover, this age group is expected to decline to under 5 percent of the population during the 1980s. In addition, many observers now see a return to traditional family lifestyles.

The net result is that "we" is in vogue in the advertising world of the 1980s. "Catch that Pepsi spirit, Drink it in" appeals to a traditional family. General Electric says "We bring you closer to the ones you love." Advertisers now refer to older consumers by such terms as "the new independents," "mature market," and the "active affluents."

The unanswered question is whether advertising is influenced by social trends or whether it creates some of these trends.

Stabilizing Sales

Sales stabilization is another promotional strategy goal. Sales contests offering prizes (such as vacation trips, color televisions, and scholarships) to sales personnel who meet certain goals are often held during slack periods of the year. Sales promotion materials—calendars, pens, and the like—are sometimes distributed to stimulate sales during off-periods. Despite shortages of antifreeze a few years ago, Union Carbide still advertised its Prestone brand heavily. Robert Cassidy, Union Carbide's marketing director, pointed out that a company should advertise when times are difficult: "We have a valuable consumer franchise and we don't intend to give it up as long as we can supply the product."[2]

A stable sales pattern allows the firm to do better financial, purchasing, and market planning; even out the production cycle; and reduce some management and production costs. The correct use of promotional strategy can be a valuable tool in accomplishing these objectives.

Television advertising often makes a lasting impression on viewers.
Reprinted by permission of Johnny Hart and Field Enterprises Inc.

Promotional strategy consists of three distinct elements—advertising, personal selling, and sales promotion. Each of these elements is important in developing a promotional strategy.

Advertising

Advertising is a nonpersonal sales presentation usually directed to a large number of potential customers. It uses various media—newspapers, magazines, television, radio, direct mail, and outdoor advertising—to relay promotional messages to widespread markets (see Focus 12–2). Newspapers receive the single largest share of total (national and local) advertising revenues. The leading national advertisers in the United States include the familiar names of Procter & Gamble, General Motors, General Mills, American Telephone & Telegraph, McDonald's, and Johnson & Johnson (see Table 12–1).

advertising
A nonpersonal sales presentation usually directed to a large number of potential customers.

FOCUS 12–2
Who Shot J. R.?

The prices that television networks charge advertisers for running their commercials is closely linked to a show's rating. Television ratings are simply the number of people who are watching a particular show. And 1980s national guessing game "Who Shot J. R.?" allowed CBS to set a new record!

The Friday, November 21, 1980, episode of the CBS nighttime soap "Dallas" set a television record as the culprit was revealed to be J. R.'s sister-in-law, Kristin. Some 41.4 million television sets, 76 percent of those that were turned on, saw this episode. The "Who Shot J. R.?" segment surpassed the final part of "Roots," the last show in "The Fugitive" series, and the various Super Bowl games. CBS was clearly the winner in this situation as Las Vegas odds makers and various contests built up nationwide interest in who had shot the Texas villain.

TABLE 12–1
The 25 Leading National Advertisers

Rank	Company	Amount Spent (in millions)
1	Procter & Gamble Co.	$614.9
2	General Foods Corp.	393.0
3	Sears, Roebuck & Co.	379.3
4	General Motors Corp.	323.4
5	Philip Morris Inc.	291.2
6	K mart Corp.	287.1
7	R. J. Reynolds Industries	258.1
8	Warner-Lambert Co.	220.2
9	American Telephone & Telegraph Co.	219.8
10	Ford Motor Co.	215.0
11	PepsiCo Inc.	212.0
12	Bristol-Myers Co.	210.6
13	American Home Products	206.0
14	McDonald's Corp.	202.8
15	Gulf & Western Industries	191.5
16	General Mills	190.7
17	Esmark Inc.	170.5
18	Coca-Cola Co.	169.3
19	Seagram Co.	168.0
20	Mobil Corp.	165.8
21	Norton Simon Inc.	163.2
22	Anheuser-Busch	160.5
23	Unilever U.S. Inc.	160.0
24	RCA Corp.	158.6
25	Johnson & Johnson	157.7

Total U.S. advertising expenditures are estimated to exceed $55 billion annually.[3] This means that about $200 is spent in advertising each year for every person in the United States.[4] The advertising expenditures for major industry groupings are presented in Table 12–2. As can be seen from the table, advertising spending can range from one-tenth of 1 percent of sales in an industry like sanitary services to 10.7 percent of sales in the motion picture production industry.

TABLE 12–2
Percentage of Sales Invested in Advertising by Major Industry Groups

Industry	Percent of Sales
Meat products	2.5
Dairy products	2.8
Bakery products	1.7
Soft drinks	5.7
Cigarettes	6.3
Soap and other detergents	6.5
Sanitary services	0.1
Household appliances	2.5
Motor vehicles and car bodies	1.7
Jewelry, precious metals	4.4
Toys, amusements, sporting goods	6.3
Retail—auto dealers, gas stations	0.5
Retail—eating places	2.9
Retail—mail order houses	5.9
Hotels, motels	2.1
Service—motion picture production	10.7

Types of Advertising

There are two basic types of advertising—product and institutional. **Product advertising** involves the nonpersonal selling of a good or service.

Institutional advertising involves the promotion of a concept, an idea, a philosophy, or the goodwill of an industry, company, organization, or government entity. "Unfair foreign competition takes jobs from American steelworkers" is a slogan used by Bethlehem Steel Corporation to present its views on steel imports. Atlanta solicited new industry by advertising its available work force with the slogan, "Come to Atlanta and we'll give you hard labor, for life!" The California Prune Advisory Board took an innovative approach to institutional advertising (see Focus 12–3).

product advertising
The nonpersonal selling of a good or service.

institutional advertising
The promotion of a concept, an idea, a philosophy, or the goodwill of an industry, company, organization, or government entity.

Sometimes product advertising may be used as institutional advertising several years later.

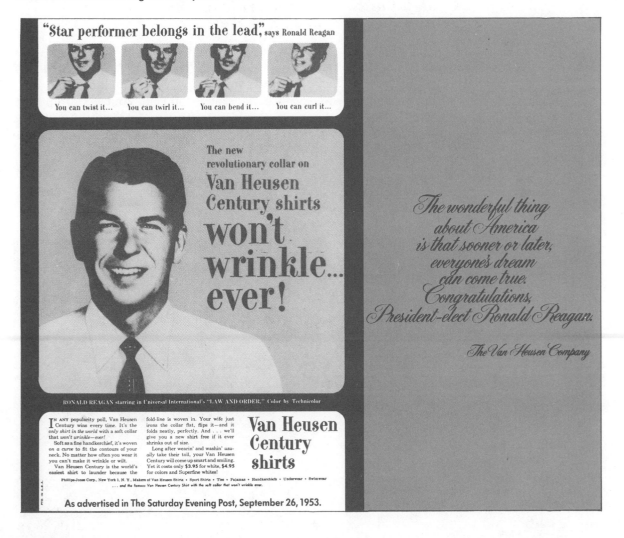

"Star performer belongs in the lead," says Ronald Reagan

You can twist it... You can twirl it... You can bend it... You can curl it...

The new revolutionary collar on
Van Heusen Century shirts won't wrinkle... ever!

RONALD REAGAN starring in Universal International's "LAW AND ORDER," Color by Technicolor

IN ANY popularity poll, Van Heusen Century wins every time. It's the *only shirt in the world* with a soft collar that *won't wrinkle—ever!*

Soft as a fine handkerchief, it's woven on *a curve* to fit the contours of your neck. No matter how often you wear it you can't make it wrinkle or wilt. Van Heusen Century is the world's easiest shirt to launder because the fold-line is woven in. Your wife just irons the collar flat, flips it—and it folds neatly, perfectly. And . . . we'll give you a new shirt free if it ever shrinks out of size.

Long after wearin' and washin' *usually* take their toll, your Van Heusen Century will come up smart and smiling. Yet it costs only **$3.95** for white, **$4.95** for colors and Superfine whites!

Van Heusen Century shirts

Phillips-Jones Corp., New York 1, N. Y., Makers of Van Heusen Shirts • Sport Shirts • Ties • Pajamas • Handkerchiefs • Underwear • Swimwear
. . . *and the famous Van Heusen Century Shirt with the soft collar that won't wrinkle ever.*

As advertised in The Saturday Evening Post, September 26, 1953.

The wonderful thing about America is that sooner or later, everyone's dream can come true. Congratulations, President-elect Ronald Reagan.

The Van Heusen Company

FOCUS 12–3
The California Prune Advisory Board

When per capita prune consumption declined to one pound annually, the California prune growers, who supply most of America's prunes, decided to take action. The California Prune Advisory Board recognized the fruit's many marketing problems. The wrinkled texture of prunes caused consumers to associate them with old age. Furthermore, most prunes were marketed for laxative purposes.

The Prune Board met its image problem head on by launching a "funny fruit" campaign featuring radio advertisements disrupted by laughter whenever someone referred to prunes. The result was a 20 percent increase in consumer awareness of the fruit.

Relationship between Advertising and the Product Life Cycle

informative advertising
The advertising approach intended to build initial demand for a product in the introductory phase of the product's life cycle.

Advertising strategy for a product varies according to its stage in the product life cycle (see Figure 12–1). **Informative advertising,** intended to build initial demand for a product, is used in the introductory phase of the product life cycle. The Australian Tourist Commission used an informative promotional campaign to get young Australians to explore their country. The campaign was based on a free, youth-oriented booklet, *Australia—A Land of Things to Do,* that listed hos-

FIGURE 12–1
Relationship between advertising and the product life cycle.

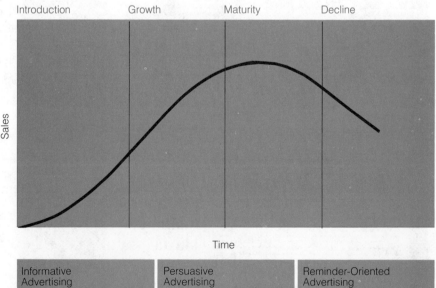

tels, watering holes (of the alcoholic variety), places to crash, surfing beaches, and the like.

Persuasive advertising attempts to improve the competitive status of a product, institution, or concept. It is used in the growth and maturity stages of the product life cycle. "Virginia is for lovers" is a persuasive institutional advertising theme.

One of the latest trends in persuasive product advertising is to make direct comparisons with competitive products. The use of **comparative advertising** has been encouraged by the Federal Trade Commission, the regulatory agency involved in such matters. The Anacin ads described in Focus 12–4 are an example of comparative advertising. It is uncertain at this point what the long-run status of comparative advertising will be in the United States and abroad, but its use has certainly changed forever the veiled comparisons that used to be made with Product X.

persuasive advertising
The advertising approach used in a product's growth and maturity stages to improve the competitive status of the product, institution, or concept.

comparative advertising
A trend in persuasive product advertising in which direct comparisons with competing products are made.

FOCUS 12–4
Your Body Knows the Difference . . .

American Home Products began to advertise that Johnson & Johnson's Tylenol lacked an anti-inflammatory action found in AHP's Anacin brand in an attempt to counter Tylenol's rapid rise to the leadership position in the huge analgesic market. A similar approach was used by Sterling Drug's Bayer and Bristol-Myers' Bufferin. The Anacin copy claimed, "Your body knows the difference between these pain removers [Tylenol and Datril were shown] and adult strength Anacin." The advertisement went on to point out the anti-inflammatory aspect of Anacin.

When Johnson & Johnson was unsuccessful in its efforts to stop the advertisements via the National Advertising Review Board and the Proprietary Association, they filed a court case. As a result of this legal action, a U.S. District judge awarded Johnson & Johnson an injunction prohibiting American Home Products from using this advertising. The authoritative trade publication *Advertising Age* reported that "this may be the first instance of a marketer knocking off a rival's advertising by going to court. . . ."

At about the same time that Johnson & Johnson was battling with American Home Products in court, Ogilvy & Mather, Inc., a leading advertising agency, was issuing a research study reporting that sponsor misidentification may result from television advertising naming the competition. The results of the study suggest that viewers of an Anacin TV ad are as likely to identify it as one for Excedrin as for Anacin! The Ogilvy & Mather research suggests that the competitive brand is the likely beneficiary of such advertising.

The moral of the story: Maybe Johnson & Johnson should have let the Anacin ads continue!

reminder-oriented advertising
The advertising approach utilized in the late maturity and decline stages of the product life cycle that attempts to keep the product's name in front of the consumer to remind people of the importance of a concept or an institution.

Reminder-oriented advertising, used in the late maturity and decline stages of the product life cycle, attempts to keep a product's name in front of the consumer or to remind people of the importance of a concept or an institution. Soft drinks, beer, toothpaste, and cigarettes are products for which reminder-oriented advertising is used. The Association of American Railroads used an advertisement that began: "Today's railroads, America's great untapped resource." Even police cars in some areas of the United States carry reminder-oriented themes such as "To protect and to serve."

Personal Selling

personal selling
A promotional presentation made on a person-to-person basis with a potential buyer.

Personal selling is a promotional presentation made on a person-to-person basis with a potential buyer. Selling, the original method of promotion, now employs over six and a half million people as salesworkers and sales managers.[5]

The sales function of most companies is changing rapidly. In some cases the change has been only cosmetic, such as when the title *salesperson* is changed to *account representative,* but the job function remains the same. Yet many companies are making significant changes in their sales forces. Sales duties have been expanded, and in some cases the function itself has actually changed. For instance, the energy crisis and shortages of some raw materials have involved sales personnel in the problems of allocating insufficient supplies. Salespeople should be advisers to their customers, helping them utilize more efficiently the items they buy.

Sales Tasks

A salesperson's work can vary significantly from one company or situation to another, but it usually includes three basic tasks—order processing, creative selling, and missionary selling. A person who sells a highly technical product may be doing 55 percent in missionary selling, 40 percent in creative selling, and 5 percent in order processing. By contrast, some retail salespeople may be doing 70 percent in order processing, 15 percent in creative selling, and 15 percent in missionary selling. Marketers often use these three sales tasks as a method of classifying a particular sales job. The designation is based on the primary task performed by the salesperson.

order processing
The sales function of simply receiving and handling an order.

Order processing. **Order processing** involves the simple receipt and handling of an order. Customer needs are identified and pointed out to the consumer, and the order is processed. Route sales personnel for such consumer products as bread, milk, and soft drinks are examples of order processors. They check a store's stock, report the inventory level to the store manager, and complete the sale.

Most sales jobs have at least a minor order-processing function. It becomes the primary duty in cases where needs are readily identified and acknowledged by the customer. Consider Danny McNaughton's sales position in Belfast, Northern Ireland. McNaughton, while working for the Chicago-based Combined Insurance Company of America, sold 208 new personal accident income protection policies in a week, averaging one sale every 12 minutes of his working day, during one period of civil unrest.[6] Belfast residents readily acknowledged the need for McNaughton's product!

Creative selling. Sales representatives for most industrial goods and some consumer goods are involved in **creative selling,** a persuasive type of promotional presentation. Creative selling is used when the benefits of a product are not readily apparent and/or its purchase is being based on a careful analysis of alternatives. New product selling is a situation where the salesperson must be very creative if initial orders are to be secured.

Missionary selling. **Missionary selling** is an indirect form of selling where the representative markets the goodwill of a company and/or provides technical or operational assistance to the customer. For example, many technically based organizations, such as IBM and Xerox, provide systems specialists who consult with their customers. These people are problem solvers and sometimes work on problems not directly involving their employer's product.

The Sales Process

Years ago sales personnel memorized a sales talk provided by their employers. Such a **canned sales presentation** was intended to provide all the information that the customer needed to make a purchase decision. The entire sales process was viewed as a situation where the prospective customer was passive and ready to buy if the appropriate information could be identified and presented by the representative.

Contemporary selling recognizes that the interaction between buyers and sellers usually rules out canned presentations in all but the simplest of sales situations. Modern sales personnel typically follow a sequential pattern, but the actual presentation varies according to the circumstances. Seven steps can be identified in the sales process— prospecting and qualifying, the approach, the presentation, the demonstration, handling objections, the closing, and the follow-up.

Prospecting and qualifying. **Prospecting** is the task of identifying potential customers. They may come from many sources, such as previous customers, friends, business associates, neighbors, other sales personnel, and other employees in the firm. **Prospects**—the potential customers—must then be **qualified** with respect to their financial ability and their authority to buy. Those who lack the necessary financial resources or who are not in a position to make the purchase decision are given no further attention.

---

creative selling
A persuasive type of promotional presentation used when the benefits of a product are not readily apparent and/or its purchase is being based on a careful analysis of alternatives.

missionary selling
An indirect form of selling where the representative markets the goodwill of a company and/or provides technical or operational assistance to the customer.

canned sales presentation
A memorized sales talk intended to provide all the information that the customer needs to make a purchase decision.

prospecting
The task of identifying potential customers.

prospects
Potential customers.

qualifying
A function of the sales presentation that enables the salesperson to identify those prospects with the financial ability and authority to buy.

The approach. Salespeople should carefully prepare their approaches to potential customers. All available information about prospects should be collected and analyzed. Sales representatives should remember that the initial impression they give prospects often affects the prospects' future attitudes.

The presentation. The presentation is the stage where the salesperson transmits a promotional message. The usual method is to describe the products' or services' major features, highlight their advantages, and cite examples of consumer satisfaction with them.

The demonstration. Demonstrations allow the prospect to become involved in the presentation. They reinforce the message that the salesperson has been communicating to the prospective buyer.

Handling objections. Many salespeople fear objections from the prospect because they view them as a rebuke. Actually, such objections should be welcomed, because they allow the salesperson to present additional points and to answer questions the consumer has about the product or service.

The closing. The closing is the critical point in selling—the time when the seller actually asks the prospect to buy the product. Several effective closing techniques have been identified. The salesperson can ask the prospect directly or propose alternative purchases. Or the salesperson may do something that implies the sale has been completed such as walking toward a cash register. This forces the prospect to say no if he or she does not want to complete the sale.

The follow-up. After-sale activities are very important in determining whether a new customer will buy again at a later date. After the prospect has agreed to buy, the salesperson should complete the order processing quickly and efficiently and reassure the customer about the purchase decision. Later, the representative should check with the customer to see that the product or service is satisfactory.

Sales Management

Consider a management problem faced by Prudential Insurance. It has a field sales force of more than 20,000 representatives. The sheer size of this sales force triggers numerous questions about organization, personnel selection, training, motivation, supervision, and evaluation. But all sales forces, regardless of size, face similar problems, which must be solved if the sales force is to be truly effective and achieve the firm's promotional strategy objectives.

A company's sales function is supervised by multiple layers of sales managers. People are usually advanced to such positions from the field sales force. The sales management organizational structure follows a format along the lines shown in Figure 12–2.

FIGURE 12–2
Typical sales management organization for a large company.

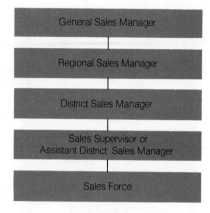

The general sales manager usually has national and sometimes international responsibilities. The rest of the market is then broken down into one or more levels such as regions and districts (the terminology varying from company to company). Some organizational structures break the market down into product or customer classifications. Figure 12–2 uses the title sales supervisor or assistant district sales manager to indicate the final level of management responsibility. Positions of this nature are often held by senior sales personnel, who are responsible for **key accounts** (major customers) and who assume some managerial duties such as sales training.

Sales managers are required to perform various managerial tasks (see Figure 12–3). They must, for example, analyze the organization's

key accounts
Major customers of a company.

FIGURE 12–3
The sales management tasks.

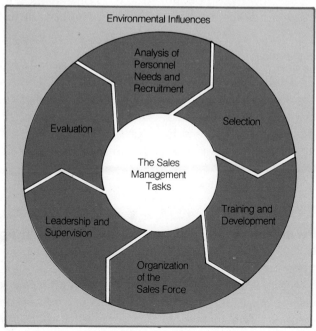

sales personnel needs and recruit the appropriate number of candidates, who are then screened for eventual selection. Sales managers are closely involved in the training and development of sales personnel and in the organizational structure. Leadership and supervision are a natural part of the sales management role. Finally, sales managers must be involved in the evaluation of their sales forces and in making decisions on salaries, promotions, and dismissals. All sales management tasks are subject to the environmental influences that exist in competitive business surroundings.

Sales Promotion

sales promotion
The forms of promotion other than advertising and personal selling that increase sales through one-time selling efforts; used to supplement other promotional strategies.

Sales promotion consists of the forms of promotion other than advertising and personal selling that increase sales through one-time selling efforts. Sales promotion techniques are used to enhance and supplement the firm's sales or advertising efforts. They are supporting aspects of a firm's promotional strategy.

Point-of-purchase Advertising

point-of-purchase advertising (POP)
A type of sales promotion that displays and demonstrates an item at a time and place close to where the actual purchase decision is made.

Point-of-purchase advertising (POP) includes displays and demonstrations promoting an item at a time and place near the location of the actual purchase decision, such as in a retail store. POP can be very effective in continuing a theme developed in some other aspect of the firm's promotional strategy. For example, the L'eggs displays in supermarkets revolutionized the pantyhose industry.

Specialty Advertising

specialty advertising
A type of sales promotion that consists of giving away items of minimal value that are imprinted with the donor's company name (for example, pens, calendars, ashtrays).

Specialty advertising is the giving away of items such as pens, calendars, and ashtrays—currently valued at less than $4—that are imprinted with the donor's company name. Specialty advertising has been around for centuries. Artisans in the Middle Ages gave knights wooden pegs bearing the artisan's name to use in hanging up their armor[7].

Trade Shows

trade shows
A type of sales promotion that uses exhibitions designed to promote products or services to retailers, wholesalers, international buyers, and other resellers in the distribution channel.

Trade shows are often used to promote products or services to resellers in the distribution channel. Retailers and wholesalers attend trade conventions and shows where manufacturers exhibit their different lines. Such shows are very important in the toy, furniture, and fashion industries. They have also been used to promote the products of one nation to buyers from another. Eastern European countries have done this very effectively in recent years.

Samples, Coupons, Premiums, and Trading Stamps

Samples are free gifts of a product. They are an attempt to gain public acceptance of the product that will result in future sales. Samples are particularly useful in promoting new products. **Coupons** are advertising inserts or package inclusions that are redeemable by the customer for cash. Offering what amounts to a small price discount, they can be helpful in getting a consumer to try a new or different product. **Premiums** are small gifts to the consumer for buying a product. They, too, are helpful in introducing a new product or getting consumers to try a different brand. **Trading stamps** are similar to premiums in that they are redeemable for additional merchandise. Historically, they have been used to build loyalty to a certain retailer or supplier.

Promotional Contests

Promotional contests offering cash or merchandise as prizes are also considered sales promotion techniques. Usually designed by specialists in this field, they are useful in getting consumers to consider new products.

Selecting a Promotional Strategy

The selection of a promotional strategy depends on a number of variables. The basic decision is whether the organization should emphasize advertising or personal selling in the strategy. Sales promotion techniques are nearly always used in a supporting role to either personal selling or advertising.

Marketers can use either a pushing or a pulling promotional strategy to achieve their goals. A **pushing strategy** is a sales-oriented approach. The product, product line, or service is marketed to the middlemen (wholesalers and retailers) in the marketing channels. Sales personnel explain to them why they should carry this particular item or service. Middlemen are usually offered special discounts, promotional materials, and **cooperative advertising** allowances. In the last case, the manufacturer shares the cost of local advertising of the product or line. All these strategies are designed to motivate the middlemen to push the product or service to their customers.

A **pulling strategy** attempts to generate consumer demand for the product, product line, or service, primarily through advertising and sales promotion appeals. Most advertising is aimed at the ultimate consumer, who then asks the retailer for the product or service; the retailer in turn requests the item or service from the supplier. The marketer hopes that strong consumer demand will literally pull the product or service through the marketing channel by forcing middlemen to carry it.

---

samples
A type of sales promotion that uses distribution of free product gifts to gain public acceptance and future sales of a new product.

coupons
A type of sales promotion that uses advertising inserts or package inclusions that are redeemable for cash and offer a small price discount.

premiums
A type of sales promotion that offers small gifts to the consumer in return for buying a product.

trading stamps
A type of sales promotion that offers stamps that are redeemable for additional merchandise.

promotional contests
Sales promotion activities that offer cash or merchandise as prizes and are useful in getting consumers to consider new products.

pushing strategy
A sales-oriented promotional strategy designed to motivate middlemen to push the product to their customers.

cooperative advertising
A promotional strategy in which the manufacturer shares the cost of local advertising of the product or line with the middleman.

pulling strategy
A promotional strategy utilizing advertising and sales promotion appeals to generate consumer demand for a product or product line.

Controversial Issue

Should Advertising Directed at Children Be Banned?

When you are finished reading this chapter, switch on your television to a commercial channel showing a children's program. Within a few minutes, a series of commercials will be broadcast. You'll see advertisements for highly sugared breakfast cereals, sugar-filled candy, and sweetened fruit drinks. After a while you may find these products hard to resist.

Now put yourself in the position of an eight-year-old child who watches up to six hours of television a day. After viewing more than 20,000 TV commercials a year, half of which advertise sugar-filled food products, you pressure your parents to buy your television favorites. The all-too-common result, in the opinion of Action for Children's Television (ACT), is an excessive number of dental cavities, obesity, and poor nutrition.

Action for Children's Television, a nonprofit consumer organization working to improve broadcasting practices related to children, has taken the position that commercial advertisements on children's television are often harmful. ACT contends that many young children do not understand that TV advertising has a selling purpose. Unable to apply adult skepticism to advertising claims, children perceive commercials as truthful and begin to pressure their parents to buy their TV favorites. Peggy Charren, a director of ACT, advocates a total ban on commercials directed at children twelve years old or under. "Before that age," says Charren, "all television advertising will inevitably deceive."

Industry spokespeople claim that they are not trying to manipulate children unfairly. Rather, they believe that children are curious about everything but naturally skeptical. Moreover, it is the industry's view that parents—not the government—should assume

Most marketing situations require the use of both strategies, although the emphasis can vary. Consumer products are often heavily dependent on a pulling strategy, while most industrial products are sold through a pushing strategy.

Summary

Most organizations use some type of promotional strategy to reach their goals. Promotional strategy has four specific objectives or goals—providing information, increasing sales, positioning the product, and stabilizing sales.

responsibility for their children's television viewing habits. More regulation, says the industry, is not necessarily better.

Industry spokespeople also dispute the negative effects of sugared breakfast cereals. Pointing to the high nutritional content, low calories, and ease of preparation of most breakfast cereals, Dr. Eugene B. Hayden, president of the Cereal Institute, feels that banning or restricting television advertising of cereals could have a "profound negative impact on children's breakfasts."

The conflict came to a head on February 28, 1978, when, in response to a petition by Action for Children's Television and the Center for Science in the Public Interest, the Federal Trade Commission (FTC) voted to investigate the propriety of children's TV advertising—especially advertisements for highly sugared foods.

The FTC proceedings—nicknamed "kidvid"—considered proposals for nutritional and health messages funded by advertisers to balance the advertising of sugared products, the disclosure of health and nutritional information in the body of ads for highly sugared products, limiting certain advertising techniques directed at children, limiting the number and frequency of advertisements directed at young children, curtailing advertisements of highly sugared products directed at all children, and more.

After three years of hearings and sometimes bitter debates, the staff of the Federal Trade Commission acknowledged that advertisements directed at children are "a legitimate cause of public concern" but that no workable solutions were possible. The staff recommended that the FTC drop any further investigation into the matter. "What the staff was saying," said one agency official, "is, 'Yes, there's a problem here, but we're not sure we can do much about it!' "

There are three distinct elements of promotional strategy—advertising, personal selling, and sales promotion. Advertising is a nonpersonal sales presentation usually directed to a large number of potential customers. The two basic types of advertising are product and institutional. Advertising strategy depends on the product's stage in the life cycle.

Personal selling is a promotional presentation made on a person-to-person basis with a potential buyer. Salespeople's tasks usually are order processing, creative selling, and missionary selling. There are seven steps in the sales process—prospecting and qualifying, the approach, the presentation, the demonstration, handling objections, the closing, and the follow-up.

Sales promotion consists of the one-time supporting aspects of a firm's promotional strategy. It includes point-of-purchase (POP) advertising, specialty advertising, trade shows, samples, premiums, trading stamps, and promotional contests. The selection of a promotional strategy is dependent on several variables. Marketers use either pushing or pulling strategies (or both) to achieve their goals.

Key Terms

promotional strategy	prospects
positioning	qualifying
advertising	key accounts
product advertising	sales promotion
institutional advertising	point-of-purchase advertising (POP)
informative advertising	specialty advertising
persuasive advertising	trade shows
comparative advertising	samples
reminder-oriented advertising	coupons
personal selling	premiums
order processing	trading stamps
creative selling	promotional contests
missionary selling	pushing strategy
canned sales presentation	cooperative advertising
prospecting	pulling strategy

Review Questions

1. Explain each of the terms listed above.

2. Outline the objectives of promotional strategy.

3. As a class project try to find examples of advertisements used by each of the leading national advertisers listed in Table 12–1.

4. Relate the various types of advertising that are used in modern business to the product life cycle.

5. What is the primary sales task involved in the following occupations?
   a. typewriter salesperson selling to local business firms
   b. counter person at Burger Chef
   c. representative for an outdoor advertising firm
   d. industrial salesperson representing Dow Chemical

6. Describe the steps in the selling process.

7. Outline the six tasks of sales management.

8. What type of sales promotion technique (if any) would you use in the following businesses?
   a. independent insurance agency
   b. Chevrolet dealership
   c. cocktail lounge
   d. grocery wholesaling

9. Differentiate between pushing and pulling promotional strategies.

10. Would you emphasize personal selling or advertising to promote the following products?
    a. drill presses
    b. imported transistor radios
    c. specialty steel products sold to manufacturers
    d. funeral services

Discussion Questions and Exercises

1. Evaluate the pros and cons of the controversial issue that appears in this chapter.

2. Trading stamps hit their peak in 1969. Some 65 percent of the nation's supermarkets offered. them. Volume exceeded $800 million annually. Today's sales volume is less than half the 1969 high. And only 20 percent of the supermarkets offer stamps. But the head of Sperry & Hutchinson's S&H Green Stamps unit believes a $1 billion dollar industry is possible by 1990–1995. Stamp companies are seeking out new markets and adopting other innovative marketing strategies. S&H, for example, has placed its stamps in Texas Pizza Huts. The company has issued a discount catalogue. Sperry & Hutchinson has also aggressively promoted its stamps to truck stops, the second largest stamp customer. One late-night radio commercial says: "See if those little green rascals don't make gettin' home a little better."[8] What is your assessment of the future use of trading stamps as a promotional tool?

3. Determining the correct level of promotional expenditures is a traditional challenge for marketers. August Busch, head of brewer Anheuser-Busch, puts it this way: "We know advertising works, but at what level those dollars become nonproductive, nobody really knows."[9] Prepare a brief research report on this topic and report to the class what you learned.

4. Divide the class into three groups. Then set up a role-playing exercise in which each student in Group A sells a product to someone in Group B. Group C is responsible for providing a critique of each of the sales interviews. Then rotate the roles among the three groups. Continue this process for three rounds, so everyone will have a chance to play each role.

5. After the U.S. Supreme Court ruled that attorneys could advertise, many law firms began to run newspaper advertisements. Only a few attorneys advertised on television. Michelle Hinson of Houston was one. Her advertisement ran during the all-night movie and a "Divorce Court" 'program. The ads began: "Divorce used to be an ugly word. Now it is often a reality. If divorce has become a reality for you and you need an attorney, call Michelle Hinson."[10] What is your opinion on the issue of advertisements by attorneys and other professionals? One way to discuss this question is to set up a class debate on the various viewpoints.

Case 12–1: The Legend of Two Fingers

"Two Fingers," the name of a legendary tequila maker, is also the name of Hiram Walker's entry into the premium tequila market. The product was test-marketed in Arizona and Colorado before being introduced elsewhere with the biggest communications budget in its marketplace.

"Two Fingers really is a new, exciting direction for us," explained Roy W. Stevens, president of Hiram Walker Incorporated. "Tequila is the fastest growing category of distilled spirits. Although there are many tequila brands, our research told us that many consumers haven't established their brand preference. We know there's plenty of opportunity in tequila for a quality brand that's contemporary and distinctive. A brand that can stand out in a crowded field."

The entire promotional effort is based on the legend of the main character, Two Fingers, a man of mystery whose real name was never known, but somehow lost two fingers of his right hand, which gave him his nickname. The story goes that he successfully sold his own tequila throughout the Southwest in the mid 1930s, traveling from town to town with his girl friend, Honey, in an old pickup truck.

Two Fingers package design is also unique in the tequila field. The bottle is deep black, slimly styled, with both white and gold lettering. A synopsis of the Two Fingers legend is on the back.

Questions

1. Briefly research the market for distilled spirits. What is the current market position of Hiram Walker's Two Fingers tequila? What other new products might the company consider?

2. What is your opinion of Hiram Walker's decision to promote the new product on the basis of a legendary figure? Can you identify other products that use a similar approach?

3. Develop an integrated promotional campaign for Two Fingers tequila.

Case 12-2: Mead Data Central

Jerome S. Rubin used his desk-top terminal to update himself on everything that had been written about the client in recent months. Then the president of Mead Data Central (MDC)—part of the Mead Corp., the papermaker—set off to call on his customer's counterpart.

MDC is in the on-line data-base service industry that provides information to clients via desk-top terminals similar to the one on Rubin's desk. The company provides ready access to information about potential customers, competitors, and buyers. The company offers an integrated service that uses Mead terminals and software and is sold by Mead sales personnel.

MDC first introduced Lexis in 1973. This system was sold to lawyers and accountants and provided access to the complete text of various laws, court decisions, and Internal Revenue Service and Securities & Exchange Commission rulings. Lexis now commands about 90 percent of the market.

Nexis was introduced in 1980. It is a new computerized research service that carries information from the news services, various news magazines, dozens of trade publications, the *Washington Post,* and other sources. This type of information is of extreme value to marketers and, in particular, field sales personnel. But while Lexis, which dominates the field, has little competition, Nexis faces considerable competition from the alternative offerings of the *New York Times* Information Bank and Dow Jones & Co.'s news retrieval service.

Direct mail was used extensively in the promotional strategy for Lexis, where the potential customers were readily identifiable. But Rubin's strategy for Nexis relies on personal selling because of the diversity of the new marketplace. Rubin nearly doubled the size of his sales force in 1980 and 1981. MDC's sales personnel concentrate on selling either Lexis or Nexis to maximize their customer and product knowledge.

Questions

1. Do you agree with Rubin's decision to emphasize personal selling in his promotional strategy for Nexis?

2. What type of objection or difficulty would you expect to encounter in selling a service like Nexis?

3. Assume you are a salesperson for MDC. What selling points would you make to a potential Nexis buyer?

13

Prices and Pricing Strategy

Learning Goals

1. To explain the societal and business importance of pricing

2. To identify the pricing objectives of different types of businesses

3. To describe how inflation is the most critical topic in pricing today

4. To describe how prices are actually determined by marketers

5. To analyze new product pricing, price lining, price-quality relationships, and psychological pricing

6. To explain the meaning of each of the key terms introduced in this chapter

Profile: Calvin Klein
Higher Pricing for Designer Labels

When Calvin Klein Ltd. opened its doors in 1968 with a total capitalization of $10,000, it was just another of the thousands of small, ready-to-wear apparel firms that dotted New York's Seventh Avenue. In an industry known for low profits and high risk, Klein's chances for making it big were not very good.

The rest is history. Calvin Klein and his business partner Barry Schwartz transformed Klein's extraordinary ability to create what American women love to wear into a $30 million a year business. Each partner earns $4 million annually from the ready-to-wear collection alone—and that's only part of the story. They also earn another $4.5 million each from their licensing operations—the selling of the Calvin Klein name and design to a manufacturer who produces and sells an item of merchandise on a mass scale—for example, Puritan Fashions manufactures Calvin Klein jeans.

How Klein and Schwartz accomplished this phenomenal success story has a lot to do with extraordinary fashion talent and business savvy and just as much with knowing how to capitalize on their status as a designer label in an industry where today it's the designer's name that counts.

Where major department stores like Saks Fifth Avenue used to sew their own status labels into their ready-to-wear garments, they now feature designer names like Calvin Klein, Halston, and Bill Blass. Consumers are willing to spend more for these labels than they are for no-name fashions—up to $300 for a Calvin Klein dress and as much as $1,000 for an evening gown.

In order to maintain the exclusive aura of the Calvin Klein name, Schwartz limits the retail outlets he sells to (in 1973, the Calvin Klein label appeared in 1,700 stores; today it appears in only 250) and the volume of total sales. Keeping a $300 million sales ceiling on the ready-to-wear collection means that Calvin Klein garments will not be seen on every woman—a situation that pleases both partners. Says Schwartz, "The Calvin Klein image is the most important thing we have."

With 250,000 pairs of jeans sold in a single week, Calvin Klein jeans, a product of one of Klein's licensing operations, are hardly rare, but they are still a status label. The Calvin Klein image is carefully cultivated on Klein's menswear, cosmetics, patterns, scarves, belts, sheets, and pillowcases as well.

Klein and Schwartz can attribute part of their success to their hard line with retailers. If a store causes problems, they stop selling to it—even if it is a prestigious account. "When we have the slightest trouble—returns, complaints, other aggravations—I say, 'Don't sell to them,'" says Schwartz. "To us, the ultimate consumer is more important than the retailer."

How much does it cost?

A question heard throughout the world.

Combien est-ce? In France.

Wieviel kostet es? In Germany.

Quanto costa? In Italy.

¿Cuánto vale? In Spain.

Skol'ko eto stoit? In Russia.

Automobile companies used to make their biggest profits from their higher-priced, full-sized models. In fact, some have accused Detroit of resisting the switch to smaller cars because of this price differential. But times have changed. The fast-selling small cars now command big prices. A 1981 Ford Escort was priced 24.6 percent higher than the Pinto it replaced. GM's 1981 X-cars sold for 54 percent more than the same model when it was first introduced two years earlier. Chrysler's 1981 K-car has a base price 23.5 percent higher than the Volare it replaced. Meanwhile, some of 1981's big, less fuel-efficient models actually sold for less than they did in 1980.[1]

The pricing strategy selected by an organization's management can have a significant impact on profits. Airlines used various discount schemes to build passenger traffic. But lower prices combined with high fuel costs cut into profit margins. So the industry began to scale back discount plans and raise prices.[2] While situations may vary, it is important that businesspeople have a clear understanding of the importance and implications of various pricing strategies.

The Meaning and Importance of Price

exchange value
The value of any item—consumer product, industrial product, or service—in the marketplace.

price
The exchange value of a product or service in the marketplace.

The value of any item—consumer product, industrial product, or service—is its **exchange value** in the marketplace. An item is worth only what someone else is willing to pay for it. In a primitive society the exchange value may be determined by trading a good for some other commodity. A horse may be worth ten coins; 12 apples may be worth two loaves of bread. More advanced societies use money as the medium of exchange. But in either case, a product's or service's **price** is its exchange value.

All goods and services offer some utility, or want-satisfying power. Individual preferences determine how much utility a consumer will associate with a particular good or service. One person may value leisure-time pursuits, while another assigns a higher priority to acquiring real assets (property, automobiles, and household furnishings).

Consumers face an allocation problem. They have a limited amount of money and a variety of possible uses for it. The price system helps them make allocation decisions. A person may prefer a new color television to a vacation; if the price of the television set rises, that person may reconsider and allocate funds to the vacation trip instead.

Prices help direct the overall economic system. A firm uses various factors of production (such as natural resources, labor, and capital) based on their relative prices. High wage rates may cause a firm to install laborsaving machinery. Similarly, high interest rates may lead management to decide against a new capital expenditure. Prices and volume sold determine the revenue received by the firm and influence its profits.

Everyone recognizes the importance of prices in daily living. Early philosophers struggled with the issue of how to define a just price. Today's consumers may want lower retail prices, yet many complain of the lack of retail services. All such services—for example, gift wrapping, delivery, and credit—have costs associated with them, and these costs must be covered by higher prices. The unanswered question is: how do we balance prices and costs?

Pricing Objectives

Management attempts to accomplish certain objectives through its pricing decisions. Research has shown that multiple pricing objectives are common among many firms. Some companies try to maximize their profits by pricing a new technological innovation very high. Others use low prices to attract new business.

Midway Airlines has used a Penny Day promotion to attract travelers to the new carrier. On these occasions, Midway priced its flights at only 1 percent of its regular fares, which are already less than other carriers. A Detroit-to-Chicago ticket, for example, went for a mere 32 cents.[3] By contrast, no one can accuse Rolls Royce of deep discounts. The firm recently introduced its first new model in 15 years. The Silver Spirit—complete with a digital thermometer to tell the driver what the temperature will be when he or she steps out of the car—is priced at $150,000. Of course, the Silver Spirit may be designed to appeal to those who cannot afford the top-of-the-line Rolls, the Camargue, priced at $220,000 per car.[4]

There are three basic categories of pricing objectives—profitability objectives; volume objectives; and social and ethical considerations, status quo objectives, and image goals.

Even when they shop for groceries, most consumers face an allocation problem and have to decide carefully what they can afford to buy each week.

Profitability Objectives

Most firms have some type of profitability objective for their pricing strategy. Management knows that

Profit = Revenue − Expenses

and that revenue is a result of the selling price times the quantity sold:

Total Revenue = Price × Quantity Sold.

Some firms try to maximize profits by increasing their prices to the point where a disproportionate decrease appears in the number of units sold. A 10 percent price hike that results in only an 8 percent volume decline increases profitability. But a 5 percent price rise that reduces the number of units sold by 6 percent is unprofitable.

profit maximization
A pricing strategy whereby management sets increasing levels of profitability as its objective.

target return goals
A pricing strategy whereby the desired profitability is stated in terms of particular goals such as a 10 percent return on either sales or investment.

sales maximization concept
A concept under which management sets an acceptable minimum level of profitability and then tries to maximize sales.

market share
The percentage of a market controlled by a certain company, product, or service.

   Profit maximization is the basis of much of economic theory. However, it is often difficult to apply in practice, and many firms have turned to a simpler profitability objective—**target return goals.** For example, a firm might specify the goal of a 9 percent return on sales or a 20 percent return on investment. Most target return pricing goals state the desired profitability in terms of a return on either sales or investment.

Volume Objectives

Another description of pricing behavior is the **sales maximization concept,** under which management sets an acceptable minimum level of profitability and then tries to maximize sales. Sales expansion is viewed as being more important than short-run profits to the firm's long-term competitive position.

   A second volume objective is **market share**—the percentage of a market controlled by a certain company, product, or service. One firm may seek to achieve a 25 percent market share in a certain industry. Another may want to maintain or expand its market share for particular products or product lines. Several brewers added seven-ounce bottles of beer to their product line in order to reach the market of female beer drinkers, who presumably want less beer per bottle than men. Anheuser-Busch, Schmidt's, and Miller Brewing joined the Latrobe Brewing Company of Pennsylvania, which has marketed seven-ounce bottles of its Rolling Rock beer since 1939. Anheuser-Busch has even advertised its Michelob version, Mich VII, in *Woman's Day* magazine.

   Market share objectives have become popular for several reasons. Perhaps one of the most important is the ease with which market share statistics can be used as a yardstick for measuring managerial and corporate performance. Another is that increased sales may lead to lower production costs and higher profits. On a per unit basis, it is cheaper to produce 10,000 pens than it is to manufacture just a few dozen.

Other Objectives

The objectives not related to profitability or sales volume—social and ethical considerations, status quo objectives, and image goals—are often used in the pricing decisions of some firms. Social and ethical considerations play an important role in some pricing situations. For example, the prices of some products and services are based on the intended consumers' ability to pay them. Medical insurance premiums, union dues, and retirement fund contributions are often related to the income of the payers. It seems reasonable to believe that social and ethical considerations will be even more important in future pricing strategies.

Many firms have **status quo pricing objectives**; that is, they are inclined to follow the leader. These companies seek stable prices that will allow them to put their competitive efforts into other areas, such as product design or promotion.

Image goals are often used in pricing strategy. The price structures of major department stores, for example, are set to reflect the high quality of the merchandise. Discount houses, however, may seek an image of good value at low prices. Thus, a firm's pricing strategy may be an integral part of the overall image it wishes to convey.

status quo pricing objectives
Objectives that reflect management's efforts to seek stable prices, enabling the company to channel competitive efforts into other areas such as product design or promotion.

image goals
Goals that are coordinated with pricing strategies to reflect an integrated company image.

Inflation's impact on pricing affects all types of marketing efforts.

Prices and Inflation

Chapter 2 noted that *inflation* can be defined in terms of either rising prices or the decreased purchasing power of a nation's currency. Inflation is certainly the most critical topic in pricing today. Many price increases are beyond the control of marketers such as those that are cost driven.

Americans are now conditioned to inflation; we expect prices to be higher in the future (see Focus 13–1). This change in consumer attitudes has been the most marked change with which pricing strategists have had to deal. But marketers must do more than just pass cost increases on in terms of higher prices. Marketers must develop innovative pricing strategies that will give the consumer maximum benefit per dollar spent under existing conditions. They must also set prices that provide a fair and reasonable return to the firm. This is often a difficult task, because inflation-conscious consumers are now resisting further price hikes to an extent not conceived of even a few years ago. Inflations' impact on pricing strategy is sure to remain one of marketing's most pressing problems in the years ahead.

THE WALL STREET JOURNAL

ENGLEMAN

"While you're sitting down, let me give you the price."

Americans are now conditioned to inflation.
Cartoon Features Syndicate

FOCUS 13–1
The Cost of Feeding GIs—1776 to the Present

Recently inflation has boosted food prices to unparalleled highs. Not long ago the U.S. Department of Agriculture estimates that a "liberal cost" diet for a 20- to 54-year-old man was about $4.54 per day. The U.S. Department of Defense spends $3.75 per day on food for each soldier.[5]

This is in remarkable contrast to the Continental Army of 1776, which allowed 11 cents per day for enlisted personnel and 33 cents for officers. George Washington was allowed the enormous sum of $5.28 daily. The American Medical Association reports that the 1776 ration included more meat than our modern diets do, but that it was deficient in vitamins A and C.[6]

Organization of the Pricing Activity

While pricing is usually regarded as a function of marketing, it also requires considerable inputs from other areas in the company. Accounting and financial managers have always played a major role in the pricing task by providing the sales and cost data necessary for good decision making. Production and industrial engineering personnel play similarly important roles. The data-processing department is usually in charge of the firm's computer-based marketing information system, which provides up-to-date information needed in pricing.

It is essential for managers at all levels to realize the importance of pricing and the contribution that can be made to correct pricing by various areas in the organization. Inflation has caused modifications in the organization of many companies. Some firms have moved the responsibility for pricing to higher levels in the organization. Ducommun, Inc., a Los Angeles metal and electronics distributor, has created a pricing "czar" within one division to review all price changes.[7] But the primary change has been that marketing executives now treat pricing as an ongoing responsibility rather than a one-time decision for the period under consideration. In this sense, inflation has probably improved the efficiency of the overall marketing effort.

Price Determination

Economic theory, assuming a profit maximization objective, says that market price will be set at the point where the amount of a product desired at a given price is equal to the amount that suppliers will provide at that price—where the amount demanded and the amount supplied are in equilibrium. In other words, there is a schedule of amounts that will be demanded at different price levels—the **demand curve.** At $3 per pound, 5,000 pounds of an industrial chemical might be sold. A price increase to $4 per pound might reduce sales to 3,200 pounds, and a $5 per pound price might result in sales of only 2,000 pounds, as some would-be customers decide to accept less expensive substitutes or to wait for the price to be reduced (see Focus 13–2). Correspondingly, there is a schedule that shows the amounts that will be offered in the market at certain prices—the **supply curve.** The intersection of these two curves is the **equilibrium price** that will exist in the marketplace for a particular good or service (see Figure 13–1).

demand curve
A schedule of amounts of a good or service that will be demanded at different price levels.

supply curve
A schedule of amounts of a good or service that will be offered in the market at certain prices.

equilibrium price
The price that exists in the marketplace for a particular good or service, determined by the intersection of the supply and demand curves. This is the point where the amount of a product desired at a given price is equal to the amount that suppliers will provide at that price.

FOCUS 13–2
British Beer Drinkers Prove Applicability of Economic Theory to Real-world Pricing Situations

A British stockbrokers' analysis of the brewing industry concluded that the United Kingdom's soaring double-digit inflation had even impacted beer consumption. A 20 percent price hike during a recent year caused beer sales to fall close to 5 percent.[8]

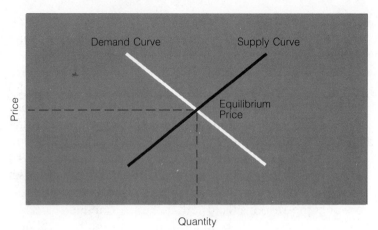

FIGURE 13–1
Demand and supply curves.

Practical Price Setting

Although this economic analysis is correct in regard to the overall market for a product, managers face the problem of setting the price of individual brands based on limited information. Anticipating the amount of a product that will be bought at a certain price is difficult, so business has tended to adopt cost-based pricing formulas. While these are simpler and easier to use, executives have to be flexible in applying them to each situation. Marketers begin the process of cost-based pricing by totaling all costs associated with offering an item in the market—including production, transportation, distribution, and marketing expenses. Then they add an amount for profit and expenses not previously considered—the **markup.** The total of this amount and the cost of the item determines the selling price. The **markup percentage,** then, is the markup divided by the price of the item:

markup
The amount added to cost for profit and expenses not previously considered. The total determines the selling price.

markup percentage
The markup divided by the price of the item.

$$\text{Markup Percentage} = \frac{\text{Amount Added to Cost (Markup)}}{\text{Price}}$$

If a game in a toy store is priced at $3, and its invoice cost (the amount the store has paid for it) is $2, then the markup percentage is 33⅓:

$$\text{Markup Percentage} = \frac{\$1}{\$3} = 33⅓$$

The firm's markup should be related to its **stock turnover**—the number of times the average inventory is sold annually (using sales figures if the inventory is recorded at retail value and cost of goods sold if the inventory is recorded at cost):

stock turnover
The number of times the average inventory is sold annually.

$$\text{Stock Turnover} = \frac{\text{Sales or Cost of Goods Sold}}{\text{Average Inventory}}$$

Markups should be lower for products with stock turnover figures above the industry average and higher for items with turnover figures below the industry average.

Marketers must be flexible, willing to adjust their markups and prices according to the demand for their products. Both costs and market demand must be considered in arriving at the price to be charged the customer.

Breakeven Analysis—An Aid to Better Pricing Decisions

Marketers often use **breakeven analysis** as a method of determining the minimum sales volume needed at a certain price level to cover all costs. It involves a consideration of various costs and total revenue. Total cost (TC) is composed of total variable costs (TVC) and total fixed costs (TFC). **Variable costs** are those that change with the level of production (such as labor and raw material costs), while **fixed costs** are those that remain stable regardless of the production level achieved (such as the firm's insurance costs). Total revenue is determined by multiplying price and the number of units sold.

Figure 13–2 shows the calculation of the **breakeven point**—the level of sales that will cover all of the company's costs (both fixed and variable). Sales beyond the breakeven point will generate profit.

breakeven analysis
A method of determining the minimum sales volume needed to cover all costs at a certain price level. A breakeven analysis considers various costs and total revenue.

variable costs
Costs that change with the level of production such as labor and raw materials.

fixed costs
Costs that remain stable regardless of the production level achieved.

breakeven point
The level of sales that will cover all the company's costs (both fixed and variable).

FIGURE 13–2
Breakeven analysis.

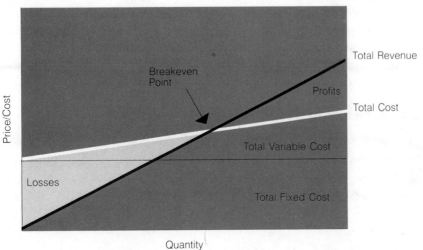

Breakeven points can also be found by using a simple formula:

$$\text{Breakeven Point (in Units)} = \frac{\text{Total Fixed Costs}}{\text{Per Unit Contribution to Fixed Costs}}$$

A product selling for $20 with a variable cost of $14 per item, produces a $6 per unit contribution to fixed costs. If total fixed costs are $42,000, then the firm must sell 7,000 units to break even:

$$\text{Breakeven Point (in Units)} = \frac{\$42,000}{\$6} = 7,000 \text{ Units}.$$

Marketers can compare the results of using various prices with breakeven analysis. Different prices produce different breakeven points, which can then be compared with what the firm's marketing research shows is the most likely sales volume. This comparison will give an indication of a realistic market price.

New Product Pricing

Pampers, the paper diapers, failed in its original market test because of pricing. Later it became Procter & Gamble's second best-selling brand (the detergent Tide is first). When it was first introduced, Pampers sold for more than the per use cost of buying a cloth diaper and washing it. When Pampers bombed in the marketplace, Procter & Gamble went to work redesigning production equipment and was able to reduce production costs to the point where per unit retail price could be slashed 40 percent. Since then, the product has become a household word in families with infants.[9]

Procter & Gamble's experience with Pampers shows how difficult it is to select a price for a new product line. Because pricing decisions are risky, it is usually best to field-test alternative prices with sample groups of consumers. Once the product is actually launched, it is difficult to modify its price during the introductory period.

New product pricing can be based on either of two strategies: the skimming price policy or the penetration price policy.

The Skimming Price Policy

skimming price policy
The strategy of setting the price of a new product relatively high compared to similar goods and then gradually lowering it.

The **skimming price policy** involves setting the price of the new product relatively high compared to similar goods and then gradually lowering it. This strategy is used where the market is segmented on a price basis—that is, where some people may buy the product if it is priced at, say, $10; a larger group may buy it at $7.50; and a still larger group may buy it at $6. Color televisions and electronic calculators are examples of the effective use of the skimming policy. Du Pont, which offers many specialty items, traditionally has followed this pattern. Du Pont's polyester fiber, Dacron, was sold at $2.25 a pound in 1953. It now goes for about 60¢ a pound. Similarly, the price of Qiana, a synthetic silklike fiber, fell 35 percent in five years.

A skimming price policy allows the firm to recover its costs rapidly by maximizing the revenue it receives. But the policy's disadvantage is that early profits tend to attract competition, and this puts eventual pressure on prices. Today most ballpoint pens sell for less than $1, but when the product was first introduced after World War II, it sold for about $20.

The Penetration Price Policy

The second strategy, the **penetration price policy,** involves pricing the new product relatively low compared to similar goods in the hope that it will secure wide market acceptance that will allow the company to raise its price. Soaps and toothpastes are often introduced this way. Penetration pricing discourages competition because of its low profits. It can also compete effectively against the skimming price policy. Dow Chemical, which sells many commodity products, tends to be a penetration pricer. Dow attempts to build its market share with lower prices and then stay in a particular market a long time.

penetration price policy
The strategy of pricing a new product relatively low compared to similar goods in the hope that it will secure wide market acceptance and allow the company to raise the price.

Price Lining

Price lining occurs when a seller decides to offer merchandise at a limited number of prices rather than price each item individually. For instance, a boutique might offer lines of women's sportswear priced at $90, $120, and $150. Price lining is a common marketing practice among retailers. The original five-and-ten-cent stores are an example of its early use.

price lining
The offering of merchandise at a limited number of prices instead of pricing each item individually.

As a pricing strategy, price lining prevents the confusion common to situations where all items are priced individually and manages the pricing function more easily. But marketers must clearly identify the market segments to which they are appealing. Three "high-price" lines might not be appropriate to a store located in an area of young couples.

A disadvantage of price lining is that it is sometimes difficult to alter the price ranges once they are set. This may be a crucial factor during a period of inflation, when the firm must either raise the price of the line or reduce its quality. Consumers may resist either of these alternatives. While price lining can be useful, its implementation must be considered carefully.

Controversial Issue

Should Supermarkets Be Required to Price Each Item or Is the Universal Product Code Enough?

Pick up almost any item on the supermarket shelf, and you will see an innocent-looking band of lines neatly tucked in the corner of the package. These lines make up the Universal Product Code (UPC) and have caused a furor among supermarket retailers, consumers, and organized labor.

An invention of the early 1970s, the UPC depends on high technology (a laser slit in the checkout counter "reads" the band of lines to identify the item, its size, and price and feeds tabulated amounts of goods sold into a central inventory computer) and big money (equipping each checkout lane with a scanner costs anywhere from $10,000 to $30,000), but the rewards are potentially enormous.

Giant Food, Inc., one of the nation's largest chains, saved nearly 1 percent of its volume each month in a typical store after the installation of UPC scanners. The bulk of the savings came from reduced cashier labor and the elimination of cashier mistakes in favor of the customer. For stores that normally operate on after-tax profits of a penny on the dollar, this saving has the potential to change the profit profile of the industry. By offering the grocers dramatic reductions in operating costs, the UPC promises to improve those intolerably low margins—at no cost to the consumer. And by giving grocers the first truly clear picture of what actually happens in their stores, scanning promises a product mix exactly tailored for maximum turnover and maximum return.

Despite these claims, consumer and labor groups wanted no part of the UPC when it was first introduced. Although the code's object was to end item pricing—the costly, hand marking of each separate package—the Consumer Federation of America viewed it as another example of big business trying to put something over

Price-quality Relationships

Numerous research studies have shown that the consumer's perception of product quality is related closely to the item's price. The higher the price of the product the better its perceived quality. One study asked 400 respondents what terms they associated with the word *expensive.* Two-thirds of the replies referred to high-quality terms such as *best* or *superior.*[10]

Most marketers believe that the price-quality relationship exists over a relatively wide range of prices, although extreme prices may be viewed as either too expensive or too cheap. Marketing managers

on the consumer. Without a price clearly printed on each item, the Federation contended, it would be just too easy to speed up price hikes. And the Retail Clerks International Union, AFL-CIO, feared massive layoffs of supermarket personnel.

The result in many states is legally mandated item pricing, which probably wipes out 20 percent of the savings expected from scanners. As more and more state legislatures jumped onto the item-pricing bandwagon, the industry feared the UPC would never survive and agreed to a self-imposed moratorium on the abandonment of individual price markings. With time, the moratorium gradually softened, and by 1981 retailers, like Giant Food, were once more committed to the elimination of item pricing.

Many consumers have reassessed their initial reactions to the UPC. They soon appreciated the price savings, speed, and efficiency that are built into the system, the itemized grocery tape that reads out each item and its cost, the inventory control that enables their market to keep their favorite items on the shelves, the system's potential to turn giant supermarkets into mom-and-pop stores by tailoring merchandise assortments to consumers' needs, and more.

The UPC will not please everyone; some consumers need to see a price on every item they buy—especially in times of high inflation. But advocates believe they can ultimately convince consumers of the system's benefits.

Whether the UPC succeeds in the long run depends on how efficiently stores maintain their shelf prices and on how much saving is ultimately passed on to the consumer. If consumer opinion is positive, one thing is certain—with only 3,000 retail stores across the nation using scanners, the UPC revolution is yet to come.

need to study and experiment with prices because the price-quality relationship can be of key importance to a firm's pricing strategy.

Psychological Pricing

Many marketers feel that certain prices are more appealing than others to buyers. Psychological pricing is used throughout the world by industry. The image pricing goals mentioned earlier are an example of psychological pricing.

Have you ever wondered why retailers use prices like $39.95, $19.98, or $9.99 instead of $40, $20, or $10? Years ago, before the

odd pricing
The practice of using uneven prices such as $1.11 or $3.22; used because retailers believe that psychologically odd prices are more attractive to consumers than even ones.

age of cash registers, this practice of **odd pricing** was employed to force clerks to make change, thereby serving as a cash control technique for retailers. It is now a common practice in retail pricing because many retailers believe that odd prices are more attractive than even ones to consumers. In fact, some stores have begun to use prices ending in 1, 2, 3, 4, 6, or 7 to avoid the look of ordinary prices like $5.95, $10.98, and $19.99. The new prices are more likely to be $1.11, $3.22, $4.53, $5.74, $3.86, or $9.97.

Many retailers believe that odd prices are more attractive to customers than even ones.

Summary

Prices can be viewed as the exchange value of goods and services in an economy. They are important because they help determine society's allocation of economic resources.

Pricing goals include profitablity objectives (profit maximization and target return goals); volume objectives (sales maximization and market share objectives); and a group of objectives not related to profitability or sales volume that includes social and ethical considerations, status quo objectives, and image goals.

Inflation, which is discussed in Chapter 2, can be defined in terms of either rising prices or the decreased purchasing power of a nation's currency. It is the most critical topic in pricing today. Marketing's challenge is to adopt pricing strategies that will be fair to both consumers and sellers.

The pricing activity in businesses has assumed new importance, with many departments contributing to pricing decisions. Price determination is based on the demand and supply curves. Where the two intersect is the equilibrium price. Businesses have also been using cost-based pricing, which involves determining the necessary markup on each product and adding it to the cost. The markup is related to the stock turnover and should be higher for low turnovers and lower for high turnovers.

Breakeven analysis is an aid in making pricing decisions. It involves total costs and total revenues. The breakeven point is determined by dividing total fixed costs by the per unit contribution to fixed costs. Anything beyond the breakeven point is profits.

New product pricing can be based on skimming price policy (setting the price relatively high compared to similar goods and then gradually lowering it) or penetration price policy (pricing the goods lower than similar goods and eventually raising the price after the product gains wide market acceptance).

Price lining refers to sellers offering merchandise at a limited number of prices. Its value lies in preventing confusion; its disadvantage is that the prices are difficult to alter once they are set.

Consumers tend to perceive a close relationship between product quality and price. The higher the price of a product the better its perceived quality. The price-quality relationship can be of key importance to pricing strategy.

Key Terms

exchange value	markup
price	markup percentage
profit maximization	stock turnover
target return goals	breakeven analysis
sales maximization concept	variable costs
market share	fixed costs
status quo pricing objectives	breakeven point
image goals	skimming price policy
demand curve	penetration price policy
supply curve	price lining
equilibrium price	odd pricing

Review Questions

1. Explain each of the terms listed above.

2. Why is pricing so important in contemporary society? Discuss this question from both business and societal viewpoints.

3. Outline the major pricing objectives sought by industry.

4. Comment on the statement: The firm's markup should be related to its sales turnover.

5. If a new automobile has a sticker price of $9,000, and the price to the dealer is $6,750, what is the dealer's markup percentage?

6. If a local music shop carries a record inventory of $15,000 and has annual sales of $120,000, what is its stock turnover?

7. Assume that a product selling for $10 has a variable cost of $6 per unit. If total fixed costs for this product are $38,000, how many units will the firm have to sell to break even?

8. Contrast the skimming and penetration viewpoints toward new product pricing. Can you make any generalization about the types of products or market situations most suitable to each strategy?

9. Comment on the statement: The consumer's perception of quality is closely related to the item's price.

10. What is meant by price lining?

Discussion Questions and Exercises

---

1. Evaluate the pros and cons of the controversial issue that appears in this chapter.

2. Many marketers have used rebates, a refund of part of the purchase price, to attract buyers. For instance, Harry I. Siegel Co.— maker of the H. I. S. label—has offered $20 rebates on men's suits.[11] Discuss the use of rebates in a firm's pricing strategy.

3. Interview executives at several local firms (preferably firms that operate in different industries). Ask them how prices are determined in their companies. Then prepare a class report on what you have learned.

4. Spend some time looking at prices used by businesses in your area. Conduct a class discussion about the use of psychological pricing.

5. Assume that you have been appointed marketing manager for a new hockey franchise. Your team will be using an arena with 3,000 first-class seats, 5,000 regular seats, and 2,000 seats behind the nets. How will you go about setting the seat prices?

Case 13—1: A Pricing Strategy to Combat the Energy Crisis

Many people believe that the best way to handle the energy crisis is through an innovative pricing strategy. Proposals vary, of course. President Reagan believes in a free-market approach where petroleum prices would move toward their natural levels. Others believe that gasoline tax hikes are the best way to discourage unnecessary consumption. For example, former congressman John Anderson proposed a 50 cent per gallon tax during his 1980 presidential campaign.

Some 1980 data revealed that a 13 percent price increase over the same time a year earlier had been responsible for an 8 percent drop in oil usage as Americans cut their driving and switched to more fuel-efficient cars.[12] An Atlantic Richfield source estimated that gasoline consumption falls 1.5–2 percent for every additional 10 cents charged at the pump.[13]

But it is a different story in France, where gasoline prices have always been high ($1 per gallon in 1960). The French now pay $3.17 a gallon, yet automobile ownership and miles driven have continued to climb. Like other Europeans, the French make extensive use of public transportation and drive very fuel-efficient cars. But high petroleum prices have not deterred them from increasing their automobile usage. One French study concluded that drivers would not alter their current patterns unless gasoline hit $5.25 to $8.20 per gallon. Claude Theirry of the French Industry Ministry commented: "We've concluded that price isn't effective in conservation. It might stun people momentarily, but the effect doesn't last."[14]

Questions

1. Relate this case to the material presented in this chapter.

2. If U.S. gasoline prices continue to escalate, do you think we will duplicate the French experience? Why? Why not?

3. What approach should the United States pursue with respect to gasoline pricing?

Case 13—2: Pricing Japanese Automobiles in the U.S.

Everyone knows that an automobile's "sticker price" (what businesspeople often call "list price") is not what you actually pay (the so-called "market price"), or is it? In 1981 U.S. pressure forced Japan to reduce automobile exports by 7.7 percent. This had a profound effect on the prices of Toyotas, Datsuns, and Hondas.

Before the cutbacks, most of the Japanese models sold at "discounts" (reductions from list price) of $100-$1000. Only a very few models sold at list price or higher. While the Japanese manufacturers did not increase their list price after the curb on exports, their U.S. dealers began to shave the discounts offered to American consumers. In other words, market prices for Japanese cars began to rise. Meanwhile, U.S. manufacturers raised their list prices 2.8–3.5 percent.

Questions

1. What is your opinion of the pricing decision of U.S. dealers of Japanese automobiles?

2. What is your opinion of the pricing decision of U.S. manufacturers?

3. Can you think of other industries that price their products through some type of list price/discount schedule/market price format?

Careers in Marketing

Marketing includes many exciting, dynamic fields, such as advertising, marketing research, personal selling, and physical distribution management. These are all areas of growing employment. Many beginning marketers start as sales personnel, then move into other positions as they gain experience. Others remain in sales roles. Still others begin their careers in different areas such as advertising or marketing research.

The Bureau of Labor Statistics has projected the employment outlook to 1990. Its forecasts for selected marketing jobs appear in the table on page 329. The bureau expects all occupations to add 20.8 percent to their work force between 1978 and 1990. Several of the marketing careers currently available appear below.

Marketing manager. The marketing manager, or marketing director, has overall responsibility for all phases of the marketing function. This person holds the highest position within the marketing area. One of the titles held by marketing managers is vice-president of marketing.

Advertising director. The advertising director is the person responsible for all aspects of the firm's advertising program. When part of the program is handled by outside agencies, the director is responsible for the contractual relationship with the agencies.

Advertising account executive. The account executive works for an advertising agency and is assigned to handle one or more of its accounts. This person is in charge of all advertising plans submitted to the clients.

Market researcher. Market researchers analyze information and data on consumers and on buying behavior. They identify facts and trends that might be relevant in developing an improved competitive strategy for the firm.

Sales manager. Sales managers are in charge of a group of sales representatives or the entire sales force. In some cases they also are involved in selling to big accounts. But the sales manager's primary job is seeing that the firm's sales personnel perform effectively.

Sales representative. Sales representatives are the people who handle the personal selling aspects of the firm's marketing program. They call on prospective buyers, explain the firm's products, and secure orders. They are also responsible for seeing that customers are satisfied with their pruchases and become repeat buyers.

Physical distribution manager. Sometimes called the traffic manager, the physical distribution manager is responsible for seeing that the firm's physical distribution function is performed effectively. Duties include transportation, shipping, warehousing, and the like.

Buyer. Buyers procure merchandise for retail stores. They usually specialize by product or department. There are furniture buyers, sportswear buyers, and so on.

Operations manager. The operations manager is the person responsible for the nonmerchandise-related activities of retailing. Duties include supervision of the receiving, shipping, delivery, service, security, and inventory control departments.

EMPLOYMENT OUTLOOK TO 1990

Marketing Occupations	Recent Employment Figures	Changes in Employment					
		Much Faster than the Average for All Occupations	Faster than the Average for All Occupations	About as Fast as the Average for All Occupations	More Slowly than the Average for All Occupations	Little Change Expected	Expected to Decline
Buyers (includes Merchandise Managers)	115,000			✓			
Marketing Research Workers	24,000	✓					
Public Relations Workers	131,000		✓				
Purchasing Agents	185,000		✓				
Automobile Sales Workers	158,000		✓				
Insurance Agents and Brokers	540,000			✓			
Manufacturer's Sales Workers	400,000		✓				
Real Estate Agents and Brokers	555,000			✓			
Retail Trade Sales Workers	2.8 million		✓				
Securities Sales Workers	110,000			✓			
Wholesale Trade Sales Workers	840,000				✓		
Travel Agents	18,500	✓					
Reservation, Ticket, and Passenger Agents	56,000			✓			

Source: U.S. Department of Labor, Bureau of Labor Statistics, *Occupational Outlook Handbook 1980–1981*, Bulletin 2075, pp. 5, 115–117, 125–127, 129–131, 190–191, 194–197, 199–202, 204–208, 247–248, 476–478.

PART
FIVE

PRODUCTION AND
INFORMATION

14

Production and Operations Management

Learning Goals

1. To be able to explain how production creates utility for the firm's customers

2. To be able to identify the three components of production and operations management: production and operations planning, installation of necessary inputs, and coordination of the production processes

3. To enumerate the major factors involved in making plant location decisions

4. To be able to explain the costs involved in maintaining inventory

5. To identify each step in the production control process

6. To explain the meaning of each of the key terms introduced in this chapter

Profile: The Entenmanns

From Family Kitchen to National Bakery

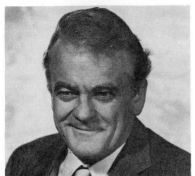

Robert Entenmann

If William Entenmann, the founder of a small neighborhood retail bake shop in Brooklyn in 1898, were alive today, he would not recognize his family business. What was once a small bakery has become a $280 million wholesale baking business producing over 200 million boxes of assorted cakes and cookies each year.

William Entenmann's son, William Jr., his wife Martha, and their three sons, Robert, now chairman of the board, William III, now president, and Charles, were responsible for this dramatic business success.

In 1957, the family decided on a major marketing shift. They became wholesalers, marketing their products through supermarkets. Demand for Entenmann's products soared, and was followed by a period of tremendous growth.

All through this period of rapid growth, Entenmann's production process played a key role in the company's success. By wisely choosing its plant locations, making well thought-out purchasing decisions, maintaining strict production and quality controls, Entenmann's established its position as the world's largest producer of fresh cakes.

According to William D. Grove, director of marketing and sales, critical marketing factors were behind the choice of their Miami and Chicago plant sites. "Our Miami plant," says Grove, "extends our distribution to the Southeast. And our Chicago facility gives us easy access to Midwestern markets." In both instances, however, the focus was on sites from which to deliver the freshest possible products.

In order to provide quality products at the lowest possible prices, all Entenmann's plants jointly purchase their raw materials. Entenmann's has found that by supplying some of its own ingredients, including vanilla and cinammon flavorings, chocolate, and apples, it can provide fresher and purer products than its competitors.

Coordinating people, ingredients, and machinery in each of Entenmann's plants is the job of the shift and plant supervisors. Working backward from a sales forecast that tells them the type and quantity of items to be produced in a given week, supervisors determine the amounts of raw materials needed. If there is a heavy demand for a particular item, supervisors can then schedule extra equipment time.

Although the Entenmann's baking process, with its huge vats of dough, conveyor belts, and giant ovens, can only be described as mass production, human contact still remains. Workers check the weight, color, and size of every cake and pie that comes down the conveyor belt and frost cakes and pack fragile donuts by hand. They also enforce strict quality control standards. "We score our products every day," says Grove, "to be sure they meet our high quality standards."

Entenmann's appeal is its "old-fashioned way of baking." As a big business using sophisticated mass production techniques, the challenge to maintain this appeal is enormous. Robert Entenmann, grandson of the company's founder, best expressed the firm's goals: "We recognize only two competitors," said Entenmann, "the neighborhood bakery and the person who bakes at home."

Production is not the application of tools to materials. It is the application of logic to work.

—Peter F. Drucker

Everything is more complicated than it seems. Nothing ever gets done as quickly as it should. If you play with a thing long enough you will break it.

—Murphy's Laws

In the early 1980s, an American sheepshearer nicknamed "Puma" arrived in Australia to work with other highly paid specialists who separate Australia's 135 million sheep from their coats. Unlike the 10,000 other shearers, Puma is a robot, trying for the first time to perform a task that until now has always been done by hand.

Robots are the latest form of automation—and although some have been around industry since the late 1950s, those old "fixed" types, best exemplified by a battery of machines designed solely to drill automobile-engine blocks, are being replaced by "programmable" or "flexible" models. These robots have capabilities far beyond those of the numerically controlled machine tools that were largely limited to metal cutting (see Focus 14–1).

Compared with their forerunners, the new robots are nimble jacks-of-all-trades. A typical model can be fitted with a variety of "hands"— for example, a mechanical "gripper" that enables it to pick up parts and pass them along, a spray head that converts it into a painter, or an arc that turns it into a welder. Such robots load and unload items from furnaces, stamping presses, and conveyors—and a few of them even perform their jobs while riding conveyors. They also quench red-hot parts, lubricate dies in stamping machines, drill holes, insert screws, grind parts, and so on.

These admittedly simple assembly chores may be the mere beginnings of what lies ahead. Robots are getting smarter all the time, and some already have a sense of "touch" as well as "sight." If researchers can overcome the remaining limitations, some of which still present formidable difficulties, truly vast horizons might open up. Contrary to general belief, 75 percent of U.S. industry's products are not mass-produced in long production runs but are assembled in small batches as styles and sizes change. At present, these products are put together largely by hand because extensive mechanization of the traditional kind does not pay. But it is now believed that robots could one day take over many of these batch-assembly jobs.[1]

But whether the employees are humans or robots, they are involved in a crucial function of any organization: the production of needed products or services.

Industrial robots look nothing like the androids of *Star Wars* fame—a distinct letdown for many aficionados—but they have grown increasingly smarter and more versatile in recent years. And in the past two years, the pace of robot evolution has quickened markedly, as the following genealogy indicates.

Industrial robots all have armlike projections and grippers that perform factory work customarily done by humans. The term is usually reserved for machines with some form of built-in control system and capable of stand-alone operation. But in Japan, it also includes manipulators operated by humans, either directly or remotely.

A pick-and-place robot is the simplest version, accounting for about one-third of all U.S. installations. The name comes from its usual application in materials handling: picking something from one spot and placing it at another. Freedom of movement is usually limited to two or three directions—in and out, left and right, and up and down. The control system is electromechanical. Prices range from $5,000 to $30,000.

A servo robot is the most common industrial robot because it can include all robots described below. The name stems from one or more servomechanisms that enable the arm and gripper to alter direction in midair, without having to trip a mechanical switch. Five to seven directional movements are common, depending on the number of "joints," or articulations, in the robot's arm.

A programmable robot is a servo robot directed by a programmable controller that memorizes a sequence of arm-and-gripper movements; this routine can then be repeated perpetually. The robot is reprogrammed by leading its gripper through the new task. The price range is $25,000 to $90,000.

A computerized robot is a servo model run by a computer. The computer controller does not have to be taught by leading the arm gripper through a routine; new instructions can be transmitted electronically. The programming for such "smart" robots may include the ability to optimize, or improve, its work-routine instructions. Prices start at about $35,000.

A sensory robot is a computerized robot with one or more artificial senses, usually sight or touch. Prices for early models start at about $75,000.

An assembly robot is a computerized robot, probably a sensory model, designed specifically for assembly line jobs. For light, batch-manufacturing applications, the arm's design may be fairly anthropomorphic [human-like].

Robots are rapidly becoming an important part of the production process.

What Is Production?

Society allows businesses to operate only so long as they make a contribution. By producing and marketing desired goods and services, businesses satisfy this commitment. They create what economists call **utility**—the want-satisfying power of a product or service. There are four basic kinds of utility—form, time, place, and ownership.

Time, place, and ownership utility are created by marketing—by having products available to consumers at convenient locations when they want to buy and at facilities where title to the products can be transferred at the time of purchase.

Form utility is created through the conversion of raw materials and other inputs into finished products or services. For example, glass, steel, fabrics, rubber, and other components are combined to form a new Fiat or Pinto. Plastics and papers are molded to produce a Frisbee. Cotton, thread, and buttons are converted into Hathaway shirts. The creation of form utility is the responsibility of the firm's production function and the subject of this chapter.

Production is the use of people and machinery to convert materials into finished products or services. This conversion of raw materials into finished products creates form utility. Figure 14–1 illustrates the production process whereby people and machinery are used to convert raw materials and component parts into finished products. Table 14–1 lists ten examples of production systems for a variety of goods and services.

The conversion process may involve major changes in raw materials or a simple combining of finished parts. The butcher performs a production function by reducing a side of beef to ground beef, steaks, chuck roasts, and so on. General Motors combines tires, spark plugs, a battery, and thousands of other components to complete a new Chevette. All these processes result in the creation of form utilty.

In many instances, the production system generates services rather

utility
The want-satisfying power of a product or service.

form utility
Utility created through the conversion of raw materials and other inputs into finished products or services.

production
The use of people and machinery to convert materials into finished products or services.

FIGURE 14–1
The production process.

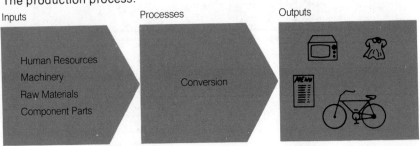

TABLE 14–1
Some Typical Production Systems

Example	Primary Inputs	Transformation	Outputs
Pet food factory	Grain, water, fish meal, personnel, tools, machines, paper bags, cans, buildings, utilities	Converts raw materials into finished goods	Pet food products
Hamburger stand	Meat, bread vegetables, spices, supplies, personnel, utilities, machines, cartons, napkins, buildings, hungry customers	Transforms raw materials into fast-food products and packages	Satisfied customers and fast-food products
Automobile factory	Purchased parts, raw materials, supplies, paints, tools, equipment, personnel, buildings, utilities	Transforms raw materials into finished automobiles through fabrication and assembly operations	Automobiles
Trucking firm	Trucks, personnel, buildings, fuel, goods to be shipped, packaging supplies, truck parts, utilities	Packages and transports goods from sources to destinations	Delivered goods
Department store	Buildings, displays, shopping carts, machines, stock goods, personnel, supplies, utilities	Attracts customers, stores goods, sells products	Marketed goods
Public accounting firm	Supplies, personnel, information, computers, buildings, office furniture, machines, utilities	Attracts customers, compiles data, supplies management information, computes taxes	Management information and tax services
Automobile body shop	Damaged autos, paints, supplies, machines, tools, buildings, personnel, utilities	Transforms damaged auto bodies into facsimiles of the originals	Repaired automobile bodies
College or university	Students, books, supplies, personnel, buildings, utilities	Transmits information and develops skills and knowledge	Educated persons
County sheriff's department	Supplies, personnel, equipment, automobiles, office furniture, buildings, utilities	Detects crimes, brings criminals to justice, keeps the peace	Acceptable crime rates and peaceful communities
National Marine Fisheries Service	Supplies, personnel, ships, computers, aircraft, utilities, office furniture, equipment	Detects offenders of federal fishery laws, brings them to justice, preserves fishery resources	Optimal stock of fish resources

than goods. Services are intangible outputs of the production system. They include outputs as diverse as trash hauling, education, haircuts, tax accounting, public and private health delivery systems, mail services, transportation, lodging, and hundreds of others. In addition to being intangible, services are often more difficult to standardize than

"YOU CAN HAVE EITHER COMFORT OR STYLE OR DURABILITY, BUT NOT ALL THREE."

The production process is intended to match products with consumer needs.
Sidney Harris

are goods. While the output of equipment-based service producers such as dry cleaners, automatic car washes, airlines, and computer time-sharing are highly standardized, there is less standardization in such services as hair care, lawn services, and professional consulting. Whether the result of the process is a tangible good or an intangible service, both are created by the conversion of inputs into outputs.

Classifying Production Processes

The methods used in producing a product or service can be classified by the means and the time used to create the product or service. The product or service results from the use of either an analytic or a synthetic system by either a continuing or an intermittent process.

An **analytic system** is one in which a raw material is reduced to its component parts in order to extract one or more products. In petroleum refining, crude oil is broken down and gasoline, wax, fuel oil, kerosene, tar, and other products are obtained. A meat-packing plant slaughters cattle and produces various cuts of meat, glue from the horns and hooves, and leather from the hides.

A **synthetic system** is the reverse of an analytic system. It combines a number of raw materials or parts into a finished product or changes raw materials into completely different finished products. On the assembly line, an automobile is produced from the combination of thousands of individual parts. Drugs and chemicals are produced by a synthetic system, as is stainless steel.

analytic system
A system in which a raw material is reduced to its component parts in order to extract one or more products.

synthetic system
A system that combines a number of raw materials or parts into a finished product or changes raw materials into completely different finished products.

Continuous process production describes a manufacturing operation where long production runs turn out finished products over a period of days, months, or even years. The steel industry provides a classic example; its blast furnaces never completely shut down unless a malfunction occurs. Petroleum refineries and nylon and other chemical manufacturers also represent continuous process production. A shutdown can ruin equipment and prove extremely costly.

Intermittent process production describes a manufacturing operation where the production run is short and machines are shut down frequently or changed in order to produce different products. When intermittent production occurs in response to a specific customer order, it is called **job-order production.** When it is used for inventory, it is called **lot-order production.**

What Is Involved in Production and Operations Management?

Obviously the process of converting inputs into finished goods and services must be managed. This, then, is the task of **production and operations management**—to manage the use of people and machinery in converting materials and resources into finished products and services. To see more clearly how this is accomplished it is useful to visit a production facility. One such facility is familiar to every college student, but few have ever thought of it as a factory: McDonald's (see Focus 14–2).

Managers of the production function are responsible for three major activities. First, production managers must make plans for production inputs. This involves determining the necessary inputs required in the firm's operations and includes such decisions as product planning, plant location, and provision for adequate supplies of raw materials, labor, power, and machinery. These plans must be completed before the conversion process from raw material to finished product or service can begin.

Second, production managers must make decisions about the installation of the necessary inputs. These include the actual design of the plant, the best types of machines to be used, the arrangement of the production machinery, and the determination of the most efficient flow of work in the plant.

Third, production managers must coordinate the production processes—the routing of material to the right places, the development of work schedules, and the assignment of work to specific employees. The objective is to promote efficiency.

continuous process
A manufacturing operation where long production runs turn out finished products over a period of days, months, or even years.

intermittent process
A manufacturing operation where the production run is short and machines are shut down frequently or changed in order to produce different products.

job-order production
The type of intermittent production that occurs in response to a specific customer order.

lot-order production
The type of intermittent production that occurs in response to inventory needs.

production and operations management
Management of the use of people and machinery in converting materials and resources into finished products and services.

Inside a Big Mac

top bun

chopped onions

meat patty

pickle slices

secret sauce and shredded lettuce

middle bun

chopped onions

meat patty

cheese

secret sauce and shredded lettuce

bottom bun

FOCUS 14–2
A Factory with Golden Arches?

A good place to start describing the production process at McDonald's is with the product itself. The McDonald's burger is a machine-stamped 1.6-ounce patty, .221 inches thick and 3.875 inches wide when raw; next comes a quarter ounce of onion, a pickle slice, and splats of ketchup and mustard. All the ingredients rest on a 4.25-inch bun.

At every McDonald's outlet, blinking lights on the grills tell the counterpersons exactly when to flip over the hamburgers. Once done, the burgers can be held under infrared warming lights for up to ten minutes—no more. After that, any burgers that have not been ordered must be thrown away. Deep fryers continuously adjust to the moisture in every potato stick to make sure that french fries come out with a uniform degree of brownness; specially designed scoops make it almost physically impossible for an employee to stuff more or fewer french fries into a paper bag than headquarters specifies for a single order. The bun has a higher-than-normal sugar content for faster browning. The whole process is dedicated to speed—turning out a burger, fries, and a shake in fifty seconds.

Professor Theodore Levitt of the Harvard Business School described McDonald's as "a machine that produces, with the help of totally unskilled machine tenders, a highly polished product. Everything is built integrally into the machine itself, into the technology of the system. The only choice available to the attendant is to operate it exactly as the designers intended."

Production Planning

Henry Ford was obsessed with a burning question: could the motor car be converted from a plaything for the rich to a replacement for the horse used by the general public? In 1893, when Ford built his first horseless carriage, the price tag was $9,000. Every piece of the automobile was hand designed, and the emphasis was on high prices for limited production runs.

Ford saw a different strategy. If the horseless carriage could be mass produced, a firm could earn small profits on each car sold and reduce the price to fit the budgets of most families. But such a production revolution would require careful planning. These plans would have to deal with *every* component of the production process if Ford's low-price, mass-production strategy was to succeed.

Ford's plans resulted in a solution for the production cost problems. He decided to use vanadium steel for automobile bodies, and he added a fast-moving assembly line. Specialists were hired, trained, and assigned specific duties on the line. Worker morale was boosted tremendously through the adoption of an eight-hour workday. Ford shocked U.S. industry by paying his employees $5 a day, more than double the prevailing wages in similar industries. And his plan worked. By 1908 his Model T carried a price tag of $850. In 1926 the price had dropped to $284. By that time nearly 15 million Model Ts had been built and sold.

Product Planning

A firm's total planning begins with the choice of products it wants to offer its customers. Plant location, machinery purchases, pricing decisions, and selection of retail outlets are all based on product planning. In a very real sense, the sole economic justification for the firm's existence is the production and marketing of want-satisfying products.

In most firms, product planning is the joint responsibility of the production and marketing departments. Because a product must be designed to satisfy consumer needs, marketing research studies are used to obtain consumer reactions to proposed products, to test prototypes of new products, and to estimate the potential sales and profitability of new products. The production department is primarily concerned with (1) converting the original product concept into the final product, and (2) designing production facilities to produce this new product as efficiently as possible. As Chapters 10–13 pointed out, the new product must not only be accepted by consumers; it must also be produced economically to assure an acceptable return on company funds invested in the project.

Service Planning

Planning the production of services involves the same considerations as planning the production of products described above. Services, like products, must be designed to satisfy consumer needs, and market research is also used to determine consumer reactions to a proposed service. The planning of the services, however, concentrates more on the personnel who will provide them than on the engineering specifications and technology that are needed to manufacture a product.

Facility Location

One of the major production decisions is the choice of plant location. The decision typically represents a long-term commitment and a substantial investment. A poor location poses severe problems in attempting to compete with better-located competitors.

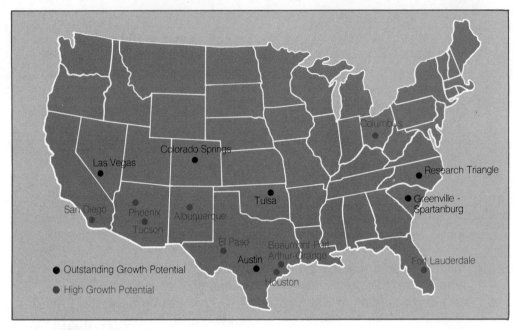

FIGURE 14–2
Cities in which sizable increases in the number of plant
locations are expected to occur during the 1980s.

On a forty-mile stretch of the Mississippi River between Baton Rouge and New Orleans, almost 60 chemical plants have been built. Gates Rubber Company discovered that it could distribute its tires to every customer in the United States within three days by using two plant locations—Denver and Cincinnati.

Figure 14–2 shows the cities where sizable increases in the number of new plant locations is expected during the 1980s. Major factors contributing to the growth of these cities include a combination of high growth potential with a high quality of life.

What Constitutes a Good Location?

Choosing a facility location is typically divided into two stages: (1) selecting a community in which the facility will be located, and (2) choosing a specific site within the community. The choice of a location should be made after considering such factors as proximity to raw materials and markets; availability of labor, transportation, and energy; local regulations; and community living conditions.

Proximity to raw materials. When raw materials are large and heavy, manufacturing firms often locate their plants near the source of these inputs. Production facilities for sheetrock are usually close to where the major ingredient, gypsum, is mined. (Mined gypsum must be dehydrated immediately in order to avoid transporting the water in it.) Trees are processed into wood products near forests, thereby eliminating the cost of transporting those parts of the log that become waste materials. Because 50,000 gallons of water are required to produce one ton of paper, paper mills must be located in areas where large quantities of clean, low-cost water are available.

Proximity to markets. If transportation costs for raw materials are not a significant part of total production costs, the plant is likely to be located near markets where the final products are to be sold. A nearby location allows the manufacturer to provide fast, convenient service for customers. Many automobile components manufacturers are located in the metropolitan Detroit area so as to provide quick service for auto assembly plants.

Several foreign manufacturers with large U.S. markets have set up production facilities in the United States. They include Volkswagen (New Stanton, Pennsylvania), Honda (Columbus, Ohio), and Volvo (Norfolk, Virginia).

Facilities that provide services, such as dry cleaners, laundromats, banks, hotels, local government offices, and hospitals, must be located near the largest concentrations of their target customers. If, for example, dry cleaners were located too far from where people live, no one would patronize them.

Availability of personnel. A third consideration in the location of production or service facilities is the availability of a qualified labor force. One early problem facing a giant shipbuilding complex in the little Gulf Coast town of Pascagoula, Mississippi, was the lack of sufficient numbers of skilled workers. Many electronics firms are located in the Boston area, which has a high concentration of skilled technicians. The same is true for Akron (tires), Hartford (insurance), Pittsburgh (steel), and Seattle (aircraft).

When unskilled workers can be used, the manufacturer has a much greater number of alternative locations. Many manufacturing plants employing unskilled labor have located in the South, where wage rates have historically been below those of the North. In the worldwide search for inexpensive labor, a number of electrical equipment manufacturers have recently begun to manufacture parts in the United States, ship them in unassembled form to the island of Taiwan, have them assembled there by low-cost workers, and then ship them back to the United States for inclusion in a finished product.

Transportation. Most manufacturing plants use transportation facilities to ship raw materials to the plant and finished products to customers. At most locations the producer can choose among several alternatives, such as trucks, railroads, ships, and airplanes. Availability of numerous alternatives can result in increased competition and lower rates for transportation users.

Service facilities also must consider available transportation. Customers must be able to get to them by either public transportation or private automobile. If cars are the primary method of transportation, then adequate parking must also be provided.

Proximity to raw materials is an important consideration when selecting a location for a production facility. For example, production facilities that process trees into wood products are usually located near forests.

Energy. While all production facilities are affected by both availability of adequate energy resources and their costs, factories producing goods tend to be more affected than service industries.

The aluminum industry began in the Tennessee Valley because the manufacture of aluminum requires great amounts of electric power. The cheap electricity provided by the Tennessee Valley Authority allows these manufacturers to produce their product at a price three to four cents lower than that for identical products manufactured in Baltimore or Philadelphia plants, where electrical rates are substantially higher. For industries such as chemicals, aluminum, and fertilizers, availability of inexpensive power supplies is a major consideration in plant location.

Local regulations. Another factor to consider in facility location is local and state taxes. Local and state governments typically impose real estate taxes on factories, equipment, and inventories. Sales taxes and income taxes may also be imposed. These taxes, which vary considerably from state to state and city to city, should be considered in making the location decision. Some states and cities attempt to entice manufacturers or service businesses into their areas by granting low taxes or temporary exemptions from taxation. However, low taxes may also mean inadequate municipal services. Taxes must be considered together with the availability and quality of needed city services.

Until recently, most communities actively competed in attracting industry, which they hoped would produce new jobs and population growth. In recent years, a countertrend has developed, as many communities reject the notion that all growth is beneficial. Most local officials are aware that more jobs also produce more demands on the public school system, more traffic congestion, increased likelihood of industrial pollution, and added pressures on police and fire departments. This awareness has resulted in numerous location constraints for manufacturers.

Both community and state pressures in Maine and New Hampshire prevented the construction of oil refineries in New England. Construction of a Miami jetport located in part on the edge of the Everglades was blocked by environmentalists. The Delaware Coastal Zone Act prevents heavy manufacturing industry from locating within two miles of the state's 115-mile coastline. State and community attitudes thus often play a role in the facility location decision.

Community living conditions. A final consideration in choosing a location is the quality of the community, as measured by its school system, colleges, cultural programs, fire and police protection, climate, spending levels of its citizens, and community attitudes toward the new facility.

The decision on plant location should be based upon a careful evaluation of all the factors discussed here (summarized in Table 14–2). Management must weigh each of these factors in the light of its own individual needs.

TABLE 14-2
Factors to Be Considered in Making the Facility
Location Decision and Examples of Affected Businesses

Location Factor	Examples of Affected Businesses
Transportation	
Proximity to markets	Baking companies or manufacturers of other perishable products, dry cleaners and hotels or other services for profit
Proximity to raw materials	Mining companies
Availability of transportation alternatives	Brick manufacturers, retail stores
Human Factors	
Labor supply	Auto manufacturers, hotels
Local regulations	Explosives manufacturers, welding shops
Community living conditions	All businesses
Physical Factors	
Water supply	Paper mills
Energy	Aluminum manufacturers

Choosing a Site

Once a community has been selected, a specific site must be chosen. Before this can be done, a number of factors must be considered: zoning regulations; availability of sufficient land; cost of the land; existence of shipping facilities, such as railroad sidings, roads, and dock facilities; and construction costs.

Most cities have developed **industrial parks**—planned site locations that provide necessary zoning, land, shipping facilities, and waste disposal outlets. These are created to entice manufacturers to locate new plants in the area by providing maximum cooperation between the firm and the local governing bodies.

Figure 14-3, which shows an industrial park between Houston and Galveston, Texas, illustrates the strengths of these planned parks.

industrial park
A planned site location that provides necessary zoning, land, shipping facilities, and waste disposal outlets.

FIGURE 14-3
Industrial park between Houston and Galveston, Texas.

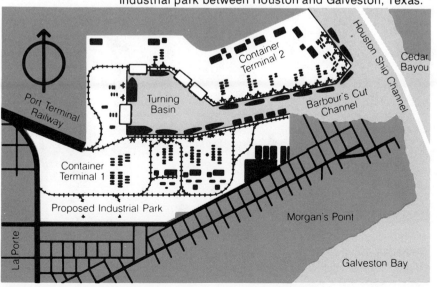

(A) A Process Layout for Producing Product X

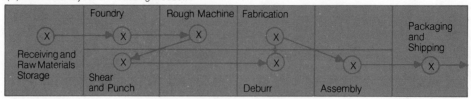

(B) Product Layout for Producing Product X

(C) Fixed-position Layout

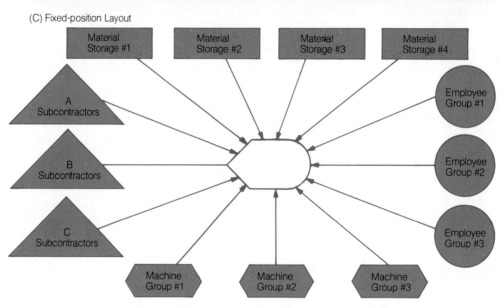

(D) Customer-oriented Layout

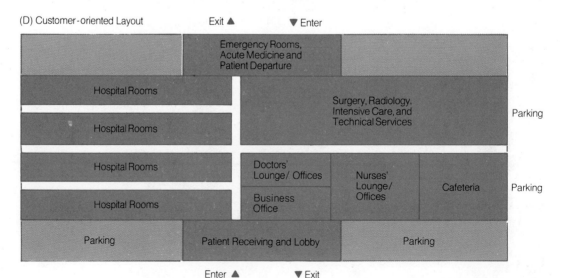

FIGURE 14-4
Basic types of facility layouts.

The land is correctly zoned for industrial production and contains an area sufficient for large facilities. It also has available rail, water, and highway transportation.

Proximity to customers or clients is often the determining factor in the location of service facilities. Service-oriented organizations as diverse as government services, health and emergency services, retailers, and profit-seeking service firms attempt to locate near their customers or clients. Locating near population concentrations allows such facilities as hospitals, fire stations, and ambulance services to provide fast service and minimize loss of life and loss of property.

Design and Layout of Production Facilities

An efficient production facility is the result of careful consideration of all phases of production and the necessary inputs at each step of the process. As Figure 14–4 indicates, a number of alternatives are available in selecting the most appropriate layout.

The first three designs are common in manufacturing facilities. A **process layout** is designed to accommodate a variety of nonstandard products in relatively small batches. Custom machine shops are typically organized in this fashion. A **product layout** is designed to accommodate only a few product designs. In the automobile industry, this type of layout allows a direct material flow through the facility to the products. A **fixed-position layout** locates the product in a fixed position, and workers, materials, and machines are transported to and from it. This approach is common in such operations as missile assembly, ship construction, large aircraft assembly, and bridge construction, where the product is very bulky, large, heavy, or fragile.

A **customer-oriented layout** is common in service facilities where the facility must be arranged to enhance the interactions of customers and the organization's services. The example of a hospital layout illustrates this approach.

process layout
A manufacturing facility design that accommodates a variety of nonstandard products in relatively small batches.

product layout
A manufacturing facility design that accommodates only a few products in relatively large quantities.

fixed-position layout
A manufacturing facility design that locates the product in a fixed position, and workers, materials, and machines are transported to and from it.

customer-oriented layout
A service facility design where the arrangement facilitates the interactions of customers and the organization's services.

Putting the Production Plan into Operation

Once the product or service decisions have been made, the production facilities developed, the necessary machinery purchased, and the most efficient facility layout determined, management must implement the production plan. Raw materials, component parts, and all other goods and services that will serve as production ingredients, from paper clips to steel bars to computers, must be purchased, inventory levels must be determined and controlled, and production schedules must be put into operation. Each of these activities will have to be performed efficiently if the production plan is to succeed.

Purchasing Decisions

The objective of purchasing is to buy the right materials in the right amounts at the right time for the right price. To achieve this goal, the purchasing department must (1) precisely determine the correct materials to purchase, (2) select the best supplier, and (3) develop an efficient ordering system (see Focus 14–3).

Too many people define the term quality as "high quality." But quality costs money, and the purchase of materials of a higher than necessary quality can adversely affect the ability of the company to price its products competitively. A minimum quality level is obviously necessary for the product to perform its functions. But the precise quality levels needed for materials to be purchased should be specified in order to assist in the purchasing process.

FOCUS 14–3
Purchasing Raw Materials for the Telephone Is a Worldwide Job

Most people think of the telephone as a U.S. institution, but it is a regular United Nations when it comes to the materials needed to make a phone.

To give you an idea of where the purchasing agent at the phone company has to look for needed materials, let's examine the telephone. The chromium used to make your finger stop on the dial comes from Africa. Nickel used in springs is mined in Canada and Norway. Indonesian or Malayan rubber finds several uses, including the phone's feet.

Of course, most of the materials are mined, grown, or made in the United States. Some of these include brass for the bells, carbon for the mouthpiece, plastics that house the insides, and steel that forms a variety of parts.

Some of the materials seem a little unlikely for a telephone. Cotton acts as an acoustical barrier in the handset. Wax fills capacitors and insulators. There is even a trace of gold and silver in the transmitter. And don't forget the paper your number is printed on. Other materials include aluminum, cobalt, copper, lacquer, lead, petroleum, rayon, silicon, tin, and zinc.

Selecting the Right Supplier

The choice of a supplier is usually made by comparing the quality, prices, availability, and services offered by competing companies. In many cases quality and price are virtually identical among suppliers, and the choice is based on factors such as the firm's previous experience with each supplier, speed of delivery, warranties on purchases, and other services.

Major purchases. Where major purchases are involved, the period of negotiations between the purchaser and potential suppliers may take several weeks or even months, and the buying decision may rest with a number of persons in the firm. The choice of a supplier for industrial drill presses, for example, may be made jointly by the production, engineering, and maintenance departments as well as by the purchasing agent. These departments have different points of view that must be reconciled before purchasing decisions are made.

Raw materials and component parts are often purchased on a long-term contractual basis. If a manufacturer requires a continual supply of materials, a one- or two-year contract with a supplier ensures that they will be available as needed.

Reciprocity. A highly controversial practice in a number of industries is **reciprocity**—the extension of purchasing preferences to those suppliers who are also customers. Reciprocal agreements are particularly common in the chemical, steel, rubber, paint, and petroleum industries. Even though the purchasing department might prefer the freedom of using suppliers of its own choosing, guaranteed sales are strong incentives for reciprocity, particularly when the prices and quality of competing offerings are similar. Both the Federal Trade Commission and the U.S. Department of Justice consider reciprocity as attempts to reduce competition and will take legal actions against any systematic use of such practices.

reciprocity
The practice of extending purchasing preferences to those suppliers who are also customers.

Inventory Control

Inventory control balances the need to have inventory on hand to meet demand with costs involved in carrying the inventory. Development of an efficient ordering system results from balancing two needs: (1) the need to have on hand sufficient supplies of raw materials and components to meet production needs and (2) the need to minimize inventory on hand in order to reduce the carrying costs.

The financial costs of carrying inventory are the funds tied up in it that cannot be used in other activities of the business. Among the expenses involved in storing inventory are warehousing, taxes, insurance, and maintenance. If the inventory on hand is excessive, these expenditures represent waste.

For example, if an automobile manufacturer were to run out of an important part, the financial impact could be quite major. Until a supply of the needed part could be obtained, assembly lines would have to be shut down, workers would be laid off, shipment schedules would not be met, relationships with dealers would be hurt, and so on. On the other hand, carrying too large an inventory of a specific part represents large costs to the firm because the purchase price would have to be financed through loans.

But a lack of needed raw materials, parts, goods, or sales often means lost production—and delays in production mean unhappy customers if the delays result in late delivery of promised merchandise.

inventory control
The balancing of the need to have inventory on hand to meet demand with the costs involved in carrying the inventory.

Firms lose business when they gain a reputation for inability to meet promised delivery dates or when their shelves are empty. These two costs must be balanced to produce acceptable inventory levels.

Control of the Production Process

Throughout this chapter, production has been viewed as a process of converting inputs into finished products and services. First, plans are made for production inputs—the products to be produced, the location of facilities, and the sources of raw materials, consumers, labor, energy, and machinery. Next, the production plans are implemented through the purchase of materials and equipment and the employment of a trained work force to convert the inputs into salable products and services. The final step in the production process is control.

What Is Production Control?

production control
A well-defined set of procedures for coordinating people, materials, and machinery to provide maximum production efficiency.

Production control is a well-defined set of procedures for coordinating people, materials, and machinery to provide maximum production efficiency.

Suppose that a watch factory has been assigned the production of 800,000 watches during the month of October. Production control executives break this down to a daily production assignment of 40,000 for each of twenty working days. The next step is to determine the number of workers, raw materials, parts, and machines needed to meet this production schedule.

Similarly in a service business, such as a restaurant, it is necessary to estimate how many meals would be served each day and then determine the number of people needed to prepare and serve the food, as well as how much food must be purchased and how often. For example, meat, fish, and fresh vegetables might have to be bought every day or every other day to ensure freshness, while canned and frozen foods might be bought less often depending on storage space.

The Five Steps in Production Control

Production control can be thought of as a five-step sequence: planning, routing, scheduling, dispatching, and follow-up.

production planning
The phase of production control that determines the amount of resources needed to produce a certain amount of goods or services.

Production planning is the phase of production control that determines the amount of resources (including raw materials and other components) needed to produce a certain amount of goods or services. If the needed amounts are not available in inventory, purchase requisitions for them are sent to the purchasing department, so they will be on hand when needed. Similar determinations are made to ensure that the necessary machines and workers are available when needed. Service-producing systems depend more on personnel than on materials.

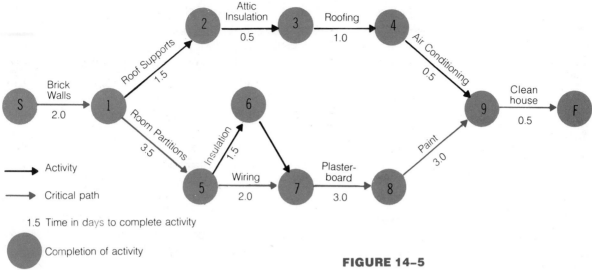

FIGURE 14-5
PERT diagram for constructing a house.

Routing is the phase of production control that determines the sequence of work throughout the facility. It specifies where and by whom each aspect of production will be performed.

Scheduling is the phase of production control involved in developing timetables that specify how long each operation in the production process takes and when it should be performed. Efficient scheduling ensures that delivery schedules are met and productive resources are efficiently used.

Scheduling is extremely important for manufacturers of complex products with large numbers of parts or production stages. A watch contains dozens of component parts, and each of them must be available at the right place, at the right time, and in the right amounts if the production process is to function smoothly.

Scheduling practices vary considerably in service-related organizations. Such small services as local trucking companies or doctors' offices may use relatively unsophisticated scheduling systems and resort to such devices as "first come, first served" rules, appointment schedules, or take-a-number systems. Part-time workers and standby equipment may be used in handling demand fluctuations. On the other hand, hospitals typically use sophisticated scheduling systems that are similar to those of a manufacturer.

A number of methods have been devised for effective scheduling of complex products. A commonly used scheduling technique designed for such complex products as ships and new airplane designs is **PERT (Program Evaluation and Review Technique).** PERT, first developed for the military, was used to produce guided missiles for the Polaris nuclear submarine. But it was quickly modified for use by industry. Figure 14–5 shows a simplified PERT diagram.

PERT is designed to minimize production delays by coordinating all aspects of the production task. The colored line in Figure 14–5

routing
The phase of production control that determines the sequence of work throughout the facility.

scheduling
The phase of production control involved in developing timetables that specify how long each operation in the production process takes.

PERT (Program Evaluation and Review Technique)
A scheduling technique (designed for complex products such as ships and new airplanes) for minimizing production delays by coordinating all aspects of the production task.

critical path
The sequence of operations in the PERT (Program Evaluation and Review Technique) diagram that requires the longest time for completion.

shows the **critical path**—the sequence of operations in the PERT diagram that requires the longest time for completion. The other operations that can be completed before they are needed by operations on the critical path have some slack time and are therefore not critical. The latter operations can be performed early or delayed until later in the production process. Some workers and machinery can be assigned to critical path tasks early, then reassigned to noncritical operations as they are needed.

In actual practice a PERT network may consist of thousands of events and cover months of time. Complex computer programs are used in developing the network and in finding the critical path among the maze of events and activities.

dispatching
The phase of production control that instructs each department on what work is to be done and the time allowed for its completion.

Dispatching is the phase of production control that instructs each department on what work is to be done and the time allowed for its completion. The dispatcher authorizes performance, provides instructions, and lists priorities for each job.

follow-up
The phase of production control that spots problems in the production process and informs management of needed adjustments.

Because even the best plans sometimes go awry, some means must be available to keep management aware of problems as they arise. **Follow-up** is the phase of production control that spots problems in the production process and informs management of needed adjustments. Problems come in many forms. Machinery malfunctions, delays in shipment of vital materials or in arrival of goods or supplies, and employee absenteeism can all result in production delays. These delays must be reported to production control so adjustments in production schedules can be made. A delay in the delivery of a particular component may require new assignments by the dispatcher to work areas affected by this delay.

Quality Control

quality control
The measurement of products and services against established quality standards.

Quality control involves measuring products and services against established quality standards. Such checks are necessary to spot defective products and to see that they are not shipped to customers. Devices for monitoring quality levels of the firm's output include visual inspection, electronic sensors, and X-rays. A high rate of rejected products can lead to necessary changes in equipment or raw materials or additional training for workers employed in the production process.

The outputs of service industries are usually intangible, and it is difficult to measure the quality of services because standards are practically nonexistent. People and facilities form the basis of most service businesses. Therefore, many service organizations have determined that the surroundings in which services are delivered are important to the customers' perception of quality. They emphasize pleasant decor, comfort, convenient parking, friendly atmosphere, cleanliness, and other features of the facility itself. However, the most important element of their quality control programs is often an intensive education and training program for their employees. An example of how a part-

FOCUS 14–4
How the Factory with the Golden Arches Practices
Quality Control

At McDonald's, quality control is summed up in the initials QSC (for Quality, Service, Cleanliness), a set of letters that every McDonald's employee learns quickly.

Cleanliness is required from the licensees. Periodic unannounced inspections are designed to produce spotless outlets. The roving inspectors (called field supervisors) make sure that the restaurant floor is mopped at proper intervals and the parking lot is tidied up hourly.

Quality control begins with raw material purchases that meet rigid headquarters specifications. The hamburger patty must be "pure" beef—that is, no lungs, hearts, cereal, soybeans, or other filler—with no more than 19 percent fat content. This compares favorably with the more than 30 percent fat in some competing hamburgers.

Once the product has been prepared to national specifications, quality is further assured by discarding hamburgers that remain unsold after ten minutes and french fries after seven. Coffee can be no more than thirty minutes old.

product, part-service organization manages quality control can be seen in Focus 14–4.

Production and Pollution

An undesirable output of many production processes is pollution, which takes many forms, including air pollution, water pollution, and noise pollution. Activities such as strip mining have produced extensive damage in West Virginia, Kentucky, Illinois, and other ore-producing states. Major oil spills in California and along the Gulf Coast have killed thousands of fish and birds and damaged beaches. Discharges from chemical plants also have meant death to fish. Atmospheric discharges by lead smelters have endangered the health of nearby residents. These undesirable outputs have resulted in the enactment of numerous state and federal laws designed to protect the environment. Efforts by manufacturers to stop pollution have resulted in the investment of billions of dollars in equipment. Expenditures to control air pollution alone will exceed $10 billion by 1990. Buyers of new cars in 1982 are paying over $300 for air pollution abatement devices. A strong commitment to protection of the environment, coupled with investments in pollution control, will be an increasingly important component of production decisions during the 1980s.

Controversial Issue

What Is the Role of Nuclear Energy in American Industry?

The availability of energy at reasonable cost is a major consideration for industry, particularly in terms of production facilities, which cannot operate without power. The Arab oil embargo of 1973 catapulted nuclear, or atomic, power into the energy spotlight. As the most powerful kind of energy known, nuclear power held the promise of an energy-rich future free of OPEC control.

By 1980, 75 nuclear power plants were in operation in the United States, producing 11.4 percent of the country's electricity needs. The predictions by nuclear industry spokespeople that nuclear power plants would provide 29 percent of the country's electricity needs by the year 2000 may be somewhat optimistic, however.

One of the major obstacles is the public's fear that nuclear energy is unsafe. This fear intensified after the accident at the Three Mile Island nuclear power plant in Pennsylvania and has been partially responsible for the fact that orders for 35 nuclear plants were canceled between 1978 and 1980. But there are other problems as well.

Regulatory delays, hold-downs on rates, the still unresolved waste disposal problem, lower than expected demand for electricity, inflation, and the lack of clear government policy have also combined to stop the nuclear power industry almost in its tracks. In addition, as delays increase, nuclear plant construction costs have skyrocketed to the point that they are now out of reach of most utilities.

As the United States takes a more cautious view of the nuclear energy issue and turns to coal as an alternate energy source, the Soviet Union and many Eastern bloc countries are expanding their nuclear potential. Currently only 4 percent of the Communist

Summary

Production creates form utility by converting human inputs, energy, raw materials, and component parts into finished products and services. Production management is responsible for three major activities: developing plans for production inputs, installing necessary production inputs and implementing production plans, and coordinating and controlling the production process.

Production planning begins with a decision on which products or services will be produced. This is a major company decision because

world's electrical needs are provided by nuclear energy. This is expected to increase to 25 percent by 1990.

Many European countries also embrace nuclear energy as the solution to the OPEC oil dilemma. Currently, nuclear energy produces 8 percent of Europe's electricity needs; but many countries, including France and Great Britain, are committed to expanding their nuclear programs. In addition, nuclear energy is an important part of Japan's energy program.

Although the potential hazards of nuclear energy, the high cost of constructing nuclear power plants, and other factors have combined to slow down the use of this source of power, proponents of nuclear energy still argue that it is a viable and necessary alternative to fossil fuels—oil and coal. They claim that the world's supply of oil may be nearly used up within the next 75 to 100 years and that even though coal is still readily available, it is an exceptionally dirty fuel to burn. On the contrary, nuclear plants require much less fuel to produce great amounts of energy, and nuclear fuel is much cleaner and, therefore, produces much less pollution than fossil fuels.

What part nuclear energy will play in the U.S. in the future is still being debated. Because of American industry's dependence on energy, it has a strong stake in the directions energy development will take. Which way energy will go depends on government support of energy programs as well as the work of energy producers themselves. The Reagan administration indicates support for nuclear power, as expressed by Energy Secretary James B. Edwards, who said, "As you look across the horizon to find the answers to our energy problems there's no real place to turn in the next 30 years other than nuclear to help keep us from being all hostages to foreign countries." Whether nuclear energy is the route that will be followed remains a highly contested question.

the firm fulfills its commitments to society by producing and marketing want-satisfying products and services. The manufacturing method may involve analytic or synthetic systems, and the production runs may be continuous or intermittent.

A second major decision is selection of a facility location. A number of factors must be considered in selecting the best location; among them are proximity to raw materials and to markets; availability of labor, transportation, and energy; local regulations; and community living conditions.

After a location has been selected, then a production facility must be designed for maximum efficiency. A number of alternatives are available in selecting the most appropriate layout, including process layout, product layout, fixed-position layout, and customer-oriented layout.

Once product, facility location, and facility layout decisions have been made, management must implement the production plan. This involves the purchase of raw materials and other components, inventory control, and the implementation of production schedules. Those responsible for purchasing attempt to buy the right materials in the right amounts at the right time for the right price. Once quality levels for materials have been determined, suppliers are contacted and orders are placed. The task of inventory control is to balance two factors: the need to maintain adequate supplies to meet production requirements and the need to minimize funds invested in inventory.

Production control attempts to provide maximum productive efficiency through the coordination of people, materials, and machinery. The production control process consists of five steps: planning, routing, scheduling, dispatching, and follow-up, as well as quality control. Coordination of each of these phases should result in improved production efficiency and lower production costs.

One undesirable output of many production processes is pollution, which manufacturers have been making efforts to stop. These efforts, however, cost a great deal of money, and some of this cost is passed along to the consumer.

Key Terms

utility
form utility
production
analytic system
synthetic system
continuous process
intermittent process
job-order production
lot-order production
production and operations management
industrial park
process layout
product layout

fixed-position layout
customer-oriented layout
reciprocity
inventory control
production control
production planning
routing
scheduling
PERT
critical path
dispatching
follow-up
quality control

Review Questions

1. Explain each of the terms listed above.

2. What utility is produced by the production function?

3. Outline the production process.

4. What is involved in production planning?

5. Discuss the factors that influence facility location decisions.

6. Describe the decision-making process involved in purchasing.

7. What costs must be considered in setting up an inventory control system?

8. List the basic steps in production control.

9. What are the chief methods of ensuring quality control?

10. Draw a PERT diagram for the completion of the course for which this book is being used.

Discussion Questions and Exercises

1. Evaluate the pros and cons of the controversial issue that appears in this chapter.

2. Name five factories and five services that are located in your community or nearby city. Identify the factors likely to have led to the location of each. Explain your choices.

3. Give two examples of production facilities in your region that use each of the following manufacturing methods:
   a. analytic processes   c. continuous processes
   b. synthetic processes   d. intermittent processes

4. Explain the concept of reciprocity, and discuss the circumstances under which it is likely to be a factor in purchase decisions. Identify several industries where reciprocity is likely to occur. Under what circumstances is it an inefficient practice?

5. Visit a local factory and observe the production operation of the plant. Then prepare a brief report on what you have learned.

Case 14–1: Robots in the Japanese Production System

Metal robots, not people, play the major role in making Datsuns at a plant 21 miles south of Tokyo. In showers of sparks, machines bearing no resemblance at all to R2-D2 or any other anthropomorphic bucket of bolts weld doors to bodies, paint, and perform other chores faster, more efficiently, and cheaper than humans.

Elsewhere in Japan, robots make electronic circuitry. Soon they will handle used nuclear rods in atomic plants and search the ocean bottom for minerals and treasure. At one plant, robots are about to begin making other robots.

Like so many other inventions over the years, from transistor radios to "instant noodles (just add water)," the robots got their start in the United States but have been refined, improved, and used more successfully in Japan.

Kanji Yonemoto, executive director of the Japanese Industrial Robot Association, estimates that at the end of 1979 "there were about 50,000 industrial robots already installed in Japan, mainly in the automobile, electronics, plastic-molding, and metal-working industries." That number includes machines that are little more than automatons, doing only one job at a time and needing a total overhaul if they have to do another job.

There are perhaps as many as 10,000 "smart" robots in Japan. With a computer for a brain, they can do such complicated tasks as figuring the difference between a two-door and four-door sedan and not putting a roof meant for a hatchback Datsun on a coupe. One brokerage firm places the 10,000 robots estimate for Japan far ahead of other industrialized countries. It lists 3,000 robots for the United States and 185 for Britain. And Japan is moving even more heavily into the field.

"Ninety-six percent of the body assembly work done at our Zama plant is performed by automated machines, highly sophisticated, precision equipment that is controlled by computer and makes no mistakes," says Nissan, maker of Datsun. The humans take over at "final assembly" time, putting on finishing touches.

Nissan began using robots in 1969 and by 1975 had 52 of them. Two years later the figure had jumped to 209, and it now has 272. "To save manpower is certainly one of the objectives" of replacing humans with robots, "but it's not all we're interested in," said company spokesman T. Etoh.

Japanese-style, Nissan began talking to its unions several years before the robots were extensively introduced. Etoh says 99 percent of Nissan's workers are graduates at least of high school or a technical school and were happy to do something besides painting or welding. "No one is willing to work eight hours a day in a paint shop, where conditions are dangerous," said Seigo Kojima, an official of the Japan Council of Metal Workers' Unions. "So we need robots. From the human being's viewpoint it's most welcome, according to some of the workers."

Teaching a robot how to paint is a scene worthy of Charlie Chaplin in an updated version of *Modern Times*. Linked to the robot behind him by wires and cables, the painter sprays from left to right, moving, stretching, bending, putting a dab in a hard-to-reach spot, adding a little bit over there. The robot mimics the man in what looks like an aberrant mating dance as the computer memorizes the sequence. The man walks away, the robot takes over, and keeps doing the job until the computer is told otherwise. The robot doesn't take coffee breaks, call in sick, or work half as well at 6 A.M. as at 11 A.M.

The Japanese government is giving tax breaks to small and medium-sized businesses to enable them to buy robots as Nissan, Toyota, and Matsushita do.

Questions

1. Develop a likely explanation for Japan's leadership in the utilization of industrial robots even though such utilization began in the United States.

2. Identify the major advantages and drawbacks of the use of robots.

Case 14—2: The Production System at Vlasic Foods

For many pickle fanciers, the word *Vlasic* is synonymous with pickle. Vlasic Foods, Inc., based in a Detroit suburb, sells approximately $150 million worth of pickles, peppers, relishes, and sauerkraut each year. The firm began as a pickle distributor to the local Polish community during the 1930s. It expanded into other products when it bought a sauerkraut plant in 1959. Vlasic now has plants in California, Connecticut, Delaware, Mississippi, and Michigan.

Vlasic produces three types of pickles. The first type, the processed dill, is really a cucumber cured in barrels of salt and spices. After curing, the dill is either sweetened or soured on the basis of its use and size. Refrigerated pickles, the second type, are not pasteurized but instead are packed into carefully prepared brines. They are kept under refrigeration to preserve the crispness of the cucumber while taking on the flavor of the brine.

The final variety, the fresh-packed pickle, undergoes a series of operations. Once the cucumbers arrive at the plant they are sized, sorted, washed, sliced, and packed into jars. Specially prepared brine containing spices is added to the sliced product, and the jars are closed. The pickle next undergoes a pasteurizing process, after which labels are affixed to the jars. The individual jars are next packaged into protective cases. The cases are then combined on shipping pallets and moved to a warehouse to await shipment to customers.

Questions

1. What type of production problems might be encountered at Vlasic Foods?

2. Draw a PERT diagram for a fresh-packed pickle. Make any necessary assumptions.

15

The Role of Computers

Learning Goals

1. To identify the elements and functions of a computer system

2. To describe what software is and to identify the most commonly used programming languages

3. To explain the major limitations of computers

4. To explain how binary arithmetic works and why it is appropriate for computers

5. To explain the meaning of each of the key terms introduced in this chapter

Profile: Kemmons Wilson
Computers Keep His Holiday Inns on Top

In 1952, Kemmons Wilson took his wife and five children on an automobile trip from their home in Memphis to Washington, D.C. Along the way he found high-priced, dirty lodgings that were unsuitable and uncomfortable for a family. The disgust Wilson felt on the trip caused him to make a fateful decision. On his return to Memphis, he vowed to build an inn that would offer clean, attractive surroundings at rates families could afford.

The first of Wilson's Holiday Inns (the name is taken from an old Bing Crosby movie) opened in 1952 on a main highway link to Memphis. Within 20 months, Wilson had constructed three almost identical inns on other major approach roads to the city. "You just had to go by a Holiday Inn to get into Memphis," said Wilson.

This was the beginning of the Holiday Inn worldwide lodging empire. Today there are more than 1,750 Holiday Inns in 59 countries throughout the world offering service to 76 million overnight guests annually.

In the early 1960s, Wilson's visionary mind understood the need to develop a computerized system for handling the millions of reservations Holiday Inns receive each year and for enabling prospective guests to make reservations at any Holiday Inn in the country through one central computerized source. On April 15, 1965, Holidex, a new computer system for reservations, was put into operation. Developed by IBM Corporation at a cost of $10 million, Holidex, the first system of its kind, changed the face of hotel and motel operations.

By 1970 Holidex was the world's largest commercial computer-controlled communications network, handling approximately 120,000 reservations a day. It gives innkeepers and guests enormous accuracy and flexibility in reserving rooms. Simply by pushing a button, the reservations clerk enters the guest's name and preferred reservation into the computer. If the room is available, a confirmation slip is generated within seconds, and the Holiday Inn where the reservation is made receives a computer-delivered written transaction notice.

Soon an even more sophisticated Holidex system will be operational. Holidex II can handle up to 900,000 messages a day and give customers faster, wider-ranging service. Each check-in desk will be equipped with a cathode ray tube terminal, which will enable staff to retrieve specific reservation information in seconds. Preprinted reservation forms will be available to reduce guest check-in time by 60 to 70 percent. A self-adjusting inventory system that will count the available rooms at each inn as reservations are made and canceled will eliminate the need for hand reservation counting, and more.

The original success of Holidex is due in large part to the hardworking, homespun philosophy of Kemmons Wilson. Said Wilson, a high-school dropout and self-made millionaire considered by the *Sunday Times* of London to be one of the 1,000 most important men of the twentieth century, "When you get an idea, you've got to think of a reason for doing it, not of a reason for not doing it."

The computer revolution is the most advertised revolution in world history. Yet one of the funny things about it is that we probably still underestimate its impact.

—Herman Kahn

First get it through your head that computers are big, expensive, fast, dumb adding-machine-typewriters. Then realize that most of the computer technicians that you're likely to meet or hire are complicators, not simplifiers. They're trying to make it look tough. Not easy. They're building a mystique, a priesthood, their own mumbo-jumbo ritual to keep you from knowing what they—and you— are doing.

—Robert Townsend

Buying a TRS 80 Model I from Tandy Corporation "was one of the best moves I ever made," declares Michael J. Rodriguez, chairman of Southern Telecom, Inc. In the year since he started his Peachtree City, Georgia, cable television business, Rodriguez has won cable franchises for 32 suburban cities and hamlets around Georgia and Tennessee—a fast start that he attributes to his personal computer. "There seems to be no end to the applications you can put on these machines," he says. "The only thing that stops me is how much of my time I can afford to spend."

Rodriguez turned to computers two years ago—when he was still an independent consultant to the cable industry—to help automate the intricate and laborious financial planning that goes into starting any cable franchise. After teaching himself programming from Radio Shack manuals, Rodriguez started writing programs to churn out the series of business projections that banks demand before they will finance cable-TV systems. Before he started using a computer, such projections took a "full week of very intensive manual work with a calculator," he recalls. The computer has cut the time to just two hours per franchise. In addition, Rodriguez can easily alter his projections to fit any new assumptions brought up by the bankers.

Rodriguez is so pleased with his computer's performance in the projection area that he is now putting it to other uses. In one case, his engineers are using the personal computer to design cable systems. They can design up to 35 miles a day compared to the two miles of cable that they could design with paper and pencil. The company recently hired a full-time programmer to write software to handle subscriber billing—a job that will require Radio Shack's more powerful small-business computer. Rodriguez has bought two of these in the last four months and plans to add four more in the next year.[1]

Computers: From Novelties to Indispensable Business Tools

Kemmons Wilson and Michael Rodriguez are just two of the millions of businesspeople, scientists, engineers, educators, and members of the general public who have replaced their awe for the computer with an ability to make it work for them. And computers can be such awesome machines. Their blinking lights, whirring reels, and chattering printouts produce both admiration and distrust in people who do not understand them.

A generation or two ago, who had even heard of computers? Today, who hasn't? They are everywhere. As tools of the greatest technological revolution in our lifetime, computers make airline and hotel reservations, keep inventory records for the local department store, monitor cardiac patients in hospitals, figure payrolls, check credit, control scientific experiments, calculate bills at some supermarkets, forecast trends in the economy, and even help educate schoolchildren.

There are two types of computers—analog and digital. **Analog computers** use continuous data—such as pressure, temperature, or voltage—in scientific or engineering applications. **Digital computers** manipulate numbers by adding, subtracting, multiplying, or dividing. Because digital computers are more commonly used in business, they are the ones to be discussed in the rest of this chapter.

analog computers
Computers that use continuous data, such as pressure, temperature, or voltage, in scientific or engineering applications.

digital computers
Computers, commonly used in business, that manipulate numbers by adding, subtracting, multiplying, or dividing.

Computers are vital tools in today's organizations.

"We're moving you out of Accounts Receivable, Dickerson. The computer doesn't like you."

Drawing by Weber; © 1978 The New Yorker Magazine, Inc.

What Is a Computer?

Computers are electronic machines that accept data and manipulate them to solve problems and produce information. They function much like the human brain. Instructions and data are received, the data are processed, and the user is provided with solutions to problems or answers to questions. Computers are known by several different names: IBM 360, 370, 3033, 303X, or System 34; CDC; Burroughs; NCR; Honeywell; and UNIVAC.

Some computers need large rooms to hold all their parts. Others fit on top of a desk. The earliest computers were gigantic beasts containing vacuum tubes. The invention of solid-state circuitry reduced their size greatly, and other technological advances have made possible the development of smaller computers. In 1955, only 244 computers were in use in the entire United States. By 1983, the number will grow to 3.7 million computers.

Minicomputers

The development of a smaller, less expensive computer by Digital Equipment Corporation in 1965 resulted in the addition of a new term: the **minicomputer**—a small computer about the size of a cash register that is used by scientists and businesspeople for solving numerous problems. Unlike the larger, so-called "mainframe" computers shown at the top of Figure 15–1 on page 366, the minicomputer is more compact and relatively low-cost but has smaller storage capabilities and slower processing speeds. These smaller versions of the regular computer systems are often used in businesses and scientific operations and in educational institutions. In many cases, they can be connected to larger, mainframe computers to utilize the greater capacity of these machines.

The technological evolution of the past two decades has blurred the distinctions between minicomputers and large-scale systems. Many of today's minicomputer systems possess more power and versatility than did the large-scale systems of the early 1960s. As a result, the term *minicomputer* now is used to refer to a number of computers of varying sizes, costs, and capabilities (*see* Focus 15–1).

Microcomputers

The **microcomputer,** the smallest type of computer, is typically a desk-top, limited-storage computer system costing from $500 to $10,000 and consisting of a visual display device called a **cathode ray tube (CRT)**—which displays data on a television screen—and a

FOCUS 15–1
Where Have All the Minis Gone?

The term *minicomputer* is rapidly becoming an anachronism. It is not that there are no longer going to be any minis, but rather, there never were any. This statement can be justified by a review of what has actually occurred in the world of the so-called "minicomputer." This focus attempts to show that providing a synthesis of available information about the application of the mini is significantly more meaningful than trying to define a mini.

The impact that was made by minicomputers began to be noticeable around the late 1960s. Since then, both in total quantity and in type, there has been a proliferation of what have been called minicomputers. Concurrently, the distinction between mini and nonmini becomes clouded.

It has been said, "a minicomputer is a marketing phenomenon." When minis first became available, the trend in computers was for bigger and faster machines. Faced with an attitude like this, the makers of computers that were smaller and slower had to come up with something that would attract attention to their technological "giant-step backward." The term *minicomputer* did just that. Once the attention of the potential user had been diverted from the bigger and the faster, the manufacturers of the slower and smaller pieces of equipment were able to show the user that in some areas of his or her business, smaller and slower were better suited and more economical than bigger and faster. And so, minis began to catch on. Yet, minis were nothing more than relatively smaller and slower computers compared to those that dominated the minds of users and the marketplace at the time. As time passed, however, minis got bigger and faster, and nonminis got smaller and, in some ways, slower.

keyboard resembling a set of typewriter keys. Development of these small systems for the home, office, or classroom was made possible by the 1971 introduction of the microprocessor. A one-quarter-inch square silicon chip contains the control unit and arithmetic logic unit of the microcomputer. The several thousand electronic components that require a cabinet the size of an ordinary desk can be etched onto such a chip at a cost as low as $10. Additional chips containing instructions and data memory are then added to convert the microprocessor into a microcomputer. Such systems, offered at relatively low prices by such retailers as Radio Shack, Sears, and specialized computer retailers, possess capabilities greater than those of the large computer systems costing as much as $1 million two decades ago.

FIGURE 15–1
Classifying computer systems by size.

Burroughs B 5930 Computer System

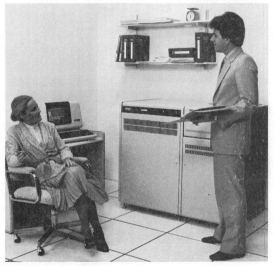

Digital Equipment Corporation's
VAX-11/750 Minicomputer

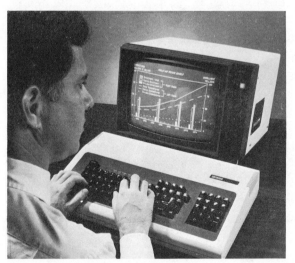

Digital Equipment Corporation's
GIGI Microcomputer

How Computers Work

Each computer system is made up of five basic elements: input, memory, arithmetic, control, and output. These are shown in Figure 15–2.

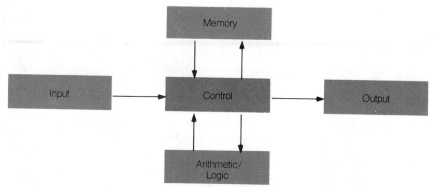

FIGURE 15–2
The basic elements of the computer system.

Input—Reading Data into the Computer

The **input** portion of the computer is responsible for converting incoming data into a form that the computer can understand. Data can be "read" into the computer in a number of forms: punched cards, machine-readable magnetic letters such as those at the bottom of checks, punched-paper tapes, magnetic tapes and disks, optical character recognition (such as the raised letters on credit cards), and typewritten instructions on a special keyboard attached to the computer.

The punched card has traditionally been the most commonly used device for inserting computer data, and it is still widely used. But punched cards are easily bent or torn (some of them even carry the warning "do not fold, spindle or mutilate"), and they take up a great deal of storage space. In recent years magnetic tapes and disks, teletype terminals, and keyboards connected to CRTs have been increasingly used as input devices. Figure 15–3 shows several ways information is fed into the computer.

Memory—Storehouse of the Computer

The **memory unit,** or storage unit, is the heart of the total computer system. It is where information is stored. This element serves as the computer's filing cabinet. Both information for solving a problem and instructions on how to use the information are stored here. The memory storage unit can be both internal and external. Computer systems contain internal memory units for the storage of instructions and data. In addition, it is possible to increase the system's computer memory capacity through the use of external memory units that can be plugged into the system. The use of such external storage units provides added flexibility for the computer system.

Arithmetic—The Computer's Adding Machine

The **arithmetic unit** is where all calculations take place. When adding, subtracting, multiplying, or dividing is required, the necessary data

input
The portion of the computer system that is responsible for converting incoming data into a form the computer can understand.

memory unit
The unit of the computer system where information is stored.

arithmetic unit
The unit in a computer system where all calculations take place.

Punched Card

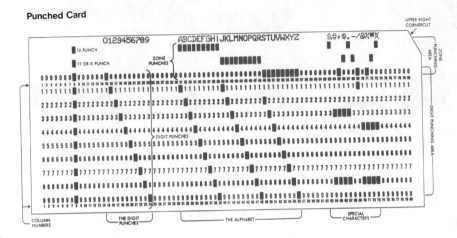

Paper Tape Code

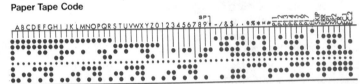

Magnetic Tape Code

CRT

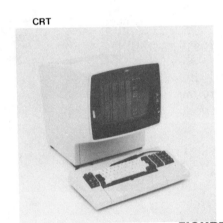

Magnetic Ink Code

FIGURE 15–3
Computer input forms.

move from the memory unit to the arithmetic unit. Once the calculations have been performed, the answers are transferred back to the memory unit. The arithmetic unit is similar to a pocket calculator but much faster.

Control—Director of Computer Operations

control unit
The unit in the computer system responsible for directing the sequence of operations, interpreting coded instructions, and guiding the computer.

The **control unit** is responsible for directing the sequence of operations, interpreting coded instructions, and guiding the computer. Control involves performing operations in the proper order. The computer must be guided every step of the way in solving a problem or per-

FIGURE 15–4
The elements of a computer system
in a modern installation.

forming an assignment such as computing the weekly payroll or print-ing paychecks. The control unit directs and coordinates both the input and the output elements of the computer system, moves data to and from memory, and directs the activities of the arithmetic unit. When incoming instructions are not in the proper form, the control unit typically rejects them.

Output—Where the Results are Produced

The **output** devices provide processed information to the user. Often output is in the form of a paper computer printout. In some cases output is simply shown on a display screen (CRT). Output may also be recorded on magnetic tapes or disks, if the data are to be reused. Sometimes it even takes the form of the spoken word! Figure 15–4 shows the elements of a large computer system in operation.

output
The device that provides processed information to the user, usually in the form of a computer printout, a CRT display, or magnetic tapes or disks.

Hardware and Software

Computer hardware consists of all of the elements of the computer system—the input devices, the machines that store and process data and perform the required calculations, and the output devices that provide the results for the information user. Computer hardware thus

computer hardware
All of the elements of the computer system.

FOCUS 15–2
A Two-Minute Lesson in Computers

What's known as a computer is really just a lot of electronic circuitry. By itself, it can't do very much. It might be likened to a radio without any speakers, knobs, or dials. In order to take advantage of the machine's gifts, a variety of additions are necessary. In technical terms, the main computer is a central processing unit (CPU), and the additions are peripherals. The two most common peripherals are the keyboard, which allows you to talk to the computer, and the display screen, which allows the computer to talk to you.

Some other peripherals can be added to make the computer even more useful. The CPU has a limited amount of storage capacity or memory. If you need to store an additional amount of data, you need additional storage. The newest generation of computers uses a disk, a hard or soft plastic platter that closely resembles a phonograph record. The disk is connected to the computer via a disk drive, which locates on the disk the specific spot where you want to deposit or retrieve information. Disks allow for random access to stored material, which means that any item on the disk can be located in equal time to all other items. With older storage systems, such as magnetic cassette and high-speed magnetic tapes, it is necessary to search for an item in the order it appears on the tape, starting at the beginning of a tape and continuing until the desired item is found; the operation is much like that of an audio tape recorder. . .

includes all the machinery and electronic gadgets that make up the computer installation.

Of equal importance in the effective use of computers is **computer software,** which consists of the instructions, or computer programs, that tell the computer what to do. Computer languages and computer programs represent software.

For more information about computer hardware and software, see Focus 15–2.

computer software
The instructions, or computer programs, that tell the computer what to do.

Advantages of Using Computers

Following are the major advantages of using computers:

1. They are fast. Calculations that take weeks to do by hand can be done in seconds by the computer. In ten seconds a person can add 4,826 to 2,739 and produce the answer, 7,565. In that same time a

Other peripherals include a printer, which enables you to print what's on the screen onto paper, and an acoustic coupler or modem, which allows you to connect a computer to a printer or another computer at a different location, using an ordinary telephone.

All of the above equipment make up the computer hardware—the physical equipment needed to do the work. What makes the equipment work is the computer's software, which comes in two varieties. The operational software, also known as the systems program, is the computer's central nervous system. It gives the computer the intelligence to carry out basic tasks, such as adding and subtracting, storing and retrieving information, and so on. The applications software consist of the instructions for the specific jobs you need to do: maintain inventory, send out bills, and so on.

The basic units of the computer's memory are bits that, when combined in configurations of up to eight bits, form bytes. A byte is a character of data—the letter "B" or the number "5," for example. Thus, the word computer consists of eight bytes. The storage capacity of a computer's memory is expressed in blocks of 1,024 bytes, abbreviated by the letter "K." For example, a 40K disk is capable of storing 40,960 bytes. A megabyte represents one million bytes. Thus, a "16K RAM" is capable of handling 16,384 bytes of *Random Access Memory* in its CPU.

There. You have just learned more about the basic components of a computer system than is understood by the majority of business executives who invest in one.

computer can add a million four-digit numbers. The Cray 1 computer, the world's most powerful computer system, can process 80 million instructions per second. IBM's 3800 system high-speed laser printer can print at speeds of up to 20,000 lines per minute.

2. They are accurate. People make mistakes, especially when they are tired. The computer never gets tired—or bored. If programs are properly written, there is almost no chance of a computer mistake.

3. They can store large quantities of information in a small space. Whole rooms of filing cabinets can be replaced by a few computer magnetic tapes. Bulky records of employee information, sales invoices, accounting records, and inventory records can be converted to compact computer storage.

4. They can make great volumes of data available for management decisions. The information retrieval function of computers allows the manager to retrieve a great deal of stored information within a few seconds.

5. They can perform much of the mechanical, often boring, routine work of recording and maintaining incoming information. These tasks are performed accurately and tirelessly, freeing people to handle more interesting and challenging assignments.

Disadvantages of Using Computers

Although computers provide a number of benefits, they also have a number of limitations:

1. They are expensive. Major computer systems may cost $100,000 or more per month to lease. Large sums of money are also required to develop the programs used in computer systems.

2. They can make disastrous mistakes when programmed incorrectly. A number of years ago a computerized defense system almost tried to shoot down the moon. At about the same time, an amazed magazine subscriber received 700 copies of a magazine in the mail. And a charge card customer realized that the only way he could prevent the computer from continuing to bill him for $0.00 was to send the store a check for $0.00.[2] All these mistakes were caused by computer programming errors. The programs contained "bugs." Computers also make mistakes when given incorrect data, and the resulting output is "garbage." The computer term for such mistakes is GIGO—garbage in, garbage out.

3. They can become a management crutch rather than a tool in decision making. Computers cannot think, and their output is only as good—or as bad—as the data fed in. The final judgment in making a decision must remain the responsibility of the manager.

4. They can be relied on too much and can alienate customers by ignoring the human element. Computerized bills are sometimes incorrect. Often, when the customer writes a letter of protest, the message is ignored, and the computer continues to send out letter after letter threatening legal action if a bill is not paid. One computer letter mailed from a Charleston, West Virginia, hospital puts out this message: "Hello, there, I am the hospital's computer. As yet, no one but me knows that you have not been making regular payments on this account. However, if I have not processed a payment from you within 10 days, I will tell a human, who will resort to other means of collection."[3]

A federal law that went into effect in 1975 requires creditors to answer any customer's inquiry about a charge within 30 days. If the bill is not explained or corrected within 90 days, the charge—if it is $50 or less—will be forfeited. In addition, the customer can sue for damages and collect a minimum of $100 from any firm that violates the law.

How to Talk to the Computer

One major advantage of computers is speed. An English mathematician named William Shanks devoted one-third of his life to computing pi to 707 decimal places (only to make a mistake at the 528th place). Today's modern computer can duplicate Shanks' work (without error) within five seconds.[4] Computers can process data so rapidly that scientists have had to dust off a little-used time measure called a **nanosecond** (one-billionth of a second)!

Binary—The Yes-no System of the Computer

The actual processing of data within the computer is much like the operation in a $10.95 calculator. Like most pocket calculators, the computer can add, subtract, multiply, and divide. (The computer typically "multiplies" by adding at incredible speeds and "divides" by subtracting at those speeds.) But there is one important difference. While the calculator uses the decimal system of the digits. 1, 2, 3, 4, 5, 6, 7, 8, 9, and 0, the computer uses the simple yes-no system of binary arithmetic.

Binary arithmetic is a special counting system that uses two digits—0 and 1. While decimal numbers are built on a base of 10, binary numbers are built on a base of 2. Base 10 means that when you move a digit one space to the left and add a zero, it is worth ten times as much. With binary numbers, every time a number is moved one space to the left, it is worth two times as much.

Then the question arises: how do you count to two without a digit 2? The answer is that the value of a binary number increases by two times as it is moved one space to the left. To produce a 2 in binary, simply move the 1 one space to the left and add 0. Thus, 10 in binary is the same as 2 in decimal—except that it does not look the same. Table 15–1 illustrates how decimal numbers can be converted to binary.

In addition to decimal numbers, letters of the alphabet and symbols can be written in binary. The binary code for the letter A is

nanosecond
A time measure now used to describe the rapidity of computer data processing that is equivalent to one-billionth of a second.

binary arithmetic
A special counting system that uses two digits—0 and 1.

TABLE 15–1
Converting Decimal to Binary Numbers

Decimal Number	Binary Number
1	000001
4	000100
7	000111
12	001100
20	010100
33	100001

bit
A binary digit—either 0 or 1.

010001; the code for the = sign is 110000. Each digit—either a 1 or a 0—is called a **bit** (for *binary digit*). All information moves through the computer one bit at a time.

Because binary exists in yes-or-no states, the computer can quickly accept incoming information simply by opening or closing an electrical circuit. A 1 is indicated when the circuit is on; a 0 is indicated when the circuit is off. For some computers, magnetizing to the left or right produces the same results.

Programming—Telling the Computer What to Do

The computer can do nothing toward solving a problem without a detailed set of instructions. It can follow instructions, but it cannot think. A **computer program** is a set of instructions that tells the computer what is to be done, how to do it, and the sequence of steps to be followed. The computer follows these directions step by step until the job is completed.

computer program
A set of instructions that tells the computer what is to be done, how to do it, and the sequence of steps to be followed.

computer programmer
The specialist who tells the computer what to do based on an analysis of the problem, a breakdown of the component parts of the problem, and an outline of steps needed for the solution.

The **computer programmer**—the specialist who tells the computer what to do—must analyze the problem, break it down into its component parts, and outline the logical steps needed to arrive at the solution. An effective way to determine these steps is to make a **flowchart**—a pictorial description of the logical steps to be taken in solving a problem. The symbols, arrows, and lines showing the step-by-step processing of information, activities, and decisions involved in issuing airline tickets is illustrated by the flowchart in Figure 15–5.

flowchart
A pictorial description of the logical steps to be taken in solving a problem.

Computer Languages

The programmer uses the flowchart to design programs that contain instructions to the computer on how to handle each step in a process. But a problem arises. The computer does not understand English. Programmers earn their salaries by writing instructions to the computer in a symbolic language that it can convert into binary. Although the language of the computer is binary arithmetic, a number of programming languages have been developed to enable the programmer to communicate with the computer in English and algebraic symbols. Four of the most commonly used computer languages are FORTRAN, COBOL, BASIC, and PL/1.

FORTRAN (FORmula TRANslation)
The dominant scientific computer language.

FORTRAN (FORmula TRANslation) was originally developed to solve mathematical equations, and it continues to be the dominant scientific computer language. It is also sometimes used for business purposes.

COBOL (COmmon Business Oriented Language)
A computer language, designed specifically for business problems, that uses English words and sentences.

COBOL (COmmon Business Oriented Language) was designed specifically for business problems. It avoids the use of symbols and algebraic notations, using English words and sentences instead.

BASIC (Beginner's All-purpose Symbolic Instruction Code)
A sophisticated computer language specifically designed for ease of use with respect to input and output operations.

BASIC (Beginner's All-purpose Symbolic Instruction Code) is a sophisticated language that is specifically designed for ease of use with respect to input and output operations, and its use is growing in both businesses and colleges and universities.

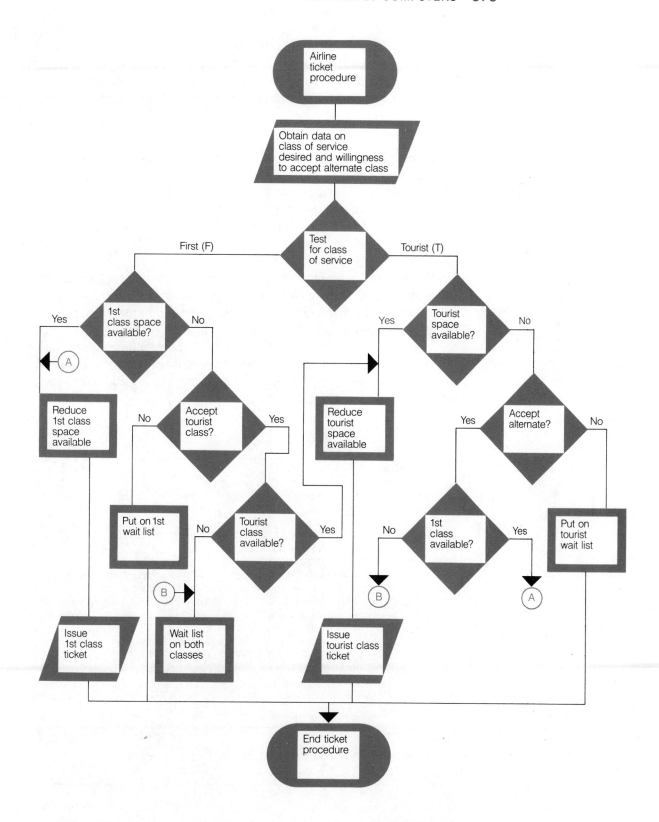

FIGURE 15–5
Flowchart for issuing airline tickets.

PL/1 (Programming Language 1)
A computer language designed for use in both scientific and business environments.

PL/1 (Programming Language 1) is a more recent computer language designed for use in both scientific and business environments. Although PL/1 was developed by IBM (in 1966) for use on IBM computers, it can be used on other computer systems as well.

Conversational Programs

A number of conversational programs have been developed to assist the manager who does not have the necessary training in writing programs to use the computer for decision making. What makes conversational programs possible are specially designed FORTRAN, COBOL, BASIC, or PL/I programs, which supply instructions to the computer on how to respond to specific questions asked by manager-users.

remote terminals
Typewriter-like machines connected to the main computer installation but located in an area physically removed from the computer.

Rather than take their programs to the computer center, executives often use **remote terminals**—typewriter-like machines connected to the main computer installation by telephone lines but located in an area physically removed from the computer. The user-manager types in instructions and receives replies either on a display screen (CRT) or in the form of typewritten output. Table 15–2 shows a series of questions asked by a business student and the computer responses to these questions.

TABLE 15–2
Conversation between Student and Computer

Student:	Hello.
Computer:	HI.
Student:	How are you this morning?
Computer:	FINE. HOW ARE YOU?
Student:	OK. Are you busy today?
Computer:	FAIRLY BUSY. I AM COMMUNICATING WITH 1263 USERS RIGHT NOW.
Student:	Will you help me with a problem?
Computer:	OF COURSE. TELL ME THE PROBLEM.
Student:	I have an item in my store that costs $18. Tell me the selling price I should charge so I will have a profit of 12% of the selling price.
Computer:	$20.45. DO YOU WANT TO KNOW HOW I COMPUTED THIS ANSWER?
Student:	No thanks. You told me what I want to know.
Computer:	DO YOU HAVE ANOTHER PROBLEM?
Student:	Yes. What should I buy my mother-in-law for her birthday?
Computer:	SORRY. I DO NOT GET INVOLVED WITH IN-LAW PROBLEMS. DO YOU HAVE ANOTHER PROBLEM?
Student:	No. Goodbye for now.
Computer:	SO LONG.

The Role of Computers in Business

Every area of business has felt the impact—and value—of computers. Banks, insurance companies, manufacturing firms, retailers, utilities, government agencies, airlines, accounting firms and departments, securities firms and stock exchanges, transportation companies—all have found important uses for computers. The following examples illustrate some of their many uses.

Record Handling

One of the earliest and most widespread uses of computers in business has been storage and processing of records. In repetitive work such as payroll accounting, inventory records, and billing, the speed and accuracy of the computer can be put to good use. The computer's

An advertisement tracing the history of the computer.

Blaise Pascal

Gottfried Leibniz

Charles Babbage

Herman Hollerith

From Abacus to Computer

Most of us think of the computer as being the unique product of twentieth century technology. Yet many of the elements which are inherent in today's computers are centuries old. The abacus, developed about 3,000 years ago, was the first digital counting machine. Since then, many other "machines and engines" were developed—all of which led to the ultimate development of the modern electronic computer. Here are just a few:

The Arithmetic Machine—1642

In the seventeenth century Blaise Pascal developed the first true calculating machine, using a technique which still is used in modern computers. A leading mathematician and philosopher in France, Pascal conceived his arithmetic machine in 1642 when he was only 19. The machine was operated by dialing a series of wheels bearing the numbers 0 to 9 around their circumferences.

The Calculating Machine—1694

Just over fifty years later Gottfried Leibniz, also a renowned mathemati-

cian and philosopher, devised a crude machine to mechanize the calculation of mathematical tables. His calculating machine was the first machine to multiply and divide directly. More complex than Pascal's arithmetic machine, it was designed to mechanize the calculation of trigonometric and astronomical tables.

The Difference Engine—1822

This was the first of several difference engines built in the nineteenth century. Developed by Charles Babbage, a British mathematician, it accumulated differences to produce tables for navigation, astronomy and even insurance. It was capable of generating tables to a 20-place accuracy. Out of his work on the difference engine, Babbage came up with the first idea for a computer, a machine which could handle any sort of mathematical computation automatically. His "analytical engine", although never built, included all those essential parts of a computer:

a stored program, an arithmetic unit and a section for data entry and output.

The Census Machine—1890

Dr. Herman Hollerith, a statistician from Buffalo, N.Y., solved a problem of major importance for the U.S. Census Bureau when he designed his electric tabulating machine in the 1880's. The problem was this: at the rate the population was growing, the eleventh census in 1890 would be obsolete before it was tabulated. Hollerith's machine solved the problem by being able to tabulate the massive amount of data electrically. The machine consisted of three parts: a tabulator which used a clock-like counting device (shown), a sorter box with compartments which were electrically connected to counters in the tabulator, and a pantographic punch, one of the first devices used to punch data onto cards.

The year 1890 marks the date the first major statistical machine was built and put into large-scale use. It was this invention of Hollerith's that launched the information-handling revolution. Afterward, many others followed who also made significant contributions leading to the development of the computer in the 1940's.

IBM.

memory can also assist management by supplying data on sales for each geographic region, for each product and brand, and for each type of customer.

Automation of Production

Computers have also taken over some production jobs that formerly were performed by hand. Continuous-process operations, such as petroleum refineries, are often run entirely by computers. At each stage of the refining process, information is fed into a computer on pressure of flows, temperature, and the like. This information is then used by the computer to send instructions to machinery that will change the temperature, increase or decrease the pressure, or take whatever action is needed to control the refining process.

Ford, General Motors, and Chrysler use about a thousand computers in their operations. Each automobile can have as many as 15,000 component parts, and computers are used to make certain that the right part is in the right place at the right time. Other computers test the engines, carburetors, distributors, and other machine parts.

Computers are also at work monitoring glass-manufacturing plants, blast furnaces, paper machines, pulp digesters, nuclear power plants, and in-warehouse inventory.

Retailing Applications

In many clothing stores an unusual price tag is attached to suits, dresses, and sportswear. The tag shows the price, but it also includes several punched holes and numbers. When the article of clothing is sold, the salesperson tears off the tag and deposits it in a special box. At the end of the day these tags are collected and taken to the computer center.

The tags are actually computer cards identifying the article of clothing and its cost and color as well as the store and the department. Processing of the cards allows inventory in the store to be automatically controlled. When inventory reaches a certain level, new shipments can automatically be made to stores, minimizing the possibility of running out of popular items.

Many cash registers have been replaced by computer terminals. The terminals are attached to computers that calculate each sale and maintain records of the store's inventory for each item carried.

Computers in the Supermarket

The latest supermarket use of the computer is the computerized checkout. The printed lines shown on the milk carton in Figure 15–6, called the Universal Product Code (UPC), are actually symbols that can be ''read'' by the optical-scanning device of a computer. As cashiers pass each item over the electronic reader, the computer instantly displays and records the sale and gives the customer a detailed receipt. The

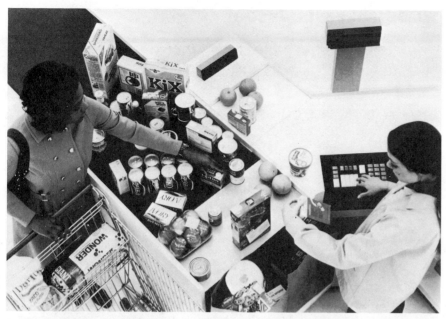

Electronic checkout equipment reduces checkout time and automatically keeps inventory records, thereby cutting labor costs.

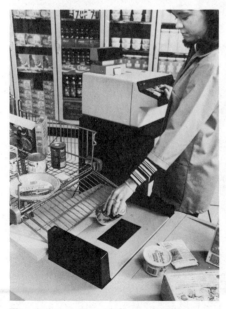

The clerk passes each item over the scanner; the scanner reads the code and records the price.

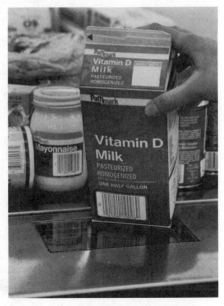

The price symbol is a series of printed lines that identify the product's name and price.

FIGURE 15–6
How computerized checkouts work.

system is expensive (between $100,000 and $150,000 per store). It is also opposed by the retail clerks union (which fears job losses) and consumer groups (which fear shopper exploitation if supermarkets stop marking prices on individual items). Still, many supermarket

Controversial Issue

Do Computers Lead to Unemployment?

Few of us would dispute the fact that computers have revolutionized American industry. But there is little agreement on the effect computer technology has had on the number and type of jobs available in the work place. Whether computers and the automation they create push people out of work or create jobs is an issue that will continue to be debated for a long time.

Many experts link the computer revolution to unemployment among blue-collar and unskilled labor. As the demands of industrial competition force businesses to computerize their traditional manufacturing techniques, semiskilled machine operators are replaced by white-collar technicians.

The plunging cost of mass-produced, programmable microprocessors is accelerating this trend, according to some observers who claim that the technology has developed to the point where it is often as flexible as the retraining of people.

On auto assembly lines, for example, human workers have been replaced by computerized robots that work double shifts at peak efficiency. In offices where productivity has risen only 4 percent in a decade, computers may someday replace secretarial and support staff. Using computerized word-processing equipment, office correspondence can be written, corrected, clean-typed, duplicated, and distributed in a fraction of the time it takes a secretary to do the same job.

Alvin Toffler, author of *The Third Wave,* paints the following picture of how tomorrow's office may operate:

> Messages and memos move silently and instantaneously. Terminals at every desk—thousands of them in any large organization—flicker quietly as information flows through the system. . .Computers link the company's files with those of other companies where necessary, and managers can call up information stored in hundreds of outside data banks.

There is little room in this picture for file clerks, stenographers, secretaries, and other back-up personnel who many believe will become obsolete and unemployable.

Few disagree with the projection that certain kinds of work will simply disappear in the computer age, but not every expert translates this into higher levels of unemployment. As the number of workers engaged in routine, repetitive, and dangerous work decreases, service and technological occupations will grow, they feel. During the 1950s and early 1960s, for example, when high technology first became a fact of life, employment expanded. The shrinkage in the manufacturing sector of the economy was more than offset by expanding white-collar and service jobs.

Experts assure us that this growth in white-collar service jobs does not mean permanent unemployment for unskilled and semi-skilled blue-collar workers. Secretaries, clerks, and stenographers may become coparticipants in office decision making along with their bosses. Or, as their skills become obsolete, they may be retrained by their corporations in computer skills so they, too, will be members of the technological elite. "The increased need for more educated manpower," says Harvard University's Program on Technology and Society, "has expanded the opportunities for upward mobility as the bottom level of the employment hierarchy contracts and the upper levels expand."

Even those who cannot read or write may benefit from the computer age, says Toffler. "Airline reservation clerks, stockroom personnel, machine operators, and repairmen may be able to function quite adequately on the job by listening rather than reading, as a voice from the machine tells them, step by step, what to do next or how to replace a broken part."

Recent data from the computer industry tell a story of expanding demand and an inadequate supply of qualified personnel. The industry now employs nearly half a million programmers and systems analysts, up from almost none in 1960. And according to a 1980 finding of the U.S. Bureau of the Census, the number of job openings for skilled computer personnel will grow at a faster rate than the rest of the labor force. According to New York personnel consultant Carl Denny, when computer programmers "walk in the door, we lay out the red carpet. In data processing, we're literally able to take almost anyone with any background or experience."

With so many factors affecting the level of employment it is difficult to determine if computer technology has increased or decreased the number of jobs available in the society. The level of employment does not simply rise or fall as computers become a part of the work place. The demand for certain skills increases; the demand for others declines. Retraining takes place until, finally, a new generation of workers is born and bred in the computer age. Although pressures on the job market may well increase dramatically in the years ahead, is it accurate to single out the computer as the primary source?

chain executives argue that the new system is a worthwhile investment. One industry spokesperson has said that the new system will cut food costs by more than $100 million a year. UPC symbols appear on an estimated 92 percent of all dry grocery products, and several thousand scanners are in use in the nation's supermarkets.[5]

Other Computer Applications

Although the impact of computers is widespread in business, virtually every phase of our society has been affected by them. Computers are regularly utilized in activities ranging from sports to education. Often the individual is affected by computers without ever knowing it. A plane trip offers numerous examples of the pervasiveness of computers:

> If, for example, you decide to make a trip by plane, your seat will probably be selected from an inventory by a computer in an automatic reservation system. To pay for your computer-recorded ticket, you might use a computer-checked credit card or a check that will be handled by a computer at your bank. You may drive to the airport in your computer-designed car over computer-designed roads and computer-controlled traffic intersections. At the airport you will take your seat in a computer-designed airplane. It will be flying with the aid of a computer-compiled weather report and a computerized ground traffic control system. If the plane is a Boeing 747, a computer coupled to the craft's autopilot might be steering the plane automatically—as you sit there in your suit made of cloth cut by a computer, reading a newspaper set in type by a computer.[6]

What's Ahead for Computers?

Few people doubt that the next 25 years of computer technology will be just as significant as the last 25 years. Technological developments will undoubtedly make computers faster and cheaper. In 1952 it cost $1.26 to do 100,000 multiplications on an IBM computer. Today this can be done for a penny. That same IBM computer could do about 2,000 multiplications a second in 1952. Today's computer can multiply at the rate of two million a second!

Microcomputers—small in size and inexpensive in price—will grow rapidly to service firms that cannot afford the larger installations or do not need the capabilities of larger computers. They will also probably replace the current use of **time-sharing**—the linking of several users through remote terminals (usually teletypewriters) to a large central computer. Companies whose volume of data is too small for them to own a computer can share costs with other users by dividing the use of a computer owned by a time-sharing company. The time-sharing firm also provides many of the necessary computer programs, thereby reducing the users' software expenses. Time-sharing is often found on

time-sharing
The linking of several users through remote terminals (usually teletypewriters) to a large central computer.

college campuses, where numerous buildings are linked to a central computer by input-output teletypewriters.

While time-sharing services continue to be popular, both the size and the price of smaller computers are declining. In time, most small firms will probably own their own computer hardware.

Software expenses are often the chief cost of a computer facility. New means will be found in the future to communicate with the computer. Future users may be able to communicate directly with the computer by using special pens or voice commands. Early strides in this direction have already been made.

Voice-input systems are still primitive, but they are already being used for a number of business activities. Bank tellers, for example, can use a special terminal to call the computer and determine whether a check should be cashed. The communication exchange goes something like this:

Computer: THIS IS THE EZ SYSTEM. WHO ARE YOU?
Teller: 201 [teller's number]. 15 [branch number].
Computer: ENTER TRANSACTION CODE.
Teller: 03 [checking account inquiry].
Computer: CENTER CHECKING ACCOUNT NUMBER.
Teller: 805-257-0.
Computer: BALANCE ON CHECKING ACCOUNT NUMBER EIGHT ZERO FIVE DASH TWO FIVE SEVEN DASH ZERO IS ONE ZERO SEVEN DOLLARS AND ZERO FIVE CENTS.[7]

Some computers are also learning to talk. One developed by Bell Laboratories has a 1,500-word vocabulary. The voice is not a tape recording but the result of a computer program that uses mathematical functions to represent the position of the tongue, lips, and palate in humans. The program is used to generate electronic speech signals that can be heard over a telephone or loudspeaker.[18]

By making direct voice contact between the user and computer possible, voice input and output systems may someday make the computer an integral tool of every manager.

Summary

Computers provide organizations with the ability to collect, analyze, store, and process information at a speed and accuracy unparalleled in history. In addition to the larger "mainframe," type of computer, minicomputers and microcomputers are available to meet all types of users' needs. The main elements of the computer are the input devices, which feed data into the computer; memory, which stores data and instructions for later use; arithmetic, which processes the data; control, which directs the sequence of operations, interprets instructions, and gives the proper commands to guide the computer; and output, which produces the requested information. These five elements represent computer hardware.

Software consists of computer languages and programs that tell the computer what to do. The most frequently used programming languages are FORTRAN, COBOL, BASIC, and PL/1. Special conversational programs have been developed to allow people with no programming abilities to use the computer.

In addition to speed and accuracy, computers provide many other advantages over hand methods of data processing. They can store large amounts of data in a small space. They can quickly make these data available for decision makers. And by performing the mechanical, routine, boring work of recording and maintaining incoming information, they can free people for more challenging work.

The major limitations of computers are cost (for both hardware and programming), computer mistakes caused by faulty programming, the tendency for management to use computers as a crutch rather than as a tool in decision making, and the potential for alienating customers by ignoring the human element in customer relations.

Computers have made contributions in every facet of business: banking, finance, marketing, manufacturing, accounting, personnel, securities markets—even the supermarket. Their contributions will increase in the future as faster and less expensive machines are developed. Continued development of microcomputers will allow smaller firms to utilize computerized operations. Software developments will increase, and software expenses will continue to decline for individual users if direct communication through voice input and output systems is refined and perfected.

Key Terms

analog computers	nanosecond
digital computers	binary arithmetic
computers	bit
minicomputer	computer program
microcomputer	computer programmer
cathode ray tube (CRT)	flowchart
input	FORTRAN
memory unit	COBOL
arithmetic unit	BASIC
control unit	PL/1
output	remote terminals
computer hardware	time-sharing
computer software	

Review Questions

1. Explain each of the terms listed on the previous page.

2. Describe each of the five basic elements of the computer.

3. What are the major advantages of computers?

4. What are the primary weaknesses of computers?

5. What is a nanosecond? What does this term imply about computer technology?

6. Distinguish between binary arithmetic and the decimal system.

7. How are flowcharts used by computer programmers?

8. What is meant by a computer language?

9. Select four or five areas of business, and list at least two computer applications for each area.

10. What advancements in computer technology can be expected in the years ahead?

Discussion Questions and Exercises

1. Evaluate the pros and cons of the controversial issue that appears in this chapter.

2. Discuss how a computer is (or could be) used in the operation of your college.

3. Using the example shown in Figure 15–5 as a basic format, draw a flowchart showing how you study for examinations in this course.

4. Convert the following decimal numbers to binary arithmetic:

104	21
16	39
11	50

5. Threshold Technology has developed and placed on the market a voice-recognition system that converts the spoken word into data that a computer can understand. More than 50 customers have each paid from $10,500 to $800,000 for this system. Customers range from United Parcel Service to the Chicago Mercantile Exchange.[9] Suggest some likely customers for the system. What major problems exist for voice-recognition systems?

Case 15-1: The Computer Invades the Home

You will awaken some morning in five years, speak a few simple instructions from your bed to your toaster, coffeepot, and frying pan, and walk into the kitchen 15 minutes later to a prepared breakfast.

The same small computer that's wired into the walls of your house and built to recognize only your voice will turn on lights when you walk into the kitchen and turn them off when you leave. It also will turn the refrigerator off when you leave for work and turn it back on before anything defrosts. Your furnace and air conditioner will respond to the same computer, driving warm or cool air into only the rooms that are occupied.

Your home computer will pay bills and balance your checkbook. It will order groceries, plan meals, and suggest recipes for dinner guests on diets or with fussy appetites. It will even open the front door, responding without locks and keys to the sound of your voice. All you'll need to say is "Open sesame."

If this *Washington Post* prediction sounds more like fantasyland than a forecast, think again. Many of the described services are available from currently tested home computers. And an estimated 100,000 U.S. households have already shelled out anywhere from $200 to $3,000 to bring one home. Retailers include Tandy Corporation's Radio Shack stores and an estimated 500 retail outlets that have opened in the past two years with such names as Computer Warehouse Store and Kentucky Fried Computers ("a computer in every pot").

The home computer looks like an electric typewriter attached to a video display screen. The user types in requests and receives output on the screen: homework problems can be checked, lawn sprinklers can be turned on and off automatically, investment portfolios can be maintained. Uses appear to be limited primarily by the user's imagination. An industry source forecast home computer sales of $2 billion by 1985; by that time most middle-income homes may come equipped with a computer.

Questions

1. Suggest additional applications of home computers.

2. Would you recommend that manufacturers of home computers attempt to market them directly to builders of new homes rather than to owners? What problems are likely to arise?

3. What do you feel are the major hurdles to be overcome in the home computer market?

Case 15–2: Computer Crimes

The explosive growth of computer technology has not only been a boon to business but has also created a new menace: a vastly expanded potential for computer crime. Among some of the wrongdoers who used a computer instead of a knife or a gun were:

An operations officer for one of the largest banks in the U.S. allegedly produced fake deposits at one branch in an account belonging to a boxing promotion outfit. He did this by using the bank's computerized interbranch account settlement process to withdraw funds from a different branch. To prevent the computer from discovering the imbalance, he created new fraudulent credits to cover the withdrawals. He allegedly kept the process going for two years and a total of $21.3 million. He denies the charges.

A computer consultant for another big bank obtained the bank's electronic funds transfer code. Later, posing as a branch manager, he called from a public telephone and used the code to send $10.3 million to a Swiss account. By the time the U.S. bank's computers discovered the fraud, he had flown to Switzerland, converted the funds into diamonds, and returned to the United States. Only when he boasted of the feat was he identified, convicted, and sentenced to prison.

The programmer in charge of payrolls at a major company decided to trim a few cents off each check and add them to his own account. Although the books balanced, this programmer was not so lucky. He now resides at the state penitentiary.

An army programmer created an entirely new (although imaginary) military base staffed by 200 nonexistent people. He then opened 200 checking accounts for their paychecks and the money rolled in. Everything went so smoothly that it took him several months to realize that he would probably never be caught *as long as the base continued to operate.* He had become—in a few months—a self-made millionaire but could think of no way to close the base! An accidental bombing, mass food poisoning, or 200 desertions all seemed too unbelievable. So finally he simply turned himself in.

Questions

1. What characteristics of the computer make it vulnerable to such crimes?

2. Suggest several procedures for preventing similar occurrences.

16

Management Information and Statistics

Learning Goals

1. To explain the purpose of a management information system and how it functions in a firm

2. To distinguish between primary and secondary data and to know the strengths and limitations of each

3. To identify each method of collecting survey data and to understand when each should be used

4. To describe how the mean, median, and mode are calculated and when each measure should be used

5. To identify the chief advantages and disadvantages of converting to the metric system

6. To explain the meaning of each of the key terms introduced in this chapter

Profile: Steven P. Jobs and Stephen G. Wozniak
Making Information Affordable for Every Firm

Steven P. Jobs

Stephen G. Wozniak

Steven P. Jobs and Stephen G. Wozniak have proven that the American dream is alive and well in the land of computers—California's "Silicon Valley." In 1976 21-year-old Jobs and 26-year-old Wozniak took six months to design their first personal computer and 40 hours to build it. Within a short time they had orders for 50 computers, which they sold unassembled, in kit form, to computer hobbyists.

To fulfill their orders, Jobs and Wozniak, who are both college dropouts, raised approximately $1,200 from the sale of a Volkswagen van and a programmable calculator to set up shop in Jobs' garage. Working 14- to 15-hour days, the partners turned their business into an overnight success. The result is a company named after the most simple, perfect, natural object they could think of—Apple Computer.

Aided by $3 million of venture capital and top-notch business management, Jobs and Wozniak moved their headquarters to Cupertino, California, where they introduced Apple II, which weighs only 12 pounds, looks like a desk-top typewriter, and is the first fully programmable computer of its size. Unlike its competitors, Apple II comes fully assembled and brings many of the ca-

pabilities of large data-processing systems to individuals and small businesses. And just as important to Apple's customers, it is easy to use and relatively inexpensive.

In May 1980, Jobs and Wozniak introduced the more sophisticated Apple III, which was designed specifically for professional and small businesses. Using Apple software, the instructions that program the computer's actions, Apple III offers small businesses previously unaffordable computer capability. Just by switching computer programs, Apple III provides a computerized accounting system, an up-to-date inventory control, a full-function word processor, a mailing list maintenance system, a Dow Jones News Service retrieval system, and more.

By 1981, riding on the wave of its latest computer success, Apple became the nation's second largest manufacturer of personal computers.

Offering an affordable personal computer to individuals and small businesses has paid off for Jobs and Wozniak. With 1.6 million personal computers expected to be in operation by 1984, up from 400,000 in 1980, the rewards are likely to be even greater in the years ahead.

*Just try explaining the value of statistical summaries
to the widow of the man who drowned crossing a
stream with an average depth of four feet.*

—Anonymous

*There are three kinds of lies: lies, damned lies, and
statistics.*

—Benjamin Disraeli

The business of bookselling was transformed during the 1970s, as major chains such as Waldenbooks, Little Professor, and B. Dalton shocked their more genteel competitors by adopting the management practices used in other more aggressive industries. Their strategies were familiar: follow the buying patterns of shoppers to the suburbs and open well-organized, cheery stores stocked with 25,000 titles and bold displays designed to attract casual readers. By 1980, Waldenbooks had established 600 units and B. Dalton was operating another 400 units. The two chains control about 20 percent of all book trade at the retail level. But here the similarities between the two major competitors end.

B. Dalton management recognized the importance of inventory control, of being able to identify quickly—and stock its stores with—fast sellers and to drop the slow movers. A decision was made to computerize book-tracking by coding each book as soon as it is ordered from the publisher. This tracking system permits corporate management to compare weekly sales reports by title and topic for every store, city, or region. These data are then used for determining restock of best-sellers and return of slow movers, as well as for selecting new books to purchase.

By contrast, Waldenbooks managers relied on a manual system and had no precise information on individual sales, titles on hand, and regional purchase patterns. Although some store managers resorted to copying manually the titles of best sellers, they frequently faced book displays that were alternately overstocked and empty. Waldenbooks decision makers were clearly in the dark about book sales, and some of their purchase decisions reflected the problem. "Because it didn't know what its inventory was, Walden often reordered on top of stock it already had, then couldn't sell the books," a sales manager of a major publisher reported. The problem was also reflected in a measure of store efficiency—sales per square foot. Dalton's $130 of sales per square foot far outdistanced the $110 generated by Walden outlets.

Waldenbooks managers recognized the competitive disadvantage of their information gap and resolved to rectify the problem. More than $4 million was invested over a two-year period in the installation of a point-of-sale terminal for each retail outlet. These terminals are connected to the corporation's central computer to generate data comparable to those available to B. Dalton managers. The expenditure should quickly pay for itself by reducing the costs of returning unsold books to publishers and by generating additional sales through making certain that books sought by consumers are available for purchase.[1]

Information: Vital Ingredient in Decision Making

The chief task of the manager is decision making. As Chapter 5 pointed out, managers earn their salaries by making effective decisions that allow their firms to solve problems as they occur. Managers must also anticipate and prevent future problems. All too often the manager is forced to make decisions with limited information or inadequate facts. If effective decisions are to be made, a system must be developed to ensure that information is available when needed and in a form suitable for analysis by the decision maker.

The Role of the Management Information System

The recipe for effective decisions was once given as "90 percent information and 10 percent inspiration." In order to obtain relevant information for decision making, most large- and medium-sized firms establish a management information system (MIS).

"What are the storage costs for Model 24?"

"What is the sales potential for our brand in the San Francisco-Oakland territory?"

"How much has Allison accomplished so far?"

"How do our wage rates compare with similar firms in Philadelphia?"

"How many units of Model 24 are there in the Denver warehouse?"

These are but a few examples of the hundreds of questions asked every day in a business operation. An effective information system

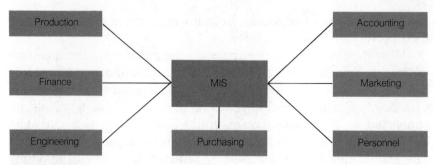

FIGURE 16–1
The MIS provides decision information for all parts of the organization.

management information system (MIS)
An organized method of providing past, present, and projected information on internal operations and external intelligence for use in management decision making.

aids decision making by having answers to such questions available for the business executive. The **management information system (MIS)** is an organized method of providing past, present, and projected information on internal operations and external intelligence for use in management decision making.[2] As Figure 16–1 indicates, the MIS can assist decision making in all major areas of the organization.

The heart of any management information system is the information itself. Decision-related information is needed for almost every company activity—whether internal or external. The latter includes information about changing consumer demands, competitors' actions, and new government regulations. If the firm knows about pending legislation, it can plan to present its viewpoint to legislators. Awareness of changing demands may result in product modifications or new marketing programs. Competitive moves may prompt the firm to make numerous decisions.

Internal Sources of Information

internal data
Data generated within the organization.

Internal data are data generated within the organization. A tremendous amount of useful information is available from financial records. Data can be obtained on changes in accounts receivable, inventory levels, loans outstanding, cash on hand, customers, product lines, profitability of particular divisions, or comparisons of sales by territories, salespeople, customers, or product lines. These records provide important insights into business operations. And because they are collected on a regular basis, the information can be added to the firm's MIS at a low cost (see Focus 16–1).

Although much of the internal information is financial, other kinds of information inputs are also available. The personnel department can supply data on employee turnover and on worker attitudes and suggestions. Quality control can supply information on the quality

FOCUS 16–1
The Sears Information System

To see how the Sears MIS works, let's follow a coffeepot as it heads for a Sears store. When the coffeepot is shipped from the warehouse, an automatic ticket-maker produces a ticket indicating the color, stock number, price, and department number in the store. When a customer takes the coffeepot to the register, the Sears clerk either keys the numbers into the register or uses a special reading wand.

The data are then stored in the store's minicomputer until nighttime, when they are automatically transferred to one of Sears's 22 regional data centers. There, one of the 33 large IBM computers processes the information. The customer's credit account is charged (if a charge sale has been made), sales and tax information are entered into the accounting department's records, and the salesperson's commission is credited to the payroll department.

Sales data are also sent to the coffeepot department's inventory management system. If the day's coffeepot sales reduce the department's inventory below a predetermined amount, the computer automatically prints a purchase order, which is sent to the department manager the next morning. If the manager decides to purchase additional coffeepots, the reorder goes to the warehouse for shipment.

At the same time, the sales data are channeled to a central data-processing department in the Chicago headquarters. Here, all sales information for the entire Sears operation is compiled. The network of 30,000 registers, 640 minicomputers, and 33 large computers allows Sears managers to monitor sales by store, region, department, and product on a daily basis.

level of materials purchased and the rejection rate of products produced by the firm. Customer complaint letters can serve as another information input.

External Sources of Information

Much of the information for the firm's MIS comes from **external data**—data generated outside the firm. This information is of two types—primary and secondary. **Primary data** consist of data being collected for the first time during a research study. In contrast, **secondary data** are previously published information. Although the re-

external data
Data generated outside the firm.

primary data
Data collected for the first time during a research study that will be used in solving a business problem.

secondary data
Previously published information that is used in solving business problems.

searcher will typically exhaust all likely sources of secondary data before deciding to begin the collection of primary data, both types offer specific benefits for the decision maker.

Secondary Data

An extremely important source of management information is secondary (previously published) data. Although considerable amounts of secondary data are available internally, even more data are available from external sources. So much is available at little or no cost that the information manager faces the problem of being overwhelmed by the sheer quantity of data that is available from many sources.

Government sources. The various levels of government are the nation's most important sources of secondary data, and the most frequently used data are census data. Although the Bureau of the Census spent slightly more than $1 per person in conducting the 1980 Census of Population, the information is available for use without charge at local libraries, or it can be purchased on computer tapes for a nominal fee.

The Census of Population is so detailed that population characteristics for large cities are available by city block. Data are available on age, sex, race, citizenship, educational levels, occupation, employment status, and income.

The Census Bureau also conducts a Census of Housing, which provides such information as the value of homes in a particular geographic area, the number of rooms, the type of structure, the occupants' race, and the years the homes were built. This information is used by numerous government agencies and departments such as the Department of Labor; the Department of Health and Human Services; and the various areas within the Department of Housing and Urban Development. It can also be used by shopping center developers to determine what sort of potential customers they will have, or by those studying potential plant sites to determine available skills in a community and the number of available workers.

Other government reports include the Census of Business, the Census of Manufacture, the Census of Agriculture, the Census of Minerals, and the Census of Government. So much data are produced by the government each year that most firms should purchase its guidebook, *Catalog of U.S. Census Publications,* in order to keep abreast of current publications. Other government sources include the *Statistical Abstract of the United States,* the *Survey of Current Business,* the monthly *Federal Reserve Bulletin,* and the *Monthly Labor Review.*

State and city governments are still other important sources of information on employment, production, and sales activities within a particular state or city.

Private sources. A number of private organizations provide information for business decision makers. Trade associations are excellent resource centers for their members. They often publish journals or newsletters containing information on production costs and wages in the industry and suggestions for improving operations. Advertising agencies continually collect information on the audiences reached by various media such as magazines, television, and radio.

Several national firms offer information to businesses on a subscription basis. The A. C. Nielsen Company collects data every 60 days on the sales of most products stocked in food stores and drugstores. *Sales and Marketing Management* magazine publishes an annual *Survey of Buying Power,* which provides detailed information on population, income, and retail sales in cities and counties for each state in the United States and in the Canadian provinces. Moody's, Dun & Bradstreet, and Standard & Poor's provide financial information on a subscription basis. The chief source of information concerning construction activities is provided by the *Dodge Reports.*

Comparing Secondary and Primary Data

The use of secondary data offers two important advantages over the use of primary data: lower cost and less time for collection and use. Even though some secondary data may require fees paid to the firm involved in the data collection, the cost is invariably less than if the firm has to collect the data itself. A considerable amount of time must be spent in determining information needs, identifying sources of data, preparing collection instruments, training researchers, and collecting and interpreting the data—all activities that are performed in obtaining primary data.

But the use of secondary data is subject to a number of important limitations. First, the data may be obsolete. The data provided by the 1980 Census of Population is already obsolete in many areas due to the substantial population shifts since 1980. Second, the classifications of secondary data may not be usable for the firm. Because the secondary data were originally collected for a specific purpose, they may not be in an appropriate form for a particular decision maker. For example, a retail merchant who is deciding whether to open a new store in a shopping mall may require data on household income for a five-mile area, but the only available data may be collected on a county basis. In still other cases, available data may be of doubtful accuracy. Errors in collecting, analyzing, and interpreting the original data may make the information inaccurate. Even the accuracy of the 1980 Census has been questioned on the grounds that information was not obtained from all members of the population. In all such instances, the firm may be forced to collect primary data.

Primary Data

As mentioned previously, primary data are data collected for the first time for use in solving a business problem. Most primary data are collected by one of two methods—observation or survey. The most efficient method depends on the particular situation.

observation method
A method of collecting primary data that involves studies conducted by actually viewing the actions of respondents either directly or through mechanical devices.

The observation method. The **observation method** involves studies that are conducted by actually viewing the actions of the respondents either directly or through mechanical devices. Quality control departments often use the observation method in checking for defective products. Traffic counts can be used to determine the best location for new fast-food franchises. Television ratings are usually determined by the Nielsen audiometer, which is attached to television sets to record when the set is turned on and which channels are being viewed (see Focus 16–2).

FOCUS 16–2
How Nielsen Determines Television Ratings

Local television stations can collect information about the characteristics of their viewers through methods such as telephone surveys and diaries (week-long listings of viewers' television choices during specified time periods). But network television ratings are determined nationally and by machine, most often by the audiometer method of the A.C. Nielsen Company. This device consists of a timer set to local time, a cartridge of film, and a lamp that lights up to expose the film when the set is turned on and a channel is selected. In some instances, the audiometer is connected directly to the central Nielsen computer to generate next-day rankings of television shows.

Network income is based primarily on the ratings of its shows, which indicate approximately how many people watch a particular program. The more people who watch a show, the more the advertisers who sponsor it can be charged. A telecast of the Super Bowl with extremely large audiences can cost advertisers as much as $375,000 for each 30-second message—as occurred during a recent Super Bowl telecast. As a result, the three major networks engage in intense competition for the largest audience for each segment of the broadcasting day and particularly for prime time in the evening.

The Nielsen method consists of a scientifically selected sample of about 1,200 homes across the nation. Each family is retained in the sample for about three years. Each participating household receives an initial payment of $25. Thereafter, it receives token payments of $1 monthly and a 50 percent reimbursement for any television set repair costs.

---

survey method
A method of acquiring primary data in which a researcher asks respondents questions to ascertain attitudes, motives, and opinions.

The survey method. Many types of primary data cannot be obtained through mere observation of actions. The researcher must ask questions. When information is needed about employee, supplier, or customer attitudes and opinions, the **survey method** must be used (see Focus 16–3).

FOCUS 16–3
The Year the Pollsters Struck Out

Every election year is filled with reports of political pollsters trying to tell us who is going to win the various elections. Such major organizations as the Harris and Gallup polls utilize a variety of data-collecting techniques to assist their clients in determining areas of strengths and weaknesses in a campaign. In the 1980s, no candidate for national office operated without the information collected by political pollsters. Increasingly, political research organizations are becoming mainstays of state and local races.

One amazing characteristic of political polling is the ability to generate precise findings based upon small samples. A second aspect of polling is the surprising accuracy of their findings. While one major pollster did pick Alf Landon back in 1936 as the presidential winner over Franklin Roosevelt, and a Chicago newspaper carried the headline "Dewey Defeats Truman" in 1948, today's general public is more often treated to precise predictions of political outcomes within minutes of the closing of voting booths.

But the 1980 election severely damaged the reputations of pollsters who labeled the Carter-Reagan race "too close to call." Months after the Reagan landslide, the pollsters were searching for the reasons for their error. Some blamed voter frustrations over the Iranian hostage crisis. Others pointed to the differences often present between a voter's expressed intentions and his or her actual behavior in the voting booth. The pollsters did agree, however, on the fact that the polls had missed something fundamental in the 1980 election, and as a result, their predictions were wrong.

Survey information is rarely gathered from all possible sources because the costs are too great. (If all sources are reached, the results are called a **census.**) Instead the researcher selects a representative group called a **sample.** If the sample is chosen in a random way so that every member of the population has an equal chance of being selected, it is called a **probability sample.** A quality control check of every hundredth item on an assembly line may give production control engineers a representative sample of the overall quality of the work. A random selection of student names from the list at the registrar's office will provide a probability sample of students at a college.

Three kinds of surveys exist: telephone, mail, and personal interview. Telephone interviews are cheap and fast for obtaining small amounts of relatively impersonal information, but they must be limited to simple clearly worded questions. Because many firms have leased Wide Area Telephone Service (WATS) lines, a survey of suppliers'

census
A primary data survey in which all possible data sources are contacted.

sample
A representative group from which data are gathered.

probability sample
A representative group selected in a random way so that every member of the population has an equal chance for inclusion in the study.

opinions on, say, a proposed payment plan could be conducted quickly and at little expense. (WATS is a telephone company service that allows a firm to make unlimited numbers of long distance calls for a fixed rate per state or region.) Telephone interviews have two major limitations: (1) it is extremely difficult to obtain personal information from respondents, and (2) the survey may be prejudiced because two important groups are omitted—those without telephones and those with unlisted numbers.

Mail interviews allow the researcher to conduct national studies at reasonable costs. Whereas personal interviews with a national sample may prove too costly, mail interviews allow the researcher to reach each potential respondent for the price of a first-class stamp. Costs can be misleading, however, because the rate of return of questionnaires in such a study may average only 15 to 25 percent, depending on the length of the questionnaire and respondent interest. Unless additional information is obtained from those not responding through a telephone interview or other method, the results are likely to be biased, because there may be important differences between the characteristics of the nonrespondents and those who took the time to complete and return the questionnaire.

Companies using mail questionnaires to collect data often try a variety of techniques to increase response rates. Some firms include research questions on warranty cards. TI Corporation received a 60 percent response to its questionnaire to stockholders by printing the questions on the back of dividend checks. Others use a coin to attract the reader's attention (as in Figure 16–2).

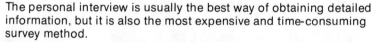

The personal interview is usually the best way of obtaining detailed information, but it is also the most expensive and time-consuming survey method.

Marketing Research Analysts

January 14, 19xx

Dear Miami resident:

We are conducting a study for a client to determine
how well Miami residents know the organizations
described in the enclosed questionnaire.

We would appreciate it if you would answer the questions
and return the questionnaire to us in the enclosed,
stamped, addressed envelope. Your reply will be
confidential, of course, and the results of this
survey will be shown in statistical form only.

Many thanks for your help. The attached coin is
intended only to gain your attention. Perhaps it
may help brighten the day for some youngster you know.

Cordially,

Margaret Carpenter
Margaret Carpenter
Director of Research

Survey Research ● Consumer Panels ● Attitude Studies ● Political Research ● AD and TV Commercial Tests

FIGURE 16–2
Use of a coin to attract attention and
increase mail survey response rates.

The personal interview is the most expensive and time-consuming survey method. It calls for well-trained and well-paid interviewers and involves expenses of traveling to the respondents' locations. (In fact, the costs are so great that officials at the Bureau of the Census collected 85 percent of the 1980 Census of Population by mail.) Still, the personal interview is typically the best means of obtaining detailed information, particularly because the interviewer can explain any questions that are confusing or vague to the respondent. The flexibility and detailed information offered by this method often more than offset the time and cost limitations.

Interpreting research findings. Considerable expertise is required in collecting primary data. Many firms have research departments staffed with specialists in designing questionnaires, training interviewers, developing representative samples, and interpreting the findings of the research study. Other organizations hire specialized research firms to handle specific projects.

Increasing the value of research findings. Because researchers are specialists who assist the line managers in their decision making, it is crucial for both parties to communicate effectively at each stage of the research process so that both agree on the studies to be conducted—and on how they will be conducted and evaluated. Too many research studies go unused because managers view the results as too restricted. This often occurs because of study summaries that include lengthy discussions of research limitations or use too many technical terms such as "confidence limits" or "Type II" errors. In such instances, the line manager may dismiss the report as too filled with research jargon and as failing to address the problem at hand.

The summary report of the research study should include recommendations for management based on research findings. Whenever possible, the researcher should make an oral report of research findings so that the written document can be explained, expanded, or clarified. This increases the likelihood of its use by management in making more informed decisions.

Statistical Analysis of Management Information

The world is filled with statistics. The distance from the earth to the sun is 93 million miles. The average family has 2.1 children. Heart disease is the number one cause of death. The episode of CBS's nighttime soap opera *Dallas* that revealed who shot J. R. attracted the largest audience in the history of television. Some 75 percent of the potential viewing audience watched at least portions of the program. Two British brothers made their fortunes by amassing thousands of statistics and publishing them as the *Guinness Book of World Records.*

When viewed as individual items such as basketball scoring averages or the quarterly earnings per share of a corporation, the term statistics refers to a collection of numerical data about some event, object, or individual. More broadly, **statistics** is the collection, analysis, interpretation, and presentation of information in numerical form. (This definition includes the first, more limited, concept.)

It is not an overstatement to say that statistics—like accounting—is a language of business. Although business executives are not ex-

statistics
The collection, analysis, interpretation, and presentation of information in numerical form.

pected to be statistical experts, they must possess some familiarity with the basic concepts and terms used in this field.

Statistical analysis is used in interpreting data obtained from research investigations. There are many methods for analyzing statistical information. Among the most often used are array and frequency distribution and measures of mean, median, and mode.

Array and Frequency Distribution

Table 16-1 is an example of secondary data from the Ford Motor Company. The table shows total production of each Ford and Lincoln-Mercury division auto model. It is an example of an **array**—a listing of items by size, from either the smallest to the largest or the largest to the smallest.

array
A listing of items by size, from either the smallest to the largest or the largest to the smallest.

TABLE 16–1
Passenger Car Production by Ford Motor Company

Model	Number of Units Produced (in thousands)
1. Mustang	370
2. Thunderbird	260
3. Ford Fairmont	210
4. LTD/LTD II	190
5. Pinto	170
6. Granada	140
7. Cougar/Cougar XR 7	140
8. Capri	110
9. Mercury Marquis	100
10. Lincoln	70
11. Mark VI/V	70
12. Zephyr	60
13. Monarch	60
14. Bobcat	40
15. Ford Club Wagon	40
16. Versailles	10
Total	2,040

In order to increase the meaning of the statistics, it is common practice to group the data into a **frequency distribution,** which shows the number of times each item appears in the data. Figure 16–3 is based on data in Table 16–1; it graphically displays the frequency

frequency distribution
The common practice of grouping data in a listing or graph to show the number of times each item appears in the data.

FIGURE 16–3
Frequency distribution of Ford Motor Company passenger car models.

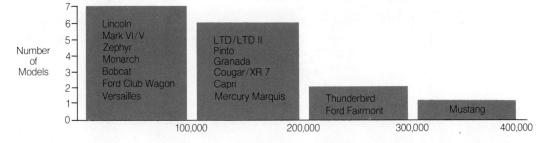

distribution of auto models and production levels. It helps summarize the data, pointing out that fewer than 200,000 units were produced for most of the Ford Motor Company auto models.

Mean, Median, and Mode

mean (average)
A statistical measure calculated by adding together all the observations and dividing by the number of observations.

median
The middle score in the distribution of observations.

mode
The most frequently occurring value in a series of observations.

Perhaps the most widely used statistical measure, the arithmetic **mean** (or average) is calculated by adding together all the observations and dividing by the number of observations. The mean number of units produced for each Ford Motor Company model in Table 16–1 is 128,000 (the 2,040,000 total divided by the 16 different auto models).

A second commonly used measure is the **median,** the middle score in the distribution. The median is the value that lies above half the observations in the distribution and below the other half. Because Table 16–1 contains 16 observations, the median is between the eighth (Capri) and ninth (Mercury Marquis) observations, or between 100,000 and 110,000 units.

A third measure is the **mode,** which represents the most frequently occurring value. As Table 16–1 indicates, the mode is not particularly useful in summarizing production data, because four production levels (140,000 for Granada and Cougar; 70,000 for Lincoln and Mark VI/ V; 60,000 for Zephyr and Monarch; and 40,000 for Bobcat and Ford Club Wagon) each occur twice.

Each of these measures has its limitations. Although the mean is the most commonly used, it is subject to distortions when extremely low or high numbers appear. The median is frequently used for in-

Statistics are an important ingredient in the presentation of information.

"That's the gist of what I want to say. Now get me some statistics to base it on."

Drawing by Joe Minachi; © 1977 The New Yorker Magazine, Inc.

come figures because the presence of a few millionaires will distort "average" income figures if the mean is utilized. A travel agent may want to use the mode to plan a package vacation tour for the next season. By knowing last year's most popular vacation area, the agent may be able to meet the desires of the firm's clients.

Presentation of Data

It is not enough that data be collected, analyzed, and interpreted. If they are to fulfill their role as decision-oriented management information, they must also be presented in a form that allows the decision maker to understand and use them.

The proper form for presenting data may vary from one executive to another or from department to department. In some situations computer printouts are the proper form. Copies of financial reports, such as income statements, may be sufficient for other users. In still other cases statistical information should be presented in tabular or pictorial form. Data can be effectively summarized and represented in graphic form by line charts, bar charts, pie charts, or pictographs. Examples of these charts are shown in Figure 16–4. The pictorial summaries serve to ensure the use of the information by the decision maker.

A New Measuring System for Management Information and Statistics

Even though the Constitution clearly gives Congress the power to "fix the standard of weights and measures" for the United States, it is clear that two systems are currently being used. Jokes such as "take me to your liter" are a result of the growth in the use of the second system. The **metric system**—the standard of weights and measures based upon the decimal system of tens and multiples—is already used throughout most of the world, and its use is growing rapidly in the United States. The "metric car," Chevette, was introduced by General Motors in 1976. Seven-Up and many other soft drinks come in one-half liter and liter bottles as a substitute for pints and quarts. Many canned and packaged foods carry metric equivalents to ounces and pounds on their labels. Mustangs equipped with 2.3 liter engines are being powered by motors designed entirely in metrics.

metric system
The standard of weights and measures based on the decimal system of tens and multiples.

FIGURE 16–4
Examples of graphic presentations of data:
A—line chart, B—bar graph, C—pie chart,
D—pictograph.

(A) Line Chart

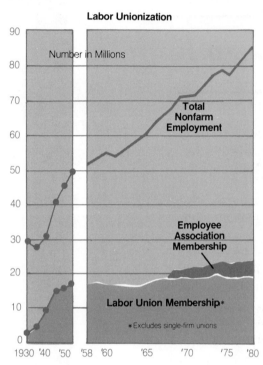

Labor Unionization

(B) Bar Graph

**Foreign Workers as Percent of
Total Employment in Host Country, 1977**

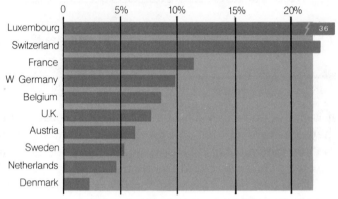

(C) Pie Chart

Population by Labor Force Status

(D) Pictograph

Number of Persons by Age and Sex: 1970
Number in Millions

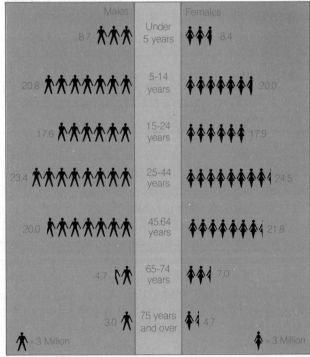

Many packaged food items now carry metric
equivalents to ounces and pounds on their labels.

While many people fail to understand the new system—and laugh
at stories of a cigarette smoker walking 1.6 kilometers for a Camel or
Reggie Jackson hitting a 112-meter home run—preparations are under way to equip the next generation with a working knowledge of
metrics. Twenty-five states and the District of Columbia have already
begun to prepare classwork in metrics. In California all elementary
school texts must include metrics. Even major league baseball clubs
are marking their stadiums in both feet and meters. The distance from
home plate to the left-field foul pole may be indicated by two numerals
painted on the stands: perhaps 330 (for feet) and 100 (for meters).

International companies are making the switch to enable them to
compete in a metric world. Firms such as Caterpillar Tractor, IBM,
Deere & Co., International Harvester, Honeywell, and Rockwell International have been using metrics for years in foreign trade. The
switch to metrics should increase export sales by smaller firms that
cannot afford to produce two sets of products—one for the U.S. market and another for export.

The current U.S. measuring system is a holdover from England,
which has already switched to the metric system. The mile, for in-

Controversial Issue

The 1980 Census Undercount: Should Statistical Tools Be Used to Estimate Those We Missed?

With 226.5 million of us officially counted by the U.S. Census Bureau, the 1980 census is complete. Or is it? Mayors of Detroit, New York, Chicago, Philadelphia, and Newark have challenged the accuracy of the census results in court, charging that blacks, Hispanics, other minority group members, and illegal aliens living in inner-city ghettos were undercounted. This is not surprising because in New York alone an estimated 8.5 percent of welfare recipients were overlooked, thousands of others complained they had never received census forms, and a significant percentage of forms were sent back by the U.S. Postal Service marked "undeliverable."

Despite all this, the United States Supreme Court ruled that the census figures could be certified to meet the year-end deadline, while the Census Bureau appealed a lower court decision requiring it to devise a plan to estimate the serious undercount of blacks and Hispanics in New York.

The Census Bureau balks at the need for using statistical devices to correct its population figures. It contends that its national population count for April 1, 1980, will prove as valid as any statistical device designed to estimate those it missed. Motivated by a court directive, however, the Bureau plans to use a demographic analysis, to match a 1978 population survey with Internal Revenue Service records, and to conduct a "postenumeration program" to estimate the number of uncounted people throughout the country. After evaluating its findings, it will recommend to the court the most precise and accurate technique for adjusting census data.

stance, is 1,000 paces stepped off by a Roman soldier. A yard, according to legend, is the distance from King Edward III's nose to the end of his outstretched hand. An acre represents the amount of ground that a yoke of oxen can plow in a day.

The metric system is based on the decimal system of tens and their multiples. These include deca (10), hecto (100), kilo (1,000), and myria (10,000). Fractions are deci (1/10th), cent (1/100th), and milli (1/1000th). A centimeter, therefore, is 1/100th of a meter.

Conversion will undoubtedly be expensive. Estimates run as high as $11 billion. But supporters of the switch argue that it will save teachers the time they now use to explain the much more complicated current system and will eliminate the need to manufacture two versions of products to meet domestic and foreign needs.

Refusal to convert to the metric system would isolate U.S. manufacturing from the rest of the world. The only nations that have not already begun to convert to metrics are Brunei, Burma, Liberia, and Yemen.[3]

In one suggested approach, officials estimate the undercount percentage for a particular group, then increase the census count proportionately across the country for that group. If, for example, 7 percent of the black population was thought to be missed, the Census Bureau would up the count of blacks in every area by 7 percent. Critics call this technique highly inaccurate because blacks were not equally undercounted in all areas. In addition census officials are having difficulty in even estimating the number of Hispanics and other minorities who were undercounted.

The Constitution calls for an "actual enumeration" of residents. If estimates were not good enough for our forefathers, legal experts tell us, they are certainly not good enough for us. In addition, under federal law, legislative redistricting, a process that adjusts the representation in the House of Representatives, must be based on actual census data.

If the current census figures hold up, 16 or more House seats will shift from the Northeast to the South and West. This means that the clout to bring some of the $50 billion in government projects back home will change hands. With such high stakes, Sun Belt politicians are sure to dig in their spurs and resist even the most sophisticated statistical techniques for revising the census.

Whether the census figures stand or some method of estimating the undercount is used, there is almost certain to be a political outcry, despite the fact that some observers believe that, even assuming an undercount, the difference would be so statistically small that it would make little difference.

Summary

Information is a vital element in management decisions. Effective decisions cannot be made without answers to questions about the internal operations of the firm and the environment in which it operates. Progressive companies are currently involved in introducing and perfecting their own planned management information system (MIS), which will enable them to provide past, present, and projected information on internal operations and external intelligence for use in making decisions. Such information systems should aid all areas of the organization—production, accounting, marketing, personnel, purchasing, engineering, and finance—in their decision-making responsibilities.

A great deal of the information in the firm's MIS is generated from internal information, much of it from accounting records. Additional internal information comes from production, personnel, employee suggestions, and other internal sources.

External information, that collected outside the firm, can be divided into two types: primary and secondary. Secondary data are those previously published. Important sources include federal, state, and local governments and firms that supply information on a subscription basis.

Primary data are collected for the first time for use in solving a business problem. They can be obtained through observation or surveys. Surveys can be conducted by telephone, mail questionnaires, or personal interviews.

Statistical analysis is used in interpreting data obtained from research investigations. Statistics involves the collection, analysis, interpretation, and presentation of information in numerical form. Data are often listed in an array or grouped into a frequency distribution. Three common statistical measures are the mean, median, and mode: they indicate the central values in a group of observations.

Effective presentation of research findings is essential if the information is to be useful in management decision making. Pictorial representations of data in the form of line charts, bar charts, pie charts, or pictographs are effective means of summarizing findings.

The metric system—the system of weights and measures based on the decimal system of ten and its multiples—will become increasingly important in future management information systems. Although the United States lags behind most other nations in converting to metrics, many firms have taken steps toward metrication. The system is especially important for companies marketing their products outside the United States, and many of them have been using metrics for several years. The metric system will become increasingly important in the decade of the 1980s.

Key Terms

management information system (MIS)
internal data
external data
primary data
secondary data
observation method
survey method
census
sample

probability sample
statistics
array
frequency distribution
mean (or average)
median
mode
metric system

Review Questions

1. Explain each of the terms listed on the previous page.

2. Explain the role of the management information system in contemporary business.

3. Identify the chief internal sources of information.

4. What are the major external sources of information?

5. Distinguish between primary and secondary data and explain the strengths and limitations of each.

6. Discuss the two chief methods of collecting primary data.

7. Identify the three methods of collecting survey data. Give an example of when each method might be used.

8. Assume that a class of 15 students received the following grades on a business examination:

100	88	82	76	76
96	86	82	76	72
92	84	78	76	66

a. What is the mean grade for this class?
b. What is the median grade?
c. What is the mode?

9. Assume that a local supermarket reported the following monthly sales figures during 1982:

Month	Sales	Month	Sales
January	$ 90,000	July	$ 70,000
February	85,000	August	80,000
March	90,000	September	105,000
April	100,000	October	100,000
May	105,000	November	130,000
June	105,000	December	140,000

a. What is the mean monthly sales figure for this store?
b. Would the median and mode be useful figures for the supermarket manager to calculate? Explain.

10. What are the major advantages and disadvantages of converting to the metric system?

Discussion Questions and Exercises

1. Evaluate the pros and cons of the controversial issue that appears in this chapter.

2. Interview a local businessperson or administrator on your campus. Ask what types of information he or she needs every day and how it is obtained.

3. Prepare a report using the following to present your data: a line chart, a pie chart, a bar chart, and a pictograph.

4. Prepare a brief report on the use of statistical analysis in business.

5. Identify several problems that will be faced by consumers if the United States switches entirely to metrics. Suggest a remedy for each problem.

Case 16–1: Fisher-Price

Fisher-Price is the nation's largest maker of toys for children under the age of six. For this reason it is not surprising to discover that its research and development building is actually a state-licensed nursery school located at the firm's East Aurora, New York, headquarters. The nursery school is run by trained teachers paid by the company. As in any nursery school, the kids finger-paint, sing, eat snacks, and read stories.

And they do other things. For Fisher-Price, the most important part of the school is the free-play time, where the three- and four-year-olds become toy-testers for the firm's proposed new toys. There they bang, poke, kick, accept—and sometimes reject—the new toys dreamed up by the firm's designers.

A new group of kids comes in every six weeks to make certain that one group's whims aren't forced on a nation of toy buyers. In the nursery, the kids are never asked such direct questions as "How do you like this toy?" or "Isn't this a cute doll, Bratina?" Instead, teachers make elaborate notes during free play and sometimes call designers to observe through one-way windows.

Children's inputs often initiate changes in successful toys. One such toy is the jack-in-the-box, a toy-business staple item. Fisher-Price built one a few years ago and tested it in the nursery school. But the teachers reported an unusual occurrence. After pressing the button to make "Jack" pop out of his box, the children invariably would gather round and talk to him. "Is it dark in the box?" they would ask; then, assuming the role of Jack, they would give each other answers. So the teacher suggested making Jack's jaws move. Designers spent another year building a lever-operated mouth, a squeaky voice, and a turntable head for the figure.

Questions

1. What type of data are obtained by Fisher-Price and through what method are they gathered?

2. What are the major advantages of this novel approach to obtaining management information? Suggest some other firms that might profitably utilize a similar approach to collecting information.

3. What are the potential disadvantages of this approach?

Case 16–2: Applying Statistical Analysis to Test Scores

"What did you get on the test?" is commonly heard in college hallways. Students usually respond with letter grades like "A," "B," and "C." These grades are often used to represent their numerical scores. But did you ever consider how these grades are determined? Grading is essentially a research assignment for the instructor.

A group of 25 students were enrolled in an introductory business class where *Contemporary Business* was the assigned textbook. They took a 50-item objective question examination. Consider the following scores achieved by these students:

Student	Score	Student	Score
Student 1	100	Student 14	72
Student 2	98	Student 15	70
Student 3	92	Student 16	70
Student 4	88	Student 17	70
Student 5	86	Student 18	68
Student 6	84	Student 19	66
Student 7	82	Student 20	66
Student 8	78	Student 21	64
Student 9	74	Student 22	60
Student 10	74	Student 23	56
Student 11	74	Student 24	48
Student 12	74	Student 25	46
Student 13	72		

Questions

1. Calculate the mean, median, and mode for this distribution of scores.

2. What letter grade would you assign to each of these scores?

17

The Role of Accounting

Learning Goals

1. To explain the functions of accounting and the role accounting plays in an organization

2. To identify the interested parties both inside and outside the firm and to show how accounting information is used by each of them

3. To explain briefly how the three key accounting statements are used to show the financial status of a firm

4. To describe the financial ratios used in interpreting financial statements

5. To explain the meaning of each of the key terms introduced in this chapter

Profile: Abraham J. Briloff
The Conscience of Accountancy

The review of corporate reports by outside accountants is a cornerstone of our financial system. Stockholders depend on this review as do stockbrokers, bankers, handlers of pension funds, government officials, and many others. The public expects that the audited reports accurately reflect what is going on.

Although Abraham J. Briloff believes that the use of generally accepted accounting principles in the preparation of financial statements usually provides reasonable and responsible reports for decision making, he also claims that the same principles may be manipulated and distorted in practice so that accountants often paint fakes.

The distortions Briloff speaks of often hide the real truth about a company's financial condition. They avoid rather than seek a full and fair disclosure. And the results can make a big difference in reported profits and resulting stock prices. By choosing one principle instead of another, charges Briloff, a company's financial picture can be made to look like something it is not.

Briloff, who is a distinguished professor of accountancy at the Baruch College of the City University of New York, has been criticizing his profession for years in books and articles. He has named names and ruffled many personal and corporate feathers in the process.

He has attacked shoddy accounting procedures that lead away rather than toward the pursuit of truth and the failure of auditors to force corporate management to institute fair accounting practices. Briloff's viewpoint is uncompromising. He thinks auditors should require their clients to state their financial facts fairly and accurately with no distortions or cover-ups. And he believes that auditors who fall short of this mark should be subject to disciplinary action by the American Institute of Certified Public Accountants or the Securities and Exchange Commission.

Citing an abuse of the public trust, Briloff personally filed disciplinary charges against Maurice Stans, former Nixon finance chief. When Stans was exonerated, Briloff saw the decision as consistent with his profession's failure to discipline powerful figures.

Even the Big Eight accounting firms have come under Briloff's attack. He charges that they are too closely aligned with corporate management. Instead of acting as independent overseers forcing management to paint a true picture of their corporate health, they have allowed management's biases to permeate their reports.

Briloff maintains that accountants handling audits must take steps to reassert their independence from corporate management and resume their role as society's trustworthy representatives in corporate affairs.

Abe Briloff has spent a lifetime revealing what other accounting professionals have been afraid to face. Now in his 60s, his determination is as strong as ever even though he suffers from glaucoma and is legally blind.

Never ask of money spent
Where the spender thinks it went.
Nobody was ever meant
To remember or invent
What he did with every cent.

—Robert Frost

Annual income twenty pounds,
annual expenditure nineteen six.
Result: happiness.
Annual income twenty pounds,
annual expenditure twenty pounds
ought and six.
Result: misery.

—Charles Dickens
David Copperfield

Simon Reynolds carried a leather attaché case to his first meeting with the president and chief officials of Computer Controls, Inc., the reportedly fast-growing company he was considering for acquisition as the fourteenth subsidiary of Reynolds Enterprises. He shook hands with everyone at the meeting and quickly went to his seat at the head of the long polished oak conference table. He immediately opened the attaché case and produced a folder containing one typewritten page. "Ladies and gentlemen," he said, "let's come right to the point. Here is the information I need immediately."
The list was a short one:

1. Did Computer Controls earn a profit last year?
2. What was the taxable income for the year?
3. How did Computer Controls raise money last year, and how was it used?
4. What were the production costs of the firm's major products?
5. What were the costs involved in marketing the products?
6. How profitable and efficient was each of the firm's three major divisions?
7. What is the overall financial position of the company?
8. How did last year's operations and current financial position compare with plans made by management at the beginning of the year?

The president of Computer Controls breathed a sigh of relief. "Thank goodness we've got a good accounting system," he said.

What Is Accounting?

Accounting, like statistics, is a language of business. It is the process of measuring and communicating financial information to enable interested parties inside and outside the firm to make informed decisions. Accountants are responsible for gathering, recording, reporting, and interpreting financial information that describes the status and operation of a firm and aids in decision making. They must accomplish three major tasks: scorekeeping, calling attention to problems and opportunities, and aiding in decision making.

accounting
The process of measuring and communicating financial information to enable interested parties inside and outside the firm to make informed decisions.

Accounting for Whom?

Who are the interested parties—inside and outside the firm—aided by accounting? Inside the firm, management uses accounting information to help plan and control both daily and long-range operations. Owners of the firm rely on accounting data to determine how well the firm is being operated. Union officials use the data in contract negotiations.

Outside the firm, potential investors use accounting information to help them decide whether to invest in the company. Bankers and other creditors find that it helps them determine the company's credit rating and gives them insight into its financial soundness. The Internal Revenue Service uses it to evaluate the company's tax payments for the year.

Accounting versus Bookkeeping

Too many people make the mistake of using the terms *accounting* and *bookkeeping* interchangeably. But they are not synonymous.

Bookkeeping is the chiefly clerical phase of accounting. Bookkeepers are responsible primarily for the systematic recording of company financial transactions. They provide the data that the accountant uses. Accounting is a much broader area. The one million accountants in the United States are responsible for developing systems to classify and summarize transactions and for interpreting financial statements.

Accountants are decision makers, while bookkeepers are trained in the largely mechanical tasks of record keeping. Accountants hold positions as chief executives in many of the largest companies and in top-level government offices.

A bookkeeper records transactions and takes care of other clerical phases of accounting such as writing payroll checks.

"One nice thing about being a C.P.A.—it's not a metaphor for anything else."

CPA has become the recognized designation for a professional accountant.

Drawing by Lorenz; © 1981 The New Yorker Magazine, Inc.

The People Who Constitute the Accounting Profession

The nearly one million accountants in the United States are employed in a variety of areas in business firms, government agencies, nonprofit organizations, and as self-employed individuals. Approximately 275,000 of these accountants are **certified public accountants (CPAs)**. The CPAs have proven their skills by successfully completing a number of rigorous tests in accounting theory and practice, auditing, and law in order to meet the legal requirements of their state. CPAs have the same professional status within their field as do attorneys in law and physicians in medicine (see Focus 17–1). Although the CPA certificate is not required for accountants, only CPAs can officially express an opinion on whether a firm's financial statements present fairly and accurately that company's financial position. Such audits of financial records are required of all publicly held corporations and are usually required by any lending agency. In Canada, the United Kingdom, and Australia, these accounting professionals are called chartered accountants (CAs).

certified public accountant (CPA)
An accountant who has met state certification requirements involving college degrees and experience and who has passed a comprehensive examination covering law, accounting theory and practice, and auditing.

FOCUS 17-1

Significant Financial Rewards in the Accounting Profession

The accounting profession has grown rapidly in size and importance, thanks to the increasing complexity of tax laws and the mass of regulations under which modern firms must operate.

There are now approximately 275,000 certified public accountants, three times as many as there were 15 years ago. And there are many more on the way. Enrollment in accounting courses has more than doubled in the past five years and is still growing. This year degrees in accounting will be awarded to approximately 50,000 undergraduate and 6,000 graduate students.

For the future CPA the next step, after getting a degree and some experience, is a grueling 2½-day national exam, which many fail on the first try. In May 1981, the largest number of candidates ever—60,000—took this exam. That was 10 percent more than in 1976. After passing the exam, CPA candidates must meet their state's residence and experience requirements before they can be fully licensed.

Behind this rush to the profession lies the lure of high salaries and challenging responsibilities. "Today's accountant does more than add up figures: he's also a problem solver, giving businesses advice on how to make maximum use of their resources and their money," says Russell E. Palmer, managing partner of Touche Ross & Company. In many cases, accountants are now included in the upper echelons of corporate management and have a voice in shaping corporate policy decisions.

The financial returns for accountants are significant. Beginners with only an undergraduate degree can expect a minimum starting salary of $17,000 to $21,500 at a large national firm, depending on where in the country the job is located. The pay climbs steeply for those accepted as partners, a move that usually comes when accountants are in their early 30s. Those who reach the top of a firm can easily earn six-figure annual salaries. Published reports from Price Waterhouse & Company revealed that Chairman John C. Biegler earned $383,000 for a single year, while the firm's two cochairmen received $361,000 and $344,000.

Eight big firms dominate the accounting business: Arthur Andersen; Arthur Young & Company; Coopers & Lybrand; Ernest & Whinney; Deloitte, Haskins & Sells; Peat, Marwick, Mitchell & Company; Price Waterhouse; and Touche Ross & Company.

Only about 11 or 12 percent of the nation's CPAs are associated with these companies. But their clients are the largest and wealthiest corporations. Of the 2,600 companies listed in the New York Stock Exchange and the American Stock Exchange, 85 percent are clients of the Big Eight.

certified management accountant (CMA)
An accountant who has met specific educational and professional requirements and has passed a series of examinations established by the National Association of Accountants for the Certificate in Management Accounting.

CPAs employed in business firms may be members of an accounting department containing a relatively new accounting professional—the **certified management accountant (CMA).** This individual has met the specific educational and professional requirements and passed a series of examinations established by the National Association of Accountants and has been awarded the Certificate in Management Accounting. The key responsibilities of the CMA are developing, generating, and analyzing information to assist management in making sound decisions.

The Accounting Process

The basic data used in accounting are financial transactions between the firm and its employees, suppliers, owners, bankers, and various government bodies. Weekly payroll checks result in cash outflows for the compensation of employees. A payment to a supplier results in the receipt of needed materials for the production process. Prompt payment of bills preserves the firm's credit rating and its ability to obtain future loans.

As Figure 17–1 indicates, these transactions must be recorded, classified, and summarized in order to produce financial statements for the firm's management and other interested parties.

The Accounting Equation

assets
Everything of value owned or leased by a business.

Assets are everything of value owned or leased by the business. Cash, accounts receivable and notes receivable (amounts owed to the business through credit sales), land, buildings, supplies, and marketable securities are all assets.

FIGURE 17–1
The accounting process.

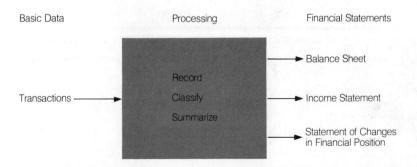

Equities are claims against the assets of a business. The two major classifications of individuals who have equities in a firm are creditors (liability holders) and owners. The **liabilities** of a business are everything owed to creditors—that is, the claims of the firm's creditors. When the firm makes credit purchases for inventory, land, or machinery, the creditors' claims are shown as accounts payable or notes payable. Wages and salaries owed to employees also represent liabilities (known as wages payable). The **owners' equity** represents the proprietor's, the partners', or the stockholders' claims against the assets of the firm or the excess of all assets over all liabilities.

Because equities by definition represent the total claims against assets, then assets must equal equities. This relationship is shown as follows:

$$\underset{\substack{\text{(Things}\\\text{of Value)}}}{\textbf{Assets}} = \underset{\text{(Claims)}}{\textbf{Equities}} \leftarrow \begin{array}{l} \textbf{Claims of Creditors} \\ \text{(Liabilities)} \\ \textbf{Claims of Owners} \\ \text{(Owners' Equity)} \end{array}$$

The basic **accounting equation** reflects the financial position of any firm at any point in time:

Assets = Liabilities + Owners' Equity.

Business assets owned equal the sources of those assets. The equation can be modified slightly to reflect the form of ownership of the firm. For a corporation the equation would be:

Assets = Liabilities + Stockholders' Equity,

and in a partnership it would be:

Assets = Liabilities + Partners' Equity.

Accounting Statements

The relationship expressed by the accounting equation is used to develop the three primary accounting statements: the balance sheet, the income statement, and the statement of changes in financial position.

The Balance Sheet

The **balance sheet** shows the financial position of a company as of a particular date. It is like a photograph in that it captures the status of the company's assets and equities at a moment in time.

equities
Claims against the assets of a business.

liabilities
Claims of the firm's creditors.

owners' equity
Claims of the proprietor, the partners, or the stockholders against the assets of the firm, or the excess of all assets over all liabilities.

accounting equation
The equation showing that assets (things of value) are equal to liabilities (claims of creditors) plus owners' equity (claims of owners).

balance sheet
A statement of a company's financial position as of a particular date.

Balance sheets should be prepared at regular intervals to provide information to management concerning the financial position of the firm. Balance sheets are provided for external users at least once a year and, more typically, quarterly. Managers are likely to receive such statements on a more frequent basis.

Figure 17–2 shows the balance sheet for Armstrong World Industries, Inc. The basic accounting equation is illustrated by Armstrong's three classifications. The assets total must equal the liabilities and stockholders' equity total.

Assets are divided into current and long-term (or noncurrent). Current assets consist of cash and other assets that can be readily converted into cash or that are expected to be used in the operation of the business within one year. They are usually listed in order of their expected **liquidity**—the speed at which they can be converted to cash. For Armstrong, the current assets are cash, temporary investments of excess or idle cash in marketable securities, accounts receivable, and inventory. Other current assets often include prepaid expenses such as insurance that have already been paid for but have not yet been used up.

liquidity
The speed at which items can be converted to money.

Net property, plant, and equipment are fixed assets to be used over a long period of time (generally more than a year) in the operation of the business. They include items such as land, factories, and machinery. Other noncurrent assets often include long-term receivables, which are debts of the firm's customers that are not due to be repaid within the next 12 months.

Like assets, liabilities are divided into current and long-term claims. Current liabilities are those claims that will be repaid within a one-year period. Accounts payable and notes payable are the liability counterparts of accounts receivable and notes receivable. **Accounts payable** represent credit purchases by the firm that must be repaid within a one-year period. **Notes payable** are loans represented by a written document, such as an IOU, and made for a period longer than one year. Notes payable due in the current year are listed as current liabilities. Notes payable that are due after one year are included on the balance sheet as long-term liabilities.

accounts payable
Credit liabilities that must be repaid within a one-year period.

notes payable
Liabilities represented by a written document that are payable in a period of time longer than one year.

Income taxes are listed on the balance sheet as both current and long-term liabilities. Because firms are required to pay a sizable portion of their estimated income taxes every three months, the $11.5 million current liability on the balance sheet is the portion still to be paid by Armstrong.

In order to encourage manufacturers to keep their plant equipment modern and efficient, tax regulations permit companies to put off certain tax payments to a future date. The $47.3 million in deferred income taxes represents the tax obligation that will come due later than twelve months in the future.

Stockholders' equity (shown in Figure 17–3) represents the claims of the firm's owners. Because Armstrong is a corporation, it uses the

FIGURE 17–2

Balance sheet for Armstrong World Industries, Inc.

Armstrong World Industries, Inc. and Subsidiaries
Consolidated Balance Sheet
December 1980

Assets	In Millions
Current assets:	
Cash	$ 6.3
Short-term securities	31.5
Accounts and notes receivable (less $10,208,000 allowance for discounts and losses)	177.1
Inventories	217.4
Other current assets	13.2
Total current assets	445.5
Property, plant, and equipment (less $379,370,000 accumulated depreciation and amortization)	436.4
Other non-current assets	9.6
	$891.5

Liabilities and Stockholders' Equity	
Current liabilities:	
Payable to banks	$23.8
Current installments of long-term debt	3.0
Accounts payable and accrued expenses	111.2
Income taxes	11.5
Total current liabilities	149.5
Long-term debt	103.8
Deferred income taxes	47.3
Minority interest in foreign subsidiaries	3.8
Stockholders' equity	587.1
	$891.5

FIGURE 17–3

Detailed breakdown of stockholders' equity portion of balance sheet.

Stockholders' Equity	In Millions
Preferred stock, $3.75 cumulative, no par value. Authorized 161,821 shares; issued 161,522 shares (at redemption price of $102.75 per share)	$ 16.6
Voting preferred stock. Authorized 1,500,000 shares	—
Common stock, $1.00 par value per share. Authorized 60,000,000 shares; issued 25,939,455 shares	25.9
Capital surplus	47.1
Retained earnings	524.2
	613.8
Less treasury stock, at cost:	
Preferred stock, $3.75 cumulative—43.373 shares	4.0
Common Stock—1,192,748 shares	22.7
	26.7
	$587.1

term *stockholders' equity* rather than *owners' equity, proprietors' equity,* or *partners' equity.*

When the corporation's stock certificates show par value (a stated amount on the stock certificate), the par value times the number of shares of stock outstanding appears in the stockholders' equity section of the balance sheet. Because Armstrong's common stock sold at a premium over the $1 par value when it was issued, an account called capital surplus (also known as paid-in capital in excess of par) is also listed on the balance sheet. When combined, the two amounts represent the stockholder contributions to the corporation over time.

The profits of the corporation can be distributed to the stockholders in the form of cash dividends, or they can be retained by the corporation and reinvested. Retained earnings can be used for expansion and growth and can be invested in such assets as land and buildings. Armstrong's retained earnings of $524.2 million represent the accumulated earnings that have been left in the firm.

A corporation may decide to repurchase some of its own stock—called treasury stock. If the corporation receives approval from the Securities and Exchange Commission, it can purchase its stock on the open market for uses such as an employee stock purchase program or bonuses for key executives. Armstrong currently holds $26.7 million of treasury stock.

The Income Statement

income statement
The financial statement that reflects the income, expenses, and profits of a company over a period of time.

While the balance sheet reflects the financial position of the company at a specific time, the **income statement** reflects the income, expenses, and profits of a company over a period of time.

The purpose of the income statement (also called a *statement of earnings* and a *profit and loss statement*) is to show the profitability (or unprofitability) of a firm during a period of time such as a year, a quarter, or a month and to provide basic data to help the investor analyze the reasons for the result. Figure 17–4 shows the 1980 income statement for Armstrong World Industries, Inc.

The income statement summarizes the income and expenses of the firm over a period of time. The basic format shows the deduction of costs and expenses, including taxes, from income in order to determine the net profit of the firm for that time period. The equation for the income statement is:

Income − Expenses = Net Profit (or Loss).

Income from sales shows the total sales to customers during the accounting period. Sales represent the major source of income for the company. Other income (or expense) represents net profit (or loss) from transactions such as the sale of machinery, rent received from property, or interest earned on investments during the period. These types of income are treated separately because they do not relate directly to the company's normal operations.

par value

Armstrong World Industries, Inc. and Subsidiaries
Consolidated Statement of Earnings
Year Ended December 31, 1980

Current Earnings	In Millions	Percent of Sales*
Net Sales	$1,323.0	. 100.0
Cost of goods sold	973.7	73.6
Gross profit	349.3	26.4
Selling and administrative expense	237.4	17.9
Earnings before other income (expense), income taxes, and extraordinary gain	111.9	8.5
Other income (expense):		
Interest expense	(14.2)	(1.1)
Unrealized foreign exchange gains (losses)	(2.7)	(0.2)
Miscellaneous, net	3.9	0.3
	(13.0)	(1.0)
Earnings before income taxes	98.9	7.5
Taxes on income	50.3	3.8
Net earnings	$ 48.6	3.7
Net earnings per share of common stock	$ 1.94	

* Percentage figures have been added to show approximate proportion of sales income represented by each item.

FIGURE 17–4
Income statement for Armstrong World Industries, Inc.

In order to determine the profit earned for the year, the expense of producing the goods sold must be deducted from income. Next, the selling and administrative expenses of the period must also be deducted from income. These expenses include advertising, sales commissions, officers' salaries, and rent.

Deduction of these expenses from income leaves income before taxes. Once taxes are deducted, the net profit (or loss) for the period remains. For Armstrong the net income or earnings for 1980 was approximately $48.6 million, or $1.94 per share of common stock.

Percentage of net sales. The use of percentages based on net sales points up the important expense items on the income statement. The percentage figures also (a) assist investors and financial analysts in comparing the income statement with similar statements for previous periods, (b) sometimes make comparisons of company operations with other firms in the industry easier, and (c) help the company compare its figures with industry averages.

LIFO versus FIFO. LIFO (Last In, First Out) is a common method of inventory accounting that assumes that the cost of goods sold is calculated on prices paid for the most recently purchased materials and parts. By using recent prices, the cost of goods sold reflects the higher prices that must be paid to purchase new raw materials. The LIFO method thus reduces profits (because it increases the cost of goods sold). But proponents argue that it provides a more accurate

LIFO (Last In, First Out)
A method of inventory accounting that assumes that the cost of goods sold is calculated on prices paid for the most recently purchased materials and parts.

FIFO (First In, First Out)
A method of inventory accounting that assumes that the first raw materials purchased are the first used in producing finished goods.

statement of profits than does the **FIFO (First-In, First-Out)** method of inventory valuation.

Under FIFO, which used to be the more common form of inventory valuation, the assumption is made that the first raw materials purchased are the first used in producing finished goods. However, as raw materials increase in cost, the FIFO method produces higher profits. Many accountants feel that these profits are unrealistic because they ignore the need to replenish inventories at higher costs; so the switch in inventory valuation methods is often made.

A switch from FIFO to LIFO can reduce profits considerably, but it has another important effect too. Reduced profits actually increase the amount of cash available to a firm because income taxes are also lowered.

Table 17–1 shows the effect on profits of this switch. It assumes a 10 percent rate of inflation and a tax rate of 50 percent. Among the many major firms switching to the LIFO method of inventory accounting during the inflationary 1970s and 1980s were Du Pont, Firestone Tire & Rubber, Armstrong World Industries, Inc., and Eastman Kodak.

TABLE 17–1
Income Statement Comparing LIFO and FIFO
Methods of Inventory Valuation

	LIFO Method	FIFO Method
Sales	$100,000	$100,000
Cost of goods sold	82,500	75,000
Profits before taxes	17,500	25,000
Income taxes	8,750	12,500
Net income after taxes	$ 8,750	$ 12,500

Statement of Changes in Financial Position

The statement of changes in financial position, which is of more recent origin than the income statement and the balance sheet, is required for almost all companies. Since 1970, the Securities and Exchange Commission has required this statement as part of the annual registration information for all companies listed on organized stock exchanges. It must also be included as part of the accounting information for firms whose financial statements are audited by public accounting firms. As its name indicates, the **statement of changes in financial position** is designed to explain the financial changes that occur in a company from one accounting period to the next. It is sometimes referred to as the "where got, where gone" statement because it presents the financing and investing activities of the firm from one operating period to the next. The 1980 statement for Armstrong World Industries, Inc. is shown in Figure 17–5.

The statement of changes in financial position reflects the firm's ability to meet its operating expenses and to purchase additional merchandise for resale. The focus of this statement is on increases or decreases in **working capital**—the difference between current assets

statement of changes in financial position
The financial statement that explains the financial changes that occur in a company from one accounting period to the next.

working capital
The difference between current assets and current liabilities.

Armstrong World Industries, Inc. and Subsidiaries
Consolidated Statement of Changes in Financial Position
Year Ended December 31, 1980

Funds Became Available From:	In Millions
Operations:	
Net earnings	$ 48.6
Add items not requiring funds:	
Depreciation and amortization	45.6
Deferred income taxes	6.9
Net loss on foreign exchange related to long-term items	2.4
Other	0.5
Total from operations	104.0
Other items	5.4
	$109.4
These Funds Were Used For:	
Additions to property, plant, and equipment	$ 64.6
Dividends to stockholders	27.7
Reduction in long-term debt	27.7
	120.0
Increase (decrease) in working capital	$(10.6)
Changes in Working Capital Consist Of:	
Increase (decrease) in current assets:	
Cash and short-term securities	$ 2.4
Receivables	11.4
Inventories	(18.4)
Other current assets	2.8
	(1.8)
Decrease (increase) in current liabilities:	
Payable to banks	(1.0)
Current installments of long-term debt	(0.2)
Accounts payable and accrued liabilities	(2.9)
Income Taxes	(4.7)
	8.8
Decrease (increase) in Working Capital	$(10.6)

FIGURE 17-5
Statement of changes in financial position for
Armstrong World Industries, Inc.

and current liabilities. In effect, working capital represents the source of assets to keep the business operating during the months ahead.

As Figure 17–5 shows, working capital is created from a number of sources. Armstrong World Industries, Inc.'s statement is similar to that of most firms in that much of it comes from company earnings. Other sources include the sale of plant or equipment, borrowed funds, and the issuance of stock. The payment of dividends to stockholders and payments for new plant, property, and equipment represent uses of working capital. In the case of Armstrong World Industries, Inc., more funds were utilized during the period than became available, resulting in a $10.6 million decrease in working capital.

The statement of changes in financial position acts as a link between the present and preceding year's balance sheets. It provides interested parties with an insight into how the firm's operations are being financed and for what its funds are being used. For these reasons, it is one of the three key accounting documents.

Interpreting Financial Statements

Once financial statements have been produced from the accounting data collected for a period, an accountant must interpret them. The fact that a firm earned a profit for the past year is of interest; of equal interest is the profit it should have earned. Over the years a number of techniques have been developed for interpreting financial information in order to aid management in planning and evaluating the day-to-day and ongoing operations of the company.

The practice of converting the various costs and expenses on the income statement to percentages of sales is a common method of interpretation that has already been discussed. Cost and expense items shown in percentage form can quickly be compared with those of previous periods or of other companies in the industry. In this way, unusually high or low expenses become immediately apparent to management, and corrective action can be taken if necessary.

A second method of interpreting financial statements is ratio analysis. By comparing the company ratios to industry standards, problem areas can be pinpointed. The six most commonly used ratios are current ratio, acid test ratio, inventory turnover, earnings per share, total debt to net worth ratio, and ratio of net income to sales.

Current Ratio

current ratio
A ratio that measures the company's ability to pay its current debts as they mature, calculated by dividing current assets by current liabilities.

The **current ratio** compares current assets to current liabilities. It measures the company's ability to pay its current debts as they mature. The current ratio of Armstrong World Industries, Inc. is computed as:

$$\text{Current Ratio} = \frac{\text{Current Assets}}{\text{Current Liabilities}} = \frac{\$445,516,000}{\$149,543,000} = 3 \text{ to } 1.$$

This means that Armstrong has $3.00 of current assets for every $1 of current liabilities. In general, a current ratio of 2 to 1 is considered to be financially satisfactory. This rule of thumb must be considered along with other factors such as the nature of the business, the season of the year, and the quality of the company's management. Armstrong World Industries' managers and other interested parties are likely to compare this 3-to-1 ratio to previous operating periods and to industry averages to determine its appropriateness.

Acid Test Ratio

acid test ratio
A ratio that measures the ability of a firm to meet its current debt on short notice, calculated by dividing quick assets by current liabilities.

The **acid test ratio** (or quick ratio) measures the ability of the firm to meet its current debt on short notice. This ratio does not include inventory or prepaid expenses; only cash, marketable securities, and accounts receivable—all highly liquid assets—are included.

The current balance sheet of Armstrong World Industries, Inc. lists the following quick assets: cash ($6.3 million), marketable securities ($31.5 million), and accounts and notes receivable ($177.1 million). Armstrong's acid test ratio is computed as:

$$\text{Acid Test Ratio} = \frac{\text{Quick Assets}}{\text{Current Liabilities}} = \frac{\$214,859,000}{\$149,543,000} = 1.5 \text{ to } 1.$$

Because the typical minimum acid test ratio is 1 to 1, Armstrong appears to be in a good short-term credit position. However, this ratio should be compared with industry averages and with previous operating periods in determining its appropriateness for Armstrong World Industries, Inc.

Inventory Turnover

The **inventory turnover ratio** indicates the number of times merchandise moves through the business. It is calculated by dividing the cost of goods sold by the average amount of inventory. The inventory turnover for a retail jeweler might be calculated as:

inventory turnover ratio
A ratio that measures the number of times merchandise moves through a business, calculated by dividing the cost of goods sold by the average amount of inventory.

$$\frac{\text{Inventory}}{\text{Turnover}} = \frac{\text{Cost of Goods Sold}}{\text{Average Inventory}} = \frac{\$285,000}{\$120,000} = 2.4 \text{ times.}$$

The turnover rate can be compared with industry standards and used as a measure of efficiency. For a jewelry store, 2.4 times is above average. For a supermarket, the turnover rate should be about 20. In general, the higher the turnover rate, the less warehouse space needed and the greater the number of sales being made.

Earnings per Share

One of the most commonly watched ratios in business is **earnings per share.** This ratio indicates the amount of profits earned by a company for each share of common stock outstanding. As Figure 17-4 indicates, the 1980 earnings per share for Armstrong World Industries, Inc. is $1.94.

earnings per share
The amount of profits earned by a company for each share of common stock outstanding, calculated by dividing net earnings (or net profits) by the average number of common shares outstanding.

Earnings per Share
$$= \frac{\text{Net Earnings} - \text{Provision for Preferred Dividends}}{\text{Average Number of Common Shares Outstanding}}$$
$$= \frac{\$48,566,000 - \$443,000}{24,746,707} = \$1.94.$$

The $1.94 earnings figure can be compared with earnings per share in previous years to provide some indication of performance at Armstrong World Industries, Inc. It can also be compared with the earnings per share of other firms in the industry to evaluate the relative performance of the firms.

Controversial Issue

Should Accountants Take Inflation into Consideration in Financial Statements?

Accountants have a chronic headache that is not likely to go away—at least not for a while. It is inflation—the uncontrollable price spiral that is rewriting every business's financial statement.

Gone are the days when the expected cost of raw materials and the market value of inventory remained relatively constant for a few months or even a year. In their place is a steady upward trend that often takes more inflated dollars out of a business than it brings in.

In the steel industry, for example, the ever-increasing cost of raw materials has put a damper on company profits. When inflated costs are considered, the adjusted, or real, earnings of the steel manufacturers are actually lower than the amount paid out in dividends.

Inflation accounting tries to deal with these fluctuations by creating a new kind of balance sheet. Plant, equipment, and inventories are adjusted upward, and these figures are then translated into a much higher depreciation expense and cost of goods sold. Financial statements that are properly adjusted for inflation give executives the information they need to plan accurately for future activities and evaluate their companies' current financial health.

Even though everyone agrees on the need for inflation accounting, there is little consensus on what an inflation-adjusted financial statement should include. The Financial Accounting Standards Board (FASB), the nation's accounting rule-making body, describes three sets of numbers that must be included in a financial statement.

First, there are the historical, or actual, cost figures of depreciation, of goods sold, and of income from continuing operation.

Debt to Net Worth Ratio

debt to net worth ratio
A ratio that measures the extent to which company operations are financed by borrowed funds, calculated by dividing total liabilities by stockholders' equity.

The **debt to net worth ratio** is designed to measure the extent to which the operations of the company are financed by borrowed funds. It indicates the amounts of funds contributed by creditors as compared with the total funds provided. The debt to net worth ratio for Armstrong World Industries, Inc. is computed as:

$$\text{Debt to Net Worth Ratio} = \frac{\text{Total Liabilities}}{\text{Stockholders' Equity}}$$
$$= \frac{\$300,630,000}{\$587,059,000} = 0.51.$$

These figures form the basis for comparison with the other two sets of numbers—the constant-dollar and the current-cost accounting figures.

Constant-dollar figures take inflation into account by making adjustments using a general price-level index such as the consumer price index. Current-cost figures, on the other hand, make adjustments using the specific index of today's replacement cost of each of the company's fixed assets and inventories.

Compiling these three sets of figures can be a monumental accounting task requiring additional time, personnel, and money. In order to simplify the problem, many executives favor the constant-dollar approach based on a single price index, in part because this method is less costly to determine than the current-cost approach. But accountants claim that the current-cost approach offers a more meaningful set of figures because it shows the changing values of specific assets.

Unfortunately for stockholders, the adjustments made for inflation generally show bad news—that is, that dividends should be drastically reduced. One accountant predicted that when current-cost income statements make their way into company annual reports, some directors may realize that their companies are slowly liquidating themselves by paying out as dividends cash that is needed to replace existing plant.

Currently the FASB requires inflation-adjusted figures for only the 1,280 largest corporations—those with assets over $1 billion. Although inflation accounting, with its increased cost and confusion, may be important for management to make corporate decisions on the basis of realistic data, stockholders are also critical to a company's success, and they are not overjoyed by the changes in dividends brought about by inflation accounting.

Ratio of Net Income to Sales

The **ratio of net income to sales** measures company profitability by comparing net income and sales. For Armstrong World Industries, Inc., the ratio is computed as:

$$\text{Ratio of Net Income to Sales} = \frac{\text{Net Income}}{\text{Sales}}$$

$$= \frac{\$48,566,000}{\$1,322,967,000} = 3.7 \text{ percent.}$$

ratio of net income to sales
A ratio that measures company profitability by dividing net income by sales.

This profitability ratio is a critical indicator for any profit-seeking firm. In the case of Armstrong World Industries, Inc., it indicates that a profit of 3.7 cents was realized for every dollar of sales. Although this ratio is below the national average of 4 to 5 percent, it should be compared with profit forecasts, past performance, and/or industry averages in determining its appropriateness. Similar profitability ratios can be computed by comparing a company's net income to assets or net worth.

Summary

Accounting is a language of business. Its purpose is to supply financial information for use in planning and evaluating the operations of a firm. Accountants are professionals who are responsible for recording, classifying, summarizing, reporting, and interpreting the financial transactions of a firm.

Accounting data are grouped into assets and equities, including liabilities and owners' equity. Assets are things of value owned or leased and used in the business. Cash, accounts and notes receivable, inventory, land, buildings, and machinery are all assets. Liabilities are claims against the assets by the creditors of the firm. The owners' claims on the assets are called owners' (or stockholders') equity. The relationship between the assets of a firm and the claims against those assets is shown by the basic accounting equation:

Assets = Liabilities + Owners' Equity.

Financial information is summarized in three key accounting statements: the balance sheet, the income statement, and the statement of changes in financial position. The balance sheet can be thought of as a photograph showing the assets, liabilities, and owners' equity of a firm at one point in time. The income statement is a motion picture designed to show the profitability of a company over a period of time such as a quarter or a year. By subtracting expenses from income, the income statement reveals the amount of profit (or loss) for that accounting period. The statement of changes in financial position explains the financial changes that occur from one accounting period to the next. It focuses on the sources and uses of funds in the firm.

Financial statements can be interpreted through the use of percentages or ratios. Such ratios as current ratio, acid test ratio, inventory turnover, earnings per share, debt to net worth ratio, and ratio of net income to sales are commonly used. The ratios assist the manager and other interested parties by making possible the comparison of current company financial information with that of previous years and with industry standards.

Key Terms

accounting

certified public accountant
(CPA)

certified management
accountant (CMA)

assets

equities

liabilities

owners' equity

accounting equation

balance sheet

liquidity

accounts payable

notes payable

income statement

LIFO (Last In, First Out)

FIFO (First In, First Out)

statement of changes in financial
position

working capital

current ratio

acid test ratio

inventory turnover ratio

earnings per share

debt to net worth ratio

ratio of net income to sales

Review Questions

1. Explain each of the terms listed above.

2. Who are the major users of accounting information?

3. Distinguish between accounting and bookkeeping.

4. Explain the concept of equities. What are the two chief types of
   equities?

5. What are the major differences between the balance sheet and
   the income statement?

6. Distinguish between current and long-term assets.

7. Briefly explain the following concepts:
   a. stockholders' equity
   b. paid-in capital in excess of par
   c. treasury stock

8. What are the major advantages of showing the various items on
   a firm's income statement in percentages based upon net sales
   rather than showing the actual figures involved?

9. Relate the statement of changes in financial position to the other
   two chief financial statements.

10. Explain the techniques used by accountants in interpreting finan-
    cial statements.

Discussion Questions and Exercises

1. Evaluate the pros and cons of the controversial issue that appears in this chapter.

2. Interview an accounting professor at your college or university. Determine the major differences between the certified public accountant (CPA) and other types of accountants.

3. A number of financial ratios are discussed in this chapter. Briefly review each ratio and include it in one of the categories listed below. Support your answer.
   a. profitability ratio
   b. liquidity ratio
   c. leverage ratio
   d. activity ratio

4. Interview a college placement officer. Determine the demand for accountants in your area, and in a brief report explain the reasons for this demand.

5. List each of the ratios covered in this chapter. Explain the value of each ratio from the viewpoint of the decision maker.

Case 17—1: Charlie's Angels

California resident Robert Wagner and his actress wife Natalie Wood were extremely pleased with the contract they had just signed with Spelling-Goldberg Productions. In exchange for their acting services in some forthcoming productions, they accepted no cash but instead received 43.75 percent of the net profits in a new television series called *Charlie's Angels*.

Their satisfaction with the agreement was based largely on the reputation of Spelling-Goldberg, which furnished the ABC network with as many as five hours a week of highly rated programs and had acquired the nickname "the hit factory." The new production, built around the story of three attractive female undercover police agents, appeared likely to join the category of hits.

And so it did. *Charlie's Angels* quickly rose in popularity and subsequently become the highest ranked prime-time television show. It continued to enjoy ratings successes for over five years.

In 1978, the Wagners were dismayed at a financial statement sent to them from Spelling-Goldberg showing that *Charlie's Angels* had lost $1 million in its first three seasons.

In perusing the financial statements, the Wagners learned that expenses of financing, producing, and promoting the series were greater than the rentals received from the networks. Future profits were possible from syndicating the series—renting the already-completed episodes to independent television networks and foreign television stations—but the Wagners' hopes of substantial financial returns were fading in red ink. The growing controversy hinges on the determination of the actual expenses involved in such productions.

In the movie business, top directors, producers, and actors often get a percentage of a film's gross profits or gross receipts, but ordinary participants must take their cuts from the net profits. A studio arrives at net profits as follows. It starts with revenues from theaters, which are about 30 to 40 percent of the box-office receipts. The studio then deducts distribution expenses (including costs of collecting from theater chains, advertising, and taxes). Then "negative costs"—all expenses associated with making the film (dressing rooms, salaries, props, and so on)—are deducted. Finally, interest on the money invested by the studio in the production is deducted.

A studio can easily direct profits away from point-holders. One way is to sell block or multiple bookings (consisting of a hit show together with less popular productions) to an exhibitor or network. Then the studio can allocate a large part of the receipts to the lesser shows, from which it gets most of the profits.

Lawsuits over these practices are usually settled out of court. In 1980, however, producer Larry Turman won a judgment against Avco Embassy Pictures, a distributor that sold his film *The Graduate* to CBS-TV in a $7 million package consisting of eight pictures. *The Graduate* had made Avco $50 million from theaters, but Avco allocated only $2 million of the proceeds of the CBS-TV sale to *The Graduate*. A jury placed the worth of the film at $4 million. Turman, as a one-sixth profit participant, was awarded $1 million, including punitive damages.

Questions

1. What characteristics of the film industry contribute to such problems in accounting? Are these situations unique, or does the possibility of unrealistic allocations of revenues and expenses exist in other industries? Explain.

2. What steps should interested parties take in the above situation to remedy the problem and minimize the possibility of future occurrences?

Case 17—2: Beatrice Foods Company

Beatrice Foods Company is a highly diversified manufacturer with headquarters in Chicago. Its product lines include dairy products (Meadow Gold, yogurt, dehydrated food items, franchising for Weight Watchers soft drinks), grocery products (La Choy, Miracle White, Clark Candy, and others), specialty meat products, warehousing, manufacturing, life insurance, and chemicals. The financial statements for the year ended February 28, 1981, are shown below.

Questions

1. Calculate the following ratios for Beatrice Foods Company:
   a. current ratio
   b. acid test ratio
   c. earnings per share
   d. debt to net worth ratio
   e. ratio of net income to sales

2. What can you conclude about the company from your analysis?

Statement of Consolidated Earnings
Year Ended February 28, 1981

Income:	In Thousands
Net Sales	$8,772,804
Interest income	40,198
Other income	25.590
Equity in net earnings of Southwestern Investment Company	—
	$8,838,592
Cost and expenses:	
Cost of sales, excluding depreciation	$6,510,782
Selling, administrative, and general expenses, excluding depreciation	1,457,158
Depreciation expense	155,373
Interest expense	96,403
	8,219,716
Earnings before income taxes and minority interests	618,876
Provision for income taxes	301,700
Earnings before income taxes	317,176
Minority interests in net earnings of consolidated subsidiaries	12,965
Net earnings	$ 304,211
Earnings per share:	
Primary	$2.94
Fully diluted	$2.79

Consolidated Balance Sheet
February 28, 1981

Assets	In Thousands
Current assets:	
Cash	$132,420
Short-term investments, at cost which approximates market	285,108
Receivables, less allowance for doubtful accounts of $26,030	834,480
Inventories	972,032
Prepaid expenses and other current assets	72,573
Total current assets	2,296,613
Investments in affiliated companies	57,021
Plant and equipment:	
Land	70,171
Buildings	529,544
Machinery and equipment	1,252,049
Capitalized leases	202,745
	2,117,509
Less accumulated depreciation	803,587
	1,313,922
Intangible assets, principally goodwill	463,369
Noncurrent receivables	80,570
Other assets	25,060
	$4,236,555
Liabilities and Stockholders' Equity	
Current liabilities:	
Short-term debt	122,410
Accounts payable	521,061
Accrued expenses	
Taxes, other than income taxes	30,252
Other accruals (principally employees' compensation)	243,880
Income taxes	112,792
Current portion of long-term debt	28,813
Current obligations of capitalized leases	15,563
Total current liabilities	1,074,771
Long-term debt	564,710
Long-term obligations of capitalized leases	126,728
Deferred items:	
Income taxes	90,963
Investment tax credits	31,870
Other	23,368
Other noncurrent liabilities	89,293
Minority interests in subsidiaries	53,407
Stockholders' equity:	
Preference stock (without par value). Authorized 20,000,000 shares. Issued and outstanding 5,010,437 at stated values with aggregate liquidation preference of $262,247	259,567
Common stock (without par value). Authorized 200,000,000 shares. Issued and outstanding 97,756,784 shares at $1.85 stated value	180,850
Additional capital	106,930
Retained earnings	1,634,098
Total stockholders' equity	2,181,445
	$4,236,555

Careers in Production, Computers, Research, and Accounting

Accounting, computers, production, and research offer considerable career opportunities for business students. People with accounting training are in high-level positions throughout most organizations. Entry-level jobs are plentiful and provide real challenges for graduates. Computers require professional personnel to assure that management gets the information needed for critical decisions. Production management positions are available in a diverse array of industries. Business researchers are also important in several areas of business; they secure and analyze the data on which decisions are based.

The Bureau of Labor Statistics has projected the employment outlook to 1990. Its forecasts for selected jobs in accounting, computers, production, and research appear in the table on page 437. The bureau expects all occupations to add 20.8 percent to their work force between 1978 and 1990. Seven of the currently available careers in these areas appear below.

Public accountant. Public accountants are independent business persons who provide accounting services to firms and individuals. These services range from setting up accounting systems to preparing tax forms. Professional certification for public accountants is indicated by the title of certified public accountant (CPA).

Auditor. An auditor is an accountant who checks the accuracy and validity of accounting records and procedures. If they conform to recognized standards, the auditor certifies them in a public statement.

Cost accountant. Cost accountants are involved in accounting for the costs of producing the firm's product and operating the enterprise. They gather, analyze, and report on cost data for management.

Production manager. The production manager is responsible for the actual manufacturing of a product. This includes engineering, production control, quality control, and other areas of administration. The production manager is sometimes referred to as the plant manager.

Programmer. A programmer is a person who gives commands to a computer through specialized computer languages and selects meaningful information out of the data stored in a computer.

Systems analyst. Systems analysts are well-trained computer experts who develop the various computer-based information systems needed in an organization. They determine which information is required and how best to obtain it.

Statistician. Statisticians apply statistical procedures to data in order to assess their validity and reliability and to analyze, predict, and evaluate in such areas as quality control, marketing research, production control, and finance.

Supervisor. A supervisor is a manager of a particular work area within a plant. This person directly supervises employees such as assembly line workers, welders, cutters, and others. The supervisor is at the first level of management in a factory.

Actuary. Actuaries calculate insurance risks. Using statistical methods, they determine the likelihood of death at a certain age or the possibility of a casualty loss under given circumstances. Once these risks are calculated, actuaries help determine the insurance rates necessary to cover the risks.

EMPLOYMENT OUTLOOK ON 1990

Changes in Employment

Occupations in Accounting, Production, Computers and Research	Recent Employment Figures	Much Faster than the Average for All Occupations	Faster than the Average for All Occupations	About as Fast as the Average for All Occupations	More Slowly than the Average for All Occupations	Little Change Expected	Expected to Decline
Blue-Collar Work Supervisors	1,670,000			X			
Bookkeeping Workers	1.8 million			X			
Inspectors (Manufacturing)	736,000			X			
Statistical Clerks	377,000			X			
Purchasing Agents	185,000		X				
Computer Operating Personnel	666,000			Mixed Employment Outlook			
Industrial Engineers	185,000		X				
Programmers	247,000		X				
Systems Analysts	182,000		X				
Actuaries	9,000		X				
Accountants	980,000		X				
Marketing Research Workers	24,000	X					
Mathematicians	33,000				X		
Statisticians	23,000		X				
Computer Service Technicians	63,000	X					

Source: U.S. Department of Labor, Bureau of Labor Statistics, *Occupational Outlook Handbook, 1980–1981,* Bulletin 2075, pp. 5, 55–56, 61–63, 79–80, 92–93, 96–101, 107–109, 113–115, 125–127, 129–131, 288–289, 305–308, 341–343.

FINANCING THE ENTERPRISE

18

Money, the Banking System, and Other Financial Institutions

Learning Goals

1. To explain the advantages of money over a barter system

2. To describe the characteristics a good money form should possess

3. To explain the functions of money

4. To analyze the Federal Reserve System and how it increases or decreases the money supply

5. To analyze the purpose and chief functions of the Federal Deposit Insurance Corporation

6. To identify the major types of financial institutions and the sources and uses of their funds

7. To explain the meaning of each of the key terms introduced in this chapter

Profile: Paul A. Volcker

Charting the Course of the Country's Economy

When 6-ft 7-in, 240–pound Paul A. Volcker presides over a meeting of the Federal Reserve Board, he dominates the room. But more than his size makes him the center of attention. As chairman of the Federal Reserve (the "Fed"), he must chart the monetary course of the nation's economy—a responsibility that is becoming increasingly difficult to achieve as the inflation rate zooms and recession threatens.

Volcker, a shy man who smokes 20-cent cigars and is known for his personal frugality, was well-prepared to take over the top post at the Fed when he was tapped in 1979 by President Carter. The son of a Teaneck, New Jersey, city manager, Volcker attended Princeton, Harvard, and the London School of Economics, where he completed his doctoral studies but not his dissertation.

Volcker then began his meteoric career as an economist. At the age of 34, he was chief financial analyst at the U.S. Treasury in Washington, D.C. From there he became Deputy Under Secretary for Monetary Affairs in the Kennedy Administration, a vice president of Chase Manhattan Bank, and Under Secretary for Monetary Affairs under President Nixon. In 1975, Volcker was appointed president of the regional Federal Reserve Bank of New York—a job he held until he became chairman of the Fed in July 1979.

Volcker took the top Fed job at a time the agency was moving from bureaucratic obscurity to high visibility as the chief instrument in the nation's anti-inflation struggle. During 1980 and 1981, Volcker presided over an unprecedented tightening of the money supply and available credit. This move made him the target of liberals, who condemned the devastating short-term effects of tight money on the middle class and poor, and conservatives, including top Reagan Administration officials, who contended that the screws on the economy must be even tighter to control spiraling inflation. Even though the Fed cannot escape this kind of political pressure, Volcker and the other members of the board of governors run the Fed essentially on their own with no budget constraints or direct accountability to the President or Congress.

In a speech to the American Bankers Association in 1979, Volcker set the tone for his tenure at the Fed: "We can no longer blithely assume we can 'buy' prosperity with a little more inflation because inflation itself is the greatest threat to economic stability."

Under Volcker, the Federal Reserve has attempted to control inflation by affecting the growth of the money supply, primarily through the purchase and sale of government securities. It buys securities when it wants to increase the money supply, and sells them when it wants a slowdown. Even though Volcker has sometimes failed to follow through consistently on his tight money policies, he and his staff are generally acknowledged as wielding the only real power at the Fed. Known for his probing mind and openness to new ideas, Volcker has shown an extraordinary ability to provide the Fed with intellectual leadership—even at times of extreme pressure. "When you get right down to it," said a Fed staff member, "this place is Volcker, Volcker, Volcker."

negotiable order of withdrawal (NOW) account
An interest-bearing checking account offered by commercial banks, savings and loan associations, and mutual savings banks that requires a minimum balance established by the individual financial institution.

A war broke out in the financial community on January 1, 1981. The general public knew the competitive conflict was approaching because of a deluge of advertising and sales promotion from the financial community during the last months of 1980. At the center of these battles was an interest-bearing checking account called **negotiable order of withdrawal (NOW).** In a move toward deregulating the banking industry, the federal government decided to permit commercial banks, savings and loan associations, and mutual savings banks to offer these accounts, which earn 5.25 percent interest.

In return for paying interest on deposits in checking accounts, the financial institutions established minimum balances for each account. Any depositor whose account drops below a specific minimum amount (typically $300 to $1,300) pays a monthly fee and perhaps an additional charge per check written. As a result, the NOW accounts are particularly attractive to those people who maintain minimum balances exceeding $1,000.

Perhaps even more significant than the payment of interest to depositors is the fact that savings and loan associations are allowed to establish checking accounts. Although these institutions previously attracted savings accounts by offering 0.25 percent higher interest than was permitted for similar accounts at commercial banks, the growth of their savings accounts and loans has been adversely affected by the desires of many people to do all of their banking in one place.

The financial battles of the early 1980s may prove to be just the start of continued competition among financial institutions. The distinctions among many of these institutions are becoming increasingly blurred as more and more institutions duplicate the service offerings of their competitors.[1]

Money: Lubricant of Contemporary Business

The competition among the various financial institutions is a competition for money. The competition is both for acquiring money in the form of deposits and for lending money to borrowers. Money is not only one of the 5*M*s of management, it is a vital resource in the operation of any organization.

In analyzing the characteristics, functions, and different types of money, it is useful to begin by defining it. **Money** is anything generally accepted as a means of paying for goods and services.

Anyone asked to define *money* will probably respond something like this: "It's the coins in my pocket and the folding kind I wish I had in my wallet and whatever is currently in my checking account." And bankers would agree: these are all money.

Money is one of the most fascinating subjects for both individuals and businesspeople. Everyone seems to need it:

> Money bewitches people. They fret for it, and they sweat for it. They devise most ingenious ways to get it, and most ingenious ways to get rid of it. Money is the only commodity that is good for nothing but to be gotten rid of. It will not feed you, clothe you, shelter you, or amuse you unless you spend it or invest it. It imparts value only in parting. People will do almost anything for money, and money will do almost anything for people. Money is a captivating, circulating, masquerading puzzle.[2]

Money Comes in Different Shapes and Sizes

Money has not always been the same to all people. Historically, objects of value were used as money. These objects can be referred to as full-bodied money, because they had a usefulness apart from their use as money. Cattle often were used this way. A cow was valuable because it could produce milk, butter, and cheese and eventually be converted into meat and hide. Its owner could also trade the cow for other goods. The list of products that have served as money is long, including such diverse items as wool, pepper, tea, fishhooks, tobacco, shells, feathers, salt (from which came "salary" and "being worth one's salt"), boats, sharks' teeth, cocoa beans, wampum beads, woodpecker scalps, and precious metals. For a number of reasons, precious metals gained wide acceptance as money. As early as 2000 B.C. gold and silver were used as money, and as late as 1933 gold coins were used as money in the United States. Figure 18–1 shows examples of different types of paper money from all over the world.

What Characteristics Should Money Possess?

Most of the early forms of money possessed a number of serious disadvantages. A cow is a poor form of money for the owner who wants only a loaf of bread and a bottle of wine. To perform its necessary functions, money should be divisible, portable, durable, and difficult to counterfeit—and it should have a stable value.

FIGURE 18–1
Examples of paper money from various countries.

Divisibility. The owner of a cow who found that a loaf of bread cost one-fiftieth of a cow was faced with a major dilemma. So were the owners of other items used as money. But gold and silver coins could be minted in different sizes with differing values in order to facilitate the exchange process.

Spanish gold doubloons were literally divided into pieces of eight. The dollar can be converted into pennies, nickels, dimes, and quarters. The pound sterling of the United Kingdom is worth 100 pence. A French franc is valued at 100 centimes. The German deutsche mark can be traded for 100 pfennigs. And these forms of money can easily be exchanged for goods ranging from chewing gum to a car.

Portability. The inhabitants of the little island community of Yap chose a unique form of money—huge round stones weighing as much as 90 pounds each. Because the stone money was often placed at the door of its owner, the wealth of the inhabitant was known to every passerby. But Yap money lacked the important characteristic of portability. The process of trading the stones for needed goods and services was difficult at best.

Modern paper currency is lightweight, which facilitates the exchange process. United States paper money comes in denominations ranging from $1 to $100,000, although the highest denomination currently being printed is $100.

Durability. Durability is a third important characteristic of money. A monetary system using butter or cheese faces the durability problem in a matter of weeks. Although coins and paper currency wear out over time, they are replaced easily with shiny new coins and crisp new paper. U.S. dollar bills have an average life of 18 months and can be folded some 4,000 times without tearing.

Stability. A good money system should have a stable value. If the value of money fluctuates, people become unwilling to trade goods and services for it. Inflation is, therefore, a serious concern for governments. When people fear their money will lose much of its value, they begin to abandon it and look for safer means of storing their wealth. Where once they accepted dollars or francs, they may now demand gold coins or they may store their wealth in the form of land, jewelry, or other physical goods. In the case of runaway inflation, where the value of money may decrease 20 percent or more in a single year, people increasingly return to a barter system, exchanging their output for the output of others.

Difficult to counterfeit. If you hold a dollar bill to the light, you will notice small red and blue silk threads imbedded in the paper. Their purpose is to make counterfeiting difficult. Theft of currency plates from government mints is a common plot for espionage and mystery novels and movies, because the production and distribution of counterfeit money could undermine a nation's monetary system by ruining the value of legitimate money. For this reason all governments make counterfeiting a serious crime and take elaborate steps to prevent it.

What Are the Functions of Money?

medium of exchange
The function performed by money in facilitating exchange and eliminating the need for a barter system.

Money serves primarily as a **medium of exchange**—the function performed by money in facilitating exchange and eliminating the need for a barter system. Rather than follow the complicated process of trading wheat directly for gasoline or clothing (the barter system), a farmer can sell the wheat and use the money from the sale to make other purchases.

unit of account
The function performed by money in serving as the common denominator for measuring the value of all products and services.

Money also functions as a **unit of account**—the common denominator for measuring the value of all products and services. A new car is worth, say, $9,500, a certain cut of beef $4, and a 40-yard-line ticket to the Oakland Raiders game $20. Using money as a common denominator aids in comparing widely different products and services.

store of value
The function performed by money in serving as a temporary store of accumulated wealth until it is needed for new purchases.

Finally, money acts as a temporary **store of value**—a way of keeping accumulated wealth until it is needed to make new purchases. Wealth can also be held in the form of stocks and bonds, real estate, antiques, works of art, houses, precious gems, or any other kind of valuable goods. The advantage of storing value in goods other than money is that they often produce additional income in the form of dividends, interest payments, rent, or increases in value. For example, paintings by Renoir, Monet, and van Gogh have greatly increased in value over the past 20 years. But money offers one substantial advantage as a store of value: It is highly liquid. An asset is said to be liquid if it can be obtained and disposed of quickly and easily.

A van Gogh painting may increase in value, but its owner can obtain money for it only after finding a purchaser. In order to exchange bonds for money, the owner must contact a broker and pay a commission. And the possibility always exists that the value of the bond may be less than when it was first purchased. The owner can then either hold the bond until maturity (at which time the corporation or government agency that issued it will pay the total amount of the bond and interest) or sell it at a loss in order to obtain the more liquid dollars. In addition to the liquidity problem, many nonmoney stores of value involve storage and insurance costs.

There are disadvantages in holding money, particularly in inflationary times. If prices double, all the dollar bills under the mattress will buy only half the clothes and movie tickets when they're pulled out to be spent. Also, unless it is held in the form of NOW account deposits or savings account deposits, money earns no interest for its owner. Its chief advantage, then, is that it is immediately available for use in purchasing products or paying debts.

Composition of the Money Supply

The United States money supply is divided into the following categories: coins, paper money, demand deposits (checking accounts), NOW accounts at commercial banks and thrift institutions (savings and loan associations and mutual savings banks), and credit union share draft accounts. About 3 percent of the total money supply is in the form of metal coins ranging from copper pennies to (partially) silver dollars. Another 25 percent of the total money supply is made up of paper money. These two components of the money supply are usually called **currency.**

currency
Two of the components of the money supply—coins and paper money.

Demand deposits. Approximately two-thirds of the money supply in the United States is in the form of **demand deposits,** the technical name for checking accounts at commercial banks and mutual savings banks. Demand deposits are considered part of the money supply because they are promises to pay immediately to the depositor any amount of money requested—as long as it does not exceed the amount in the person's checking account.

demand deposits
The technical name for checking accounts, which are promises to pay immediately to the depositor any amount of money requested as long as it does not exceed the checking account balance.

Nearly 95 percent of the dollar value of all financial transactions in the U.S. is conducted with checks rather than currency. Americans write and cash more than 1,000 checks a second. There are several explanations for this frequent use of checks:

1. A check is a more convenient form of payment for large or odd-numbered purchases. Writing a check for a $93.60 jacket is more convenient than handing the salesperson four $20s, a $10, three dollars, two quarters, and a dime.

2. It reduces the possibility of theft or loss of currency.

3. It makes payment by mail easier and safer.

Even though an estimated 40 percent of the people in the United States deal almost exclusively in cash, the use of checkbook money offers the advantages of convenience and safety. In addition to checkbook money, many people also use credit cards as a substitute for cash (see Focus 18–1).

Other forms of money. Because the depositor can write what are essentially checks on these accounts, NOW accounts, automatic transfer service accounts, and credit union share draft accounts are also considered as part of the money supply. These newer types of deposits provide their owner with interest payments on deposited funds while also permitting immediate payment upon request. NOW accounts offered by commercial banks, savings and loan associations, and mutual savings banks typically earn slightly above 5 percent. **Automatic transfer system accounts (ATS),** frequently referred to as "interest/checking plans," are similar to NOW accounts in that all deposited funds earn interest at the bank's regular savings rate. As checks are written, funds equal to the amount of the check are trans-

automatic transfer system accounts (ATS)
Accounts in which all deposited funds earn interest at the bank's regular savings rate because money is transferred from savings to checking accounts only when checks are written; also known as interest/checking plans.

In this era of plastic money, credit cards are often used as a substitute for cash.

FOCUS 18–1
Plastic Money as a Substitute for Cash

The era of plastic money has arrived. With growing frequency, people are using credit cards as substitutes for cash.

At least half of all U.S. families hold one or more credit cards. More than 17 million of them use three or more cards, and about 6 million use nine or more. Consumers owe $68 billion on credit card accounts of all types, roughly $540 per family.

A major reason for the tremendous increase in credit card business is the amazing growth in the use of bank cards—particularly those issued by Master Card and VISA, which together claim more than 90 million cardholders. About 11,000 U.S. banks offer credit card services.

While credit cards have traditionally been used for such travel-related purchases as airline tickets, gasoline, auto rentals, and motel charges, retail store charge cards continue to be the most widely used type of credit cards in the United States.

But new areas of credit card use are rapidly developing. In California, a holder of a credit card can pay property taxes, state income taxes, motor vehicle license fees, even car and home insurance, simply by making a phone call.

Doctors and dentists, hospitals, colleges and universities, utilities, and even mortuaries are accepting credit cards for payment in many parts of the country. Some churches and political parties hand out "pledge" cards with spaces for credit card numbers.

Even though department store charge cards and some of the bank credit cards are provided at no charge to consumers (unlike American Express, Diners Club, and Carte Blanche, which charge an annual membership fee), they generally do lead to higher retail prices. Goods and services at many stores that honor the cards are priced higher to cover the service cost charged by the credit card companies. These fees range from 2 to 9 percent.

share draft accounts
Accounts similar to ATS accounts used by depositors at credit unions.

time deposits
The technical name for savings accounts, which are not in the form of NOW or ATS accounts at commercial banks and thrift institutions; the institution is permitted to require prior withdrawal notice or to assess an early withdrawal penalty.

ferred from the depositor's savings account to his or her checking account. **Share draft accounts** are used in a similar manner by depositors at credit unions who wish to earn slightly greater interest rates on their funds yet still have immediate access to their funds. Such drafts are payable through banks and operate much like checks.

Near-monies

In addition to the money supply, a number of assets exist that are almost, but not quite, money. These include **time deposits**—the technical name for savings accounts not in the form of NOW or ATS accounts—at commercial banks and thrift institutions, United States government bonds, and money market mutual fund shares. Such assets are called **near-monies** because they are almost as liquid as checking accounts, NOW and ATS accounts, and share draft accounts but cannot be used directly as mediums of exchange. Such savings accounts permit the financial institution to require one or two months' notice prior to withdrawal, or to assess a penalty for early withdrawal in the form of losing some of the interest already accrued. Money market mutual funds represent an increasingly popular means of earning high interest rates through the purchase of shares in a mutual fund which, in turn, buys short-term notes of government agencies and major corporations. Because they are purchasing short-term debts, such mutual funds earn high interest during such inflationary periods as the early 1980s. In addition, they can be quickly converted to money. These funds are discussed in Chapter 19.

near-monies
Assets that are almost as liquid as checking accounts but that cannot be used directly as a medium of exchange.

The U.S. Commercial Banking System

The heart of the U.S. banking system is the approximately 14,500 commercial banks.

Commercial banks are profit-making businesses that perform two basic functions:

1. They hold the deposits of individuals and business firms in the form of checking or savings accounts.

2. They use these funds to make loans to individuals and businesses.

commercial banks
Profit-making businesses that hold deposits of individuals and businesses in the form of checking or savings accounts and that use these funds to make loans to individuals and businesses.

Commercial banks provide a number of services to their customers.
Drawing by Mort Geiberg; © 1979 The New Yorker Magazine, Inc.

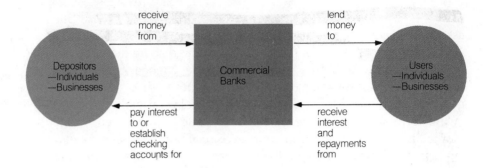

FIGURE 18-2
The operations of commercial banks.

Figure 18–2 shows how commercial banks perform these two functions. Another view of banks follows:

> Like frisbee manufacturers, bankers buy inputs, massage them a bit, burn a little incense, say the magic words, and out pops some output from the oven. If their luck holds, they can sell the finished product for more than it cost to buy the raw materials and process them through the assembly line.
>
> For a banker, the raw material is money. He buys it at a long counter he sets up in the store, then rushes around to the back, polishing it on his sleeve as he goes, sits down behind a huge desk (a little out of breath), and sells it as soon as he can to someone else. . . .
>
> About the only way you can tell whether a banker is buying money or selling it is to observe him in his native habitat and see whether he's standing up or sitting down. For some unknown reason, probably an inherited trait, bankers always stand up when they buy money (take your deposit), but invariably sit down when they sell it (make loans or buy securities).[3]

Types of Commercial Banks

state banks
Commercial banks chartered by individual states.

national banks
Commercial banks chartered by the federal government.

Most commercial banks are **state banks**—commercial banks chartered by individual states. Approximately one-third are **national banks**—commercial banks chartered by the federal government. These tend to be larger in size, and they hold approximately 60 per-

---

FOCUS 18–2
How Much Is $1 Billion?

Students of business and economics become so accustomed to seeing terms like *billions of dollars* that they often have no conception of just how much money they are discussing. But suppose you were given the task of spending $1 billion. At the rate of $100,000 per day, you would be spending money for more than 26 years!

TABLE 18-1

The 15 Largest Commercial Banks in the United States

Rank	Company	Deposits (in billions)
1	BankAmerica Corp. (San Francisco)	$ 88.4
2	Citicorp (New York)	71.8
3	Chase Manhattan Corp. (New York)	56.8
4	Manufacturers Hanover Corp. (New York)	41.7
5	J. P. Morgan & Co. (New York)	35.6
6	Chemical New York Corp.	30.1
7	Continental Illinois Corp. (Chicago)	27.3
8	Western Bankcorp. (Los Angeles)	24.9
9	Bankers Trust New York Corp.	23.9
10	First Chicago Corp.	21.4
11	Security Pacific Corp. (Los Angeles)	21.2
12	Wells Fargo & Co. (San Francisco)	16.2
13	Crocker National Corp. (San Francisco)	14.9
14	Irving Bank Corp. (New York)	14.2
15	Marine Midland Banks (Buffalo)	14.2

cent of the total commercial bank deposits. While the regulations affecting state and national banks vary slightly, in practice there is little difference between the two from the viewpoint of the individual depositor or borrower.

Table 18-1 lists the 15 largest banks in the United States. The BankAmerica Corp. in California is the largest, with deposits of $88 billion. More than 50 banks in the United States have deposits of more than $2 billion each (see Focus 18-2).

The Federal Reserve System

Banks use deposits as the basis of the loans they make to individual and business borrowers. Because their income is derived from loans, banks lend most of the currency obtained from their checking and savings account depositors to borrowers at interest rates higher than the rates paid to depositors. Approximately 15 percent of the total deposits are kept on hand at the bank or at the nearest Federal Reserve District Bank to cover withdrawals; the remainder is used for loans.

The Coming of the Federal Reserve System

What would happen if all the bank's depositors decided to withdraw their funds at once? The bank would be unable to return the depositors' money—unless it could borrow the needed funds from another bank. But if the demand for currency instead of checking and savings accounts spread to other banks, the result would be a bank panic. Banks would have to close their doors (sometimes referred to as a bank holiday) until they could obtain loan payments from their borrowers. Such panics in the past resulted in the failure of numerous commercial banks and plunged the economy into major depressions.

Economic depressions occurred in the United States four times between the end of the Civil War and 1907, and most of them began with bank panics. The severe depression of 1907 prompted Congress to appoint a commission to study the banking system and make recommendations for changes. The commission's recommendations became the basis of the Federal Reserve Act, which President Woodrow Wilson signed two days before Christmas in 1913 to create the Federal Reserve System.

The Structure of the Federal Reserve System

Federal Reserve System
A system of regulating banking in the United States through 12 regional banks controlled by a board of governors.

The **Federal Reserve System** is a system of regulating banking in the United States through twelve regional banks controlled by a board of governors. Figure 18–3 indicates the twelve regions and the cities in which the regional banks are located.

In practice, the Federal Reserve System (the "Fed") is a banker's bank. It holds the deposits of member banks, acts as a clearing house for checks, and regulates the commercial banking system.

The Federal Reserve System is controlled by a board of governors in Washington, D.C. The board consists of seven members appointed by the President and confirmed by the Senate. Political pressures are reduced by a 14-year term of office for each member, with one term expiring every two years.

While all national banks are required to be members of the Federal Reserve System, membership is optional for state-chartered banks. In all, there are approximately 5,500 member banks.

FIGURE 18–3
Map of the Federal Reserve System.

■ Boundaries of Federal Reserve Districts.
  The San Francisco District includes Alaska and Hawaii
● Federal Reserve Bank Cities
★ Board of Governors of the Federal Reserve System

Control of the Money Supply: The Fed's Basic Function

The most essential function of the Federal Reserve System is to control the supply of credit and money in order to promote economic growth and a stable dollar, both at home and in international markets.[4] It performs this function through the use of three important tools: reserve requirements, open market operations, and the discount rate.

Reserve requirements. The strongest weapon in the Federal Reserve System's arsenal of tools to control the money supply is the **reserve requirement**—the percentage of a bank's checking and savings accounts that must be kept in the bank or on deposit at the local Federal Reserve District Bank. By changing the percentage of required reserves the Federal Reserve System can directly affect the amount of money available for making loans. Should the board of governors choose to stimulate the economy by increasing the amount of funds available for borrowing, it can lower the reserve requirement.

Changing the reserve requirement is such a powerful means of changing the money supply that it was seldom used prior to the unprecedented inflationary period of the late 1970s and early 1980s. Even a 1 percent variation in the reserve requirement means a potential fluctuation of billions of dollars in the money supply. Because of this the board of governors would prefer to rely more often on the other two weapons at its disposal—open market operations and changes in the discount rate.

Open market operations. A far more common method used by the Federal Reserve System to control the money supply is **open market operations**—the technique of controlling the money supply by purchasing and selling government bonds. When the board of governors decides to increase the money supply, it buys government bonds on the open market. The exchange of money for bonds places more money in the economy and makes it available to member banks. A decision to sell bonds serves to reduce the overall money supply.

Control of the money supply through open market operations is often exercised by the board when small adjustments are desired. These operations do not produce the psychological effect that often results from announcements of changes in reserve requirements. Such announcements make newspaper headlines and are widely interpreted by commercial banks, businesspeople, and the stock market as a signal by the Federal Reserve System of "tighter" or "easier" money. Over the years, open market operations have been increasingly used as a flexible means of expanding and contracting the money supply.

The discount rate. Earlier the Federal Reserve System was referred to as a "banker's bank." When member banks need extra money to lend, they turn to a Federal Reserve bank, presenting either

reserve requirement
The percentage of a bank's checking and savings accounts that must be kept in the bank or on deposit at the local Federal Reserve District Bank.

open market operations
The technique of controlling the money supply through the purchase and sale of government bonds by the Federal Reserve System.

discount rate
The interest rate charged by the Federal Reserve System on loans to member banks.

IOUs drawn against themselves or promissory notes from their borrowers. The interest rate charged by the Federal Reserve System on loans to member banks is called the **discount rate.**

Commercial banks choose to borrow from the Federal Reserve System when the discount rate is lower than rates charged by other sources of funds. A high discount rate may motivate bankers to reduce the number of new loans to individuals and businesses due to the higher costs of obtaining loanable funds.

The Federal Reserve banks may choose to stimulate the economy by reducing the discount rate. Because the rate is treated as a cost by commercial banks, a rate reduction encourages them to increase the number of loans to individuals and businesses.

The discount rate has been used a number of times during the past few inflation-plagued years in controlling the money supply and attempting to curb the nation's inflation. Like the reserve requirement, it is a blunt instrument with considerable impact on such interest-sensitive industries as automobiles and housing.

A second reason for the increased use of the discount rate in recent years has been to communicate to banks and to the general public the attitude of the board of governors concerning the money supply. An announcement of a reduction in the discount rate is interpreted as an indication by the Federal Reserve System that the money supply should be increased and credit should be expanded.

Table 18–2 shows how each of the tools of the Federal Reserve System can be used to stimulate or slow the economy.

Check Processing: Another Role of the Fed

check
A piece of paper addressed to a bank on which is written a legal authorization to withdraw a specified amount of money from an account and to pay that amount to someone.

Figure 18–4 is a **check**—a piece of paper addressed to a bank on which is written a legal authorization to withdraw a specified amount of money from an account and to pay that amount to someone. Because $19 of every $20 of business transactions are in the form of checks, it is important to understand how they are processed and the role played by the Federal Reserve System in the processing.

In this case, Louis E. Boone has authorized the Florida National Bank of Orlando, Florida, to reduce his checking account by $30 by paying this amount to *Sports Illustrated* magazine for renewing his subscription. If both parties have checking accounts in the same bank, check processing becomes a simple matter of increasing the checking

TABLE 18–2
The Tools of the Federal Reserve System and How They Affect the Economy

Tools	Stimulate the Economy	Slow the Economy
Reserve requirement	Lower	Raise
Open market operations	Buy	Sell
Discount rate	Lower	Raise

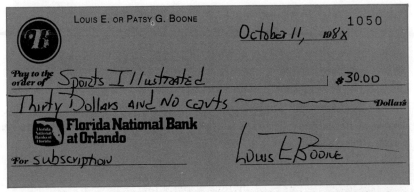

FIGURE 18–4
A sample check.

account of *Sports Illustrated* by $30 and reducing Boone's account
by that amount.

But suppose *Sports Illustrated*'s publisher, Time, Inc., has a checking account in Chicago. In this situation the Federal Reserve System
enters the picture to act as collector for intercity transactions. The
Federal Reserve handles millions of checks every day. Figure 18–5
shows the journey of Boone's check through the system. Whenever
you write a check, you can trace the route it has taken by examining
the endorsement stamps on the back of it.

FIGURE 18–5
Journey of a check through the Federal Reserve System.

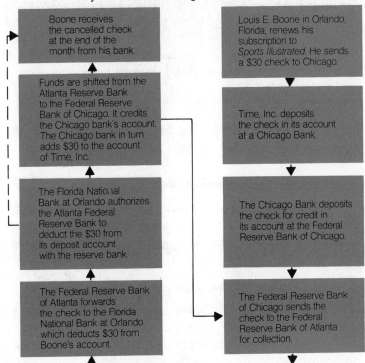

Providing Insurance for Depositors: The FDIC

Prior to 1934, bank failures were both common and catastrophic for depositors. In the depression year of 1933 alone, nearly 4,000 banks collapsed. Both individuals and businesses feared the loss of their deposits and looked for means of protecting them.

Federal Deposit Insurance Corporation (FDIC)
A corporation that insures bank depositors' accounts up to a maximum of $100,000 and sets requirements for sound banking practices.

The **Federal Deposit Insurance Corporation (FDIC)** began operating on January 1, 1934. It insures depositors' accounts up to a maximum of $100,000 and sets requirements for sound banking practices. All commercial banks that are members of the Federal Reserve System must subscribe to the FDIC, and most nonmember banks are also covered. In fact, only about 300 commercial banks in the entire United States are not covered.

Insurance coverage cannot be increased by holding accounts in a different name or by opening accounts in other branches of the same bank. Deposits in different banks are separately insured, however, so there is no limit to the number of $100,000 deposits that can be fully protected in different banks in the same town or scattered throughout the country.

The FDIC has made major contributions to improving the stability of the commercial banking system. Since it began operations, fewer than 700 banks have failed.

When the Franklin National Bank of New York, the twentieth largest bank in the United States, failed in the mid-1970s, the FDIC quickly stepped in and arranged for the European-American Bank & Trust Company to take over the banking operations. Depositors lost no money, and consumer installment loans were continued by European-American. As far as the general public was concerned, only the name of the bank had changed.[5] Such actions by the FDIC and the Federal Reserve System contribute to the general public's confidence in the banking system by guaranteeing depositors' savings.

Electronic Funds Transfer Systems and Other Efficient Bank Services

In a single year, U.S. businesses handle between 35 and 40 billion checks. The huge costs associated with processing these checks have led companies and the banking system to explore methods of reducing the number of checks being written.

electronic funds transfer system (EFTS)
A computerized system of reducing check-writing through electronic depositing and withdrawal of funds.

The long-awaited "cashless society" may already have begun in the form of **electronic funds transfer systems (EFTS)**—computerized systems of reducing check-writing through electronic depositing and withdrawal of funds. EFTS include automatic 24-hour banking stations where holders of specially coded bank cards can make deposits, withdraw cash, and pay utility bills. Automatic cash dispensers are being installed in shopping centers, major department stores, even super-markets—where consumers write the greatest number of checks. The cash dispenser is connected to the bank's computer, which checks the validity of the card, reduces the cardholder's checking account total by the amount of cash requested, and provides the cash and a printed receipt—all within 20 seconds. In addition, some stores have point-of-sale (POS) terminals similar to cash registers. By inserting the cus-tomer's card into the terminal and punching in the data relating to a purchase, the amount of the purchase can be transferred via computer from the customer's account to the retail store's account. EFTS offer advantages for both businesses and consumers. Merchants can reduce their bad check losses, banks can save on paperwork costs, and con-sumers can get money instantly.

Other bank services also provide consumer convenience and im-prove the efficiency of banking operations. Employers, for example, can automatically deposit employees' checks in their bank accounts. Also, for a number of years banks have enabled depositors to auto-matically pay utility bills and make home mortgage and even insur-ance payments. With the depositor's preauthorization, such creditors bill the bank directly. The bank then reduces the depositor's checking account total by the amount of the payments and sends the person a receipt at the end of the month showing the amount of each bill paid.

With competition for customers growing, many banks are initiating even greater convenience services for consumers. For example, Chase Manhattan Bank in New York now has a bank-by-telephone service that enables members who maintain checking accounts at the bank to pay their bills by telephone. The service eliminates the need to write and mail checks. All members have to do is call the special toll-free number and give their payment instructions. The fee is $1.50 a month no matter how many bills a member pays. Citicorp in New York has started what it calls PassWord Service, which enables mem-bers to buy Citicorp travelers checks by toll-free telephone, 24 hours a day, 365 days a year, from anywhere in the continental United States. Enrollment in the service is free, and members get electroni-cally presigned travelers checks delivered anywhere they wish for the standard 1 percent travelers check fee.

Other Financial Institutions

A number of financial institutions other than commercial banks exist as both sources and users of funds. **Savings and loan associations** accept time deposits from businesses and individual investors and pay interest at rates that are slightly higher than those paid by commercial banks. These deposits are then used to purchase corporate bonds,

savings and loan associations
Financial institutions that pay slightly higher interest rates on time deposits and lend money for residential construction and commercial purposes.

Controversial Issue

Should Interstate Banking Be Permitted?

A bank customer in Great Britain has the luxury of depositing money in one bank branch and withdrawing it from another branch located in a distant corner of the country. This is not yet possible in the United States.

The Pepper-McFadden Act, passed in 1927, prevents U.S. banks from having offices in more than one state unless specifically authorized by state law, and requires banks to adhere to the branch banking laws of the state. In some states, these laws prohibit statewide branch banking, and in 12 states, including Oklahoma, no branches are permitted even within the same city. Only South Dakota allows out-of-state banks to establish offices within its boundaries.

For years the banking community has struggled with the issue of interstate banking and the sides in the controversy are clearly drawn. The nation's 2,000 largest banks, with assets of $50 million or more, strongly support interstate banking, while the 13,000 smaller banks, which make up the bulk of the nation's banking industry, bitterly oppose any change. The controversy was heated up by a report recommending the end to interstate banking barriers issued during the last days of the Carter Administration. John F. McGillicuddy, chairman of the Manufacturers Hanover Trust Company, the nation's fourth largest bank, echoed the sentiments of the entire banking community when he said, "The issue of nationwide banking is not one that is going to go away."

Opponents of interstate banking fear that the nation's 12 to 15 largest banks such as New York's Citibank, Chase Manhattan, and Manufacturers Hanover Trust and California's Bank of America would quickly seize control of the entire banking industry and eliminate small, local competition. They also fear that large out-of-state banks would show little interest in small communities and would concentrate their holdings in large cities.

Supporting the interests of the politically powerful small banks, Senator Jake Garn (R-Utah), chairman of the Senate Banking Committee, has, as he put it, "a rather large bias against interstate banking." Senator Garn fears that medium-sized banks

home mortgages, and government securities. Nearly half of all new homes are financed by funds from savings and loan associations.

Approximately 30 percent of the nation's 4,500 savings and loan associations are incorporated under federal regulations and must use the word *federal* in their names. The remaining 70 percent are state-chartered. Deposits in 90 percent of the savings and loans are insured by the Federal Savings and Loan Insurance Corporation (FSLIC).

Mutual savings banks were first established to provide interest on savings accounts. The early U.S. banks did not provide such accounts, and the first mutual savings banks were organized in the early

mutual savings banks State-chartered banks located primarily in the northeastern section of the United States whose operations are similar to those of savings and loan associations.

would be the most seriously hurt by a change in the law. They would be "caught between very small, personalized service and the big boys," said Garn. He also believes that interstate banking would mark the end to the kind of banking service that people have grown to expect. "Once all the small people are squeezed out," warns Garn, "what level of service do you get?"

Those who support the end to interstate banking restrictions see little risk of diminished competition. In their view, the new law would have little effect on the concentration of economic power. Moreover, supporters claim that changing the law would allow them to do what other nonbanking businesses are permitted to do. Firms like American Express, and Merrill Lynch, Pierce, Fenner and Smith are not subject to the same legal restrictions as banks, and they offer the equivalent of checking and savings accounts and other services on a nationwide scale. In addition, foreign banks, which are free from federal banking restrictions, have already set up interstate operations.

Supporters also point to the new electronic banking technology, which makes the status quo even more anachronistic. Within days after the relaxation of interstate banking barriers, says the *New York Times* "a California bank could place machines in New York through which a New Yorker would be able to get cash, make deposits, or take out loans." Currently these machines are considered branch offices and are subject to the same prohibitions on interstate banking as the banks themselves.

In addition, analysts believe that competitive pressures and changes in federal laws eliminating the ceiling on the amount of interest banks may pay on consumer accounts may encourage many banks to welcome the chance of selling out. With their costs rising, many small banks have already found themselves in need of an emergency bail-out.

The issues are clearly drawn. On one side stand the nation's small and midsized banks who fear that interstate banking means an end to their economic viability. On the other side are large banking institutions who are straining to loosen the tethers of federal law. It will be up to Congress to decide which side states its case more strongly.

1800s in Philadelphia and Boston. They operate in much the same way as savings and loan associations by investing deposits in mortgages and bonds to generate sufficient revenues to pay interest to depositors and earn a profit. Although they are state-chartered, their deposits are insured up to $100,000 per account by the Federal Deposit Insurance Corporation. Mutual savings banks are located primarily in the northeastern section of the United States.

In 1981 savings and loan associations and mutual savings banks began offering interest-bearing NOW accounts in direct competition with commercial banks.

credit unions
Financial institutions typically sponsored by companies, unions, or professional or religious groups that pay interest to their member depositors and make loans to members.

insurance companies
Businesses that provide protection for individual and business policyholders in return for payment of premiums and that use these premiums to make long-term loans for corporations, commercial real estate mortgages, and government bonds.

pension funds
Funds set up to guarantee members a regular monthly income on retirement or on reaching a certain age that often utilize surplus cash for investment in corporate securities.

The nation's 22,500 **credit unions** serve as sources for short-term consumer loans at competitive rates for their members. Credit unions are typically sponsored by companies, unions, and professional or religious groups; they pay interest to their member depositors. Credit unions today have outstanding loans of more than $42 billion.

Other sources of funds include insurance companies and pension funds. **Insurance companies** provide protection for insured individual and business policyholders in return for payment of premiums. They are major sources of long-term loans for corporations, commercial real estate mortgages on major commercial buildings and shopping centers, and government bonds. These funds are generated through the premiums paid by policyholders. **Pension funds** are established to guarantee members a regular monthly income on retirement or on reaching a certain age. Total assets of all private, state, and local government pension plans are approximately $300 billion. Most pension funds invest surplus cash in corporate securities.

Summary

Money serves as the lubricant for modern industrial society. In order to perform its necessary functions, money should possess the following characteristics: divisibility, portability, durability, stability, and difficulty of counterfeiting. These characteristics allow money to perform its functions as a medium of exchange, a unit of account (or common denominator of measuring the value of different products), and a temporary store of value.

The money supply is composed of several ingredients: coins, paper money, demand deposits, NOW and ATS accounts, and credit union share draft accounts. Demand deposits (checking accounts) make up the great majority of the U.S. money supply. Items such as time deposits, United States government bonds, and money market fund shares are called near-monies. Because they cannot be used directly as a medium of exchange, they are not money. But they are highly liquid and can easily be converted into money.

The U.S. commercial banking system is made up of 14,500 commercial banks, which serve two important functions. They hold the deposits of individuals and business firms, and they use these funds to make loans to others.

The regulation of the commercial banking system is the responsibility of the Federal Reserve System, which has three major weapons that can be used to control the money supply: the reserve requirement, open market operations, and the discount rate. Increases in the reserve requirement or the discount rate have the effect of reducing the money supply. Decreases in these rates have the opposite effect.

Open market operations—the purchase and sale of government bonds—are the most commonly used tool. Purchases of government bonds by the Federal Reserve System have the effect of placing more money in circulation. Sales of bonds act to reduce the money supply. Another function of the Federal Reserve System is to assist in processing checks written on commercial banks throughout the United States.

The Federal Deposit Insurance Corporation (FDIC) is an agency that regulates the banking system. It establishes rules for sound banking practices and insures deposits up to a maximum of $100,000. The FDIC has substantially reduced the number of bank failures and, through insuring deposits, has strengthened the general public's confidence in the banking system.

For many years banks have enabled depositors to pay bills automatically and have allowed employers to deposit employees' checks directly in their bank accounts. Now banks are offering electronic funds transfer systems—computerized systems of reducing check-writing through electronic depositing and withdrawal of funds—and other services to their customers.

Other financial institutions that exist as both sources and users of funds include savings and loan associations, mutual savings banks, credit unions, insurance companies, and pension funds. These institutions pay interest to depositors, make loans for residential and commercial buildings, and purchase corporate bonds and government securities.

Key Terms

---

negotiable order of withdrawal (NOW) account

money

medium of exchange

unit of account

store of value

currency

demand deposits

automatic transfer system accounts (ATS)

share draft accounts

time deposits

near-monies

commercial banks

state banks

national banks

Federal Reserve System

reserve requirement

open market operations

discount rate

check

Federal Deposit Insurance Corporation (FDIC)

electronic funds transfer system (EFTS)

savings and loan associations

mutual savings banks

credit unions

insurance companies

pension funds

Review Questions

1. Explain each of the terms listed on the previous page.

2. What characteristics should money possess?

3. What are the functions of money?

4. Describe the composition of the money supply in the United States.

5. Why are most of the financial transactions in the United States conducted with checks rather than currency?

6. Why are near-monies not included in the money supply?

7. Identify the major types of financial institutions, the types of loans typically made by each, and the types of accounts provided by each institution.

8. Describe the operation of a commercial bank.

9. Describe each of the tools used by the Federal Reserve System to control the economy.

10. Outline the processing of checks by the banking system in the United States.

Discussion Questions and Exercises

1. Evaluate the pros and cons of the controversial issue that appears in this chapter.

2. Invite a local bank executive to speak to your class. Ask the person to explain the role his or her bank plays in the local community.

3. What is the current status of EFTS in your community? Why do merchants prefer this instant transfer of funds?

4. Prepare a brief report on the most recent economic policy actions of the Federal Reserve System. Your research should include recent newspaper and magazine accounts of Federal Reserve decisions.

5. Ask a local bank for permission to observe its operations for a few hours. Then report to the class on what you observed.

Case 18–1: The S & L Crisis

The savings and loan associations of America are in serious trouble. In 1981, an estimated 90 percent of the 4,560 S & Ls lost money. The reason for their troubles is a savings revolution that is sweeping the U.S. Americans are withdrawing billions of their savings from traditional checking accounts, Christmas Clubs, and passbook savings accounts and reinvesting them in higher interest-paying accounts. During the first five months of 1981, $43 billion flowed into these new accounts. As *Time* magazine points out, depositors have a variety of savings options:

Never before have Americans faced such an array of savings choices. Some of the options:

The Mattress. Keeping cash at home ensures that it will always be close at hand and safe, assuming that it is protected from theft and fire. Disadvantage: at current rates of inflation, the money will lose about 10% in value each year.

Savings Account. Money deposited in a savings account can be easily withdrawn at any time and is insured by the Federal Government for up to $100,000. Disadvantage: the interest is a low 5.25% at a bank or 5.5% at a savings and loan or savings bank.

Savings Certificates. Time deposits offered by banks and S and Ls pay more interest than a savings account, and they are still insured by the Government. . . . Disadvantage: if the money is withdrawn early, the saver loses a substantial part of his interest.

Money-Market Certificate. This six-month, Government-insured time deposit in a bank or thrift institution pays high interest. . . . Disadvantage: $10,000 minimum and a penalty for early withdrawal.

Treasury Bills. Known as T-bills, these are securities sold by the Government to finance the national debt. Since they are backed by the U.S. Treasury, they are safe and the interest is not taxed by state or local governments. They usually have a maturity of three months to a year. . . . Disadvantage: the minimum denomination is $10,000.

Money-Market Funds. These are portfolios of high-interest securities sold to investors as a mutual fund. The customer can usually write checks against the account. The deposits are not insured by the Government, but the funds are generally sound. Disadvantage: interest rates fluctuate on a daily basis, and thus the current high yields . . . would fall sharply and quickly if general interest rates come down.

Commercial Paper. This is a short-term corporate IOU that is not backed by any collateral. The safety depends on the soundness of the corporation issuing it. Commercial paper and large certificates of deposit currently pay the highest rate of interest available. . . . Disadvantage: the minimum investment is usually $100,000.

The S & Ls face the dilemma of a portfolio of long-term loans (particularly home mortgage loans) earning an average of 9 to 10 percent and a current cost of funds ranging as high as 16 percent in mid-1981. A new law, the Depository Institutions Deregulation and Monetary Control Act of 1980, removed some of the constraints on lending and permitted the offering of NOW accounts. By 1986, it will abolish all ceilings on interest that can be paid by commercial banks and thrift institutions. Such deregulation would permit S & Ls to compete with the high interest rates offered by major borrowers.

Questions

1. What is the major cause of the loss of earnings by financial institutions? What changes in lending practices have occurred in recent years to overcome this problem?

2. Evaluate the changes in mortgage loan terms that have occurred since 1980. How do these changes aid and hurt borrowers?

Case 18–2: "Will That Be VISA or Cashcard?"

Many observers have pointed out that the United States has become a credit-card economy. Consumer installment debt is over $300 billion, and the widespread use of credit cards continues to be an important feature of modern retailing.

Credit-card companies charge retailers from 2 to 9 percent for handling their charge sales. This cost is then passed on to consumers in the form of higher prices—unless the retailer can generate enough added sales through the convenience of offering credit-card service to cover the added costs. Both cash and credit-card customers pay any higher prices that might occur.

Even though the Fair Credit Billing Act of 1975 legalized discounts of up to 5 percent for cash purchases, few retail stores offer such discounts. Many people consider charging identical prices to both cash and credit-card customers discriminatory. The result has been the formation of cash-discount organizations. These groups provide for 3 to 10 percent discounts at participating retailers when the cardholder pays by check or in cash.

Questions

1. Do you think charge cards result in discriminatory pricing?

2. Why would a retailer oppose a two-price system for cash and credit-card customers?

19

Financial Management: Obtaining and Using Money

Learning Goals

1. To describe the important functions the financial executive performs in the operation of the firm

2. To describe the likely sources of short-term and long-term funds for the business

3. To determine how money is used by business firms for both long-term and short-term purposes

4. To evaluate the three basic sources of funds for the business

5. To explain the meaning of each of the key terms introduced in this chapter

Profile: John Z. De Lorean
The Dream That Became a Nightmare

To many, former General Motors (GM) executive John Zachary De Lorean's dream was an impossible one. How could any single individual raise nearly $300 million required to design, build, and sell an expensive, futuristic sports car that would bear his own name. But build it he did . . . at least for a time.

De Lorean's reputation at General Motors was built on such engineering successes as the Pontiac Firebird and the Chevrolet Camaro—sporting cars that excited the buying public. Promoted up the ladder of corporate management, De Lorean soon missed the freedom of designing the kinds of cars he wanted Americans to drive. In 1973, he left his $650,000-per-year job at GM with the dream of forming his own auto company. Two years later the De Lorean Motor Company was in operation.

From that point on, De Lorean put his efforts into taking the "De Lorean" from the drawing board onto the roadway. With a fiberglass underbody, a brushed stainless-steel finish, a chassis of steel dipped in epoxy, leather upholstery, stereo system, and a price tag of $26,000, De Lorean's luxury sports car was designed for the rich. When it rolled off the assembly line in 1981, De Lorean had convinced the public to buy his car—a relatively easy challenge compared to his struggles to raise the initial capital investment for his auto plant.

When De Lorean started his fund-raising efforts, he did not know how difficult it would be to reach the $270 million figure needed to design and operate the auto assembly plant. He risked $4 million of his own money; set up a limited partnership that raised an additional $15.5 million; and convinced investors like Johnny Carson, brokerage giant Merrill Lynch, and 339 GM dealers, each of whom purchased $25,000 in company stock and agreed to buy between 50 and 150 cars, to back his efforts. All these millions did not even bring him halfway to his goal.

De Lorean knew early on that without another benefactor willing to risk nine figures on his flying-wedge-shaped automobile, his dream would die. He also knew that the only one around who would give him that kind of money was government. Ours. Theirs. Anyone's.

In July 1978, Great Britain made De Lorean an offer he could not turn down: $146.9 million in loans, grants, and equity participation for the 2,000 jobs he promised to bring to West Belfast, Northern Ireland. De Lorean promised to build his assembly plant in Dunmurry, a Belfast suburb with a 13 percent unemployment rate. The British had good reason for making this offer. Employed Irish Catholics were less likely to kill British soldiers.

The early successes in 1981 quickly turned sour as the worst recession since the 1930s took hold. Sales slowed for the expensive De Lorean, but the firm had no alternative models to offer an increasingly economy-minded market. In early 1982, production was increased at the Dunmurry plant, even though inventory was growing and no cars had been sold at full price since March 1982. With more funds being poured into production and less being realized from auto sales, the De Lorean financial plan began to unravel.

On October 18, 1982, the British government stepped in with an announcement that it was closing the Northern Ireland assembly plant. Six hours later, the business world was shocked to learn of the arrest of John De Lorean by federal narcotics agents in Los Angeles. The founder and chief executive officer of De Lorean Motor Company was charged with trafficking in narcotics when he was arrested with $24 million in cocaine in his possession.

Though my bottom line is black,
I am flat upon my back,
My cash flows out and customers pay slow. The
growth of my receivables is almost unbelievable;
The result is certain—unremitting woe! And I
hear the banker utter an ominous low mutter,
"Watch cash flow."

—Herbert S. Bailey, Jr.
with apologies to Edgar Allan Poe's "The Raven"

A billion dollars is not what it used to be.

—Bunker Hunt, after failing to corner the world's
silver market

He was 41 years old, a skilled sailor, and he had a plan. By plotting a new nautical trade route, he could bring back wealth in the form of gold, gems, drugs, and spices. He would also be honored for the rest of his life. But the axiom "it takes money to make money" applied to his plan, and he would need at least $14,000 to finance the venture. His own meager savings were totally inadequate and no commercial lender would provide the funds. A formal request for funding from the Portuguese government was rejected.

Finally, almost in desperation, he dispatched his brother Bartholomew to London and Paris to seek financing from the English and French governments. He decided to handle personally the presentation of his proposal to the Spanish government. It took five years, but finally the leaders of the Spanish government accepted his ideas and agreed to back the venture. The government agreed to provide the necessary funds for the implementation of the plan, to grant him a percentage in any ensuing trade that might develop, to award him the title of Admiral, and to make him governor of any new lands he might discover.

He invested the $14,000 in hiring a crew, purchasing the necessary provisions, and preparing a fleet of three ships that would subsequently become famous: the flagship *Santa Maria,* and the two smaller vessels, the *Nina* and the *Pinta.* Although the venture did not prove to be a financial success for Christopher Columbus, his voyages to the West Indies rank among the most important events in history. And finance made them possible.

What Is Finance?

Finance is the business function of effectively obtaining and using funds.

On numerous occasions this text has stressed the two primary functions that must be performed by a business to satisfy its customers: production and marketing of needed or desired products and services. But a third—and equally critical—function must also be performed. Unless adequate funds are available for the purchase of materials and equipment and the hiring of production and marketing personnel, management may find itself in bankruptcy proceedings.

Finance—A Popular Route to the Top in the Corporate World

In the business world of the 1980s effective financial decisions are increasingly becoming synonymous with corporate success. Greater priority already is being placed on measuring—and reducing—the costs of doing business. As a result, the financial manager is emerging as one of the most important people on the corporate scene. "Ten years ago, our financial capacity seemed unlimited," says Kenneth S. Axelson, finance vice-president of J. C. Penney. "Today it is strictly limited."[1]

The growing importance of financial managers is reflected in the number of chief executives who were promoted from financial positions. Firms with financial people at the top include such giants as General Motors, Singer, FMC Corporation, Fruehauf, and Pfizer. Figure 19–1 shows the main career emphasis of chief executives of the top 802 corporations in the United States.

As Figure 19–1 indicates, finance is the most common background of chief executives in major U.S. corporations. Approximately one chief executive officer in five has a finance background and another 10 percent have backgrounds in banking, bringing the total to 30 percent with finance or finance-related backgrounds.

This represents a major change in the past 25 years. Production, engineering, research, and operations were the dominant routes to the top a generation ago. But, increasingly, the extensive financial planning and control required in managing multiproduct, multinational companies have brought managers from finance and marketing to the helm.

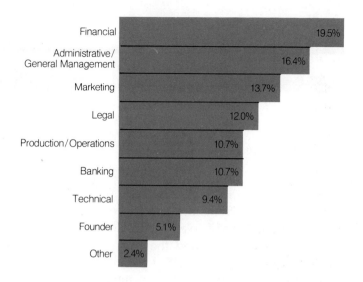

FIGURE 19–1
Backgrounds of chief executives in
802 leading U.S. corporations.

The Financial Manager—Guardian of the Firm's Purse Strings

The chief function of the financial manager is to decide on sources and uses of funds. Simply stated, **financial managers** are responsible for both raising and spending money. They must have funds available to make purchases and pay bills. They must evaluate alternative sources of funds to determine the least expensive ones. Their responsibilities also extend to a continual monitoring of the level of the firm's cash, inventories, and unpaid bills in order to ensure that excessive funds are not tied up in these items. Although financial managers do not directly control many of these areas, they must act as "watchdogs" over them to be sure that cash is being used efficiently. They do this by setting up a financial plan for the company.

The organization's financial plan is built on answers to two vital questions:

1. How much funds are required for the firm during the next period of operations?

2. How will the necessary funds be obtained?

As Figure 19–2 indicates, it is the financial manager's responsibility to consider these two questions carefully and then to decide on the best sources of funds and how they should be used.

financial manager
A manager whose chief responsibilities involve the raising and spending of money.

FIGURE 19–2
The financial manager and the two
key ingredients of the financial plan.

Some funds will be obtained through sale of the firm's products and services. But funds are needed in different amounts at different times, and the financial plan must reflect both the amount of inflows and outflows of funds and their timing. Profitable firms often face financial squeezes as a result of the need for funds when sales lag or when customers are slow in making payments. The financial plan should indicate when the flows of funds entering and leaving the organization will occur and in what amounts.

Sources of Funds

debt capital
Funds obtained through borrowing.

equity capital
Funds provided by the firm's owners through additional investment, plowing back earnings, or the sale of stock.

Needed funds for implementing the organization's financial plan come from two major sources: debt and equity. **Debt capital** represents funds obtained through borrowing. **Equity capital** consists of funds provided by the firm's owners through the sale of stock or additional investment by the current owners. In addition, equity funds can be generated by plowing back the earnings of the firm. These alternative sources are shown in Figure 19–3.

Unless financial managers are able to generate adequate funds through plowing back earnings, they will be forced to choose between

FIGURE 19–3
Sources of funds.

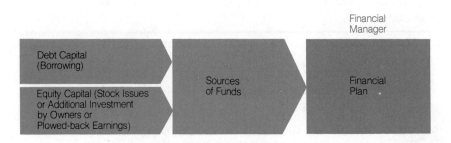

funds provided by borrowing debt capital and funds provided by the firm's owners through sale of stock or additional investment by the current owners in the business (equity capital). As Table 19–1 shows, debt and equity can be compared on the basis of maturity, claim on assets, claim on income, and right to a voice in the management of the firm.

TABLE 19–1

Comparison of Debt and Equity Financing

Factor	Debt	Equity
Maturity	Has a specific date when it must be repaid.	Has no maturity date.
Claim on assets	Company lenders have prior claims on assets.	Stockholders have claims only after claims to lenders have been paid.
Claim on income	Lenders have prior claim on a fixed amount of interest, which must be paid before dividends can be paid to stockholders. Interest payments are a contractual obligation of the borrowing firm.	Stockholders have a residual claim after all creditors have been paid. While common stockholders may receive large dividends when the company prospers, dividends are paid only when the board of directors of the firm chooses. Dividends are *not* a contractual obligation of the firm.
Right to a voice in management	Lenders are creditors, not owners. They have no voice in company affairs unless interest payments are not received.	Stockholders are the owners of the company, and most are given a voice in the operation of the firm. Common stockholders normally have voting rights, while preferred stockholders generally are not given this privilege.

Short-term Sources of Funds

It is convenient to distinguish between short- and long-term sources of funds. Short-term sources are those that must be repaid within a one-year period. Long-term sources must be repaid over a period of one year or more. The four major sources of short-term loans for business firms are trade credit, unsecured bank loans, commercial paper, and secured short-term loans.

Trade Credit

trade credit
The short-term source of funds from making purchases on credit or open account.

Most firms not only sell on credit, they also make purchases on credit, or open account. These open account purchases, called **trade credit,** represent the major source of short-term financing by most business firms.

Trade credit typically does not involve a formal contract. The purchaser who accepts shipped merchandise in effect agrees to pay the supplier for the goods. The credit terms are stated on the supplier's invoice (or bill), which accompanies the shipment (see Focus 19–1).

FOCUS 19–1
Why Purchasers Should Take Advantage of Cash Discounts

The supplier's invoice includes credit terms; it lists the period of time for which credit is extended, the size of the discount offered if the purchaser pays cash, and the date the credit period begins. A cash discount is a reduction of the purchase price of products, provided the purchaser pays for the goods within a specific time period.

A typical supplier's credit terms may be stated as "2/10 net 30." The purchaser reads these terms as "a 2 percent discount will be allowed if I pay the invoice within 10 days. Otherwise the bill is due in 30 days." But why should the firm pay quickly in order to take advantage of the 2 percent discount? Assume the local Pizza Hut has been extended credit terms of 2/10 net 30 on a $1,000 paper supplies purchase made March 16. By deciding to take the discount the Pizza Hut manager will pay $980 ($1,000 less 2 percent) on March 25. By ignoring the discount offer, the manager will pay $1,000 on April 15.

The decision not to take the discount means that the manager is paying $20 to keep the money for an extra 20 days (March 26 to April 15). Because there are slightly more than eighteen 20-day periods in a year, the interest cost—on an annual basis—amounts to more than 36 percent. It is wise for the Pizza Hut manager (or any other financial manager) to borrow money from the bank if necessary to take advantage of cash discounts.

Unsecured Bank Loans

unsecured loan
A short-term source of funds from a loan in which the borrower does not pledge any assets as collateral but is given the loan on the basis of credit reputation and previous experience with the lender.

A second major source of short-term funds is **unsecured loans** from commercial banks. These loans are called *unsecured* because the borrower firm does not pledge any assets (such as accounts receivable or inventory) as collateral. Commercial banks make short-term loans on the basis of previous experience in dealing with the firm and the

THE WALL STREET JOURNAL

"You have an honest face, Mr. Ferndale. But of course our computer doesn't know that."

Commercial banks make short-term loans on the basis of previous experience with the borrower and the borrower's credit reputation.

Cartoon Features Syndicate

firm's credit reputation. They lend unsecured short-term funds in three basic forms: promissory notes, lines of credit, and revolving credit agreements.

Promissory notes. A **promissory note** is a traditional loan whereby the borrower signs a note that states the terms of the loan, including its length and the interest rate charged. It is to be used for a specific purpose such as a temporary increase in inventory for the "back to school" sales season. Figure 19–4 shows a typical promissory note. The note states the terms of the loan, including the length of time for which the loan is made and the interest rate charged. Most promissory notes have maturities of 30 to 90 days.

For major business firms with high credit standings, the interest rate is at or near the **prime interest rate**—the lowest rate of interest charged by commercial banks for short-term loans. The prime rate shifts on the basis of availability of funds and demand for short-term funds, as well as on the basis of changes in the Federal Reserve discount rate. Each fluctuation of the prime rate makes news headlines, because it indicates the relative availability of funds.

Line of credit. A **line of credit** is an agreement between a commercial bank and a business firm that states the amount of unsecured short-term credit the bank will make available to the borrower—provided the bank has enough funds available for lending. A line of credit is not a guaranteed loan. It typically represents a one-year agreement that if the bank has enough available funds, it will allow the firm to borrow the maximum stated amount of money. The presence of a line of credit speeds the borrowing process for both the bank and the borrowing firm because the bank does not have to examine the cred-

promissory note
A traditional bank loan for which the borrower signs a note that states the terms of the loan, including its date of repayment and interest rate.

prime interest rate
The lowest rate of interest charged by commercial banks for short-term loans to major business firms with high credit standings.

line of credit
An agreement between a commercial bank and a business firm that states the amount of unsecured short-term credit the bank will make available to the borrower—provided the bank has enough funds available for lending.

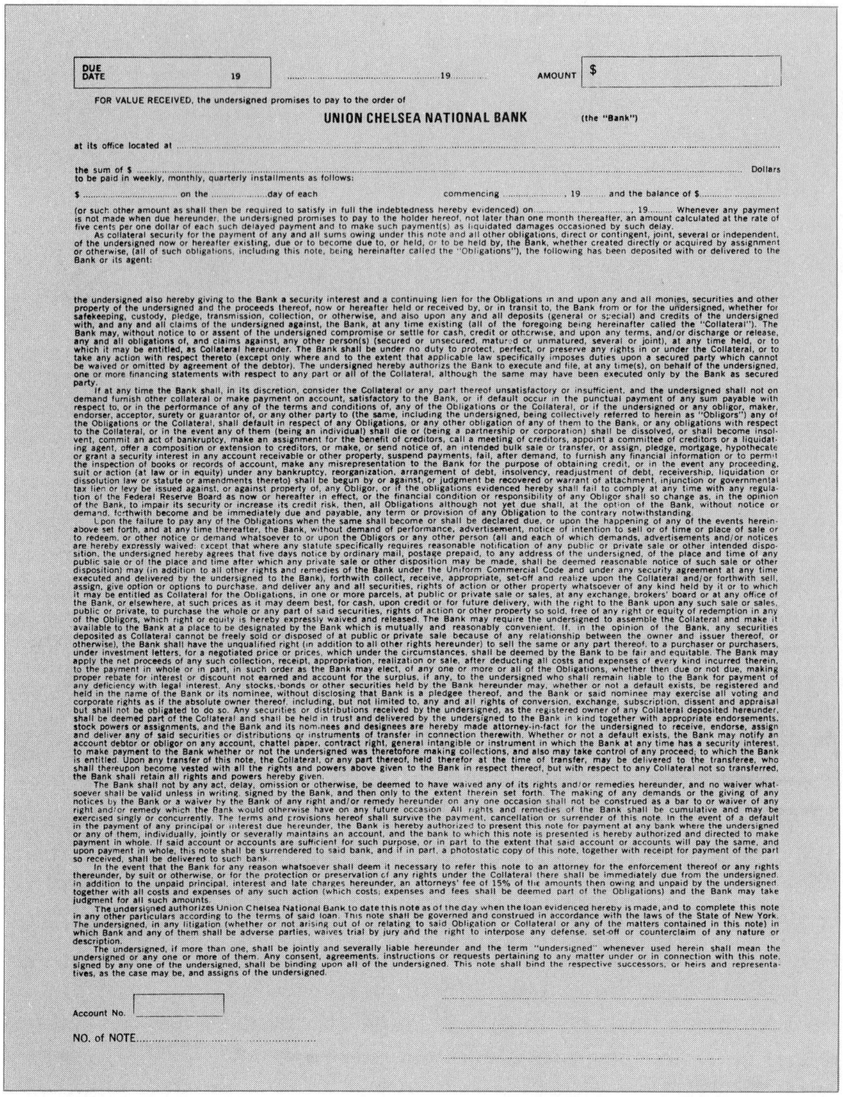

DUE DATE 19 .... 19 .... AMOUNT $

FOR VALUE RECEIVED, the undersigned promises to pay to the order of

UNION CHELSEA NATIONAL BANK (the "Bank")

at its office located at ....

the sum of $ .... Dollars
to be paid in weekly, monthly, quarterly installments as follows:

$ .... on the .... day of each commencing ...., 19 .... and the balance of $ ....

(or such other amount as shall then be required to satisfy in full the indebtedness hereby evidenced) on ...., 19 .... Whenever any payment is not made when due hereunder, the undersigned promises to pay to the holder hereof, not later than one month thereafter, an amount calculated at the rate of five cents per one dollar of each such delayed payment and to make such payment(s) as liquidated damages occasioned by such delay.

As collateral security for the payment of any and all sums owing under this note and all other obligations, direct or contingent, joint, several or independent, of the undersigned now or hereafter existing, due or to become due to, or held, or to be held by, the Bank, whether created directly or acquired by assignment or otherwise, (all of such obligations, including this note, being hereinafter called the "Obligations"), the following has been deposited with or delivered to the Bank or its agent:

the undersigned also hereby giving to the Bank a security interest and a continuing lien for the Obligations in and upon any and all monies, securities and other property of the undersigned and the proceeds thereof, now or hereafter held or received by, or in transit to, the Bank from or for the undersigned, whether for safekeeping, custody, pledge, transmission, collection, or otherwise, and also upon any and all deposits (general or special) and credits of the undersigned with, and any and all claims of the undersigned against, the Bank, at any time existing (all of the foregoing being hereinafter called the "Collateral"). The Bank may, without notice to or assent of the undersigned compromise or settle for cash, credit or otherwise, and upon any terms, and/or discharge or release, any and all obligations of, and claims against, any other person(s) (secured or unsecured, matured or unmatured, several or joint), at any time held, or to which it may be entitled, as Collateral hereunder. The Bank shall be under no duty to protect, perfect, or preserve any rights in or under the Collateral, or to take any action with respect thereto (except only where and to the extent that applicable law specifically imposes duties upon a secured party which cannot be waived or omitted by agreement of the debtor). The undersigned hereby authorizs the Bank to execute and file, at any time(s), on behalf of the undersigned, one or more financing statements with respect to any part or all of the Collateral, although the same may have been executed only by the Bank as secured party.

If at any time the Bank shall, in its discretion, consider the Collateral or any part thereof unsatisfactory or insufficient, and the undersigned shall not on demand furnish other collateral or make payment on account, satisfactory to the Bank, or if default occur in the punctual payment of any sum payable with respect to, or in the performance of any of the terms and conditions of, any of the Obligations or the Collateral, or if the undersigned or any obligor, maker, endorser, acceptor, surety or guarantor of, or any other party to (the same, including the undersigned, being collectively referred to herein as "Obligors") any of the Obligations or the Collateral, shall default in respect of any Obligations, or any other obligation of any of them to the Bank, or any obligations with respect to the Collateral, or in the event any of them (being an individual) shall die or (being a partnership or corporation) shall be dissolved, or shall become insolvent, commit an act of bankruptcy, make an assignment for the benefit of creditors, call a meeting of creditors, appoint a committee of creditors or a liquidating agent, offer a composition or extension to creditors, or make, or send notice of, an intended bulk sale or transfer, or assign, pledge, mortgage, hypothecate or grant a security interest in any account receivable or other property, suspend payments, fail, after demand, to furnish any financial information or to permit the inspection of books or records of account, make any misrepresentation to the Bank for the purpose of obtaining credit, or in the event any proceeding, suit or action (at law or in equity) under any bankruptcy, reorganization, arrangement of debt, insolvency, readjustment of debt, receivership, liquidation or dissolution law or statute or amendments thereto) shall be begun by or against, or judgment be recovered or warrant of attachment, injunction or governmental tax lien or levy be issued against, or against property of, any Obligor, or if the obligations evidenced hereby shall fail to comply at any time with any regulation of the Federal Reserve Board as now or hereafter in effect, or the financial condition or responsibility of any Obligor shall so change as, in the opinion of the Bank, to impair its security or increase its credit risk, then, all Obligations although not yet due shall, at the option of the Bank, without notice or demand, forthwith become and be immediately due and payable, any term or provision of any Obligation to the contrary notwithstanding.

Upon the failure to pay any of the Obligations when the same shall become or shall be declared due, or upon the happening of any of the events hereinabove set forth, and at any time thereafter, the Bank, without demand of performance, advertisement, notice of intention to sell or of time or place of sale or to redeem, or other notice or demand whatsoever to or upon the Obligors or any other person (all and each of which demands, advertisements and/or notices are hereby expressly waived: except that where any statute specifically requires reasonable notification of any public or private sale or other intended disposition, the undersigned hereby agrees that five days notice by ordinary mail, postage prepaid, to any address of the undersigned, of the place and time of any public sale or of the place and time after which any private sale or other disposition may be made, shall be deemed reasonable notice of such sale or other disposition) may (in addition to all other rights and remedies of the Bank under the Uniform Commercial Code and under any security agreement at any time executed and delivered by the undersigned to the Bank), forthwith collect, receive, appropriate, set-off and realize upon the Collateral and/or forthwith sell, assign, give option or options to purchase, and deliver any and all securities, rights of action or other property whatsoever of any kind held by it or to which it may be entitled as Collateral for the Obligations, in one or more parcels, at public or private sale or sales, at any exchange, brokers' board or at any office of the Bank, or elsewhere, at such prices as it may deem best, for cash, upon credit or for future delivery, with the right to the Bank upon any such sale or sales, public or private, to purchase the whole or any part of said securities, rights of action or other property so sold, free of any right or equity of redemption in any of the Obligors, which right or equity is hereby expressly waived and released. The Bank may require the undersigned to assemble the Collateral and make it available to the Bank at a place to be designated by the Bank which is mutually and reasonably convenient. If, in the opinion of the Bank, any securities deposited as Collateral cannot be freely sold or disposed of at public or private sale because of any relationship between the owner and issuer thereof, or otherwise), the Bank shall have the unqualified right (in addition to all other rights hereunder) to sell the same or any part thereof, to a purchaser or purchasers, under investment letters, for a negotiated price or prices, which under the circumstances, shall be deemed by the Bank to be fair and equitable. The Bank may apply the net proceeds of any such collection, receipt, appropriation, realization or sale, after deducting all costs and expenses of every kind incurred therein, to the payment in whole or in part, in such order as the Bank may elect, of any one or more or all of the Obligations, whether then due or not due, making proper rebate for interest or discount not earned and account for the surplus, if any, to the undersigned who shall remain liable to the Bank for payment of any deficiency with legal interest. Any stocks, bonds or other securities held by the Bank hereunder may, whether or not a default exists, be registered and held in the name of the Bank or its nominee, without disclosing that Bank is a pledgee thereof, and the Bank or said nominee may exercise all voting and corporate rights as if the absolute owner thereof, including, but not limited to, any and all rights of conversion, exchange, subscription, dissent and appraisal but shall not be obligated to do so. Any securities or distributions received by the undersigned, as the registered owner of any Collateral deposited hereunder, shall be deemed part of the Collateral and shall be held in trust and delivered by the undersigned to the Bank in kind together with appropriate endorsements, stock powers or assignments, and the Bank and its nominees and designees are hereby made attorney-in-fact for the undersigned to receive, endorse, assign and deliver any of said securities or distributions or instruments of transfer in connection therewith. Whether or not a default exists, the Bank may notify an account debtor or obligor on any account, chattel paper, contract right, general intangible or instrument in which the Bank at any time has a security interest, to make payment to the Bank whether or not the undersigned was theretofore making collections, and also may take control of any proceeds to which the Bank is entitled. Upon any transfer of this note, the Collateral, or any part thereof, held therefor at the time of transfer, may be delivered to the transferee, who shall thereupon become vested with all the rights and powers above given to the Bank in respect thereof, but with respect to any Collateral not so transferred, the Bank shall retain all rights and powers hereby given.

The Bank shall not by any act, delay, omission or otherwise, be deemed to have waived any of its rights and/or remedies hereunder, and no waiver whatsoever shall be valid unless in writing, signed by the Bank, and then only to the extent therein set forth. The making of any demands or the giving of any notices by the Bank or a waiver by the Bank of any right and/or remedy hereunder on any one occasion shall not be construed as a bar to or waiver of any right and/or remedy which the Bank would otherwise have on any future occasion. All rights and remedies of the Bank shall be cumulative and may be exercised singly or concurrently. The terms and provisions hereof shall survive the payment, cancellation or surrender of this note. In the event of a default in the payment of any principal or interest due hereunder, the Bank is hereby authorized to present this note for payment at any bank where the undersigned or any of them, individually, jointly or severally maintains an account, and the bank to which this note is presented is hereby authorized and directed to make payment in whole. If said account or accounts are sufficient for such purpose, or in part to the extent that said account or accounts will pay the same, and upon payment in whole, this note shall be surrendered to said bank, and if in part, a photostatic copy of this note, together with receipt for payment of the part so received, shall be delivered to such bank.

In the event that the Bank for any reason whatsoever shall deem it necessary to refer this note to an attorney for the enforcement thereof or any rights thereunder, by suit or otherwise, or for the protection or preservation of any rights under the Collateral there shall be immediately due from the undersigned, in addition to the unpaid principal, interest and late charges hereunder, an attorneys' fee of 15% of the amounts then owing and unpaid by the undersigned, together with all costs and expenses of any such action (which costs, expenses and fees shall be deemed part of the Obligations) and the Bank may take judgment for all such amounts.

The undersigned authorizes Union Chelsea National Bank to date this note as of the day when the loan evidenced hereby is made, and to complete this note in any other particulars according to the terms of said loan. This note shall be governed and construed in accordance with the laws of the State of New York. The undersigned, in any litigation (whether or not arising out of or relating to said Obligation or Collateral or any of the matters contained in this note) in which Bank and any of them shall be adverse parties, waives trial by jury and the right to interpose any defense, set-off or counterclaim of any nature or description.

The undersigned, if more than one, shall be jointly and severally liable hereunder and the term "undersigned" whenever used herein shall mean the undersigned or any one or more of them. Any consent, agreements, instructions or requests pertaining to any matter under or in connection with this note, signed by any one of the undersigned, shall be binding upon all of the undersigned. This note shall bind the respective successors, or heirs and representatives, as the case may be, and assigns of the undersigned.

Account No.

NO. of NOTE ....

FIGURE 19–4
A promissory note.

itworthiness of the firm each time it borrows money. Lines of credit are available to individuals as well as businesses (see Focus 19–2).

revolving credit agreement
A guaranteed line of credit.

Revolving credit agreement. A **revolving credit agreement** is simply a guaranteed line of credit. The commercial bank guarantees that the amount shown in the credit agreement will be available to the borrower. For guaranteeing availability, the bank usually charges a commitment fee which applies to the unused balance of the revolving credit agreement.

FOCUS 19-2
Bank Credit Cards: Lines of Credit for Individuals

The Bank of America and its affiliated commercial banks that issue VISA cards provide a service similar to a line of credit for individual cardholders. Each cardholder is allowed to make credit purchases of up to the authorized amount. Similar services are provided to Master Card cardholders. The services even extend to the purchase of money from the local bank that handles the bank card. Cardholders can automatically withdraw $50 to $100 without a credit check being made.

Commercial Paper

Commercial paper consists of short-term notes issued by major corporations with very high credit standings. It is backed solely by the reputation of the corporation, and it may have a maturity of anywhere from 3 to 270 days. It can be both a use of cash for firms with excess funds and a source of funds for major corporations attempting to raise money.

Because commercial paper is unsecured—backed only by the reputation of the issuing firm—only very large firms with unquestioned financial stability are able to issue it. Even with large companies, risk is present. Holders of Penn Central commercial paper found these unsecured loans worth very little when the ailing railroad giant defaulted on several million dollars' worth of them in the early 1970s. Commercial paper is typically sold in denominations of $25,000 with a maturity of nine months or less. Using commercial paper to raise funds directly from large lenders is usually 1 or 2 percent cheaper than using short-term bank loans.

commercial paper
Short-term promissory notes issued by major corporations with high credit standings and backed solely by the reputation of the issuing firms.

Secured Short-term Loans

As the firm continues to borrow money, it soon reaches a limit beyond which no additional unsecured loans will be made. Indeed many companies, especially smaller ones, are unable to obtain any short-term unsecured money. For them, secured loans are the only source of short-term borrowed funds.

Secured loans require the borrower to pledge collateral such as accounts receivable or inventory. The agreement between lender and borrower lists the amount of the loan, the interest rate and due date, and the pledged collateral. A copy of the agreement is filed with the state, usually at a state or county office. The filed agreement provides to future lenders information about which assets of the borrower are still free to be used as collateral.

Commercial banks and commercial finance companies, such as CIT Financial Corporation and Commercial Credit Corporation, usually extend loans backed by pledges of accounts receivable or inventory. Both assets are usually highly liquid and are therefore an attractive form of short-term collateral.

Factoring—Outright Sale of Accounts Receivable

factor
A financial institution that purchases at a discount the accounts receivable of retailers such as furniture and appliance dealers.

Instead of using accounts receivable as collateral for loans, some firms sell them to a **factor**—a financial institution that purchases at a discount the accounts receivable of firms such as furniture and appliance dealers, for whom credit sales are common. Selling the accounts receivable to a factor means that every sale is a "cash" sale and the firm is thus freed from the necessity of collecting payments from customers. In many instances, sales finance companies perform the role of a factor, as do some commercial banks.

Accounts receivable that are factored are sold at a discount, with the factor typically assuming all credit risks. Once the factor has purchased the accounts, customers are notified to make future payments directly to that company. Although factoring is an expensive method of raising short-term funds, it is often used in retailing because it reduces the need for major record keeping and for maintaining a collection department.

Floor-planning—The Automobile Dealer's Friend

floor-planning
The assignment of inventory title (collateral) to financing agencies in return for short-term loans.

The automobile industry uses a special type of financing called **floor-planning**—the assignment of inventory title (collateral) to financing agencies in return for short-term loans. This practice is commonly used by retailers who handle identifiable, expensive goods such as automobiles, furniture, and major appliances.

An auto dealer who receives a shipment of new cars may sign an agreement with a local commercial bank or other financing agency for a loan in the amount of the shipment. Title to the cars passes to the lender, but the cars themselves (the inventory) remain with the dealer. The lender periodically checks the dealer's inventory to make sure that all the required collateral is still in the borrower's hands. As cars are sold, the dealer pays a portion of the sales price plus interest to the lender.

Some automobile manufacturers allow their own financing subsidiaries to make floor-plan loans. The local Chevrolet dealer may have the alternative of floor-planning through a local commercial bank or through General Motors Acceptance Corporation (GMAC), the financial subsidiary of General Motors.

Long-term Sources of Funds

While short-term sources of cash prove satisfactory in financing current needs for cash or inventory, major purchases of land, plant, and equipment require funds for a much longer period of time. The business firm has three long-term financing sources available: long-term loans, bonds, and equity financing.

Long-term Loans

Long-term loans are made by various financial institutions to business firms, primarily for purchasing machinery and equipment. They generally have maturities of five to twelve years. Although shorter maturities are available, the minimum of five years is most common. Long-term loans are made by financial institutions such as commercial banks, insurance companies, and pension funds; some are also made by the U.S. Small Business Administration. In some cases equipment manufacturers may allow their customers to make credit purchases over a period of several years.

The cost of long-term loans is generally higher than that of short-term loans due to greater uncertainty about the future. Long-term financing agreements include the length of time for repaying the loan, the interest rate, the timing of payments, and the dollar amount of the payments. Quarterly interest payments are normally required.

Sales of Bonds

A **bond** represents a method of long-term borrowing by corporations or government agencies. The corporate bond is issued according to the terms of a legal contract called the bond indenture, which contains the provisions of the loan—amount, interest rate, and maturity date. Figure 19–5 shows a corporate bond.

Bonds are typically sold in denominations of $1,000. They are purchased by commercial banks, insurance companies, pension funds, and even individuals. Like stocks, they are actively traded and can be bought and sold through any stockbrokerage firm. Their current market prices are quoted daily in the financial sections of newspapers. Issuing bonds to raise money is generally reserved only for larger companies with regional or national reputations.

Equity Funds

Equity funds are obtained by selling stock in the company or by reinvesting company earnings. They differ from debt in that there is no maturity date. Sale of ownership shares (the subject of Chapter

bond
A certificate of indebtedness sold to raise long-term funds for corporations or government agencies.

equity funds
Funds obtained by selling stock in the company or by reinvesting company earnings.

FIGURE 19–5
A corporate bond.

20) is an important company decision. Such sales provide cash inflows for the firm and a share in ownership for stock purchasers. Because most shares are traded on organized security exchanges, stockholders can easily sell their stock. Neither source of equity funds is used by all firms. Stock sales, for example, can be used only by corporations. Each source must be evaluated by the financial manager of a business.

Sales of stock. The sale of stock—both preferred and common—represents the true source of equity funds to the business firm. **Stocks** are shares of ownership in the corporation, and stockholders are considered the real owners of the firm. However, they are not guaranteed dividend payments. Stockholders receive dividends only after bondholders of the company are paid. Even then, dividend payments must be decided by the firm's board of directors. Subject to certain legal requirements, any corporation can sell stock to raise new funds.

stocks
Shares of ownership in the corporation.

Retained earnings. Another source of funds is the reinvestment of earnings in the firm. A company may have funds available after paying all claims, including taxes. One choice is to distribute the earnings to stockholders in the form of cash dividends. But seldom are all earnings paid out as dividends; at least a portion is usually kept to finance future growth. A company, such as Walt Disney Enterprises, typically distributes less than 10 percent of its annual earnings in the form of dividends. On the other hand, such mature public utilities as AT&T pay out as much as 80 percent of their profits in the form of dividends.

How Borrowed Funds Produce Leverage

Raising needed cash by borrowing allows the firm to benefit from the principle of **leverage**—a technique of increasing the rate of return on investment through the use of borrowed funds. Table 19–2 shows two identical firms that chose to raise money in different ways. The Leverage Corporation obtained 90 percent of its funds through issuing bonds. The Equity Corporation raised all its needed funds through the sale of shares of stock in the firm. Although each company earned the same profits, stockholders of the Leverage Corporation received a 210 percent return on their $10,000 investment—even after paying $9,000 in interest to bondholders. The $30,000 earned by the Equity Corporation represents only a 30 percent return on its stockholders' investment of $100,000.

leverage
A technique of increasing the rate of return on investment through the use of borrowed funds.

TABLE 19–2
Simplified Income Statements for the Leverage Corporation and the Equity Corporation

Leverage Corporation		Equity Corporation	
Common stock	$ 10,000	Common stock	$100,000
Bonds (at 10% interest)	90,000	Bonds	0
	$100,000		$100,000
Earnings	$ 30,000	Earnings	$ 30,000
Less bond interest	9,000	Less bond interest	0
	$ 21,000		$ 30,000
Return to stockholders $\dfrac{\$\,21{,}000}{\$\,10{,}000}=210\%$		Return to stockholders $\dfrac{\$\,30{,}000}{\$100{,}000}=30\%$	

As long as earnings exceed interest payments on borrowed funds, the application of leverage allows the firm to increase the rate of return on stockholders' investments. But leverage also works in reverse. If company earnings drop to $5,000 in the example, the Equity Corporation will earn a 5 percent return on its stockholders' investment. But because bondholders must be paid $9,000 in interest at the Leverage Corporation, what appears to be a $5,000 gain is actually a $4,000 loss for its stockholders.

Uses of Funds

So far we have focused on the first half of the definition of finance—the alternative sources of funds. But sources represent a financial means to the accomplishment of the goals of the organization. Every bit as vital to the firm's financial plan is the efficient utilization of funds. Like the sources of funds, uses of funds may be classified as either short term or long term.

current assets
Items of value expected to be converted into cash within a period of one year.

Short-term uses are often referred to as **current assets.** As Chapter 17 explained, *assets* are items of value, and *short term* indicates that they are expected to be converted into cash within a period of one year. Short-term funds are critical in the day-to-day operations of the business firm because they provide the firm with the ability to pay bills, extend credit, and promptly deliver merchandise to its customers.

fixed assets
Items of value not expected to be converted into cash within a one-year period.

The largest dollar investment of many firms takes the form of long-term, or **fixed, assets.** The key long-term uses of funds are for items of value not expected to be converted into cash within a one-year period, such as land, buildings, machinery, and equipment. Figure 19–6 focuses on the part of the financial plan devoted to the uses of current and fixed assets.

FIGURE 19–6
Uses of funds.

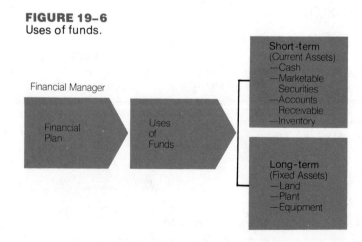

Short-term Uses of Funds

A number of short-term uses of funds are present in any organization. Some funds must be held in the form of cash to meet day-to-day requirements. Other short-term uses include short-term investments in marketable securities, accounts receivable, and funds invested in inventory.

Cash—The Ultimate in Liquidity

Some of the firm's funds are held in the form of cash, the majority of which is in the firm's checking account for use in paying bills and meeting payrolls. But because the firm cannot receive any interest from checking or savings accounts, the financial manager tries to avoid carrying large balances in them.

The general principle underlying cash management is the minimization of the amount of cash required for business operations, thereby allowing a maximum amount of funds to be used in interest-producing investments. In order to minimize the firm's cash needs, the financial manager should pay bills as late as possible and collect money as early as possible. As long as these actions can be taken without damaging the firm's credit standing and without costing more than they save, they lead to efficient cash management. The First National Bank in St. Louis advertisement shown in Figure 19–7 emphasizes efficient management of cash.

Marketable Securities as Substitutes for Cash

Financial managers performing a balancing act between liquidity and profitability have an alternative to holding excessive amounts of cash. They can invest the cash in marketable securities, which, because of their marketability and easy conversion into cash, are often considered near-money. A number of different types of marketable securities are available for purchase. Three of the most common are treasury bills, commercial paper, and certificates of deposit.

Treasury bills. United States **treasury bills** are issued each week on a competitive bid basis to the highest bidder. Most of them are short-term U.S. Treasury borrowings, usually for 91 or 182 days—although one-year bills are occasionally sold. The smallest denomination of treasury bills is usually $10,000. Because treasury bills are issues of the U.S. government, they are considered virtually riskless. Because of their riskless nature and ease of resale, treasury bills are the most popular marketable security.

treasury bills
Short-term U.S. Treasury borrowings that are issued each week on a competitive bid basis and are virtually riskless and easy to resell.

FIGURE 19–7
Efficient cash management.

Commercial paper. Commercial paper, discussed earlier in the chapter, is riskier than treasury bills, and does not have a well-developed secondary market for resale prior to maturity. However, it does pay the purchaser a higher rate of interest. The smallest denomination is normally $25,000.

certificate of deposit (CD)
A short-term, high-interest note issued by a commercial bank.

Certificates of deposit. A **certificate of deposit (CD)** is a short-term note issued by a commercial bank. The size and maturity date of a CD are often tailored to the needs of the investor. Normally, the smallest denomination is $10,000, and the minimum maturity is 30 days. CDs are easily resold, and their interest rate is typically higher than treasury bills but lower than commercial paper.

Accounts Receivable—Credit Sales to the Firm's Customers

In order to retain their present customers and attract new ones, most companies find it necessary to allow at least some credit purchasing by their customers. For many firms, **accounts receivable**—credit sales to customers—make up 15 to 20 percent of all assets. Because accounts receivable represent sales for which payment has yet to be received, they are another use of funds. That is, the company has its money invested in products that it no longer owns.

A firm usually devotes a great deal of attention to the efficient management of credit sales. The decision of whether to sell on credit to another firm is usually based on past dealings with that firm and on financial information provided by such credit-rating agencies as Dun & Bradstreet and Retail Credit Company. (Figure 19–8 shows a sample Dun & Bradstreet report.) The objective is to collect accounts as promptly as possible while allowing credit terms that will attract the desired level of sales.

accounts receivable
Credit sales to customers for which payment has yet to be received.

Inventory—A Major Use of Cash

The subject of inventory management was first discussed in Chapter 14. Because most firms hold inventory in order to satisfy customer demands quickly, it represents a major dollar investment. Cash is continuously invested in raw materials, work-in-process (goods in various stages of production), and finished goods inventory (see Focus 19–3).

The amount of money invested in inventory may vary during the year. Retail stores increase their inventories considerably just before the Christmas selling period and reduce them beginning on December 26. When the next selling season approaches, inventories are again increased.

Long-term Uses of Funds

For many companies, particularly manufacturing firms, the largest dollar investments take the form of long-term, or fixed, assets, which are needed to produce salable products. Fixed assets include land, plant, and equipment.

Land owned by the firm is considered a fixed asset with an unlimited life. As a result, the firm receives no tax benefits for income tax purposes. Plant refers to buildings owned by the firm. Because buildings are likely to deteriorate over time, their owners are allowed to deduct a certain percentage of the purchase price from income each

© Dun & Bradstreet, Inc.

This report has been prepared for:

BE SURE NAME, BUSINESS AND ADDRESS MATCH YOUR FILE.

ANSWERING INQUIRY

SUBSCRIBER: 008-001042

THIS REPORT MAY NOT BE REPRODUCED IN WHOLE OR IN PART IN ANY MANNER WHATEVER.

CONSOLIDATED REPORT

DUNS: 00-647-3261
BEAUMONT & HUNT INC

120 LEMOINE AVE
AUGUSTA, GA 30901
TEL: 404 872-9664

DANIEL T BEAUMONT, PRES

DATE PRINTED
OCT 15 198-
DEPARTMENT STORE

SIC NO.
53 11

SUMMARY

RATING	BB1
STARTED	1956
PAYMENTS	SEE BELOW
SALES	$1,600,000
WORTH	F $261,791
EMPLOYS	20
HISTORY	CLEAR
CONDITION	STRONG
TREND	UP

SPECIAL EVENTS

09/10/8- Kevin Hunt, Sec-Treas, reported a $3,000 merchandise loss in Sep 8 burglary. Loss is fully insured.

05/17/8- CHANGES: Subject recently expanded its line of merchandise with the addition of sporting goods.

PAYMENTS (Amounts may be rounded to nearest figure in prescribed ranges)

REPORTED	PAYING RECORD	HIGH CREDIT	NOW OWES	PAST DUE	SELLING TERMS	LAST SALE WITHIN
09/8-	Disc	15000	5000	-0-	2 10 N30	1 Mo
08/8-	Ppt	7500	500	-0-	30	2-3 Mos
	Ppt	5000	2500	-0-	30	1 Mo
07/8-	Disc	10000	2500	-0-	30	2-3 Mos
	Ppt	2500	1000	-0-	30	2-3 Mos
	Ppt	1000	-0-	-0-	EOM	2-3 Mos
02/8-	Disc	10000	500	-0-	2 10 N30	1 Mo
	Ppt	2500	500	-0-	2 10 N30	1 Mo
	Ppt	1000	-0-	-0-	30	2-3 Mos

FINANCE

02/15/8- Fiscal statement dated Oct 31 198–.

Cash	$ 75,000	Accts Pay	$ 140,510
Accts Rec	110,746	Accruals	48,636
Inventory	285,465	Fed & Other Taxes	26,714
Prepaid	1,240		
Current	472,451	Current	215,860
Fixt & Equip	5,200	CAPITAL STOCK	50,000
		RETAINED EARNINGS	211,791
Total Assets	477,651	Total	477,651

Annual sales $1,600,000; net income $48,000; monthly rent $2,500. Lease expires 198–. Fire insurance on mdse & fixt $300,000.

Accountant: Fred Mitchell, Augusta, GA. Prepared from books without audit.

--0--

UPDATE: On Aug 10 198-, Daniel T Beaumont, Pres, said nine months sales through July 31 were up 10%, profits rising. Concern now employs 20.

On Feb 14, 198- Kevin J Hunt reported sales and profits in fiscal quarter ended Jan 31 as above those of prior year period because of an upsurge in local economy. He expects full year sales to exceed $1.7 million.

PUBLIC FILINGS

03/25/8- On Mar 17 198 , a suit in the amount of $250 was entered against subject by A Henry Associates, Augusta, GA (Docket #27511). Cause of action goods sold and delivered.

05/28/8- On May 21 198-, a financing statement (#741170) was filed listing subject as debtor and NCR Corp, Dayton, OH as secured party. Collateral consists of equipment.

08/10/8- Kevin J Hunt reported action filed by A Henry Associates was due to defective merchandise and had been settled. Court records reveal the suit was withdrawn.

BANKING

02/15/8- Balances average moderate five figures. Non-borrowing account. Relations satisfactory. Account opened Jun 1956.

(CONTINUED)

THIS REPORT, FURNISHED PURSUANT TO CONTRACT FOR THE EXCLUSIVE USE OF THE SUBSCRIBER AS ONE FACTOR TO CONSIDER IN CONNECTION WITH CREDIT, INSURANCE, MARKETING OR OTHER BUSINESS DECISIONS, CONTAINS INFORMATION COMPILED FROM SOURCES WHICH DUN & BRADSTREET, INC. DOES NOT CONTROL AND WHOSE INFORMATION, UNLESS OTHERWISE INDICATED IN THE REPORT, HAS NOT BEEN VERIFIED. IN FURNISHING THIS REPORT, DUN & BRADSTREET, INC. IN NO WAY ASSUMES ANY PART OF THE USER'S BUSINESS RISK, DOES NOT GUARANTEE THE ACCURACY, COMPLETENESS, OR TIMELINESS OF THE INFORMATION PROVIDED, AND SHALL NOT BE LIABLE FOR ANY LOSS OR INJURY WHATEVER RESULTING FROM CONTINGENCIES BEYOND ITS CONTROL OR FROM NEGLIGENCE. 9 R2-3(741212)

FIGURE 19–8
Sample Dun & Bradstreet report.

year. These deductions, commonly called depreciation, result in lowering the firm's tax payments. Equipment refers to all items used in production, from drill presses to forklift trucks, and from typewriters to computers. Because equipment is also expected to deteriorate with use, business firms are permitted to depreciate it on their tax forms, thereby reducing the amount of taxes they pay. Because each of the fixed assets is likely to represent major purchases, the financial manager usually plays a major role in the decision process associated with their purchase.

FOCUS 19–3
Inventory as an Investment

Inventory is obviously an investment in the sense that it requires the firm to tie up its money. A useful technique for illustrating its investment nature is inventory turnover, which represents the number of times the average amount of a firm's inventory is used (or sold) each year. A high rate of inventory turnover means that the firm can reduce the amount of investment for inventory. Let's see how this works.

The Dryden Press is currently evaluating its textbook inventory in order to determine how much money it will save by increasing inventory turnover from four to six times a year. The increase in turnover is possible through the use of a new, fully automated method of filling book orders within 24 hours after they are received.

Dryden expects to continue to move $1.8 million in books through its inventory next year. The average amount of inventory carried under the current and new plans can be calculated by dividing the annual sales by the turnover rate:

$$\text{New Plan: } \frac{\$1.8 \text{ million}}{6} = \$300,000$$

$$\text{Old Plan: } \frac{\$1.8 \text{ million}}{4} = \$450,000$$

Use of the new plan means that Dryden will tie up only $300,000 in inventory instead of the current $450,000. The extra $150,000 can be used elsewhere. If Dryden can earn 12 percent on the $150,000, the reduction in average inventory investment will produce $18,000 (12 percent × $150,000) in new profits. Dryden's management understands that inventory is a major investment.

Who Has the Authority to Purchase Fixed Assets?

Companies typically delegate fixed asset purchasing authority on the basis of certain dollar limits. They usually make major purchases the responsibility of the board of directors, while lesser purchases are delegated to lower levels in the organization. Table 19–3 illustrates how fixed asset purchasing authority might be delegated in a typical company. It indicates that as the dollar value of the purchase decreases, the decision-making authority moves to lower levels. The actual breakdown of this decision-making authority differs for each company.

Controversial Issue

Should the Government Have Bailed Out Chrysler?

In late 1979 Congress authorized a $1.5 billion loan guarantee for the ailing Chrysler Corporation and another $400 million in 1980. These guarantees saved the nation's number 3 automaker from certain bankruptcy. Even after the loans were granted, the debate over the government's role continued. Here is a sampling of how government, economic, and auto industry experts viewed the bail-out decision:

Senator William Proxmire of Wisconsin, Chairman of the Senate Banking Committee, believed that loan guarantees undermine those principles of the free enterprise system that say that poor management and skill deserve to fail. As the senator pointed out, thousands of smaller firms employing hundreds of thousands of workers fail each year and the government does not step in. "By giving such a large sum now," said Senator Proxmire, "the government is essentially saying that any firm can get government assistance if it is big and powerful and has a strong union."

Senator Donald W. Riegle, Jr., of Michigan saw "no other responsible course of action" open to the government than granting the loan guarantees. Senator Riegle argued that as the nation's tenth largest manufacturing firm, Chrysler's collapse would have a catastrophic effect on the nation's economy: the loss of as many as 600,000 jobs, a decline in income, production, and tax revenues, and an increase in federal unemployment and food stamp pay-

TABLE 19–3
Typical Delegation of Authority to Make Fixed Asset Purchases

Size of Purchase	Decision-making Authority
More than $200,000	Board of directors or specified top management committee
$90,000 to $200,000	President and/or chairman of the board of directors
$30,000 to $89,999	Vice-president in charge of a division
$5,000 to $29,999	Plant manager
Less than $5,000	Persons specified by plant manager

Summary

Finance is the business function of effectively obtaining and using funds. The financial manager plays an important role in the operation of the firm. The firm's financial plan must include a systematic approach to the acquisition of funds and the best uses of them.

Sources of funds include borrowing (debt capital), sales of stock in the firm (equity capital), and reinvesting company earnings. Short-

ments. Moreover, in the senator's view, the loss of Chrysler would mean even more money flowing out of the country for foreign cars—a situation that would make our bad balance of payments problem even worse.

William E. Simon, former Secretary of the Treasury, saw the danger of a Chrysler-type bail-out infecting and destroying the free market economy. "If we don't stop this soon," said Simon, "we will become an inefficient, bungling nation where profits will be reaped by a diminished group of shareholders, and losses will be borne by all the rest of us."

Douglas Fraser, President of the United Auto Workers, viewed the Chrysler bail-out as a continuation of a long-standing federal policy to aid financially beleaguered firms. He pointed to hundreds of millions of dollars of federal loan guarantees already granted steel and heavy industry, farming, and small business. In addition, Fraser saw a Chrysler failure as contributing to the decrease of competition among U.S. automakers—a situation that could pose serious antitrust problems.

Despite all the debate and the government's action, the question still remains of whether the government should step in and bail out a company in trouble because of poor financial management and planning, or whether the free enterprise system should be left to operate on its own.

term sources available to the financial manager include the use of the trade credit provided by suppliers, unsecured bank loans, commercial paper, and secured short-term loans. Secured loans are those backed by pledges of company assets such as accounts receivable or inventory. Some firms sell their accounts receivable directly to financial institutions called factors, which purchase the accounts at a discount. Retailers of furniture and appliances often sell accounts receivable to factors.

Long-term sources of funds include long-term loans, bonds, and equity financing. Both long-term loans and bonds represent debt (or borrowed) capital. Equity financing—whether from the sale of stock or the plowing back of company earnings—represents ownership capital.

Uses of funds can be distinguished by time. Short-term uses are purchases of assets that will be converted into cash within a one-year period. Long-term uses are purchases of assets that will be used for one year or more. Short-term uses include cash, marketable securities, accounts receivable, and inventory. Long-term uses include fixed assets such as land, plant, and equipment.

Key Terms

finance	factor
financial manager	floor-planning
debt capital	bond
equity capital	equity funds
trade credit	stocks
unsecured loan	leverage
promissory note	current assets
prime interest rate	fixed assets
line of credit	treasury bills
revolving credit agreement	certificate of deposit (CD)
commercial paper	accounts receivable

Review Questions

1. Explain each of the terms listed above.

2. What are the major functions of the financial manager?

3. Explain the two key ingredients of the financial plan.

4. Identify the major sources of funds.

5. Compare debt financing and equity financing.

6. What is meant by the term *retained earnings?*

7. Outline the uses of funds.

8. What role do firms like Dun & Bradstreet and Retail Credit Company play in financial management?

9. How do borrowed funds produce leverage?

10. Identify the basic principle underlying efficient cash management. What dangers exist if this principle is carried too far?

Discussion Questions and Exercises

1. Evaluate the pros and cons of the controversial issue that appears in this chapter.

2. The Equal Credit Opportunity Act of 1977 was designed to improve women's ability to obtain credit. The law allows a woman who has a joint account with her husband to obtain a separate credit rating on request. It also requires creditors to consider the woman's income when a married couple applies for joint credit, and it prohibits the refusal of credit based on a change in marital status. Discuss the likely reasons for discriminatory credit practices based on sex.

3. Cash discounts to businesses for immediate payment are a good arrangement for the purchaser. Why do suppliers choose to offer businesses such generous discounts?

4. Identify several firms that are likely to use floor-planning. Explain why this type of financing developed.

5. Lenders often develop rating systems to help them make decisions about business and personal loans. Table 19–4 shows how an individual might be scored as a credit risk. What items are likely to appear on a credit risk form for a business borrower?

TABLE 19–4
How Do You Score as a Credit Risk?

Lenders increasingly are using sophisticated scoring systems to rate borrowers. In this simplified illustration, which does not take income into account, an applicant could receive a top score of 215 points.

Home phone	Points	Occupation	
Yes	36	Professional	27
No	0	Technical	5
		Proprietor	−3
Residence		Clerical, sales	12
Owner	34	Craft, laborer	0
Renter	0	Supervisory	26
		Service worker	14
Time at current address		Farm worker	3
Under 6 months	0		
6 months–3 years	11	**Years on present job**	
3–6 years	19	Under 1	0
6–9 years	27	1–5	7
Over 9 years	35	5–8	11
		8–14	15
Any other finance-company loans		Over 14	19
Yes	−12		
No	0	**Bank acounts**	
		None	0
Any bank credit cards		Checking or savings	13
Yes	29	Both	19
No	0		
		Age	
		Under 30	6
		30–40	11
		41–50	8
		Over 50	16
		Maximum Score	215

Case 19–1: The Financial Crisis at Chrysler

In 1981, the United States government rescued Chrysler Corporation from imminent bankruptcy by approving up to $400 million in federal loan guarantees. Approval came on a unanimous vote by the Chrysler Loan Guarantee Board, which said that new cash infusion gives the company "reasonable prospects" of becoming financially viable over the long run. But the board added that this is no sure thing.

In return for receiving the loan guarantees, the board wrestled unprecedented concessions from Chrysler's workers, lenders, and suppliers.

The United Auto Workers agreed to a wage freeze and other wage concessions for the duration of the contract, including giving up the cost-of-living adjustments after March 1981. Chrysler workers saw increases in pensions scheduled for August 1981 delayed until 1982, and all paid personal holidays eliminated during the remainder of the contract. In addition, Chrysler workers agreed that during the next contract, which begins September 15, 1982, wage increases would be in line with the cost of living at the time. This was another way of saying the union would not try to seek catch-up pay for accepting a wage freeze.

Suppliers had to freeze prices at the January 1, 1981, level throughout 1981, as well as give Chrysler a 5 percent discount on purchases during the first quarter.

The board urged the company to press ahead with a satisfactory capital infusion program as quickly as possible.

Chrysler submitted an operating plan calling for eliminating 1,700 jobs and cutting indirect expenses and taking other measures to save $3 billion. Of this, $2 billion would be saved by reducing spending on new models, $300 million by refinancing assets, and up to $320 million by selling 51 percent of Chrysler Financing Corporation, the company's financial arm.

Although no one was willing to admit that Chrysler's problems were over, Chairman Lee Iacocca called a news conference in July 1981 and presented small bottles of ink to the members of Congress who had voted for the guarantees. Each bottle of black ink was labeled *Now being used by the Chrysler Corp.* Chrysler had just earned its first quarterly profit in 27 months.

Questions

1. Resorting to direct assistance by the federal government is both extraordinary and a major distress signal for any firm. Relate spe-

cifically the problems faced by Chrysler to the components of the financial plan shown in Figure 19–2.

2. In return for the government bail-out, Chrysler management agreed to an operating plan designed to severely curtail outflows of funds. Classify each of these steps utilizing the system shown in Figure 19-3.

3. How should federal loan guarantees assist Chrysler? Base your answer on the text discussion of sources of funds.

Case 19–2: After Six, Inc.

After Six, Inc. generates annual revenues of $70 million in a relatively stable business—tuxedos. Yet despite the stability of its market, After Six faced a severe financial crisis during 1981 as a result of record interest rates. Although the firm earned a profit of $4.8 million from operations the previous year, its interest expenses reduced overall net income to a miniscule $264,000. The market price of the firm's stock skidded to only 25 percent of book value. A total of $29 million in outstanding loans was payable in 1981, equalling 40 percent of sales and 108 percent of shareholders' equity.

After Six's financial problems were caused by the fact that only 15 percent of its revenues were generated by direct retail sales. The remaining 85 percent came from credit sales to retail stores. Because these stores tended to be undercapitalized, After Six provided them with 90-day credit at an annual interest rate of 6 percent. Such generous credit terms provided the necessary inducement for retail purchasers, but they were painfully expensive. Because After Six was borrowing funds at the market rate, during the early 1980s it found itself paying three times as much in interest as it was charging its retail customers.

Reducing interest expense was clearly the major challenge facing After Six's management. In fact, their earnings per share would rise from a mere 13 cents to $1.00 if they could cut interest expenses in half.

Questions

1. Relate the problems faced by After Six's financial managers to the information presented in this chapter.

2. What recommendations would you make to the chief executive officer of After Six?

3. Identify two or three other firms in different industries that face similar financial problems. What can be learned from these situations?

20

The Securities Markets

Learning Goals

1. To distinguish among common stock, preferred stock, and bonds and to understand the reasons for an investor's preferring each type of security

2. To identify investors' three basic objectives and to be able to recommend which securities should be purchased by an investor seeking a particular objective

3. To explain the steps involved in selling or purchasing a security listed on the organized stock exchanges

4. To explain the meaning of the information included in stock and bond quotations

5. To evaluate the major features of state and federal laws protecting investors

6. To explain the meaning of each of the key terms introduced in this chapter

Profile: E. F. Hutton

When E. F. Hutton Talks, Everybody Listens

When the late Edward F. Hutton opened the doors to his brokerage house in 1904, he had some innovative ideas in mind. He saw a future in providing a complete range of brokerage services to the West Coast—an area of the country long ignored by every New York-based brokerage house.

For Hutton's San Francisco office to succeed, it required dependable, fast communication, so Hutton advanced $50,000 to Western Union for the completion of the first private, direct coast-to-coast wire. With instant communication at his fingertips, Hutton was able to establish a reputation for speed of service. Orders taken in San Francisco were transmitted, executed, and reported in New York in less than three minutes.

Hutton's ability to operate under pressure was put to the test by two different crises: the San Francisco earthquake and the Crash of 1929. On April 18, 1906, the San Francisco earthquake all but destroyed Hutton's offices, yet all the books and records were left untouched. When the manager of the San Francisco office wired E. F. Hutton with the news of the quake, Hutton knew that it would create panic among investors with money in San Francisco-based businesses. So acting in behalf of clients who could not be reached, Hutton sold their West Coast stock before news of the quake reached Wall Street—a move that reinforced his reputation for always acting in the best interests of his clients.

Twenty-three years later, Edward F. Hutton withstood another crisis—the stock market crash of 1929. Where most firms were left holding the bag on customers' credit accounts, Hutton's total loses amounted to less than $50,000. This conservative investment approach enabled Hutton to guide his company through the depression years.

All through his life E. F. Hutton had a powerful belief in business and the free marketplace—a belief that prompted one observer to describe him as a man who could "look back upon a long life of dedication to the American principle of enterprise." He expressed this commitment in a personal advertisement published in the *New York Times* on October 7, 1947:

"We Americans will always drop an inferior product for a better one, patronize a better shop, try to buy a better light, get a better job, cheer for a better team, buy a better automobile. That kind of thinking and doing has made us what we are.

"Please God, as a prayer, may we never accept any foreign 'ism'—totalitarianism, collectivism—for Americanism."

Today, E. F. Hutton, the company that Edward F. Hutton founded, is the second largest investment firm in the world. Under the leadership of Robert Fomon, earnings reached a record high in 1980 of $82.6 million, while revenues peaked at $1.1 billion, exceeding $1 billion for the first time in the firm's history. The 249 branch offices may be a far cry from the single room in New York's Financial District that served as Edward F. Hutton's first office. But the commitment to a complete range of services to investors and a strong financial base are the same.

How to get rich in the stock market:

Take all your savings and buy some good stock and hold it till it goes up and then sell it. If it don't go up, don't buy it.

—Will Rogers

October 14, 1980, was a day in which dreams appeared to become reality for both the small firm issuing the stock and for the investors who bought it. The corporation was Genentech, Inc., a four-year-old genetic engineering firm headquartered in San Francisco. Although the gene-splitting pioneer had not proven a huge success in terms of profits in its short existence, the prospects of manufacturing modified life forms by moving genes from one organism to another had caught the attention of many people. Genentech's research efforts placed it in competition with such industry giants as Du Pont, Exxon, Corning Glass, Monsanto, and General Electric. In order to compete, management needed money. The firm decided to raise these needed funds through a public offering of ownership shares. The offering of one million shares raised $35 million at $35 per share. It was so successful that on the day of the offering, purchasers of the shares could resell them to other buyers within hours at prices as high as $89 per share. By utilizing the securities markets to generate equity capital, Genentech, Inc., acquired needed funds for further development and expansion, and investors had the opportunity to own part of this potentially profitable operation.

Securities: Stocks and Bonds

securities
Stocks and bonds that represent obligations on the part of the issuers to provide purchasers with an expected or stated return on funds invested.

The previous chapter discussed two sources of funding for long-term capital: equity capital and debt capital. Equity capital takes the form of stocks—shares of ownership in the corporation. Long-term debt capital exists in the form of corporate bonds. Stocks and bonds are commonly referred to as **securities** because both represent obligations of their issuers to provide purchasers with an expected or stated return on the funds invested.

Stocks: Shares of Ownership in the Corporation

Stocks are units of ownership in a corporation. Although many corporations issue only one type of stock, two types exist: common stock and preferred stock.

Common stock. The basic form of corporate ownership is **common stock.** Purchasers of common stock are the true owners of a corporation; in return for their investment they expect to receive payments in the form of dividends and/or capital gains resulting from increases in the value of their stock holdings.

Holders of common stock vote on major company decisions, such as the purchase of other companies or the election of the board of directors. They benefit from company success, and they risk the loss of their investment if the company fails. Creditors and preferred stockholders are paid before common stockholders. Common stock is sold on either a par or no-par value basis. **Par value** is the value printed on the stock certificates of some companies. In some states, par value is used as the basis for paying state incorporation taxes. Because the par value is highly arbitrary, most corporations now issue no-par value stock. In either case, the total number of shares outstanding represents the total ownership of the firm, and the value of an individual stockholder's investment is based on the number of shares owned and their market price rather than on an arbitrary par value.

Sometimes confusion results over two other types of value: market value and book value. **Market value**—the price at which a stock is currently selling—is easily determined by referring to the financial page of the daily newspaper. It usually varies from day to day, depending on company earnings and investor expectations about future prospects for the firm. **Book value** is determined by subtracting what the company owes (its liabilities) from its assets minus the value of any preferred stock. When this net figure is divided by the number of shares of common stock, the book value of each share is known.

What happens when the corporation decides to raise additional long-term funds through the sale of additional stock? In most cases current stockholders are given the opportunity to purchase a proportionate share of new stock issues—their **preemptive right.** Without this right a stockholder owning 6 percent of a company's stock would find his or her share of the company diluted to 3 percent if it decided to double the amount of stock. An illustration of a stock certificate is shown in Figure 20–1.

Preferred stock. In addition to common stock, many corporations issue **preferred stock**—stock whose owners receive preference in the payment of dividends. Also, if the company is dissolved, preferred

common stock
Stock whose owners have only a residual claim (after creditors and preferred stockholders have been paid) on the firm's assets but who have voting rights in the corporation.

par value
The value printed on the stock certificates of some companies.

market value
The price at which a security is currently selling.

book value
The value of stock determined by subtracting a company's liabilities from its assets (minus the value of any preferred stock).

preemptive right
The right of current stockholders to purchase a proportionate share of new stock issues.

preferred stock
Stock whose owners receive preference in the payment of dividends and have first claim to the corporation's assets after all debts have been paid but who usually do not have voting rights in the corporation.

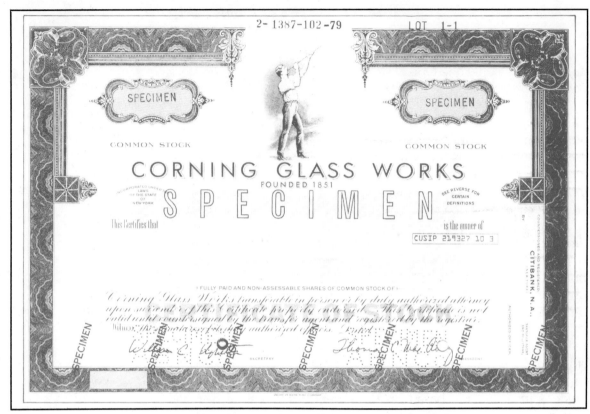

FIGURE 20–1
A stock certificate.

stockholders usually have a claim on its assets prior to any claim by common stockholders.

In return for this preference, preferred stockholders usually do not have voting rights. And even when they do exist, voting rights are typically limited to such important proposals as mergers, sales of company property, and dissolution of the company itself. Although preferred stockholders are granted certain privileges over common stockholders, they are still considered owners of the firm, and their dividends are therefore not guaranteed.

Preferred stock can be cumulative or noncumulative. In the case of **cumulative preferred stock,** stockholders must be paid a dividend for each year before dividends can be paid to common stockholders. If, for example, RCA's board of directors decides one year to omit the $4.00 dividend to preferred shareholders because of poor earnings, it cannot pay any dividends to the common stockholders the following year until dividends of $8 are paid to each preferred stockholder. Omitted dividends accumulate automatically and must be paid before common stockholders can receive any dividends at all. Owners of **noncumulative preferred stock,** on the other hand, need be paid

cumulative preferred stock
Preferred stock whose owners are entitled to the automatic payment of accumulated dividends, when the company omits a dividend payment, before common stockholders can receive any dividends at all.

noncumulative preferred stock
Preferred stock whose owners are entitled only to the current year's dividend before common stockholders receive their dividends.

only the current year's dividend before common stockholders receive their dividends.

Preferred stock is often issued with a conversion privilege. This **convertible preferred stock** gives stockholders the option of having their preferred stock converted into common stock at a stated price.

Preferred stock is usually issued to attract conservative investors, who want the margin of safety in having preference over common stock. Although preferred stock represents equity capital, many companies consider it a compromise between bonds and common stock.

convertible preferred stock
Preferred stock whose owners have the option of converting their preferred stock into common stock at a stated price.

Bonds

Bondholders are creditors, not owners, of a corporation. In Chapter 19 bonds were introduced as a means of obtaining long-term debt capital for the corporation and as sources of funds for municipal, state, and federal government units. Bonds are issued in denominations of $1,000, $5,000, and even $50,000. They indicate a definite rate of interest to be paid to the bondholder and the **maturity date**—the date at which the loan must be repaid. Because bondholders are creditors of the corporation, they have a claim on the firm's assets prior to any claims of preferred and common stockholders in the event of the firm's dissolution.

maturity date
The date at which a loan must be repaid.

Types of bonds. The potential bondholder has a variety of bonds from which to choose. Some bonds are **secured**—backed by specific pledges of company assets, including real property and personal property such as furniture, machinery, and even stocks and bonds of other companies owned by the borrowing firm. Railroads, which often raise 40 to 45 percent of their long-term funds through issuing bonds, often use rolling stock (locomotives and rail cars) as collateral.

secured bond
A bond backed by specific pledges of company assets.

Other companies issue **debentures**—bonds backed by the reputation of the issuing corporation rather than by specific pledges of assets. Only major corporations with extremely sound financial reputations can find buyers for their debentures. AT&T, the parent company of Bell Telephone system, has successfully raised billions of dollars from debentures in the past 30 years. Bond purchasers have been willing to buy AT&T unsecured bonds because of their faith in the ability of the issuing company.

debenture
A bond backed by the reputation of the issuing corporation rather than by specific pledges of assets.

In order to entice more speculative purchasers, **convertible bonds** are sometimes issued. These are bonds with the option of being converted into a specific number of shares of common stock. The number of shares of stock exchanged for each bond is included in the **bond indenture**—the legal contract containing all provisions of the bond. A $1,000 bond might be convertible into 50 shares of common stock. If the common stock is selling at $18 when the bonds are issued, the

convertible bonds
Bonds that offer the option of being converted into a specific number of shares of common stock.

bond indenture
The legal contract containing all provisions of a bond.

conversion privilege has no value. But if the stock rises in price to $30, the value of the bond increases to $1,500.

How bonds are retired. Because bonds have a maturity date, the issuing corporation must have the necessary funds available to repay the principal when the bonds mature. The two most common methods of repayment are serial bonds and sinking-fund bonds.

In the case of **serial bonds,** a corporation simply issues a large number of bonds that mature at different dates. If a corporation decides to issue $4.5 million in serial bonds for a 30-year period, the maturity dates may be established in such a manner that no bonds mature for the first 15 years. Beginning with the sixteenth year, $300,000 in bonds mature each year until all the bonds are repaid at the end of the 30-year period. Serial bonds are often issued by city governments.

A variation of the concept of serial bonds is **sinking-fund bonds.** Under this plan, the issuing corporation makes annual deposits of funds for use in redeeming the bonds when they mature. These deposits are made with a **bond trustee**—usually a major bank with the responsibility of representing bondholders. The deposits must be large enough so that with accrued interest they will be sufficient to redeem the bonds at maturity.

Callable bonds have provisions that allow the issuing corporation to redeem them prior to their maturity dates if a premium is paid. For instance, a 20-year bond may not be callable for the first ten years. Between 11 and 15 years it can be called at a premium of perhaps $50, and between 16 and 20 years it can be called at its face value.

Table 20–1 summarizes the characteristics of the most important types of bonds.

serial bonds
A large number of bonds that are issued at the same time but mature at different times.

sinking-fund bonds
Bonds whose issuing corporation makes annual deposits of funds for use in redeeming them when they mature.

bond trustee
An individual, major bank, or other financial institution that has the responsibility of representing bondholders.

callable bonds
Bonds that have provisions allowing the issuing corporation to redeem them prior to their maturity date (ordinarily at a premium).

TABLE 20–1

Types and Characteristics of Bonds

Types of Bonds	Characteristics
Secured bonds	Backed by specific pledges of company assets—real or personal property
Unsecured bonds (debentures)	Backed not by specific pledges of assets but by the financial reputation of the issuing corporation
Convertible bonds	Can be converted into common stock at the option of the bondholder
Serial bonds	A large issue, parts of which mature at different dates
Sinking-fund bonds	Yearly deposits by the corporation of funds sufficient to redeem the bonds when they mature
Callable (or redeemable) bonds	Gives the issuing corporation the option of redeeming the bonds (usually at a premium) prior to their maturity date

Why Do People Purchase Stocks and Bonds?

Chapter 19 focused on why businesses issue securities. But why do people purchase them?

Speculation

For some people the motivation for purchasing stocks is **speculation**—the hope of making a large profit on stocks within a short time period (see Focus 20–1). Speculation may take the form of high-risk stocks, such as low-priced penny stocks (so called because they sell for less than a dollar per share). Shareholders pray that their 50-cent stock will soar to $5, giving them ten times the amount of their purchase price in return. Penny stocks include inactive uranium mining companies, Canadian exploration companies, and numerous small oil-drilling firms. Most of them show no current profits and have little prospect of future profits.

speculation
Purchasing stocks in anticipation of making a large profit within a short time period.

FOCUS 20–1
How $300 Turned into $3 Million

Most investors dream of an investment like the one Dave Thurmond's great grandfather made more than 60 years ago. Thurmond decided to invest $300 (at $1 per share) in a little sandpaper manufacturer called the Minnesota Mining and Manufacturing Company. By the time Dave Thurmond inherited the stock, its original value had increased from $300 to nearly $3 million! In addition, Dave Thurmond received approximately $100,000 a year in dividends. As someone once remarked, "Thrift is an important virtue—especially in an ancestor."

Investment

In contrast to speculation, **investment** is the purchase of stocks and bonds that assure some safety for the investment and that provide satisfactory dividends and interest as payment for the risk taken (see Focus 20–2). Investors may also be interested in growth—increases in the value of a stock due to the company's success. The investor's objectives include one or more of these three goals: growth in the value of the investment, income, or safety.

investment
The purchase of stocks and bonds with the hope of getting satisfactory dividends and interest as payment for the risk taken.

FOCUS 20–2
A Profile of the U.S. Investor

The New York Stock Exchange's (NYSE) 1980 Shareownership Survey disclosed a dramatic resurgence of shareownership in the United States between mid-1975 and mid-1980. A net increase of 4.6 million shareowners raised the total to 29.8 million individuals—or 18.1 percent above the 1975 figure—after a similar percentage drop during the 1970 to 1975 period. Shareownership among adults increased from one-in-six in 1975 to one-in-five in the latest survey.

The largest numerical increase was in ownership of NYSE-listed stocks. Nearly 79 percent of all shareowners owned at least one NYSE-listed issue in 1980 compared with 71 percent in 1975. The net addition of 5.6 million shareowners represented an increase in NYSE-listed shareownership.

Adult male shareowners slightly outnumbered adult female shareowners in 1980 (14.0 million to 13.5 million). This reversed the 1975 findings, when women held a slight edge. The median age of shareowners also ran counter to the trend of the previous five years by dropping sharply from 52½ years to 45½ years—from the highest to the lowest recorded in any NYSE shareownership surveys. This decrease is mostly due to the 6½ million new shareowners who came into the market for the first time between 1975 and 1980 and who had a median age of only 36 years.

People who invest in stocks for income are interested in the dividends the company will pay.
Drawing by Ross; © 1976 The New Yorker Magazine, Inc.

"The choice is yours, ladies and gentlemen. Will you take the regular dividend or will you take whatever is behind that curtain?"

Growth. Investors who choose growth as a primary goal will select companies whose earnings have increased and are expected to continue growing at a rate faster than that of other companies. They are likely to own shares of companies in industries such as electronics, drugs, and energy, which typically pay out only small amounts in the form of dividends. Most of their earnings are reinvested in the company to finance further growth. Investors should benefit from this growth through increases in the value of their shares.

Income. Some investors use stocks and bonds as a means of supplementing their income. When income is the major goal, investors concentrate on the dividends of prospective companies. Because dividends are paid from company earnings, investors consider the company's past record for paying dividends, its current profitability, and its prospects for future earnings. Purchasers of income stocks are likely to own shares of companies in industries such as banking, insurance, and public utilities. Table 20–2 lists 17 companies that have paid dividends consistently for more than 125 years.

TABLE 20–2

Companies with Uninterrupted Dividend Payments for More than 125 Years

Company	Year Dividend Payments Began
Bank of New York Co., Inc.	1784
First National Boston Corp.	1784
Industrial National Corp.	1791
Citicorp	1813
First National State Bancorporation	1813
Chemical New York Corporation	1827
First Pennsylvania Corporation	1828
J. P. Morgan & Co., Inc.	1840
Chase Manhattan Corporation	1848
Connecticut Natural Gas Corporation	1851
Manhattan Life Corporation	1851
Bay State Gas Co.	1852
Manufacturers Hanover Corporation	1852
Washington Gas Light Co.	1852
Cincinnati Gas & Electric Co.	1853
Continental Corporation	1853
Scovill Inc.	1856

The income received from securities is called the investor's return, or **yield.** Yield is expressed as a percent. Assume that a potential investor plans to purchase $1,500 in stocks. She is interested in four companies: B. F. Goodrich, Walt Disney Productions, McDonald's, and Middle South Utilities. Their recent market prices and dividend rates are shown in Table 20–3.

yield
The income received from securities; calculated by dividing dividends by market price.

TABLE 20-3
Market Price and Annual Dividend for Selected Companies

Company	Recent Market Price	Recent Annual Dividend
B. F. Goodrich	$22	$1.56
Walt Disney Productions	50	1.00
McDonald's	54	.80
Middle South Utilities	11	1.62

The yield (annual dividend divided by current market price) for B. F. Goodrich is 7 percent, for Disney 2 percent, for McDonald's 1.5 percent, and for Middle South 14.7 percent. For the investor seeking immediate income from securities, a utilities stock such as Middle South may be appropriate.

The yield from any particular security varies with the market price and the dividend payments. If the market price of Middle South rises to $20, the yield for a prospective investor will be 8 rather than 14.7 percent. Thus, even though the $1.62 dividend return remains the same, the yield changes.

Safety. In many cases investors are unwilling to risk the potential reverses of common stock. Neither their blood pressure nor their bank account is able to endure fluctuations such as those that occurred in recent years. In a single 12-month period during 1980, Xerox stock prices fluctuated between 48 and 71, IBM from 50 to 72, Polaroid from 19 to 32, McDonald's from 36 to 56, and Eastman Kodak from 42 to 75. Investors whose primary objective is safety for their original investments are likely to purchase high-quality bonds and preferred stocks. These securities offer substantial protection and are likely to continue paying a good return on the investment.

Most investors have more than one investment goal. Investors who emphasize safety of principal may buy preferred stocks, which can grow in market value. Those who buy growth stocks may choose stocks paying at least a 3 percent yield in order to receive some short-term return on the investment. Table 20-4 is a useful guide for evaluating stocks and bonds in terms of the three investment objectives.

Whatever their investment goals, individual investors are most likely to own one or more of the popular stocks listed in Table 20-5. These ten companies have the largest number of stockholders in the United States.

TABLE 20-4
Comparison of Securities with Investment Objectives

Security	INVESTMENT OBJECTIVE		
	Safety	Income	Growth
Bonds	Best	Very steady	Usually none
Preferred stocks	Good	Steady	Variable
Common stocks	Least	Variable	Best

TABLE 20–5
The Ten Companies with the Largest Number of Stockholders

Company	Number of Stockholders
American Telephone & Telegraph	3,026,000
General Motors	1,191,000
International Business Machines	737,000
Exxon	697,000
General Electric	524,000
General Telephone & Electronics	486,000
Texaco, Inc.	394,000
Sears, Roebuck	350,000
Ford Motor	346,000
Southern Company	345,000

stock exchanges
The locations at which stocks and bonds are bought and sold.

The Securities Exchanges

Securities exchanges are the marketplaces for stocks and bonds. The **stock exchanges** are the locations at which stocks and bonds are bought and sold. Although corporations' securities are traded, the corporations themselves are not directly involved, and they receive no proceeds from the sales. The securities traded at organized exchanges have already been issued by corporations. The sales are between individual and corporate investors.

The New York Stock Exchange (NYSE)

When investors talk about the stock market, they are usually referring to the New York Stock Exchange. The "Big Board," as it is sometimes called, is the largest and best known of all stock exchanges. In order to transact business on the NYSE a brokerage firm must be a member. There are 1,366 "seats," and potential members must purchase seats from current members and be approved by the 33-member governing board. Memberships have varied considerably in price, ranging from a high of $625,000 in 1929 to a low of $17,000 in 1942.

Approximately 1,600 stocks and 2,700 bonds are listed (traded) on the NYSE (see Focus 20–3). These securities represent 90 percent of the market value of all outstanding stocks in the United States. In addition to the ten companies shown in Table 20–5, NYSE-listed stocks include such major corporations as Sears, RCA, Mobil Oil, Du Pont, Xerox, Eastman Kodak, and TWA. Foreign stocks such as Canadian Pacific (Canada), KLM Royal Dutch Airlines (Netherlands), Sony (Japan), ASA Limited (South Africa), and British Petroleum (United Kingdom) are also listed.

The New York Stock Exchange.

Activity on the floor of the American Stock Exchange.

FOCUS 20–3
Requirements for Listing on the New York Stock Exchange

To qualify for listing on the NYSE a company must meet the following minimum standards:

1. Annual earnings for the most recent year must be at least $2.5 million before taxes, and for each of the two preceding years they must be $2 million.

2. At least 1 million common shares must be publicly held.

3. At least 2,000 investors must hold 100 shares or more.

4. The outstanding common stock must have a market value of at least $8 million.

5. The company must have net tangible assets of at least $16 million.

Once these requirements are met, the governing board determines on a case-by-case basis whether the securities of applicant corporations will be listed.

The American Stock Exchange (AMEX)

Second in size and importance to the New York Stock Exchange is the American Stock Exchange. The AMEX, as it is called, is also located in New York and has approximately 500 full members and 400 associate members. Approximately 1,000 stocks are traded on the AMEX, including such well-known companies as Ozark Airlines, the New York Times, Hormel Meat Packing, and Bic Pen.

Regional and Local Exchanges

In addition to the two major exchanges, a number of regional and local exchanges operate throughout the United States. The largest of the regional exchanges is the Midwest Exchange in Chicago. Others include the Philadelphia-Baltimore-Washington Stock Exchange, the Cincinnati Stock Exchange, and the Pacific Coast Stock Exchange (which has operations in both San Francisco and Los Angeles). Local exchanges operate in Boston, Pittsburgh, Detroit, Salt Lake City, Richmond, Spokane, Honolulu, Colorado Springs, and Wheeling. The total activity on the regional stock exchanges accounts for only about 7 percent of the annual volume on the organized exchanges.

Approximately 500 companies are listed on each of the regional exchanges; each of the local exchanges usually lists slightly more than 100 firms. These exchanges were originally established to trade the shares of smaller firms operating within a limited geographic area. While many of the listed companies continue to be smaller corporations, the regional exchanges now also list many of the major corporations. As the volume of trading on the regional exchanges increased, larger firms decided to list their shares there. Today, about half of all the companies listed on the New York Stock Exchange are also listed on one or more regional exchanges.

Foreign Stock Exchanges

Stock exchanges are not a creation of the United States. The world's oldest exchange is the Amsterdam Stock Exchange, which began operations in 1611. The London Stock Exchange, which lists more than 10,000 stocks, traces its beginnings to before the American Revolution. Other important foreign exchanges are located in Paris, Tokyo, Zurich, Frankfort, Johannesburg, Melbourne, Copenhagen, Montreal, and Toronto. Major U.S. corporations are frequently listed and traded on foreign exchanges.

The Over-the-counter (OTC) Market

The investor who decides that the "Rocky Mountain spring water" image of Coors beer is likely to result in continued growth from Adolph Coors Brewing Co. will not find the stock listed on the New York Stock Exchange. It is not on the American Stock Exchange or on any of the other regional exchanges. Adolph Coors is one of the nearly 60,000 securities traded in the **over-the-counter (OTC) market.** Actually, the OTC market is not a real place at all. It is simply a method of trading unlisted securities outside the organized securities exchanges. It is a network of approximately 5,000 brokers scattered throughout the United States who buy and sell unlisted stocks and bonds by telephone. These brokers are in regular contact with one another, and the prices of the securities they trade are established by supply and demand.

over-the-counter market (OTC)
A method of trading unlisted securities outside the organized securities exchanges.

Security dealers in the OTC market often purchase shares in their own names. When a prospective buyer appears, they sell these shares at a profit. A broker who has none of the wanted shares in inventory will call other brokers to make purchases at the lowest possible price for resale.

The OTC market includes trading in the shares of most insurance companies and banks and in the bonds issued by many city and state government units. It trades stocks in a variety of firms, including such companies as Dunkin' Donuts, Bekins, National Lampoon, Tampax, and Pabst Brewing Company.

How Securities Are Bought and Sold

If you decide to invest the $1,000 your grandmother presented to you as a birthday present, you first must contact a **stockbroker** (or account

stockbroker
A middleman who buys and sells securities for clients.

executive)—a middleman who buys and sells securities for clients. If you do not already have a stockbroker, you should probably contact one of the stockbrokerage firms listed in the *Yellow Pages* of your local telephone directory. Most cities have offices of major brokerage firms, such as Merrill Lynch; E. F. Hutton; Paine Webber; and Bache, as well as smaller firms.

Once you have contacted a broker, your next step is a discussion of your investment objectives. Then you and your broker can discuss a number of stocks and bonds that appear to meet your investment goals.

If Exxon common stock meets your dual goals of income and growth, the broker can determine the current market price of the stock by typing the Exxon symbol (XON) on an electronic device at his desk. These devices—called Telequote, Ultronic Stockmaster, or Quotron—are linked to the national stock exchanges in New York and can provide immediate information on current stock prices, dividends paid, and the high and low prices for the year. Many brokerage firms also have **ticker tapes**—electronic screens that show trades of securities. All securities, both listed and over-the-counter, are shown on the ticker tape. OTC trades are indicated by the letter *T* following the price of the transaction. In many cities with cable television service, one of the channels shows the ticker tape—providing maximum convenience and immediate information for the investor-viewer. Focus 20–4 shows a segment of a ticker tape and explains how to read it.

ticker tapes
Large screens that electronically display actual transactions on the New York and American stock exchanges and over-the-counter transactions.

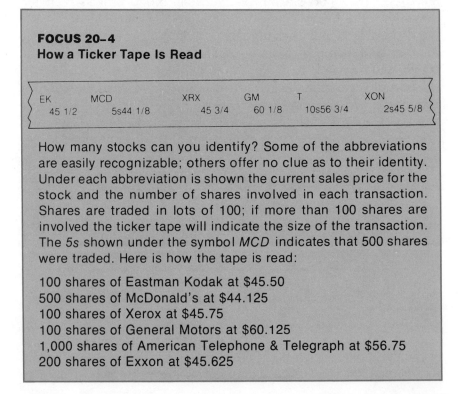

FOCUS 20–4
How a Ticker Tape Is Read

EK	MCD	XRX	GM	T	XON
45 1/2	5s44 1/8	45 3/4	60 1/8	10s56 3/4	2s45 5/8

How many stocks can you identify? Some of the abbreviations are easily recognizable; others offer no clue as to their identity. Under each abbreviation is shown the current sales price for the stock and the number of shares involved in each transaction. Shares are traded in lots of 100; if more than 100 shares are involved the ticker tape will indicate the size of the transaction. The *5s* shown under the symbol *MCD* indicates that 500 shares were traded. Here is how the tape is read:

100 shares of Eastman Kodak at $45.50
500 shares of McDonald's at $44.125
100 shares of Xerox at $45.75
100 shares of General Motors at $60.125
1,000 shares of American Telephone & Telegraph at $56.75
200 shares of Exxon at $45.625

Placing an Order

If the investor decides to purchase Exxon common stock, he or she instructs the broker, who then teletypes the order to the firm's member on the floor of the New York Stock Exchange. The New York representative goes directly to the location on the floor of the exchange where Exxon is traded and attempts to make the purchase.

Market orders and limit orders. An investor request that a stock purchase or sale be made at the current market price is a **market order.** The NYSE floor member quickly makes the purchase on a "best price" basis, and the investor is notified of the purchase price within a matter of minutes. (Figure 20–2 illustrates how stocks are bought and sold on the NYSE.) An investor request that a stock purchase or sale be made at a specified price is a **limit order.** In this case a notation of the limit order is made at the post that handles the stock transactions, and if the price drops to the specified price, the purchase is made.

Round lots and odd lots. As Focus 20–4 indicates, stock trading is conducted in quantities of 100 shares, called **round lots.** But because 100 shares of Exxon costs more than $7,000, how can you invest your $1,000 in Exxon stock? The answer is through **odd lots** —purchases or sales of fewer than 100 shares of stock that are grouped together to make up one or more round lots. The stocks are then distributed to the various odd-lot purchasers when the transaction is completed.

Bulls and bears. The two most frequently mentioned stock market terms refer to investor attitudes. **Bulls** are investors who expect stock prices to rise. They buy securities in anticipation of the increased market prices. When stock market prices continue to rise, market observers call it a bull market.

    Bears are investors who expect stock prices to decline. They are likely to sell their securities because they expect market prices to fall. When market prices steadily decline, the market is labeled a bear market.

The Cost of Trading

Buyers and sellers of securities pay commissions to brokerage firms for their services. Commission charges vary among brokerage firms, but they generally range from 1 to 2 percent of the total value of the stock transaction. A slightly higher fee is often charged when shares are traded in odd lots. The percentage charged typically declines as the dollar value of the transaction increases. Large business investors, such as insurance companies, mutual funds, and pension funds, can often negotiate major reductions in commissions because of the competition among brokerage firms for their business.

---

market order
An investor request that a stock purchase or sale be made at the current market price.

limit order
An investor request that a stock purchase or sale be made at a specified price.

round lots
Quantities of 100 shares of stock purchased or sold.

odd lots
Purchases or sales of fewer than 100 shares of stock that are grouped together to make up one or more round lots.

bulls
Investors who expect stock prices to rise and buy securities in anticipation of the increased market prices.

bears
Investors who expect stock prices to decline and sell their securities in expectation of declining market prices.

1. The account executive receives a customer's order by phone.

2. The order is conveyed to the stock exchange via a communications terminal.

3. The firm's floor broker executes the sale.

4. The confirmation is teletyped back to the broker.

5. The account executive notifies the customer that the transaction has been made.

FIGURE 20–2
How stocks are bought and sold on the New York Stock Exchange.

In recent years, approximately 50 "discount" brokerage firms have been established to provide price competition to the traditional full-service brokerage firms. Such operations are able to offer lower commissions by providing fewer investor services. They ordinarily provide no research services and simply handle purchases and sales for their clients.

Reading the Financial News

At least two or three pages of most major daily newspapers are devoted to reporting current financial news, which typically focuses on the previous day's securities transactions. Stocks and bonds traded on the NYSE and AMEX are listed alphabetically in the newspaper. Information is provided on the volume of sales and the price of each security.

Stock Quotations

Figure 20–3 on page 510 is reproduced from the *Wall Street Journal,* a newspaper published each weekday that contains detailed information on financial and business news. To see how to read these stock quotations, focus on the ninth stock: Abbott Laboratories. The highest price for Abbott in 1981 was $32.25 per share; the lowest was $22.50. Abbott pays annual dividends of $.72. Its **price-earnings ratio**—current market price divided by annual earnings per share—is 15. A total of 77,200 shares changed owners in the day's trading. The highest price paid for the stock was $27.75, and the lowest was $27.25. When the trading stopped for the day, Abbott was being traded for $27.75, which amounted to $.50 more than the closing price on the previous day.

price-earnings ratio
The current market price divided by annual earnings per share.

A careful inspection of the sample quotations reveals additional information. The symbol *pf* indicates preferred stock. Lower-case letters following the dividend listing on some stocks refer the reader to special information at the bottom of the page. For example, the symbol *e* following a dividend listing of 4¢ means that this is the dividend payment for the previous 12 months.

Bond Quotations

The right half of Figure 20–3 shows a number of bond quotations. To see how bond quotations are read, focus on the Aetna Life Insurance bond. Most bonds are issued in denominations of $1,000; thus, bond prices must be read differently from stock prices. Although the closing price for Aetna reads 59¼, this does not mean $59.25. Because bond prices are quoted as a percentage of the $1,000 price, 59¼ means $592.50.

Stocks

52 Weeks High	52 Weeks Low	Stock	Div.	Yld %	P-E Ratio	Sales 100s	High	low	Close	Net Chg.
		— A—A—A —								
14¾	9⅞	AAR	.44	4.4	7	22	10	9⅞	10	.....
52¼	35¼	ACF	2.76	6.5	12	246	42⅞	42½	42¾	+ ¼
27	15⅜	AMF	1.24	5.7	10	165	21⅞	21⅝	21⅞	+ ⅜
24¾	10⅞	AM Intl		..	..	89	12¾	12½	12½	− ⅛
10¼	5¾	APL		..	..	2	6	6	6	.....
37⅝	28½	ARA	1.94	6.0	6	66	32⅛	31⅞	32⅛	+ ½
91½	42¼	ASA	5a	10.	..	291	48⅛	47¼	47⅝	+ ⅛
45	20⅛	AVX	.32	1.3	16	593	24¾	22¾	23¾	+ ⅞
32¼	22½	AbtLb s	.72	2.6	15	772	27¾	27¼	27¾	+ ½
35⅝	23	AcmeC	1.40	5.8	7	x2	24¼	24¼	24¼	− ⅛
6¾	3⅝	AdmDg	.04	.7	7	7	5⅜	5¼	5⅜	.....
17	13⅛	AdaEx	1.88e	13.	..	32	14⅜	14⅛	14⅛	− ⅛
7½	4⅝	AdmMI	.20e	3.1	7	39	6½	6	6⅜	+ ⅜
44½	20	AMD s		..	17	733	20½	20	20	− ⅝
44	30	AetnLf	2.32	6.1	6	420	38¼	38	38	− ⅛
24¾	15⅞	Ahmns	1.20	7.3	17	124	16⅞	16½	16½	− ⅛
6⅛	2⅞	Aileen		..	17	31	3⅜	3⅛	3¼	.....
54¼	36¾	AirPrd	.80	2.1	9	246	37⅜	37⅛	37¼	+ ¼
26½	11¾	AirbFrt	.60	4.4	13	22	13¾	13⅝	13⅝	.....
15½	10	Akzona	.80	5.8	36	25	13⅞	13⅝	13¾	− ⅛
22½	19¾	AlMoa n		..	..	371	21¼	20⅝	21	+ ⅜
26⅜	24⅝	AlaP pfA	3.92	16.	..	28	25⅜	25	25⅛	− ¼
7¼	5½	AlaP dpf	.87	15.	..	10	6	5⅞	5⅞	.....
74½	56	AlaP pf	9	15.	..	z170	59	58½	58½	+ ½
17	14⅜	Alagsco	1.60	11.	6	21	15	14⅝	15	+ ⅜
40⅛	22	AlskInt	.60	2.2	9	635	28	26⅞	27	.....

Bonds

Bonds	Cur Yld	Vol	High	Low	Close	Net Chg.
AMInt 9⅜95	17.	1	53¾	53¾	53¾	.....
AetnLf 8⅛07	14.	25	59¼	59¼	59¼	− 1¼
AlaP 9s2000	15.	26	60	59¾	59¾	.....
AlaP 7¾s02	15.	11	54½	52	52	− 1
AlaP 8⅞s03	16.	51	58⅝	57¼	57¼	− ¾
AlaP 8¼s03	16.	14	53½	53	53	− 1
AlaP 9¾s04	16.	36	62⅞	61⅛	62⅞	+ 1⅞
AlaP 10½05	16.	18	66	66	66	+ ⅝
AlaP 8¾07	15.	5	58½	58½	58½	+ 1¼
AlaP 9¼07	15.	5	61¼	61¼	61¼	+ 1¾
AlaP 9½08	16.	22	61	61	61	+ ½
AlaP 9⅝08	16.	3	61	61	61	.....
AlaP 15¼10	17.	19	90⅞	90⅜	90⅞	.....
AlaP 17⅜11	18.	80	99⅞	99	99¼	.....
AlskH 16¼94	16.	6	99¼	99¼	99¼	+ ¼
AlskH 16¼99	16.	6	99	99	99	.....
Allgl 10¾99	16.	2	66¼	66¼	66¼	.....
AlldPd 7s84	9.2	2	76	76	76	+ ⅞
AlldSt 4½92	cv	1	124½	124½	124½	.....
AlsCha 16s91	16.	5	98⅜	98⅜	98⅜	− ⅛
Alcoa 4¼s82	4.5	3	94 9-32	94 9-32	94 9-32	+ 23-32
AMAX 8s86	10.	6	78¾	78¾	78¾	.....
AFoP 4.8s87	8.0	4	60⅛	60⅛	60⅛	− ¼
AForP 5s30	12.	3	40⅜	40⅜	40⅜	+ ⅝
AAirl 4¼92	9.2	3	46	45½	46	+ 1

FIGURE 20–3
Stock and bond quotations from the *Wall Street Journal*.

The symbols to the right of the Aetna Life Insurance name indicate that the bonds pay an annual interest rate of 8.125 percent and that the maturity date for this issue is 2007. Because the bond is currently selling below its original $1,000 face value, the yield is 14 percent—considerably more than the 10 percent stated interest rate. The Allied Stores bond listed shows the symbol *cv* instead of a yield, indicating that it is a convertible bond.

A total of $25,000 worth of the Aetna Life Insurance bonds were traded during the day, with no variation in the $592.25 price. The closing bond price was $125 less than the previous day's closing price.

Stock Averages

Dow-Jones Averages
Stock averages that use three indexes based on the market prices of 30 industrial, 20 transportation, and 15 utility stocks to provide a general measure of market activity for a given time period.

Standard & Poor's Index
An index developed from the market performance of 425 industrial, 25 rail, and 50 utility stocks that reflects the general activity of the stock market.

A feature of most daily newscasts is the report of current stock averages. The two most familiar stock averages are the **Dow-Jones Averages** and the **Standard & Poor's Index.** Both are indexes that have been developed to reflect the general activity of the stock market.

The Dow-Jones Averages are actually three different indexes based on the market prices of 30 industrial, 20 transportation, and 15 utility stocks. The Standard & Poor's Index is developed from the market performance of 425 industrial, 25 rail, and 50 utility stocks.

The Dow-Jones Industrials include a cross-section of major corporations such as AT&T, Du Pont, Procter & Gamble, General Electric, Eastman Kodak, and Sears. While individual stocks may rise when the Dow-Jones Index falls, the index does provide a general measure of market activity for a given time period.

Mutual Funds—Another Approach to Investing

Many investors recognize that they have neither the time nor the knowledge to analyze continually stock market developments. These people often concentrate their investments in **mutual funds**—companies that sell shares of their own stock in order to raise money to invest in the securities of other firms. In so doing, investors obtain diversification in their portfolio of stocks and the professional management of the mutual fund. Investors who buy shares of stock in a mutual fund become part owners of a large number of companies, thereby spreading the risk.

mutual funds
Companies that sell shares of their own stock in order to raise money to invest in the securities of other firms.

Mutual funds are managed by trained, experienced professionals whose careers are based on success in analyzing the securities markets and specific industries and companies. Mutual funds attempt to accomplish for the individual investor what he or she might do with enough time, inclination, background, experience, and money to spread the investment among many businesses.

Nearly nine million people in the United States currently own shares in one or more of the 600 mutual funds. Total mutual fund assets are more than $51 billion.

Just as individual investor goals differ, so do the objectives of mutual funds. Growth funds emphasize the purchase of growth companies. Income funds emphasize high dividends. Balanced funds diversify their holdings by purchasing all types of securities—common and preferred stocks and corporate bonds. Money market funds emphasize returns to investors through investment in short-term debt instruments such as certificates of deposit, commercial paper, and treasury bills. Specialty funds concentrate on particular industries such as gold, real estate, or banking.

Regulating Securities Transactions

Both the federal government and state governments have enacted legislation regulating the sale of securities. Early laws were passed at the state level, beginning with Kansas in 1911. While the proposed law was under consideration, one state legislator remarked that some unscrupulous securities promotors would sell stock in the "blue sky." And the name **blue-sky laws** was quickly applied to the early state

blue-sky laws
Early state laws regulating securities transactions.

Controversial Issue

Dividend Reinvestment Plans: Bonus or Paper Gain?

In 1969 the stockholders of Allegheny Power were given the option of reinvesting their cash dividends in company stock rather than taking cash payments. This was the first dividend reinvestment plan (DRP).

Over a decade later DRPs have become an established part of the investment scene. Over 900 companies offered this option to their shareholders in 1979—and, as the figures show, they had good reason. They realized approximately $2 billion in reinvestment income; AT&T alone raised $967 million in equity capital.

In the earliest dividend reinvestment plans, companies purchased shares on the open market at the going rate per share to provide shares to those investors who had chosen dividend reinvestment. In 1972 Long Island Lighting began to issue new shares to stockholders who wished to reinvest their dividend income. In 1975, to encourage greater participation in its reinvestment program, AT&T gave shareholders the option of reinvesting their dividend income at a 5 percent price discount. Many companies have followed this lead and are also offering discounts on shares purchased through reinvestment.

Supporters of dividend reinvestment programs believe they offer many advantages to individual investors. Such plans enable stockholders who lack additional ready cash to increase their equity in the company, often at reduced rates. They also provide the small investor the chance to begin an investment program without large outlays of cash, to save brokerage charges, and to evaluate the future as it becomes clearer.

laws regulating securities transactions. Eventually, every state except Nevada passed laws to protect stock purchasers.

These laws typically require that most securities sold in the state be registered with an appropriate state official—usually the secretary of state. Annual licenses are usually required for securities dealers and salespeople. But additional protection was needed for *interstate* sales of securities.

Securities Act of 1933

Securities Act of 1933
A federal law designed to protect investors by requiring full disclosure of relevant financial information from companies desiring to sell new stock or bond issues to the general public; also known as the Truth in Securities Act.

The **Securities Act of 1933,** often called the Truth in Securities Act, is a federal law designed to protect investors through requiring full disclosure of relevant financial information by companies desiring to sell new stock or bond issues to the general public. This information takes two forms: a registration statement containing detailed company

Institutional investors, such as pension funds, are taking advantage of these plans as well. Because they are bound by a responsibility to make the best investments possible, pension fund administrators see dividend reinvestment plans as a deal they cannot pass up.

From the issuing company's point of view, DRPs are a painless way to raise needed capital. In a study done by the Salomon Brothers investment firm, companies that would have paid out 61.5 percent of net earnings in dividends actually paid only 47.1 percent—the difference being attributed to reinvested dividends. Utilities find DRPs particularly attractive as they search for additional capital to meet rising energy and construction costs.

Critics who question the ethics of these plans charge that they mislead shareholders into believing that their equity has increased when in fact the firm's earnings have simply been divided among a greater number of shares. The net effect of DRPs, they say, is to divide the company pie into a greater number of pieces. Critics also point to the inevitability of paying more dividends as larger numbers of shares are issued through reinvestment programs. In addition, the start-up costs and annual maintenance expenses of these programs often prove extremely costly to companies.

As more and more firms encourage their stockholders to reinvest their dividend income, the benefits and drawbacks of these plans will come into sharper focus. Whether companies are giving shareholders a bonus or diluting the earnings of existing shares will be the subject of many heated debates.

information, which is filed with the Securities and Exchange Commission, and a condensed version of the registration statement in a booklet called a *prospectus*, which must be furnished to each purchaser.

Securities Exchange Act of 1934

One year after the passage of the Securities Act of 1933, Congress enacted the **Securities Exchange Act of 1934.** This federal law created the Securities and Exchange Commission (SEC) to regulate the national stock exchanges. All companies with securities listed on the NYSE or the AMEX are required to file registration statements with the SEC and to update them annually. Brokerage firms and individual brokers are regulated by the SEC, and brokers selling listed securities are required to pass an examination.

Securities Exchange Act of 1934
The federal law that created the Securities and Exchange Commission (SEC) to regulate the national stock exchanges.

Other Federal Legislation

Maloney Act of 1938
An amendment to the Securities Exchange Act of 1934 that authorized self-regulation of over-the-counter securities operations.

National Association of Securities Dealers (NASD)
An association created by the Maloney Act of 1938 that is responsible for regulating over-the-counter securities operations.

Investment Company Act of 1940
The federal law that brought the mutual fund industry under the jurisdiction of the Securities and Exchange Commission in order to protect investors from possible trading abuses and stock manipulation.

The **Maloney Act of 1938,** an amendment to the Securities Exchange Act of 1934, authorized self-regulation of over-the-counter securities operations. This led to the creation of the **National Association of Securities Dealers (NASD),** which is responsible for regulating OTC businesses. Written examinations are now required of all new brokers and dealers selling OTC securities. The **Investment Company Act of 1940** brought the mutual fund industry under SEC jurisdiction. Mutual funds are now required to register with the SEC. The state and federal laws mentioned protect investors from the securities trading abuses and stock manipulations that occurred prior to the 1930s.

Summary

Securities represent obligations on the part of their issuers to provide purchasers with an expected or stated return on the funds invested. Securities are issued in the form of stocks or bonds. Stocks are units of ownership in a corporation and may be either common or preferred. Bondholders are creditors, not owners, of a corporation.

People and corporations investing in the stock market have diverse reasons for doing so. Speculators purchase securities in the hope of making large profits in a short time. Investors purchase them to achieve one or more of the following objectives: growth in the value of the original investment, income, and safety.

Bonds provide the most safety and common stocks the least. Bonds usually do not grow in value, but they do give a steady income. Common stocks are likely to be purchased by investors seeking growth. Many investors consider preferred stocks a compromise investment between common stocks and bonds.

Common and preferred stocks and the bonds of most major corporations are traded through organized securities exchanges. Unlisted stocks of smaller companies, banks, and insurance firms and government bonds are traded on the over-the-counter market through a network of 5,000 securities dealers and brokers located in cities throughout the United States.

Securites purchases and sales are handled by a trained specialist called a stockbroker or account executive. The stockbroker receives a commission for the services given in handling these transactions. Current prices of securities, sales volume, and information on dividends are reported in the financial sections of most daily newspapers and in such financial newspapers as the *Wall Street Journal.*

Investors who are unwilling or unable to spend the necessary time to analyze individual companies, and who want to spread their investment risks by owning a number of different companies, may choose to purchase shares of mutual funds. These are professionally managed investment companies that own shares in a large number of different companies. The investor who purchases shares in a mutual fund has partial ownership of many companies.

The Securities Act of 1933 and the Securities Exchange Act of 1934 provide the mechanism for regulating organized securities exchanges and for protecting investors by requiring disclosure of relevant financial information from companies that issue stocks and bonds. The Securities and Exchange Commission (SEC), created by the Securities Exchange Act of 1934, enforces these acts and regulates brokerage firms and individual brokers. Other legislative acts have extended the SEC's powers to include the reglation of mutual funds.

Key Terms

securities
common stock
par value
market value
book value
preemptive right
preferred stock
cumulative preferred stock
noncumulative preferred stock
convertible preferred stock
maturity date
secured bond
debenture
convertible bonds
bond indenture
serial bonds
sinking-fund bonds
bond trustee
callable bonds
speculation
investment
yield

stock exchanges
over-the-counter market (OTC)
stockbroker
ticker tapes
market order
limit order
round lots
odd lots
bulls
bears
price-earnings ratio
Dow-Jones Averages
Standard & Poor's Index
mutual funds
blue-sky laws
Securities Act of 1933
Securities Exchange Act of 1934
Maloney Act of 1938
National Association of
    Securities Dealers (NASD)
Investment Company Act of
    1940

Review Questions

1. Explain each of the terms listed on the previous page.

2. What is common stock?

3. How are common stocks valued?

4. How are preferred stocks different from common stocks?

5. Explain this statement: bondholders are creditors, not owners, of the corporation.

6. How are bonds retired?

7. Discuss the three major goals of investors.

8. Compare different types of securities with the three basic investment objectives.

9. How does the New York Stock Exchange operate?

10. How does an investor go about placing an order for a common stock?

Discussion Questions and Exercises

1. Evaluate the pros and cons of the controversial issue that appears in this chapter.

2. Ask a local stockbroker to talk to your class about setting up an investment program.

3. Assume you have just inherited $20,000 from a rich aunt and her will stipulates that you must invest all the money until you have completed your education. Prepare a report on how you will invest the money.

4. Record for 30 days the daily price movements of a group of three to five common stocks. At the end of this period prepare a brief report on what you think influenced the price movements in these issues.

5. Assume you are an investment counselor who has been asked to set up some general investment goals for the following individuals, each of whom has adequate current income and about $30,000 to invest. Prepare a short report outlining the proposed investment goals for each person:
   a. a 56-year-old retired army officer
   b. a 40-year-old divorced woman with two children
   c. a wealthy 19-year-old college student

Case 20–1: Calculating Yields and Price-earnings Ratios

Year	Name of Company	Average Price per Share	Earnings per Share	Average Dividend per Share
Year 1	Cities Service Oil	$ 60	$ 5.12	$ 2.70
	IBM	268	13.35	10.00
	McDonald's	42	2.17	.05
	Playboy	6	.12	.08
	Texaco	30	3.06	1.70
Year 2	Cities Service Oil	59	7.98	2.80
	IBM	275	15.94	10.00
	McDonald's	45	2.72	.06
	Playboy	8	.22	.10
	Texaco	29	3.20	1.80
Year 3	Cities Service Oil	61	9.00	3.00
	IBM	260	17.50	10.00
	McDonald's	40	3.40	.10
	Playboy	7	.80	.12
	Texaco	27	3.75	2.00

Questions

1. Calculate the dividend yield and the price-earnings ratio for each stock for each of the three years.

2. On the basis of the above data, evaluate the potential risk of each of the five securities. Match each security with a specific investment objective.

3. Insert current data for each stock and calculate dividend yields and price-earnings ratios for the five companies. Are the matches you calculated in Question 2 still appropriate? Explain.

Case 20–2: The Perils and Pleasures of Penny Stocks

Kathy Foley, 33, is a suburban Denver mother, a flight attendant for United Airlines—and a feverish speculator. About a year ago she began playing the flourishing penny-stock market in Denver, where shares of high-risk companies are traded over the counter for a few cents a share or, at most, a dollar or two. So far Foley has parlayed her original ante of $1,500 into an ever-changing portfolio of a dozen volatile issues that is now worth $23,000 on paper. "I made $5,000 just today," she exulted recently. "I guess you would say I'm addicted."

Foley's success may be unusual, but her addiction isn't. Thousands of Rocky Mountain executives, waitresses, cops, and housewives are hooked on the red-hot Denver market, which is enjoying one of its periodic bursts of wild action—this time in fledgling energy and high-tech stocks. Switchboards in brokerage offices along Seventeenth Street, Denver's mini-equivalent of Wall Street, are overloaded with incoming calls. Daily trading volume in the market's 250 or so issues often exceeds 20 million shares, and obscure Colorado-based companies occasionally dominate the daily national listings of most active over-the-counter issues.

Everybody is playing—and at the moment many seem to be winning. Gains of 500 percent in penny stocks are common, with some soaring 1,000 percent and more. The stock price of U.S. Minerals Exploration Co., for example, has increased thirteenfold in just four months; similarly, shares in Key Exploration, another tiny energy company, are now trading at 80 cents, against a dime a share at the public offering earlier this month. Given such profits, local underwriters are straining to bring out new issues fast enough to satisfy the speculators' lust. Thirty-six new issues were offered in the third quarter alone—and 34 of those have since risen in price, with the average gain running nearly 200 percent. "Absolute craziness," says one broker.

Questions

1. What types of firms are likely to fall into the category of penny stocks? Categorize the types of investors who are likely to be attracted to such offerings.

2. Many organized securities exchanges establish minimum market prices for traded stocks. Should these penny stocks be prohibited from over-the-counter trading? Defend your answer.

21

Risk Management and Insurance

Learning Goals

1. To explain the meaning of risk and to distinguish between the two types of risk faced by individuals and businesses

2. To explain each of the four methods of dealing with risk

3. To analyze the law of large numbers and how it makes insurance possible

4. To identify each of the several types of property and casualty insurance and to describe their importance to a business

5. To analyze each of the types of life insurance a firm might offer its employees

6. To explain the meaning of each of the key terms introduced in this chapter

Profile: Cyndi Dietz
One of Allstate's Fighting Females

Cyndi Dietz could have picked an easier town than Columbus, Ohio, in which to sell insurance. With 35 insurance company home offices located in Columbus, says Dietz, "Everyone and his or her brother are in the business."

Yet Dietz has no problem selling clients the property and casualty, life, health, and commercial insurance offered by her employer, Allstate Insurance. With over 1,400 active accounts in 1980, 26-year-old Dietz is a young woman on the move.

"To get where I am now," says Dietz, "in only four years with Allstate, I've had to put in a lot of time and hard work. Many of my clients have been burned by insurance agents—they trust them just about as much as used-car salespeople. I have to overcome that image before I can even hope to make a sale."

"Even when I convince people to buy a policy," continues Dietz, "they usually start small. People aren't anxious to buy all their insurance from me until I build some kind of track record with them. As the years pass, they realize that what I've told them is true and that when they're in a jam, I'm there to help them out. I've taken the customer's side with our claims department, for example, and I feel no mixed loyalties about it. In the long run, a satisfied customer is in Allstate's best interest, too."

Being a young woman has made some of Dietz's initial business contacts with men more difficult. "I've had to overcome some men's reluctance to let women handle their finances," says Dietz. "To make a sale I have to prove that I know more than a male agent. If I can do that, then the same male client who didn't want any part of me because I'm a woman is likely to give me more business because I'm a woman. I guess some men feel special having a competent woman handling their insurance."

Dietz attributes part of her success to the reputation Allstate has built as the nation's second largest insurance company. "Allstate's advertising often gets me through the door," admits Dietz. "Our TV and radio exposure makes the company a household word people can trust. Once I get into someone's living room, however, I represent the company, and people's perception of my honesty—not the company's—takes over. With inflation tightening everyone's belt, people are a lot more cautious than ever before about where they put their insurance dollars. If they don't trust what I tell them, they'll just go somewhere else."

Having learned most of what she knows on the job (she was a physical education major in college and is still about 30 credits short of graduation), Dietz feels that you don't need a degree to make money in insurance sales. But, she adds, "you have to like your work and know how to persevere."

Nothing is ever gained without risk. You can't steal second base with one foot on first.

—*Anonymous*

Never invest in anything that eats or needs repainting.

—*Billy Rose*

Most people my age are dead.

—*Casey Stengel, at 80*

A small family-owned company in Newark, New Jersey, had been producing and marketing soup for more than a hundred years until the day in 1971 when its name became a household word. The company was the Bon Vivant Soup Company, and the day was July 1, 1971. That day the Food and Drug Administration notified Bon Vivant—and the world—that a New York man had died and his wife was paralyzed from botulism caused by eating a can of Bon Vivant's vichyssoise soup.

Although Bon Vivant quickly traced the problem to a single crate of 460 cans of soup, the FDA recalled all of the 52 varieties of Bon Vivant soup. Over 4 million cans of soup had been manufactured by Bon Vivant in 1971.[1]

The next month Bon Vivant was in bankruptcy court. A lawyer for the company reported that the total recall of the firm's products resulted in no money coming in with which to pay debts. In November 1972 the company resumed operations under a new name—Moore & Company Soups. The FDA continued to keep a close watch on the company's products as they reached the grocers' shelves in early 1973. The new company manufactured five soups. Vichyssoise was not one of them.[2]

The Concept of Risk

Risk is a daily fact of life for both individuals and businesses. Automobile accidents take the lives of 50,000 people in the United States each year. In 1981 the collapse of a sky bridge walkway at Kansas

City's Hyatt Regency Hotel cost 111 lives, injured another 186 guests, and produced lawsuits totaling $750 million. A total of 54 "catastrophes" occurred in 1979, and three disasters produced over $100 million in insured losses: Hurricane Frederic ($753 million); a Wichita Falls, Texas, tornado ($240 million); and Hurricane David ($122 million). Fifteen California physicians each paid more than $1 million in a single year as a result of malpractice suits. Fires take their toll in lives and property damage each year.

Businesses face these catastrophes and more. They run the risk of injury to their employees in job-related accidents, of changing consumer tastes transforming their profits into losses (see Focus 21–1), and of faulty products causing lawsuits and loss of business.

FOCUS 21–1
The Watch Industry: Changing Demands Produce Business Risk

At the beginning of the twentieth century the individual's treasured timepiece was likely to be a pocket watch. Retirement from the company or the railroad was frequently the occasion for presenting the retiree with an engraved (often gold) pocket watch.

But times changed, and the 1920s witnessed the popularity of new wristwatches. Pocket watches were old fashioned, and companies (such as Waltham) that were unwilling to convert their production to the manufacture of wristwatches eventually closed due to lack of demand. (Waltham was so well known, however, that the name was sold to another watch manufacturer to use on its products.) People in the 1920s and 1930s wore their wristwatches with pride. These watches typically bore the name of manufacturers such as Bulova and Elgin.

Today's watch market has two major segments. One can be called the disposable watch market. Many people have a number of watches for different occasions and may choose watches to fit their wardrobes. These watches are inexpensive—often costing from $20 to $50—and usually bear a name such as Timex.

Many of the watches in the lower-price market not only function as an accurate timepiece but also as a stopwatch and, in some instances, as a calculator as well.

The second segment is the quality market. Watches designed for this segment are likely to be both luxurious and expensive. Manufacturers stress the accuracy of the timepiece and the good taste of its owner. Prices range from $175 to more than $5,000. Bulova's Accutron, Cartier, and the top-quality quartz watches are examples of this kind of product.

Types of Risk

Risk is uncertainty about loss or injury. The business firm's list of risk-filled decisions is long. The warehouse faces the risk of fire, burglary, water damage, and physical deterioration. Accidents, judgments due to lawsuits, and nonpayment of bills by customers are other risks. Two major types of risk exist: speculative risk and pure risk.

risk
Uncertainty about loss or injury.

Speculative risk. In the case of **speculative risk** the firm or individual has the chance of either a profit or a loss. Purchasing shares of stock on the basis of the latest hot tip can result in profits or in potential losses. Expansion of operations in a new market may mean higher profits or the loss of invested funds. Karl Wallenda's performances on the high wire exposed him to the risk of death as the price for failure—and in 1978 that risk became a reality as Wallenda plunged to his death while walking a wire stretched between two buildings during high winds. But his years of risk taking had brought him lucrative earnings and admiration as rewards for his successes.

speculative risk
A type of risk where the firm or individual has the chance of either a profit or a loss.

Pure risk. With speculative risk there is a chance of profit and a chance of loss. **Pure risk** involves only the chance of loss. Automobile drivers always face the risk of accidents. If they occur, the drivers (and others) may suffer financial and physical loss. If they do not occur, however, there is no gain. Insurance is often used to protect against the financial loss resulting from pure risk.

pure risk
A type of risk involving only the chance of loss.

Dealing with Risk

Because risk is an unavoidable part of business, management must find ways of dealing with it. Recognition of its presence is an important first step. Once this occurs, the manager has four methods available for dealing with it: avoiding the risk, reducing the frequency and/or severity of the risk, self-insuring against the risk, or shifting the risk to insurance companies.

Avoiding Risk

Chapter 20 dealt with different types of investors. Some were willing to take high risks as the price for potentially high rewards, and others were not. The same is true for companies. Some firms are, for example, unwilling to risk the costs involved in developing new and untried products. They may know that Du Pont's attempt to develop a leather substitute called Corfam resulted in losses of more than $100 million and that Ford's unhappy experiences with the Edsel cost over $200 million.

Companies unwilling to assume risk are content to produce and market products that have a stable demand and offer an adequate profit margin. This strategy ensures profitability, but it stifles innovation. Companies whose managers seek to avoid most risk are rarely leaders in the industry. Even though Corfam was a market failure, the Du Pont product development record is an enviable one, with such contributions as cellophane, nylon, Dacron, and Teflon.

Reducing Risk

Many types of risk can be reduced or even eliminated through eliminating hazards. Safety programs are often begun to educate employees about potential hazards and the proper methods of performing specific tasks. Safety glasses and safety shoes may be required for workers performing certain activities. Danger areas within a factory may be marked with red lines or special caution signs.

Other steps can be taken to reduce risks. Guard dogs and 24-hour security patrols may minimize burglaries. Installation of fire-retardant building materials and an automatic sprinkler system can help protect a warehouse from fire. Preventive maintenance lessens the risk of defective machinery. Adequate credit checks allow managers to make careful decisions on which customers should be extended credit.

All these actions can reduce the risk involved in business operations; they cannot, however, eliminate all risk. Preventive maintenance greatly reduces the possibility of plane crashes due to mechanical problems, but such disasters do occur. The risk of loss—although greatly reduced—is still there.

Requiring workers to wear special safety equipment while performing certain jobs is one method companies use to reduce risk.

Self-insuring against Risks

Instead of purchasing insurance against certain risks, some multiplant, geographically scattered firms accumulate funds to cover losses. This is called **self-insurance.** Firms that self-insure set aside cash reserves on a periodic basis to be drawn upon only in the event of a financial loss resulting from the assumption of a pure risk.

Federated Department Stores owns 175 stores in cities throughout the United States. Included in the chain are famous stores such as Abraham & Straus and Bloomingdale's in New York, I. Magnin in San Francisco, Foley's in Houston, Filene's in Boston, Sanger-Harris in Dallas, Burdines in Miami, Shilito's in Cincinnati, and Gayfers in cities along the Gulf Coast. Rather than purchase fire insurance for the various stores, the firm's management may choose to self-insure. Because there are many stores scattered throughout the United States, self-insurance or establishment of a fire reserve fund may be cheaper than paying insurance premiums.

The alternative of self-insurance can be a realistic choice for large multiplant companies, because the likelihood of several fires is small, and the likelihood of one can be calculated. For the single-plant firm, one fire can prove disastrous, and contributions to a reserve fund for large potential fire damage can be prohibitively high. As a result, small firms with concentrated facilities and the possibility of being forced out of business by a major fire or accident usually shift the risk to others through the purchase of insurance.

self-insurance
The practice of some multiplant, geographically scattered firms of assuming risks by developing a system, such as accumulating funds, in order to absorb possible losses.

Shifting the Risk to Insurance Companies

Although steps can be taken to avoid or reduce risk, the most common method of dealing with it is to shift it to others in the form of **insurance**—the process by which a firm (the insurance company) for a fee (the insurance premium) agrees to pay another firm or individual (the insured) a sum of money stated in a written contract (the policy) if a loss occurs. Thus, insurance is the substitution of a small known loss (the insurance premium) for a larger unknown loss that may or may not occur. In the case of life insurance, the loss (death) is a certainty; the uncertainty is the date of occurrence.

insurance
The process by which a firm (the insurance company) for a fee (the premium) agrees to pay another firm or individual (the insured) a sum of money stated in a written contract (the policy) if a loss occurs.

The Importance of Insurance Companies

The importance of insurance companies in dealing with risk is best illustrated by a single statistic. Total premiums paid to commerical insurance companies by individuals and businesses for casualty and property insurance coverage is now $80 billion annually.[3]

The premiums accumulated by insurance companies are designed to cover eventual losses. However, as Chapter 19 indicated, these funds are carefully invested to generate additional returns for the company. The returns from insurance company investments may be utilized in reducing premiums, generating a profit for those companies organized as profit seeking, or both. Insurance companies represent a major source of long-term financing for other businesses.

Insurance Basics

Insurance companies are professional risk takers. They serve society, for a fee, by accepting the risk of loss or damage to businesses and individuals. Three basic principles operate in insurance: the concept of insurable interest, the concept of insurable risks, and the law of large numbers.

Insurable Interest

insurable interest
An insurance concept wherein the policyholder must stand to suffer financial loss due to the occurrence of fire, accident, or lawsuit.

In order to purchase insurance, an applicant must demonstrate that he or she has an **insurable interest** in the property or life insured. That is, the policyholder must stand to suffer financial loss due to the occurrence of fire, accident, or lawsuit. However, for life insurance, a blood relative may have an insurable interest even though no financial loss occurs in the event of the insured's death.

A businessperson can obtain fire insurance for property. An individual can purchase life insurance for herself or himself or for members of the family. Because top managers are important assets to a firm, the corporation can purchase key-executive insurance. But a businessperson cannot collect on insurance to cover damage to the property of competitors when no insurable interest exists. Nor can an individual purchase an insurance policy on the life of the United States president. In these two cases an insurable interest is not present.

Insurable Risks

insurable risk
The requirements that a risk must meet in order for the insurance company to provide protection against its occurrence.

An **insurable risk** should meet a number of requirements in order for an insurance company to provide protection against its occurrence:

1. The likelihood of loss should be predictable. Insurance companies know approximately how many fires will occur each year, how many people of a certain age will die, how many burglaries will occur, and how many traffic accidents and job-related injuries will take place. Knowledge of the numbers of such losses and of their average size allows the insurance company to determine the amount of premiums necessary to repay those companies and individuals who suffer losses.
2. The loss should be financially measurable. In order to determine the amount of premium income necessary to cover the costs of losses, the dollar amount of losses must be known. For this reason life in-

surance policies are purchased in specific dollar amounts, which eliminates the problem of determining the value of a person's life. Many health insurance policies list the dollar value for specific medical procedures. Some policies have no schedule of benefits for such procedures but pay, say, 80 or 100 percent of the cost.

3. The loss should be fortuitous or accidental. Losses must happen by chance and must not be intended by the insured. The insurance company is not required to pay for damages caused by a fire if the insured is guilty of arson. Similarly, life insurance policies typically exclude the payment of proceeds if the insured commits suicide in the first year of the policy's coverage.

4. The risk should be spread over a wide geographic area. An insurance company that concentrates its coverage in one geographic area risks the possibility of a major catastrophe affecting most of its policyholders. A major Louisiana hurricane, California earthquake, or Midwest tornado might bankrupt the company.

5. The insurance company has the right to set standards for accepting risks. The company may refuse insurance coverage to individuals with heart disease or to those in dangerous occupations—such as fire fighters, test pilots, and crop dusters. Or the company may choose to insure these people at considerably higher rates due to the greater risks involved. In the same manner, fire insurance rates may be different for residences and commercial buildings.

The Law of Large Numbers

Insurance is based on the law of averages (or statistical probability). Insurance companies have studied the occurrence of deaths, injuries, lawsuits, and all types of hazards. From their investigations they have developed the **law of large numbers**—a probability calculation of the likelihood of the occurrence of perils on which premiums are based. They also use actuarial tables to predict the number of fires, automobile accidents, plane crashes, and deaths that will occur in a given year.

law of large numbers A probability calculation of the likelihood of the occurrence of perils on which premiums are based.

Table 21–1 is an actuarial table indicating the number of deaths per thousand persons that will occur this year for each age category, and the number of additional years people in each category are expected to live. For 33-year-olds, deaths average slightly less than one per thousand, and people in this age group are expected to live another 44 years.

No one can predict which two persons per thousand will die; the insurance companies only know that an average of two per thousand will do so. Armed with knowledge, the company can determine the size of premium necessary to pay the beneficiaries of its policies when claims arise. The longer the life expectancy, the lower the premiums. The same type of calculation is also made to determine premiums for automobile (see Focus 21–2) or fire insurance. The law of large numbers is the basis of all insurance premium calculations.

TABLE 21–1

Mortality Table for Males and Females through Age 50*

Age	Male Deaths per 1,000	Expectation of Life (Years)	Female Deaths per 1,000	Expectation of Life (Years)
0	13.37	70.2	10.58	77.8
1	1.01	70.1	0.71	77.6
2	0.75	69.2	0.56	76.7
3	0.59	68.3	0.46	75.7
4	0.49	67.3	0.38	74.8
5	0.43	66.3	0.33	73.8
6	0.40	65.4	0.29	72.8
7	0.37	64.4	0.26	71.8
8	0.33	63.4	0.23	70.8
9	0.28	62.4	0.21	69.9
10	0.24	61.5	0.19	68.9
11	0.24	60.5	0.18	67.9
12	0.33	59.5	0.21	66.9
13	0.51	58.5	0.26	65.9
14	0.77	57.5	0.34	64.9
15	1.06	56.6	0.44	64.0
16	1.33	55.6	0.52	63.0
17	1.55	54.7	0.58	62.0
18	1.69	53.8	0.61	61.1
19	1.78	52.9	0.61	60.1
20	1.85	52.0	0.61	59.1
21	1.93	51.1	0.61	58.2
22	1.96	50.2	0.61	57.2
23	1.93	49.3	0.61	56.2
24	1.87	48.4	0.62	55.3
25	1.79	47.5	0.62	54.3
26	1.72	46.5	0.62	53.3
27	1.66	45.5	0.62	52.4
28	1.62	44.7	0.64	51.4
29	1.61	43.8	0.66	50.4
30	1.60	42.8	0.69	49.5
31	1.60	41.9	0.72	48.5
32	1.63	41.0	0.76	47.5
33	1.68	40.0	0.80	46.6
34	1.76	39.1	0.85	45.6
35	1.86	38.2	0.90	44.6
36	1.99	37.2	0.98	43.7
37	2.13	36.3	1.07	42.7
38	2.29	35.4	1.19	41.8
39	2.47	34.5	1.33	40.8
40	2.68	33.6	1.49	39.9
41	2.93	32.6	1.66	38.9
42	3.22	31.7	1.85	38.0
43	3.58	30.8	2.06	37.1
44	3.99	29.9	2.28	36.1
45	4.44	29.1	2.52	35.2
46	4.93	28.2	2.78	34.3
47	5.48	27.3	3.06	33.4
48	6.08	26.5	3.34	32.5
49	6.73	25.6	3.65	31.6
50	7.46	24.8	3.98	30.7

*The numbers in this table are for white males and females. For blacks and others, the number of expected deaths per 1,000 is somewhat higher, and the expectation of life is somewhat lower.

FOCUS 21–2
**Insurance Companies: Reflecting Different Degrees
of Risk in Premiums Charged**

Although the law of large numbers is used by insurance companies in designing policies, they often divide individuals and industries into different risk categories and attempt to match premiums to the risk involved. A good example is automobile insurance.

Insurance claims statistics reveal that for every $100 in bodily injury losses caused by the adult pleasure-use car owners, the unmarried man under 25—as owner or principal operator—generates $306 in claims. The second highest claim group is unmarried women under age 21, at $181, with adult business use, specifically corporate-owned cars, third at $180. As a result, youthful male drivers pay the highest insurance premiums.[4]

In an attempt to inform the motoring public of the rationale for differing rates, the American Insurance Association recently initiated an advertising campaign. The message shown below appeared in a number of general-interest magazines.

Some people feel...

"So what if I'm young. I've never had an accident or even gotten a ticket. Why should I pay the highest insurance rates?"

That's why we want you to know...

We understand how you feel. You've got a good driving record, and that's great. And you don't expect to have an accident. No one does. But the fact is that good drivers as well as bad have accidents. That's why insurance protection exists.

No one can predict which <u>individual</u> is going to have an accident. But we can predict the accident potential for <u>groups</u> of drivers who share similar characteristics. This is the only way possible to make auto insurance rates.

Insurance companies set their rates to reflect how often they have to pay claims of insured groups and how much those claims cost. This is done for each state and for each rating territory within the state.

Year after year, without exception, statistics show a consistent pattern: <u>younger</u> drivers have more accidents than <u>older</u> drivers. Young <u>males</u> have more accidents than young females. And young <u>unmarried</u> males have more accidents than young <u>married</u> men.

The fairest way to distribute accident costs is for each driver to pay an insurance rate that reflects as closely as possible the exposure to loss of his or her group. Of course, differences within the groups also are taken into account. Among them are the age and type of car and how the car is used (whether for business, pleasure or commuting).

But take heart. If you have a good driving record, you will pay less than others in your group who have been involved in serious accidents or who have been guilty of major traffic law violations. And, as you get older, the accident potential of your group will decline, and so will your rates.

We're working to keep insurance affordable.

This message presented by the **American Insurance Association**, 85 John Street, NY, NY 10038

Types of Insurance Companies

Insurance companies are typically categorized by ownership. Two types of companies exist: mutual companies and stock companies.

Mutual Companies

mutual insurance company
An insurance company owned by its policyholders.

A **mutual insurance company** is actually a type of cooperative; it is owned by its policyholders. The mutual company is chartered by the state and governed by a board of directors elected by the policyholders.

Unlike the stock company, the mutual company earns no profits for its owners. Because it is a nonprofit organization, any surplus funds remaining after operating expenses, payment of claims, and establishment of necessary reserves are returned to the policyholders in the form of dividends or premium reductions.

Mutual companies are found chiefly in the life insurance field. Although they account for slightly less than 10 percent of the approximately 1,800 life insurance companies in the United States, they sell more than half of all the life insurance in force. As Table 21–2 indicates, many of the major life insurance companies are mutuals.

TABLE 21–2
The 15 Largest Life Insurance Companies in the United States
(Ranked by Assets)

Rank	Company	Assets (in Billions)	Life Insurance in Force (in Billions)
1	Prudential (Newark)	$ 59.8	$ 406.6
2	Metropolitan (New York)	48.3	349.2
3	Equitable Life Assurance (New York)	34.6	197.3
4	Aetna Life (Hartford)*	22.3	144.2
5	New York Life	19.7	122.8
6	John Hancock Mutual (Boston)	18.8	133.7
7	Connecticut General Life (Bloomfield)*	13.8	80.4
8	Travelers (Hartford)*	13.4	104.4
9	Northwestern Mutual (Milwaukee)	11.4	61.3
10	Teachers Insurance & Annuity (New York)*	9.7	7.6
11	Massachusetts Mutual (Springfield)	9.1	50.9
12	Mutual of New York	8.0	38.0
13	Bankers Life (Des Moines)	7.9	35.1
14	New England Mutual (Boston)	6.8	31.7
15	Mutual Benefit (Newark)	5.9	40.2

* Aetna Life, Connecticut General Life, Travelers, and Teachers Insurance & Annuity are stock companies. The other 11 companies are mutuals.

Stock Companies

Stock insurance companies are insurance companies operated for profit. Stockholders do not have to be policyholders; they invest funds in the stock company in order to receive dividends from company earnings. Profits earned by the company come from two sources: (a) insurance premiums in excess of claims and operating costs, and (b) earnings from company investments in stocks, bonds, and real estate.

Insurance companies—whether stock or mutual companies—are interested in the objective of minimizing the premiums necessary to cover operating expenses and to pay for personal or property losses. Accident claim data are studied carefully in an attempt to spot problem areas and to adjust coverage costs accordingly. Such data provide expected reasons for accidents—excessive speed, alcohol, equipment malfunction, and inattentiveness, among others (see Focus 21–3).

stock insurance company
An insurance company operated for profit.

FOCUS 21–3
"Did You Hear the One about the Invisible Car?"

The explanations for accidents given by Metropolitan Life Insurance Co. auto insurance claimants were sometimes bizarre:

"An invisible car came out of nowhere, struck my car and vanished."

"The other car collided with mine without warning me of its intention."

"I had been driving my car for 40 years when I fell asleep at the wheel and had the accident."

"As I reached an intersection, a hedge sprang up obscuring my vision."

"I pulled away from the side of the road, glanced at my mother-in-law, and headed over the embankment."

"The pedestrian had no idea which direction to go, so I ran over him."

"The telephone pole was approaching fast. I attempted to swerve out of its path when it struck my front end."

"The guy was all over the road. I had to swerve a number of times before I hit him."

"The indirect cause of this accident was a little guy in a small car with a big mouth."

The major difference between stock and mutual companies is that stockholders seek profits from stock insurance companies. Even so, there is no clear indication that the insurance premiums of stock companies are greater than those of mutual companies. Although mutual companies dominate the life insurance field, the majority of all other types of insurance is written by stock companies. The efficiency of a particular company appears to depend on its management ability.

A general liability and automobile insurance policy issued for a New York City firm.

Types of Insurance

Although literally hundreds of different types of insurance policies are available for purchase by individuals and businesses, they can be conveniently divided into two broad categories: (1) property and casualty insurance and (2) life insurance.

Property and Casualty Insurance

Eight types of property and casualty insurance exist: fire insurance; automobile insurance; burglary, robbery, and theft insurance; workers' compensation insurance; health insurance; marine insurance; fidelity, surety, title, and credit insurance; and public liability insurance. Table 21–3 discusses the purposes of each type.

TABLE 21–3
The Eight Types of Property and Casualty Insurance and Their Functions

Type of Insurance	Protection Against
Fire insurance	Losses due to fire
Automobile insurance	Losses due to automobile theft, fire, or collision; claims resulting from damage to other property due to collision or injury or death of another person resulting from an automobile accident
Burglary, robbery, and theft insurance	Losses due to the unlawful taking of the insured's property, either by force or by burglaries
Workers' compensation insurance	Medical expenses and partial salary payments for workers injured on the job
Health insurance	Medical and surgical expenses and lost income due to sickness or accidents
Marine insurance	Losses to property that is being shipped from one location to another
Fidelity, surety, title, and credit insurance	Misappropriation of funds (fidelity bond); failure to perform a job (surety bond); loss due to a defective title to land or other property (title insurance); failure to repay loans (credit insurance)
Public liability insurance	Claims against property owner for injuries or damage to property of others caused by falls, malpractice, negligence, or faulty products

fire insurance
Insurance coverage for losses due to fire and—with extended coverage—windstorms, hail, water, riot, and smoke damage.

Fire insurance. Every 13 seconds a fire starts somewhere in the United States. Fires will cause more than $3.5 billion in property losses this year. Many businesspeople and individuals purchase **fire insurance** to cover losses due to fire and—with extended coverage—windstorms, hail, water, riot, and smoke damage.

Fire insurance rates vary according to the risks involved. Homes and buildings located in cities with adequate fire protection have lower rates than those in rural areas. Frame buildings have higher rates than brick or metal structures.

Standard fire insurance policies protect only against damage by fire or lightning; therefore, policyholders commonly purchase added coverage to protect them against perils such as windstorms, hail, water, riot, and smoke damage. This supplementary coverage is called extended coverage.

Because most fires result in less than total destruction, many businesspeople insure their property for less than its total value. For example, a $100,000 building may carry insurance of $80,000. Because insurance companies extend coverage on the entire building and receive premiums on only a fraction of the value of the building, they protect themselves by including a **coinsurance clause** in the policy. This clause requires that the insured carry fire insurance of some minimum percentage of the actual cash value of the property (usually 80 percent) in order to receive full coverage of a loss.

The coinsurance clause works this way. If the owner of a $50,000 building suffers a $20,000 fire loss, the amount the insurance company will repay depends on the value of the fire insurance policy. Should the owner have $30,000 in fire insurance, the insurance company will pay only three-fourths of the damage. Why? Because the coinsurance clause requires the owner to have a minimum of $40,000 insurance (80 percent of the $50,000 actual cash value of the building), the $30,000 policy amounts to 75 percent of the required insurance. The insurance company calculates its share of the loss as:

$$\frac{\text{Amount of Insurance Carried}}{\text{Amount of Insurance Required}} \times \text{Loss} = \frac{\text{Insurance Company's}}{\text{Share of the Loss}}$$

$$\frac{\$30,000}{\$40,000} \times \$20,000 = \$15,000$$

The remaining $5,000 of the loss must be absorbed by the insured. In many states the coinsurance clause applies to residential property.

Automobile insurance. The National Safety Council regularly advertises to inform the public of the risk involved in driving automobiles—with good reason. Automobile accidents have killed more people than all the armed forces battles since the Revolutionary War. Every 16 seconds someone is injured in an automobile accident; every 19 minutes someone dies in an automobile accident. The automobile injury toll last year was 2 million.

Most **automobile insurance** includes coverage for losses due to automobile theft, fire, or collision and claims resulting from damage to the property or person of others involved in an automobile accident. The automobile owner protects against these risks through the purchase of comprehensive fire and theft, collision, and liability insurance.

Comprehensive coverage protects the insured's car against damage caused by fire, theft, hail, falling objects, and a variety of other

coinsurance clause
An insurance policy clause requiring that the insured carry fire insurance of some minimum percentage of the actual cash value of the property (usually 80 percent) in order to receive full coverage of a loss.

automobile insurance
Insurance coverage for losses due to automobile theft, fire, or collision and for claims resulting from damage to the property or person of others involved in an automobile accident.

Many businesspeople purchase fire insurance to cover losses due to fire, smoke damage, and other hazards.

perils. Contents of the car are also usually covered if the car is locked. In recent years insurance companies have been forced to exclude stereo tape decks and CB radios (or to issue special policies at a separate premium) due to the ease of their detachment from the car and their attractiveness to thieves.

Collision insurance pays for damage caused by collision with another vehicle or a stationary object. Most policies list a deductible amount ranging from $50 to $200 or $300 that the insured must pay. Most automobile insurance policies provide both comprehensive and collision coverage for a single premium.

Liability insurance covers both property damage and bodily injury. Bodily injury liability insurance is usually stated on the policy as $20,000/$40,000, $25,000/$50,000, $100,000/$300,000, or more. The first amount listed is the maximum amount the insurance company will pay for the injury or death of one person. The second is the maximum amount the insurance company will pay for a single accident. Property damage liability insurance covers any damage to other automobiles or property caused by the insured's automobile. Liability insurance also typically includes a medical payments endorsement, which pays hospital and doctor bills up to a specified amount for any persons injured in the insured's car.

Uninsured-motorist insurance covers the policyholder who is injured in an accident by a driver who has no liability insurance and is at fault. This type of insurance also protects the insured against losses caused by hit-and-run drivers.

As automobile insurance premiums soar and the delays in settling claims lengthen, states have begun to look for new ways of insuring motorists. In 1971 Massachusetts became the first state to enact a **no-fault insurance plan**—a state law requiring that claims payments by the policyholder's insurance company be made without regard to fault, and limiting the right of victims to sue. Florida, Connecticut, New Jersey, Michigan, New York, Utah, and Kansas quickly followed. As Figure 21-1 shows, fifteen states now have no-fault laws.

Although the laws are not identical, all have the following features:

1. Insurance is required for all drivers of private automobiles. That is, all motorists must carry liability insurance to cover medical costs resulting from accidents involving themselves and other passengers in their cars.
2. Payments for financial losses are made, without regard to fault, to any driver, passenger, or pedestrian injured in an auto accident. These payments are made by the policyholder's insurance company, not by the company of the person ruled at fault.
3. All victims are automatically limited in their right to sue. As a rule, lawsuits are barred except in cases where medical expenses exceed a set amount (which varies from state to state) or where the accident results in death, dismemberment, disfigurement, or certain other serious injuries.

no-fault insurance plan
An insurance plan, created by state law, that requires claims payments to be made by the policyholder's insurance company without regard to fault and that limits the right of victims to sue.

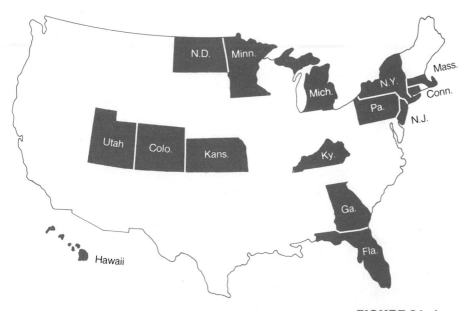

FIGURE 21–1
The 15 states where no-fault automobile insurance
systems are operating.

Proponents of no-fault insurance argue that it will lead to lower premiums. Although it appears to be too early to make a final judgment, the impact of such laws upon premiums has been mixed. Although Michigan, New York, and Minnesota have enjoyed some success in modifying rate increases, Nevada decided to repeal its six-year-old plan after premiums rose 81 percent in a two-year period.[5]

Burglary, robbery, and theft insurance. Although burglary, robbery, and theft are all crimes, each has a different meaning, and the insurance rate for each crime is different. The act of taking property from an unlocked building is theft, not burglary. **Burglary insurance** provides coverage for losses due to the taking of property by forcible entry. **Robbery insurance** provides coverage for losses due to the unlawful taking of property from another person by force or the threat of force. **Theft** (or larceny) **insurance** gives coverage for losses due to the unlawful taking of property. Theft insurance provides the broadest coverage and is, therefore, the most expensive of all insurance coverages for crime.

Workers' compensation insurance. Workers' compensation insurance—insurance provided by employers under state law to guarantee payment of medical expenses and salaries to employees who are injured on the job—exists in all 50 states. Premiums are based on the company's payroll, and rates depend on the hazards present on the job and the safety record of the employer. Payments are usually set at a fraction of the employee's regular wage (usually one-half to

burglary insurance
Insurance coverage for losses due to the taking of property by forcible entry.

robbery insurance
Insurance coverage for losses due to the unlawful taking of property from another person by force or the threat of force.

theft insurance
Insurance coverage for losses due to the unlawful taking of property.

workers' compensation insurance
Insurance provided by employers under state law to guarantee payment of medical expenses and salaries to employees who are injured on the job.

two-thirds of the weekly salary). In addition, workers' compensation typically reimburses the injured worker for medical and rehabilitation expenses. A waiting period of a few days to two weeks is usually provided to discourage claims for minor accidents.

Health insurance. One out of every seven people in the United States was hospitalized in 1981. Without insurance, family incomes can be cut off, a lifetime of savings can be wiped out, and a business can face the loss of a valuable employee. Because of these severe risks, 90 percent of the people in the United States have some form of **health insurance**—insurance that provides coverage for losses due to sickness or accidents.

Most businesses offer health and accident insurance for their workers as part of their fringe benefit programs. This insurance typically covers hospital, surgical, and other medical expenses; loss of income for a certain period of time; loss of an eye, a hand, or a foot; and death benefits, if death results from an accident.

Health insurance is sold by regular insurance companies and by nonprofit associations such as Blue Cross and Blue Shield. The federal government has become increasingly involved with health insurance through its Medicare and Medicaid programs and through the disability provisions of the Social Security Act. More than 21 million people are covered by Medicare.

Marine insurance. Marine insurance is the oldest form of insurance, dating back at least 5,000 years. It is used as a means of insuring ships and their cargoes. **Ocean marine insurance** protects shippers from losses of property due to damage to a ship or its cargo while at sea or in port. **Inland marine insurance** covers losses of property due to damage while goods are being transported by truck, ship, rail, or plane.

Fidelity, surety, title, and credit insurance. Fidelity bonds protect employers from employees' dishonesty. They are commonly used by banks, loan companies, and other businesses to cover cashiers and other employees who handle company funds. The employer is guaranteed against loss up to the amount of the policy.

Surety bonds are designed to protect people or companies against losses resulting from nonperformance of a contract. A building contractor who agrees to construct a new city library may be required to furnish a surety bond that the library will be erected according to specifications and completed within the time limit of the contract.

Title insurance protects real estate purchasers against losses that might be incurred because of a defect in the title to the property. It eliminates the purchaser's need to investigate legal records in order to determine the true owner of the property and the presence of any claims against it. This insurance is often purchased by a person buying a new home.

health insurance
Insurance coverage for losses due to sickness or accidents.

ocean marine insurance
Insurance that covers shippers for losses of property due to damage to a ship or its cargo while at sea or in port.

inland marine insurance
Insurance coverage for losses of property due to damage while goods are being transported by truck, ship, rail, or plane.

fidelity bonds
Bonds that protect employers from employees' dishonesty.

surety bonds
Bonds that protect people or companies against losses resulting from nonperformance of a contract.

title insurance
Insurance protection for real estate purchasers against losses that might be incurred because of a defect in the title to the property.

Credit insurance protects lenders against losses from bad debts. Most credit insurance policies do not protect against all unpaid debts, because the premiums would be too expensive. Instead they usually define normal losses from bad debts and cover any in excess of the norm.

credit insurance
Insurance protection for lenders against losses from bad debts.

Public liability insurance. Public liability insurance is designed to protect businesses and individuals against claims caused by injuries to others or damage to the property of others. Most homeowners' insurance policies include liability coverage for claims such as those by people injured in falls or bitten by pets. Businesses purchase this insurance to cover possible injuries to customers in their stores or arising out of their operations. Physicians commonly purchase malpractice insurance to protect themselves against charges of incompetence or negligence. In a recent year, some California surgeons paid annual malpractice premiums of more than $30,000.

public liability insurance
Insurance protection for businesses and individuals against claims caused by injuries to others or damage to the property of others.

Product liability insurance (which comes under the general heading of public liability insurance) is designed to protect businesses against claims for damages resulting from the use of the company's products. It covers, for example, a druggist being sued by a customer who claims that a prescription was prepared improperly, or a manufacturer accused of producing and selling unsafe products.

product liability insurance
Insurance protection for businesses against claims for damages resulting from the use of the company's products.

Malpractice insurance protects physicians against charges of incompetence.

"Now your medical history—any lawsuits?"

Cartoon Features Syndicate

Product liability insurance has become increasingly necessary in recent years. The number of product liability cases increased by 500 percent during a five-year period in the late 1970s, and the average amount sought rose from $476,000 to $1.7 million over this period. The record judgment for product liability was set in the late 1970s when a jury awarded a judgment of $128 million against Ford Motor Company in a case involving a Ford Pinto accident. Ford appealed and eventually settled out of court for a small fraction of this amount. Premiums for product liability insurance are rising at an alarming rate, and in some cases coverage is hard to obtain. Several manufacturers of football helmets discontinued production in recent years due to the unavailability of product liability insurance.[6]

Relative importance of each type of property and casualty insurance. Each type of property and casualty insurance has been developed to protect individuals and businesses against specific types of losses. As Table 21–4 indicates, automobile insurance is the most frequently purchased property and casualty insurance, followed by workers' compensation and homeowners' insurance. The rankings are based on the amount of annual premiums paid by policyholders.

Life Insurance

Life insurance is different from all the other types of insurance coverage described in this chapter. It deals with a risk that is certain—death. The only uncertainty is when it will occur. Life insurance is a common fringe benefit in most firms because its purchase provides financial protection for the family of the policyholder and, in some instances, an additional source of retirement income for employees

TABLE 21–4
Property and Casualty Insurance Ranked
in Order of Total Annual Premiums

Type of Insurance	Percentage of Total Annual Premiums	
Automobile		40.7
Liability	24.6	
Physical damage	16.1	
Medical malpractice		1.3
Other liability		7.3
Fire insurance and allied lines		
(extended coverage)		5.3
Homeowners' multiple peril		9.8
Farmowners' multiple peril		0.8
Commercial multiple peril		7.4
Workers' compensation		14.6
Marine		3.4
Inland	2.3	
Ocean	1.1	
Surety and fidelity		1.3
Burglary and theft		0.2
Accident and health		3.5
Miscellaneous		4.4
Total		100.0

and their families. An immediate estate is created by the purchase of a life insurance policy. Because the need for financial security is great in most families, approximately two out of every three people in this country are covered by life insurance. Some 150 million people are covered by $12.5 trillion of insurance. As Figure 21–2 indicates, the average amount of life insurance coverage per family in 1979 was $38,500—more than eight times as great as in 1950.

Group or individual insurance. Life insurance policies can be purchased on an individual basis for almost any amount. Unlike property and casualty insurance, the life insurance purchases are limited only by the amount of premiums people can afford to pay—provided that purchasers qualify medically. Insurance companies have paid as much as $8 million in death benefits on a single policy.

Most businesses purchase employee life insurance on a group basis as a company fringe benefit. Employees may be required to contribute a portion of the cost of the insurance, or the employer may pay the total cost. **Group life insurance** for company employees is typically written under a single master policy, and covered employees are not normally required to undergo medical examinations. Because selling costs and administrative expenses are much lower for group insurance, this type is usually much cheaper than individual insurance.

group life insurance
Life insurance for company employees that is typically written under a single master policy.

The mortality table. The **mortality table,** first introduced in Table 21–2, is based on past experience with large numbers of policyholders. It is used to predict the number of people in each age category who will die in a given year. Once this is known, the premiums for a life insurance policy can be calculated to provide sufficient income to pay death benefits, company operating expenses, and profits (if the company is a stock company).

mortality table
The table, based on past experience, which is used to predict the number of persons in each age category who will die in a given year.

FIGURE 21–2
Life insurance per family in the United States, 1930–1979.

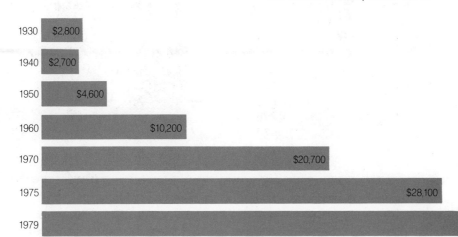

1930	$2,800
1940	$2,700
1950	$4,600
1960	$10,200
1970	$20,700
1975	$28,100
1979	$38,500

Controversial Issue

Is No-fault Automobile Insurance Working?

Faced with the highest automobile insurance premiums in the nation, Massachusetts drivers were fed up. They demanded a change and got it in the form of the country's first no-fault insurance system.

That was 1971. Since then 14 other states have adopted no-fault plans. Why they have done it and why others have not is what we will examine here.

No-fault automobile insurance is at one and the same time a common and revolutionary concept. Like homeowners', hospitalization, and income disability insurance, it offers protection under the policyholder's own insurance plan. When an accident occurs, each driver simply files a claim with his or her own insurance company to collect compensation for injury-related costs. This avoids the costly and time-consuming litigation, which characterizes traditional auto insurance coverage. Assigning blame for the accident is simply not an issue in the no-fault system.

Most state no-fault plans cover medical expenses, lost income, the cost of hiring help—a housekeeper, for example—and funeral expenses. They do not exclude litigation when an accident results in death, permanent injury, or disfigurement, or when a specific amount of medical expenses, referred to as the threshold for suit, has been incurred.

Supporters of no-fault insurance claim that it has transformed an inhumane and unresponsive system into one that deals equitably with accident cases. Proving the other driver at fault in order to collect has placed many accident victims in the unfortunate position of collecting no compensation at all. This can happen when both drivers are partially at fault, when negligence is impossible to prove, or in single-vehicle accidents. Moreover, damages that are collected under a fault system are often too small to cover the victim's real costs. The amount a victim ultimately gets is diminished by any contributory role he or she may have had in the accident, and by legal fees, which can take between 20 and 50 percent of the settlement.

Supporters also claim that no-fault insurance pays accident victims faster than traditional insurance plans. Eighty-one percent of accident victims in no-fault states get their money within three months, and 90 percent collect within six months, says the All-Industry Research Advisory Committee, an insurance-industry group. These figures outstrip those in states without no-fault in-

Insurance premiums for a 40-year-old female are usually greater than for a 20-year-old, because the number of deaths per thousand increases from 0.61 to 1.49. As the age of the insured increases, the length of expected life decreases and life insurance premiums rise.

surance, where only 46 percent of accident victims collect within three months and 62 percent within six months. In addition, supporters point to states like Michigan, considered the model no-fault state, where the cost of bodily injury insurance has declined and compensation to accident victims has increased dramatically since no-fault insurance became law. According to the Michigan Insurance Bureau, no-fault is "paying more benefits to more accident victims in a more timely manner than any other automobile insurance system in the country."

Opponents of the no-fault system cite a variety of problems—not the least of which is the system's failure to reduce the cost of insurance premiums. In Massachusetts, for example, coverage may cost up to three times more than it does in other states. The problem of soaring rates became so severe in Nevada that the state's no-fault law was repealed six years after it was passed. Critics also charge that initial premium reductions, which supporters point to with pride, are only temporary because they are due to limits on recovery and increased risk spreading.

Part of the reason for uncontrollable rate hikes, say no-fault opponents, is dollar thresholds that are too low to discourage lawsuits. When lawsuits are possible after expenses exceed $200, for example, minor cases are once again subject to litigation.

According to the Association of Trial Lawyers of America (ATLA), one of the chief opponents of the no-fault system, no-fault is an industry scam. In effect, says the ATLA, it makes people pay twice for the same insurance. Their auto insurance under a no-fault plan simply duplicates their health and disability coverage. In addition, opponents charge that no-fault robs accident victims of their right to sue for pain and suffering—a right that victims of nonautomobile accidents retain. And it is also inherently unfair. "Under a system of fault-based liability," says congressional representative Robert Krueger of Texas, "a motorist's premiums will be a function of his or her propensity to cause accidents. Under a no-fault system, a motorist's premiums will be a function of his or her propensity to be involved in an accident whether or not the motorist was at fault. Bad drivers are the greatest beneficiaries of the no-fault concept."

Whether or not the no-fault system takes hold in more states depends on state legislators' perceptions of its effectiveness, speed, and cost benefits. The debate is complex, and the issues are not always clear.

Types of life insurance. The four basic types of life insurance are term, whole life, limited payment, and endowment. A company can choose one type or a combination of them as part of its total fringe benefit package for its employees.

term insurance
Insurance coverage protecting the individual for a specified period of years that has no value at the end of that period.

credit life insurance
A special form of term insurance purchased by persons who are buying a home or other major item that repays the balance owed on these items if the policyholder dies.

whole life insurance
Insurance providing both protection and savings for the individual who pays premiums throughout life and builds up a cash surrender value in the policy.

cash surrender value
The savings portion of a life insurance policy that can be borrowed by the policyholder at low interest rates or paid to the policyholder if the policy is canceled.

limited payment life insurance
A variation of whole life insurance for which the policyholder pays all premiums within a designated period such as 20 or 30 years.

single payment policy
A variation of whole life insurance that consists of a large premium paid in a lump sum at the time the insurance is purchased.

endowment policy
A type of insurance policy that provides coverage for a specified period after which the face value is refunded to the policyholder.

Term insurance provides protection for the individual for a specified period of years, but it has no value at the end of that period. It is "pure" insurance with no savings features. Some term policies give the policyholder the right to convert to whole life insurance at a higher rate. Term insurance is most often purchased by young married couples who want protection in the early years of marriage against the possibility of an early death of one partner. Term insurance offers low-cost protection for the one or two decades before the family can develop financial security through savings and investments.

A special form of term insurance, **credit life insurance,** is often purchased by persons buying a home or other major item. It repays the balance owed on these items if the policyholder dies, thereby protecting both the family and the lender. Credit life insurance decreases in value as the loan is repaid. In 1981 more than $100 billion in credit life insurance was in force.

Whole life insurance, the most popular form of life insurance, is a combination of protection and savings. It provides protection for the individual, who pays premiums throughout a lifetime, and also builds up a cash surrender value in the policy. This **cash surrender value** is the savings portion of a life insurance policy: it can be borrowed by the policyholder at low interest rates or paid to the policyholder if the policy is canceled.

Several variations of whole life insurance exist. Many companies offer **limited payment life insurance**—whole life insurance for which the policyholder pays all premiums within a designated period such as 20 or 30 years. An extreme variation is the **single payment policy,** which consists of a large premium paid in a lump sum at the time the insurance is purchased.

Endowment policies place more emphasis on savings than do whole life policies. The purchaser of an endowment policy gets coverage for a specified period, usually 20 years or until the age of 65. After this period the face value of the policy is refunded to the policyholder. Endowment insurance is considered forced saving and is commonly used as a portion of a family's retirement income plan.

Which type of life insurance policy is best? The answer to the question "Which type of life insurance policy is best?" must be "It depends." Table 21–5 compares the typical annual premiums for $1,000 worth of insurance for each of the four types of life insurance policies.

Individuals must carefully study their personal situations with the aid of a qualified insurance agent. Factors such as the costs of different policies, the insured's age, family responsibilities, health, and future expectations must be considered. While Table 21–5 provides an illustration of cost comparisons among the different types of life insurance, each person must determine the proper balance between savings and protection that is best for the household.

TABLE 21-5
Comparison of Sample Annual Premiums
per $1,000 in Insurance

Bought at Age	Straight Life	Limited Payment (20 Years)	Endowment (20 Years)	Renewable-Convertible Term (5 Years)
18	$11.95	$20.15	$43.17	$ 5.35
20	12.54	20.93	43.20	5.38
25	14.27	23.11	43.43	5.50
30	16.60	25.83	43.68	5.68
40	23.32	32.87	45.20	7.96
50	34.51	43.06	48.91	14.21

Rates shown are approximate premium rates for nonparticipating life insurance policies for men. Rates for women are somewhat lower because of women's somewhat lower mortality. Rates of participating policies would be slightly higher, but the cost would be lowered by annual dividends. The premium rates shown here are per $1,000 of protection if the policies are purchased in units of $10,000.

Summary

Risk is part of the daily life of both the individual and the business firm. It comes in different forms: property damage, dishonesty, death, injury to employees or customers, sickness, lawsuits, and nonpayment of debts. The four methods of dealing with risk are avoiding it, reducing it through effective management and elimination of perils, assuming it through self-insurance, and shifting it to insurance companies.

Insurance is based on the concepts of insurable interest, insurable risks, and the law of large numbers. Insurance companies are professional risk takers who operate by charging premiums that are large enough to repay insurance claims and cover operating expenses. There are two basic types of insurance companies: nonprofit mutual insurance companies, which are primarily involved in the life insurance field, and profit-seeking stock insurance companies.

Insurance can be divided into two categories: property and casualty insurance and life insurance. Property and casualty insurance includes protection against fire losses; protection against automobile accident losses; protection against burglary, robbery, and theft losses; workers' compensation; health insurance; marine insurance; fidelity, surety, title, and credit insurance; and public liability insurance.

Life insurance can be purchased by individuals or on a group basis by employers at rates lower than those for individuals. Four basic types of life insurance are available. Term insurance provides pure protection for a specific period of time. Whole life insurance provides a combination of protection and savings for the policyholder, who pays premiums throughout a lifetime. Limited payment insurance is similar to whole life, except that the policyholder pays all premiums within a designated time period. Endowment life insurance policies are a type of forced savings; they provide protection for a specified time period and then return the face value of the policy to the policyholder.

Each type of life insurance has merits and shortcomings. The choice of the best type or types must be made by the individual, who should consider factors such as his or her own age, the size of the family and the ages of its members, personal health, and future job expectations.

Key Terms

risk	health insurance
speculative risk	ocean marine insurance
pure risk	inland marine insurance
self-insurance	fidelity bonds
insurance	surety bonds
insurable interest	title insurance
insurable risk	credit insurance
law of large numbers	public liability insurance
mutual insurance company	product liability insurance
stock insurance company	group life insurance
fire insurance	mortality table
coinsurance clause	term insurance
automobile insurance	credit life insurance
no-fault insurance plan	whole life insurance
burglary insurance	cash surrender value
robbery insurance	limited payment life insurance
theft insurance	single payment policy
workers' compensation insurance	endowment policy

Review Questions

1. Explain each of the terms listed above.

2. Explain the concept of risk as it relates to business.

3. What methods are available to the manager for dealing with risk?

4. Discuss the three basic principles of insurance.

5. Identify the various types of property and casualty insurance.

6. Describe the relative importance of each type of property and casualty insurance.

7. How is life insurance different from other types of insurance?

8. Identify and describe the four basic types of life insurance.

9. What types of insurance should a small family-owned bakery carry?

10. Why does group insurance cost less than individual insurance?

Discussion Questions and Exercises

1. Evaluate the pros and cons of the controversial issue that appears in this chapter.

2. What types of insurance does your college or university provide as a fringe benefit for its employees? What other types of insurance would you recommend?

3. Identify and give an example of each of the methods by which risk can be reduced.

4. Discuss the concept of self-insurance as it relates to each type of insurance. Give an example of a firm that would be likely to self-insure for each type of insurance.

5. Insurance companies typically charge higher automobile insurance rates for people under 25 than they do for older persons. Do you think this is a fair policy? Explain. Can you think of any situations where younger people receive more favorable insurance rates than older ones?

Case 21–1: Lloyd's of London

The concept of insurable risk and the law of large numbers are rules to live by for most insurance companies. The typical insurance company requires that the likelihood of a loss be predictable, that the risk be spread over a wide geographic area, and that standards of acceptable risk be established. But Lloyd's of London is hardly a typical insurance company.

Lloyd's is actually not an insurance company at all, but an association of individual insurers who agree to insure risks that are not acceptable to more conventional insurance companies. The association has a colorful history that spans nearly three centuries since its beginning in a London coffeehouse in 1689. Today, Lloyd's is comprised of more than 400 separate risk-taking syndicates who share profits in good years and divide losses in bad years. The syndicates, in turn, are made up of from 20 to 1,000 mostly nonprofessional investors in whose ranks are included some 1,200 Americans, 40 Arabs, titled British aristocracy, and the Pink Floyd rock group.

Although the traditional emphasis at Lloyd's has been marine insurance, it is best known throughout the world for providing insurance against extremely unusual risks. Lloyd's has insured body parts such as Jimmy Durante's nose and Marlene Dietrich's legs. It has agreed to pay $2 million if the Loch Ness monster is captured. Most of the major bridges in the United States are insured by Lloyd's. Because bridges are usually built by the issuance of bonds, the insurance covers not only damage to the bridges but also losses in revenue that the tolls would have provided.

Lloyd's has paid off numerous claims involving extremely large sums of money. When the *Titanic* sank in 1912, Lloyd's lost $3 million (a huge loss for that time). Hurricane Betsy resulted in a $100 million loss in 1965. But until recently, the syndicates who make up Lloyd's had enjoyed considerable profits. In 1976, they divided premium incomes of $281 million. But Lloyd's has fallen on hard times recently, and many of the syndicate members, who face unlimited liability for the losses, are also threatened with personal bankruptcy.

In some instances, the string of losses results from what appears to be several cases of bad luck. When the U.S. chose not to participate in the 1980 Moscow Olympics, Lloyd's paid off on a $40 million policy purchased by NBC against cancellation. It underwrote most of the $50 million baseball strike insurance purchased by major league club owners prior to 1981's strike. But the biggest loss of all resulted from computer-lease cancellation contracts. Lloyd's incurred an estimated $340 million in such losses when IBM introduced an improved model. Policies were written on about $2.4 billion worth of such equipment on the highly unrealistic assumption that the equipment would be worth 40 percent of its purchase price at the expiration of the lease.

Another recent concern of Lloyd's has been the approximately $50 million in fire losses suffered by one of its syndicates. In one two-year period, this syndicate paid out 1,300 claims for $22 million in fire losses, many of them in the arson-plagued South Bronx of New York. Although only the members of this syndicate are liable for the loss, it has caused serious damage to Lloyd's reputation. And while Lloyd's admits that its only responsibility is to provide professional underwriters to assess the risks and establish policy premiums, members of many syndicates argue that more internal controls should be established.

Questions

1. How can an organization such as Lloyd's ignore such concepts as the law of large numbers and insurable risk and expect to earn profits? Upon what principles would such an organization be based?

2. What types of industries are likely to purchase insurance from such an organization?

3. Recommend some possible reforms that would allow Lloyd's to continue to operate while reducing the risk exposure of its affiliates.

Case 21-2: Medical Malpractice Insurance

Malpractice insurance is carried by physicians to protect them from lawsuits by patients who allege that the treatment led to some avoidable injury or loss. It pays for damage awards that may result from these lawsuits. Similar types of insurance are carried by lawyers, corporate officers and directors, ministers, travel agents, certified public accountants, and others who provide professional services.

A major nationwide insurance crisis began in 1975. Lawsuits for medical malpractice cases had resulted in rapidly rising payments, many of which were in amounts of several hundred thousand dollars. As a result, the insurance companies raised their malpractice insurance rates to a point where some physicians are paying over $30,000 a year in premiums. Furthermore, as the risks mounted, some insurance companies refused even to issue new insurance or renew existing policies. By 1978 only 5 to 10 percent of the nation's insurers were writing any kind of malpractice policies.

The malpractice insurance crisis resulted in doctor strikes in California, New York, and elsewhere. State legislatures began immediate consideration of the problem. Some states decided to limit damage awards in medical malpractice cases. Others became involved in insuring physicians.

Questions

1. What is the current status of the medical malpractice controversy?

2. How did your state approach the malpractice insurance crisis? Do you agree with its approach?

3. Is it likely that similar insurance crises in other professions will occur in the future? How can this problem be avoided?

Careers in Banking, Finance, Investments, and Insurance

All enterprises and many individuals require financial services. This means that there is a wide array of potential career fields for people interested and qualified in the area of finance. These careers are exciting and challenging, and they provide excellent advancement possibilities into top management.

The Bureau of Labor Statistics has projected the employment outlook to 1990. Its forecasts for some selected jobs in finance, banking, investments, and insurance appear in the table on page 549. The bureau expects all occupations to add 20.8 percent to their work force between 1978 and 1990. Seven of the careers currently available in these areas appear below.

Finance director. The finance director is the chief financial officer of any organization, with the responsibility for all aspects of the finance function. Two titles for this person are vice-president of finance and treasurer.

Financial analyst. A financial analyst is someone who studies and analyzes data, then prepares reports for management that outline various financial strategies that can be taken by the firm. Financial analysts are very important in any enterprise.

Banker. The term *banker* applies to a number of people in banking positions. Most top bank executives have had experience in all aspects of bank management and operations. Banking is a prestigious, rewarding career field.

Stockbroker. Stockbrokers are agents in the purchase and sale of securities—generally common and preferred stocks and bonds. They work for brokerage houses, providing information and advice to clients about their investments. Stockbrokers execute the buy and sell orders for securities.

Portfolio manager. Portfolio managers are financial consultants to investors. They supervise investments and often have legal authority to buy and sell securities for a client. Individuals, pension funds, banks, trust funds, colleges, insurance companies, and private foundations all employ portfolio managers.

Underwriter. Underwriters evaluate insurance applications to determine the risks involved for the insurer. They specialize in various types of insurance, such as life and casualty. After assessing the insurance application, the underwriter assigns the proper rate (price) to the new policy. If the risks are too great for the insurer, the underwriter rejects the application.

Insurance agent. Insurance agents are insurance consultants and sales representatives. They evaluate people's insurance needs and recommend the best type of coverage. If the prospect agrees, they complete the sales transaction. Insurance agents can either work for a particular company or represent several companies as independent agents.

EMPLOYMENT OUTLOOK TO 1990

Occupations in Finance, Banking, Investment, and Insurance	Recent Employment Figures	Changes in Employment					
		Much Faster than the Average for All Occupations	Faster than the Average for All Occupations	About as Fast as the Average for All Occupations	More Slowly than the Average for All Occupations	Little Change Expected	Expected to Decline
Collection Workers	78,000	Generally good employment outlook					
Bank Clerks	500,000	■					
Bank Tellers	410,000		■				
Actuaries	9,000		■				
Bank Officers and Managers	330,000	■					
Claim Representatives	169,000		■				
Underwriters	28,000		■				
Credit Managers	49,000					■	
Insurance Agents and Brokers	540,000			■			
Securities Sales Workers	110,000				■		
Economists	130,000		■				

Source: U.S. Department of Labor, Bureau of Labor Statistics, *Occupational Outlook Handbook 1980–1981,* Bulletin 2075, pp.5, 102–112, 120–121, 194–195, 204–205, 419–421.

PART
SEVEN

ADDITIONAL DIMENSIONS

22

International Business

Learning Goals

1. To evaluate the importance of international business

2. To describe the concept of international business and to analyze why countries tend to specialize in certain goods

3. To describe the different levels of involvement in international business

4. To distinguish among the various obstacles to effective international business

5. To explain multinational economic integration, the role of the multinational corporation, and the status of the United States as a foreign market

6. To explain the meaning of each of the key terms introduced in this chapter

Profile: William Blackie

Building Caterpillar Tractor into a Multinational Firm

For many years, the name William Blackie was synonymous with Caterpillar Tractor's bright yellow earth-moving machines found on construction sites and farms all over the world. The identification was well deserved.

As Caterpillar's board chairman between 1966 and 1972, Blackie led his company through a period of rapid international expansion. His organizational genius and insistence on locating manufacturing plants overseas in order to compete with foreign manufacturers propelled Caterpillar into a position as one of the world's leading multinational companies.

A multinational corporation, says Blackie, "trades internationally, has manufacturing sources in several different countries and employs nationals in those countries." Under Blackie's leadership Caterpillar operated factories in 11 foreign countries, including France, Scotland (Blackie's birthplace), Australia, and Brazil. With a major factory located close to almost every foreign market and the ability to avoid the cost of duties and transportation from the United States, Caterpillar increased its ability to defend its markets against competition and to expand.

Moreover, says Blackie, "because of our investment overseas we have increased our [U.S.] exports to every country in which we have created a subsidiary . . . Multinational companies which are undertaking investment abroad are also increasing employment and investment within the United States at a greater rate than the average American company is."

One of the major reasons Caterpillar thrived as a multinational corporation was its ability to anticipate demand. In the mid-1960s Caterpillar officials foresaw an increase in the construction of large projects, including hydroelectric and irrigation dams, pipelines, and roads to new oil and gas regions and to newly developed farm areas, to help meet growing demands for food and energy. Such projects, the company assumed, would mean increased demand for large earth-moving machines. So expansion became the goal.

While most companies pulled back during the 1970–71 recession, Caterpillar expanded rapidly and capitalized on its investments during the 1973–74 Arab oil embargo. Caterpillar machines were needed for pipeline construction, stepped-up drilling for gas and oil, and rapid industrialization of the oil-rich Middle Eastern and North African countries.

Blackie's insistence on producing a quality machine played an important part in Caterpillar's success. "The idea of quality has permeated us in all aspects of the business," says Blackie, "in the type of dealerships we have, in the way we do things. We believe that in our kind of machinery, which is subject to severe usage under all kinds of conditions, anything less than a quality product would be worse than useless."

Part of William Blackie's philosophy in managing a multinational corporation is that a worldwide interchange of goods and services breeds greater world understanding and cooperation. Multinationals teach people how similar they are, insists Blackie, and it helps minimize their differences.

In matching our products and services against sophisticated, world-scale competitors abroad, we have three things going against us: higher labor costs in absolute terms, lower rates of productivity improvement in relative terms, and higher inflation than all but a few of the leading industrial nations. These three factors combined put us at a tremendous disadvantage.

*—Phillip Caldwell
Chairman, Ford Motor Co.*

Pepsi is so popular in the Soviet Union that it is served at formal dinners.

In the past decade, imported beers (those produced abroad) have already quadrupled their share of the U.S. beer market. While foreign beer still constitutes only 2.6 percent of the U.S. market, American acceptance of brands like Heineken (the leading import), Beck, Guiness, Foster, and Carta Blanca illustrates how even a traditional product like beer is seeing increased international competition.

Molson—Canada's biggest brewer and the oldest one in North America—typifies the increased competition for domestic brewers. Molson, which sells three of its 22 brands in the U.S., is the number two imported beer. U.S. marketing efforts are conducted through a wholly owned subsidiary, Marlatt Importing Co., Inc., of Great Neck, New York. Molson's primary market target are young, affluent males and college students.

Molson's competitive strategy includes pricing their brand between the domestics and the European imports. The firm concentrates its advertising in radio and print media rather than television. Product quality is stressed. The emphasis is on providing a product with a wider, more flavorful taste than domestic brands.[1] Molson's phenomenal rise in the imported beers segment attests to the Canadian firm's ability in international business activities.

The Importance of International Business

Evidence of the growing importance of world business is everywhere. The United States is both a seller and a purchaser in the world marketplace. Some U.S. firms, like their counterparts elsewhere, view the world as their market. About 25,000 U.S. firms are engaged in some type of international business activity (see Focus 22–1).

How about Another Round, Nikita?

The plant manager says his product will "quench the thirst, invigorate the body, and raise the tone." Is he describing a new wonder drug? No, he is talking about a traditional favorite—Pepsi-Cola! The speaker is Russian, and he manages PepsiCo's plant in Novorossisk, a Black Sea port. PepsiCo beat its rival, Coca-Cola, into the Russian market with an agreement under which PepsiCo imports Russian vodka, wine, and champagne into the United States and in return supplies Russia with Pepsi concentrate and equipment. Over 50 million bottles of Pepsi are sold annually in the Soviet Union.

How did the deal originate? In 1959, Pepsi executive Donald M. Kendall, now chairman, persuaded then Vice-president Richard Nixon to bring Nikita Khrushchev into the Pepsi kiosk at the Moscow Trade Fair. The Soviet leader liked Pepsi so much that he drank eight bottles. Today, Pepsi is so popular in Russia that only three of each five bottles purchased are returned to the bottler; the rest are kept as souvenirs, even though they carry a twelve-cent deposit. Not all Russians drink Pepsi straight. Some are reported to mix it fifty-fifty with their national favorite, vodka.

TABLE 22-1
Importance of Foreign Markets to Selected U.S. Firms

Company	Percentage of Revenue Received from Foreign Sources
American Brands, Inc.	64.1
Bendix Corporation	33.8
Black and Decker Manufacturing Company	61.5
Caterpillar Tractor Co.	57.1
The Coca-Cola Company	44.7
Colgate-Palmolive Company	61.4
H. J. Heinz Company	41.0
Ingersoll-Rand Company	37.2
Kimberly-Clark Corporation	37.4
NCR Corporation	55.0
Pfizer, Inc.	56.8
R. J. Reynolds Industries, Inc.	34.1
The Singer Company	43.4
Squibb Company	36.1
Standard Brands Incorporated	41.5
Sunbeam Corporation	40.2
Texas Instruments Incorporated	34.3
Warner-Lambert Company	45.8

Some U.S. companies depend heavily on the ability to sell their products overseas (see Table 22–1 on p. 555). All of the companies listed in Table 22–1 receive over a third of their revenues from abroad. American Brands gets over two-thirds of its revenues from overseas; Black and Decker, Caterpillar Tractor, Colgate-Palmolive, NCR, and Pfizer receive at least 50 percent of their revenues from abroad.

Foreign trade is important to the United States from two viewpoints—**exporting**—selling goods abroad—and **importing**—buying foreign goods and raw materials. The United States is both the largest exporter and the largest importer in the world. But foreign trade is less critical to the United States than it is to such countries as the United Kingdom and New Zealand, which are heavily dependent on international trade. The leading trade partners of the United States are shown in Table 22–2.

World business allows a nation to sell abroad products not needed domestically and to import products not produced or in short supply

exporting
Selling domestic goods abroad.

importing
Buying foreign goods and raw materials.

A ship carrying Honda motorcycles being imported is being unloaded in Seattle.

TABLE 22-2
Major U.S. Trade Partners

Leading Customers for U.S. Merchandise	Billions
Canada	$33.1
Japan	17.6
United Kingdom	10.6
Mexico	9.8
Federal Republic of Germany	8.5
Netherlands	6.9
France	5.6
Belgium and Luxembourg	5.2
Saudi Arabia	4.9
Italy	4.4
Republic of Korea	4.4
Venezuela	3.9
Switzerland	3.7
Australia	3.6
Soviet Union	3.6

Leading Venders to the U.S.	Billions
Canada	$38.1
Japan	26.2
Federal Republic of Germany	11.0
Mexico	8.8
Nigeria	8.2
Saudi Arabia	8.0
United Kingdom	8.0
Taiwan	5.9
Libya	5.3
Venezuela	5.2
Algeria	4.9
Italy	4.9
France	4.8
Republic of Korea	4.0
Hong Kong	4.0

TABLE 22-3
Some Leading Commodities in U.S Foreign Trade

Exports	Billions
Chemicals	$17.3
Grains and preparations	14.5
Road motor vehicles	13.8
Aircraft, civilian, and parts for all aircraft	8.8
Metals and manufactures	7.9
Automotive parts	6.1
Soybeans	5.7
Agricultural machines, tractors, parts	3.8
Coal, coke, and briquettes	3.5
Pulp, paper, and manufactures	3.4

Imports	Billions
Petroleum, crude and partially refined	$46.1
Machinery	28.5
Transport equipment	25.1
Automobiles, new	14.8
Petroleum products	9.9
Chemicals	7.5
Iron and steel mill products	6.8
Pulp, paper, and manufactures	4.9
Nonferrous base metals	4.7
Coffee	3.8

locally. For example, New Zealand imports all its motor vehicles. Some leading U.S. exports and imports are shown in Table 22–3. Petroleum is the leading import, and chemicals are the leading export.

The Concept of International Business

International business activity is the result of several factors—some economic, others political or traditional. To understand international business it is essential to understand the concepts of balance of trade and balance of payments.

Balance of Trade

A country's **balance of trade** is determined by the relationship between its exports and its imports. A favorable balance of trade, or export surplus, occurs when exports exceed imports, because, other things being equal, new money flows into the economic system. An unfavorable balance of trade, or import surplus, occurs when imports exceed exports, because, other things being equal, the net money flow is outward. In 1980 the United States had an unfavorable balance of trade of approximately $32 billion.[2]

balance of trade
The relationship between a country's exports and imports.

Balance of Payments

A country's balance of trade plays a key role in determining its **balance of payments**—the flow of money into or out of the country. A

balance of payments
The relationship between a country's inward and outward money flows.

favorable balance of payments means a net flow into the country, while an unfavorable balance of payments means a net outflow.

But balance of payments is affected by other factors, too, such as tourism, military expenditures abroad, investment abroad, and foreign aid. A money outflow caused by these factors may erase the money inflow from a favorable balance of trade and leave a country with an unfavorable balance of payments.

The Exchange Rate

The value of a nation's currency is sometimes changed by a governmental action or by market conditions. **Devaluation** is the reduction in value of a country's currency in relation to gold or to some other currency. Devaluation of the dollar would have the effect of lowering the cost of U.S. goods abroad and making trips to the United States cheaper for foreign tourists. **Revaluation,** a less typical case, is the upward adjustment in value of a country's currency. In either situation, the country adjusts its **exchange rate**—the rate at which its currency can be exchanged for other currencies or gold. Most nations, including the U.S., have now adopted a **floating exchange rate** which is allowed to vary in accordance with market conditions.

devaluation
The reduction in value of a country's currency in relation to gold or to some other currency.

revaluation
An upward adjustment in the value of a country's currency.

exchange rate
The rate at which a country's currency can be exchanged for other currencies or gold.

floating exchange rate
An exchange rate that varies according to market conditions.

Specialization among Countries

Australia has vast grazing lands, while Hong Kong's estimated 5 million people live in a small area that has become one of the most urbanized territories in the world. Hong Kong is a world trader as well as a source of foreign exchange for the People's Republic of China. Kuwait has rich oil fields but few other industries or resources.

These situations suggest that countries are usually better off if they specialize in certain products or commerical acitivities. By doing what they do best, they are able to exchange products not needed domestically for foreign-made goods that are needed. This allows a higher standard of living than would be possible if the country tried to produce everything itself. But specialization by countries sometimes produces odd situations.

Consider these cases. Holland has sold sand to the desert kingdom of Saudi Arabia because Saudi sand does not work well in swimming pool filters.[3] The Saudis are also water poor and once spent $1 million on a feasibility study on hauling Antarctic icebergs to one of their ports. The Saudis and other Middle Eastern nations are now buying fresh water from Japan. Tankers bringing oil to Japan are loaded with water for the return trip.[4] The concepts of absolute and comparative advantage play a crucial role in the specialization among countries.

Absolute Advantage Concept

A country has an **absolute advantage** in the marketing of a product if it has a monopolistic position or if it produces the item at the lowest cost. Examples of absolute advantage are rare, because few countries are sole suppliers and because economic conditions rapidly alter production costs.

absolute advantage
The situation where a country has a monopolistic position in the marketing of a product or if it produces at the lowest cost.

Comparative Advantage Concept

A more realistic approach to international specialization is that of comparative advantage. A country has a **comparative advantage** in an item if it can supply that item more efficiently and at a lower cost than it can supply other products. Nations usually produce and export those goods in which they have the greatest comparative advantage or least comparative disadvantage. Countries tend to import those items in which they have the least comparative advantage or greatest comparative disadvantage.

comparative advantage
A country's ability to supply a particular item more efficiently and at a lower cost than it can supply other products.

Table 22-3 suggests how the comparative advantage concept is applied in the United States. The export commodities tend to be those in which the United States has a comparative advantage over its trading partners. Being a highly industrialized nation with good natural and agricultural resources, the United States tends to export manufactured items, food products, and natural resources such as coal. By contrast, countries with low-cost labor often specialize in products that require a significant amount of labor such as shoes and clothing.

Australia's vast grazing lands enable her to export sheep to the United States.

The Self-sufficiency Argument

Some countries refuse to specialize their productive efforts because they want to be self-sufficient. The communist nations have typically followed this pattern, as has Israel. Other countries subscribe to the self-sufficiency viewpoint only for commodities that they regard as strategic to their long-run development, such as energy in the United States.

In most cases, countries that seek to be self-sufficient do so for reasons of military preparedness, fear of economic reprisal from other countries, and nationalism. They see noneconomic advantages as being more important to the national welfare than the economic advantages of specialization.

Levels of Involvement in International Business

International business involvement is an evolving process for many firms. A company usually starts exporting on a small scale, then expands its overseas efforts as management gains confidence and the ability to operate well abroad.

There are five levels of involvement in world business: casual or accidental exporting, active exporting, foreign licensing, overseas marketing by the firm, and foreign production and foreign marketing.[5]

Casual or Accidental Exporting

Some firms sell goods abroad without being aware of it. Buyers for foreign firms often purchase the goods in the United States and then ship them overseas, but the U.S. company considers the transaction a domestic sale. U.S. purchasers of a supplier's goods sometimes export them for inclusion in an item manufactured overseas. Casual exporting is thus quite common, but it is not a real commitment to international trade.

Active Exporting

Once a firm decides to enter the export market, it must invest two company resources—capital and managerial effort. The export operation may be handled within the organization by an "export manager," or the company may elect to engage an outside firm that specializes in this activity. Active exporting is distinguished from casual exporting by the company's commitment to seek foreign sales. In some cases active exporting may evolve from a casual exporting experience. Boeing leads the list of major U.S. exporters reported in Table 22-4.

Foreign Licensing

Another approach is to license foreign manufacturers to produce an item rather than to export it. Licensing is often selected because of high shipping costs, tariff barriers or trade restrictions, or nationalistic markets. Sometimes it is chosen because the licensee can provide considerable marketing expertise.

Overseas Marketing by the Firm

Overseas marketing involves setting up a foreign sales organization. While the goods may come from a variety of sources—including plants, licensees, or contract manufacturers—foreign marketing is controlled directly by the parent company operating abroad.

Foreign Production and Foreign Marketing

Total international business involvement exists when a company starts or acquires both a foreign manufacturing organization and a foreign marketing organization. In either case the firm is totally committed to doing business abroad.

TABLE 22-4
The 25 Leading Exporters

Rank	Company	Products	Exports (in Billions)
1	**Boeing** (Seattle)	Aircraft	3,967,900
2	**General Electric** (Fairfield, Connecticut)	Generating equipment, aircraft engines	2,772,100
3	**Caterpillar Tractor** (Peoria, Illinois)	Construction equipment, engines	2,499,900
4	**McDonnell Douglas** (St. Louis)	Aircraft	1,788,425
5	**E.I. du Pont de Nemours** (Wilmington, Delaware)	Chemicals, fibers, plastics	1,764,000
6	**United Technologies** (Hartford)	Aircraft engines, helicopters	1,417,257
7	**Weyerhaeuser** (Tacoma, Washington)	Pulp, logs, lumber, wood products	978,000
8	**Lockheed** (Burbank, California)	Aircraft and related support services	956,000
9	**Westinghouse Electric** (Pittsburgh)	Generating equipment, defense systems	879,840
10	**Raytheon** (Lexington, Massachussetts)	Electronic equipment	734,000
11	**Northrop** (Los Angeles)	Aircraft and related support services	701,577
12	**Union Carbide** (New York)	Chemicals, plastics	602,000
13	**Archer-Daniels-Midland** (Decatur, Illinois)	Soybean meal and oil, wheat, corn	564,808
14	**Signal Companies** (Beverly Hills, California)	Trucks, engines, chemicals	544,700
15	**Rockwell International** (Pittsburgh)	Electronic, automotive, and industrial equipment	536,000
16	**Philip Morris** (New York)	Tobacco products	521,235
17	**Occidental Petroleum** (Los Angeles)	Agricultural and chemical products, coal	499,000
18	**Kaiser Aluminum & Chemical** (Oakland, California)	Aluminum	496,800
19	**Textron** (Providence)	Helicopters, chain saws, metal products	489,000
20	**Deere** (Moline, Illinois)	Farm equipment	480,000
21	**R.J. Reynolds Industries** (Winston-Salem, North Carolina)	Tobacco products	476,000
22	**FMC** (Chicago)	Industrial and farm equipment	462,398
23	**International Harvester** (Chicago)	Farm equipment, trucks	447,000
24	**Dresser Industries** (Dallas)	Oil-field and industrial equipment	435,500
25	**Monsanto** (St. Louis)	Herbicides, textile fibers, specialty chemicals	406,400

Obstacles to International Business

Various barriers to effective world business exist. Some are minor and can be overcome easily; others are nearly impossible to bridge. But either way, business executives must expect and learn to handle a multitude of problems in attempting to reach international markets.

Economic, Societal, and Cultural Obstacles

Numerous economic, societal, and cultural obstacles can interfere with a firm's attempt to sell its product in countries other than the U. S.

Mistakes in translation are common in international business. Parker Pen's Latin American advertising company once claimed that a new ink warded off unwanted pregnancies. Similarly, a Venezuelan ad once called a U.S. auto battery "highly overrated." Specialist firms and individual consultants are now available to help U.S. companies avoid such costly translation mistakes.[6]

Economic conditions also play an important part in international business. The economic status of a country influences whether it can be a viable candidate for economic expansion. But, as Culligan International discovered, per capita income figures alone cannot always be depended on in assessing a market's potential. When Culligan

FOCUS 22–2
The Tokyo Round

The Tokyo Round was named for the city where it was decided to start the talks, but the negotiations actually took place in Geneva. Ninety-nine nations participated in this complex debate.

The chart shown below indicates that the Tokyo Round will result in considerable tariff reductions throughout the world. These cuts, expected to average 33 percent during the next eight years, will affect about 5,700 products.

Numerous nontariff barriers have also been reduced. With the exception of Japan, the participating governments agreed to change their procurement regulations to allow foreign marketers to bid on government purchases. The new pact reduced each nation's ability to use custom valuations or product standard regulations to discriminate against foreign goods. It also reduced restrictions on the international sale of civil aircraft and restricted government subsidies to exporters.

Early assessments of the Tokyo Round suggest that it could lead to a considerable increase in international trade. A Brookings Institution representative estimated that the United States will gain $4.5 billion in exports annually—which will help offset the nation's enormous trade deficit.

Cuts in tariffs and nontariff barriers . . .

**Total trade between industrial
countries covered by tariff cuts** .... **$200 billion**

personnel discussed the possibility of selling their water softener in France, the American Embassy's commercial attaché discouraged them by observing that the product—unknown in France—would be priced higher than the country's annual per capita income. The Culligan manager persisted in his belief that an adequate market did exist in France, and Culligan's French operation became one of its most successful overseas ventures.[7]

U.S. products do not always meet the needs of foreign consumers. The products of U.S. automobile manufacturers have traditionally been called "Yank Tanks" by Australians, who must travel vast distances on narrow roads. Similarly, some foreign products do not meet U.S. needs. Japanese machine tool producers found that U.S. firms, with higher labor costs, used machines intensively and could afford little time for maintenance. Thus, the Japanese had to alter both their product and their service programs.[8]

These examples suggest the importance of economic, societal, and cultural factors in the success of international business. Business managers who want to operate in an overseas market should consider these factors before beginning their ventures.

Tariffs	Average reduction
Between the U.S. and EC	35% each way
Between the U.S. and Canada	40% each way
On U.S. imports into Japan	40%
On Japanese imports into the U.S.	30%

Nontariff barriers	New rules
Government procurement code	Opens $20 billion annually in foreign official purchasing to bids by U.S. suppliers
Customs valuation code	Establishes the invoice price as basis for valuing imports
Product standards code	Requires public procedures and encourages uniformity in setting standards and certifying products
Civil aircraft code	Eliminates 5% U.S. import tariff; eases government preferences, "offsets," and other restrictions by other countries
Subsidies and countervailing duties code	Requires governments to take account of trade effects of domestic subsidies and authorizes countermeasures by injured countries

...should spur continued growth in trade

World exports (billions of current dollars)

Tariffs and Trade Restrictions

International business is also affected by tariffs and related trade restrictions. **Tariffs** are taxes levied against products imported from abroad. Some are a set amount per pound, gallon, or other unit; others are figured on the value of the imported product. Tariffs can be classified as either revenue or protective. **Revenue tariffs** are designed to raise funds for the government. **Protective tariffs,** which are usually higher than revenue tariffs, are designed to raise the retail price of imported products. In earlier days it was believed that a country should protect its "infant industries" by using tariffs to keep out foreign-made products. Although some foreign goods would enter the country, the high tariff payment would make domestic products competitive. Recently it has been argued that such tariffs should be used to protect employment and profits in domestic U.S. industry.

The **General Agreement on Tariffs and Trade (GATT),** an international trade accord, has sponsored various tariff negotiations that have led to cuts in the overall level of tariffs throughout the world. The most recent (1974–1979) produced some significant changes (see Focus 22-2). While the general movement has been toward tariff

tariffs
Taxes levied against products from abroad.

revenue tariffs
Tariffs designed to raise funds for the government.

protective tariffs
Tariffs designed to raise the retail price of imported products to the level of products produced domestically.

General Agreement on Tariffs and Trade (GATT)
An international trade accord that has sponsored various tariff negotiations leading to cuts in the overall level of tariffs throughout the world.

import quotas
Limitations on the number of products in certain categories that can be imported with the objective of protecting domestic industries and preserving foreign exchange.

embargo
A complete ban on certain imported products.

exchange control
The allocation, expansion, or restriction of foreign exchange according to existing national policy.

reduction, economic downturns always bring calls for economic protection of domestic industries.

There are also other forms of trade restrictions. **Import quotas** set limits on the number of products in certain categories that can be imported. The objective of such quotas is to protect domestic industries and their employees and preserve foreign exchange. Sometimes the threat of mandatory import quotas causes a nation to change its export policies. The Japanese agreed to limit automobile exports to the United States in face of such a threat. The ultimate quota is the **embargo**—a complete ban on certain products. In the past the United States prohibited the importation of products from some communist countries.

Foreign trade can also be regulated by exchange control through a central bank or government agency. Under **exchange control**, firms must buy and sell foreign exchange through the central bank or government agency. The government can then allocate, expand, or restrict foreign exchange according to existing national policy.

Political and Legal Obstacles

Political factors certainly influence international business. For example, Colgate's popular Irish Spring soap was introduced in England with a political name change. Britain knows it as Nordic Spring.[9]

Many nations try to achieve political objectives through international business activities. Like it or not, firms operating abroad often end up involved in or influenced by international relations. U.S. companies have been boycotted, burned, bombed, and banned by people who object to U.S. foreign policy. A dynamic political environment is a fact of life in international business.

Legal requirements also complicate international business. Liquor sales in Sweden are a government monopoly. The Netherlands requires that candy commercials on television carry tooth decay warnings. Many nations have local laws specifying the portion of a product that must come from domestic sources. These examples suggest that managers involved in international business must be well versed in legislation affecting their industry.

The legal environment for U.S. firms operating abroad consists of three dimensions: U.S. law, international law, and the legal requirements of host nations.[10] Firms in the United States are subject to comprehensive U.S. business legislation. International operations are also subject to various trade regulations, tax laws, and import-export requirements. One of the best-known U.S. laws in this area is the **Webb-Pomerene Act** of 1918, which exempted from antitrust laws certain combinations of U.S. firms acting together to develop export markets. The intent was to give U.S. industry economic power equal to that possessed by **cartels**—the monopolistic organizations of foreign firms. Companies operating under the Webb-Pomerene law

Webb-Pomerene Act
Federal legislation exempting from antitrust laws certain combinations of U.S. firms acting together to develop export markets.

cartels
Monopolistic organizations of foreign firms.

must not reduce competition within the United States and must not use unfair methods of competition.

International law can be seen in the various agreements existing among nations. The United States has many **friendship, commerce, and navigation (FCN) treaties** with other nations. Such treaties include many aspects of international business relations such as the right to conduct business in the treaty partner's domestic market. The **International Monetary Fund (IMF)** was established to lend foreign exchange to countries that require assistance in conducting international trade. This facilitates the entire process of international business. Other international business agreements concern standards for products, patents, trademarks, reciprocal tax treaties, export control, international air travel, and international communications.

The legal requirements of host nations often affect foreign marketers. Japan, for example, is cited as having complex import requirements. Other nations limit foreign ownership in their business sectors.

The majority of international businesspeople realize the importance of obeying the laws and regulations of the countries within which they operate. Violations of these legal requirements are setbacks for international business as a whole and should be carefully avoided.

Multinational Economic Communities

Several multinational economic communities have been formed since World War II.[11] The European Community (EC)—also known as the Common Market—is the most widely publicized of them. Some of the participants in such regional associations (shown in Table 22–5) have strong political as well as economic ties.

Three basic formats for economic integration exist: the free trade area, the customs union, and the common market or economic union. Within the **free trade area,** participants agree to allow trading among themselves without any tariffs or trade restrictions. Under the **customs union,** a free trade area is established for member nations, with a uniform tariff imposed on trade with nonmember nations. The **common market** or economic union maintains a customs union and seeks to bring all government trade rules into agreement. The EC, the best example of a customs union, is moving in the direction of a common market.

Regardless of their approach, it seems certain that multinational economic communities will play a significant role in international business during the next decade. U.S. firms invested heavily in Western Europe in the 1960s basically because of the attraction of large markets offered by the EC. Multinational economic integration is forcing management to adapt its operations to meet the requirements of the economic associations.

friendship, commerce, and navigation (FCN) treaties
Treaties with other nations that include many aspects of international business relations such as the right to conduct business in a treaty partner's domestic market.

International Monetary Fund (IMF)
A fund established to lend foreign exchange to countries that require assistance in conducting international trade.

free trade area
A basic format for economic integration within which participants agree to allow trading among themselves without any tariffs or trade restrictions.

customs union
A basic format for economic integration within which a free trade area is established for member nations and a uniform tariff is imposed on trade with nonmember nations.

common market
A basic format for economic integration that maintains a customs union and seeks to bring all government trade rules into agreement.

TABLE 22–5

Regional Economic Associations

Name	Membership	Date of Origin
ANCOM: Andean Development Corporation (also called the Andean Common Market)	Bolivia, Colombia, Ecuador, Peru, Venezuela	1969
Council of Arab Economic Unity	Iraq, Jordan, Kuwait, Syria, Egypt, Sudan, Libya, Mauritania, Palestine Liberation Organization, Somalia, United Arab Emirates, Yemen Arab Republic, Yemen People's Democratic Republic	1964
ASEAN: Association of Southeast Asian Nations	Indonesia, Malaysia, Philippines, Singapore, Thailand	1967
Benelux	Belgium, Luxembourg, the Netherlands	1960
CACM: Central American Common Market	Costa Rica, El Salvador, Guatemala, Honduras, Nicaragua	1960
CARICOM: Caribbean Common Market	Antigua, Barbados, Dominica, Belize, Grenada, Guyana, Jamaica, Montserrat, St. Christopher-Nevis-Anguilla, St. Lucia, St. Vincent and the Grenadines, Trinidad, and Tobago	1973
CEAD: Communaute Economique de L'Afrique de L'ouest (West African Economic Community)	Ivory Coast, Mali, Mauritania, Niger, Senegal, Upper Volta (Observers are Benin and Togo.)	1974
CMEA: Council for Mutual Economic Assistance (also called COMECON)	Bulgaria, Czechoslovakia, East Germany, Hungary, Mongolian People's Republic, Poland, Romania, USSR, Cuba, Vietnam	1949
EC: European Community (also called the Common Market)	Belgium, France, West Germany, Italy, Luxembourg, the Netherlands, Denmark, Ireland, United Kingdom, Greece	1958
ECOWAS: Economic Community of West Africa States	Benin, Cape Verde, Gambia, Ghana, Guinea, Guinea-Bissau, Ivory Coast, Liberia, Mali, Mauritania, Niger, Nigeria, Senegal, Sierra Leone, Togo, Upper Volta	1975
EFTA: European Free Trade Association	Austria, Norway, Portugal, Sweden, Switzerland, Iceland, Finland (associate member)	1960
ALADI: Asociacion Latino-Americana de Integracion (Latin American Integration Association)	Argentina, Bolivia, Brazil, Chile, Colombia, Ecuador, Mexico, Paraguay, Peru, Uruguay, Venezuela	1980 (Replaced Lafta)
The Nordic Council	Denmark, Finland, Iceland, Norway, Sweden	1953
OCAM: Organisation Commune Africaine et Mauricienne	Central African Republic, Ivory Coast, Mauritius, Niger, Rwanda, Senegal, Togo, Upper Volta, Benin	1965
RCD: Regional Cooperation for Development	Iran, Pakistan, Turkey	1964
UDEAC: L'union Douaniere et Economique de L'Afrique Centrale (Customs and Economic Union of Central Africa)	Cameroon, Central African Republic, Congo, Gabon	1964

The Multinational Corporation

When IBM developed the System/360 computers, it followed a completely multinational approach by giving its United Kingdom, French, and German subsidiaries major responsibilities in the project. This international specialization speeded the overall task and generated enthusiasm in the participating subsidiaries.

A **multinational corporation** is one that operates on an international level. Ideally, the corporation should standardize its product lines to maximize production efficiency. Parts manufacturing should be done where it is most economical, and sales efforts should be concentrated where the market is growing fastest. Currently, four of the five leading U.S. multinationals are oil companies. Exxon heads the list, followed by Mobil, Texaco, Ford, and Standard Oil of California.[12]

multinational corporation A corporation that operates on an international level.

Ford Motor Company discovered that there are many problems in managing a multinational enterprise. Ford of Europe, the umbrella organization for an integrated manufacturing/marketing operation in Europe, is headquartered near London. It has large manufacturing plants in Britain and Germany and smaller factories in Belgium, France, Ireland, the Netherlands, and Portugal. The Ford organization has had to face, among other problems, British complaints that German-designed parts were too precise and German complaints that strikes in Britain delayed shipments. Still, Ford remains committed to the multinational approach. It seems likely that most major U.S. companies will follow the example set by Ford and continue to develop an international approach to their operations.

Multinational corporations have become so dominant in some foreign markets that they are now the object of close political and economic scrutiny. These firms have been criticized for their profit margins, investment policies, employment practices, market positions, and the like.

It seems likely that the multinational corporation will continue to be criticized in several areas, sometimes justifiably, sometimes not. Companies operating abroad must be sure that they act as fairly and responsibly overseas as they do at home.

The United States as a Foreign Market

The United States is a foreign market to many other countries. Our importation of huge quantities of oil highlights the importance of foreign resources to the U.S. economy. But the United States also depends on overseas firms for a variety of other goods and services. The Japanese, for example, have achieved a considerable share of U.S. electronics and automobile markets. The plant shutdown of the Youngstown Sheet and Tube Company in Youngstown, Ohio, symbolized to many the substantial inroads of foreign steel into the United States.

Foreign sellers can employ any of the five levels of international business involvement noted earlier. Some sellers—like the Japanese—have become major forces in a variety of markets. Direct foreign investments in the United States have increased substantially. Table 22–6 shows the 10 largest foreign investors in the United States. Foreign capital is evident everywhere in the United States, with investors constantly seeking out attractive opportunities.

A & P, Korvettes, Liggett, and Howard Johnson are now controlled by foreign interests.[13] And Texans were shocked when a sheik wanted to buy the Alamo for his son.

Many foreign nations actually conduct or coordinate their sales

TABLE 22–6
The Ten Largest Foreign Investors in the U.S.

Rank	Foreign Investor	Country	U.S. Company	Percent Owned	Industries
1	Anglo American Corporation of South Africa Ltd.	South Africa	Engelhard Mining & Chemical	29	Industrial materials
			Inspiration Consolidated Copper	50	Copper
			Terra Chemicals International	51	Fertilizer
			AMCON Group	100	Mining exploration, steel, scrap
			ARC America Corp.	100	Construction materials
			SKYTOP Brewster Rig	100	Oil rig manufacturing
			King Oil Tools	100	Oilfield equipment
			Mechanical Seal & Service	100	Oilfield equipment
2	Royal Dutch/ Shell Group	Netherlands United Kingdom	Shell Oil	69	Oil
			Scallop Holding	100	Oil, coal
3	British Petroleum Ltd.	United Kingdom	Standard Oil Ohio	53	Energy
4	Tengelmann Group	Germany	Great A&P Tea	47	Supermarkets
5	Friedrich Flick Group	Germany	WR Grace	27	Chemicals, consumer products
			US Filter	35	Pollution control, chemicals
6	B. A. T Industries Ltd.	United Kingdom	BATUS	100	Paper, retailing, tobacco
			Germaine Monteil	NA	Cosmetics
7	Générale Occidentale S.A.	France	Grand Union	100	Supermarkets
			J. Weingarten	100	Supermarkets
8	Beneficiaries of US Philips Trust	Netherlands	North American Philips	62	Electronics
9	Nestlé S.A.	Switzerland	Nestlé Co	100	Food
			Libby, McNeill & Libby	100	Food
			Stouffer Corp.	100	Food, restaurants
			Alcon Laboratories	100	Pharmaceuticals
			Beech-Nut Corp	100	Baby foods
10	Unilever N.V.	Netherlands	Lever Brothers	100	Consumer goods
			Thomas J. Lipton	100	Food
			National Starch & Chemical	100	Chemicals, starch

efforts in the United States through an agency or corporation of their own government. Agricultural and primary products are often marketed in this way.

People have shown a preference for some foreign products over their domestic competitors. Foreign cars, English china, Sony products, and French wine all have sizable shares of the U.S. market. Some foreign products, such as Mercedes automobiles, sell well in the United States because they have a quality image. Others sell well because they have a price advantage over domestic competitors.

What Is Dumping?

Just a few years ago almost no one knew what the term *dumping* meant. Now dumping is viewed as a threat to our economic system. **Dumping** is selling goods abroad at a price lower than that used for the domestic market. U.S. law specifically requires that imported items be sold for at least production costs plus 10 percent overhead plus 8 percent profit margin. If dumping is proved, punitive tariffs may be assigned to the dumped imports.

dumping
Selling goods abroad at a price lower than that charged in the domestic market.

But dumping is difficult to prove. Japanese steel firms, for instance, have balked at providing cost data essential to investigations in that industry. Furthermore, dumping complaints sometimes take up to 15 months to resolve. But more and more complaints are being filed with

Although the importation of foreign-made products is often blamed for the United States' economic problems, many people prefer certain foreign goods over their domestic competitors.

Reprinted by permission of Chronicle Features

Controversial Issue

Should the United States Limit the Import of Foreign Cars?

With thousands of auto workers out of work, with foreign car sales skyrocketing to 22 percent of all cars sold in the United States, with the Chrysler Corporation facing possible bankruptcy and Ford and General Motors reporting huge losses, the time is right to limit the import of foreign cars. Or is it?

The move to reduce the number of foreign car imports is primarily directed at Japan, which controls 78 percent of the U.S. auto import market. Spearheaded by the UAW, which has a vested interest in limiting foreign car imports, the import-restriction lobby points to a 25 percent projected drop in auto industry employment from now through 1985.

Part of the reason for skyrocketing foreign car sales is their lower sticker price. Where U.S. auto makers spend approximately $16 an hour per employee to build their cars, the Japanese spend only $8. The question of whether the production of smaller cars by increasingly automated systems will enable U.S. auto makers to offset their higher labor costs and compete with Japanese imports still gnaws at the industry's future. Auto analysts doubt whether this is possible without import curbs. The Department of Transportation warned that the current problems in Detroit posed a threat to national security and urged limits on Japanese imports.

Those in favor of import restraints point to government regulations that have increased car production costs. According to Ford Motor Company officials, if 18 emission and safety standard regulations were eliminated, the company would save $500 million over the next five years—a saving that would enable it to compete more effectively with the Japanese. Even if these regulations were eliminated (President Reagan proposed regulation relief), the need for import curbs still remains, say auto industry spokespeople. An import reduction would give the industry the time and financial backing it needs to retool for smaller, more fuel-efficient cars and help it equalize the $1,000 to $1,500 a car cost disadvantage it now faces.

Those who oppose restraints on foreign imports as a restriction of free trade believe that the U.S. auto industry has its own self-interest at heart and cares little for the plight of the American car buyer. They point to recent price increases that made Detroit's

the U.S. Treasury Department. Steel is the best-known battleground, although dumping has been alleged to occur in the sale of TV sets, CB radios, microwave ovens, and motorcycles.

Dumping is viewed by many people as an unfair business practice. While the United States remains committed to a free-trade philosophy, pressures exist to protect basic industries from unfair foreign compe-

ability to compete even less likely. While the Japanese held their 1980 price hikes to less than 5 percent, U.S. auto makers raised their base prices as high as 20 percent over 1979 prices.

With import curbs in place critics warn of increasing inflationary pressures. By raising the tariff on foreign cars from 2.9 percent to 20 percent, the price of a $7,000 Japanese import would increase by $500. In addition, fewer imports would also reduce competition and allow U.S. auto makers to raise the prices of their vehicles.

Those opposed to import curbs contend that by rewarding Detroit for its mistakes, we encourage mismanagement and incompetence instead of forcing the industry to take a long, hard look at its future needs. In addition, opponents charge, import restraints reward highly paid U.S. auto workers instead of forcing them to scale down their wage and benefit demands. Even with a two-year freeze in place, Chrysler workers earn considerably more than the average industrial wage. In the end, auto import restraints would cost American consumers more than $1 billion—a high price to pay to save 20,000 jobs. Opponents also fear that auto import quotas would encourage other industries to turn to the government for similar protectionist plans.

Whether the desire to protect the U.S. auto industry from increasing foreign competition is strong enough to convince Washington to tamper with the forces of the free marketplace depends largely on the country's economic health. Whatever the country's mood, both sides agree that it is preferable to negotiate a voluntary limit of Japanese imports and avoid legislation restricting the number of imports to 1.6 million cars a year for three years. Such a compromise would prevent protectionist repercussions from Western Europe and Japan and strained relations among Western trading partners.

After months of negotiations, the United States and Japan agreed on voluntary auto import limits on May 1, 1981. The agreement curbs the number of auto imports to 1.68 million for the first year and links second- and third-year imports to the growth of the U.S. auto market.

"Buy American" may have been the rallying cry of those favoring protective tariffs, but although protectionism might give Detroit some temporary relief from tough competition, is it really the way to cure the ills of the American auto industry?

tition, sometimes from firms actually owned by foreign governments. Another worry is that dumping complaints may lead to extensive trade warfare. It seems certain that the question of dumping will remain a vital public issue as long as the United States has massive trade deficits, relatively high unemployment, economically threatened industries, and related economic ills.

Government policy and public opinion on imports have varied over time. Relatively high unemployment usually leads to calls for higher tariff walls and severe import restrictions to protect U.S. industry and its employees. This economic protection argument has been voiced by both corporate management and labor union executives. The import market has often been used to accomplish economic and political objectives. For example, the Australian government once revalued its dollar upward to attract cheaper imports in an attempt to combat severe inflation.

It appears likely that imported goods will continue to grow in importance in the United States. The long-run trend is toward increased international trade. The Eastern countries are trading more even though it is contrary to their ideology. They seem to realize they are better off with increased trade.

Summary

International business is growing in importance. The United States is both the biggest exporter and the biggest importer in the world. About 25,000 U.S. firms are engaged in some type of international business activity.

The concept of international business includes the concepts of balance of trade (the relationship between exports and imports) and balance of payments (the difference between inward and outward cash flows).

Countries are usually better off if they specialize in certain products or commercial activities. A country has an absolute advantage in marketing a product if it is in a monopolistic position or produces the item at lowest cost. It has a comparative advantage if it can supply the product more efficiently or at lower cost than it can supply other products. Some countries refuse to specialize because they want to be self-sufficient, particularly in certain strategic areas.

The five levels of involvement in world business are casual or accidental exporting, active exporting, foreign licensing, overseas marketing by the firm, and foreign production and foreign marketing. The three primary obstacles to world business are economic, societal, and cultural obstacles; tariffs and trade restrictions; and political and legal obstacles.

There has been a movement toward multinational economic integration in many parts of the world. Three basic formats exist: the free trade area, the customs union, and the common market or economic union.

Multinational corporations—those operating internationally—have become so dominant in foreign markets that in several countries they are now the object of close scrutiny. Companies operating abroad should act fairly and responsibly.

The United States serves as a foreign market to other countries. In fact, many people show a preference for some foreign goods over their domestic counterparts. Some foreign products sell well because of their high-quality image, others because they are lower priced than domestic products.

Dumping—the selling of goods abroad at a price lower than they are sold domestically—is viewed as a great threat to the economic system. It is difficult to prove, however, and complaints take a long time to be resolved.

Key Terms

exporting
importing
balance of trade
balance of payments
devaluation
revaluation
exchange rate
floating exchange rate
absolute advantage
comparative advantage
tariffs
revenue tariffs
protective tariffs
General Agreement on
  Tariffs and
  Trade (GATT)

import quotas
embargo
exchange control
Webb-Pomerene Act
cartels
friendship, commerce, and navigation
  (FCN) treaties
International Monetary Fund (IMF)
free trade area
customs union
common market
multinational corporation
dumping

Review Questions

1. Explain each of the terms listed above.

2. Is it possible for a nation to have a favorable balance of trade and an unfavorable balance of payments? Explain.

3. Discuss the growing importance of international business.

4. Distinguish between the concepts of absolute advantage and comparative advantage.

5. Outline and discuss the five possible levels of involvement in international business.

6. Explain the difference between a revenue tariff and a protective tariff.

7. Describe the three basic formats for multinational economic integration.

8. Discuss the United States as a foreign market for overseas competitors.

9. What types of products does the United States export? What types does it import?

10. Outline the major obstacles to international business.

Discussion Questions and Exercises

1. Evaluate the pros and cons of the controversial issue that appears in this chapter.

2. Prepare a report on the use of import quotas and embargoes by the United States from its founding to the present.

3. Prepare a report on the operation of the International Monetary Fund.

4. Many people believe that we should limit automobile imports in order to protect the jobs of U.S. workers and restore domestic manufacturers to profitability. On the other hand, the Federal Trade Commission estimates that limiting imports would increase consumer costs $3–$5 billion. Similarly, the commission estimates that a 20 percent tariff—rather than the existing 2.9 percent levy—would cost American consumers $5.6–$6.6 billion.[14] Set up a classroom debate on the question: whom should we protect—American workers or American consumers?

5. Prepare a report about the alleged dumping by the international steel industry on the U.S. domestic market. What are your major conclusions?

Case 22–1: PRA—A Fact of Life in International Business

PRA refers to political risk assessment. With the recent political turmoil in Iran, El Salvador, South Korea, and Nicaragua, many U.S. firms are seeking out research analyzing the relative risks of doing business abroad. Political risk assessment (PRA) is available from several sources. Business Environment Risk Index (BERI) ranks the risk of doing business in a certain country on a 1–100 scale. Frost & Sullivan's World Political Risk Forecasts (WPRF) assign a probability to future losses. Business International provides a Country Assessment Service analysis for 71 countries around the globe. And many large firms like American Can, General Electric, TRW, and General Motors have now set up in-house PRA departments.

The trend toward political risk assessment has been criticized in that the subjective opinion of informed observers is often quantified when reported to management, which implies a precision that isn't really there. There is also often considerable divergence in PRA ratings among consultants. Another criticism is that a PRA may not provide plans for dealing with a perceived risk.

Despite the criticisms, more and more companies are subscribing to the PRA services. The annual cost (BERI, $500; WPRF, $1500) is minimal considering the overseas investments made by many firms. Another indication of the growing importance of the field is the formation of a professional organization—Association of Political Risk Analysts (APRA).

Questions

1. Assume you have been hired by a small multinational corporation as an internal PRA analyst. How would you go about your task?

2. To what uses do you feel a PRA report might be put by the management of a multinational corporation?

3. Discuss the possible conflicts between private political risk assessment and the work of the U.S. Department of State. Why are many companies seeking their own analysis rather than relying on that available from the government?

Case 22–2: The Thai Industrial Standards Institute

Many Thailand businesspeople are impressed with the fact that Japan's success in international business is often credited to its national policies regulating standardization and quality control. The lack of adequate product standards has been a traditional problem for Thai executives. Thai pineapples and tapioca exports failed on U.S. and European markets because they did not meet recognized packing standards.

The Thai Industrial Standards Institute is trying to correct this situation with assistance from the United Nations Development Program and the United Nations Industrial Development Organization. Fourteen products are subject to mandatory standards. Export products where safety is an important factor are among those with required standards.

The Institute is now trying to get other Thai industries to accept voluntary standards. The program is backed by regular government inspections. The Institute, which uses a mark to identify approved products, has also launched a domestic campaign to inform Thai consumers of the value of its program. The Institute can point to some success stories such as the fish sauce producer that overwhelmed the competition when the company qualified for and used the Institute's standards compliance mark.

Questions

1. Why would this type of program be so important to Thai exporters?

2. Can you think of other situations where quality standards have had a major impact on international business?

3. How would you assess the strengths and weaknesses of U.S. exporters in this area?

23

Business and the Legal System

Learning Goals

1. To explain the meaning of law and the nature of business law

2. To analyze the structure of the judicial system

3. To identify the major aspects of business life

4. To describe how competition is regulated in the United States

5. To explain key federal business regulations

6. To explain the meaning of each of the key terms introduced in this chapter

Profile: Anthony L. Lanese, Jr.
Maraschino Cherries and the FDA

Anthony L. Lanese, Jr., knows what it's like to have to comply with government regulations—even when the rules he's forced to follow almost destroy his business.

Lanese's business is the Genoa Cherry Company located in West New York, New Jersey. As manufacturers of maraschino cherries since 1931, Genoa Cherry used food, drug, and cosmetic (FD&C) red dye No. 4 as its coloring agent—a dye the Food and Drug Administration (FDA) took off the market because of lack of proven safety.

Genoa Cherry, like all the other firms in the maraschino cherry industry, was forced to comply with the FD&C red No. 4 ban, even though it considered the ruling completely unjust. To continue in operation, the firm turned to FD&C red No. 40, a color approved by the FDA. The change from one dye to another threw Genoa Cherry and the entire maraschino cherry industry into a state of financial havoc—a situation that resulted in lost sales and lost profits to some firms and the closing down of others.

"When the government came out with its first statements about the safety of FD&C red No. 4, there were about 50 firms in the maraschino cherry business," says Lanese. "Today, there are about 25." According to Lanese, "the small firms didn't have the technological know-how or the capital to make the change to FD&C red No. 40. Even mid-size firms like us had to struggle. It took us years to work through the problems with FD&C red No. 40. Our first tries were disastrous. The color was wrong—our cherries even changed color on the shelves. The smaller businesses that waited for the last minute to make the change never had a chance.

"The ironic thing about the whole problem," continues Lanese, "is that we were hit hardest before the actual delisting took place. Our business dropped 26 percent when the government put FD&C red No. 4 on provisional status—a status that only means that more tests are being run to prove product safety. People panicked when they heard words like bladder lesions and adrenal atrophy thrown around. They avoided our product like the plague. It took us nine years to get our sales back to where they were."

Lanese points out that because of the FDA's controversial actions, the maraschino cherry industry never reached its growth potential, even though the firms that survived did well. "Each of the businesses that made it through this period got a greater share of the pie. They simply took up the slack left by the firms that failed. But these gains had nothing to do with greater public demand, and that fact hurts our future growth."

Lanese is angry about the FDA's power to turn an industry inside out even when, according to him, they have no hard proof of product danger. "When a regulatory agency makes a decision like this, an industry may never recover. The stigma often lasts forever. People will always think of us whenever any food additive gets bad press."

"In the end," says Lanese sadly, "regulatory actions that cause this kind of fallout hurt business badly. And if you think about it, the public loses too."

Anyone who sells butter containing stones or other things [to add to the weight] will be put into our pillory, then said butter will be placed on his head until entirely melted by the sun. Dogs may lick him and people offend him with whatever defamatory epithets they please without offense to God or King. If the sun is not warm enough, the accused will be exposed in the great hall of the gaol in front of a roaring fire, where everyone will see him.

—*Edict of Louis XI, King of France, 1481*

U.S. Senator John Melcher of Montana has firsthand knowledge of the extent of business law and regulation—much of it created by Congress and other legislative bodies. Melcher still continues to receive Census Bureau letters threatening a $500 fine if he does not provide information about his veterinary practice—a business he closed in 1969.[1] While the Census Bureau may have been a little overzealous in Senator Melcher's case, the legal system is a pervasive aspect of contemporary business.

Business must operate within the legal framework of federal, state, and local governments, and business law is playing an increasingly important role in the private enterprise system. Executives are not expected to be attorneys, but they should be aware of the various legal requirements that affect their management decision making.

What Is Law?

Law is the standards set by government and society in the form of either legislation or custom. Arising from state and federal constitutions that originally established the forms of government, our complex body of law consists primarily of legislation and legal decisions (see Focus 23–1). The laws are enforced through a judicial system, and citizens who do not obey them are subject to legal action by that system.

This broad body of principles, regulations, rules, and customs that governs the actions of all members of society, including business, is derived from several sources. **Common law** refers to the body of law arising out of judicial decisions related to the unwritten law the United States inherited from England. This unwritten law is based on custom and court decisions of early England.

law
Standards set by government and society in the form of either legislation or custom.

common law
The body of law arising out of judicial decisions related to the unwritten law the United States inherited from England.

FOCUS 23–1
Our Amusing Legal System

The American legal system is well known for its complexity. It seems that we have regulated almost everything at one time or in one place. And many of these laws remain on the books today. Consider the following:

1. Louisiana prohibits gargling in public.

2. Orlando, Florida, prohibits snake charming within the city limits.

3. Dyersburg, Tennessee, forbids women to call men for a date.

4. Sault Ste. Marie, Michigan, outlaws spitting into the wind.

5. Ashland, Wisconsin, prohibits children from playing marbles for keeps.

6. Windemere, Florida, forbids bartenders to serve a man if a written warning has been received from the man's wife, children, or parents.

7. The Commonwealth of Kentucky does not allow men to marry their wives' grandmothers.

8. Michigan does not permit crocodiles to be hitched to fire hydrants.

9. Lexington, Kentucky, does not allow people to carry ice cream cones in their pockets.

10. Oxford, Ohio, forbids women to undress in front of a man's photograph.

11. Auchula, Florida, forbids its citizens to criticize the city.

12. Hammond, Indiana, has made the throwing of watermelon seeds on the sidewalk illegal.

But perhaps Helena, Montana, has gone the farthest in regulating its citizens. Helena has outlawed "unrestrained giggling." Perhaps Helena's residents have just too many of the laws by which Americans are expected to live.

statutory law
Written law that includes state and federal constitutions, legislative enactments, treaties of the federal government, and ordinances of towns, cities, and other local governments.

While common law plays an important role in today's legal system, the primary sources of law now are the statutory rules of the 50 state legislatures and the various acts passed by the U.S. Congress. **Statutory law,** or written law, includes state and federal constitutions, legislative enactments, treaties of the federal government, and ordinances of towns, cities, and other local governments. There is now less reliance on the unwritten, common law and more on statutory or written law as legislative bodies enact new rules in most areas of legal and governmental concern.

Of course, statutory law should not be regarded as a set body of rules and regulations. Statutes must be drawn in a precise and reasonable manner in order to be constitutional (and thus enforceable), but courts are frequently called upon to interpret their intention and meaning. The court rulings result in statutory laws being expanded, contracted, modified, or even discarded altogether.

Law also changes as the nation and society change. No system of law, written or unwritten, is permanent. Laws reflect the beliefs of the people they regulate, and both courts and legislatures are aware of this fact. Laws are constantly being added, repealed, or modified as the requirements of society and government dictate.

The Nature of Business Law

In a broad sense all law is business law, because all business entities—however they are organized—are subject to the entire body of law in the same manner as citizens are. But in a narrower sense, **business law** consists of those aspects of law that most directly and specifically influence and regulate the management of various types of business activity.

business law
Those aspects of law that most directly and specifically influence and regulate management of various types of business activity.

The term *business law* includes all law that is of concern to business, although particular areas of legal emphasis vary widely from business to business and from industry to industry. Laws affecting small firms are different from those governing large corporations. The legal interests of the automobile industry differ from those of real estate developers.

The Internal Revenue Code is an example of a law written by Congress that has universal application. However, numerous federal laws regulate only one industry such as oil and gas drilling or television communications. State and local laws also have varying applications. Some state statutes effectively regulate all business conduct in a particular state, regardless of the size or nature of the enterprise. Workers' compensation laws, which govern payments to workers for injuries incurred on the job, are an example. Other state statutes control only certain businesses or business activities: the so-called blue laws, which regulate the extent to which businesses—particularly retailers—can operate on Sundays, are an example of this kind of narrow control.

Law is important to all aspects of business. No owner, manager, or employee can conduct any type of business activity without reference to some laws. All business decisions must take into account the legal consequences. Some decisions must involve in-depth legal planning and review, while others need have only an implied or subconscious reference to the law.

Business decision makers gain experience and expertise in applying legal standards to their decisions in much the same manner as they develop any other management skill—through constant use and refinement. When legality cannot be determined through the experience and judgment of the businessperson, other professionals—such as lawyers, government employees, and elected officials—must be consulted. Generally, the more complex the business objective, the more complex is the role of law.

The Court System

judiciary
The branch of government charged with deciding disputes among parties through the application of laws.

The **judiciary,** or court system, is that branch of government charged with deciding disputes among parties through the application of laws. The judiciary is comprised of several types and levels of courts, each with specific jurisdiction. Court systems are organized at the federal, state, and local levels. Administrative agencies also have some limited judicial functions, but these agencies are more properly regarded as belonging to the executive or legislative branches of government.

Trial Courts

trial courts
Courts of general jurisdiction operating at both the federal and state levels that hear a wide range of cases.

At both the federal and state levels there are **trial courts**—courts of general jurisdiction—that hear a wide range of cases. Unless a case is assigned by law to another court or to an administrative agency, the court of general jurisdiction is empowered to hear it. The majority of cases, both criminal and civil, are heard by these courts. Within the federal system the trial courts are known as United States district courts, and at least one such court exists in each state. In the state court systems the general jurisdiction courts are known as circuit courts, and in most states there is one for each county. Some states call their general courts by other names such as superior courts, common pleas courts, or district courts.

The state judiciary systems also have a wide range of courts of lesser or specific jurisdiction. These courts have limited jurisdiction in that they hear only a certain size or type of case, as set forth by statute or constitution. In most states decisions of the lesser courts can be appealed to the general jurisdiction courts. Examples of lesser courts are probate courts (where deceased persons' estates are settled) and small claims courts (where people can represent themselves in suits involving small amounts of damage).

Appellate Courts

appellate courts
Courts that hear appeals from the general trial courts.

Both the federal and the state systems have **appellate courts** that hear appeals from the general trial courts. An appeal usually is filed when the losing party feels that the case was wrongly decided by the judge or jury.

The appeals process allows a higher court to review the case and correct any lower court error complained of by the **appellant,** the party making the appeal. The federal appeals system, together with that of most states, consists of two tiers of courts. The courts at the federal intermediate level are called U.S. circuit courts of appeal, and each such court hears cases from the U.S. district courts of several states. The intermediate level of state appellate courts—if it exists—is known as the court of appeals or the district court of appeals in most states.

appellant
The party making an appeal for a higher court to review a case.

Appeals from the U.S. circuit courts of appeal can go to the highest court of the land, the U.S. Supreme Court. Appeals from the state courts of appeal are heard by the highest court in each state, usually called the state supreme court. In states without intermediate courts, the state supreme court hears appeals directly from the trial courts. Parties not satisfied by the verdict of a state supreme court can appeal to the U.S. Supreme Court, if grounds for such an appeal exist and if the Supreme Court considers the case significant enough to be heard. In a typical year, the U.S. Supreme Court usually decides to hear about 155 of the 5,500 appeals filed.[2]

While the great majority of cases are resolved by the system of courts described here, certain highly specialized cases require the expertise of special courts. Such cases are assigned to the special courts by constitutional provision or statute. Examples of specialized federal courts are the U.S. Tax Court (which hears tax cases) and the U.S. Court of Claims (which hears claims against the U.S. government itself). Similar specialized courts exist in many of the state court systems.

Administrative Agencies

Administrative agencies—also known as bureaus, commissions, or boards—are organized at all levels of government. Their powers and responsibilities are sometimes derived from constitutional provisions, but usually they come from state or federal statutes. Administrative agencies decide a variety of cases. Technically, they conduct hearings or inquiries rather than trials. But the parties are often represented by attorneys, evidence and testimony are included, and the agencies issue legally binding decisions based on the regulations involved.

administrative agencies
Government agencies at all levels that are empowered (by state or federal statutes and constitutional provisions) to hear and decide a variety of cases.

Examples of federal administrative agencies with extensive powers are the Federal Trade Commission, the National Labor Relations Board, and the Federal Power Commission. The major federal administrative agencies are described in Figure 23–1. Examples at the state level are public utility commissions, boards that govern the licensing of various trades and professions, and other state regulatory bodies. At the local (city or county) level are zoning boards, planning commissions, boards of appeal, and other administrative agencies concerned with similar matters.

THE MAJOR FEDERAL REGULATORS

 Federal Communications Commission
FCC
Founded in 1934

Seven Commissioners license radio and television stations and oversee interstate and international telephone and telegraph operations.

 Federal Power Commission
FPC
Founded in 1920

Five Commissioners set wholesale rates for the interstate transportation and sale of natural gas and for interstate transmission of electricity.

 Civil Aeronautics Board
CAB
Founded in 1938

Five Commissioners determine interstate airline routes, passenger fares and freight rates.

 Securities and Exchange Commission
SEC
Founded in 1934

Five Commissioners regulate securities issues, supervise stock exchanges and regulate holding and investment companies.

 Federal Reserve Board
FRB
Founded in 1913

Seven-member Board of Governors sets monetary and credit policy and regulates commercial banks belonging to the Federal Reserve System.

 Equal Employment Opportunity Commission
EEOC
Founded in 1964

Five Commissioners investigate and rule on charges of racial and other discrimination by employers and labor unions.

 Environmental Protection Agency
EPA
Founded in 1970

An Administrator develops and enforces environmental-quality standards for air, water and noise pollution and for toxic substances and pesticides.

 Food and Drug Administration
FDA
Founded in 1931

A Commissioner in the Department of Health, Education and Welfare sets standards for certain foods and drugs and issues licenses for the manufacturing and distribution of drugs.

 Federal Trade Commission
FTC
Founded in 1914

Five Commissioners enforce some antitrust laws, protect businesses from unfair competition and enforce truth-in-lending and truth-in-labeling laws.

 Interstate Commerce Commission
ICC
Founded in 1887

Eleven Commissioners set rates, routes and practices for interstate railroads, truckers, bus companies and pipelines.

 Consumer Product Safety Commission
CPSC
Founded in 1972

Five Commissioners set product-safety standards and initiate recall notices for defective products.

 Federal Aviation Administration
FAA
Founded in 1948

An Administrator in the Department of Transportation certifies airworthiness of aircraft, licenses pilots and sets safety standards for airports.

 Federal Energy Administration
FEA
Founded in 1974

An Administrator regulates price and allocation controls of petroleum products.

 Nuclear Regulatory Commission
NRC
Founded in 1975

Five Commissioners issue licenses for the design, construction and operation of nuclear power plants.

FIGURE 23–1
The major federal regulators.

The decisions of most administrative agencies can be appealed to the courts of general jurisdiction or to other specified appellate courts. Many businesses have regular contact with federal, state, and local administrative agencies, even though they have almost no contact with the regular court system.

Important Aspects of Business Law

Most laws affect business in some manner, whether directly or indirectly. But certain laws are so vital to business enterprises that every businessperson should understand their roles in the legal framework.

Contract Law

Contract law is important because it affects most aspects of any business operation. It is the legal foundation on which normal business dealings are constructed.

A **contract** is an agreement that the law will enforce.[3] The key element is that there must be an agreement among the parties as to the act or thing specified. In order for such an agreement, or contract, to be valid and enforceable through the courts, **consideration**—the value or benefit that a party provides to the others with whom the contract exists—must be furnished by each party to the contract. Legal consideration for a contract exists when, for example, A agrees to work for B and B agrees to pay A a certain salary. The contract is just as valid if B actually pays A at the time A agrees to work. Similarly, valid consideration exists even if no promises are exchanged but A works for B and B pays A for the work.

In addition to consideration, an enforceable contract must involve a legal and serious agreement. Agreements made in a joking manner or relating to purely social matters or involving the commission of a crime are not enforceable as legal contracts. An agreement between two competitors to fix the prices for their products is not enforceable as a contract, because the subject matter is illegal and because the performance of the agreement will violate the law.

The last element of a legally enforceable contract is the capacity of each party to make the agreement. **Capacity** is the legal ability of a party to enter into agreements. The law does not permit certain persons, such as those judged to be insane, to enter into legally enforceable contracts.

Contracts are used in almost all types of business activities. Generally, they are created and executed by the firms with little notice or concern on the part of the contracting parties. Examples of valid contracts are purchase agreements with suppliers, labor contracts, group insurance policies for employees, franchise agreements, and sales contracts.

Sales Law

The law of sales is an offspring of contract law. But the sales agreement, or sales transaction, is a special kind of contract that is entered into millions of times each day throughout the economic system. **Sales law** involves the sale of goods or products for money or on credit. As an economic transaction, sales can be of services or real estate as well as goods, but the law of sales is concerned only with the transfer of tangible personal property. The law involved with intangible personal property and real estate will be examined later in the chapter.

Executives must be concerned not only with the body of general contract law but also with the specifics of sales law. Sales law has evolved in a distinct manner. It goes back to ancient English law that consisted largely of the customs of merchants and included a system

---

contract law
The legal foundation on which normal business dealings are constructed.

contract
An agreement among two or more parties regarding a specified act or thing that the law will enforce.

consideration
The value or benefit that one party provides to the others with whom a contract is made. Each party to the contract must furnish consideration in order for the agreement to be valid and enforceable.

capacity
The legal ability of a party to enter into agreements.

sales law
An offspring of contract law that involves the sale of goods or products for money or credit.

of merchant courts to resolve disputes. Many of these customs and practices were adopted in the United States as part of common law. Later, the Uniform Commercial Code provided uniformity in all commercial law, including sales law.

The **Uniform Commercial Code (UCC),** originally drafted in 1952, is a comprehensive commercial law that has been adopted by all states except Louisiana. The UCC covers the law of sales as well as other specific areas of commercial law.

Article 2 of the UCC specifies the circumstances under which sales contracts are entered into by seller and buyer. Ordinarily such agreements are based on the express conduct of the parties. Under the UCC, enforceable sales contracts must also generally be in writing if goods worth more than $500 are involved. The formation of the sales contract is quite flexible, because certain missing terms in the written contract or other ambiguities do not keep it from being legally enforceable. A court will look to past dealings, commercial customs, and other standards of reasonableness in evaluating the existence of a legal contract.

These variables will also be considered by a court when either the buyer or the seller seeks to enforce his or her rights against the other party where the sales contract has not been performed or has been only partially performed or where performance has been defective or unsatisfactory. The UCC's remedies in such cases consist largely of monetary damages awarded to the injured party. The UCC defines the rights of the parties to have the contract specifically performed, to have it terminated, and to reclaim the goods or have a lien placed against them.

Article 2 also sets forth the law of warranty for sales transactions. There are two basic types of warranties. **Express warranties** are specific representations made by the seller regarding the goods. **Implied warranties** are those legally imposed on the seller. Generally, unless implied warranties are disclaimed by the seller in writing, they are automatically effective. Other provisions of Article 2 govern the rights of acceptance, rejection, and inspection of the goods by the buyer; the rights of the parties during manufacture, shipment, delivery, and the passing of title to goods; the legal significance of sales documents such as bills of lading; and the placing of the risk of loss in the event of destruction or damage to the goods during manufacture, shipment, or delivery.

Two decades of court interpretation of UCC provisions have substantially cleared up the problem areas that exist in any new statutory law. On balance, the UCC has been a major step forward in sales law.

Property Law

Property law is not only an important part of the private enterprise system, it is also a key feature of the democratic way of life. **Property**

Uniform Commercial Code (UCC)
A comprehensive commercial law adopted by all states except Louisiana that covers the law of sales as well as other specific areas of commercial law.

express warranties
Warranties with specific representations made by the seller regarding the goods.

implied warranties
Warranties legally imposed on the seller and, generally, automatically effective unless disclaimed by the seller in writing.

property
Something for which people have the unrestricted right of possession or use.

refers to the unrestricted right to possess and use something. Property rights are guaranteed and protected by the U.S. Constitution.

Property can be divided into several categories. **Tangible personal property** consists of physical things such as goods and products. Every business is concerned with this kind of property, which includes equipment, supplies, and delivery vehicles.

Intangible personal property is property that is most often represented by a document or other instrument in writing, although it may be as vague and remote as a bookkeeping or computer entry. Certain intangible personal properties such as personal checks and money orders are well known. Others, although less widespread or well known, are important to the businesses or individuals who own and utilize them. Examples are stocks, bonds, treasury bills and notes, letters of credit, and warehouse receipts. Mortgages are also technically intangible personal property.

The last major branch of property law is that of **real property,** or real estate. Some real property customs have been formalized in statutes. There is also case law to guide real-property owners in their transactions and conduct. All firms have some concern with real estate law because of the need to own or occupy the space or building where business is conducted. The real estate needs of national retail chains or major manufacturing companies are indeed considerable. Some businesses are created to serve the real estate needs of others. Real estate developers, builders, contractors, brokers, mortgage companies, and architects are all concerned with various aspects of real property law.

The Law of Agency

Agency describes a legal relationship in which two parties, the principal and the agent, "agree that one will act as a representative of the other. The **principal** is the person who wishes to accomplish something, and the **agent** is the one employed to act in the principal's behalf to achieve it."[4]

While the agency relationship can arise as simply as one family member acting on behalf of another, the legal concept is most closely associated with business relationships. This is true because all types of firms conduct business affairs through a variety of agents—among them partners, directors, corporate officers, and sales personnel.

The law of agency is based on common law principles and case decisions of the state and federal courts. Relatively little agency law has been enacted into statute. The law of agency is important because the principal is generally bound by the actions of the agent.

The legal basis for holding the principal liable for acts of the agent is the Latin maxim of *respondeat superior* ("let the master answer"). In cases involving agency law, the courts must decide the rights and obligations of the various parties. Generally, the principal is held liable where an agency relationship existed and the agent had some general

tangible personal property
Physical things, such as goods and products.

intangible personal property
Property most often represented by a document or other instrument in writing, although it may be as vague and remote as a bookkeeping or computer entry.

real property
Real estate.

agency
A legal relationship between two parties, principal and agent, who agree that one will act as a representative of the other.

principal
The person who, wishing to accomplish something, hires an agent to act on his behalf.

agent
The person employed to act in the principal's behalf.

authority to do the wrongful act. The agent in such cases is liable to the principal for any damages caused to that person. Principals have no responsibility for the acts of persons who are not their agents.

The Law of Torts

tort
A civil wrong inflicted on other persons or their property.

Torts (French for "wrongs") refers to civil wrongs inflicted on other persons or their property.[5] The law of torts is closely related to the law of agency, because the business entity, or principal, can be held liable for the torts committed by its agents in the course of business dealings. Tort law differs from both criminal and contract law. While criminal law is concerned with crimes against the state or society, tort law deals with compensating injured persons who are the victims of noncriminal wrongs. For example, the Elliot-Hamil Funeral Home of Abilene, Texas, filed a $311,000 lawsuit against Southwestern Bell, when the telephone company listed the mortuary under "Frozen Foods–Wholesale" in the *Yellow Pages,* causing a rash of crank calls.[6]

intentional torts
Civil wrongs purposely inflicted on other persons or their property, such as assault, embezzlement, slander, or libel.

Many torts, such as assault, are intentional actions carried out by the wrongdoer (although sometimes the person argues that while the actions were intentional the damages were not). Examples of **intentional torts** are embezzlement, trespass, slander, libel, and fraud. Business can become involved in such cases through the actions of both owners and employees. The supermarket clerk who manhandles a suspected shoplifter and holds the suspect in the manager's office for questioning may have committed a tort if the conduct is excessive or otherwise unjustified. Under agency law, the store owner can be held liable for any damages or injury caused to the suspect.

negligence
A tort based on careless rather than intentional behavior that causes injury to another person.

The other major group of torts is **negligence.** This type of tort is based on careless (rather than intentional) behavior that causes injury to another person. Under agency law, businesses are held liable for the negligence of their employees or agents. The delivery truck driver who kills a pedestrian while delivering goods creates tort liability for the employer if the accident is a result of negligence. Similarly, an airline is liable if a plane crashes because of faulty maintenance, pilot error, or other negligence.

products liability
An area of tort law developed by both statutory and case law to hold business liable for negligence in the design, manufacture, sale, and use of products.

An area of tort law known as **products liability** has been developed by both statutory and case law to hold business liable for negligence in the design, manufacture, sale, and use of products. An Oklahoma court awarded $125,000 to a man who had drunk over half of a soft drink before discovering that the bottle also contained a dead rat.[7]

strict products liability
A legal concept that extends the tort theory to cover injuries caused by products regardless of whether the manufacturer is proven negligent.

Some states have extended the theory of tort to cover injuries by products regardless of whether the manufacturer is proven negligent. Under this legal concept, known as **strict products liability,** the injured party need only show "(1) that the product was defective, (2) that the defect was the proximate cause of injury, and (3) that the defect caused the product to be unreasonably dangerous."[8]

Careful supervision of employees and careful conduct by employees in their duties are the best means of avoiding most tort liability. However, with tort damages running higher and higher, most firms have turned to liability insurance for protection.

Even the U.S. Consumer Product Safety Commission has been affected by this area of law. The commission once had to recall 80,000 lapel buttons promoting safe toys because of sharp edges, high levels of lead content in the paint, and clips that could break off in a child's mouth and be swallowed.[9]

Bankruptcy Law

Bankruptcy—the legal nonpayment of financial obligations—is a common occurrence in contemporary society. Some 355,000 bankruptcies (usually of individuals rather than companies) were filed in 1980. The previous high was 254,484 filings in 1975.[10] Lenders lose an estimated $1 to $2 billion annually to bankruptcies. The tremendous increase in bankruptcies was attributed to 1980's poor economic climate, a recession coupled with tighter credit restrictions, and a new law that made bankruptcy a more realistic alternative for many people.

The days of debtor prisons and deportation are long past. Federal legislation passed in 1918 and revised in 1938 and 1978 provides for an orderly handling of bankruptcies by the federal court system. The bankruptcy procedure allows the individual or company to get a fresh start. Two types of bankruptcies are recognized. Under voluntary bankruptcy, a person or firm asks to be judged bankrupt because of an inability to pay off creditors. Under involuntary bankruptcy, the creditors may request that a party be judged bankrupt.

The Federal Bankruptcy Reform Act of 1978

The latest revision to bankruptcy law—the **Federal Bankruptcy Reform Act of 1978**—is the subject of considerable debate (see case 23–1). The new law was designed to help people get out from under excessive debts often caused by circumstances beyond their control such as job layoffs. The lending industry believes that the reform goes too far in permitting people to escape their debts.

Changes in personal bankruptcies. It costs $60 to file for bankruptcy in a U.S. district court. The entire process can often be concluded in 90 days. Two options are available. Chapter 13 of the new law—the wage-earner plan—allows a person to set up a three-year debt repayment plan. Debtors often end up repaying only 10

bankruptcy
The legal nonpayment of financial obligations.

Federal Bankruptcy Reform Act of 1978
The latest version of the bankruptcy law designed to help people combat excessive debts caused by circumstances beyond their control through a three-year debt repayment plan or a liquidation plan.

percent of what they owe. The other alternative—Chapter 7—is a liquidation plan where the assets are divided among the creditors. Initial selection of Chapter 13 does not preclude a later switch to Chapter 7.

The new law liberalized the property that is not subject to the claims of creditors. These exemptions are:

1. House equity of $7,500.
2. Motor vehicle equity of $1,200.
3. $200 on each personal item such as household furnishings, clothes, books, and so on.
4. $500 of personal jewelry.
5. Another $400 of any other property.
6. Tools of one's trade or prescribed health items up to $750.

Husbands and wives filing jointly can double the amounts noted above. And individual states can set even higher allowances. California, for example, allows a head of household to exempt $30,000 in home equity.

Changes in business bankruptcies. While the personal bankruptcy changes have attracted the most attention, the recent reform has also had an impact on business bankruptcies. The primary differences are that the 1978 bill toughened the rules against hiding assets from creditors and made it easier for creditors to force involuntary bankruptcy.

Negotiable Instruments

negotiable instruments
Forms of commercial paper that are transferable among individuals and businesses.

Negotiable instruments are forms of commercial paper that are transferrable among individuals and businesses. The most commonplace example of a negotiable instrument is a check; drafts, certificates of deposit, and notes are also sometimes considered negotiable instruments.

Article 3 of the UCC specifies that a negotiable instrument must be written and must:

1. Be signed by the maker or drawer.
2. Contain an unconditional promise or order to pay a certain sum in money.
3. Be payable on demand or at a definite time.
4. Be payable to order or to bearer.

indorsement
The procedure that renders commercial paper transferable when the payee signs the back of the instrument.

Checks and other forms of commercial paper are transferred when the payee signs the back of the instrument, a procedure known as **indorsement.** The four basic kinds of indorsement described by Article 3 of the UCC are:

1. Blank indorsement, which consists only of the name of the payee. All that is required to make a blank indorsement is to sign the back

of the instrument. This makes it payable to the bearer. A blank indorsement should not be used if the instrument is to be mailed.

2. Special indorsement, which specifies the person to whom the instrument is payable. With this kind of indorsement, only the person whose name appears after "Pay to the order of . . ." can further the negotiability of the instrument.

3. Qualified indorsement, which contains wording that the indorser is not guaranteeing payment of the instrument. The qualified indorsement of "Without recourse, (signed) . . ." will limit the indorser's liability in the event the instrument is not backed by sufficient funds.

4. Restrictive indorsement, which limits the negotiability of the instrument. One of the most common restrictive indorsements is "For deposit only." Its value is great in the case of a lost or stolen instrument, because it means that the instrument, usually a check, can only be deposited to the indicated account; it cannot be cashed.[11]

Patents, Trademarks, and Copyrights

Patents, trademarks, and copyrights are important legal protection for key business assets, and they are carefully guarded by their owners.

Patents guarantee inventors exclusive rights to their inventions for 17 years, provided the inventions are accepted by the U.S. Patent Office. Along with copyrights, patents have a constitutional basis. The Constitution specifies that the federal government has the power "to promote the progress of science and useful arts, by securing for limited Times to Authors and Inventors the exclusive Right to their respective Writings and Discoveries." Patent owners sometimes license the use of the patent to others for a fee.

patents
Guarantees to inventors of exclusive rights to their inventions for 17 years, provided the inventions are accepted by the U.S. Patent Office.

Trademarks (and brand names) are words, symbols, or other designations used by businesses to identify their products. The Lanham Act (1946) provides for federal registration of trademarks, which, once registered, are protected for as long as the registrant desires. However, if a trademark becomes the generic term for a class of products, then the registrant loses this important protection. Aspirin, nylon, kerosene, linoleum, shredded wheat, and milk of magnesia were once the exclusive properties of their manufacturers, but they became generic terms, and now anyone can use them.[12] Some firms take unique steps to protect their trademarks. Wham-O Manufacturing Company once sent a Pittsburgh newspaper a hundred flying saucers labeled "pittsburgh press" after the paper had failed to capitalize their trademark name Frisbee.[13]

Trademarks can become very valuable assets. Faberge reportedly paid $200,000 to a California cosmetic firm in order to be able to use the trademark Macho for a new men's cologne.[14]

Copyrights are filed with the Library of Congress. Under the 1978 revision to the copyright law, authors or their heirs hold exclusive rights to their published or unpublished works for the author's lifetime

copyrights
Protection of an individual's exclusive rights to materials such as books, photos, and cartoons.

plus 50 years. Works for hire and anonymous or pseudonymous works receive copyright protection for a period of 75 years from publication or 100 years from creation, whichever is shorter. Copyrights protect written material such as this textbook, designs, cartoon illustrations, photos, and so on.

Regulation of Competition

The legal framework influences and regulates business in many areas, including that of competition. Effective and ongoing competition is the cornerstone of the private enterprise economy. The laissez-faire ("hands off") doctrine in effect during the first hundred years of the existence of the United States was ideal for the rapid growth of the nation—geographically, politically, and economically.

But as the country developed and matured, economic abuses and an overconcentration of economic power in a few hands crept into the private enterprise system, and the result was monopolization of certain basic industries. Mergers of powerful groups of companies and industries further concentrated economic power and caused problems that led directly to government intervention.

When government regulation of competition and other commercial activity came about in the late 1800s, it took two broad forms—the regulation of industry and the enactment of statutes concerning competition. In **regulated industries,** competition is either limited or eliminated altogether, and close government control is substituted for the market controls of free competition. Examples of regulated industries are the public utilities and other industries that are closely tied to the "public interest." In these industries, competition is restricted or eliminated because it tends to become wasteful or excessive. Only one telephone company is permitted to serve a given geographical area or market. The large capital investment required to operate an airline route, to construct a pipeline or electric transmission line over great distances, or to build and operate a nuclear power plant makes this type of regulation economically reasonable. But the lack of competition can sometimes cause deterioration in services and performance.

Statutes affecting competition and various commercial practices exist at both the state and federal levels. The first effort by the federal government to regulate competition came with the **Sherman Antitrust Act** of 1890. This act, drawn in a broad and general manner, prohibits every contract or conspiracy in restraint of trade and declares illegal any action that monopolizes or attempts to monopolize any part of trade or commerce.

regulated industries
Industries in which competition is either limited or eliminated altogether and close government control substitutes for the market controls of free competition.

Sherman Antitrust Act
Federal antitrust legislation that prohibits every contract or conspiracy in restraint of trade and declares illegal any action that monopolizes or attempts to monopolize any part of trade or commerce.

The act is enforced by the antitrust division of the U.S. Department of Justice. Violators are subject not only to criminal fines or imprisonment but also to civil damage suits by competitors or other parties. In some cases the government allows the accused firm to enter into a **consent order,** under which it agrees voluntarily to cease the conduct the government is alleging to be an inappropriate action.

Another major federal statute is the **Clayton Act** of 1914, which forbids trade restraints such as tying contracts, interlocking directorates, and certain anticompetitive stock acquisitions. A **tying contract** requires a person who wishes to be the exclusive dealer for a manufacturer's product to carry other products of the manufacturer in inventory. The legality of a tying contract is based on whether it restricts competitors from major markets. **Interlocking directorates** exist where competitive companies have identical or overlapping boards of directors. The acquisition of stock in another company is also forbidden if it lessens competition.

The **Robinson-Patman Act** of 1936 outlaws price discrimination that is not based on quality or quantity differences and that injures competition. The **Celler-Kefauver Act** of 1950 amends the Clayton Act to include major asset purchases that decrease competition in an industry.

Another major statute is the **Federal Trade Commission Act** of 1914. This law, which set up the Federal Trade Commission (FTC) to administer various statutes applicable to business, bans unfair competitive practices. The powers and investigative capacities of the FTC have grown rapidly over the years. Today it is a vigorous and aggressive "watchdog" agency of the government. It can sue violators or enter into consent orders with those that agree to cease the questionable practices. The FTC is now the major regulatory and enforcement agency in the area of competitive practices. In fact, the FTC's aggressive posture on many regulatory issues led to 1980 legistation giving Congress 90 days to veto any FTC ruling.[15]

Other Business Regulations

Besides knowing about all the legislation already discussed here and elsewhere in *Contemporary Business,* the businessperson should become familiar with the following specific federal laws:

1. **Pure Food and Drug Act** of 1906, which prohibits the adulteration and misbranding of foods and drugs. This act was stengthened by the Food, Drug, and Cosmetic Act of 1938 and by the Kefauver-Harris drug amendments of 1962. The latter resulted from the uproar over

consent order
An order under which an accused firm agrees voluntarily to cease the conduct the government is alleging to be an inappropriate action.

Clayton Act
A federal statute that forbids trade restraints such as tying contracts, interlocking directorates, and certain anticompetitive stock acquisitions.

tying contract
A contract that requires a person who wishes to be the exclusive dealer for a manufacturer's product to carry other products of the manufacturer in inventory.

interlocking directorates
Identical or overlapping boards of directors for competitive companies.

Robinson-Patman Act
A federal statute outlawing price discrimination that is not based on quality or quantity differences and that injures competition.

Celler-Kefauver Act
A federal statute that amended the Clayton Act to include major asset purchases that decrease competition in an industry in its general prohibition of trade restraints.

Federal Trade Commission Act
A federal law that set up the Federal Trade Commission (FTC) as a federal agency and gave it administrative powers to ban unfair competitive practices among businesses.

Pure Food and Drug Act
A federal law prohibiting the adulteration and misbranding of foods and drugs.

Controversial Issue

Deregulation: Boon or Boondoggle?

In October 1978, Congress passed the Airline Deregulation Act, which was designed to encourage competition among airlines by allowing them to set their own rates and add and subtract routes based on their profitability. The act stripped the Civil Aeronautics Board of much of its power.

The Staggers Rail Act of 1980 fundamentally altered the Interstate Commerce Commission's power to regulate rail traffic. The law gave rail lines greater freedom to set rates for their freight-hauling operations, to sign long-term contracts with freight shippers, and to eliminate unprofitable routes.

The federal government also has loosened its grip on the trucking industry, enabling it to adjust its rates to meet market demand and to create new kinds of trucking services.

These examples of reduced federal regulatory control over the transportation industry may be a harbinger of things to come in other industries as well. The Reagan administration has pledged an all-out effort to decrease the government's role in such mainstays of American business as transportation, energy, and communications.

The proposal to deregulate air travel evoked fears of reduced competition. Critics worried that when price regulations were lifted and companies were allowed to charge whatever they wished to increase their share of the market, the large air carriers would slash their prices so much that weaker carriers would have no chance of surviving short of merger. Ultimately, the argument continued, prices would skyrocket because of a lack of competition. In fact, when the Airline Deregulation Act was passed, air fares plummetted, carriers experienced huge operating losses, and mergers became common.

Opponents also feared that deregulation would cause carriers

Wheeler-Lea Act
The federal law that both amends the Federal Trade Commission Act to further outlaw unfair or deceptive acts and practices in business and gives the FTC jurisdiction over false and misleading advertising.

Fair Packaging and Labeling Act
A federal law that requires certain kinds of information on packages or labels—including product identification, name and address of the producer or distributor, and quality information.

deformed babies whose mothers had taken the drug thalidomide during their pregnancies.

2. **Wheeler-Lea Act** of 1938, which amends the Federal Trade Commission Act to further outlaw unfair or deceptive acts or practices in business. This act gives the Federal Trade Commission jurisdiction over false and misleading advertising.

3. **Fair Packaging and Labeling Act** of 1967, which requires that certain kinds of information be disclosed on packages or labels—including product identification, name and address of the producer or distributor, and quality information.

to abandon or cut back unprofitable routes. Their fear turned out to be well founded. Out from under the yoke of deregulation, major airlines pulled out of many of the nation's small cities and towns, leaving small carriers to take up the slack.

Supporters of deregulation argue that a change in the type of service available to smaller cities and towns is inevitable but that service will continue. They claim that small carriers meet passengers' needs in a way that makes economic sense.

Deregulation supporters also argue that unrestrained price increases are not a serious threat. Says Richard Fischer, a rail and trucking analyst with Merrill Lynch, Pierce, Fenner and Smith, "You can't just go out willy-nilly and start raising your rates. If you do, you're going to find out that someone is going to take business away from you."

In addition, supporters claim that the increased competition that is a part of deregulation encourages the creation of new services. The trucking and rail industries, for example, have initiated a piggyback system of freight hauling in which trucks haul their freight over intercity highways for part of the route and transfer their trailers onto flatbed rail cars for the remaining distance.

Whether the deregulation of the transportation industry turns out to benefit both business and consumers and whether the same benefits will also apply to other industries are still unclear. For example, will oil deregulation increase competition and the search for new energy sources? And will the deregulation of the Bell System's long-distance phone service, which has brought new competing companies into the market, mean lower rates and better service ten years from now? The trend toward more deregulation represents a return to a purer free enterprise system. How much it will actually benefit businesses and consumers remains to be seen.

4. **Consumer Credit Protection Act** of 1968, known as the Truth in Lending Act, which requires lenders to specify the exact interest charges a borrower will have to pay. This law affects banks, loan companies, and other providers of consumer credit.

5. **Fair Credit Reporting Act** of 1970, which allows people to see the credit reports prepared about them and to insist on the correction of inaccurate information.

6. **Environmental Protection Act** of 1970, which set up the Environmental Protection Agency (EPA), giving it the authority to deal with various types of pollution.

Consumer Credit Protection Act
A federal law, often known as the "Truth in Lending Law," that requires lenders to specify the exact interest charges a borrower will have to pay.

Fair Credit Reporting Act
A federal law that allows people to see credit reports prepared about them, and to insist on the correction of inaccurate information.

Environmental Protection Act
A federal statute that set up the Environmental Protection Agency, giving it the authority to deal with various types of pollution.

THE WALL STREET JOURNAL

"Federal labeling laws don't apply to homemade meat loaf."

The Fair Packaging and Labeling Act of 1967 requires that certain information be disclosed on packages or labels.

Cartoon Features Syndicate

Fair Debt Collection Practices Act
A federal law aimed at prohibiting debt-collecting agencies from using harassing, deceptive, and unfair collection practices.

7. **Fair Debt Collection Practices Act** of 1978, which is aimed at prohibiting debt-collecting agencies from using harassing, deceptive, and unfair collection practices. The act—which exempts "in-house" debt-collection organizations such as banks, retailers, and attorneys—provides for a maximum $1,000 civil penalty for violations. Specific prohibitions include threats of violence, obscene language, and misrepresentation of consumer legal rights.

Many specific state and local regulations are important to businesses. Management must be aware of these laws and their implications if the firm is to succeed in the competitive marketplace.

Summary

Law can be defined as the standards set by government and society in the form of either legislation or custom. Business law consists of those aspects of law that most directly and specifically influence and regulate the management of various types of business activity. It is administered through a series of trial courts, appellate courts, and administrative agencies that exist at all levels of government.

Contract law is the legal foundation on which normal business dealings are constructed. The elements of enforceable contracts are consideration, legality and seriousness of the agreement, and the parties' capacity to make the agreement.

Sales law is an offspring of contract law. It involves the sale of goods or products for money or on credit. The latest evolution in sales law is the Uniform Commercial Code (UCC). Article 2 of the UCC specifies the circumstances under which sales contracts can be entered into. It also sets forth the law of warranty. The two basic types of warranties are express and implied.

Property law is a key feature of the legal system. Property can be divided into three categories: tangible personal property, intangible personal property, and real property.

Agency law is based primarily on common law principles. An agency is a relationship in which two parties, the principal and the agent, agree that one will act as a representative of the other. The principal in any agency relationship is responsible for the actions of the agent.

The law of torts deals with compensating injured persons who are the victims of noncriminal wrongs. It is closely related to the law of agency. The three major areas of this law are intentional torts, negligence, and products liability.

Bankruptcy law provides for an orderly handling of bankruptcies by the federal court system. Two types of bankruptcies are recognized—voluntary and involuntary.

Negotiable instruments are forms of commercial paper that are transferable among individuals and businesses. Article 3 of the UCC gives specifications for negotiable instruments and describes the four basic kinds of indorsement for them: blank indorsement, special indorsement, qualified indorsement, and restricitve indorsement.

Patents guarantee inventors exclusive rights to their inventions for a period of 17 years. Trademarks are words, symbols, or other designations used to identify products. When registered they give their owner protection for an unlimited time period. Copyrights give exclusive rights to a published or unpublished work to an author or the author's heirs during the author's lifetime and for a period of 50 years after the author's death.

Government regulation of competition became necessary in the late 1800s, when mergers and monopolization began to cause problems in certain industries. This regulation took two broad forms— regulation of industry and enactment of statutes concerning competition. The first act regulating competition was the Sherman Anti-Trust Act of 1890. Since then, many more acts have been drafted to further regulate this area. Other acts cover a number of business areas, and the effective businessperson will become familiar with many of them. However, there is no way for a businessperson to find out about all the rules and regulations created by the various levels of government; when in doubt, the businessperson should consult an attorney.

Key Terms

law
common law
statutory law
business law
judiciary
trial courts
appellate courts
appellant
administrative agencies
contract law
contract
consideration
capacity
sales law
Uniform Commercial Code (UCC)
express warranties
implied warranties
property
tangible personal property
intangible personal property
real property
agency
principal
agent
tort
intentional torts
negligence
products liability
strict products liability
bankruptcy

Federal Bankruptcy
   Reform Act of 1978
negotiable instruments
indorsement
patents
copyrights
regulated industries
Sherman Antitrust Act
consent order
Clayton Act
tying contract
interlocking directorates
Robinson-Patman Act
Celler-Kefauver Act
Federal Trade
   Commission Act
Pure Food and Drug
   Act
Wheeler-Lea Act
Fair Packaging and
   Labeling Act
Consumer Credit
   Protection Act
Fair Credit Reporting
   Act
Environmental
   Protection Act
Fair Debt Collection
   Practices Act

Review Questions

1. Explain each of the terms listed above.

2. Trace how business law has evolved over the years.

3. Why is an understanding of business law important to business-people?

4. Describe the organization of the U.S. court system.

5. Explain the law of contracts.

6. Discuss the law of sales.

7. Why is the law of property so critical in the private enterprise system?

8. What is meant by the law of agency?

9. Explain the concept of negotiable instruments.

10. How is competition regulated in the United States?

Discussion Questions and Exercises

---

1. Evaluate the pros and cons of the controversial issue that appears in this chapter.

2. Set up a classroom debate on the question: should attorneys be required to have some training in business administration?

3. A prepaid legal services plan negotiated with Chrysler Corporation has become operational at some United Auto Workers locals. It is possible that such a plan could eventually be extended to all of the UAW's nearly two million members and retirees. Many attorneys in Michigan (where almost a third of the UAW people reside) pro-tested the setting up of a staff of UAW lawyers to provide these services; they would rather have union members select their own legal counselors.[16] Evaluate the impact of large-scale prepaid legal services plans.

4. Various sources note that the United States has become a litigation-oriented society. More and more lawsuits are filed each year. Many people question the reasons and validity of some of this litigation. A Pennsylvania woman, who filed 20 lawsuits against her ex-hus-band, was convicted of barratry, the criminal charge of filing unjust lawsuits.[17] Why is litigation on the rise in the United States? Is this a favorable or unfavorable development for our society?

5. Ask an attorney to speak to your class about law careers, partic-ularly those dealing with business matters.

Case 23-1: The Federal Bankruptcy Reform Act of 1978

The Federal Bankruptcy Reform Act of 1978 liberalized what a debtor could retain while discharging his or her debts through bankruptcy. However, items like taxes, alimony, and child support cannot be voided by bankruptcy. The new law also retained the earlier provision specifying six years between bankruptcies.

A new type of bankruptcy petitioner has emerged as a result of the 1978 law. The National Consumer Finance Association reports the following cases:

• A heart surgeon declared bankruptcy during a short interval while he switched hospitals. He was guaranteed a $10,000 per month income in his new job but wanted to eliminate a $45,000 debt in addition to a $100,000 mortgage.

• A police lieutenant in New York retired and because he was required to wait about 18 months for his pension to begin, he filed for bankruptcy to wipe out his debts.

• Husband and wife psychiatrists, grossing about $80,000 a year, filed for bankruptcy to eliminate a $22,000 debt.

Opinions about the new law vary. Many lawyers and jurists support the act as a needed reform, but creditors argue that the measure goes too far in permitting people to duck their financial responsibilities. Detroit attorney Laurence Snider calls bankruptcy ". . . a valuable right, one that should not be taken lightly." Bankruptcy Judge George Brody says: "We now have a debtor-oriented statute. One of the purposes of going through bankruptcy is rehabilitation, and under the new law there's a better chance of that happening because it allows the debtor to keep more of his (or her) property." A contrasting view comes from William R. Moroney, speaking for the National Consumer Finance Association, "Under the new code, there are more benefits to the debtor at the creditor's expense."

Many lenders blame the legal profession for the rapid escalation of bankruptcy petitions. Many attorneys—now free of prohibitions against advertising—are openly soliciting new bankruptcy clients. Walter B. Kurth, president of the National Consumer Finance Association, puts it this way, "Some lawyers' advertising actually encourages consumers to take bankruptcy when alternatives such as budgeting, credit counseling or refinancing could be better." And for those a little down on their luck, a San Francisco organization now offers do-it-yourself bankruptcy kits.

Questions

1. Explain your viewpoints toward the Federal Bankruptcy Reform Act of 1978.

2. What other arguments either pro or con can be raised about this legislation?

3. Should attorneys be permitted to advertise for bankruptcy clients?

Case 23-2: The New Jersey Alcoholic Beverage Control Deregulates

---

The legal environment can have a sizeable impact on business firms. Consider the case of New Jersey liquor retailers when the state deregulated the pricing of alcoholic beverages in 1980. This action by the New Jersey Alcoholic Beverage Control (ABC) was in line with a 1980 U.S. Supreme Court decision against California's controls on wine prices. Prior to 1980, the ABC set minimum price levels, outlawed quantity discounts, and required wholesalers to sell at the same prices.

These regulations did not permit aggressive competition and tended to guarantee profit margins to liquor stores. In fact, one retailer described the pre-1980 era this way: "Owning a liquor store was like being a civil servant." But now many New Jersey retailers have become discounters, slashing their margins in an attempt to build volume. Still other liquor store owners have lobbied for a return to a more regulated business environment.

Questions

1. Would you favor deregulation of liquor prices? Why? Why not?

2. Can you think of other industries that have experienced similar situations when prices were decontrolled?

3. Should all prices be deregulated, allowing them to be set by free-market conditions? What is the proper role of the legal system in the regulation of the pricing mechanism?

24

The Future of
U.S. Business

Learning Goals

1. To explain why it is so difficult to predict the future

2. To analyze the accelerating pace of change

3. To describe the current trends affecting business in the United States

4. To discover which challenges will confront management in the future

5. To explain the meaning of each of the key terms introduced in this chapter

Profile: Ned Coffin
Enertech Takes on OPEC

Ned Coffin is doing his share to break OPEC's stranglehold on the American economy. As chairman of the Enertech Corporation of Norwich, Vermont, Coffin has helped popularize an alternate energy source that dates back to fourth-century Persia—the windmill.

Enertech does not even try to compete with companies like General Electric and Grumman Aerospace, which develop the large-scale windmills used by utilities. Enertech has a different market in mind. Their small wind machines are designed for home and farm use.

"At this stage," says Coffin, "the majority of buyers tend to be pioneering types concerned with energy, who have a certain amount of disposable income." For a price between $4,000 and $8,000 for the windmill alone plus the cost of the tower and installation but minus some fairly generous tax credits that are now available, Coffin's customers experience the pleasure of using the wind to power their homes and, on a brisk day, of feeding their home-grown energy back into the local power grids.

Even though home windmills are limited to certain regions of the country (they must have an exposed wind site on a hilltop, seacoast, or on a windy plain), Coffin is optimistic about the future of the industry and his own company. Enertech is the leader in home and remote-site windmill sales. To keep up with this demand, Enertech has increased the number of employees in its labor force from 8 in 1979 to 70 at present. The key to Enertech's success in Coffin's view is reliability. Enertech's goal is to provide customers with a worry- and maintenance-free wind system at the lowest possible cost.

Enertech is one of 23 companies in the home- and remote-site windmill industry. According to Ben Wolff, director of the American Wind Energy Association, only a handful of these companies will survive the competition during the early 1980s. Wolff predicts that each company that remains will sell more than 1,000 units a year. Total industry sales have recently been about 500 units annually.

Other projections are more optimistic. One government-sponsored study estimated that there could be 93 million kilowatts of installed wind power sometime in the next century from wind machines of 10 kilowatts or less. Translated, that comes to 18 million small windmills by the twenty-first century—a staggering figure to a society born and bred on oil.

Even if more conservative government estimates are correct, and only 30,000 small windmills are in operation by the year 2000, the business of bringing innovative technology to the people will have changed America's energy profile.

I believe the choice is still open to us, that we can still decide, you and I and our fellow citizens, whether we want to return to the path that made this the great land of opportunity for millions of people or whether instead we want to continue down the road toward a destruction of both liberty and prosperity.

—*Milton Friedman*

Nearly half of the United States population attended 1939's twin world's fairs in New York and San Francisco. The theme dealt with what the future would hold for America. Some of the predictions (or nonpredictions) of the 1939 world's fairs are quite interesting:

1. Nonpolluting liquid air would be the fuel of the future.
2. The United States would be at peace (World War II was actually two years away) with no internal social or racial conflicts. The economy would be prosperous, and slums would be eliminated.
3. The nation would be crisscrossed by seven-lane highways carrying 100 MPH vehicles. Control towers would monitor the traffic flow.
4. Railroads would continue to play a major role in U.S. transportation.
5. Buildings would reach 1,500 feet into the sky.
6. Rocket ships would carry travelers, but regular air transportation would still be propeller driven, and the best the world's fairs could foresee with respect to moon exploration was a telescope 100 times more powerful than its 1939 cousin.
7. Neither of the expositions predicted modern society's reliance on computers.
8. Women were assured that synthetic silk stockings that lasted three months were right around the corner.
9. Television was foreseen as a mere curiosity in the future. But picture telephones would be commonplace. And radio signals would print newspapers right in the typical American home.

Some of the 1939 predictions—such as the elaborate highway system—approached contemporary reality. But others, such as the minimal influence of television, were far from the truth. Everyone must be concerned with the future, but the margin of error in predicting it is often wide and deep.[1]

The Problems of Prediction

It is important to stress how difficult it is to predict trends. If society cannot correctly assess broad economic, societal, and cultural movements, how can business managers forecast future directions?

Detroit sadly missed the mark on its forecast of small-car demand. When small-car sales captured more than half the total automobile market, the car manufacturers admitted that their predictions had been inadequate. Since then, because of their failure to recognize changing consumer tastes, they have had to take drastic action to get smaller cars on the market. The trend toward smaller cars actually began in the mid-1960s, but it received a big push by the recent energy crisis.[2] Later, the downsizing—the industry term for the designing of smaller cars—became necessary because of government mandates on increasing fuel efficiency.

Another example of a situation where some firms did not correctly predict the future is that of the calculator industry. Bowmar Instruments, the second largest minicalculator manufacturer in the United States, went into bankruptcy. The cause: poor forecasting! Bowmar began to increase its production of pocket calculators and make substantial investments in new markets—such as microwave ovens and digital watches—at the time when increased competition was driving down the price of calculators.[3] But Bowmar's failure was not unique. Several other calculator producers failed as the prices of some models dropped to less than $10.00.

Businesspeople are often required to predict future conditions for their industries and companies. No one should underestimate the problems involved in this important task or the speed at which such predictions must be made.

The Accelerating Pace of Change

Prediction is often difficult because of the accelerating pace of change. Business is no longer able to assume that what happened yesterday or today will be true tomorrow. Alvin Toffler's bestseller, *Future Shock,* pointed out that our 50,000 years of existence can be divided into 800 lifetimes of about 62 years each. The first 650 of these lifetimes were spent in caves. Writing has existed for only the last 70 lifetimes. Most of the products used today have been developed within the present lifetime.[4]

Things are changing rapidly even within our own lifetime! Modern management must deal with an endless parade of crucial events—

among them inflation, shortages, and the rapid growth of technology. Most people agree that change is inevitable and that its pace is quickening. Today's managers must be trained and ready to deal with it.

Current Trends Affecting Business

Several societal trends are currently influencing business. Effective managers must recognize these trends, determine how they affect their businesses, and develop appropriate strategies for dealing with the changed environment.

Population Changes

population explosion
The rapid growth in the world's population.

It has been estimated that the world's population will rise to 6.2 billion by the year 2000, compared to its current 4.5 billion. The so-called **population explosion** is a well-documented fact. In 1750 the world's population stood at about 800 million. It doubled by 1900 and doubled again by 1964. Probably it will stabilize at 11 billion![5]

Economically disadvantaged nations traditionally have higher birthrates. The population of less developed countries is rising at a rate faster than that of economically advanced nations such as the United States, the United Kingdom, the Federal Republic of Germany, Japan, France, and the USSR.[6] But people in developed nations typically have longer life expectancies. For example, a white male in the United States is expected to live to 76.8 and a white female to 81.9.[7] By contrast, in India, for example, men are expected to live to 41.9 and women to 40.6,[8] and in Bangladesh both men and women have a life expectancy of 47.[9]

Population growth in the United States and elsewhere has always meant expanding markets for business. The 1980 census set the United States population at 226,504,825.[10] It is expected to hit 245 million by 2000. But the composition of the U.S. population will change even more significantly.

1. A lowered birthrate means that the U.S. will have an aging population. People entering the 30–49 age group will account for 80 percent of the population growth. An older population will produce several effects: increased financial pressure on private pension plans and social security, possible labor shortages (some have forecast the necessity of a peacetime draft by the mid 1980s to keep the armed services at required staffing levels), and marketing's gradual move away from youth-oriented advertising.
2. About 50 percent of the U.S. population increase will come from immigration. A government study suggests this massive immigration will change the ethnic composition of the United States by the year 2080. It is predicted that today's minorities—blacks, Hispanics, and

Asiatics—will constitute 50 to 60 percent of the U.S. population in the year 2080. In fact, Hispanics are expected to become the nation's biggest minority group by 1990. This change will have a significant impact on business and other institutions in society.

Lifestyle Changes

Lifestyle is the way a person lives; it includes work, leisure time, hobbies, other interests, and personal philosophy. One person's lifestyle may be dominated by work, with few social activities. Another's may involve hobbies, recreation, or personal philosophy.

lifestyle
The way a person lives, including work, leisure time, hobbies, other interest, and personal philosophy.

There is little doubt that lifestyles are changing and that these changes will have an impact on the way business operates in the years ahead. Several factors are causing lifestyle changes in U.S. society.

First, there is more leisure time than ever before. The workweek is now less than 40 hours, as compared to 70 hours a century ago. Some experts believe it will be 25 hours or less before the year 2000.[11] Several firms have adopted four-day workweeks with more hours per day. Others have cut the number of hours worked each week. Reduced work schedules mean increased leisure time.

Second, families have fewer children than before—and young couples are postponing childbirth instead of having their children early in the marriage. This trend has forced many businesses to modify their competitive strategies. Gerber Products Company used to advertise "babies are our business—our only business." Now Gerber products include infant and toddler clothing, stuffed animals, and accessories such as bottles, bassinets, and baby powder.[12]

Third, people are better educated and more prosperous now than they were earlier. These advantages bring with them the freedom to question current lifestyles and examine new ones. Inquiries of this nature have sometimes led to personal lifestyle changes. Today's youth, for example, are not only better educated but more independent and individualistic than past generations.

Fourth, more women, both single and married, with and without children, are working full time. In 1950, only 22 percent of the work force was female as compared to 42.4 percent in 1980.[13] This trend is certainly important for business. As the needs of working women and their families change, the products and services to meet these needs are also changing.

Business is only beginning to realize how people's lifestyles can influence their behavior as employees, consumers, and members of society.

Economic Changes

The past decade has witnessed sweeping economic changes that are altering the course of U.S. business. Oil boycotts, inflation, unemployment, recession, currency fluctuations, and energy resource allocation have all had a profound impact.

People are becoming more conscious than they were a decade ago about how economic factors affect everyday life. Some are

More women are working full time—a trend that is likely to continue.

alarmed by the high unemployment and double-digit inflation of recent years. Others fear economic domination by Japanese and German firms or the oil-rich Arab states. But statistics show that the United States is still the world's wealthiest nation and an effective competitor in the world marketplace.

Still, the economic changes noted above indicate the importance of businesspeoples' thoroughly understanding the competitive system. No firm is far removed from the basic economic changes that occur in society, and effective managers must be aware of current economic events affecting their businesses (see Focus 24–1).

Technological Changes

technology
The innovations, methods, practices, systems, and equipment (and related operational knowledge) applicable to the industrial setting.

Technology is the innovations, methods, practices, systems, equipment, and related operational knowledge applicable to the industrial setting. New technology is being introduced at a rate far faster than that of even a decade ago.

Technological changes require other changes. Production methods must be updated, employees retrained, and management thinking restructured. Knowledge acquired in school is outdated within ten years after graduation, and certain jobs become obsolete. Society has thus begun to emphasize lifelong education and training so people can remain productive for more than a few years.

Some people worry that technology is out of control. A few even believe that humans will someday be the slaves of computers or of "super machines." Most business executives, however, believe that technology has been and will continue to be a way of improving the standard of living and the quality of life (see Focus 24–2). But they also point out that technological improvements will fail to win public support if they are too expensive.

Societal Changes

Many societal changes affecting business involve either social responsibility or the quality of life. People want socially responsibile decisions from executives and have begun to protest actions that are not in line with this thinking. U.S. citizens have filed lawsuits against producers of poor products, picketed supermarkets, boycotted firms, and demanded stronger legislation to control certain business practices.

They also are increasingly concerned about the quality of life. While most people still seek material possessions, there is now a greater interest in living fuller, more personally rewarding lives. Individuals must decide on the lifestyle that is right for them.

Business Strategy Changes

Changes in business strategy over the years have had a direct effect on how firms operate today. Some of these changes include:

FOCUS 24–1
Auburn Automobile Company

Auburn, Indiana, is a quiet peaceful community of 8,000, the county seat of DeKalb County. Its residents work at local plants like Dana, Borg-Warner, and Cooper Industrial Products, or commute to Fort Wayne, a half-hour drive away. It is difficult to envision today's Auburn as an industrial center. But in 1931 it was the home of Auburn Automobile Co., makers of the famed Cords and Auburns. The firm was part of Cord Corp., an early conglomerate that was involved in industries like shipbuilding and aircraft manufacturing.

Auburn had leaped into thirteenth place in the automobile sales derby. The 1931 sales rankings are shown in the table below. The local plant employed 900 people out of the town's population of 5,000. Cords were selling for $3,000 each and Auburns for $2,200. The company's officers were in a brand-new art deco building. Executives worked in an atmosphere of imported chandeliers, terrazzo floors, and beamed ceilings.

Auburn's 1931 Sales

Rank	Make	Sales
1	Chevrolet	627,104
2	Ford	541,615
3	Plymouth	106,259
4	Buick	88,417
5	Pontiac-Oakland	86,307
6	W-O/Whippet	74,750
7	Hudson-Essex	57,825
8	Dodge	56,003
9	Chrysler	52,819
10	Studebaker-Rockne	48,921
11	Oldsmobile	48,000
12	Nash	39,616
13	Auburn	32,301
14	DeSoto	29,835
15	Hupmobile	17,456
16	Cadillac-LaSalle	15,012
17	Packard	13,123
18	Durant	7,000
	Sales Total	1,942,363

The Auburn had a market share of 1.7%.

As the Great Depression came, the local economy was cushioned by the resilience of nearby farms. The town's banks also survived while many similar institutions were failing all across the country. But things turned sour at Auburn Automobile Company. By 1936, the company folded, and its entire work force became victims of the depression. The saga of the Auburn Automobile Company shows how difficult it is to predict economic changes. Many once-prosperous firms—like Auburn—are now a mere footnote in business history.

FOCUS 24–2
Herman Kahn Speaks Out

Herman Kahn is one of the world's leading futurists—a researcher who studies future trends. Kahn, founder of Hudson Institute—a research group—believes that future technological change is stymied by red tape. In answer to the question, What do you believe is the major challenge that the U.S. will face in the 1980's, Kahn replied:

Various social-limits-to-growth movements remain the biggest obstacle to progress. Many of these limits are encouraged by what I call the "health-and-safety fascists"—the people who are almost religiously antitechnological, self-righteously superior in their judgments. They won't let you build a road or a refinery or a port without running a regulatory gauntlet.

If you look at how difficult it is to get anything done today, you see the problem. It used to take the U.S. government 30 months to put up a building. Now it takes 10 years for the same building. Things like the U-2 spy plane flew nine months after being authorized. Today, it would take nine years to get the same plane in the air, starting from scratch. That kind of red tape strangles the system and discourages innovation.

1. Computer-based management information systems (MIS). An efficient MIS is one that gets the appropriate data (and only the appropriate data) to the responsible decision maker in time for a considered decision. It is now estimated that 80 to 90 percent of the work force will be employed in information-processing activities in the year 2030.[14]

automation
The replacement of people with machines that can perform tasks faster or cheaper than humans.

2. **Automation**—the replacement of people with machines that can perform tasks faster or cheaper than humans. Most experts point out that because workers are required to make the new machines, the labor force stays constant. The problem is that the displaced workers may not be qualified to handle the new jobs.

3. More extensive cost control programs, within which accountants and other managers find new ways to hold down the rising costs of doing business. These programs are very important, especially during periods of inflation or sales decline.

4. New ways of acquiring the energy and materials necessary to operate business. The importance of this change is obvious, because shortages of energy and many raw materials have been experienced by U.S. businesses recently.

5. Management awareness and understanding of the attitudes and problems of workers. The labor force is composed of a multitude of different groups requiring different managerial approaches. Management must be sure that leadership styles match the work situation.

Balancing the Positive and Negative Aspects of Change

Assessments of the future of business often assign more importance to negative influences than to positive ones.[15] Indeed, many factors and circumstances may well have an adverse impact on forecasts: inflation, unemployment, and bureaucratic red tape are but a few. Still, there are favorable situations balancing the negative inputs to assessments of our future, including:

1. Recognition of the importance of continued capital investment is strong. Some recent tax proposals illustrate this vital concern.

2. Expanding foreign investment in the United States suggests that we are still the world's standard for economic stability and business opportunities.

3. Communist nations, such as China and the Eastern European bloc, are viewed as excellent spots for future business invesments and marketing efforts.

4. Experts believe that the U.S. agricultural sector may become the source of much of the world's food supply. A Department of Agriculture agency forecasts that even without improved technology we may produce 9 billion bushels of corn, 2.3 billion bushels of wheat, and 2.3 billion bushels of soybeans by 1985—all considerably higher than the record crops to date.

5. New research efforts concerning energy and various raw materals are quite hopeful. Many people believe that by 1988 the United States will be considerably more self-sufficient in these areas than it is now.[16]

On balance, these and other factors indicate that U.S. business and the private enterprise economic system face a bright future.

Business continues to face a bright future.
Drawing by Ed Arno; © The New Yorker Magazine, Inc.

Controversial Issue

Who Should Rebuild America's Cities: Private Enterprise or the Public?

Despite the spurt of interest and activity in revitalizing America's cities, the nation's oldest cities are still facing problems. And conditions may be getting worse. In a highly publicized 1980 study conducted by Richard P. Nathan of Princeton University and James W. Fossett of the University of Michigan, cities like St. Louis, Boston, Newark, Detroit, Cincinnati, and Minneapolis were found to be suffering from a decline in population and per capita wealth. The study came to the following conclusion: "By almost any reasonable measure of the prosperity of places—levels of population, income, employment activity and concentration of low-income households—more distressed cities were appreciably worse off . . . than they were . . . earlier."

Only after a visit to New York City's south Bronx with its burnt-out tenements and empty lots strewn with filth and debris or to Detroit with its army of unemployed auto workers can one realize how hopeless America's inner cities really are.

Doing something to revive blighted big-city neighborhoods has been a concern of government for many years. Since 1967 the government has spent $76 billion in revenue-sharing and community-development funds on urban development projects and $67 billion on jobs programs, yet the decline continues. Partially due to a general tightening of the federal purse strings, more and more attention has been paid to the role private industry can play in the rebuilding process.

When President Carter came into office, he was faced with an enormous consolidated urban aid program called community de-

Tomorrow's Challenges

Many of today's challenges will be present tomorrow. But management must also watch for the new challenges that will appear. Some of today's vexing situations may seem minor when compared to the complexities to be faced in the future.

Tomorrow's challenges require today's preparation. Business executives must learn to adapt to events that may be unheard of now. Management must be flexible, prepared to meet new situations with strategies designed for the future—an approach requiring a sound education. Qualified executives must have a solid understanding of the business system and must be able to adapt to change.

The only thing constant about U.S. business, in fact, is change! It is a vital part of everyday business life. Change was yesterday's challenge. It is today's challenge. And it will be tomorrow's challenge.

velopment blocks, which provided cities with about $3.5 billion in urban aid and social services each year. In order to involve the private sector in the urban revitalization effort, Carter created a new program called Urban Development Action Grants, which used federal dollars to encourage private investment. This program was enthusiastically received by big-city mayors, who called it one of the best federal programs ever initiated. Between 1978 and 1981, more than 1,000 grants worth approximately $2 billion were awarded. These grants generated $12 billion in private funds.

The Reagan administration does not share the enthusiasm for action grants. Nor does it favor CETA, the Comprehensive Employment and Training Act. It appears likely that Reagan will de-emphasize government support of urban development projects and move toward encouraging increased private investments through programs like "enterprise zones."

Enterprise zones are one- to two-square-mile areas in blighted neighborhoods that would lure businesses to build labor-intensive factories through sizable tax breaks, eased zoning restrictions, reduced government regulations, and relief from customs duties. In return businesses would be required to hire at least 50 percent of their employees from within the zone—a move that would give hope to the hard-core unemployed.

The fact that the cities are in need of help cannot be disputed. Where this help should come from is still a subject of debate.

Can and should the government turn the problem over to private industry? Will and should private industry accept the responsibility? Or should urban revitalization be the responsibility of a joint effort between the two?

One critical question remains: What will be your role in facing tomorrow's challenges? Virtually every sector of society and every career field is influenced by contemporary business—directly or indirectly. And business offers exciting opportunities for a rewarding future. Now that you have an overview of the business system, in the next chapter you will learn about where you fit in it.

Summary

It is difficult to predict the future of U.S. business. In some ways, we often miss even broad economic, societal, and cultural changes that will affect business. Prediction is also difficult because of the accelerating pace of change and trends such as population changes, lifestyle changes, economic changes, technological changes, societal changes, and business strategy changes.

All these changes have had a significant impact on the way business operates today. While many changes are negative, they are balanced by positive ones in any assessment of the future.

The only thing constant about U.S. business is change. It is a challenge now, and it will be one in the future. One unanswered question about the future is: what will be your role in it?

Key Terms

population explosion   technology
lifestyle   automation

Review Questions

1. Explain each of the terms listed above.

2. Assess the accuracy of the various predictions made in the 1939 world's fairs.

3. Why is it difficult to predict the future course of U.S. business?

4. What can be learned about predicting the future from the two examples given in the chapter—the Detroit automakers and Bowmar Instrument Corporation?

5. Identify the current trends affecting business.

6. Why are population changes particularly significant for the less developed nations?

7. How have the lifestyles of college students changed over the past few years?

8. Identify the economic changes that affect business.

9. What business strategy changes have occurred in recent years?

10. What positive factors are likely to affect the future of U.S. business and the private enterprise economic system?

Discussion Questions and Exercises

1. Discuss the pros and cons of the controversial issue that appears in this chapter.

2. Prepare a one-page report on a person who has influenced the future of U.S. business.

3. Comment on the statement: The only thing constant about U.S. business is change.

4. The median U.S. income is now about $19,000. And the average American household has net assets of $83,500.[17] Assess the likely financial prospects for the average American during the next year. You will want to consult a variety of forecasts and statistical sources in making your evaluation.

Case 24–1: The Third Wave

Author Alvin Toffler argues that civilization is now entering a third era. The so-called first wave in history occurred when permanent settlements replaced nomadic lifestyles. The second wave began with the industrial revolution. Work was shifted out of the home and into factories and offices. Families also changed. First-wave families consisted of several generations. Toffler labels the second-wave family the nuclear family. He says it is characterized by a working husband, housekeeping wife, and two children.

Toffler's book *The Third Wave* tells of another sweeping change impacting society. He points out that the nuclear family is no longer the norm. In fact, only 7 percent of the U.S. population lives in a nuclear family today. The best-selling author goes on to document the tremendous increase in single-person households, the popularity of childless marriages, the tremendous growth of the service-oriented economy, and other factors that are causing this third wave in human history. Toffler also concludes that work, often computer based, will begin to shift back into the home, similar to the pattern that existed in the first wave. Jobs will be shared; children will be exposed to work, unlike the situation in the second wave; and the changed work/living environment will impact male-female relationships. Nonfamily members will enter households as part of the new work organizations, forming a new version of the extended family. And the home will in fact become an electronic cottage.

Questions

1. Do you agree with Alvin Toffler's view of the future?

2. What other changes do you predict for the work place?

3. Research and report on other forecasts of how people will live and work in the future.

Case 24–2: Grade Inflation and the "Bottom Line"

College officials throughout the United States and elsewhere have bemoaned the evil of grade inflation, a trend toward giving higher college grades than in the past. Academic administrators, legislators, parents, writers, and the general public have all pointed to the inconsistency of falling national test scores and rising grades. In short, society is asking: if Susie and Johnnie can't read, write, and calculate effectively, why do they get better grades?

To many, the answer is a general lowering of quality standards on the part of our educational system. In other words, we are permitting students to perform at levels lower than those required a few years ago. While other explanations are offered, the lowering of quality standards is widely accepted. The root causes of this situation are varied. Parents, legislators, and the public often blame the apathy of college faculties. Instructors often blame the economic pressures that increase their class sizes. Regardless of the explanation or cause, grade inflation is viewed as a serious academic problem.

Tomorrow's managers must be as aggressive and effective as those of yesterday. Management must be "bottom line" oriented—that is, must adhere to performance standards and goal achievement. Some businesspeople openly fear that today's students are being ill-prepared for future managerial responsibility. Despite the assurance of college instructors, the business community remains skeptical: if Susie and Johnnie aren't required to produce now, how will they ever understand the bottom line?

Questions

1. How do you explain the discrepancy between grading trends and national test scores?

2. Do you believe that lower academic standards (if this is actually true) will adversely affect tomorrow's bottom line?

3. Is grade inflation a problem at your school? If so, do you think it will affect the future productivity of your classmates? Explain.

4. What grade do you expect to earn in this class? Do you think it is the one you deserve? Explain.

25

Your Career in Business

Learning Goals

1. To discover how to start your career in business

2. To explain current employment trends

3. To describe how knowing yourself is an important part of career development

4. To analyze the job search process, placement files, resume preparation, interviewing, and interviewer strategy

5. To discover the sources of career information, the financial rewards of top management, and the special problems of women choosing business careers

6. To explain the meaning of each of the key terms introduced in this chapter

Profile: Anne Gados

Helping Cuyahoga Students Find the Right Job

Anne Gados may well be the perfect role model for the students she counsels at the Western Campus of Cuyahoga Community College in Parma, Ohio. Not because of her position as director of the Career Services and Placement Center but because of how she got there. Gados' career path shows an amazing mixture of adaptability, ingenuity, and determination—qualities that have become more and more valuable in today's business world.

Gados spent many of her early adult years with no clearly thought-out career of her own. She worked in her husband's real estate business, was a credit clerk, and served as an assistant to a maitre d'hotel. "Things changed," says Gados, "about 17 years into my marriage when my husband became ill. It was at that point I decided to go back to school for a degree."

While completing a master's degree in student personnel administration, Gados interned at Cuyahoga's Western Campus. Asked to remain as student consultant on a part-time basis after graduation, Gados became an assistant to the placement and financial aid director—a position she used eventually to gain a challenging, new career slot for herself. "I wrote a proposal suggesting that the financial aid and career areas be split apart," says Gados. "When the college accepted my idea, I got the job of career services and placement director."

Many of the students Gados now counsels will make similar career changes. "We're finding graduates who are unhappy with their work coming back to us for job counseling and career direction advice," says Gados. "The job of the placement office is to be responsive to these people—to help them find the door through which they can reenter the work world. It is also to help undergraduates find out what they really want before they take their first active career step. We do this by giving students current, factual career information as well as self-assessment skills, and the knowledge of where and how to look for a job."

Under Gados' direction, Cuyahoga's Career Services and Placement Center offers students and graduates a variety of services to help them in their career goals. Campus recruitment is a major part of this program. "We have a recruitment week every month," explains Gados, "which is expected to attract 150 companies in 1981.

"Many of the companies are looking for entry-level management trainees," says Gados. "When they're filling nontechnical slots, they want people with general backgrounds. A prime candidate has one or two basic business courses—introduction to business and management, for example—and several English courses. Companies want people with good communications skills whom they can train on the job."

Many students take jobs they learn about through Anne Gados' placement office. "I encourage students to take advantage of all the college and community agencies that can help them find the right work and, above all, to be adaptable and flexible in their job search."

My philosophy of life is that if we make up our mind what we are going to make of our lives, then work hard toward that goal, we never lose— somehow we win out. . . .

—Ronald Reagan
From a 1942 letter to
a young fan

Becky Young wanted to study journalism, but she became a business student at Oklahoma State University instead. As a high school senior, Becky decided that her future career should offer variety and a chance to meet people. Journalism was her choice, until she attended a state-wide meeting of school newspaper editors that led her to conclude the field was too crowded. She then considered a teaching career in French or the humanities.

By the next fall, Becky was enrolled in Tulsa Junior College. She later transferred to Oklahoma State University. After a friend mentioned that the college had a career center, Becky decided to see what guidance she could get. This decision led her to Systems Interactive Guidance Information (SIGI), a computer program developed by the Educational Testing Service of Princeton, New Jersey, and used at Becky's college, among many others.

SIGI asks students to rate ten values—including income, security, variety, and leisure—and then to compare them with job selections. This helps the students assess their value decisions. For example, a person who gives income a high rating but who consistently picks jobs that offer employment security and low income should reconsider the importance supposedly attached to income. SIGI next helps students locate the best possible career by listing jobs that match each person's five highest values.

Through SIGI, students acquire information about the educational requirements for a job, its potential income, its geographical location, and the like. The result of Becky Young's experience with SIGI was that she decided on a career at an administrative level offering the chance for leadership, independence, variety, and meeting people. She became a business student![1]

What Is a Career Cluster?

How should you approach your career in business, especially your first **entry-level job**—that is, your first permanent kind of employment after leaving school? First, you should become aware of employment

entry-level job
The first permanent kind of employment after leaving school.

projections and trends. Suppose you are interested in teaching. You should know that many areas of this field are faced with an oversupply of trained people.

Bureau of Labor statistics projections to 1990 show that faster than average job growth will occur for accountants, systems analysts, industrial engineers, health services administrators, actuaries, marketing research workers, purchasing agents, public relations workers, city managers, and bank officers and administrators. Slower than average growth is expected for sociologists, mathematicians, credit managers, securities sales workers, and transportation, communications, and public utilities managers and administrators.[2] While the above projections are just a sampling of the forecasts produced by the Bureau of Labor Statistics, they do suggest the need to study such trends and projections.

In an employment area where the supply of workers exceeds the demand, many qualified individuals will still be able to obtain employment, but some will have to accept alternative jobs. Therefore, students should select and prepare for a group of related jobs—a **career cluster**—that offers positive employment opportunities.

career cluster
A group of related jobs.

The notion of a career cluster is not difficult to understand. Changing technology and changing demands for goods and services make it difficult to forecast what employment opportunities in a specific job will be. It is estimated that as much as three-fourths of our 1990 labor force will be working on products and services not now in existence. According to B. Edward Berman, a psychologist and job counselor, up to 45 percent of the U.S. work force will switch occupations at least once by the year 2000—and job obsolescence will be the key factor.[3] This startling prediction suggests that it is easier to estimate job trends in a cluster of related occupations than job by job.

Because each entry-level job requires specific skills and knowledge, students are wise to select a primary job interest. But they should also acquire the broad base of knowledge and skills associated with an overall career cluster. This kind of preparation allows for greater flexibility in seeking entry-level jobs.

The U.S. Office of Education has identified 15 career clusters, including business and office, marketing and distribution, marine science, and health.[4] All of them require business knowledge and skills. For example, in the hospitality and recreation, health, and transportation clusters, most jobs require some basic understanding of effective management, sound accounting practices, legal concepts, and marketing skills.

In most colleges the business curriculum is organized around the key courses of accounting, management, marketing, business law, finance, economics, statistics, and computers. These courses deal with the common knowledge required in any meaningful entry-level business position. Students then acquire more specialized knowledge by taking advanced classes in each area. This background, along with a positive attitude, provides the initial flexibility needed for many kinds of business jobs. More knowledge can be acquired at any time by anyone valuing personal and professional improvement. Many business jobs are in high demand, but those who have a good understanding of the basic business subjects can gain entry-level employment in several areas.

Employment Trends

A knowledge of general employment trends is important to college students. Figure 25–1 shows that employment growth will vary considerably from industry to industry. The service industries will grow by about 53 percent during the 1978–1990 period, while agriculture will decline by about 12 percent. According to the U.S. Bureau of Labor Statistics, by 1990 the following industries will grow more than 25 percent: services, trade, finance, insurance, and real estate.

The majority of the U.S. labor force is in service-producing industries (including government). Goods-producing industries (including agriculture and manufacturing) now account for less than one-third of the total labor force. The Bureau of Labor Statistics expects faster job growth in the service area than in the goods-producing sector through 1990.[5]

Business careers are available in virtually every industry. Accountants, managers, and computer programmers, for example, are needed in such diverse areas as government and manufacturing. The general employment trends are very favorable to business students. Well-qualified graduates are not only in immediate demand; they also have an excellent long-term career prognosis.

FIGURE 25–1
Employment growth by industry.

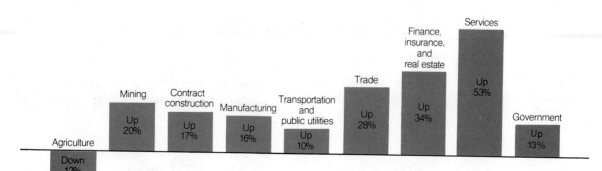

Knowing Yourself Is Part of Career Development

In order to become successful in a particular job, a person needs to enjoy and value the tasks required by that job. While some individuals do not, it makes sense for most people to select a line of work that provides such satisfaction.

In addition to analyzing the demand for employment, people must understand themselves. The process of doing so will enhance their career development. Following are some questions aimed at generating this self-understanding:

1. What motivates you to do something?
2. What type of lifestyle do you want?
3. What do you want to be 15 years from now?
4. What do you like and dislike?
5. What do you fear?
6. What personal values do you hold?
7. What is your honest opinion of yourself?

Finally, people must understand the job requirements if they are to do well in any job. The goal of career development, in fact, is to match individuals with compatible jobs. This is what SIGI did for Becky Young. After all, people are more likely to succeed if they are in a position they enjoy.

Most people need help in both self-analysis and job analysis. College students can find considerable information and personal assistance in their school library, at their counseling center, and at career guidance or placement offices. During recent years there has been a major trend toward career education. Most schools now have materials explaining how to analyze strengths and weaknesses, personal value structures, and job interests.

Obtaining the Right Position

What is the best way to find the right job for you? While there is no single approach, there are some general principles that can be followed.

The job search process is hard work. Good entry-level positions are highly sought after, so there is a lot of competition. But the best first step is to locate available positions that interest you. Then, be resourceful! Your success depends on gathering as much information as possible. Register at your school's placement office. Establish a placement or credentials file including letters of recommendation and supporting personal information. Become familiar with how the placement office conveys employment information. Most placement offices send out a monthly list of new job vacancies, so be sure your name and address are on their mailing list. If possible, visit the placement office regularly. Check out new job information. Meet the people who work in the office—both secretaries and counselors. They can prove invaluable in your job search.

Preparing Your Placement Materials

Most placement or credentials files include the following information: (1) letters of recommendation from people who know you—professors, employers, and others; (2) transcripts of your academic work to date; (3) a personal data form reporting factual information about yourself; and (4) a statement of career goals. The placement office will provide special forms to be used in setting up your placement file. These forms should be completed neatly and accurately. Employers are extremely interested in the ability to communicate in writing. The written narrative in your file should be clear, logical, and creative. Give yourself ample time to write several drafts and to polish the final copy. Be sure to prepare the best possible set of credentials. Let other people read and criticize your work. Keep a copy of the final file for later use in preparing similar information for other employment sources. Check back with the placement office to be sure that your file is in order.

Reference letters are very important. Be selective in securing recommendations, and try to include a business professor in your list of references. The people you ask for recommendations should be familiar with both your strengths and your career goals. But remember that these people are usually busy and cannot be expected to meet short deadlines. Allow them adequate time to prepare their reference letters; then follow up on missing ones.

Always ask people personally if they will write a letter of recommendation for you. Be prepared to give them a brief outline of your academic preparation along with information concerning your entry-level job preferences and your career objectives. This will help them prepare the letter and may enable them to respond quickly.

Finding Employment Sources

Another step in the process of identifying job openings involves seeking out additional job sources, including educational placement offices and private and public employment agencies.

If you have completed formal academic course work with more than one college or university, check with each of them about setting up a placement file. Some colleges have a reciprocity agreement that permits a student who has completed course work at several schools to establish a file with each placement office.

The Sunday edition of metropolitan newspapers is often a rich source of job leads.

resume
A written summary of one's personal, educational, and professional achievements.

Private employment agencies can also be useful in your job search. These agencies, which often specialize in certain types of jobs, perform several services for both employers and job candidates that are not provided elsewhere. For example, some private agencies interview, test, and screen job applicants.

Many agencies have established good relationships with employers who are looking for particular types of workers. They also can offer candidates valuable counseling on how to "market" skills to employers.

Be sure you find out the details of any agreement with an employment agency, because their services can be expensive. Many charge between 5 and 10 percent of the first year's salary of anyone who obtains a job as a result of these services. An 8 percent fee on a $20,000 salary means a cost of $1,600. Find out who is responsible for paying the fee—employer or employee. No blanket rule exists, so be sure to check carefully.

State employment agencies can also be effective in providing employment leads. However, in many states these public agencies process unemployment compensation along with other related work. Because of this mix of duties, some people view state employment agencies as providing services for semiskilled or unskilled workers. But these agencies also list jobs in many professional categories.

Other sources that can help in identifying job openings are: (1) newspaper employment advertisements (the Sunday edition of metropolitan newspapers is often a rich source of job leads); (2) trade journals or magazines; (3) college professors and administrators; (4) community organizations, such as the local chamber of commerce; and (5) friends. Another approach is to identify all the organizations where you think you would like to work. Mail a letter of inquiry and your resume to these companies. If possible, direct these documents to a specific person who has the authority to hire new employees. The letter should ask briefly about employment opportunities in a particular line of work. It should also ask for a personal interview.

Preparing Your Resume

Regardless of how you identify job openings, you must learn how to develop and use a **resume**—a written summary of your personal, educational, and professional achievements. The resume is a very personal document, covering your educational background, work experience, career preference, major interests, and other personal information. It should also include basic information such as your age, address, and telephone number.

The primary purpose of a job resume is to highlight your qualifications. In general, a resume for a person seeking entry-level employment should be only one page long. Information in a job resume should therefore be as concise as possible. An attractive layout will facilitate the employer's review of your qualifications.

There are several acceptable ways of preparing a job resume. Some use narrative sentences to explain job duties and career goals; others are in outline form. If the job resume is being sent with the credentials file, the resume can be quite short. Remember, too, that it should be designed around your own needs and objectives. Figure 25–2 shows a very simple job resume.

Studying Your Employment Opportunities

You should carefully study the various employment opportunities you have found. Obviously you will prefer some opportunities over others, but you should consider a variety of factors as you assess each job possibility: (1) the actual job responsibilities, (2) industry characteristics, (3) the nature of the company, (4) geographical location, (5) salary and advancement opportunities, and (6) the job's contribution to your long-run career objectives.

Too many graduates consider only the most striking features of a job—perhaps the location or the salary. However, a comprehensive

FIGURE 25–2
Sample resume.

```
PERSONAL INFORMATION

Albert W. Belskus                    Date of Birth:  1/30/60
901 North Elm
Hinsdale, Illinois 60521             Excellent health, 5'11", 185 lbs.
302/999-1111

EDUCATION

Cook County Community College        Associate of Arts in Business (1980)

Illinois Metropolitan University     Bachelor of Business Administration (1983)

Combined grade point average is 3.01 on a 4.0 scale.

EXTRACURRICULAR ACTIVITIES

Accounting Club        1979-80
Glee Club              1980-82
Accounting Honorary Society 1981-82

BUSINESS EXPERIENCE

Room Clerk, Town Center Motel, Oak Park, Illinois, 1979-80
Accounts Payable Clerk, St. Anthony's Hospital, Chicago, Illinois, 1980-82
Earned 80 percent of my educational expenses; balance was in part from
 personal loans.

REFERENCES

Complete credentials file is available from two sources:

Placement Center                     Center for Career Guidance
Cook County Community College        Illinois Metropolitan University
Cookville, Illinois 69998            Chicago, Illinois 69999

ADDITIONAL REFERENCES

Professor Edward Van Allan           Professor C. Carson Jones
Business Department                  Department of Accounting
Cook County Community College        Illinois Metropolitan University
Cookville, Illinois 69998            Chicago, Illinois 69999

Mrs. Helen Steinmetz                 Mr. H. Fred Matson
Manager, Town Center Motel           Accounting Supervisor
Hinsdale Road                        St. Anthony's Hospital
Oak Park, Illinois 69997             Chicago, Illinois 69999

CAREER OBJECTIVE

To obtain a challenging position in industrial accounting in the Chicago area.
```

"YOUR RESUME IS VERY IMPRESSIVE, MR. FINWICK, BUT THE JOB CALLS FOR SOMEONE WITH A LITTLE MORE SELF-CONFIDENCE."

Although a good resume is necessary for job-hunting, the impression made during an interview is equally important.

Ralph Dunagin/Orlando Sentinel Star

review of job openings should provide a balanced perspective of the overall employment opportunity, including long-run as well as short-run factors.

A number of information sources are useful in ranking job prospects. Annual reports, financial summaries, and other data can usually be obtained from libraries, stockbrokers, and placement offices. In addition, your placement office or employment agency may be familiar with the companies on your list. If possible, try to visit each of these companies for firsthand impressions. Ask your friends and associates what they know about any companies you are studying.

The Personal Interview

The initial objective of a job search is to obtain an appointment with prospective employers. Once this has been accomplished, you should begin planning for the interview. You will want to enter the interview with a good understanding of the company, its industry, and its competition. Preparation includes obtaining essential information about the company, including:

1. How was the company founded?
2. What is its current position in the industry?
3. What is its financial status?
4. Which markets does it compete in?
5. How is the firm organized?
6. What is its competition?
7. How many people does it employ?
8. Where are its plants and offices located?

This information is useful in several ways. First, it helps you gain a feeling of confidence during the personal interview. Second, it can keep you from making an undesirable employment choice. Third, it can impress interviewers, who often try to determine how much applicants know about the company as a way of assessing their interest level. Candidates who do not make the effort to obtain such information are often eliminated from further consideration.

Where do you get this preinterview information?

1. Check with your placement office or employment agency. It should be able to tell you something about the company and to provide published material.
2. Check with business instructors at your school.
3. Go to the library and investigate the company in the standard financial guides. If necessary, ask your librarian for help.
4. Contact a stockbroker and ask for information about the company.
5. Ask friends who have dealt with the company either as customers or as workers.
6. Contact the local chamber of commerce office.

These techniques should produce all the information you will need.

Interviewers report that many students fail during the interview process for two reasons: inadequate preparation for the interview and lack of confidence. Both factors prevent effective communication. Remember that the interviewer will first determine whether you can communicate effectively. You should be specific in answering and asking questions and should clearly and positively express your concerns.

Most people who conduct initial employment interviews work in the personnel division of organizations. They are in a staff position, which means that they can make recommendations to other managers about which individuals should be employed. Line managers get involved in interviewing at a later stage of the hiring process. In many instances the decision is made by personnel people and the immediate supervisor of the prospective employee. In other cases it is made entirely by the immediate supervisor. Rarely does the personnel department have sole hiring authority.

Interviewers use a number of techniques to elicit information. If you are interested in a job as a supervisor, for example, the company will want to know how you cope with conflict. To find out, it may put pressure on you by creating a crisis situation—the **stress interview.** The interview may begin with a harsh criticism of your academic record or lack of practical experience. You may also be faced with a series of rapid-fire questions about how you would handle a hypothetical situation. It is important to retain your composure and communicate in a clear and precise manner.

Another, more common, technique is for the interviewer not to talk much during the interview. This type of **open-ended interview** is designed to study your thought processes. It forces you to open up and talk about yourself and your goals. If you appear unorganized,

stress interview
An interview that creates a crisis situation by putting pressure on the interviewee in order to determine how that person copes with conflict.

open-ended interview
An interview designed to study the thought processes of interviewees by forcing them to open up and talk about themselves and their goals.

the interviewer may eliminate you as a possible employee. When faced with this type of situation, be sure to express your thoughts clearly and keep the conversation on target. Talk for about ten minutes; then ask some specific questions of the interviewer. Listen carefully to the responses. Remember that if you are prepared for a job interview, it will involve a mutual exchange of information.

If the initial interview is satisfactory, you will probably be invited to come back for another interview. Sometimes you will also be asked to take a battery of intelligence or aptitude tests. Most students do very well on these tests, because they have had plenty of practice in college!

The Employment Decision

Now let's consider the actual hiring interview. By this time the company knows a lot about you from your placement file, resume, and initial interview. You should also know a lot about the company. The primary purpose of the second interview is to determine whether you can work effectively with your potential superior and with your peers.

If you create a positive impression during your second interview, you may be offered employment. Again, your decision to accept the offer should depend on the closeness of the match between career opportunities and career objectives. If there appears to be a good match, your work is just beginning.

Make the best entry-level job decision you can; then get on with your career plan. Learn your job responsibilities as quickly and thoroughly as possible; then start looking for other ways to improve your performance and that of your company. Remember . . . your first promotion is just around the corner, so be sure not to miss the opportunity in your lifelong career development plan.

Sources of Career Information

There are numerous sources of career information, ranging from government reports to career-counseling centers to professional associations (see Focus 25–1). Following is a selected list of organizations providing such information:

Air Transport Association of America
1709 New York Avenue NW
Washington, DC 20006

American Advertising Federation
1225 Connecticut Avenue NW
Washington, DC 20036

American Bankers Association
1120 Connecticut Avenue NW
Washington, DC 20036

American Bar Association
Information Services
1155 East 60th Street
Chicago, IL 60637

American Council of Life Insurance
1850 K Street NW
Washington, D.C. 20006

American Federation of Information
Processing Societies
210 Summit Avenue
Montvale, NJ 07645

American Hotel and Motel
Association
Educational Institute
Stephan S. Nisbet Building
1407 South Harrison Road
East Lansing, MI 48823

American Institute of Certified Public
Accountants
1211 Avenue of the Americas
New York, NY 10036

American Management Association
135 West 50th Street
New York, NY 10020

American Personnel and Guidance
Association
5203 Leesburg Pike
Falls Church, VA 22041

American Planning Association
1776 Massachusetts Avenue NW
Washington, DC 20036

American Society for Personnel
Administration
1140 Connecticut Avenue NW
Washington, DC 20036

Association for Computing Machinery
Information Services
1133 Avenue of the Americas
New York, NY 10036

Association of University Programs in
Health Administration
1755 Massachusetts Avenue NW
Washington, DC 20036

Business-Professional Advertising
Association
205 East 42nd Street
New York, NY 10017

College Placement Council
62 Highland Avenue
Bethlehem, PA 18001

Direct Mail/Marketing Educational
Foundation
6 East 43rd Street
New York, NY 10017

Financial Executives Institute
633 Third Avenue
New York, NY 10017

Independent Insurance Agents of
America
85 John Street
New York, NY 10038

Institute of Internal Auditors
International Headquarters
249 Maitland Avenue
Altamonte Springs, FL 32701

National Association of Accountants
919 Third Avenue
New York, NY 10022

National Association of Life
Underwriters
1922 F Street NW
Washington, DC 20006

National Automobile Dealers
Association
Career Booklet
8400 Westpark Drive
McLean, VA 22101

National Consumer Finance
Association
1000 16th Street NW
Washington, DC 20036

National Institute for the Food Service
Industry
20 North Wacker Drive
Chicago, IL 60606

National Society of Public
Accountants
1010 North Fairfax Street
Alexandria, VA 22314

Public Relations Society of America
845 Third Avenue
New York, NY 10022
(25 cents for brochure)

Sales and Marketing Executives
International
Career Education
380 Lexington Avenue
New York, NY 10068

Society of Actuaries
208 South LaSalle Street
Chicago, IL 60604

U.S. Department of Commerce
Employment Information Center
Room 1050
14th and Constitution Avenue NW
Washington, DC 20030

FOCUS 25–1
"Discover" Is Another Source of Career Information

Students considering the future can now consult a computer.

The computer counseling system, called Discover, can provide a blizzard of information on a college or a career.

International Business Machines sells the service . . . . The system uses a video screen with a keyboard underneath and a light pen which the user touches to the screen to call up information.

The Discover system allows a student to delve as deeply as he or she wants into the prospects for a future in, for example, nursing.

Schools offering nursing training, job prospects on graduation, wages in different parts of the country as well as drawbacks of the profession can all be called up on the television screen for study and a hard copy printout of the information can also be made.

Blasch said school districts, charged $900 a month, have access to an IBM databank in Los Angeles containing information on more than 1,500 four-year colleges, 1,000 two-year colleges, over 600 types of jobs, 450 military training programs and some 1,000 technical and specialized schools.

The system was developed by career counselors JoAnn Bowlsbey and James Boyd, along with IBM experts.

Ms. Bowlsbey, now a counselor at Western Maryland College, said "the system supplements the work of the guidance counselor but it doesn't replace the counselor."

"It's intended," said Boyd, technical director of the Discover program at the College of Du Page in Glen Ellyn, Ill., "to do four things: help a student help himself; help him understand the decision-making process; help him understand the world of work and his relationship to it; and help him to identify training paths related to occupations."

In some districts, students who might feel shy or confused in front of a counselor can sit down at the computer screen located in the school library or learning center, and daydream about the future with no pressure.

Blasch said the system has proved especially helpful to middle-aged mothers and housewives entering the job market for the first time. In some areas, local jobs currently available are also listed.

The Financial Reward at the Top

People who make it to the top of their business are well rewarded for their efforts. Table 25–1 shows the 25 highest-paid executives in the United States in 1980. As the table illustrates, some of these individuals received substantial payments beyond their base salaries.

One study of top corporate executives found that the median pay for board chairmen was $399,301; for presidents, $321,649; and for vice-presidents, $228,187.[6] Extensive benefits are also common. They include insurance programs, attractive retirement plans, automobiles, private airplanes, financial and tax planning, expense accounts, club memberships, and **stock options**—company plans that enable executives to buy the firm's stock at a set price often lower than the current market price. While top-level managers are certainly well paid, college students should neither envy nor be otherwise swayed by this. Top management is an elite group screened by years of hard work and

stock options
Company plans that enable executives to buy the firm's stock at a set price often lower than the current market price.

TABLE 25–1
Earnings of 25 Top Executives in 1980

Rank	Executive	Company	Salary	Bonus	Total
1	Milton F. Rosenthal	Engelhard Minerals & Chemicals	—	—	$2,301,592
2	Donald P. Kelly	Esmark	—	—	1,647,204
3	Rawleigh Warner, Jr.	Mobil	$498,350	$ 957,000	1,455,350
4	Thomas H. Wyman	CBS	201,923	1,158,840	1,360,763
5	Steven J. Ross	Warner Communications	350,000	999,675	1,349,675
6	Fred L. Hartley	Union Oil	440,000	806,154	1,246,154
7	William Tavoulareas	Mobil	416,804	817,000	1,233,804
8	Clifton C. Garvin, Jr.	Exxon	640,000	590,551	1,230,551
9	Jack A. Vickers	Vickers Energy	201,206	1,000,000	1,201,206
10	Thomas D. Barrow	Kennecott	365,000	813,125	1,178,125
11	Michel C. Bergerac	Revlon	583,333	500,000	1,083,333
12	Rand V. Araskog	ITT	461,250	554,057	1,015,307
13	Saul P. Steinberg	Reliance Group	507,308	500,000	1,007,308
14	Reginald H. Jones	General Electric	—	—	1,000,000
15	Justin Dart	Dart Industries	—	—	1,000,000
16	John M. Seabrook	IU International	—	—	959,970
17	Donald T. Regan	Merrill Lynch	—	—	954,986
18	James H. Evans	Union Pacific	385,096	550,000	935,096
19	David Mahoney	Norton Simon	500,000	432,692	932,692
20	Thomas V. Jones	Northrop	—	—	931,537
21	Harry J. Gray	United Technologies	—	—	915,000
22	H. J. Haynes	Standard Oil of California	450,000	448,343	898,343
23	Irving Shapiro	Du Pont	—	—	872,757
24	F. T. Cary	IBM	—	—	870,649
25	Robert Anderson	Rockwell International	—	—	865,000

effort. Heidrick & Struggles, a management consulting firm, has come up with this profile for a typical chief executive officer (CEO):

> The individual began working at age 23, moving to a supervisor's position within four years. The CEO, who has been with the current employer for over 22 years, is now age 57. The CEO spends 60 hours a week on the job plus an additional 5 hours in a community service activity. These individuals also typically hold 3 outside directorships and give 20 speeches annually.[7]

Critics sometimes point out that corporate executives earn substantially more than the president of the United States, who draws only a $200,000 annual salary.[8] Admittedly, Ronald Reagan and his predecessors have not earned as much as individuals occupying corporate executive slots. But neither the president nor the typical top executive earns as much as some professional athletes, popular writers, entertainment personalities, lawyers, and physicians. In fact, President Reagan earned more in other endeavors than he now does as President. Earnings vary from one occupational group to another because of such factors as market demand, the price-setting mechanism employed, and societal standards.

Many highly paid corporate leaders made substantial financial sacrifices when they accepted government posts. Alexander M. Haig, Jr., gave up $738,750 a year from United Technologies to become Secretary of State. Donald T. Regan gave up $954,986 per year when he left Merrill Lynch to become Treasury Secretary. Their new salaries as cabinet members are $69,630.[9]

Corporate leaders are among the best-qualified people in our society to serve either business or government. Top executives earn substantial sums, but their contributions are extraordinary.

The Special Problems of Women Choosing Business Careers

Women now account for about 42.4 percent of the U.S. labor force.[10] This figure is expected to top 60 percent by 1990.[11] While the number of employed women has increased substantially over the years, women are only now opening the doors to executive office suites.

Traditionally, women entered careers such as teaching, nursing, and secretarial slots. While many were truly oriented to such careers, others may have selected them because of societal and family pressure and outright bias in other fields. The situation has changed considerably today. Women are entering many fields previously closed to them. Business administration classrooms, for instance, are full of women aspiring to high-level careers in private enterprise. In fact, the number of college women majoring in business now exceeds those majoring in education. Over a recent 12-year period, female business majors climbed 300 percent, while female education majors declined 21 percent.[12]

Retailing has long been a favorite industry for women seeking business careers. Other choices have included consumer goods and service industries. Now these traditional career areas are being shunned by some women who are performing well in industrial sales, public accounting, and the like.

Personnel is another favored area for women managers. A survey by National Personnel Associates reveals that the most management women are hired in this area, although many are also being hired in sales, accounting, data processing, and engineering.[13]

Relatively few women hold top management jobs. This situation can be explained in part by the fact that relatively few women have acquired the experience necessary to assume such posts. It is reasonable to believe that as today's young businesswomen progress in organizations, many will eventually become corporate officers. However, they will probably face many career obstacles that cannot be overlooked if contemporary business is to reach its goal of equal employment opportunity.

What are some of the special problems that face women choosing a business career? Heidrick & Struggles, management consultants, asked 148 female corporate officers about the factor that most impeded their careers. The largest number, 48.5 percent, cited discrimination. When asked what factor most contributed to their own success, 48 percent of the women answered "hard work," another 21 percent said "ability," and 10 percent named "luck."[14]

Women often lack the sort of career development model that is commonplace for men. Young women entering industry today are often their family's first generation of female businesspeople. They often lack the career perspectives that business executives provide their sons. Once employed, they sometimes lack peers on which to base a career development pattern. In the past, women tended to enter business with educational backgrounds in such nonbusiness areas as elementary education and home economics. They lacked business-oriented associations from their college days. Finally, the limited number of female executives provide few career models for young women advancing in a company, so businesswomen break new ground at each stage of their careers.

Male co-workers can also create special problems for female executives. Unaccustomed to working with women of equal or higher managerial rank, men are sometimes ill at ease in such situations. Some even attempt to disregard or circumvent directives or suggestions by female executives. As more women enter executive ranks, these incidents are expected to decline.

Public accounting is one of the many new career areas in which women are finding jobs.

Controversial Issue

Mentors and Networking: Are They Career Advancement Answers for Women?

For years, women have been treated like outsiders in the world of business. One of the major reasons for this is their lack of professional contacts: When push came to shove and a big business deal or job opportunity was on the line, they simply did not know the people in power.

A new phenomenon called networking may be changing all that. Networking is a means of developing and using contacts to get ahead in business. New job leads, information and advice about business deals, and interdepartmental information are all passed on through an informal network of coworkers. As Mary Scott Welch, author of *Networking: The Great New Way for Women to Get Ahead*, explains, networking can give women the same winning edge as men who have always depended on their male associates for information, feedback, and perhaps, most importantly, future alliances. It is an informal tie-line to what is *really* going on in the company.

Can networking work for women in the same way it has for men? In order to develop an effective networking system of their own, women must be willing to provide information even when they gain nothing for themselves in return. For women who were raised to compete with each other for the attention of men rather than to work as a team toward a common goal, this kind of communication may not come easily. Ironically, even though networking can give women the same winning edge as men, many women fear and mistrust it. This mistrust can destroy the whole system, for only women who approach each other openly, as if they were members of the same team, can make networking a success.

Networking may also break down because of the scarcity of women in high executive positions. No matter how willing women are to share information with each other and to help each other along, without political clout they may not be very effective.

To solve this problem, women may have to turn to men, who are well entrenched in the corporate power structure, as their net-

Married women face the dilemma created by their spouse's career aspirations and their own family responsibilities. This problem should become easier to solve as more husbands and wives consider both careers in making their decisions. While such situations can force difficult choices, successful executives do cope with the problems and go on to pursue their own professional goals. Success in any field has always required hard work and tough decisions, and contemporary businesswomen are proving that they can and will make the sacrifices necessary to succeed.

working sources. They may meet stiff opposition here, too, for in order to work, male-female networking must break down traditional barriers. Men are used to talking to other men about business but may be unwilling to do the same with women.

The mentor system takes the concept of networking one step further. It provides promising but inexperienced women with a kind of godfather—a senior executive in the company who takes a protégé under his wing and teaches her all he knows about business and business politics. For example, when M. Kathryn Eickhoff joined the economic consulting firm of Townsend-Greenspan as a research assistant trainee in 1962, she began a long working relationship with the economist Alan Greenspan, who became her mentor. She describes Greenspan as supportive, demanding, and passionately involved with his work. He demanded the same passion from his protégé. Eickhoff is now executive vice president of the firm.

In their study of 25 female executives, Margaret Henning and Ann Jardim, authors of *The Managerial Woman,* found that mentors were crucial to women's ability to achieve success in male-dominated business fields.

Unfortunately, many women may find it difficult to seek out the ties they need with a senior executive to take advantage of this informal opportunity for career growth. Going to an older, more experienced man for help may feel too much like going to father, and women may simply not take the first step. Even if they do, many male executives may not be willing to reach out to an up-and-coming woman and guide her along.

In the world of business, where males still dominate and the "old boy" system is strong, networking and mentors give women a way to equalize their chances for success. Only time will tell whether women will be able to take advantage of these resources and whether men at the top of corporations will respond with a helping hand or a turned back.

A Final Note . . . The Authors' View

We believe that choosing a career is the most important, and often the roughest, decision you will ever have to make. There is little room for error; your future happiness depends on a wise, thoughtfully considered choice.

Do not procrastinate or trust others to make this decision for you. Follow the steps outlined here or in other sources, and make your own decision. Your instructors, parents, friends, and advisers will be willing to help in a multitude of ways. But in the end, the bottom line is your own personal decision.

We hope this textbook has opened a panorama of business- and management-oriented careers for you. Probably most of your classmates will work for a business firm when they leave school. But whatever your own decision, be sure it is right for you. As the old saying goes, "You pass this way only once." Enjoy!

Summary

When approaching a career in business, students should become aware of projected employment trends and should prepare for a group of related jobs—a career cluster—that offers good employment and career opportunities. A good business background along with a positive attitude will pave the way for many entry-level jobs.

Besides analyzing the demand for people in certain areas, students should learn about themselves. Help is available from school libraries, counseling centers, and career guidance or placement offices.

Obtaining the right job is difficult. Some ways to begin the search are:

1. Locate available jobs that interest you.
2. Register with your placement office—and make sure you are on its mailing list for new job opportunities.
3. Prepare a placement or credentials file, including letters of recommendation from instructors and others who know you well, transcripts of your academic work, other factual information about yourself, and a statement of career goals.
4. Seek out job sources such as educational placement offices at other colleges you have attended, private employment agencies, and public employment agencies. Look at newspaper ads and trade journals and magazines. Talk to your professors and to school administrators, community organizations, and friends. Try writing directly to a company that interests you.
5. Prepare a resume, with the following information: personal, educational, and professional achievements; age; address; telephone number; and references.
6. Study your employment opportunities and consider many factors in assessing them rather than only the most striking features.
7. Be well prepared for the personal interview with a prospective employer. Know as much as you can about the company, its industry, and its competition. Be confident and communicate effectively. Retain

your composure even under the pressure of a stress interview. If the interview is open-ended, talk for about ten minutes, then begin asking questions.

Once you have been hired, begin looking for ways to improve yourself and your company. This is the beginning of your lifelong career development plan.

There are many sources of career information, ranging from government reports to career counselors and professional associations.

People who make it to the top in business are well paid and receive many other benefits. They also work hard to get to the top—and to stay there.

Women have a number of problems in their business careers. Among the problems women face are the following:

1. Women lack the kinds of career development models that have been commonplace for men.
2. They are discriminated against by male co-workers.
3. Married women are caught in the dilemma of allocating priorities among their spouse's career aspirations, family responsibilities, and their own career goals.

Choosing a career is the most important and often the most difficult decision to make—but it should always be your own.

Key Terms

entry-level job	stress interview
career cluster	open-ended interview
resume	stock options

Review Questions

1. Explain each of the terms listed above.

2. Explain the importance of the career cluster concept.

3. Why do many people switch careers several times?

4. Trace the major employment trends outlined in this chapter.

5. Why is knowing yourself such a critical part of overall career development?

6. Outline the contents of a typical placement or credentials file.

7. What employment sources are available to you?

8. Prepare a written outline of the job search procedure you plan to use when you enter the labor market or switch jobs.

9. What are the special career development problems facing women?

10. Discuss the financial compensation packages provided for management. Compare them with the compensation for other successful people such as entertainers, politicians, and the self-employed.

Discussion Questions and Exercises

1. Evaluate the pros and cons of the controversial issue that appears in this chapter.

2. Construct your own resume following the procedure outlined in this chapter. Ask your instructors, friends, relatives, and associates to criticize it. Then revise the resume.

3. Contact the campus office that can arrange for you to take tests that will help you select a career field. Take one of the tests, and prepare a report on what you learn from it.

4. Set up job interviews in your class. Designate one person (perhaps your instructor) as the interviewer who announces an available position. Then, randomly select students to apply for the job. Prepare a brief critique of the way the interviews are conducted.

5. Select a career cluster that interests you, and prepare a report on future career opportunities and employment trends affecting this cluster.

Case 25-1: Occupation— The Main Status Symbol

Donald Treiman, a UCLA sociologist, has published a status scale for various occupations. Treiman has developed an international occupational prestige ranking, with 0 to 100 ratings for 509 separate endeavors. Physicians and university professors rank highest, while persons living on public assistance score lowest. Here are some of the ratings:

Occupation	Rating	Occupation	Rating
University professors	78	Farmers	47
Physicians	78	Construction workers	46
Lawyers	71	Office clerks	43
Dentists and heads of large		TV repair personnel	42
business firms	70	Police officers	40
Professional accountants	68	Soldiers	39
Business executives	67	Receptionists	38
High school teachers	64	Models	36
Veterinarians	61	Plumbers	34
Clergy	60	Sales clerks	34
Persons living off income property	57	Truck drivers	33
Journalists	55	Assembly line workers	30
Nurses	54	Taxi drivers	28
Secretaries	53	Janitors	21
Real estate agents	49	Laborers	19
Bank tellers	48	People living on public assistance	16

Questions

1. Explain why professors and physicians rank at the top of the prestige scale.

2. Discuss the rankings of various business-oriented occupations, such as business executives, professional accountants, real estate agents, and the like.

3. Relate Treiman's study to the career development process explained in this chapter.

Case 25–2: What Makes an Executive Tick?

What makes an executive work the long hours required for business success? Certainly, the pay at the top of the management ladder is an incentive. Six-digit compensation figures are common at these levels. While money is important, it appears to be secondary to the satisfaction inherent in managerial work. A study by management consultants Heidrick & Struggles found that the chief executive officers tended to enjoy work more than most of their associates, and they preferred business activities over other activities.[15] Another study, by Paul R. Ray & Co. of Fort Worth, Texas, concluded that a love of work was the primary motivating factor for business executives. Two-thirds of the respondents in this study said they would continue to work even if they were financially independent.[16]

Questions

1. Relate the studies reported here to points raised in the chapter.

2. What do the findings presented in this case imply for your own career development?

Careers in International Business, Business Law, and Selected Industries

International business, business law, and certain industries all offer career opportunities. International business includes many careers, both at home and abroad. Attorneys assist management and often become actively involved in the operation of a firm. Some work directly for companies, but most contract their services to businesses.

The Bureau of Labor Statistics has projected the employment outlook to 1990. Its forecasts for selected jobs in international business, business law, and certain industries appear in the following table. The bureau expects all occupations to add 20.8 percent to their work force between 1978 and 1990. Five of the careers available in these areas appear below.

Importer. Importers are individuals who buy foreign products and then resell them in their home country. Their field is interesting because of the many new product ideas with which they are involved.

Export manager. Export managers direct the foreign sales of a company. They are responsible for marketing, distribution, financing, and after-sale servicing. Their position is important because foreign sales represent a significant proportion of many firms' revenues.

International manager. When a company has multinational operations a separate international unit is usually set up. The international manager is the chief executive for this unit and has overall responsibility for its operations.

Attorney. Most legal firms are extensively involved in business problems. Some attorneys work directly for a firm, but most are independent contractors. Because so much of most attorneys' work is in business law, it is advisable for them to have a business as well as a legal education.

EMPLOYMENT OUTLOOK ON 1990

Occupations in World Business, Business Law, and Selected Industries	Recent Employment Figures	Changes in Employment					
		Much Faster than the Average for All Occupations	Faster than the Average for All Occupations	About as Fast as the Average for All Occupations	More Slowly than the Average for All Occupations	Little Change Expected	Expected to Decline
Hotel Managers and Assistants	168,000				X		
Lawyers	480,000		X				
Health and Regulatory Inspectors (Government)	100,000		X				
Occupational Safety and Health Workers	80,000	X					
Manufacturing Industry Managers and Administrators	1,250,000	Mixed Employment Outlook					
Wholesale and Retail Trade Managers and Administrators	3,686,000			X			
Transportation, Communications, and Public Utilities Managers and Administrators	531,000				X		
Finance, Insurance and Real Estate Mangers and officers	Not Available	Mixed Employment Outlook					

Source: U.S. Department of Labor, Bureau of Labor Statistics, *Occupational Outlook Handbook 1980–1981*, Bulletin 2075, pp. 5, 121–125, 165–170, 348–350, 501–502, 569–570, 592, 599–600.

Appendix: Selected Readings

This appendix contains a list of readings that should prove worthwhile to business students. The selections, from well-known sources, were chosen because of their relevance to contemporary business.

Business and its Environment

Bohlander, George W. "Declining Productivity: Trends and Causes." *Arizona Business,* February 1981, pp. 3–13.

Chatov, Robert. "What Corporate Ethics Say." *California Management Review,* Summer 1980, pp. 20–29.

Graham, Roberta. "Small Business: Beset, Bothered, and Beleaguered by Five Big Problems." *Nation's Business,* February 1980, pp. 22–26, 27–31.

Herschman, Arlene, and Mark Levenson. "The Reindustrialization of America." *Dun's Review,* July 1980, pp. 34–39, 43.

Jones, Thomas M. "Corporate Social Responsibility Revisted, Redefined." *California Management Review,* Spring 1980, pp. 59–67.

Kuntz, Edwin C., Banwari L. Kedia, and Carlton J. Whitehead. "Variations in Corporate Social Performance." *California Management Review,* Summer 1980, pp. 30–36.

Louviere, Vernon. "Let's Rebuild America!" *Nation's Business,* November 1980, pp. 32–34, 36–38, 40, 45.

McKenna, Jack F., and Paul L. Oritt. "Small Business Growth: Making a Conscious Decision." *Advanced Management Journal,* Spring 1980, pp. 45–53.

Podhoretz, Norman. "The New Defenders of Capitalism." *Harvard Business Review,* March–April 1981, pp. 96–106.

Schwartz, Felice N. "Invisible Resource: Women for Boards." *Harvard Business Review,* March–April, 1980, pp. 6–8, 12, 14, 18.

Weber, James. "Institutionalizing Ethics into the Corporation." *MSU Business Topics,* Spring 1981, pp. 47–52.

Wilson, Erika. "Social Responsibility of Business: What Are the Small Business Perspectives?" *Journal of Small Business Management,* July 1980, pp. 17–24.

Organization and Management of the Enterprise

Andrews, Kenneth R. "Directors' Responsibility for Corporate Strategy." *Harvard Business Review,* November–December 1980, pp. 30, 32, 36, 40, 42.

Charan, Ram, Charles W. Hofer, and John F. Mahon. "From Entrepreneur to Professional Management: A Set of Guidelines." *Journal of Small Business Management,* January 1980, pp. 1–10.

Gabarro, John J., and John P. Kotter. "Managing Your Boss." *Harvard Business Review,* January–February 1980, pp. 92–100.

Greenwood, Ronald G. "Management by Objectives: As Developed by Peter Drucker, Assisted by Harold Smiddy." *The Academy of Management Review,* April 1981, pp. 225–230.

Koontz, Harold. "The Management Theory Jungle Revisited." *The Academy of Management Review,* April 1980, pp. 175–187.

Leontrades, Milton. "The Dimension of Planning in Large Industrialized Organizations." *California Management Review,* Summer 1980, pp. 82–86.

McMurray, Robert N. "What to Do about Executives Who Can't Delegate and Won't Decide." *Nation's Business,* May 1980, pp. 70, 72, 73.

Norgaard, Connie T. "Problems and Perspectives of Female Managers." *MSU Business Topics,* Winter 1980, pp. 23–28.

Piercy, James E., and J. Benjamin Forbes. "Industry Differences in Chief Executive Officers." *MSU Business Topics,* Winter 1981, pp. 17–29.

Rousch, Charles H., Jr., and Ben C. Ball, Jr. "Controlling the Implementation of Strategy." *Managerial Planning,* November–December 1980, pp. 3–12.

Sasser, W. Earl, Jr., and Frank S. Leonard. "Let First-Level Supervisors Do Their Job." *Harvard Business Review,* March–April 1980, pp. 113–121.

Whetten, David A. "Organizational Decline: A Neglected Topic in Organizational Science." *Academy of Management Review,* October 1980, pp. 577–588.

Management of Human Resources

Alpander, Guvenc G. "Human Resource Planning in U.S. Corporations." *California Management Review,* Spring 1980, pp. 24–32.

Burns, John L. "Benefits of Training the Hard-to-Employ." *Harvard Business Review,* May–June 1980, pp. 141–151.

Cook, Curtis W. "Guidelines for Managing Motivation." *Business Horizons,* April 1980, pp. 61–69.

Imberman, Woodruff. "Are Strikes Avoidable?" *Business Horizons,* April 1980, pp. 43–48.

Kelley, Joe, and Kamran Khozan. "Participative Management: Can It Work?" *Business Horizons,* August 1980, pp. 74–79.

Klein, Gerald D. "Beyond EOE and Affirmative Action." *California Management Review,* Summer 1980, pp. 74–81.

Millard, Cheedle W., Diane L. Lockwood, and Fred Lultrans. "The Impact of a Four Day Workweek on Employees." *MSU Business Topics,* Spring 1980, pp. 31–37.

Pate, Gopal C., and John I. Atkins. "Hire the Handicapped—Compliance Is Good Business." *Harvard Business Review,* January–February 1980, pp. 14–15, 18, 20, 22.

Runcie, John F. "By Days I Make the Cars." *Harvard Business Review,* May–June 1980, pp. 106–115.

Summers, Clyde W. "Protecting *All* Employees Against Unjust Dismissal." *Harvard Business Review,* February–March 1980, pp. 132–139.

Teel, Kenneth S. "Performance Appraisal: Current Trends, Persistent Progress." *Personnel Journal,* April 1980, pp. 296–301, 316.

Vosburgh, Richard M. "The Annual Human Resource Review (A Career-Planning System)." *Personnel Journal,* October 1980, pp. 830–837.

Marketing Management

Barkesdale, Hiram C., and William D. Perreault, Jr. "Can Consumers Be Satisfied?" *MSU Business Topics,* Spring 1980, pp. 19–30.

Bloom, Paul N., and William D. Novelli. "Problems and Challenges in Social Marketing." *Journal of Marketing,* Spring 1981, pp. 79–88.

Donath, Bob. "Sniffing Out the Elusive Hot Sales Lead." *Industrial Marketing,* May 1980, pp. 46–47, 50, 54, 58–59.

Doyle, Stephen X., and Benson P. Shapiro. "What Counts Most in Motivating Your Sales Force?" *Harvard Business Review,* May–June 1980, pp. 133–140.

Faris, Paul W., and Mark S. Albion. "The Impact of Advertising on the Price of Consumer Products." *Journal of Marketing,* Summer 1980, pp. 17–35.

Kleinberg, Ellen M. "Trademarks: The Care and Feeding of Brand Name Identities." *Industrial Review,* October 1980, pp. 56, 58, 62–63.

La Barbera, Priscilla A., and Larry J. Rosenberg. "How Marketers Can Better Understand Consumers." *MSU Business Topics,* Winter 1980, pp. 29–36.

Lawton, Leigh, and A. Parasuraman. "The Impact of the Marketing Concept on New Product Planning." *Journal of Marketing,* Winter 1980, pp. 19–25.

McNeal, James U., and Landa M. Zeren. "Brand Name Selection for Consumer Products." *MSU Business Topics,* Spring 1981, pp. 35–39.

McNiven, Malcom A. "Plan for More Productive Advertising." *Harvard Business Review,* March–April 1980, pp. 13–136.

Michman, Ronald D. "The Double Income Family: A New Marketing Target." *Business Horizons,* August 1980, pp. 31–37.

Rosenberg, Larry J., and Elizabeth C. Hirschman. "Retailing Without Stores." *Harvard Business Review,* July–August 1980, pp. 103–112.

Production and Information

Anthony, Robert N. "Making Sense of Nonbusiness Accounting." *Harvard Business Review,* May–June 1980, pp. 83–93.

Buchanan, Jack R., and Richard G. Linowes. "Understanding Distributed Data Processing." *Harvard Business Review,* July–August 1980, pp. 143–153.

Greiner, Larry E., and Alan L. Scharff. "The Challenge of Cultivating Accounting Firm Executives." *Journal of Accountancy,* September 1980, pp. 57–58, 59–61.

Groves, Ray J. "Corporate Disclosure in the 1980s." *Financial Executive,* June 1980, pp. 14–19.

Halladay, Maurice E. "Improve ADP Software Development: Ask the Data Providers." *Business Horizons,* August 1980, pp. 48–55.

Janson, Robert L. "Graphic Indications of Operations." *Harvard Business Review,* November–December 1980, pp. 164–170.

Leone, Robert A., and John R. Myer. "Capacity Strategies for the 1980s." *Harvard Business Review,* November–December 1980, pp. 133–140.

Leontrades, Milton. "Evaluating a Firm's Performance Potential." *Business Horizons,* August 1980, pp. 61–66.

Mechlin, George F., and Daniel Berg. "Evaluating Research—ROI Is Not Enough." *Harvard Business Review,* September–October 1980, pp. 93–99.

Neumann, Seev, and Michael Hadass. "DSS and Strategic Decisions." *California Management Review,* Spring 1980, pp. 77–84.

Rappapat, Alfred. "The Strategic Audit." *Journal of Accountancy,* June 1980, pp. 71–74, 76–77.

Richardson, Peter R., and John R. M. Gordon. "Measuring Total Manufacturing Performance." *Sloan Management Review,* Winter 1980, pp. 47–58.

Financing the Enterprise

Bonocore, Joseph J. "Getting a Picture of Cash Management." *Financial Executive,* May 1980, pp. 30–33.

Corr, Arthur V. "Capital Investment Planning." *Financial Executive,* August 1980, pp. 12–15.

Farrelly, Gail. "A Behavioral Science Approach to Financial Research." *Financial Management,* Autumn 1980, pp. 15–22.

Hershlman, Arlene. "Bring Back the Gold Standard." *Dun's Review,* April 1980, pp. 58–61, 64–66.

Long, John D. "What Should Insurance Companies Do About Soaring Insurance Costs?" *Business Horizons,* April 1980, pp. 22–30.

Perham, John C. "Stockholders Attack Nuclear Power." *Dun's Review,* April 1980, pp. 91–93, 96–97.

Reckers, Phillip M. R., and A. J. Stagliano. "How Good Are Investors' Data Sources." *Financial Executive,* April 1980, pp. 26, 28, 30, 32.

Reilly, Robert F. "A Cost of Funds Employed Method in Lease vs. Buy Analysis." *Financial Executive,* October 1980, pp. 14–17.

Stetson, Charles P., Jr. "The Reshaping of Corporate Financial Services." *Harvard Business Review,* September–October 1980, pp. 134–142.

Waldron, Dorothy, and Leslie D. Ball. "The Bottom Line on Checkless Banking." *Across the Board,* August 1980, pp. 34–41.

Wilkens, Maurice C., Jr. "Financial Flexibility in the 1980s." *Harvard Business Review,* March–April 1980, pp. 103–105.

Wynant, Larry. "Essential Elements of Project Financing." *Harvard Business Review,* May–June 1980, pp. 165–173.

Additional Dimensions

Badway, M. K. "Styles of Mideastern Managers." *California Management Review,* Spring 1980, pp. 51–58.

Bartolome, Fernando, and Paul A. Lee Exons. "Must Success Cost So Much?" *Harvard Business Review,* March–April 1980, pp. 137–148.

Berry, Leonard Eugene, and Gordon B. Harwood. "Using Accounting Information to Make Better Decisions." *Business,* March–April 1981, pp. 24–27.

Friedman, Hershey H. "Futuristics: Reducing Marketing Myopia." *Business Horizons,* August 1980, pp. 17–20.

Hall, William K. "Survival Strategies in a Hostile Environment." *Harvard Business Review,* September–October 1980, pp. 75–85.

Lambert, Douglas M., and Jeffrey G. Towle. "A Theory of Return for Deposit." *California Management Review,* Summer 1980, pp. 65–73.

Levinson, Harry. "When Executives Burn Out." *Harvard Business Review,* May–June 1981, pp. 72–81.

March, Robert M. "Foreign Firms in Japan." *California Management Review,* Spring 1980, pp. 42–50.

Milbourne, Gene, Jr., and Richard Cuba. "What Blacks Want from Their Jobs—And What They Get." *Advanced Management Journal,* Autumn 1980, pp. 50–60.

Perham, John. "Top Management Views the 1980's." *Dun's Review,* January 1980, pp. 68–69, 73.

Tuthill, Mary. "Where the Jobs Are." *Nation's Business,* September 1980, pp. 24–26, 28, 30, 32.

Whalen, Richard. "No American Business is an Island." *Across the Board,* July 1980, pp. 40–51.

Chapter 1

1 The saga of the WFL is told in Glenn Drosendahl, "Here Lies the Late, Almost Great WFL," *Journal-American,* October 21, 1980, p. B1.

2 Nancy Way, "Firm Capitalizes on Shortage of Post Office Boxes," *Journal-American,* January 12, 1981, pp. D1, D2.

3 "U.S. Has 2nd Lowest Gain in Productivity, Study Says," *Detroit News,* May 25, 1980, p. 17-C.

4 Ibid.

5 "Survey Says Public Poor on Economic Knowledge," *Advertising Age,* December 29, 1980.

6 A. F. Ehbar, "A Strong Start on the Economy," *Fortune,* March 23, 1981, p. 51.

7 The term five *M*s of management was first suggested by L. T. White, a leading small business proponent. See U.S. Small Business Administration, *Strengthening Small Business Management: Collections from the Papers of L. T. White,* Joseph C. Schabacker, ed., (Washington, D.C.: Government Printing Office, 1971), p. 21.

8 "Big Loss, Bigger Bailout," *Time,* November 12, 1979, p. 100.

Chapter 2

1 Robert E. Vanderbeek, "Social Responsibility Can Be Profitable, Too," *Response,* May 1980, pp. 8–9.

2 Ralph E. Winter, "Furor Over a Plant on Lake Superior Is Warning to Industry," *Wall Street Journal,* August 25, 1974.

3 See the *1980 General Motors Public Interest Report,* April 7, 1980.

4 These examples are from William Guttmann, "You Can't Beat Inflation," *The Age,* September 28, 1974, p. 11.

5 These estimates are reported in Raymond F. DeVoe, Jr., "Inflation: 1990 Style," *Barron's,* January 28, 1980, pp. 27–28, 36.

6 Reported in W. Howard Chase, "Adjusting to a Different Business/Societal Climate," *Administrative Management,* January 1979, p. 30.

7 Ronald G. Shafer, "Inflation Is Eroding the Ability of Many to Buy Own Home," *Wall Street Journal,* September 5, 1974.

8 See Byron Klapper, "Encouraged by Lenders and Retailers, More People Use Credit and Regret It," *Wall Street Journal,* August 17, 1974.

9 These examples are from Gail Bronson, "Profit-pinched Firms Extend Cost Cutting Down to Paper Clips," *Wall Street Journal,* January 30, 1975.

10 "While Consumers Squirm, Many Firms Prosper, "*U.S. News & World Report,* October 1, 1979, p. 50.

11 Quoted in "Federal Agencies—Which Are Worst?" *U.S. News & World Report,* November 14, 1977, p. 42.

12 Reported in Edward M. Syring, "Realizing Recycling's Potential," *Nation's Business,* February 1976, pp. 68, 70.

13 *The Age,* August 13, 1974, p. 1.

14 Farish A. Jenkins discusses these rights in "Business, Government, and Consumer," *Journal of Business,* December 1969, pp. 25–29.

15 "Olympia to Use Beer, Wastes to Brew Ethanol," *Seattle Times,* November 12, 1980, p. A 22.

16 Based on dates reported in *World Energy Outlook,* Exxon Background Series, January 1980, pp. 26–27.

17 Michael A. Robinson, "The Ups and Downs of Fuel Crisis," *Detroit News,* June 22, 1980, pp. 1-J, 2-J.

18 Reported in *Wall Street Journal,* July 10, 1979.

19 This study is discussed in Max Ways, "Business Faces Growing Pressures to Behave Better," *Fortune,* May 1974, p. 310.

Chapter 3

1 Stanton H. Patty, "Merger May Englarge Native Corporation," *Seattle Times,* November 23, 1980, p. B 5.

2 Rate A. Howell, John R. Allison, and Nate T. Henley, *Business Law, Text and Cases* 2d ed. (Hinsdale, Ill.: Dryden Press, 1981), p. 1014.

3 Census estimates for 1980 are contained in "Profile of America: What '80 Census Will Show," *U.S. News & World Report,* April 7, 1980, p. 67.

4 *American Telephone and Telegraph: 1980 Annual Report,* p. 28.

5 Max Ways, "Business Faces Growing Pressure to Behave Better," *Fortune,* May 1974, p. 316.

Chapter 4

1 "OMBE Client Installs White House Solar System," *Access,* July–August 1979, pp. 4–5, 14.

2 These statistics are reported in "Why Small Firms Find Inflation Hard to Lick," *U.S. News & World Report,* June 25, 1979, p. 61 and in Fern S. Schumer, "Planning Is Key to Opening a Small Business," *Orlando Sentinel Star,* October 12, 1980, p. 1-D.

3 Reported in "The Little Engines of Growth," *Time,* January 26, 1981, p. 52.

4 Reported in "The 500 Largest Industrial Corporations," *Fortune,* May 5, 1980, pp. 280, 282.

5 U.S. Bureau of the Census, *Statistical Abstract of the United States: 1980,* 101st ed. (Washington, D.C.: Government Printing Office, 1980), p. 556.

6 "Small Business Defined and Defended," *CPA Client Bulletin,* April 1980, p. 1.

7 These features are suggested in *Meeting the Special Problems of Small Business* (New York: Committee for Economic Development, 1947), p. 14.

8 Statistics taken from "Service Industries: Growth Field of '80s," *U.S. News & World Report,* March 17, 1980, pp. 80–81. Data from U.S. Department of Commerce and the Conference Board.

9 Marilyn Chase, "Venture Capitalists Rush in to Back Emerging High-technology Firms," *Wall Street Journal,* March 18, 1981, Section 2, p. 25.

10 McDaniel's story is told in "The Little Engines of Growth," *Time,* January 26, 1981, p. 52.

11 David M. Elsner, "A Small Cereal-maker Has a Tough Struggle in a Big Guy's World," *Wall Street Journal,* April 26, 1977.

12 Marilyn Kirkly, "She Traded Dance Shoes for a Needle and Thread," *Seattle Times,* December 4, 1980, p. E 6.

13 "When Everyone Can List Causes of Failure, Why Is Success Not Guaranteed to All?" *CPA Client Bulletin,* November 1980, p. 2.

14 "Doyle Hoyt Survives Bankruptcy, Succeeds Second Time Around," *Wall Street Journal,* November 29, 1977.

15 U.S. Small Business Administration, *SBA: What It Does,* p. 4.

[16] "Carter to Aids: Keep Small Business in Mind," *CPA Client Bulletin,* February 1980, p. 4.

[17] "Now It's Young People Making Millions: The Way Eight Did It," *U.S. News & World Report,* February 24, 1974, p. 48.

[18] U.S. Bureau of the Census, *Statistical Abstract of the United States: 1980,* 101st ed. (Washington D.C.: Government Printing Office, 1980), p. 558.

[19] Lester Books, "Guess Who's Coming to Sell Us," *Exxon USA,* Third Quarter 1977, p. 7.

[20] Ibid.

[21] "Small Business: Washington Begins to Take It More Seriously," p. 77.

[22] These activities are described in U.S. Small Business Administration, *SBA: What It Does.*

[23] This program is described in the U.S. Small Business Administration brochure "You Can Have Personalized Management Assistance Counseling."

[24] See "On The Way: New Round of Help for Small Business," *U.S. News & World Report,* August 30, 1976, p. 40.

Chapter 5

[1] See "Corporate Culture," *Business Week,* October 27, 1980, pp. 158, 160 and Earl C. Gottschalk, "Fox Film's Fortunes Soaring on the Wings of 'Star Wars' Movie," *Wall Street Journal,* January 12, 1978, p. 1.

[2] Fred Feidler, *A Theory of Leadership Effectiveness* (New York: McGraw-Hill, 1967).

Chapter 6

[1] The immense organizational tasks involved in landing an astronaut on the moon are described in *Man and the Organization* (New York: Time-Life Books, 1975), pp. 88–99. This quotation is from page 88.

[2] "Translating Bureaucratese," *U.S. News & World Report,* October 3, 1977, p. 26.

[3] C. Northcote Parkinson, *Parkinson's Law and Other Studies in Administration* (Boston: Houghton Mifflin, 1957), p. 2.

[4] Ibid., pp. 7–11.

[5] Ibid., pp. 4–7.

[6] See Frederick W. Taylor, *The Principles of Scientific Management* (New York: Harper & Bros., 1916).

[7] A thorough discussion of the matrix organization structure is contained in Stanley M. Davis and Paul R. Lawrence, *Matrix* (Reading, Mass.: Addison-Wesley, 1977).

[8] Robert Townsend, *Up the Organization* (New York: Knopf, 1970), p. 134.

[9] Keith Davis, *Human Relations at Work* (New York: McGraw-Hill, 1972), pp. 261–273.

Chapter 7

[1] The Kockums decisions are described in Bowen Northrup, "More Swedish Firms Attempt to 'Enrich' Production-line Jobs," *Wall Street Journal,* October 25, 1974.

[2] Stuart Chase, *Men at Work* (New York: Harcourt, Brace & World, 1941), pp. 21–22.

[3] Abraham H. Maslow, "A Theory of Human Motivation," *Psychological Review,* July 1943, pp. 370–396.

[4] Ibid., pp. 394 and 382, respectively.

[5] Robert Louis Stevenson, *Familiar Studies of Men and Books* (1882).

[6] Douglas McGregor, *The Human Side of Enterprise* (New York: McGraw-Hill, 1960), pp. 33–34.

[7] Ibid., pp. 47–48.

[8] Frederick Herzberg, *Work and the Nature of Man* (Cleveland: World Publishing, 1966).

[9] Peter Drucker, *The Practice of Management* (New York: Harper & Bros., 1954), pp. 128–129.

[10] Charles R. Walker and Robert Guest, *Man on the Assembley Line* (Cambridge, Mass.: Harvard University Press, 1952), p. 19.

[11] William J. Paul, Jr., Keith B. Robertson, and Frederick Herzberg "Job Enrichment Pays Off," *Harvard Business Review,* March–April 1969, p. 61.

[12] "The New Industrial Relations," *Business Week,* May 11, 1981, pp. 85–98 and "Workers Don't Give a Damn? Chrysler Thinks They Do, If—," *Ward's Auto World,* June 1972, p. 43.

[13] Personal interview with Randy Castelluzzo, manager of personnel services, General Foods Corporation, May 1981.

[14] Robert N. Ford, *Motivation Through the Work Itself* (New York: American Management Association, 1969).

[15] M. D. Kilbridge, "Do Workers Prefer Larger Jobs?" *Personnel,* September–October 1960, pp. 45–48.

[16] William E. Reif and Peter P. Schoderbek, "Job Enlargement: Antidote to Apathy," *Management of Personnel Quarterly,* Spring 1966, pp. 16–23.

Chapter 8

[1] Jerry Kirshenbaum, ed., "Scorecard," *Sports Illustrated,* January 26, 1981, p. 9.

[2] U.S. Equal Employment Opportunity Commission, *Affirmative Action and Equal Employment: A Guidebook for Employers* (Washington, D.C.: Government Printing Office, 1974).

[3] The mandatory retirement controversy is discussed in "After All the Fuss About Forced Retirement," *U.S. News & World Report,* December 11, 1978, pp. 91–92; "New Retirement Rules: Their Impact on Business, Workers," *U.S. News & World Report,* November 7, 1977, pp. 71–73; and "The Ax for Forced Retirement," *Business Week,* September 19, 1977, pp. 38–39.

[4] "A Work Force Wins a Travel Bonus," *Business Week,* January 10, 1977, p. 29.

[5] This section is based primarily on U.S. Department of Labor, Occupational Safety and Health Administration, *All About OSHA* (Washington, D.C.: Government Printing Office, n.d.).

[6] An interesting summary of alternative benefit programs is included in "How to Size Up Your Company Fringe Benefits," *Business Week,* May 12, 1980, pp. 136–138.

Chapter 9

[1] The Polish government-union disputes are discussed in "In Poland, Solidarity Walks a Tightrope," *U.S. News & World Report,* January 12, 1981, pp. 31–32; "Solidarity Wins a Round," *Newsweek,* November 24, 1980, pp. 74, 76; and "The Government Gets Tough," *Time,* January 26, 1981, pp. 42–43.

[2] James A. Barnes, *Wealth of the American People: A History of Their Economic Life* (New York: Prentice-Hall, 1949), pp. 286–290.

[3] Quoted in Campbell R. McConnell, *Economics* (New York: McGraw-Hill, 1975), p. 754.

[4] This section is adapted from Heinz Kohler, *Economics: The Science of Scarcity* (Hinsdale, Ill.: Dryden Press, 1970), pp. 449–451.

[5] U.S. Department of Labor, *Employment and Training Report of the President* (Washington, D.C.: Government Printing Office, 1977), p. 259.

6 "Unions on the College Campus: The Struggle Gets Sharper," *U.S News & World Report,* August 22, 1977, pp. 59–60.

7 "Organized Labor's New Recruits," *Time,* September 15, 1980, p. 62 and "Labor's Big Swing from Surplus to Shortage," *Business Week,* February 20, 1978, pp. 75–77.

Chapter 10

1 Stuart Elliot, "Is that Staid, Old Kellogg Gambling at the Big-money Table?" *Detroit Free Press,* July 20, 1980, pp. 6, 8, 12, 14.

2 Committee on Definitions, *Marketing Definitions: A Glossary of Marketing Terms* (Chicago: American Marketing Association, 1960), p. 15.

3 Robert J. Keith, "The Marketing Revolution," *Journal of Marketing,* January 1960, p. 36.

4 Reported in Thomas Joffe, "Who's Got Heinz in a Pickle," *Forbes,* August 15, 1977, pp. 63–64.

5 This definition is offered in Laurence A. Klatt, *Small-business Management* (Belmont, Cal.: Wadsworth Publishing, 1973), p. 157.

6 The figures in this paragraph are from *The World Almanac & Book of Facts 1981* (New York: Newspaper Enterprise Associates, Inc., 1981), pp. 442, 544.

7 *Monthly Vital Statistics* (Washington, D.C.: U.S. Department of Health and Human Services, Public Health Service, Office of Health Research, Statistics, and Technology, March 18, 1981), p. 1.

8 See June Kronholz, "Stagnant Birth Rate is Expected to Climb within a Few Years," *Wall Street Journal,* July 29, 1977.

9 "The Census: Southwestward Ho!" *Newsweek,* December 29, 1980, p. 20.

10 The statistical estimates in this section come from U.S. Bureau of the Census, *Statistical Abstract of the United States: 1980,* 101st ed. (Washington, D.C.: Government Printing Office, 1980), pp. 30–31.

11 Committee on Definitions, *Marketing Definitions,* p. 17.

12 The convenience, shopping, and specialty goods categories were first suggested by Melvin T. Copeland. See his *Principles of Merchandising* (New York: McGraw-Hill, 1924). A later commentary on this system appears in Richard H. Holton, "The Distinction between Convenience Goods, Shopping Goods, and Specialty Goods," *Journal of Marketing,* July 1958, pp. 55–56.

13 Peter Vanderwicken, "P & G's Secret Ingredient," *Fortune,* July 1974, p. 78.

14 Ibid., p. 79.

15 Committee on Definitions, *Marketing Definitions,* pp. 9–10.

16 See Kenneth Uhl and Carl Block, "Some Findings Regarding Recall of Brand Marks: Descriptive Marks vs. Non-descriptive Marks," *Southern Journal of Business,* October 1969, pp. 1–10.

17 "How Coke Protects Its Good Name," *Business Week,* November 4, 1972, p. 66.

18 William B. Meade, "What's in a Name Brand," *Money,* February 1974, p. 40.

Chapter 11

1 The birth of the supermarket is described in Stuart Elliot, "Supermarkets' 50th Isn't Very Happy," *Detroit Free Press,* July 20, 1980, pp. 1, 6 and "Fifty Years of Supermarketing: 1930–1980," advertising supplement to *Time,* October 27, 1980.

2 The K mart and W. T. Grant sagas are detailed in various sources. See for example, "How W. T. Grant Lost $175 Million Last Year," *Business Week,* February 24, 1975, pp. 74–76; Stanley Slom and Karen Rothmyer, "W. T. Grant Co. Files Bankruptcy Petition, Marketing Failure of Its Turnaround Efforts," *Wall Street Journal,* December 4, 1975; "Dividing What's Left of Grant's," *Business Week,* March 1, 1976, p. 21; Ruth Loving, Jr., "W. T. Grant's Last Days—As Seen From Store 1192," *Fortune,* April 1976, pp. 108–112, 114; and Eleanore Carnith, "K mart Has to Open Some New Doors on the Future," *Fortune,* July 1977, p. 144.

3 U.S. Bureau of the Census, *Statistical Abstract of the United States: 1980,* 101st ed. (Washington, D.C.: Government Printing Office, 1980), p. 557.

4 The wheel of retailing, originally proposed by M. P. McNair, is discussed in Stanley C. Hollander, "The Wheel of Retailing," *Journal of Marketing,* July 1960, pp. 37–42. Some of the material in this section is based on the Hollander article.

5 The Smitty's example is reported in Bill Hendrickson, "Supermarkets Realize That Usual Food Items Won't Sustain Profits," *Wall Street Journal,* July 18, 1980.

6 John McAllenan, "Dental Service at Ward's Puts Bite on Inflation," *Detroit News,* June 14, 1980, p. 1-D.

7 U.S. Bureau of the Census, *Statistical Abstract of the United States: 1980,* p. 639.

8 Ibid.

9 Ibid.

10 Ibid.

11 Ibid.

12 Reported in Edwin G. Pipp, "1,700-seat Jetliners Due in 50 Years?" *Detroit News,* March 3, 1976.

Chapter 12

1 Stan Issacs, "Mean Joe: Goliath Plays Othello," *Sports Illustrated,* December 12, 1979, p. 61.

2 "Antifreeze Marketers Set Major Winter Ad Campaigns," *Advertising Age,* September 16, 1974, p. 2.

3 Robert J. Coen, "Ad Growth Predicted to be 'Fair' In 1980," *Advertising Age,* October 10, 1979, pp. 3, 45.

4 Michael Thornyn, "Advertising: Never Have So Many Sold So Much to So Many," *Nation's Business,* November 1979, p. 85.

5 U.S. Bureau of the Census, *Statistical Abstract of the United States: 1980,* 101st ed. (Washington D.C., Government Printing Office, 1980), p. 419.

6 "Labor Letter," *Wall Street Journal,* September 14, 1971.

7 Walter Gaw, "Specialty Advertising," Specialty Advertising Association, 1970, p. 7.

8 Jeffrey H. Birnbaum, "Industry Blues Fail to Deter S & H Stamps," *Wall Street Journal,* August 5, 1980, p. 31.

9 Quoted in Thomas O'Hanlon, "August Busch Brews Up a New Spirit In St. Louis," *Fortune,* January 15, 1974, p. 100.

10 "Lawyers Advertising Expected to Pick Up As States Set Rules," *Wall Street Journal,* September 9, 1977.

Chapter 13

1 Price data is from Debra Whitefield, "Have Auto Makers Priced Their Cars Too High?" *Seattle Times,* October 4, 1980, p. C 1.

2 Airline industry pricing is discussed in "Belt-tightening," *Seattle Times,* October 23, 1980, p. D 1; "The Rate War in the Skies," *Newsweek,* August 11, 1980, p. 62; and "An Airline Fare Warning," *Newsweek,* November 24, 1980, p. 90.

[3] "A Real Trip: 32 cents for Flight to Chicago," *Detroit News,* January 26, 1980, p. 15 A.
[4] "For Those Who Can Afford It, There's a New Rolls Royce Out," *Seattle Times,* October 4, 1980, p. C 4.
[5] The cost estimates in this paragraph were provided by the Federal Information Center, General Services Administration, May 1981.
[6] "Food was 11¢ a Day in 1776," *Ypsilanti Press,* February 11, 1974.
[8] "Beer Too Expensive; Britons Drink Less," *Seattle Times,* November 13, 1980, p. A 23.
[9] Peter Vanderwicken, "P & G's Secret Ingredient," *Fortune,* July 1974, p. 78. According to a P & G spokesperson, Tide was still its best-selling brand as of June 1, 1981.
[10] James H. Myers and William H. Reynolds, *Consumer Behavior and Marketing Management* (Boston: Houghton Mifflin, 1967), p. 47.
[11] Katrinka W. Leefmaus, "Business Bulletin," *Wall Street Journal,* January 10, 1980, p. 1.
[12] "U.S. Oil Consumption Drops 6.5 Percent," *Journal-American,* October 18, 1980, p. A 12.
[13] "Reduced Gasoline Use Cuts into Tax Levies, Hurts Many Businesses," *Wall Street Journal,* April 3, 1980, p. 1.
[14] June Kronholz, "Europe's Drivers Don't Reduce Gasoline Use Despite Soaring Prices," *Wall Street Journal,* May 12, 1980, pp. 1, 20.

Chapter 14
[1] Gene Bylinsky, "Those Smart Young Robots on the Production Line," *Fortune,* December 17, 1979, p. 90.

Chapter 15
[1] "How Personal Computers Speed Executives' Tasks," *Business Week,* December 1, 1980, p. 92.
[2] "When Computers Goof—Consumers Air Their Frustrations," *U.S. News & World Report,* May 2, 1977, pp. 61–62.
[3] "Between the Lines," *Journal of Insurance,* March/April 1975, p. 17.
[4] Donald H. Sanders, *Computers and Management* (New York: McGraw-Hill, 1970), p. 16.
[5] Kenneth P. Partch, "UPC Scanners Bloom, Promise Vast New Retail Data," *Advertising Age,* October 24, 1977, pp. 38, 50.
[6] *The Computer: How It's Changing Our Lives* (Washington, D.C.: U.S. News & World Report, 1972), p. 72.
[7] Elias M. Awad, Business Data Processing (Englewood Cliffs, N.J.: Prentice-Hall, 1975), pp. 315–316.
[8] Susan Rakowski, "Its Master's Voice: To a New Computer, Your Word Is Law," *Wall Street Journal,* April 13, 1977.
[9] Ibid.

Chapter 16
[1] The competition between B. Dalton and Waldenbooks is described in "Waldenbooks: Countering B. Dalton by Aping Its Computer Operations," *Business Week,* October 8, 1979, pp. 116, 121. The quotation is from this article.
[2] This definition is based on Walter J. Kennevan, "MIS Universe," *Data Management,* September 1970, p. 63.
[3] See Janet Novack, "Multinationals Lead as U.S. Slowly Turns to the Metric System," *Wall Street Journal,* August 20, 1976 and Arlen J. Large, "The Slow March to Metric," *Wall Street Journal,* November 16, 1977.

Chapter 18
[1] NOW accounts are discussed in "If You're Thinking about a NOW Account," *U.S. News & World Report,* December 22, 1980, p. 45.
[2] "Creeping Inflation," *Federal Reserve Bank of Philadelphia Business Review,* August 1957, p. 3. Quoted in Campbell R. McConnell, *Economics* (New York: McGraw-Hill, 1975), p. 289.
[3] Lawrence S. Ritter and William L. Silber, *Principles of Money, Banking and Financial Markets* (New York: Basic Books, 1974), pp. 385–386.
[4] Board of Governors of the Federal Reserve System, *The Federal Reserve System: Purposes and Functions* (Washington, D.C.: Government Printing Office, 1967), p. 1.
[5] See "The Safety of Your Savings," *U.S. News and World Report,* May 12, 1980, p. 74.

Chapter 19
[1] "Why the Financial Man Calls the Plays," *Business Week,* April 8, 1972, p. 55.

Chapter 21
[1] Mary Bralove, "Sales of Canned Gourmet Soups Fall Sharply after Death Laid to Bon Vivant Vichyssoise," *Wall Street Journal,* August 3, 1971.
[2] "Bon Vivant Changes Name and Resumes Operations," *Wall Street Journal,* November 15, 1972.
[3] Patrick J. Davey, *Managing Risks Through Captive Insurance Companies* (New York: The Conference Board, Inc., 1979), p. 2.
[4] Insurance claims data are from *The Journal of Insurance,* March/April 1979, p. 13.
[5] "Has No-fault's Time Come—and Gone?" *U.S News & World Report,* November 12, 1979, p. 63.
[6] See William L. Trombetta, "Products Liability: What New Court Rulings Mean for Management," *Business Horizons,* August 1979, pp. 67–72.

Chapter 22
[1] Based on Bernard F. Whalen, "Imported Beer Sales Up, But Domestics Aren't Worried," *Marketing News,* October 17, 1980, Section 2, pp. 6–7, 10 and "Molson's Marketer: American Beer Too Bland; Consumers Want Flavor, Big Rich Taste," *Marketing News,* October 17, 1980, Section 2, p. 6.
[2] "Trade Deficit Up, But Less Than Last Year," *Seattle Times,* November 29, 1980, p. A 3.
[3] "Sandbagger," *Detroit News,* September 6, 1979, p. 1-A.
[4] "Periscope," *Newsweek,* March 31, 1980, p. 21.
[5] The rest of this section is based on Vern Terpstra, *International Marketing,* 2d ed. (Hindsdale, Ill.: Dryden Press, 1978), pp. 11–14.
[6] G. Christian Hill, "More Firms Turn to Translation Experts to Avoid Costly, Embarrassing Mistakes," *Wall Street Journal,* January 13, 1977.
[7] Donald M. Hintz, "Overseas, Culligan Found Water Hard, Marketing Easier," *Marketing News,* November 4, 1977, p. 3.
[8] Terpstra, *International Marketing,* p. 250.
[9] "Off the Record," *Detroit News,* February 28, 1975.
[10] This section is based on information from Terpstra, *International Marketing,* pp. 127–147.
[11] This section is based on Terpstra, *International Marketing,* pp. 41–46.
[12] "The 100 Largest U.S. Multinationals," *Forbes,* July 7, 1980, p. 102.

13 "U.S. Business," *U.S. News & World Report,* July 28, 1980, p. 53.
14 This data is reported in John Hein, "Paging Adam Smith," *Across the Board,* January 1981, pp. 46–47.

Chapter 23
1 Reported in "Washington Whispers," *U.S News & World Report,* August 6, 1979, p. 12.
2 Rate A. Howell, John R. Allison, and Nate T. Henley, *Business Law Text and Cases 2d ed.* (Hinsdale, Ill.: Dryden Press, 1981), p. 24.
3 Ibid., p. 140. The various elements of a legally enforceable contract are also explained in this volume.
4 Ibid., p. 503.
5 Ibid., p. 115.
6 "The Cold Facts," *Seattle Times,* October 10, 1980.
7 "Man Wins Suit over Rat in Drink," *Seattle Times,* November 23, 1980, p. A 7.
8 Howell, Allison, and Henley, *Business Law,* p. 129.
9 *The Age,* November 23, 1974, p. 1.
10 "Debtors File for Bankruptcy at a Record Rate, Spurred by New Code, Recession, Tight Credit," *Wall Street Journal,* June 30, 1980, p. 30.
11 Based on Howell, Allison, and Henley, *Business Law,* p. 429–433.
12 Reported in Joseph J. Joyce, "How to Select and Protect a Trademark," *Product Marketing,* May 1979, p. 28.
13 Ibid., p. 31.
14 Ibid., p. 28.
15 Louis Mleczko, "FTC Faces Constraints," *Detroit News,* May 25, 1980, p. 1-B.
16 The Chrysler—UAW Plan is described in Al Stark, "UAW's Legal Plan Makes Lawyers Fret," *Detroit News,* November 29, 1977.
17 "Dubious 'First' for a Woman," *Detroit News,* June 16, 1979, p. 16-A

Chapter 24
1 These predictions are outlined in "Crystal Gazers of '39: How Near the Mark," *U.S. News & World Report,* April 16, 1979, pp. 72–74 and Merrill Shiels, "The Cracked Crystal Ball," *Newsweek,* November 19, 1979, p. 133.
2 An excellent update is contained in William Serrin, "Detroit Strikes Back," *New York Times Magazine,* September 14, 1980, pp. 26–30, 32, 95–98, 100–101, 104–105.
3 "A Price War Staggers Bomar," *Business Week,* February 24, 1975, p. 28.
4 Alvin Toffler, *Future Shock* (New York: Random House, 1970), p. 14.
5 Warren Talbat, "Next Century Offers Chance for Man to Soar or to Stumble," *Sentinel Star,* November 25, 1979, p. 1-D and a speech by Robert S. McNamara, former president of the World Bank, at the Massachusetts Institute of Technology, excerpted in "How to Defuse the Population Bomb," *Time,* October 24, 1977, p. 93.
6 See, for example, data in *World Bank Atlas* (Washington, D.C., World Bank, 1975), p. 6.
7 Reported in "Tomorrow," *U.S. News & World Report,* October 17, 1977, p. 22.
8 *The World Almanac & Book of Facts 1981* (New York: Newspaper Enterprise Associates, Inc., 1981), p. 544.
9 "If You Live in Bangladesh and Want Some 40 More Years," *Forbes,* July 6, 1981, p. 24.

10 This section is based on: "226.5 Million Tallied in Census" *Seattle Times,* January 1, 1981, p. 2 A; "Immigrants to Flood into U.S.—MSU Expert," *Plymouth Observer,* July 7, 1980, p. 8A; James Coates, "Population Expert Predicts Whites Will Become Minority," *Sentinel Star,* December 13, 1980, p. 13-A; "Taking Shape: A Bigger, Different Population," *U.S. News & World Report,* October 15, 1979, p. 47; and "Census: Nation Adds 21 Million People," *Seattle Times,* December 25, 1980, p. A 21.
11 Ella Mae Howay, "Business in the Year 2000," *Carroll Business Bulletin,* Fall 1974, pp. 18–19.
12 "Gerber Products Grows Up With Infant-related Interests," *Detroit News,* June 18, 1978.
13 U.S. Bureau of the Census, *Statistical Abstract of the United States: 1980,* 101st ed. (Washington, D.C. Government Printing Office, 1980), p. 394.
14 Juan Cameron, "Forecast: A Look at Industrial America 2030," *Seattle Times,* September 28, 1980, p. H 1.
15 This situation is noted in William Lazar, "The 1980's and Beyond: A Perspective," *MSU Business Topics,* Spring 1977, p. 21.
16 These positive factors were offered in Charles L. Lapp, "Future Needn't Be Dismal; Key Lack: Investment Capital," *Marketing News,* September 23, 1977, p. 4.
17 Cameron, "Forecast: A Look at Industrial America 2030," p. H 1.

Chapter 25
1 Adapted with permission from Judy Randle, "Computers Help TJC Students Evaluate Career Goals," *Tulsa World,* November 6, 1977.
2 U.S. Department of Labor, Bureau of Labor Statistics, *Occupational Outlook Handbook, 1980–1981* (Washington, D.C.: Government Printing Office, 1980).
3 These estimates are cited in William Dunn, "Updated Skills Called Key to Jobs of Future," *Detroit News,* March 14, 1977.
4 "What's Job Clustering All About?" *Occupational Outlook Quarterly,* Winter 1973, p. 17.
5 *Occupational Outlook Handbook, 1980–1981,* pp. 18–20.
6 "Who Gets the 7-figure Paychecks," *U.S. News & World Report,* June 9, 1980, p. 75.
7 Reported in "What It Takes to Run a Big Company," *U.S. News & World Report,* December 12, 1977, p. 69.
8 Related issues are discussed in Frank Trippett, "The Big Puzzle: Who Makes What and Why," *Time,* July 13, 1977, pp. 83–84.
9 "Washington Whispers," *U.S. News & World Report,* May 4, 1981, p. 15.
10 U.S. Bureau of the Census, *Statistical Abstract of the United States: 1980,* 101st ed., (Washington, D.C.: Government Printing Office, 1980), p. 394.
11 Joyce Lain Kennedy, "The 1980's: Just Who Will be Working?" *Seattle Times,* October 5, 1980, p. H 1.
12 "Women Abandoning Traditional Majors," *Journal-American,* September 10, 1980, p. C 10.
13 These survey results were reported in "Where Women Work," *Wall Street Journal,* November 1, 1977.
14 This research is discussed in "Women Still Struggle in Work World," *Detroit News,* September 24, 1977.
15 Reported in "What It Takes To Run a Big Company," *U.S. News & World Report,* December 12, 1977, P. 69.
16 Reported in "Labor Letter," *Wall Street Journal,* November 15, 1977.

Glossary

absolute advantage The situation where a country has a monopolistic position in the marketing of a product it produces at the lowest cost. (p. 559)

accountability The liability of a manager for carrying out activities for which he or she has the necessary authority and responsibility. (p. 137)

accounting The process of measuring and communicating financial information to enable interested parties inside and outside the firm to make informed decisions. (p. 415)

accounting equation The equation showing that assets (things of value) are equal to liabilities (claims of creditors) plus owners' equity (claims of owners). (p. 419)

accounts payable Credit liabilities that must be repaid within a one-year period. (p. 420) *See also* accounts receivable; notes payable.

accounts receivable Credit sales to customers for which payment has yet to be received. (p. 483) *See also* accounts payable; notes payable.

acid test ratio A ratio that measures the ability of a firm to meet its current debt on short notice, calculated by dividing quick assets by current liabilities. (p. 426)

Active Corps of Executives (ACE) Groups of volunteer management consultants who assist people with small business problems. A program of the SBA. (p. 96)

administrative agencies Government agencies at all levels that are empowered (by state or federal statutes and constitutional provisions) to hear and decide a variety of cases. (p. 583)

advertising A nonpersonal sales presentation usually directed to a large number of potential customers. (p. 293)

affirmative action programs Programs set up by businesses with the assistance of the EEOC to increase job opportunities for women and minorities through analysis of the present work force and formulation of goals for hiring and promotion within target dates. (p. 187)

agency A legal relationship between two parties, principal and agent, who agree that one will act as a representative of the other. (p. 587)

agency shop A place of employment where all qualified workers can be hired but those not joining the union are required to pay the union a fee equal to union dues. (p. 216) *See also* closed shop; union shop.

agent The person employed to act in the principal's behalf. (p. 587) *See also* principal.

agent wholesalers Independent wholesalers who take possession of goods but do not hold legal title to them (typically acting as sales agents). (p. 270) *See also* merchant wholesalers.

alien corporation A corporation organized in another country but operating in the United States. (p. 70) *See also* domestic corporation; foreign corporation.

American Federation of Labor (AFL) A national union made up of affiliated individual craft unions that later joined with the Congress of Industrial Organizations (CIO) to become the AFL-CIO. (p. 211) *See also* Congress of Industrial Organizations.

analog computers Computers that use continuous data, such as pressure, temperature, or voltage, in scientific or engineering applications. (p. 363) *See also* digital computers.

analytic system A system in which a raw material is reduced to its component parts in order to extract one or more products. (p. 338) *See also* synthetic system.

antitrust laws Laws that prohibit attempts to monopolize or dominate a particular market. (p. 12)

appellant The party making an appeal for a higher court to review a case. (p. 583)

appellate courts Courts that hear appeals from the general trial courts. (p. 582)

apprenticeship training An employee training program in which the new worker serves as an assistant to a trained worker for a relatively long time period. (p. 189)

arbitration The process of bringing an impartial third party, called an arbitrator, into a union-management dispute to render a binding, legally enforceable decision. (p. 220) *See also* mediation.

arithmetic unit The unit in a computer system where all calculations take place. (p. 367) *See also* control unit; input; memory unit; output.

array A listing of items by size from either the smallest to the largest or the largest to the smallest. (p. 401)

assets Everything of value owned or leased by a business. (p. 418) *See also* liabilities.

authority The power to act and make decisions in carrying out assignments. (p. 136)

autocratic leaders Leaders who make decisions without consulting others. (p. 121) *See also* democratic leaders; free-rein leaders.

automatic transfer system accounts (ATS) Accounts in which all deposited funds earn interest at the bank's regular savings rate because money is transferred from savings to checking accounts only when checks are written; also known as interest/checking plans. (p. 447)

automation The replacement of people with machines that can perform tasks faster or cheaper than humans. (p. 610)

automobile insurance Insurance coverage for losses due to automobile theft, fire, or collision and for claims resulting from damage to the property or person of others involved in an automobile accident. (p. 533)

balance of payments The relationship between a country's inward and outward money flows. (p. 557)

balance of trade The relationship between a country's exports and imports. (p. 557)

balance sheet A statement of a company's financial position as of a particular date. (p. 419)

bankruptcy The legal nonpayment of financial obligations. (p. 589)

BASIC (Beginner's All-purpose Symbolic Instruction Code) A sophisticated computer language specifically designed for ease of use with respect to input and output operations. (p. 374) See also COBOL; FORTRAN; PL/1.

bears Investors who expect stock prices to decline and sell their securities in expectation of declining market prices. (p. 507) See also bulls.

binary arithmetic A special counting system that uses two digits—0 and 1. (p. 373)

bit A binary digit—either 0 or 1. (p. 374)

blue-sky laws Early state laws regulating securities transactions. (p. 511)

board of directors The governing authority of a corporation (most states require a minimum of three directors and at least one annual meeting of the board) elected by the stockholders. (p. 72)

bond A certificate of indebtedness sold to raise long-term funds for corporations or government agencies. (p. 477)

bond indenture The legal contract containing all provisions of a bond. (p. 497)

bond trustee An individual, major bank, or other financial institution that has the responsibility of representing bondholders. (p. 498)

bonuses Additions to a salary or time or piece wage that are intended as incentives to increase productivity or as rewards for exceptional performance. (p. 196)

book value The value of stock determined by subtracting a company's liabilities from its assets (minus the value of any preferred stock). (p. 495) See also market value; par value.

boycott An attempt to keep people from purchasing goods or services from a company. (p. 223) See also primary boycott; secondary boycott.

brand A name, term, sign, symbol, design, or some combination used to identify the products of one firm and to differentiate them from competitive offerings. (p. 255)

brand name That part of the brand consisting of words or letters that make up a name used to identify and distinguish the firm's offerings from those of competitors. (p. 255)

breakeven analysis A method of determining the minimum sales volume needed to cover all costs at a certain price level. A breakeven analysis considers various costs and total revenue. (p.319)

breakeven point The level of sales that will cover all the company's costs (both fixed and variable). (p. 319)

bulls Investors who expect stock prices to rise and buy securities in anticipation of the increased market prices. (p. 507) See also bears.

burglary insurance Insurance coverage for losses due to the taking of property by forcible entry. (p. 535)

business All profit-seeking activities and enterprises that provide goods and services necessary to an economic system. (p. 7)

business law Those aspects of law that most directly and specifically influence and regulate management of various types of business activity. (p. 581)

callable bonds Bonds that have provisions allowing the issuing corporation to redeem them prior to their maturity date (ordinarily at a premium). (p. 498)

canned sales presentation A memorized sales talk intended to provide all the information that the customer needs to make a purchase decision. (p. 299)

capacity The legal ability of a party to enter into agreements. (p. 585)

capital The funds necessary to finance the operation of a business. (p. 14)

capital items Relatively long-lived industrial products that usually cost large sums of money. (p. 253) See also expense items.

capitalism The system founded on the principle that competition among business firms best serves the needs of society (also called the private enterprise system). (p. 11) See also communism; mixed economies; socialism.

career cluster A group of related jobs. (p. 620)

cartels Monopolistic organizations of foreign firms. (p. 564)

cash surrender value The savings portion of a life insurance policy that can be borrowed by the policyholder at low interest rates or paid to the policyholder if the policy is cancelled. (p. 542)

cathode ray tube (CRT) A visual display device that projects data onto a television screen. (p. 364)

Celler-Kefauver Act A federal statute that amended the Clayton Act to include major asset purchases that decrease competition in an industry in its general prohibition of trade restraints. (p. 593) See also Clayton Act.

census A primary data survey in which all possible data sources are contacted. (p. 397) See also sample.

centralization The practice of managers' dispersing very little authority throughout the organization. (p. 139) See also decentralization.

certificate of deposit (CD) A short-term, high-interest note issued by a commercial bank. (p. 482)

certified management accountant (CMA) An accountant who has met specific educational and professional requirements and has passed a series of examinations established by the National Association of Accountants for the Certificate in Management Accounting. (p. 418) See also certified public accountant.

certified public accountant (CPA) An accountant who has met state certification requirements involving college degrees and experience and who has passed a comprehensive examination covering law, accounting theory and practice, and auditing. (p. 416) See also certified management accountant.

check A piece of paper addressed to a bank on which is written a legal authorization to withdraw a specified amount of money from an account and to pay that amount to someone. (p. 454)

classroom training An employee training program that uses classroom techniques to teach employees difficult jobs requiring high levels of skill. (p. 189)

Clayton Act A federal statute that forbids trade restraints such as tying contracts, interlocking directorates, and certain anticompetitive stock acquisitions. (p. 593) *See also* Celler-Kefauver Act.

closed corporation A corporation owned by relatively few stockholders, who control and manage the corporation's activities. (p. 70) *See also* open corporation.

closed shop A place of employment where management cannot hire nonunion workers; prohibited by the Taft-Hartley Act. *See also* agency shop; union shop. (p. 216)

coaching A management development program in which a junior executive works directly under a senior executive. (p. 190)

COBOL (Common Business Oriented Language) A computer language, designed specifically for business problems, that uses English words and sentences. *See also* BASIC; FORTRAN; PL/1.

coinsurance clause An insurance policy clause requiring that the insured carry fire insurance of some minimum percentage of the actual cash value of the property (usually 80 percent) in order to receive full coverage of a loss. (p. 533)

collective bargaining A process of negotiation between management and union representatives for the purpose of arriving at mutually acceptable wages and working conditions for employees. (p. 218)

commercial banks Profit-making businesses that hold deposits of individuals and businesses in the form of checking or savings accounts and that use these funds to make loans to individuals and businesses. (p. 449)

commercial paper Short-term promissory notes issued by major corporations with high credit standings and backed solely by the reputation of the issuing firms. (p.475)

committee organization The organization structure wherein authority and responsibility are jointly held by a group of individuals rather than by a single manager. (p. 144) *See also* functional organization; line organization; line-and-staff organization; matrix organization.

common carrier A transportation company that performs services within a particular line of business for the general public. (p. 278) *See also* contract carrier; freight forwarder; private carrier.

common law The body of law arising out of judicial decisions related to the unwritten law of the United States inherited from England. (p. 579) *See also* statutory law.

common market A basic format for economic integration that maintains a customs union and seeks to bring all government trade rules into agreement. (p. 565)

common stock Stock whose owners have only a residual claim (after creditors and preferred stockholders have been paid) to the firm's assets but who have voting rights in the corporation. (pp. 71, 491) *See also* preferred stock.

communism An economic theory, developed by Karl Marx, under which private property is eliminated and goods are owned in common. (p. 20) *See also* capitalism; socialism.

comparative advantage A country's ability to supply a particular item more efficiently and at a lower cost than it can supply other products. (p. 559)

comparative advertising A trend in persuasive product advertising in which direct comparisons with competing products are made. (p. 297) *See also* advertising; informative advertising; persuasive advertising; reminder-oriented advertising.

competition The battle among businesses for consumer acceptance. (p. 9)

compulsory arbitration Arbitration to which both union and management representatives must submit, usually required by a third party (such as the federal government). (p. 220) *See also* voluntary arbitration.

computer hardware All of the elements of the computer system. (p. 369) *See also* computer software.

computer program A set of instructions that tells the computer what is to be done, how to do it, and the sequence of steps to be followed. (p. 374)

computer programmer The specialist who tells the computer what to do based on an analysis of the problem, a breakdown of the component parts of the problem, and an outline of steps needed for the solution. (p. 378)

computer software The instructions, or computer programs, that tell the computer what to do. (p. 370) *See also* computer hardware.

computers Electronic machines that accept data and manipulate them to solve problems and produce information. (p. 364) *See also* microcomputer; minicomputer.

Congress of Industrial Organizations (CIO) A national union made up of affiliated individual industrial unions that later joined with the American Federation of Labor (AFL) to become the AFL-CIO. (p. 212) *See also* American Federation of Labor.

consent order An order under which an accused firm agrees voluntarily to cease the conduct the government is alleging to be an inappropriate action. (p. 593)

conservation The preservation of declining energy resources. (p. 48)

consideration The value or benefit that one party provides to the others with whom a contract is made. Each party to the contract must furnish consideration in order for the agreement to be valid and enforceable. (p. 585)

Consumer Credit Protection Act A federal law, often known as the "Truth in Lending Law," that requires lenders to specify the exact interest charges a borrower will have to pay. (p. 595)

consumer goods Products and services purchased by the ultimate consumer for his or her own use. (p. 243)

consumerism The demand that businesses give proper consideration to consumer wants and needs in making their decisions. (p. 46)

containerization Putting packages, usually made up of several unitized loads, into a form that is relatively easy to transfer. (p. 283) *See also* unitization.

continuous process A manufacturing operation where long production runs turn out finished products over a period of days, months, or even years. (p. 339) *See also* intermittent process.

contract An agreement among two or more parties regarding a specified act or thing that the law will enforce. (p. 585)

contract carrier A transportation company that carries goods for hire by individual contract or agreement and not for the general public. Their services meet the special needs of their customers. (p. 278) *See also* common carrier; freight forwarder; private carrier.

contract law The legal foundation on which normal business dealings are constructed. (p. 585)

control unit The unit in the computer system responsible for directing the sequence of operations, interpreting coded instructions, and guiding the computer. (p. 368) *See also* arithmetic unit; input; memory unit; output.

controlling The management function involved in evaluating the organization's performance to determine whether it is accomplishing its objectives. (p. 118) *See also* directing; organizing; planning.

convenience goods Products that consumers seek to purchase frequently, immediately, and with a minimum of effort. (p. 252) *See also* shopping goods; specialty goods.

convertible bonds Bonds that offer the option of being converted into a specific number of shares of common stock. (p. 497)

convertible preferred stock Preferred stock whose owners have the option of converting their preferred stock into common stock at a stated price. (p. 497)

cooling-off period An 80-day suspension of threatened strikes that can be called for by the President of the United States under the Taft-Hartley Act if the threatened strikes could imperil the national health and safety. (p. 218)

cooperative An organization whose owners band together to operate collectively all or part of their company or industry. (p. 76)

cooperative advertising A promotional strategy in which the manufacturer shares the cost of local advertising of the product or line with the middlemen. (p. 303)

copyrights Protection of an individual's exclusive rights to materials such as books, photos, and cartoons. (p. 591) *See also* patents.

corporation An association of persons created by statute as a legal entity with authority to act and to have liability separate and apart from its owners. (p. 66) *See also* partnership; sole proprietorship.

cost-push inflation Results when a rise in operating costs is passed along to the consumer. (p. 41) *See also* demand-pull inflation; inflation; stagflation.

countervailing powers Big business, big labor, and big government are the countervailing powers that balance the economy so that no single sector will ever totally dominate the society. (p. 24)

coupons A type of sales promotion that uses advertising inserts or package inclusions that are redeemable for cash and offer a small price discount. (p. 303)

craft union A labor union consisting of skilled workers in a specific craft or trade. (p. 209) *See also* industrial union.

creative selling A persuasive type of promotional presentation used when the benefits of a product are not readily apparent and/or its purchase is being based on a careful analysis of alternatives. (p. 299) *See also* missionary selling; order-processing.

credit insurance Insurance protection for lenders against losses from bad debts. (p. 537)

credit life insurance A special form of term insurance purchased by persons who are buying a home or other major item that repays the balance owed on these items if the policyholder dies. (p. 542)

credit unions Financial institutions typically sponsored by companies, unions, or professional or religious groups that pay interest to their member depositors and make loans to members. (p. 460)

critical path The sequence of operations in the PERT (Program Evaluation and Review Technique) diagram that requires the longest time for completion. (p. 352) *See also* PERT.

cumulative preferred stock Preferred stock whose owners are entitled to the automatic payment of accumulated dividends, when the company omits a dividend payment, before common stockholders can receive any dividends at all. (p. 496) *See also* noncumulative preferred stock; preferred stock.

cumulative voting The practice of enabling stockholders to combine their votes in selecting the board of directors. (p. 71)

currency Two of the components of the money supply—coins and paper money. (p. 447)

current assets Items of value expected to be converted into cash within a period of one year. (p. 480) *See also* fixed assets.

current ratio A ratio that measures the company's ability to pay its current debts as they mature, calculated by dividing current assets by current liabilities. (p. 426)

customer departmentalization Departmentalization organized on the basis of customer segments. (p. 135) *See also* departmentalization; functional departmentalization; geographic departmentalization; process departmentalization; product departmentalization.

customer-oriented layout A service facility design where the arrangement facilitates the interactions of customers and the organization's services. (p. 347) *See also* fixed-position layout; process layout; product layout

customs union A basic format for economic integration within which a free trade area is established for member nations and a uniform tariff is imposed on trade with nonmember nations. (p. 565)

debenture A bond backed by the reputation of the issuing corporation rather than by specific pledges of assets. (p. 497)

debt capital Funds obtained through borrowing. (p. 470) *See also* equity capital.

debt to net worth ratio A ratio that measures the extent to which company operations are financed by borrowed funds, calculated by dividing total liabilities by stockholders' equity. (p. 428)

decentralization The practice of managers' dispersing great amounts of authority to subordinates. (p. 139) *See also* centralization.

decision making Choosing among two or more alternatives by following these steps: recognizing the problem, identifying and evaluating alternatives, selecting and implementing alternatives, and obtaining follow-up on the effectiveness of the decision. (p. 114)

delegation The act of assigning part of the manager's activities to subordinates. (p. 136)

demand curve A schedule of amounts of a good or service that will be demanded at different price levels. (p. 317) *See also* law of supply and demand; supply curve.

demand deposits The technical name for checking accounts, which are promises to pay immediately to the depositor any amount of money requested as long as it does not exceed the checking account balance. (p. 447)

demand-pull inflation A rise in prices caused when consumer demand for a product exceeds its supply. (p. 41) *See also* cost-push inflation; inflation; stagflation.

democratic leaders Leaders who involve their subordinates in making decisions. (p. 121) *See also* autocratic leaders; free-rein leaders.

departmentalization The subdivision of work activities into units within the organization. (p. 135) *See also* customer departmentalization; functional departmentalization; geographic departmentalization; process departmentalization; product departmentalization.

devaluation The reduction in value of a country's currency in relation to gold or to some other currency. (p. 558)

digital computers Computers, commonly used in business, that manipulate numbers by adding, subtracting, multiplying, or dividing. (p. 363) *See also* analog computers.

directing Guiding and motivating subordinates to accomplish organizational objectives. (p. 117) *See also* controlling; organizing; planning.

discount rate The interest rate charged by the Federal Reserve System on loans to member banks. (p. 454)

dispatching The phase of production control that instructs each department on what work is to be done and the time allowed for its completion. (p. 352) *See also* follow-up; production control; production planning; routing; scheduling.

distribution strategy The part of marketing decision making that involves the physical distribution of goods, the selection of marketing channels, and the organization of wholesalers and retailers who handle distribution. (p. 251) *See also* marketing mix; pricing strategy; product strategy; promotional strategy.

distribution warehouse A place used to store products for a short period of time; usually used to gather and redistribute products. (p. 282) *See also* storage warehouse.

dividend Payment from earnings of a corporation to its stockholders. (p. 68)

domestic corporation A firm doing business in the state in which it is incorporated. (p. 70) *See also* alien corporation; foreign corporation.

"doughnut" structure An organization chart made up of concentric circles that represent top management, staff personnel, and functional areas and that reflect a more flexible structure. (p. 146)

Dow-Jones Averages Stock averages that use three indexes based on the market prices of 30 industrial, 20 transportaion, and 15 utility stocks to provide a general measure of market activity for a given time period. (p. 510) *See also* Standard and Poor's Index.

dumping Selling goods abroad at a price lower than that charged in the domestic market. (p. 569)

earnings per share The amount of profits earned by a company for each share of common stock outstanding, calculated by dividing net earnings (or net profits) by the average number of common shares outstanding. (p. 427)

ecology The relationship between people and their environment. (p. 45)

electronic funds transfer system (EFTS) A computerized system of reducing check-writing through electronic depositing and withdrawal of funds. (p. 456)

embargo A complete ban on certain imported products. (p. 564)

employers' associations Cooperative efforts on the part of employers to present a united front in dealing with labor unions. (p. 224)

endowment policy A type of insurance policy that provides coverage for a specified period after which the face value is refunded to the policyholder. (p. 542)

energy crisis The world's diminished ability to provide for its current and future energy needs. (p. 47)

entrepreneur A risk taker in the private enterprise system. (p. 10)

entrepreneurship The taking of risks to set up and run a business. (p. 14)

entry-level job The first permanent kind of employment after leaving school. (p. 619)

Environmental Protection Act A federal statute that set up the Environmental Protection Agency, giving it the authority to deal with various types of pollution. (p. 595)

Equal Employment Opportunity Commission (EEOC) A federal commission created to increase job opportunities for women and minorities and to assist in ending job discrimination based on race, religion, color, sex, or national origin in hiring, promotion, firing, compensation, and other terms and conditions of employment. (p. 186)

equilibrium price The price that exists in the marketplace for a particular good or service, determined by the intersection of the supply and demand curves. This is the point where the amount of a product desired at a given price is equal to the amount that suppliers will provide at that price. (p. 317)

equities Claims against the assets of a business. (p. 419)

equity capital Funds provided by the firm's owners through additional investment, plowing back earnings, or the sale of stock. (p. 470) *See also* debt capital.

equity funds Funds obtained by selling stock in the company or by reinvesting company earnings. (p. 477)

esteem needs The human needs for a sense of accomplishment, a feeling of achievement, and the respect of others. (p. 164) *See also* need; physiological needs; safety needs; self-actualization needs; social needs.

exchange control The allocation, expansion, or restriction of foreign exchange according to existing national policy. (p. 564)

exchange rate The rate at which a country's currency can be exchanged for other currencies or gold. (p. 558) *See also* floating exchange rate.

exchange value The value of any item—consumer product, industrial product, or service—in the marketplace. (p. 312)

exclusive distribution The opposite of intensive distribution; occurs when the manufacturer gives a retailer or wholesaler the exclusive right to sell its products in a specific geographical area. (p. 277) *See also* intensive distribution; selective distribution.

expense items Usually less costly industrial products than capital items, consumed within a year of their purchase. (p. 253) *See also* capital items.

exporting Selling domestic goods abroad. (p. 556) *See also* importing.

express warranties Warranties with specific representations made by the seller regarding the goods. (p. 586) *See also* implied warranties.

external data Data generated outside the firm. (p. 393) *See also* internal data.

factor A financial institution that purchases at a discount the accounts receivable of retailers such as furniture and appliance dealers. (p. 476)

factors of production The basic inputs into the private enterprise system, including natural resources, labor, capital, and entrepreneurship. (p. 13)

Fair Credit Reporting Act A federal law that allows people to see credit reports prepared about them and to insist on the correction of inaccurate information. (p. 595)

Fair Debt Collection Practices Act A federal law aimed at prohibiting debt-collecting agencies from using harassing, deceptive, and unfair collection practices. (p. 596)

Fair Labor Standards Act A federal law that sets a minimum wage and maximum basic hours for workers employed in industries engaged in interstate commerce. (p. 215)

Fair Packaging and Labeling Act A federal law that requires certain kinds of information on packages or labels—including product identification, name and address of the producer or distributor, and quality information. (p. 594)

featherbedding A situation where workers are paid for work not done. (p. 217)

Federal Bankruptcy Reform Act of 1978 The latest version of the bankruptcy law designed to help people combat excessive debts caused by circumstances beyond their control through a three-year debt repayment plan or a liquidation plan. (p. 589)

Federal Deposit Insurance Corporation (FDIC) A corporation that insures bank depositors' accounts up to a maximum of $100,000 and sets requirements for sound banking practices. (p. 456)

Federal Reserve System A system of regulating banking in the United States through 12 regional banks controlled by a board of governors. (p. 452)

Federal Trade Commission Act A federal law that set up the Federal Trade Commission (FTC) as a federal agency and gave it administrative powers to ban unfair competitive practices among businesses. (p. 593)

fidelity bonds Bonds that protect employers from employees' dishonesty. (p. 536) *See also* surety bonds.

FIFO (First In, First Out) A method of inventory accounting that assumes that the first raw materials purchased are the first used in producing finished goods. (p. 424) *See also* LIFO.

finance The business function of effectively obtaining and using funds. (p. 468)

financial manager A manager whose chief responsibilities involve the raising and spending of money. (p. 469)

fire insurance Insurance coverage for losses due to fire and—with extended coverage—windstorms, hail, water, riot, and smoke damage. (p. 532)

five *Ms* The basic resources of any firm—manpower, materials, money, machinery, and management. (p. 27)

fixed assets Items of value not expected to be converted into cash within a one-year period. (p. 480) *See also* current assets.

fixed costs Costs that remain stable regardless of the production level achieved. (p. 319) *See also* variable costs.

fixed-position layout A manufacturing facility design that locates the product in a fixed position, and workers, materials, and machines are transported to and from it. (p. 347) *See also* customer-oriented layout; process layout; product layout.

floating exchange rate An exchange rate that varies according to market conditions. (p. 558) *See also* exchange rate.

floor-planning The assignment of inventory title (collateral) to financing agencies in return for short-term loans. (p. 476)

flowchart A pictorial description of the logical steps to be taken in solving a problem. (p. 374)

follow-up The phase of production control that spots problems in the production process and informs management of needed adjustments. (p. 352) *See also* dispatching; production control; production planning; routing; scheduling.

foreign corporation A corporation doing business in a state other than the one in which it is incorporated. (p. 70) *See also* alien corporation; domestic corporation.

form utility Utility created through the conversion of raw materials and other inputs into finished products or services. (p. 336) *See also* ownership utility; place utility; time utility; utility.

FORTRAN (FORmula TRANslation) The dominant scientific computer language. (p. 374) *See also* BASIC; COBOL; PL/1.

franchisee The dealer in a franchise operation; a small businessperson who is allowed to sell a product or service of a supplier, or franchisor, in exchange for some payment—usually a flat fee plus future royalties or commissions. (p. 90)

franchising A contractual arrangement between a manufacturer or other supplier and a dealer that sets the methods to be used in selling a product. (p. 90)

franchisor The supplier of a franchise who typically provides building plans, site selection research, managerial and accounting procedures, and other services to assist the franchisee—and who receives payment, usually in the form of a flat fee and royalties or commissions. (p. 90)

free-rein leaders Leaders who believe in minimal supervision and who leave most decisions to their subordinates. (p. 121) *See also* autocratic leaders; democratic leaders.

free trade area A basic format for economic integration within which participants agree to allow trading among themselves without any tariffs or trade restrictions. (p. 565)

freight forwarder A common carrier that purchases bulk space from other carriers by lease or contract and resells this space to small-volume shippers. The forwarder picks up, loads and delivers the merchandise, and takes care of the billing. (p. 278) *See also* common carrier; contract carrier; private carrier.

frequency distribution The common practice of grouping data in a listing or graph to show the number of times each item appears in the data. (p. 401)

friendship, commerce, and navigation (FCN) treaties Treaties with other nations that include many aspects of international business relations such as the right to conduct business in a treaty partner's domestic market. (p. 565)

fringe benefits Nonmonetary employee benefits such as pension plans, health and life insurance, sick-leave pay, credit unions, and health and safety programs. (p. 197)

functional departmentalization Departmentalization based on the various departments of an organization. (p. 135) *See also* departmentalization; customer departmentalization; geographic departmentalization; process departmentalization; product departmentalization.

functional organization The organization structure based on a direct flow of authority for each work activity or function. (p. 142) *See also* committee organization; line organization; line-and-staff organization; matrix organization.

General Agreement on Tariffs and Trade (GATT) An international trade accord that has sponsored various tariff negotiations leading to cuts in the overall level of tariffs throughout the world. (p. 563)

general partnership A partnership in which all partners carry on the business as co-owners and are liable for the business's debts. (p. 64) *See also* limited partnership; partnership.

geographic departmentalization Departmentalization organized by regions of the country. (p. 135) *See also* customer departmentalization; departmentalization; functional departmentalization; process departmentalization; product departmentalization.

grapevine The informal communications network found in most organizations. (p. 148)

great man theory Leadership theory emphasizing that only an exceptional person is capable of playing a prominent leadership role. (p. 120)

grievance An employee or union complaint that management is violating some provision of the union salary, or to a time or piece wage.

group life insurance Life insurance for company employees that is typically written under a single master policy. (p. 539)

Hawthorne studies A series of investigations that revealed money and job security are not the only sources of employee motivation and that lead to the development of the human relations approach to employee motivation. (p. 161)

health insurance Insurance coverage for losses due to sickness or accidents. (p. 536)

hierarchy of organizational objectives Levels of objectives that progress from the overall objectives of the firm to the specific objectives established for each employee. (p. 134)

hiring from within A policy whereby a firm first considers its own employees for new job openings.(p. 186)

image goals Goals that are coordinated with pricing strategies to reflect an integrated company image. (p. 315)

implied warranties Warranties legally imposed on the seller and, generally, automatically effective unless disclaimed by the seller in writing. (p. 586) *See also* express warranties.

import quotas Limitations on the number of products in certain categories that can be imported with the objective of protecting domestic industries and preserving foreign exchange. (p. 564)

importing Buying foreign goods and raw materials. (p. 556) *See also* exporting.

incentive compensation Rewarding an employee for exceptional performance by adding something extra to a salary or to a time or piece wage. (p. 196)

income statement The financial statement that reflects the income, expenses, and profits of a company over a period of time. (p. 420)

indorsement The procedure that renders commerical paper transferable when the payee signs the back of the instrument. (p. 590)

industrial distributors Wholesalers of industrial goods. (p. 268)

industrial goods Products purchased to be used either directly or indirectly in the production of other goods for resale. (p. 243)

industrial park A planned site location that provides necessary zoning, land, shipping facilities, and waste disposal outlets (p. 345)

Industrial Revolution The shift to a factory system of manufacturing that began in England around 1750–1775. (p. 17)

industrial union A labor union consisting of all of the workers in a given industry regardless of their occupations or skill levels. (p. 209) *See also* craft union.

inflation A decrease in the purchasing power of a nation's currency, often defined in terms of rising prices. (p. 41) *See also* cost-push inflation; demand-pull inflation, stagflation.

informal organization A self-grouping of employees in the organization who possess informal channels of communication and contact. (p. 147)

informative advertising The advertising approach intended to build initial demand for a product in the introductory phase of the product's life cycle. (p. 296) *See also* advertising; comparative advertising; persuasive advertising; reminder-oriented advertising.

injunction A court order prohibiting some practice.(p. 224)

inland marine insurance Insurance coverage for losses of property due to damage while goods are being transported by truck, ship, rail, or plane. (p. 536) *See also* ocean marine insurance.

input The portion of the computer system that is responsible for converting incoming data into a form the computer can understand. (p. 367) *See also* arithmetic unit; control unit; memory unit; output.

institutional advertising The promotion of a concept, an idea, a philosophy, or the goodwill of an industry, company, organization, or government entity. (p. 295) *See also* product advertising.

insurable interest An insurance concept wherein the policyholder must stand to suffer financial loss due to the occurence of fire, accident, or lawsuit. (p. 526)

insurable risk The requirements that a risk must meet in order for the insurance company to provide protection against its occurrence. (p. 526)

insurance The process by which a firm (the insurance company) for a fee (the premium) agrees to pay another firm or individual (the insured) a sum of money stated in a written contract (the policy) if a loss occurs. (p. 525)

insurance companies Businesses that provide protection for individual and business policyholders in return for payment of premiums and that use these premiums to make long-term loans for corporations, commerical real estate mortgages, and government bonds. (p. 460)

intangible personal property Property most often represented by a document or other instrument in writing, although it may be as vague and remote as a bookkeeping or computer entry. (p. 587) *See also* real property; tangible personal property.

intensive distribution A strategy used to achieve saturation market coverage by placing a product in nearly every available outlet; requires a maximum distribution effort and involves low-priced convenience goods like chewing gum and newspapers. (p. 276) *See also* exclusive distribution; selective distribution.

intentional torts Civil wrongs purposely inflicted on other persons or their property such as assault, embezzlement, slander, or libel. (p. 588)

interlocking directorates Identical or overlapping boards of directors for competitive companies. (p. 593)

intermittent process A manufacturing operation where the production run is short and machines are shut down frequently or changed in order to produce different products. (p. 339) *See also* continuous process.

internal data Data generated within the organization. (p. 392) *See also* external data.

International Monetary Fund (IMF) A fund established to lend foreign exchange to countries that require assistance in conducting international trade. (p. 565)

inventory control The balancing of the need to have inventory on hand to meet demand with the costs involved in carrying the inventory. (p. 349)

inventory turnover ratio A ratio that measures the number of times merchandise moves through a business, calculated by dividing the cost of goods sold by the average amount of inventory. (p. 427)

investment The purchase of stocks and bonds with the hope of getting satisfactory dividends and interest as payment for the risk taken. (p. 499) *See also* speculation.

Investment Company Act of 1940 The federal law that brought the mutual fund industry under the jurisdiction of the Securities and Exchange Commission in order to protect investors from possible trading abuses and stock manipulation. (p. 514)

invisible hand of competition Description by Adam Smith of how competition regulates the private enterprise system and assures that consumers receive the best possible products and prices. (p. 12)

job analysis A systematic, detailed study of jobs based on identification and examination of job characteristics and the requirements of the person assigned the job. (p. 184)

job description A document specifying the objectives of a job, the work to be performed, the responsibilities involved, the skills needed, the relationship of the job to other jobs, and the working conditions. (p. 185)

job enlargement A method of increasing the number of tasks performed by a worker in order to make the job more psychologically rewarding. (p. 173)

job enrichment Giving workers more authority to plan their work and to decide how it is to be accomplished and allowing them to learn related skills or to trade jobs with others. (p. 172)

job evaluation A method of determining wage levels for different jobs by comparing each job on the basis of skill requirements, education requirements, responsbilities, and physical requirements. (p. 195)

job-order production The type of intermittent production that occurs in response to a specific customer order. (p. 339) *See also* lot-order production.

job rotation A management development program that familiarizes junior executives with the various operations of the firm and the contributions of each department through temporary assignments in various departments. (p. 190)

job specification The written description of the special qualifications required of a worker who fills a particular job. (p. 185)

joint venture A partnership in which two or more people form a temporary business for a specific undertaking. (p. 64)

judiciary The branch of government charged with deciding disputes among parties through the application of laws. (p. 582)

jurisdictional strikes Strikes resulting from disputes between two unions fighting each other for jurisdiction over a group of workers. (p. 216)

key accounts Major customers of a company. (p. 301)

labor All individuals who work for a business. (p. 14)

labor union A group of workers who have banded together to achieve common goals in the key areas of wages, hours, and working conditions. (p. 209)

Landrum-Griffin Act A federal law requiring regularly scheduled elections of union officers by secret ballot and increased regulation of the handling of union funds. (p. 218)

law Standards set by government and society in the form of either legislation or custom. (p. 579)

law of large numbers A probability calculation of the likelihood of the occurrence of perils on which premiums are based. (p. 527)

law of supply and demand An economic law that says market price is determined by the intersection of the supply and demand curves. (p. 15) *See also* demand curve; supply curve.

layoffs Temporary separations due to business slowdowns. (p. 192)

leadership The act of motivating or causing others to perform activities designed to achieve specific objectives.(p. 120)

leverage A technique of increasing the rate of return on investment through the use of borrowed funds. (p. 479)

liabilities Claims of the firm's creditors. (p. 419) *See also* assets.

lifestyle The way a person lives, including work, leisure time, hobbies, other interests, and personal philosophy. (p. 607)

LIFO (Last In, First Out) A method of inventory accounting that assumes that the cost of goods sold is calculated on prices paid for the most recently purchased materials and parts. (p. 423) *See also* FIFO.

limit order An investor request that a stock purchase or sale be made at a specified price. (p. 507) *See also* market order.

limited partnership A partnership composed of one or more general partners and one or more limited partners (those whose liability is limited to the amount of capital contributed to the partnership). (p. 64) *See also* general partnership; partnership.

limited payment life insurance A variation of whole life insurance for which the policyholder pays all premiums within a designated period such as 20 or 30 years. (p. 542)

line-and-staff organization The organization structure that combines the direct flow of authority present in the line organization with staff departments that service,

advise, and support the line departments. (p. 143) *See also* committee organization; functional organization; line-and-staff organization; matrix organization.

line of credit An agreement betwen a commerical bank and a business firm that states the amount of unsecured short-term credit the bank will make available to the borrower—provided the bank has enough funds available for lending. (p. 473)

line organization The organization structure based on a direct flow of authority from the chief executive to subordinates. (p. 141) *See also* committee organization; functional organization; line-and-staff organization; matrix organization.

liquidity The speed at which items can be converted to money. (p. 420)

lockout A management method to bring pressure on union members by closing the firm. (p. 224)

lot-order production The type of intermittent production that occurs in response to inventory needs. (p. 339) *See also* job-order production.

maintenance factors Job-related factors, such as salary, working conditions, and job security, that must be present in order to prevent worker dissatisfaction but which are not strong motivators. (p. 167) *See also* motivational factors.

Maloney Act of 1938 An amendment to the Securities Exchange Act of 1934 that authorized self-regulation of over-the-counter securities operations. (p. 514)

management The achievement of organizational objectives through people and other resources. (p. 109)

management by objectives (MBO) A program designed to improve employees' motivation through having them participate in setting their own goals and letting them know in advance precisely how they will be evaluated. (p. 170)

management development programs Employee training programs designed to improve the skills and broaden the knowledge of present managers as well as to provide training for employees with management potential.(p. 189)

management information system (MIS) An organized method of providing past, present, and projected information on internal operations and external intelligence for use in management decision making. (p. 392)

management pyramid The various levels of management, or hierarchy, in an organization—supervisory, middle, and top management. (p. 110)

market People with the necessary authority, financial ability, and willingness to purchase goods and services. (p. 243)

market order An investor request that a stock purchase or sale be made at the current market price. (p. 507) *See also* limit order.

market segmentation The process of dividing the total market into groups with similar characteristics. (p. 244)

market share The percentage of a market controlled by a certain company, product, or service. (p. 314)

market target A group of consumers toward which a firm decides to direct its marketing effort. (p. 248)

market value The price at which a security is currently selling. (p. 495) *See also* book value; par value.

marketing The performance of business activities that direct the flow of goods and services from producer to consumer or user. (p. 241)

marketing channels The paths that goods and title to them follow from producer to consumer; the means by which all businesses and public organizations distribute the products or services they are producing and marketing. (p. 266) *See also* middlemen; retailers; wholesalers.

marketing concept A business philosophy advocating that all activities and functions of the organization be directed toward the identification and satisfaction of consumer wants. (p. 19)

marketing mix The combination of the four strategies of market decision making (product strategy, distribution strategy, promotional strategy, and pricing strategy) in order to satisfy chosen consumer segments. (p. 250) *See also* distribution strategy; pricing strategy; product strategy; promotional strategy.

marketing research The systematic gathering, recording, and analyzing of data about problems relating to the marketing of goods and services. (p. 248)

markup The amount added to cost for profit and expenses not previously considered. The total determines the selling price. (p. 318)

markup percentage The markup divided by the price of the item. (p. 318)

materials handling The moving of items within the customer's warehouse, terminal, factory, or store. (p. 282)

matrix organization The organization structure in which specialists from different parts of the organization are brought together to work on specific projects. It is usually used in conjunction with a traditional line-and-staff structure. (p. 144) *See also* committee organization; functional organization; line organization; line-and-staff organization.

maturity date The date at which a loan must be repaid. (p. 497)

mean (average) A statistical measure calculated by adding together all the observations and dividing by the number of observations. (p. 401) *See also* median; mode.

median The middle score in the distribution of observations. (p. 401) *See also* mean; mode.

mediation The process of bringing in a third party to make recommendations for the settlement of union-management differences. (p. 220) *See also* arbitration.

medium of exchange The function performed by money in facilitating exchange and eliminating the need for a barter system. (p. 446) *See also* store of value; unit of account.

memory unit The unit of the computer system where information is stored. (p. 367) *See also* arithmetic unit; control unit; input; output.

merchant wholesalers Independent wholesalers who take legal title to goods. (p. 270) *See also* agent wholesalers.

merger The event that occurs when one firm buys the assets and liabilities of another. (p. 73)

metric system The standard of weights and measures based on the decimal system of tens and multiples. (p. 403)

microcomputer A desk-top, limited storage computer system consisting of a visual display device and a keyboard that, due to its small size, can be easily used in the home, office, or classroom. (p. 364) *See also* computers; minicomputer.

middle management The second level of the management pyramid, including executives, such as plant managers and department heads who are responsible for developing detailed plans and procedures to implement the general plans of top management and are involved in specific operations within the organization. (p. 110) *See also* management pyramid; supervisory management; top management.

middlemen Persons or firms, including wholesalers and retailers, that operate between the producer and the consumer or industrial purchaser. (p. 267) *See also* marketing channels; retailers; wholesalers.

minicomputer A small computer about the size of a cash register that is used by scientists and businesspeople for solving numerous problems. (p. 364) *See also* computers; microcomputer.

Minority Business Development Agency An agency of the U.S. Department of Commerce that provides financial assistance and advice to minority-owned businesses; often encourages minority businesspeople to enter more profitable fields. (p. 94)

missionary selling An indirect form of selling where the representative markets the goodwill of a company and/or provides technical or operational assistance to the customer. (p. 299) *See also* creative selling; order-processing.

mixed economies Economies consisting of a mix of socialism and private enterprise. (p. 22) *See also* capitalism; communism; socialism.

mode The most frequently occurring value in a series of observations. (p. 402) *See also* mean; median.

money Anything generally accepted as a means of paying for goods and services. (p. 443) *See also* medium of exchange.

monopolistic competition A situation where somewhat fewer firms than would exist in perfect competition produce and sell goods that are different from those of their competitors. (p. 15) *See also* perfect competition.

monopoly A market situation where there are no direct competitors. (p. 16) *See also* oligopoly.

morale The mental attitude of employees toward their companies and their jobs. (p. 168)

mortality table The table, based on past experience, which is used to predict the number of persons in each age category who will die in a given year. (p. 539)

motivational factors Job-centered characteristics, such as the work itself, recognition, responsibility, advancement, and growth potential, which are the key sources of employee motivation. (p. 168) *See also* maintenance factors.

motive The inner state that directs the individual toward the goal of satisfying a felt need. (p. 162)

multinational corporation A corporation that operates on an international level. (p. 567)

mutual funds Companies that sell shares of their own stock in order to raise money to invest in the securities of other firms. (p. 511)

mutual insurance company An insurance company owned by its policyholders. (p. 530)

mutual savings banks State-chartered banks located primarily in the northeastern section of the United States whose operations are similar to those of savings and loan associations. (p. 458)

nanosecond A time measure now used to describe the rapidity of computer data processing that is equivalent to one-billionth of a second. (p. 373)

National Association of Securities Dealers (NASD) An association created by the Maloney Act of 1938 that is responsible for regulating over-the-counter securities operations. (p. 514)

national banks Commerical banks chartered by the federal government. (p. 450)

National Labor Relations Board (NLRB) An agency set up by the Wagner Act for the purpose of supervising union elections and prohibiting unfair labor practices on the part of management. (p. 215)

natural resources Everything useful as a productive input in its natural state, including land and everything that comes from the land. (p. 14)

near-monies Assets that are almost as liquid as checking accounts but that cannot be used directly as a medium of exchange. (p. 449)

need The lack of something useful; a discrepancy between a desired state and the actual state. (p. 162) *See also* esteem needs; physiological needs; safety needs; self-actualization needs; social needs.

negligence A tort based on careless rather than intentional behavior that causes injury to another person. (p. 588)

negotiable instruments Forms of commercial paper that are transferrable among individuals and businesses. (p. 590)

negotiable order of withdrawal (NOW) account An interest-bearing checking account offered by commercial banks, savings and loan associations, and mutual savings banks that requires a minimum balance established by the individual financial institution. (p. 442)

no-fault insurance plan An insurance plan, created by state law, that requires claims payments to be made by the policyholder's insurance company without regard to fault and that limits the right of victims to sue. (p. 534)

noncumulative preferred stock Preferred stock whose owners are entitled only to the current year's dividend before common stockholders receive their dividends. (p. 496) *See also* cumulative preferred stock; preferred stock.

Norris-La Guardia Act Early federal legislation aimed at protecting unions through greatly reducing management's ability to obtain injunctions halting union activities. (p. 214)

notes payable Liabilities represented by a written document that are payable in a period of time longer than one year. (p. 420) *See also* accounts payable; accounts receivable.

objectives Guideposts used by managers to define standards of what the organization should accomplish in areas such as profitability, customer service, and social responsibility. (p. 112)

observation method A method of collecting primary data that involves studies conducted by actually viewing the actions of respondents either directly or through mechanical devices. (p. 396) *See also* survey method.

Occupational Safety and Health Administration (OSHA) A federal agency created by the Occupational Safety and Health Act to assure safe and healthful working conditions for the U.S. labor force. (p. 197)

odd lots Purchases or sales of fewer than 100 shares of stock that are grouped together to make up one or more round lots. (p. 507) *See also* round lots.

odd pricing The practice of using uneven prices such as $1.11 or $3.22; used because retailers believe that psychologically odd prices are more attractive to consumers than even ones. (p. 324)

ocean marine insurance Insurance that covers shippers for losses of property due to damage to a ship or its cargo while at sea or in port. (p. 536) *See also* inland marine insurance.

oligopoly A market where there are few sellers. (p. 16) *See also* monopoly.

on-the-job training An employee training program in which the worker actually performs the required tasks under the guidance of an experienced employee. (p. 189)

open corporation A large corporation where ownership is widely diversified. (p. 70) *See also* closed corporation.

open-ended interview An interview designed to study the thought processes of interviewees by forcing them to open up and talk about themselves and their goals. (p. 627)

open market operations The technique of controlling the money supply through the purchase and sale of government bonds by the Federal Reserve System. (p. 453)

order processing The sales function of simply receiving and handling an order. (p. 298) *See also* creative selling; missionary selling.

organization A structured process in which people interact to accomplish objectives. (p. 133)

organization chart The formal outline of authority and responsibility relationships in an organization. (p. 145)

organizing The means by which management blends human and material resources through the design of a formal structure of tasks and authority. (p. 117) *See also* controlling; directing; planning.

output The device that provides processed information to the user, usually in the form of a computer printout, a CRT display, or magnetic tapes or disks. (p. 369) *See also* arithmetic unit; control unit; input; memory unit.

outside director A member of the board of directors of a corporation who is not employed by the organization. (p. 73)

over-the-counter market (OTC) A method of trading unlisted securities outside the organized securities exchanges. (p. 505)

owners' equity Claims of the proprietor, the partners, or the stockholders against the assets of the firm, or the excess of all assets over all liabilities. (p. 419)

ownership utility Utility created by arranging for the transfer of title from seller to buyer. (p. 242) *See also* form utility; place utility; time utility; utility.

par value The value printed on the stock certificates of some companies. (p. 495) *See also* book value; market value.

parent company A corporation that owns all or a majority of another corporation's stock (called a subsidiary). (p. 73)

Parkinson's Law A theory that claims "Work expands so as to fill the time available for its completion." (p. 140)

partnership An association of two or more persons who operate a business as co-owners by voluntary legal agreement. (p. 64) *See also* corporation; general partnership; limited partnership; sole proprietorship.

patents Guarantees to inventors of exclusive rights to their inventions for 17 years, provided the inventions are accepted by the U.S Patent Office. (p. 591) *See also* copyrights.

penetration price policy The strategy of pricing a new product relatively low compared to similar goods in the hope that it will secure wide market acceptance and allow the company to raise the price. (p. 321) *See also* skimming price policy.

pension funds Funds set up to guarantee members a regular monthly income on retirement or on reaching a certain age that often utilize surplus cash for investment in corporate securities. (p. 460)

perfect competition A situation where the firms in an industry are so small that none of them can individually influence the price charged in the marketplace. (p. 15) *See also* monopolistic competition.

personal selling A promotional presentation made on a person-to-person basis with a potential buyer. (p. 298)

personnel management The recruitment, selection, development, and motivation of human resources.(p. 184)

persuasive advertising The advertising approach used in a product's growth and maturity stages to improve the competitive status of the product, institution, or concept. (p. 297) *See also* advertising; comparative advertising; informative advertising; reminder-oriented advertising.

PERT (Program Evaluation and Review Technique) A scheduling technique (designed for complex products such as ships and new airplanes) for minimizing production delays by coordinating all aspects of the production task. (p. 351) *See also* critical path.

physical distribution The actual movement of goods from producer to user; covers activities such as transportation, warehousing, and materials handling.(p. 277)

physiological needs The primary needs for food, shelter, and clothing that are present in all humans and that must be satisfied before higher-order needs can be considered. (p. 163) *See also* esteem needs; need; safety needs; self-actualization needs; social needs.

picketing Workers marching at the entrances of an employer's plant as a public protest against some management practice. (p. 223)

piece wage Employee compensation based on the amount of output produced by a worker. (p. 196) *See also* time wage.

PL/1 (Programming Language 1) A computer language designed for use in both scientific and business environments. (p. 376) *See also* BASIC; COBOL; FORTRAN.

place utility Utility created by having the product available at a convenient location when the consumer wants to buy it. (p. 242) *See also* form utility; ownership utility; time utility; utility.

planning The management function concerned with anticipating the future and determining the best courses of action to achieve organizational objectives. (p. 115) *See also* controlling; directing; organizing.

point-of-purchase advertising (POP) A type of sales promotion that displays and demonstrates an item at a time and place close to where the actual purchase decision is made. (p. 302)

pollution The tainting or destroying of a natural environment. (p. 45)

population explosion The rapid growth in the world's population. (p. 606) *See also* zero population growth.

positioning The promotional strategy that concentrates on specific market segments rather than on trying to achieve a broad appeal; often used for products that are not leaders in their particular fields. (p. 291)

preemptive right The right of current stockholders to purchase a proportionate share of new stock issues.(p. 495)

preferred stock Stock whose owners receive preference in the payment of dividends and have first claim to the corporation's assets after all debts have been paid but who usually do not have voting rights at stockholder meetings. (pp. 71, 495) *See also* common stock; cumulative preferred stock; noncumulative preferred stock.

premiums A type of sales promotion that offers small gifts to the consumer in return for buying a product.(p. 303)

price The exchange value of a product or service in the marketplace. (p. 312)

price-earnings ratio The current market price divided by annual earnings per share. (p. 509)

price lining The offering of merchandise at a limited number of prices instead of pricing each item individually. (p. 321)

pricing strategy The part of marketing decision making that deals with the methods of setting profitable and justifiable prices. Consideration is given to government regulations and public opinion. (p. 251) *See also* distribution strategy; marketing mix; product strategy; promotional strategy.

primary boycott A boycott in which union members are told not to patronize the boycotted firm. (p. 223) *See also* boycott; secondary boycott.

primary data Data collected for the first time during a research study that will be used in solving a business problem. (p. 393) *See also* secondary data.

prime interest rate The lowest rate of interest charged by commercial banks for short-term loans to major business firms with high credit standings. (p. 473)

principal The person who, wishing to accomplish something, hires an agent to act on his or her behalf. (p. 587) *See also* agent.

private brands Products that are not identified as to manufacturer but instead carry the retailer's label (often known as house, distributor, or retailer brands). (p. 258)

private carrier A company that carries its own property in its own vehicles. (p. 278) *See also* common carrier; contract carrier; freight forwarder.

private enterprise system The system under which firms operate in a dynamic environment where success or failure is determined by how well they match and counter the offerings of competitors. (p. 9) *See also* capitalism.

private property Property that can be owned, used, bought, sold, and bequeathed under the private enterprise system. (p. 13)

probability sample A representative group selected in a random way so that every member of the population has an equal chance for inclusion in the study. (p. 397)

process departmentalization Departmentalization based on the activities being performed. (p. 135) *See also* customer departmentalization; departmentalization; functional departmentalization; geographic departmentalization; product departmentalization.

process layout A manufacturing facility design that accomodates a variety of nonstandard products in relatively small batches. (p. 347) *See also* customer-oriented layout; fixed-position layout; product layout.

product advertising The nonpersonal selling of a good or service. (p. 295) *See also* institutional advertising.

product departmentalization Departmentalization organized on the basis of products. (p. 135) *See also* customer departmentalization; departmentalization; functional departmentalization; geographic departmentalization; process departmentalization.

product layout A manufacturing facility design that accommodates only a few products in relatively large quantities. (p. 347) *See also* customer-oriented layout; fixed-position layout; process layout.

product liability insurance Insurance protection for businesses against claims for damages resulting from the use of the company's products. (p. 537)

product life cycle A series of stages from initial appearance to death that all products pass through: introduction, growth, maturity, decline, and termination. (p. 253)

product strategy The part of marketing decision making that deals with package design, brand, trademarks, warranties, guarantees, product cycles, and new product development. (p. 251) *See also* distribution strategy; marketing mix; pricing strategy; promotional strategy.

production The use of people and machinery to convert materials into finished products or services. (p. 336)

production and operations management Management of the use of people and machinery in converting materials and resources into finished products and services. (p. 339)

production control A well-defined set of procedures for coordinating people, materials, and machinery to provide maximum production efficiency. (p. 350) *See also* dispatching; follow-up; production planning; routing; scheduling.

production era The early part of the twentieth century, when business managers concentrated almost solely on the firm's production tasks. (p. 19)

production planning The phase of production control that determines the amount of resources needed to produce a certain amount of goods or services. (p. 350) *See also* dispatching; follow-up; production control; routing; scheduling.

productivity A measure of the efficiency of production. It relates to the amount of goods or services a worker produces in a given period of time. (p. 14)

products liability An area of tort law developed by both statutory and case law to hold business liable for negligence in the design, manufacture, sale, and use of products. (p. 588) *See also* strict products liability.

profit The difference between a company's revenues (receipts) and expenses (expenditures). (p. 7)

profit maximization A pricing strategy whereby management sets increasing levels of profitability as its objective. (p. 314)

profit-sharing A type of incentive compensation program where a percentage of company profits is distributed to employees involved in producing these profits. (p. 196)

promissory note A traditional bank loan for which the borrower signs a note that states the terms of the loan, including its date of repayment and interest rate. (p. 473)

promotional contests Sales promotion activities that offer cash or merchandise as prizes and are useful in getting consumers to consider new products. (p. 303)

promotional strategy The function of informing, persuading, and influencing a consumer decision; the part of marketing decision making that blends personal selling, advertising, and sales promotion tools to produce effective communication between the firm and the marketplace. (pp. 251, 290) *See also* distribution strategy; marketing mix; pricing strategy; product strategy.

promotions Upward movements in an organization to positions of greater authority and responsibility and higher salaries. (p. 190)

property Something for which people have the unrestricted right of possession or use. (p. 586)

prospecting The task of identifying potential customers. (p. 299)

prospects Potential customers. (p. 299)

protective tariffs Tariffs designed to raise the retail price of imported products to the level of products produced domestically. (p. 563) *See also* revenue tariffs.

proxy Authorization by stockholders for someone else to vote their shares, as instructed, at stockholder meetings. (p. 71)

public liability insurance Insurance protection for businesses and individuals against claims caused by injuries to others or damage to the property of others. (p. 537)

public ownership The ownership and operation of an organization by a government unit or its agency on behalf of the population served by that unit. (p. 74)

pulling strategy A promotional strategy utilizing advertising and sales promotion appeals to generate consumer demand for a product or product line. (p. 303) *See also* pushing strategy.

Pure Food and Drug Act A federal law prohibiting the adulteration and misbranding of foods and drugs. (p. 593)

pure risk A type of risk involving only the chance of loss. (p. 523)

pushing strategy A sales-oriented promotional strategy designed to motivate middlemen to push the product to their customers. (p. 303) *See also* pulling strategy.

qualifying A function of the sales presentation that enables the salesperson to identify those prospects with the financial ability and authority to buy. (p. 299)

quality control The measurement of products and services against established quality standards. (p. 352)

ratio of net income to sales A ratio that measures company profitability by dividing net income by sales. (p. 429)

real property Real estate. (p. 587) *See also* intangible personal property; tangible personal property.

reciprocity The practice of extending purchasing preferences to those suppliers who are also customers. (p. 349)

recycling The reprocessing of used materials for reuse. (p. 45)

regulated industries Industries in which competition is either limited or eliminated altogether and close government control substitutes for the market controls of free competition. (p. 592)

reminder-oriented advertising The advertising approach utilized in the late maturity and decline stages of the product life cycle that attempts to keep the product's name in front of the consumer to remind people of the importance of a concept or an institution. (p. 298) *See also* advertising; comparative advertising; informative advertising; persuasive advertising.

remote terminals Typewriter-like machines connected to the main computer installation but located in an area physically removed from the computer. (p. 376)

reserve requirement The percentage of a bank's checking and savings accounts that must be kept in the bank or on deposit at the local Federal Reserve District Bank. (p. 453)

responsibility The obligation of a subordinate to perform assigned duties. (p. 136)

resume A written summary of one's personal, educational, and professional achievements. (p. 624)

retailers Firms that sell products to individuals for their own use rather than for resale. (p. 267) *See also* marketing channels; middlemen; wholesalers.

revaluation An upward adjustment in the value of a country's currency. (p. 558)

revenue tariffs Tariffs designed to raise funds for the government. (p. 563) *See also* protective tariffs.

revolving credit agreement A guaranteed line of credit. (p. 474)

right-to-work laws State laws prohibiting compulsory union membership. (p. 217)

risk Uncertainty about loss or injury. (p. 523)

robbery insurance Insurance coverage for losses due to the unlawful taking of property from another person by force or the threat of force. (p. 535)

Robinson-Patman Act A federal statute outlawing price discrimination that is not based on quality or quantity differences and that injures competition. (p. 593)

round lots Quantities of 100 shares of stock purchased or sold. (p. 507) *See also* odd lots.

routing The phase of production control that determines the sequence of work throughout the facility. (p. 351) *See also* dispatching; follow-up; production control; production planning; scheduling.

safety needs The second level of human needs in Maslow's hierarchy, which includes job security, protection from physical harm, and avoidance of the unexpected. (p. 163) *See also* esteem needs; need; physiological needs; self-actualization needs; social needs.

salary Employee compensation calculated on a weekly, monthly, or annual basis. (p. 194) *See also* wage.

sales branches Manufacturer-owned wholesalers who stock the items they distribute and process orders from their inventory; often specialize in large-volume, complex, perishable, or highly competitive products. (p. 270)

sales law An offspring of contract law that involves the sale of goods or products for money or credit. (p. 585)

sales maximization concept A concept under which management sets an acceptable minimum level of profitability and then tries to maximize sales. (p. 314)

sales offices Manufacturer-owned offices for salespeople that provide close local contacts for potential purchasers. (p. 270)

sales promotion The forms of promotion other than advertising and personal selling that increase sales through one-time selling efforts; used to supplement other promotional strategies. (p. 302)

sample A representative group from which data are gathered. (p. 397) *See also* census.

samples A type of sales promotion that uses distribution of free product gifts to gain public acceptance and future sales of a new product. (p. 303)

savings and loan associations Financial institutions that pay slightly higher interest rates on time deposits and lend money for residential construction and commercial purposes. (p. 457)

scheduling The phase of production control involved in developing timetables that specify how long each operation in the production process takes. (p. 351) *See also* dispatching; follow-up; production control; production planning; routing.

scrambled merchandising Diversification of products offered for sale by retailers in order to preserve or increase their sales volume. (p. 272)

secondary boycott A boycott or work stoppage intended to force an employer to cease dealing in the product of another firm involved in a labor dispute. (p. 218) *See also* boycott; primary boycott.

secondary data Previously published information that is used in solving business problems. (p. 393) *See also* primary data.

secured bond A bond backed by specific pledges of company assets. (p. 497)

securities Stocks and bonds that represent obligations on the part of the issuers to provide purchasers with an expected or stated return on funds invested. (p. 494)

Securities Act of 1933 A federal law designed to protect investors by requiring full disclosure of relevant financial information from companies desiring to sell new stock or bond issues to the general public; also known as the Truth in Securities Act. (p. 512)

Securities Exchange Act of 1934 The federal law that created the Securities and Exchange Commission (SEC) to regulate the national stock exchanges. (p. 513)

selective distribution A degree of market coverage somewhere between intensive and exclusive distribution; occurs when a limited number of retailers are selected to distribute a firm's product lines. (p. 277) *See also* exclusive distribution; intensive distribution.

self-actualization needs The needs for fulfillment, for realizing one's potential, and for totally using one's talents and capabilities. (p. 164) *See also* esteem needs; need; physiological needs; safety needs; social needs.

self-insurance The practice of some multiplant, geographically scattered firms of assuming risks by developing a system, such as accumulating funds, in order to absorb possible losses. (p. 525)

seniority The privileges attained as a result of the length of time an employee has worked at a particular job or in a particular department. (p. 190)

separations Employee movements resulting from resignations, retirements, layoffs, and terminations. (p. 191)

serial bonds A large number of bonds that are issued at the same time but mature at different times. (p. 498)

Service Corps of Retired Executives (SCORE) Groups of volunteer management consultants who assist people with small business problems. A program of the SBA. (p. 96)

share draft accounts Accounts similar to ATS accounts used by depositors at credit unions. (p. 448)

Sherman Antitrust Act Federal antitrust legislation that prohibits every contract or conspiracy in restraint of trade and declares illegal any action that monopolizes or attempts to monopolize any part of trade or commerce. (p. 592)

shopping goods Products purchased only after the consumer has compared competing goods in competing stores on bases such as price, quality, style and color. (p. 252) *See also* convenience goods; specialty goods.

single payment policy A variation of whole life insurance that consists of a large premium paid in a lump sum at the time the insurance is purchased.(p. 542)

sinking-fund bonds Bonds whose issuing corporation makes annual deposits of funds for use in redeeming them when they mature. (p. 498)

skimming price policy The strategy of setting the price of a new product relatively high compared to similar goods and then gradually lowering it. (p. 320) *See also* penetration price policy.

small business A business that is independently owned and operated, is not dominant in its field, and meets a variety of size standards. (p. 84)

Small Business Administration (SBA) The principal government agency concerned with small U.S. firms. Set up in 1953, it provides financial assistance and offers management training and consulting and other services to small businesses in order to preserve free competitive enterprise. (p. 95)

Small Business Development Centers Centers that are part of a federal program aimed at using qualified faculty personnel and others to assist small businesses through research and consulting activities. (p. 97)

Small Business Institute (SBI) An organization (part of the SBA) that sends out senior and graduate business students as consultants on small business problems at no cost to the firm. (p. 97)

social (belongingness) needs The desire to be accepted by members of the family and other individuals and groups. (p. 164) *See also* esteem needs; need; physiological needs; safety needs; self-actualization needs.

social responsibility Consideration by management of social as well as economic effects in its decision making. (p. 38)

socialism An economic system that advocates government ownership and operation of all basic industries (with private ownership continuing to exist in smaller businesses). (p. 22) *See also* capitalism; communism; mixed economies.

sole proprietorship Ownership (and usually operation) of an organization by a single individual. (p. 62) *See also* corporation; partnership.

span of control The optimum number of subordinates a manager can effectively manage. (p. 138)

specialty advertising A type of sales promotion that consists of giving away items of minimal value that are imprinted with the donor's company name (for example, pens, calendars, ashtrays). (p. 302)

specialty goods Products particularly desired by the purchaser who is willing to make a special effort to obtain them and is familiar with the items sought. (p. 252) *See also* convenience goods; shopping goods.

speculation Purchasing stocks in anticipation of making a large profit within a short time period. (p. 499) *See also* investment.

speculative risk A type of risk where the firm or individual has the chance of either a profit or a loss. (p. 523)

stagflation The dual economic problem of high unemployment and a rapidly rising price level. (p. 42) *See also* cost-push inflation; demand-pull inflation; inflation.

Standard & Poor's Index An index developed from the market performance of 425 industrial, 25 rail, and 50 utility stocks that reflects the general activity of the stock market. (p. 510) *See also* Dow-Jones Averages.

state banks Commercial banks chartered by individual states. (p. 450)

statement of changes in financial position The financial statement that explains the financial changes that occur in a company from one accounting period to the next. (p. 424)

statistics The collection, analysis, interpretation, and presentation of information in numerical form. (p. 400)

status quo pricing objectives Objectives that reflect management's efforts to seek stable prices, enabling the company to channel competitive efforts into other areas such as product design or promotion. (p. 315)

statutory law Written law that includes state and federal constitutions, legislative enactments, treaties of the federal government, and ordinances of towns, cities, and other local governments. (p. 580) See also common law.

stock exchanges The locations at which stocks and bonds are bought and sold. (p. 503)

stock insurance company An insurance company operated for profit. (p. 531)

stock options Company plans that enable executives to buy the firm's stock at a set price often lower than the current market price. (p. 631)

stock turnover The number of times the average inventory is sold annually. (p. 318)

stockbroker A middleman who buys and sells securities for clients. (p. 505)

stockholders The people who acquire the shares (and therefore are the owners) of a corporation. (p. 70)

stocks Shares of ownership in the corporation. (p. 479) See also common stock; preferred stock.

storage warehouse A place used to store products for a relatively long period of time; usually used for seasonal products. (p. 282) See also distribution warehouse.

store of value The function performed by money in serving as a temporary store of accumulated wealth until it is needed for new purchases. (p. 446) See also medium of exchange; unit of account.

stress interview An interview that creates a crisis situation by putting pressure on the interviewee in order to determine how that person copes with conflict. (p. 627)

strict products liability A legal concept that extends the tort theory to cover injuries caused by products regardless of whether the manufacturer is proven negligent. (p. 588) See also products liability.

strike A temporary work stoppage by employees until a dispute has been settled or a contract signed. (p. 222)

Subchapter S corporation A corporation that can elect to be taxed as a partnership while maintaining the advantages of incorporation. (p. 68)

subsidiary A corporation with all or a majority of its stock owned by another corporation. Management is appointed by the chief executive of the parent company subject to the approval of the parent's board of directors. (p. 73)

supervisory management The third level of the management pyramid, including people who are directly responsible for the details of assigning workers to specific jobs and evaluating performance. (p. 112) See

also management pyramid; middle management; top management.

supply curve A schedule of amounts of a good or service that will be offered in the market at certain prices. (p. 317) See also demand curve; law of supply and demand.

surety bonds Bonds that protect people or companies against losses resulting from nonperformance of a contract. (p. 536) See also fidelity bonds.

survey method A method of acquiring primary data in which a researcher asks respondents questions to ascertain attitudes, motives, and opinions. (p. 396) See also observation method.

synthetic system A system that combines a number of raw materials or parts into a finished product or changes raw materials into completely different finished products. (p. 338) See also analytic system.

Taft-Hartley Act A federal law designed to balance the power of unions and management by prohibiting a number of unfair union practices. (p. 216)

tangible personal property Physical things such as goods and products. (p. 587) See also intangible personal property; real property.

target return goals A pricing strategy whereby the desired profitability is stated in terms of particular goals such as a 10 percent return on either sales or investment. (p. 314)

tariffs Taxes levied against products from abroad. (p. 563)

technology The innovations, methods, practices, systems, and equipment (and related operational knowledge) applicable to the industrial setting. (p. 608)

term insurance Insurance coverage protecting the individual for a specified period of years that has no value at the end of that period. (p. 542)

terminations Permanent separations resulting from inability to perform the work, repeated violations of work rules, excessive absenteeism, elimination of jobs, or the closing of work facilities. (p. 192)

theft insurance Insurance coverage for losses due to the unlawful taking of property. (p. 535)

Theory X The traditional managerial assumption that employees dislike work and must be coerced, controlled, or threatened to motivate them to work. (p. 165) See also Theory Y.

Theory Y The newer managerial assumption that workers do not dislike work and that under proper conditions they accept and seek out responsibilities in order to fulfill their social, esteem, and self-actualization needs. (p. 166) See also Theory X.

ticker tapes Large screens that electronically display actual transactions on the New York and American stock exchanges and over-the-counter transactions. (p. 506)

time deposits The technical name for savings accounts, which are not in the form of NOW or ATS accounts at commercial banks and thrift institutions; the institution is permitted to require prior withdrawal notice or to assess an early withdrawal penalty. (p. 448)

time-sharing The linking of several users through remote terminals (usually teletypewriters) to a large central computer. (p. 382)

time utility Utility created by having the product available when the consumer wants to buy it. (p. 242) *See also* form utility; ownership utility; price utility; utility.

time wage Employee compensation based on the amount of time spent on the job. (p. 196) *See also* piece wage.

title insurance Insurance protection for real estate purchasers against losses that might be incurred because of a defect in the title to the property. (p. 536)

top management The highest level of the management pyramid, comprised of the president and other key company executives who develop long-range plans for the company and interact with the government and community. (p. 110) *See also* management pyramid; middle management; supervisory management.

tort A civil wrong inflicted on other persons or their property. (p. 588)

trade credit The short-term source of funds from making purchases on credit or open account. (p. 472)

trade shows A type of sales promotion that uses exhibitions designed to promote products or services to retailers, wholesalers, international buyers, and other resellers in the distribution channel. (p. 302)

trademark A brand that has been given exclusive legal protection—protection includes not only the pictorial design but also the brand name. (p. 255)

trading stamps A type of sales promotion that offers stamps that are redeemable for additional merchandise. (p. 303)

transfers Horizontal movements in the organization at about the same wage and the same level. (p. 190)

treasury bills Short-term U.S. Treasury borrowings that are issued each week on a competitive bid basis and are virtually riskless and easy to resell. (p. 481)

trial courts Courts of general jurisdiction operating at both the federal and state levels that hear a wide range of cases. (p. 582)

tying contract A contract that requires a person who wishes to be the exclusive dealer for a manufacturer's product to carry other products of the manufacturer in inventory. (p. 593)

Uniform Commerical Code (UCC) A comprehensive commercial law adopted by all states except Louisiana that covers the law of sales as well as other specific areas of commercial law. (p. 586)

union shop A place of employment where all qualified employees can be hired but where they must join the union within a specified time period. (p. 216) *See also* agency shop; closed shop.

unit of account The function performed by money in serving as the common denominator for measuring the value of all products and services. (p. 446) *See also* medium of exchange; store of value.

unitization Combining as many packages as possible into one load that can be handled by a forklift truck. (p. 282) *See also* containerization.

unsecured loan A short-term source of funds from a loan in which the borrower does not pledge any assets as collateral but is given the loan on the basis of credit reputation and previous experience with the lender.(p. 472)

utility The want-satisfying power of a product or service. (pp. 242, 336) *See also* form utility; ownership utility; place utility; time utility.

variable costs Costs that change with the level of production such as labor and raw materials. (p. 319) *See also* fixed costs.

venture capitalists Groups of private individuals or business organizations that invest in promising new businesses. Sometimes they loan money, and sometimes they become part owners of the firm. (p. 90)

vestibule schools Company-established schools where workers are given instruction in the operation of equipment similar to that used in their new jobs and are exposed to facsimiles of their actual work areas. (p. 189)

voluntary arbitration Arbitration where both union and management representatives decide to present their unresolved issues to an impartial third party. (p. 220) *See also* compulsory arbitration.

wages Employee compensation based on the number of hours worked or on the amount of output produced. (p. 193) *See also* salary.

Wagner Act A federal law that made collective bargaining legal and required employers to bargain with the elected representatives of their employees; also known as the National Labor Relations Act. (p. 214)

warehousing The storage of products. (p. 282)

Webb-Pomerene Act Federal legislation exempting from antitrust laws certain combinations of U.S. firms acting together to develop export markets. (p. 564)

Wheeler-Lea Act The federal law that both amends the Federal Trade Commission Act to further outlaw unfair or deceptive acts and practices in business and gives the FTC jurisdiction over false and misleading advertising. (p. 594)

wheel of retailing A concept that explains how the retail structure is continually evolving as new retailers enter the market by offering lower prices through reductions in service; as the new entries add services and grow, they become targets for competitive assault. (p. 272)

whole life insurance Insurance providing both protection and savings for the individual who pays premiums throughout life and builds up a cash surrender value in the policy. (p. 542)

wholesalers Persons or firms who sell primarily to retailers and to other wholesalers or industrial users. (p. 267) *See also* marketing channels; middlemen; retailers.

workers' compensation insurance Insurance provided by employers under state law to guarantee payment of medical expenses and salaries to employees who are injured on the job. (p. 535)

working capital The difference between current assets and current liabilities. (p. 424)

yield The income received from securities; calculated by dividing dividends by market price. (p. 501)

zero population growth The point where live births equal the current death rate. (p. 245) *See also* population explosion.

Chapter 1

Chapter 2

Solution," *Detroit News*, Jan. 7, 1976, p. 1; and Ralph E. Winter, "Furor Over a Plant on Lake Superior Is Warning to Industry," *Wall Street Journal*, Aug. 25, 1974, p. 1. Photo, p. 46, by Grant Heilman. Focus 2–2 source, p. 49: "High Voltage," *Time*, Oct. 6, 1980, p. 33, reprinted by permission from TIME, The Weekly Newsmagazine, copyright TIME, Inc., 1980. Advertisement, p. 50, courtesy Ford Consumer Appeals Board. Controversial Issue sources, pp. 52–53: "U.S. and Hooker in Accord on Cleaning Up Waste Site," *New York Times*, Jan. 20, 1981, p. B–6; "An Alarming Silence on Chemical Wastes," *Business Week*, May 7, 1979, pp. 44, 46; Michael H. Brown, "Love Canal, U.S.A.," *New York Times Magazine*, Jan 21, 1979, pp. 23, 38, 39, 44, 45; and "Labors of Love," *Newsweek*, Dec. 11, 1978, pp. 16–17. Case 2–1 source, pp. 56–57: Margaret Yao, "Civic Duties Become a More Beastly Burden for Chief Executives," *Wall Street Journal*, June 11, 1980, pp. 1, 18, reprinted by permission of the Wall Street Journal, © Dow Jones & Company, Inc., 1980, all rights reserved. Case 2–2 source, pp. 57–58: "Economics: A Triple Whammy on Charities," *Business Week*, Mar. 23, 1981, pp. 117–118; the issues in regard to corporate giving are discussed in Ellen K. Coughlin, "How Charitable Should American Corporations Be?" *Chronicle of Higher Education*, Oct. 31, 1977, p. 12; and Norman Sinclair, "Dow Cuts Aid Over Talk by Fonda," *Detroit News*, Oct. 29, 1977.

Chapter 3

Photos, p. 60, courtesy Sears, Roebuck & Company. Profile source, p. 60, "Merchant to the Millions," © Copyright 1978, Sears, Roebuck & Company. Kingen quote source, p. 61: Alf Collins, "Red Robbins' Main Man Bob-Bobbing Along," *Seattle Times*, Nov. 25, 1980, p. B–1. Photo, p. 61, copyright Paul Sequeira from Rapho/Photo Researchers, Inc. Photo, p. 65, copyright Raphael Macia/Photo Researchers, Inc. Table 3–2 source, p. 67: "Corporate Scoreboard: How 1200 Companies Performed in 1980," *Business Week*, Mar. 16, 1981, p. 65, reprinted from the Mar. 16, 1981 issue of *Business Week*, by special permission, © 1981 by McGraw-Hill, Inc., New York, N.Y., 10020, all rights reserved. Figure 3–1 source, p. 68: U.S. Bureau of the Census, *Statistical Abstract of the United States: 1979*, 100th ed. (Washington, D.C.: Government Printing Office, 1979), p. 553. Focus 3–2 source, p. 76: Debbie Carlton, "R.E.I.: New President Sparks Turnaround at Cooperative," *Journal American*, Bellevue, Wash., Now. 3, 1980, p. D–1. Case 3–1 sources, p. 79: Allan Sloan, "Wait 'til Next Year," *Forbes*, Aug. 4, 1980, pp. 46–47 and Alex Ben Block, "So You Want to Own a Ballclub," *Forbes*, Apr. 1, 1977, pp. 37–40. Case 3–2 source, p. 80: Maureen Baily, "That's Entertainment?" *Barron's*, Oct. 22, 1979, pp. 9, 18, 22.

Chapter 4

Photo, p. 82, by Brian R. Wolfe for Business Week. Profile source, p. 82: "Corporate Woman: Women Rise as Entrepreneurs," *Business Week*, Feb. 25, 1980, pp. 85–86; reprinted from the Feb. 25, 1980 issue of *Business Week* by special permission, © 1980 by McGraw-Hill, Inc., New York, N.Y. 10020, all rights reserved. Smith quote source, p. 83: Art Runde, "A Pipeline to Prosperity," *Money*, Jan., 1980, p. 80. Photo, p. 84, © Inger McCabe from Rapho/Photo Researchers, Inc. Top photo, p. 85, © Beryl Goldberg. Bottom photo, p. 85, by Jon Rawle/Stock, Boston. Focus 4–1 source, p. 90: "That New Santa Fe Travail," *Time*, May 5, 1980, p.

85; reprinted by permission from TIME, The Weekly Newsmagazine; copyright TIME, Inc., 1980. Photo, p. 92, by Lucinda Fleeson/Stock, Boston. Table 4–2 source, p. 92: adapted from U.S. Bureau of the Census, *Statistical Abstract of the United States: 1980*, 101st ed. (Washington, D.C.: Government Printing Office, 1980) p. 558. Photo, p. 95, by Sybil Shelton/Monkmeyer Press Photo Service. Controversial Issue sources, pp. 96–97: Roberta Graham, "Small Business: Fighting to Stay Alive," *Nation's Business*, July, 1980, pp. 33–36; "How Small Companies Can Survive Hard Times," *U.S. News & World Report*, May 19, 1980, p. 76; "Those Small Business Blues," *Time*, May 5, 1980, pp. 84–85; "How Government Helps Small Business in the U.S.A.," *Director*, Feb., 1980, pp. 47–48; and "Why Small Firms Find Inflation Hard to Lick," *U.S. News & World Report*, June 25, 1979. Case 4–1 source, pp. 100–101: "Two Cash In on Game about Business," Associated Press Newsfeature as it appeared in the *Journal American*, Bellevue, Wash., Dec. 1, 1980, p. B–7. Case 4–2 source, p. 101: Tom Corddry, "Speakerlab Turns Up the Profits with Financial Goals," *Seattle Business Journal*, Dec. 8, 1980, pp. 10–11.

Chapter 5

Photo, p. 107, courtesy of CBS, Inc. Profile sources, p. 107: "Why Paley's Heir May Have What It Takes," *Business Week*, June 9, 1980, p. 24; "CBS 'I' Strikes Again," *Newsweek*, June 2, 1980, p. 66; and Tony Schwartz, "New Chief's Road to CBS," *New York Times*, May 23, 1980, pp. D–1, D–9. Focus 5–1 sources, p. 112: reprinted by permission of the publisher from Wylie A. Walthall, *Getting Into Business*, (New York: Harper & Row, 1979), pp. 98–99; findings based on Margaret Henning and Anne Jardim, *The Managerial Woman*, (Garden City: Anchor Press/Doubleday, 1977) and Betty Lehan Harragan, *Games Mother Never Taught You: Corporate Gamesmanship for Women*, (New York: Rawson Associates, 1977). Focus 5–2 sources, p. 116: "Communes: A More Businesslike Style," *U.S. News & World Report*, March 3, 1980, p. 67, reprinted from "U.S. News & World Report," copyright 1980, U.S. News & World Report, Inc.; the description of the Twin Oaks Commune is reprinted from "What's This? Distasteful As It Is, Many Communes Turn to Business Techniques," *Wall Street Journal*, Dec. 22, 1971, p. 1, reprinted by permission of the Wall Street Journal, © Dow Jones & Company, Inc., 1971, all rights reserved. Photo, p. 117, courtesy of Avery Fisher Hall/Marianne Barcelona. Figure 5–5 source, p. 118: reprinted by permission of John Wiley and Sons, Inc. from Bertram Schoner and Kenneth P. Uhl, *Marketing Research: Information Systems and Decision Making*, p. 13, copyright © 1975 John Wiley and Sons, Inc. Focus 5–3 source, p. 119: "News You Can Use in Your Personal Planning," *U.S. News & World Report*, Jan. 12, 1981, p. 69, reprinted by permission from U.S. News & World Report, copyright 1981, U.S. News & World Report. Figure 5–7 source, p. 121: adapted with permission from Robert Tannenbaum and Warren H. Schmidt, "How to Choose a Leadership Pattern," *Harvard Business Review*, May–June, 1973, p. 164, copyright © 1973 by the President and Fellows of Harvard College, all rights reserved. Controversial Issue sources, pp. 122–123: "What the Companies are Doing," *Response*, Nov., 1980, p. 5; *1980 Social Report of the Life and Health Insurance Business*, Clearinghouse on Corporate Social Responsibility, Washington, D.C., Oct.,

1980; Mary Ann Bird, "Businesses Are Stepping Up Their Roles in Social Problems of Cities," *New York Times,* Feb. 4, 1979, p. 44; and Stanley G. Karson, "Insurance Industry and Social Responsibility: A Successful Effort," *Journal of Contemporary Business,* Graduate School of Business Administration, University of Washington, Seattle, Vol. 8, No. 1, Spring, 1979. Case 5–2, p. 128, excerpted from "Consensus in San Diego," *Time,* Mar. 30, 1981, p. 58, reprinted by permission from TIME, The Weekly Newsmagazine, copyright TIME, Inc., 1981.

Chapter 6
Photo, p. 131, United Press International. Photo, p. 132, courtesy NASA. Figure 6–4 source, p. 136, Robert D. Hay, *Introduction to Business* (New York: Holt, Rinehart and Winston, 1968) p. 102, reprinted by permission of the author. Focus 6–1 source, p. 137: William M. Carley, "TWA Will Slash Salaries of Management Up to 25% of Amounts Exceeding $35,000," *Wall Street Journal,* Feb. 1, 1980, p. 8, reprinted by permission of the Wall Street Journal, © Dow Jones & Company, Inc., 1980, all rights reserved. Figure 6–8 source, p. 145: *Management: Theory, Process and Practice,* 2nd edition, by Richard M. Hodgetts, copyright © 1979 by W. B. Saunders Company, copyright 1975 by W. B. Saunders Company, reprinted by permission of Holt, Rinehart and Winston. Controversial Issue sources, pp. 148–149: Irwin Ross, "How Lawless Are Big Companies?" *Fortune,* Dec. 1, 1980, pp. 57–64 and Nick Galluccio, "The Boss in the Slammer," *Forbes,* Feb. 5, 1979, pp. 61–62. Case 6–1 source, pp. 152–153: *Management: Theory, Process and Practice,* 2nd edition, by Richard M. Hodgetts, copyright © 1979 by W. B. Saunders Company, copyright 1975 by W. B. Saunders Company, reprinted by permission from Holt, Rinehart and Winston.

Chapter 7
Profile sources, p. 159: Alexander Stuart, "U.S. Home's Management Religion," *Fortune,* Dec. 4, 1978, pp. 66–78 and information from Tina Schiebl, Manager of Media Communications, U.S. Home Corporation, Houston, Texas. Lafferty quotation source, p. 160: Dale D. McConkey, "Participative Management: What It Really Means in Practice," *Business Horizons,* October, 1980, p. 68. Figure 7–1 source, p. 162: adapted by permission from James H. Donnelly, Jr., James L. Gibson, and John M. Ivancevich, *Fundamentals of Management,* (Dallas: Business Publications, 1975) p. 130. Focus 7–1 source, p. 165: reprinted from "World Business," *U.S. News & World Report,* Sept. 19, 1977, p. 54, copyright 1977, U.S. News & World Report, Inc. Focus 7–2 sources, p. 167: current statistics from *The Hammond Almanac: 1981,* (Maplewood, N.J.: Hammond Almanac, Inc., 1981). "Drive to Organize G.I.'s Picks Up Steam," *U.S. News & World Report,* Mar. 28, 1977, p. 50; and Bowen Northrup, "This Is an Army? Well, It Has Arms, Marches . . . Sort Of." *Wall Street Journal,* Oct. 1, 1974, p. 1. Photo, p. 167, United Press International. Figure 7–3 source, p. 168: *Human Behavior at Work* by Keith Davis, © Copyright 1979 by McGraw-Hill Book Company, used with permission of McGraw-Hill Book Company. Tables 7–1 and 7–2 source, p. 169: reprinted by permission of the publisher from "What Makes a Good Job," by Lawrence Lindahl, *Personnel,* Jan., 1949. © 1949 by American Management Association, Inc., p. 265, all rights reserved. Controversial Issue sources, p. 174: "Aide Calls Sex

Harassment Cases 'Tip of Iceberg,' " *New York Times,* April 22, 1981, p. C–8 and Phyllis Gillis, "Sexual Harassment—No Longer a Dirty Joke," *Parents Magazine,* Aug., 1980, pp. 24, 28, 30. Case 7–1 source, p. 178: Joe L. Welch and David Gordon, "Assessing the Impact of Flexitime on Productivity," *Business Horizons,* Dec., 1980, pp. 61–65 and Robert J. Kuhne and Courtney O. Blair, "Flexitime," *Business Horizons,* Apr., 1978, pp. 42–44. Case 7–2 source, p. 179: "Lumber Company Includes 'Well Pay' in Health Program," *Sentinel Star,* Orlando, FL, May 2, 1980.

Chapter 8
Photo, p. 181, Wide World Photos. Profile sources, p. 181: Curry Kirkpatrick, "Hallelujah, He's, Uh, Bum," *Sports Illustrated,* Oct. 27, 1980, pp. 68–82 and Mark Goodman, "The Wit and Whimsey of Coach Bum Phillips," *Family Weekly,* Nov. 30, 1980, p. 13. Sanders quote source, p. 182: Christopher Evans, "Col. Sanders Dies at 90 from Leukemia, Pneumonia," *Sentinel Star,* Orlando, FL, Dec. 17, 1980, p. 15–A. Lincoln quote source, p. 182: a Lincoln National Life Insurance ad that appeared in *Journal American,* Bellevue, Wash., Nov. 15, 1980, p. B–11. Table 8–1 source, p. 183: reprinted by permission of Delbert J. Duncan, Charles F. Phillips, and Stanley C. Hollander, *Modern Retailing Management* (Homewood, Ill.: Richard D. Irwin, 1972), p. 184. Photo, p. 185, © 1980 Ellis Herwig/Stock, Boston. Table 8–2 source, p. 185: based on U.S. Department of Labor, Employment and Training Administration, *Dictionary of Occupational Titles* (Washington, D.C.: Government Printing Office, various years). Photo, p. 187, by Hugh Rogers/Monkmeyer Press Photo Service. Photo, p. 188, by Hugh Rogers/Monkmeyer Press Photo Service. Focus 8–2 source, p. 193: courtesy Rockwell World Industries. Focus 8–3 source, pp. 194–195: Pamela Reeves, "Women Still Earn Less Than Men," *Sentinel Star,* Orlando, FL, Mar. 24, 1980, p. B–2, reprinted by permission of United Press International. Table 8–4 source, p. 197: "Where the Benefits Go," *U.S. News & World Report,* Jan. 19, 1981, p. 66, reprinted from "U.S. News & World Report," copyright 1981, U.S. News & World Report, Inc., basic data obtained from a survey of 922 companies by the Chamber of Commerce of the United States. Photo, p. 197, by Joe Rychetnik/Photo Researchers, Inc. Controversial Issue sources, pp. 198–199: "Job 'Quotas' to Fight Bias—Furor Goes On," *U.S. News & World Report,* July 7, 1980, pp. 45–47; Herbert Hill, "A Blow to Minorities," *Commonweal,* Sept. 2, 1977, pp. 552–555; and "The Court Strikes a Blow for Seniority," *Time,* June 13, 1977, p. 60. Case 8–1 source, p. 204: Martha M. Hamilton, "Lower Wages for Teen-agers? A Bonanza for Fast-food Firms," *Sentinel Star,* Orlando, FL, Dec. 29, 1980, p. D–8. Case 8–2 source, pp. 204–205: "New Benefits, New Lifestyles," reprinted from the Feb. 11, 1980 issue of *Business Week* by special permission, © 1980 by McGraw-Hill, Inc., New York, N.Y. 10020, all rights reserved.

Chapter 9
Photo, p. 207, United Press International. Profile sources, p. 207: Robert L. Simison, "Chrysler Lauds Strong Performance of UAW's Fraser as Board Member," *Wall Street Journal,* March 12, 1981, pp. 33, 49; "Labor's Voice on the Board," *Newsweek,* May 26, 1980, p. 13; "UAW's Fraser—Can He Serve Two Masters?" *U.S. News*

& World Report, May 26, 1980, p. 8; and "Blue Collars in the Board Room," Time, May 19, 1980, p. 78. Leontief quote source, p. 208: Adam Smith, "The Big Picture," Esquire, Feb., 1981, p. 11. Marshall quote source, p. 208: "When Pro Athletes Carry Union Cards," U.S. News & World Report, March 31, 1980, p. 79. Photo, p. 209, Culver Pictures, Inc. Table 9–1 source, p. 214: The Hammond Almanac: 1981 (Maplewood, N.J.: Hammond Almanac, Inc., 1981) p. 205. Focus 9–4 source, p. 217: Robert Townsend, Up The Organization (New York: Knopf, 1970) p. 93. Photo, p. 219, © Michael Hayman, Photo Researchers, Inc. Photo, p. 222, by Barbara Alper/Stock, Boston. Photo, p. 224, © Marjorie Pickens 1980. Focus 9–5 source, p. 227: reprinted from "New Breed of Workers," U.S. News & World Report, Sept. 3, 1979, p. 35, copyright U.S. News & World Report, Inc., 1979. Controversial Issue sources, pp. 228–229: "Work for Robots is Picking Up," New York Times, Nov. 28, 1980, pp. D-1, D-3; John Hilton, "Report From the Assembly Line," Newsweek, June 30, 1980, p. 11; and Douglas Colligan, "The Robots Are Coming," New York Magazine, July 30, 1979, pp. 40–44. Case 9–1 sources, pp. 231–232: Richard M. Hodgetts, Management Theory, Process and Practice (Philadelphia: W. B. Saunders, 1979) pp. 334–335; and "How IBM Avoids Layoffs Through Retraining," Business Week, Nov. 10, 1975, pp. 110, 112. Case 9–2 source, p. 233: courtesy of Dunbar Furniture Corporation.

Chapter 10
Photo, p. 239, by Alan Zanger/United Press International. Profile sources, p. 239: "Bio," People, Feb. 11, 1980, pp. 86–90; Vartan Kupelian, "Jerry Buss: Charismatic Owner in a Class by Himself," Detroit News, Oct. 30, 1979, pp. C-1, C-5; and William Oscar Johnson, "Jerry Is Never Behind the Eight Ball," Sports Illustrated, June 18, 1979, pp. 22, 24, 29. Harness quote source, p. 240: John H. Pressto, "At Proctor and Gamble, Success is Largely Due to Heeding Consumer," Wall Street Journal, April 29, 1980, p. 16. Focus 10–1 source, p. 241: reprinted from Edward G. Harness, Chairman of the Board of Proctor and Gamble, "Some Basic Beliefs About Marketing," a talk to the annual marketing meeting of the Conference Board, New York City, 1976, courtesy of the Proctor and Gamble Company. Advertisement, p. 241, courtesy of the Proctor and Gamble Company. Photo, p. 243, © Ray Ellis from Rapho/Photo Researchers, Inc. Photo, p. 244, by Peter Southwick/Stock, Boston. Figure 10–1 source, p. 245: adapted from "The Census: Southwestward Ho!" Newsweek, Dec. 29, 1980, p. 20, copyright 1980, Newsweek, Inc., all rights reserved, reprinted by permission. Figure 10–2 source, p. 246: U.S. Bureau of the Census, Statistical Abstract of the United States: 1980, 101st ed. (Washington, D.C.: Government Printing Office, 1980) pp. 30–31. Advertisement, p. 247, courtesy of Johnson & Johnson. Focus 10–2 source, p. 248: "Dual Incomes Will Lift More Families to Middle Class Affluence in The Decade," Wall Street Journal, June 27, 1980, p. 1, reprinted by permission of the Wall Street Journal, © Dow Jones and Company, Inc., 1980. Focus 10–3 source, p. 249: adapted from William H. Reynolds, "The Edsel Ten Years Later," Business Horizons, Fall, 1967, pp. 39–46, copyright 1967 by The Foundation for the School of Business at Indiana University, reprinted by permission. Photo, p. 251, by Beryl Goldberg. Photo, p. 252, by Sybil Shelton/Monkmeyer Press Photo

Service. Figure 10–5 source, p. 254: Contemporary Marketing, 3rd edition, by Louis E. Boone and David L. Kurtz, copyright © 1980 by The Dryden Press, a division of Holt, Rinehart and Winston, reprinted by permission of Holt, Rinehart and Winston. Controversial Issue sources, pp. 256–257: Richard Severo, "Sharp Decrease in U.S. Reported in Toxic Shock Syndrome Cases," New York Times, Jan. 30, 1981, pp. A-1, D-15; "Tampon Tussle," Time, Nov. 3, 1980, p. 86; "A New Warning for Tampon Users," Newsweek, Oct. 6, 1980, pp. 105–106; and "Rely Advertisements Will Advise Women to Quit Product," Wall Street Journal, Sept. 29, 1980, p. 20. Case 10–1 source, pp. 261–263: reprinted with permission from the Dec. 5, 1980 issue of Advertising Age, copyright 1980 by Crain Communications, Inc. Case 10–2 sources, p. 263: adapted from Richard D. James, "Levi Strauss Builds Its Success on a 'Fad' That Has Not Faded," Wall Street Journal, Feb. 7, 1977, reprinted by permission of the Wall Street Journal, © Dow Jones & Company, Inc., 1977, all rights reserved and "The Jeaning of America," Newsweek, Oct 6, 1980, pp. 83, 85.

Chapter 11
Photo, p. 265, courtesy of Ike Antebi. Woolworth quote source, p. 266: B. C. Forbes, Men Who Made America Great (Brookfield, WI: The Hamilton Press), originally published in 1917 as Men Who Are Making America Great. Top photo, p. 271, © Donald Dietz 1980/Stock, Boston. Bottom photo, p. 271, by Randy Matusow. Table 11–1 source, p. 272: Anne Pillsbury, "The 50's: The Fortune Directory of the Largest Non-industrial Companies," Fortune, July 13, 1981, p. 122, reprinted by permission of FORTUNE Magazine, © TIME Inc. Focus 11–1 source, p. 273: condensed from "Death of a Salesman," Newsweek, Aug. 15, 1977, p. 64, copyright 1977 by Newsweek, Inc., all rights reserved, reprinted by permission. Focus 11–2 source, p. 274: excerpted by permission from Joseph Barry Mason, "Retailing Strategies for 1980," Alabama Business, April 1977, vol. 47, no. 8, p. 5, published by the Center for Business and Economic Research, The University of Alabama. Photo, p. 274, © 1980 Marjorie Pickens. Photo, p. 275, by Peter Vandermark/Stock, Boston. Focus 11–3 source, p. 276: Laurence Ingrassin, "A Bag from Byerly's is the Stylish Place to Stow the Garbage," Wall Street Journal, June 4, 1980, pp. 1, 25, reprinted by permission of the Wall Street Journal, © Dow Jones & Company, Inc., 1980, all rights reserved. Photo, p. 279, © Jan Lukas from Rapho/Photo Researchers, Inc. Case 11–1 sources, pp. 285–286: "Dr. Pepper Agrees to Produce and Sell Welch Soft Drinks," Wall Street Journal, May 26, 1981, p. 14, reprinted by permission of the Wall Street Journal, © Dow Jones & Company, Inc., 1981, all rights reserved, and Phil Fitzell, "Distribution: How Welch Cracked the Soft Drink Market," Product Marketing, June, 1977, pp. 19–23, reprinted with permission, Product Marketing Magazine. Case 11–2 source, pp. 285–286: reprinted as adapted from "Coal Mainly Stands and Waits," Time, Sept. 1, 1980, p. 50, used by permission from TIME, The Weekly Newsmagazine, copyright TIME, Inc., 1980.

Chapter 12
Photo, p. 289, courtesy of Proctor and Gardner. Profile source, p. 289: Ricki L. Francke, "Proctor Takes a Gamble and Hits the Jackpot," Working Woman, Aug. 1979, pp. 19–20, reprinted by permission of Ricki F.

Pollack. Photo, p. 291, by Mimi Forsyth/Monkmeyer Press Photo Service. Focus 12–1 source, p. 291: Randall Pol, "Ads Togetherness Pitches May Be Ringing in 'We' Decade." *Sentinel Star*, Orlando, FL, Dec. 2, 1980, pp. 1–B, 6–B. Focus 12–2 sources, p. 292: "J. R. Mystery Resolved in 41.4 Million Homes," *Journal American*, Bellevue, Wash., Nov. 26, 1980, p. B–5 and "Huge Dallas Audience Saw Kristin Shoot J. R.," *Seattle Times*, Nov. 23, 1980, p. A–4. Table 12–1 source, p. 294: reprinted with permission from the Sept. 11, 1980 issue of *Advertising Age*, copyright 1980 by Crain Communications, Inc. Table 12–2 source, p. 294: "Percentages of Sales Invested in Advertising by Major Industry Groups," courtesy of Schonfeld and Associates, Inc., Chicago, Il. Advertisement, p. 295, Van Heusen Shirt Company. Focus 12–3 source, p. 296, adapted from "Business Bulletin," *Wall Street Journal*, Feb. 21, 1974, reprinted by permission of the Wall Street Journal, © Dow Jones & Company, Inc., 1974, all rights reserved. Focus 12–4 sources, p. 297: Nancy Giges, "Judge Rules for Tylenol: Anacin Ordered to Halt Inflammation Ad Claims," *Advertising Age*, August 22, 1977, pp. 1, 62 and "Business Bulletin," *Wall Street Journal*, Aug. 11, 1977. Figure 12–3 source, p. 301: adapted with permission from Albert H. Dunn, Eugene M. Johnson, and David L. Kurtz, *Sales Management: Concepts, Practices and Cases* (Morristown, N.J.: General Learning Press, 1974), p. 45. Controversial Issue sources, pp. 304–305: A. O. Sulzberger, Jr., "F.T.C. Staff Urges End to Child TV Ad Study," *New York Times*, April 3, 1981, p. 27; Harold V. Semling, Jr., "Food Industry Spokesmen/Opponents Square Off on 'Children's Advertising,' Sugared Cereals," *Food Processing Magazine*, May, 1979, pp. 10, 12, 16, 17; Christopher Demuth, "Hands Off Children's TV, *Advertising Age*, May 7, 1979, pp. 65, 66; and promotional brochure of Action For Children's Television (ACT), Newtonville, MA. Case 12–1 source, p. 308: courtesy of Hiram Walker Company. Case 12–2 source, p. 309: Thayer C. Taylor, "Mead Data Lays It on the Line," *Sales and Marketing Management*, April 6, 1981, pp. 42–43, 45, reprinted by permission from Sales and Marketing Management Magazine, copyright 1981.

Chapter 13
Photo, p. 311, courtesy of Calvin Klein, Ltd. Profile source, p. 311: Walter McQuade, "The Bruising Businessman Behind Calvin Klein," *Fortune*, Nov. 17, 1980, pp. 106–109, 116, 118. Photo, p. 313, © 1981 Ira Berger. Photo, p. 315, © Paul Sequeira/Photo Researchers, Inc. Focus 13–1 source, p. 316: "Food Was 11¢ a Day in 1776," *Ypsilanti Press*, Feb. 11, 1974. Controversial Issue sources, pp. 322–323: Joseph S. Coyle, "Scanning Lights Up a Dark World for Grocers," *Fortune*, March 27, 1978, pp. 76–78, 80; "Breaking the Code," *Forbes*, March 6, 1978, p. 50; and "Computerized Grocery Check-outs," *Better Homes and Gardens*, Feb. 1976, p. 111. Photo, p. 324, © Herman LeRoy Emmet 1980/Photo Researchers, Inc. Case 13–1 sources, pp. 326–327: "U.S. Oil Consumption Drops 6.5%," Associated Press Newsfeature, *Journal American*, Bellevue, Wash., Oct. 18, 1980, p. A–12; June Kronholz, "Europe's Drivers Don't Reduce Gasoline Use Despite Soaring Prices," *Wall Street Journal*, May 12, 1980, pp. 1, 20; and "Reduced Gasoline Use Cuts Into Tax Levies, Hurts Many Businesses," *Wall Street Journal*, April 3, 1980, p. 1. Case 13–2 source, p. 327: "U.S. Dealers of Japanese Autos Dump Discounts as Shortage Looms,"

Associated Press Newsfeature, *Journal American*, Bellevue, Wash., May 19, 1981, p. B–6.

Chapter 14
Photo, p. 333, courtesy of Warner Lambert. Profile sources, p. 333: News releases from Entenmann's, Inc.; Brenda Holland, "Entenmann's on the Rise," *Advertising Age*, April 27, 1981, pp. S–31, 32; and Jean Bergantini Grillo, "Let 'em Eat Cake (and Pies, and Doughnuts . . .)," *New York Magazine*, April 16, 1979, pp. 44–46. Focus 14–1 source, p. 335: "Robots Join the Labor Force," reprinted from the June 9, 1980 issue of *Business Week* by special permission, © 1980 by McGraw-Hill, Inc., New York, N.Y. 10020, all rights reserved. Photo, p. 335, courtesy of Unimation. Table 14–1, p. 337, from *Production and Operations Management: A Problem-Solving and Decision-Making Approach*, by Norman Gaither, copyright © 1980 by Dryden Press, a division of Holt, Rinehart and Winston Publishers, reprinted by permission of Holt, Rinehart and Winston. Focus 14–2 source, p. 340: *Big Mac* by Max Boas and Steve Chain, copyright © 1976 by Max Boas and Steve Chain, reprinted by permission of the publisher, E. P. Dutton. Illustration, p. 340, from "The Burger That Conquered the Country," *Time*, Sept. 17, 1973, p. 85, reprinted by permission of TIME, The Weekly Newsmagazine, copyright Time, Inc., 1973. Figure 14–2 source, p. 342: these cities are discussed in Sam Allis, "Those Who Rate Cities as Business Sites Like Mid-sized Sun Belt Ones," *Wall Street Journal*, March 14, 1980, pp. 1, 26. Photo, p. 343, © Jacques Jangoux/Peter Arnold, Inc. Figure 14–3, p. 345, reproduced through the courtesy of *Port of Houston Magazine*. Figure 14–4 source, p. 346: *Production and Operations Management: A Problem-Solving and Decision-Making Approach*, by Norman Gaither, copyright © 1980 by Dryden Press, a division of Holt, Rinehart and Winston Publishers, reprinted by permission of Holt, Rinehart and Winston. Focus 14–3 source, p. 348: adapted with permission from *Telephone Talk*, southwestern Bell, St. Louis, 1975. Figure 14–5 source, p. 351: *Fundamentals of Modern Business* by Robert E. Swindle, © 1977 by Wadsworth Publishing Company, Inc., Belmont, CA 94002, reprinted by permission of the publisher. Focus 14–4 source, p. 353: *Big Mac* by Max Boas and Steve Chain, copyright © 1976 by Max Boas and Steve Chain, reprinted by permission of the publisher, E. P. Dutton. Controversial Issue sources, pp. 354–355: Anthony J. Parisi, "Hard Times for Nuclear Power," *New York Times Magazine*, April 12, 1981, pp. 36, 38, 40, 42, 44, 46, 48; Robert D. Hershey, Jr., "Can Reagan Lift the Cloud Over Nuclear Power?" *New York Times*, March 8, 1981, sec. 3, pp. 1, 22; Erick Morganthaler, "Soviet Bloc Is Pushing Nuclear Power Plants Even as U.S. Pulls Back," *Wall Street Journal*, Jan. 4, 1980, pp. 1, 23; and "Nuclear Power on the Ropes," *Newsweek*, April 16, 1979, pp. 41–42, 44. Case 14–1 source, p. 357–358: "Leave It to Japan to Employ Best Workers Money Can Build," *Sentinel Star*, Bellevue, Wash., Jan. 10, 1981, p. D–10, reprinted by permission of United Press International.

Chapter 15
Photo, p. 361, courtesy of Holiday Inns, Inc. Profile sources, p. 361: Holiday Inns, Inc., news releases; "Marketing Observer," *Business Week*, Feb. 17, 1975, p. 48; "Holiday Inns Take a New Road to Profits," *Business Week*, Sept. 7, 1974, p. 88; Marilyn Bender, "The

Hospitality Crusade," The New York Times, Aug. 26, 1973, Sec. 3, p. 11; and "Meet the Host With the Most," The Readers Digest, September, 1972, pp. 165–170: Kahn quote source, p. 362: Hesh Weiner, "Computers and the Future of America," Computer Decisions, Jan., 1977. Townsend quote source, p. 362: Robert Townsend, Up the Organization (New York: Alfred A. Knopf, 1970). Focus 15–1 source, p. 365: Myles E. Walsh, "Where Have All the Minis Gone?" INFOSYSTEMS, July, 1978, reprinted with permission from The Hitchcock Publishing Company, copyright 1978 by the Hitchcock Publishing Company. Top left photo, p. 366, courtesy of the Burroughs Corporation. Top right and bottom photos, p. 366, courtesy of the Digital Equipment Corporation. Figure 15–3, p. 368, courtesy of International Business Machines Corporation. Figure 15–4, p. 369, courtesy of International Business Machines Corporation. Focus 15–2 source, pp. 370–371: Joel Makower, "Computing in the 80's," Flightime, May, 1980, pp. 42, 44. Figure 15–5 source, p. 375: reproduced by permission from Gordon B. Davis, Computer Data Processing, (New York: McGraw-Hill, 1973) p. 233. Table 15–2 source, p. 376: reprinted by special permisssion from Donald D. Spencer, Introduction to Information Processing (Columbus, Ohio: Charles E. Merrill Publishing, 1977) p. 640. Advertisement, p. 377, reprinted by permission from International Business Machines Corporation. Figure 15–6 source, p. 379: top two photos courtesy of International Business Machines Corporation; bottom photo reprinted from the Dec. 30, 1974 issue of U.S. News and World Report, copyright 1974, U.S. News and World Report, Inc. Controversial Issue sources, pp. 380–381: Alvin Toffler, The Third Wave (New York: Bantam Books, 1981); Peter F. Drucker, "The 'Re-industrialization' of America," Wall Street Journal, June 13, 1980 p. 10; Fred Lamond, "Europeans Blame Computers," Datamation, Nov. 1, 1978, pp. 107, 110, 114; and Herbert A. Simon, "What Computers Mean for Man and Society," Science, vol. 195, March 18, 1977, pp. 1186–1190. Case 15–1 source, p. 386: quoted and adapted from Thomas O'Toole, "Breakfast? Just Tell Your Computer," a Washington Post article reprinted in the Detroit News, June 10, 1977, © The Washington Post, reprinted by permission. Case 15–2 source, p. 387: adapted by permission from Susan Wooldrige and Keith London, THE COMPUTER SURVIVAL HANDBOOK, revised edition (Ipswich, Ma.: Gambit, Inc. Publishers, 1979), pp. 162–163.

Chapter 16

Profile photo, p. 389, courtesy of Apple Computer. Profile sources, p. 389: "Discovering a Vast Potential Market," Business Week, Dec. 1, 1980, pp. 91–92, 97; Apple Computer news releases, Oct., 1980; Philip Shenon, "Investment Climate Is Ripe for Offering by Apple Computer," Wall Street Journal, Aug. 20, 1980, p. 17; "Shiny Apple," Time, Nov. 5, 1979, p. 84; and Dan Dorfman, "Move Over, Horatio Alger," Esquire, June 6, 1978, p. 9. Focus 16–1 source, p. 393: based on information from "How Giant Sears Grows and Grows," Business Week, Dec. 16, 1972, pp. 54–55. Focus 16–3 source, p. 397: Evans Witt, "What Went Wrong?" Associated Press Newsfeature, Journal American, Bellevue, Wash., Nov. 8, 1980, p. A–11. Photo, p. 398, by Sybil Shelton/Peter Arnold, Inc. Table 16–1 and Figure 16–3 sources, p. 401: The Hammond Almanac: 1981 (Maplewood, N.J.: Hammond Almanac, Inc. 1981), p. 203 and production data from 1979 supplied by the Motor Vehicle Manufacturers Association of the United Sates, Inc. Figure 16–4 sources, p. 404: (A) reprinted by permission from The Conference Board, "Labor Unionization," Union Membership #1882, July, 1980; (B) reprinted by permission from The Conference Board, "Foreign Workers as Percentage of Total Employment in Host Country, 1977," International Labor Migration #1890–1891, Nov., 1980; (C) reprinted by permission from The Conference Board, "Population by Labor Force Status," Characteristics of Job Seekers #1889, Oct., 1980; (D) "Number of Persons by Age and Sex: 1970," Your Guide to Census '80, U.S. Department of Commerce, Bureau of the Census (Washington, D. C.: Government Printing Office, 1979). Photo, p. 405, by Randy Matusow. Controversial Issue sources, pp. 406–407: Arnold H. Lubasch, "Census's Count of Welfare Roles Missed by 8.5%," New York Times, Jan. 26, 1981, p. B–3; "How to Count Up the Uncounted," Newsweek, Oct. 6, 1980, p. 52; "Why the Census May Turn Up a Miscount," Business Week, June 16, 1980, p. 72; 'Let the Great Headcount Begin," Time, March 31, 1980, pp. 24–25, 27; Carol Simons, "Everyone Figures in the Greatest U.S. Enumeration," Smithsonian, March, 1980, pp. 93–99; and Andrew Hacker, "The No-account Census," Harpers, March, 1980, pp. 28–32. Case 16–1 source, p. 410: adapted from Jim Hyatt, "At One Toy Company, The Guys in Research are 3 and 4 Years Old," Wall Street Journal, Dec. 20, 1971, reprinted with permission of the Wall Street Journal, © Dow Jones & Company, Inc. 1971, all rights reserved.

Chapter 17

Profile photo, p. 413, by Paul Schumach/Metropolotan Photo Service, Inc. Profile sources, p. 413: personal interview with Abraham J. Briloff and Floyd Norris, Assocated Press feature story, "Number Tricks Don't Fool Blind Accountant," Bergen County Record, Feb. 20, 1981, p. C–9. Robert Frost quote source, p. 414, from The Poetry of Robert Frost, edited by Edward Connery Lathem, copyright © 1936 copyright © 1964 by Lesley Frost Ballantine, copyright © 1969 by Holt, Rinehart and Winston, reprinted by permission of Holt, Rinehart and Winston, publishers. Photo p. 415 © Ginger Chih 1978/ Peter Arnold, Inc. Focus 17–1 sources, p. 417: 1981 Accounting and Finance Salary Survey (Chicago: Source Finance, 1981), pp. 4–12 and correspondence with American Institute of Certified Public Accounts, June, 1981; the quotation is from "Accountants—Clearing Up America's Mystery Profession," U.S. News & World Report, Dec. 19, 1977, p. 40. Figures 17–2 and 17–3 sources, p. 421: courtesy of Armstrong World Industries, Inc. Figure 17–4 source, p. 422: courtesy of Armstrong World Industries, Inc. Figure 17–5 source, p. 425: courtesy of Armstrong World Industries, Inc. Case 17–2 source, p. 434: courtesy of Beatrice Foods Company.

Chapter 18

Profile photo, p. 441, Wide World Photos. Profile sources, p. 441: Steven Rattner, "A Look Inside Paul Volcker's Fed," New York Times, May 3, 1981, Sec. 3, pp. 1, 8, 9; Nicholas von Hoffman, "Can Volcker Stand Up to Inflation?" New York Times Magazine, Dec. 2, 1979, pp. 11–12, 22–24; and "Defender of the Dollar," Time, Oct. 22, 1979, p. 23. Figure 18–1 source, p. 444: © Paolo

Koch 1978/Photo Researchers, Inc. Photo, p. 448, by Randy Matusow. Focus 18–1 sources, p. 448: "Withdrawal Pains for Credit Card Holders," *U.S. News & World Report,* March 31, 1980, p. 29 and "Credit Cards: Great Strides Yet to be Made," *Nation's Business,* June, 1978, p. 59. Table 18–1 source, p. 451: *The Hammond Almanac:1981* (Maplewood, N.J.:Hammond Almanac Inc., 1981), p. 200, basic data from *Fortune,* reprinted by permission. Figure 18–3 source, p. 452: The Federal Reserve System. Controversial Issue sources, pp. 458–459: Clyde Farnsworth, "Washington Watch, Bank Battle Shaping Up," *New York Times,* March 2, 1981, p. D–2; Glenn Ritt, "Garn Admits 'Bias' Against Interstate Banking Growth," *New York Post,* Feb. 24, 1981, p. 44; Clyde Farnsworth, "More Bank Competition Suggested," *New York Times,* July 14, 1980, pp. D–1, D–5; Chauncey E. Schmidt, "The Fed Brings Nationwide Banking One Stage Nearer," *Euromoney,* May, 1980, pp. 87–88, 90; "U.S. Bank Regulators Ask Emergency Power for Interstate Sales," *Wall Street Journal,* April 10, 1980, p. 4; "Regulators May Seek Power to Approve Emergency Interstate Bank Acquisitions," *Wall Street Journal,* April 9, 1980, p. 7; and Stephen A. Rhoades, "The Competitive Effects of Interstate Banking," *Federal Reserve Bulletin,* Jan., 1980, pp. 1–7. Case 18–1 source, p. 463: "Money Havens," *Time,* June 8, 1981, p. 65, reprinted by permission from TIME, The Weekly Newsmagazine, copyright TIME, Inc., 1981.

Chapter 19

Profile photo, p. 466, Wide World Photos. Profile sources, p. 466: "A Company Star in Business for Himself," *Fortune,* March 9, 1981, p. 52; "Classy Chassis," *Time,* Oct. 13, 1980, p. 106; and William Flanagan, "The Dream Car of John De Lorean," *Esquire,* June 19, 1979, pp. 75–80, 84. Baily quote source, p. 467: *Forbes,* Feb. 2, 1981, p. 69. Hunt quote source, p. 467: *Time,* Dec. 29, 1980, p. 51. Figure 19–1 source, p. 469: Louis E. Boone and James C. Johnson, "The 801 Men (and One Woman) at the Top: A Profile of the CEOs of the Largest U.S. Corporations," *Business Horizons,* Feb. 1980, p. 50, copyright 1980 by the Foundation of the School of Business at Indiana University, reprinted by permission. Figure 19–4 source, p. 474: courtesy of Union Chelsea National Bank. Figure 19–5 source, p. 478: by Omikron/Photo Researchers, Inc. Figure 19–7 source, p. 482: courtesy of First National Bank in St. Louis. Figure 19–8, p. 484: reproduced by permission of Dun and Bradstreet, Inc. Table 19–4 source, p. 489: "If You Want a Bank Loan—New Tests You Have to Pass," *U.S. News & World Report,* Aug. 22, 1977, p. 65, reprinted from *"U.S. News & World Report,"* copyright 1977, U.S. News & World Report, Inc. Case 19–1 source, p. 490: "$400 Million Federal Loan Guarantee to Help Bail Out Sinking Chrysler," *Sentinel Star,* Orlando, FL, Jan. 20, 1981, p. 7–A, copyrighted, 1981, Chicago Tribune, used with permission. Case 19–2 source, p. 491: Newcomb Stillwell, "Dark Nights at After Six," *Forbes,* Jan. 19, 1981, p. 72.

Chapter 20

Profile photo, p. 493, by Randy Matusow. Profile sources, p. 493: E. F. Hutton recruiting package, Dec. 23, 1980; E. F. Hutton 1979 annual report; and "Founder of Brokerage Firm Here Was Chairman of General Foods until '35," *New York Times,* July 12, 1962, p. 29. Figure

20–1, p. 496, courtesy of Corning Glass Works. Focus 20–2 source, p. 500: adapted by permission from *Fact Book 1980* (New York: New York Stock Exchange, 1980), p. 49. Table 20–2 source, p. 501: reprinted by permission from *Fact Book 1981* (New York: New York Stock Exchange, 1981), p. 28. Table 20–5 source, p. 503: reprinted by permission from *Fact Book 1981* (New York: New York Stock Exchange, 1981), p. 35. Photo, p. 503, © 1978 Jan Lukas/Photo Researchers, Inc. Focus 20–3 source, p. 504: reprinted by permission from *Fact Book 1981* (New York: New York Stock Exchange, 1981), pp. 29–31. Photo, p. 504, © Sherry Suris 1975/Photo Researchers, Inc. Figure 20–2 sources, p. 508: photos 1, 2, 4, and 5 courtesy of Loewi Financial Companies, Ltd.; photo 3 by Edward C. Topple, courtesy of the New York Stock Exchange. Figure 20–3 source, p. 510: *Wall Street Journal,* July 21, 1981. Reprinted by permission of the Wall Street Journal, © Dow Jones & Company, Inc., 1981, all rights reserved. Controversial Issue sources, pp. 512–513: H. Kent Baker and William H. Seippel, "Dividend Reinvestment Plans Win Wide Currency," *Harvard Business Review,* Nov.–Dec., 1980, pp. 182, 184, 186; "Statistical Spotlight," *Forbes,* September 15, 1980, "The Boom in Reinvestment," *U.S. News & World Report,* May 5, 1980, p. 86; "Substituting Shares for Dividends," *Business Week,* Aug. 27, 1979, p. 105; Grant F. Winthrop, "Buying Discount Stock with Dividends," *Fortune,* Oct. 9, 1978, pp. 193–196; "Buying Shares at a Discount," *Dun's Review,* Oct., 1978, p. 112; and "Dividend Reinvestment Catches On," *Business Week,* Sept. 4, 1978, pp. 82–83. Case 20–2 source, p. 517: "Playing Penny Ante," *Newsweek,* Dec. 1, 1980, p. 67, copyright © 1980 Newsweek, Inc., all rights reserved, reprinted by permission.

Chapter 21

Profile source, p. 520: personal interview. Stengel quote source, p. 521: *Bits and Pieces* (Fairfield, N.J.: The Economics Press, Nov. 1980), p. 13. Photo, p. 524, © Josephus Daniels/Rapho/Photo Researchers, Inc. Table 21–1 source, p. 528: *Statistical Abstract of the United States, 1980,* 101st ed. (Washington, D.C.: Government Printing Office, 1980), p. 73. Focus 21–2 source, p. 529: the insurance claims data are listed in *The Journal of Insurance,* March/April, 1979, p. 13. Advertisement, p. 529, courtesy of The American Insurance Association. Table 21–2 source, p. 530: *The Hammond Almanac: 1981,* p. 201, basic data from *Fortune,* reprinted by permission. Focus 21–3 source, p. 531: "Phantom Cars, Speeding Poles Head Insurance List," as it appeared in *Tulsa World,* Jan. 21, 1979, reprinted by permission of United Press International. Photo p. 532, © Van Bucher 1978/Photo Researchers, Inc. Photo, p. 533, © Ronny Jacques/Photo Researchers, Inc. Table 21–4 source, p. 538: information from *Insurance Facts 1980–81* (New York: Insurance Information Institute, 1980), p. 12, used with permission. Figure 21–2 source, p. 539: *1980 Life Insurance Fact Book* (Washington, D.C.: American Council of Life Insurance, 1980) p. 24. Controversial Issue sources, pp. 540–541: Associated Press feature "Insurance Hikes No-fault's Fault?" as it appeared in the *New York Daily News,* Feb. 14, 1981; "No-fault Car Insurance Works in Michigan," *Changing Times,* August, 1979, pp. 25–29; Associated Press feature "No-fault Meets Mixed Success," as it appeared in the *San Diego Union,* June 24, 1979, pp. A–22–23, A–25; *Insurance for the Car* (New York: Insurance Information Institute, 1979); and "No-fault Automobile Insurance," bulletin of the Office of Public and Consumer Affairs, U.S. Dept. of Transportation, Washington, D.C., July, 1978, pp. 1–6. Table 21–5, p. 543, reprinted by permission from *Policies for Protection* (Washington, D.C.: American Council of Life Insurance, 1977), p. 7. Case 21–1 source, pp. 545–547: "Lloyd's Biggest Disaster," *Forbes*, May 28, 1979, p. 38, reprinted by permission.

Chapter 22
Profile photo, p. 553, Wide World Photos. Profile sources, p. 553: "A revved-up Market for Diesel Engine Makers," *Business Week*, Feb. 5, 1979, pp. 76–79; "Butterflies at Caterpillar," *Forbes*, April 17, 1978, pp. 62–63; "Caterpillar in the Land of Nod," *Forbes*, Aug. 1, 1976, p. 43; Harlan S. Byrne, "A Leaping Caterpillar is a Wondrous Thing, Even If Its Rivals Agree," *Wall Street Journal*, April 19, 1976, pp. 1, 18; "William Blackie of Caterpillar Tractor," *Nation's Business*, August, 1972, pp. 38–43; "William Blackie Looks at Company's Multinational Future," *Cat World*, June/July, 1972, pp. 16–19; Tom Pugh, "Blackie's Legacy," *Peoria Journal Star*, May 28, 1972, p. C–1; and "Can 'Cat' Move the World?" *Dun's Review*, May, 1970, pp. 34, 36, 100. Caldwell quote source, p. 554: from Phillip Caldwell, "Management Opinion," *Administrative Management*, Sept., 1979, p. 100. Photo, p. 554, by Burt Glinn/Magnum Photos. Table 22–1 sources, p. 555: 1980 annual reports. Photo, p. 556, © Josephus Daniels/Rapho/Photo Researchers, Inc. Table 22–2 source, p. 556: Bureau of the Census, *Statistical Abstract of the United States, 1980*, 101st ed. (Washington, D.C.: Government Printing Office, 1980), pp. 874–877. Table 22–3 source, p. 557: Bureau of the Census, *Statistical Abstract of the United States, 1980*, 101st ed. (Washington, D.C.: Government Printing Office, 1980), p. 878. Photo, p. 559, by Joe Munroe/Photo Researchers, Inc. Table 22–4, p. 561, adapted with permission from "The 50 Leading Exporters," *Fortune*, Sept. 22, 1980, p. 115. Focus 22–2 source, p. 564: "How the U.S. Scored on Trade," *Business Week*, May 7, 1979, p. 35, reprinted from the May 7, 1979, issue of *Business Week* by special permission, copyright © 1979 by McGraw-Hill, Inc., New York, N.Y. 10020, all rights reserved; data from Gatt and the United Nations. Table 22–5 source, p. 566: compiled by Professor Paul F. Jenner, Institute of International Business, Georgia State University, from information in *The Europa Year Book 1981, A World Survey, Vol. I* (London: Europa Publications, Ltd., 1981). Table 22–6, p. 568, based on information from "The 100 Largest Foreign Investments in the U.S.," *Forbes*, July 7, 1980, pp. 90–91. Controversial Issue sources, pp. 570–571: Henry Scott Stokes, "Japan's Amazing Auto Machine," *New York Times*, Jan. 18, 1981, Sec. 3, pp. 1, 22; Robert D. Hershey, Jr., "Ailing Auto Industry Called Peril to U.S.," *New York Times*, Jan. 14, 1981, pp. A–1, D–14; "Tiffs on Trade," *Time*, Oct. 20, 1980, p. 77; Patrick Bedard, "Protect Us, Oh Lord, From Protective Tariffs," *Car and Driver*, Oct., 1980, p. 18; "Thinking the Unthinkable," *Forbes*, Sept. 1, 1980, p. 133; and "Why Detroit Could Turn Protectionist," *Business Week*, Nov. 5, 1979, pp. 92, 97, 100. Case 22–1 sources, p. 575: "Foreign Investment: The Post-Shah Surge in Political Risk Studies," *Business Week*, Dec. 1, 1980, p. 69; and Grant F. Winthrop, "Can a Computer Tell the Ratio of Risk?" *Fortune*, March 24, 1980, p. 95.

Chapter 23
Photo, p. 578, courtesy of Anthony L. Lanlese, Jr. Profile source, p. 578: personal interview. Focus 23–1 source, p. 580: Jeffrey Zaslow, "Looney Laws That Will Leave You Speechless," Orlando *Sentinel Star*, May 11, 1981, pp. B–1, B–6. Figure 23–1 source, p. 584: "Federal Regulators: Impact on Every American," *U.S. News & World Report*, May 9, 1977, P. 62, reprinted from "U.S. News & World Report," copyright 1977 U.S. News & World Report, Inc., used with permission. Controversial Issue sources, pp. 594–595: Lindley A. Clark, Jr., "It's a Long, Long Way to Deregulation," *Wall Street Journal*, Feb. 3, 1981, p. 33; "Talking Business," *New York Times*, Jan. 13, 1981, p. D–2; "Dogfight in the Sky for More Passengers," *U.S. News & World Report*, July 21, 1980, pp. 35–36; "For Airlines, Boom Times Near an End," *U.S. News & World Report*, Nov. 5, 1979, p. 86; "If You're Confused About Airline Fares . . ." *U.S. News & World Report*, April 23, 1979, pp. 30–32; and "Deregulating the Airlines," *U.S. News & World Report*, March 30, 1978, p. 56. Case 23–1 sources, p. 599: "Bankruptcy: New Law Makes New Start Easier," *Journal American*, Bellevue, Wash., Oct. 27, 1980, p. D–3; "A Rush to Personal Bankruptcy," *Newsweek*, Aug. 11, 1980. pp. 59–60; and Ronald L. Russell, "When All Else Fails . . . Try Bankruptcy," *Detroit News*, Nov. 26, 1979, pp. 1–C, 4–C. Case 23–2 source, p. 600: Sanford L. Jacobs, "Deregulation Forces Owners of Liquor Stores to Adjust," *Wall Street Journal*, March 16, 1981, p. 29, reprinted by permission of the Wall Street Journal, © Dow Jones and Company, Inc., 1981, all rights reserved.

Chapter 24
Profile photo, p. 603, courtesy of Enertech. Profile sources, p. 603: information from Ned Coffin; Andrea Aurichio, "Energy: Reaping the Wind," *New York Times*, June 15, 1980, pp. 1, 11; Frank Farwell, "New Energy: A Burgeoning Business in Windmills," *New York Times*, April 27, 1980, p. F–3; and Sharon Churcher, "The Answer is Blowin' in the Wind," *New York Magazine*, Oct. 23, 1978, pp. 92–95. Photo, p. 607, © Bruce Roberts 1978/Photo Researchers, Inc. Focus 24–1 and Table 24–1 source, p. 608: Frederick C. Klein, "How Depression Shook One Town—And Sank Its Luxury Car Maker," *Wall Street Journal*, Sept. 6, 1979, pp. 1, 16, reprinted by permission of the Wall Street Journal, © Dow Jones and Company, Inc., 1979, all rights reserved. Focus 24–2 source, p. 610: "Next Decade Will Be Sobering 80s," *U.S. News & World Report*, August 20, 1979, p. 53, reprinted with permission from "U.S. News & World Report," copyright 1979 U.S. News & World Report, Inc. Controversial Issue sources, pp. 612–613: Steven R. Weisman, "Reagan is Reportedly Ready to Eliminate Urban Aid Program," *New York Times*, Feb. 4, 1981, pp. A–1, B–4; "How Reagan Plans to Turn America Around," *U.S. News & World Report*, Jan. 12, 1981, pp. 17–21; "Next: Let Old Cities Fade Away?" *U.S. News & World Report*, Jan. 12, 1981, p. 8; "It's a Renaissance on the Waterfront," *U.S. News & World Report*, Sept. 29, 1980, pp. 65–66; John Herbers, "Study Says Old Cities Continue to Decline Despite Rejuvenation," *New York Times*, July 7, 1980, pp. A–1, A–13; Kathleen Teltsch, "Foundation and Businesses Start Self-Help Corporation," *New York Times*, May 23, 1980, p. B–3; Roger Wilkins, "Urban Development Grant: Spur to Private Investment," *New York Times*, June 8, 1979, Sec. 4, p. 15; and Robert Reinhold, "Federal Neighborhood

Panel Urges New Policies to Help Communities," *New York Times,* March 16, 1979, p. 18. Case 24–1 sources, p. 615: Alvin Toffler, *The Third Wave* (New York: William Morrow, 1980); and *Detroit News Magzine,* June 1, 1980, pp. 22–34.

Chapter 25
Profile source, p. 618: personal interview. Reagan quotation source, p. 619: "Fan Values 1942 Letter," United Press International story which appeared in the *Seattle Times,* Nov. 30, 1980, p. A–2. Figure 25–1 source, p. 621: U.S. Department of Labor, Bureau of Labor Statistics, *The Occupational Outlook Handbook, 1980–81* (Washington, D.C.: Government Printing Office, 1980), Bulletin 2075. Photo, p. 624, © Van Bucher 1979/ Photo Researchers, Inc. Focus 25–1 source, p. 630: reprinted as adapted from "Computers Can Help You Pick Your College and Your Future," United Press International story which appeared in the *Times-Picayune,* Nov. 23, 1980, sec. 3, p. 2. Table 25–1 source, p. 631: "Corporate Chiefs' Pay: Up, Up—and Away," *U.S. News & World Report,* May 18, 1981, p. 82, reprinted from "U.S. News & World Report," copyright 1981 U.S. News & World Report Inc. Controversial Issue sources, pp. 634–635: George Dullea, "On Ladder to Top, A Mentor is Key Step," *New York Times,* May 21, 1981, sec. 3, p. 2; Phyllis Gillis, "The New Girl Network," *Parents Magazine,* Nov., 1980, pp. 35–36, 38, 40; and Mary Scott Welch, "Networking: It Could Be Your Key To Job Survival, Success," *Vogue,* March, 1980, pp. 155–156. Case 25–1 source, pp. 638–639: Adapted from Donald Treiman, *Occupational Prestige in Comparative Perspective,* (New York: Academic Press, 1977), used with permission of Academic Press and Donald Treiman.

Subject Index

Name and Company Index